Portugal

PEDROSA

Also available by Pedrosa:
Equinoxes

See previews, get exclusives and order from:
NBMPUB.COM

We have over 200 graphic novels available.
Catalog available upon request.
NBM
160 Broadway, Suite 700 East,
New York, NY 10038

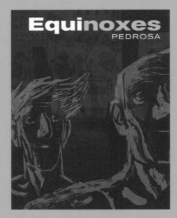

ACKNOWLEDGEMENTS

To those who share my life, thank you for your support, in every sense of the term, during the two long years I was immersed in the making of this book.

Many of the digital files in the first part were patiently "cleaned up" by Sarah Mattey and Anthony Neaulleau. The Portuguese dialogue in the third part was translated by Helder Wasterlain. Sylvie Duvelleroy carried out the final review of all the texts in Portuguese. My thanks goes out to all four of them for their invaluable assistance.

Abraço to Luis Beira and the organizers of the Festival de Sobreda, for that is where it all began. Thank you to Licinia for the tomatoes, cabbages, carrots, for the sound of her voice and her smile in the morning.

A huge thank you goes out to Malvildia, Cristina, Daniel, Magdalena, and Carolina, as well as Carlos, Teresa and Diogo, for their warm and generous welcome.

It cannot be said enough that the colors in the second part of this book were done by the talented, inventive, and patient Ruby.

Finally, this story could not have been told in the form I wanted without the unfailing support of José-Louis Bocquet, who maintained the courage of his convictions throughout the entire process. Thank you.

Até já.

Cyril Pedrosa

ISBN 9781681121475
Library of Congress Control Number: 2017953030
Originally published in French
© Dupuis 2011, by Pedrosa: All rights reserved.
© Dupuis 2015 for the English translation
Translation by Montana Kane
Lettering by Calix Ltd.

1st printing December 2017 in China

This graphic novel is also available as an e-book

Portugal

PEDROSA

Color by Pedrosa and Ruby

nbm GRAPHIC NOVELS

Nantier • Beall • Minoustchine
NEW YORK

According to Simon

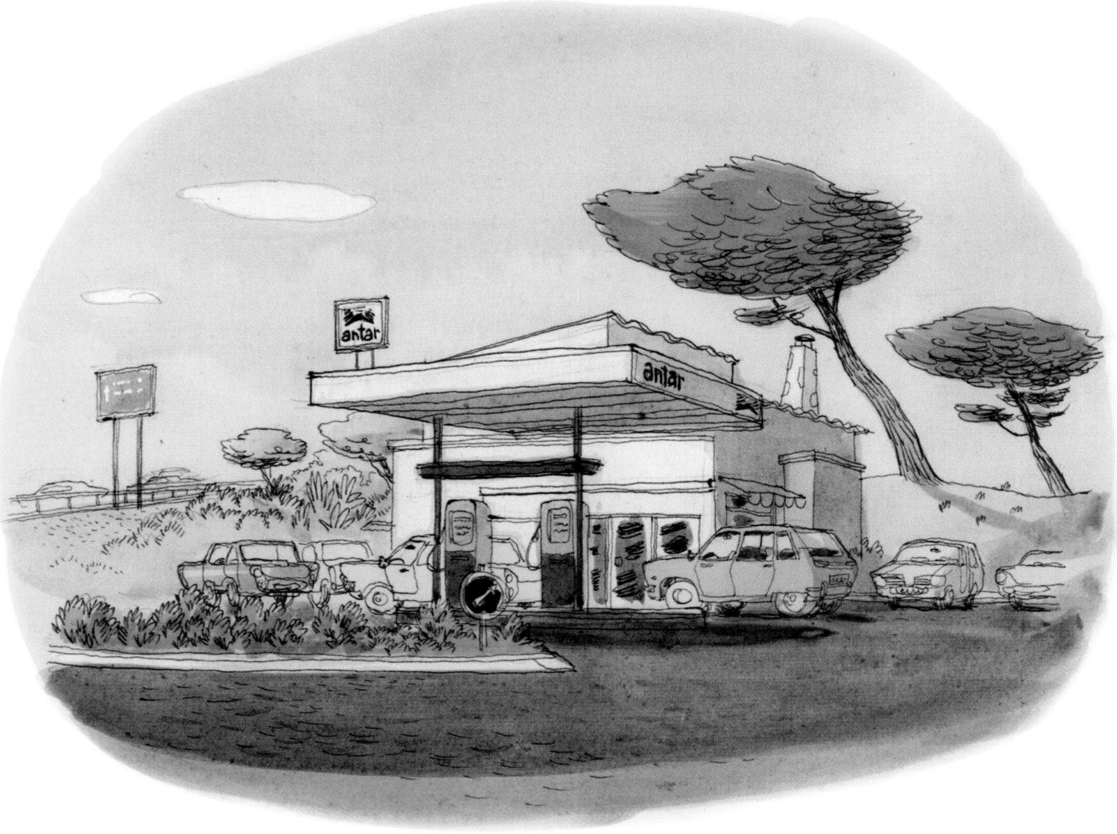
antar
antar

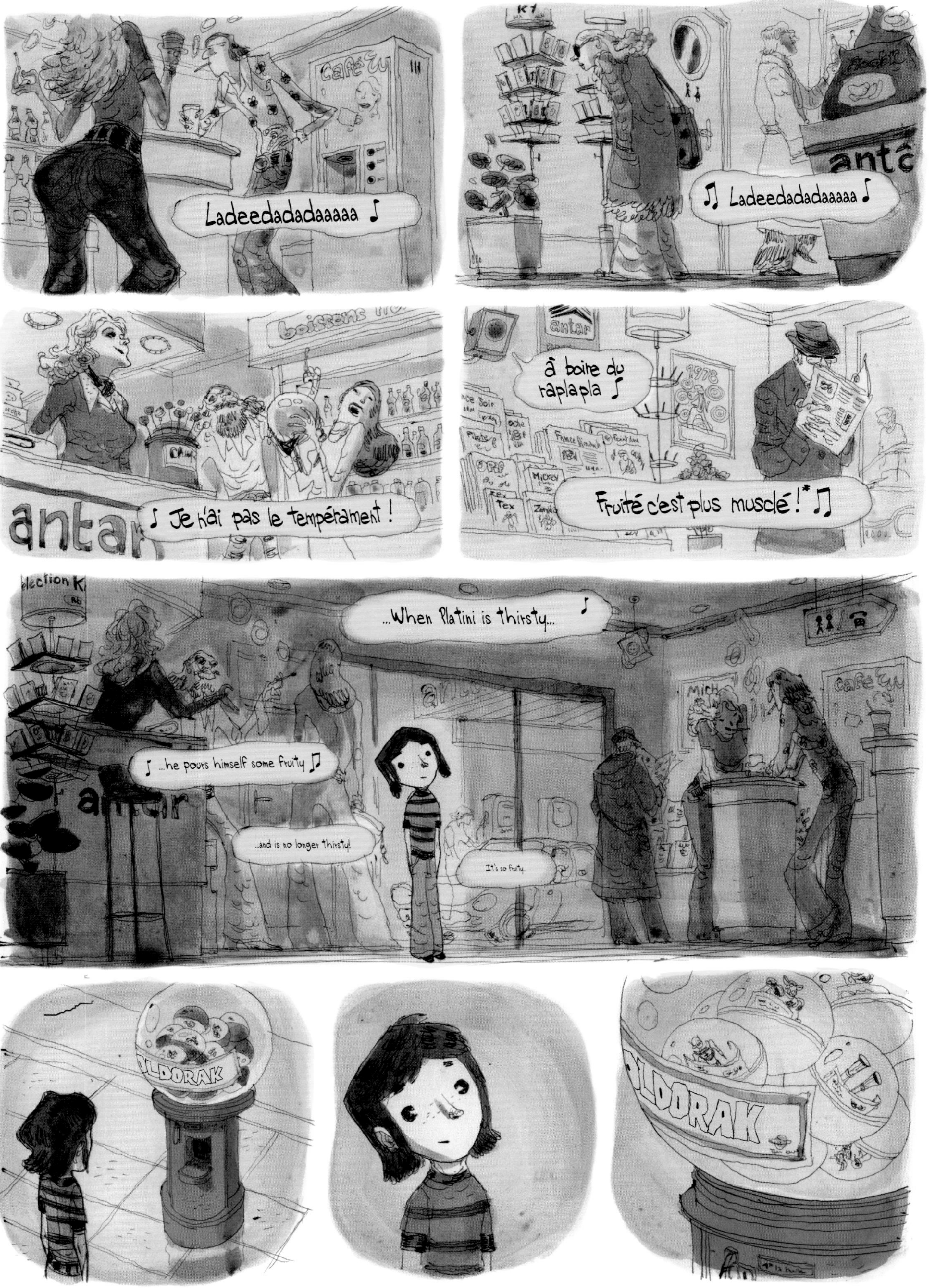
Ladeedadadaaaaa ♪
♫ Ladeedadadaaaaa ♪
♪ Je n'ai pas le tempérament !
â boire du raplapla ♪
Fruité c'est plus musclé !* ♫
...When Platini is thirsty... ♪
♪ ...he pours himself some fruity ♫
...and is no longer thirsty!
It's so fruity...
OLDORAK
OLDORAK

*Song featured in French fruit juice advert. 'I can't drink just any old juice. Fruité packs a punch!'

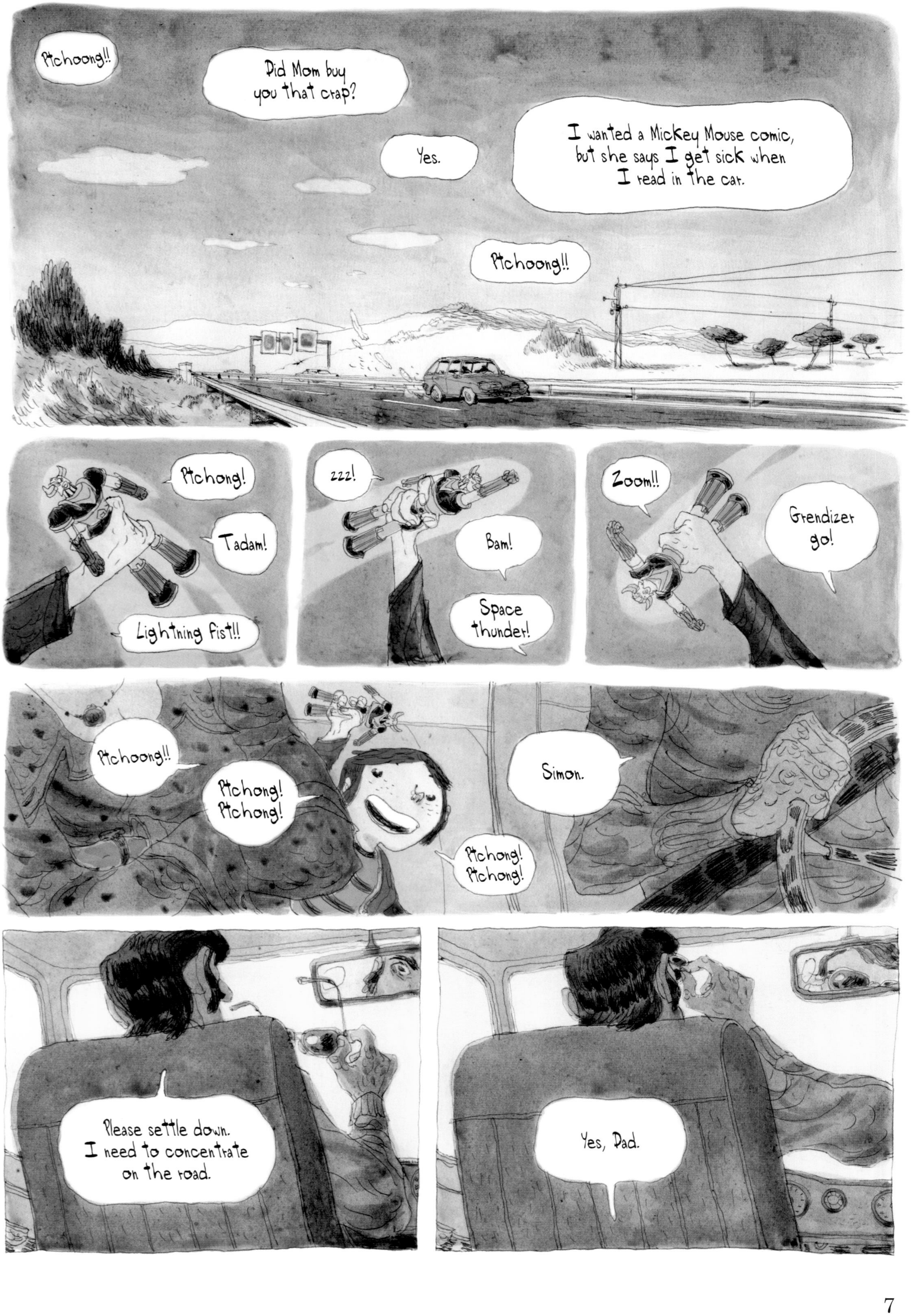
Ptchoong!!
Did Mom buy you that crap?
Yes.
I wanted a Mickey Mouse comic, but she says I get sick when I read in the car.
Ptchoong!!
Ptchong!
Tadam!
Lightning fist!!
zzz!
Bam!
Space thunder!
Zoom!!
Grendizer go!
Ptchoong!!
Ptchong! Ptchong!
Ptchong! Ptchong!
Simon.
Please settle down. I need to concentrate on the road.
Yes, Dad.

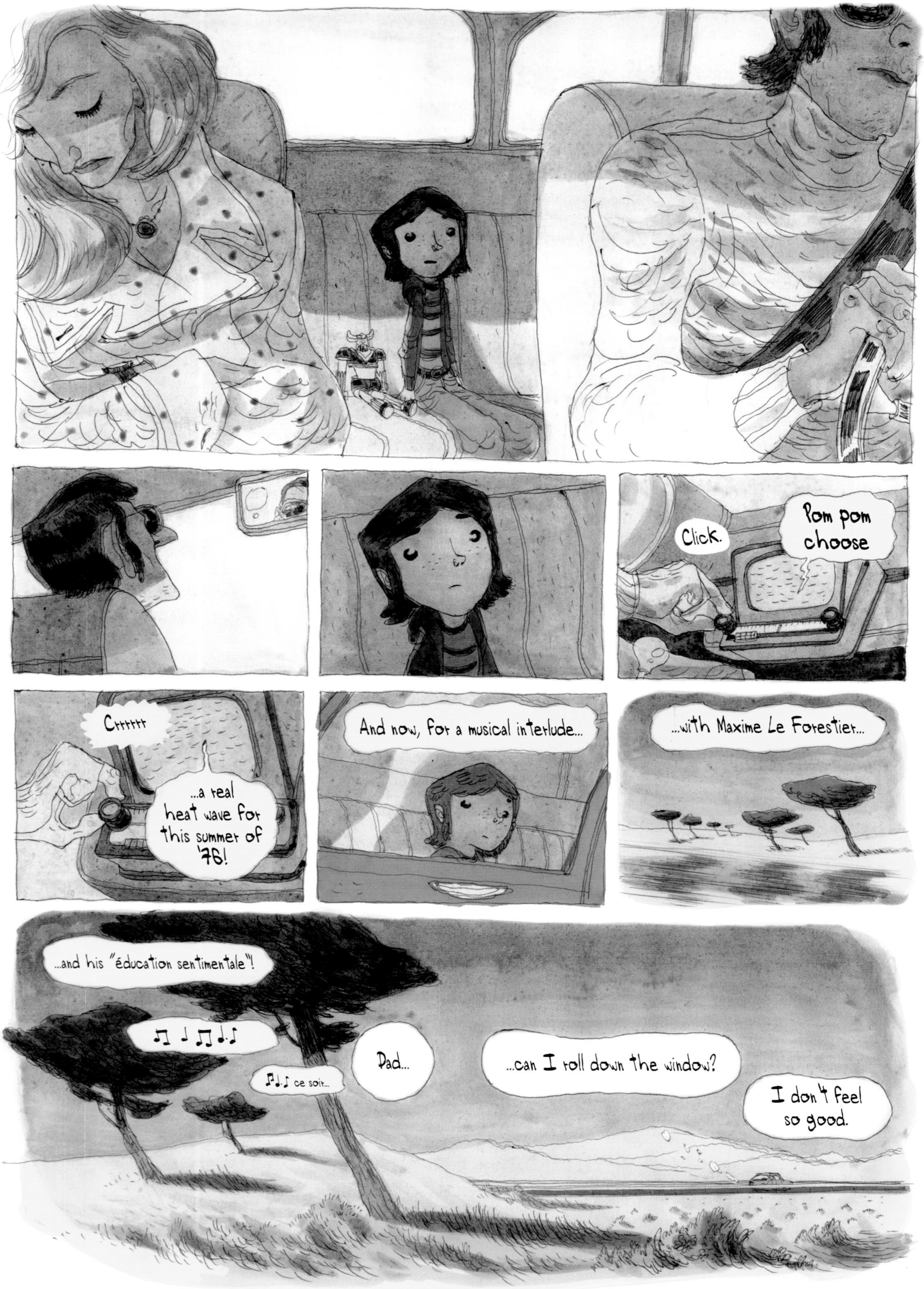
Click.
Pom pom choose
Crrrrrr
...a real heat wave for this summer of '76!
And now, for a musical interlude...
...with Maxime Le Forestier...
...and his "éducation sentimentale"!
ce soir...
Dad...
...can I roll down the window?
I don't feel so good.

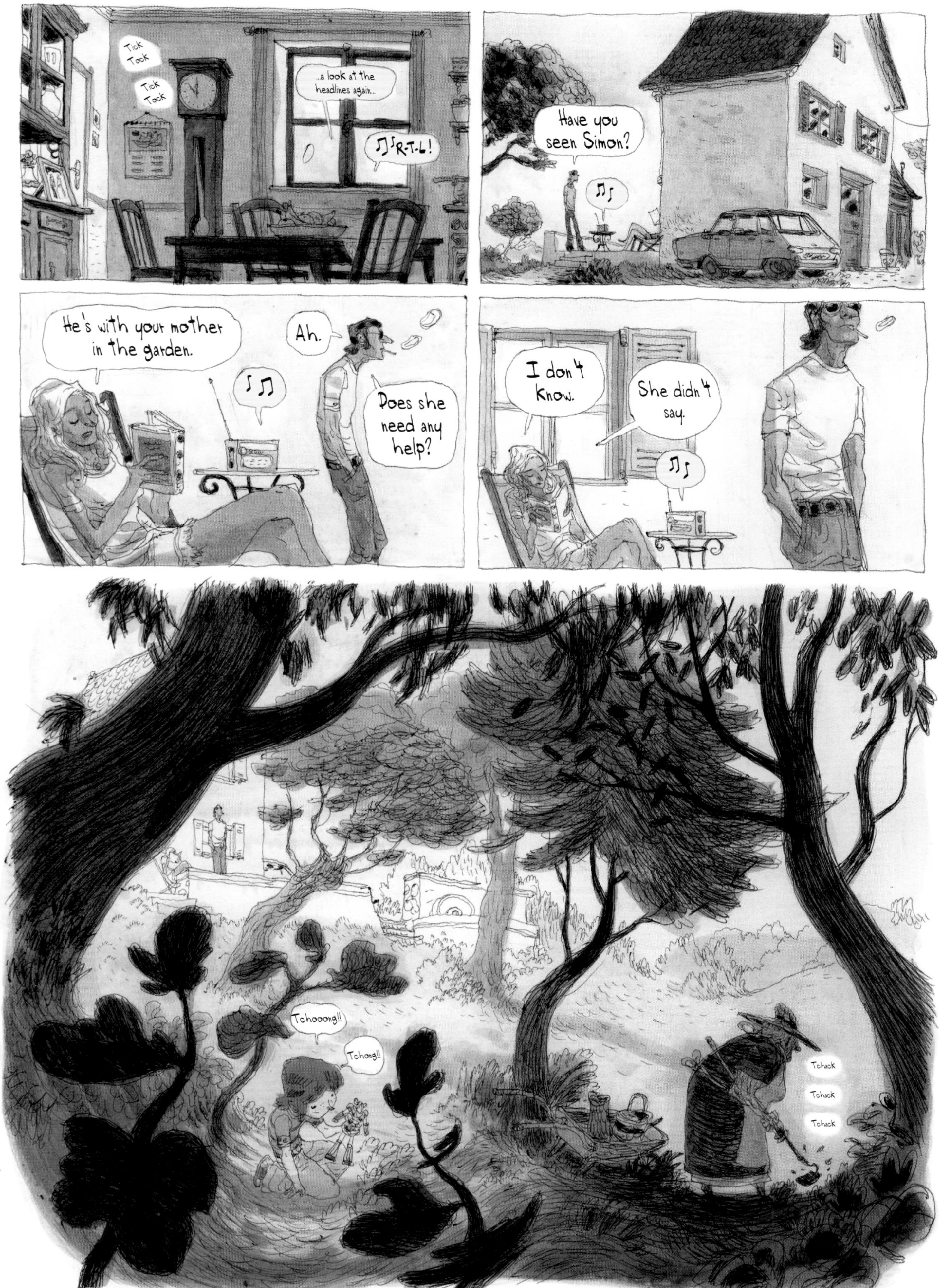
Tick Tock
Tick Tock
...a look at the headlines again...
R-T-L!
Have you seen Simon?
He's with your mother in the garden.
Ah.
Does she need any help?
I don't know.
She didn't say.
Tchooong!!
Tchong!!
Tchack
Tchack
Tchack

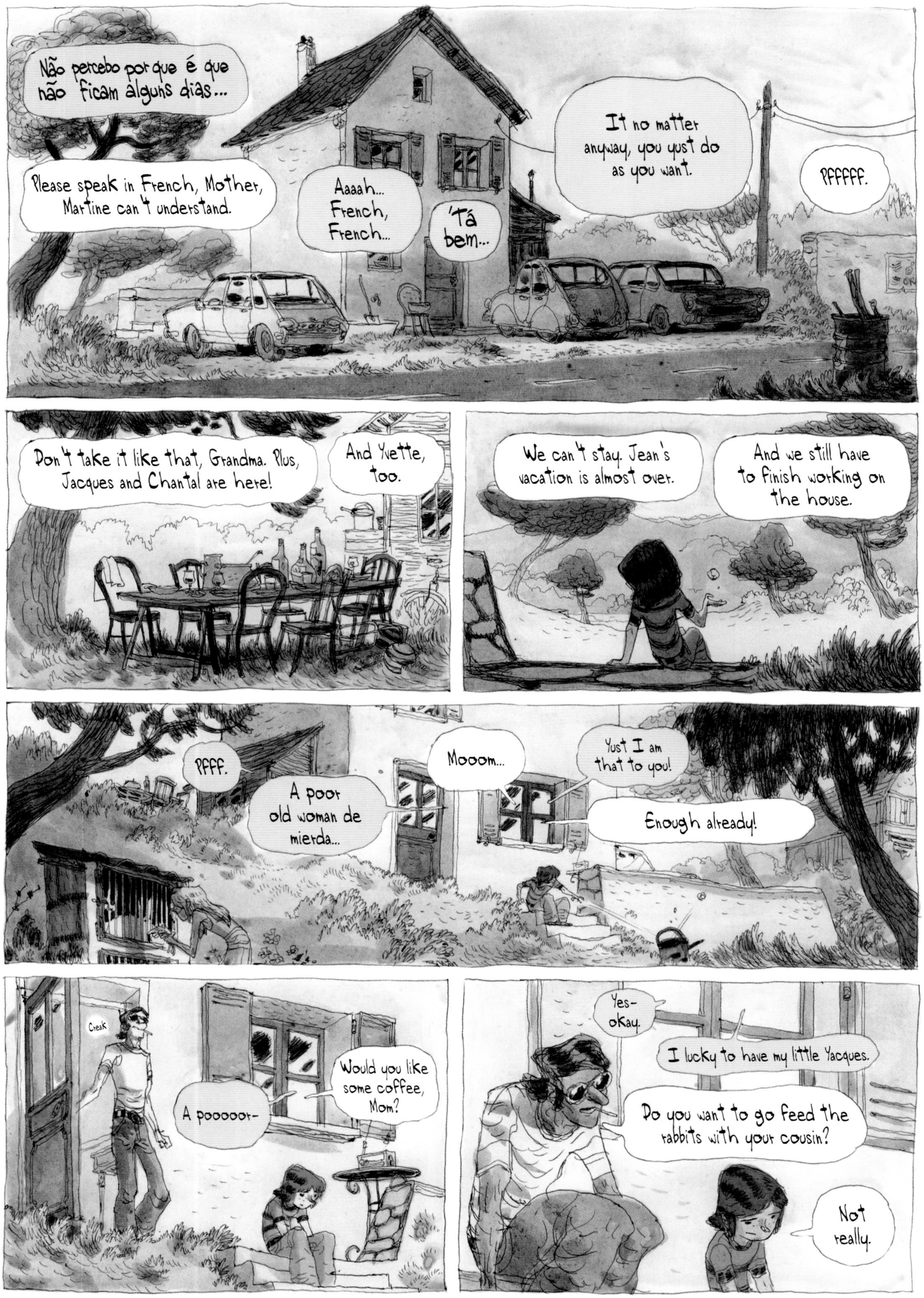

Não percebo por que é que não ficam alguns dias...
Please speak in French, Mother, Martine can't understand.
Aaaah... French, French...
'Tá bem...
It no matter anyway, you yust do as you want.
PFFFFF.
Don't take it like that, Grandma. Plus, Jacques and Chantal are here!
And Yvette, too.
We can't stay. Jean's vacation is almost over.
And we still have to finish working on the house.
PFFF.
A poor old woman de mierda...
Mooom...
Yust I am that to you!
Enough already!
Creak
A poooooor-
Would you like some coffee, Mom?
Yes-okay.
I lucky to have my little Yacques.
Do you want to go feed the rabbits with your cousin?
Not really.

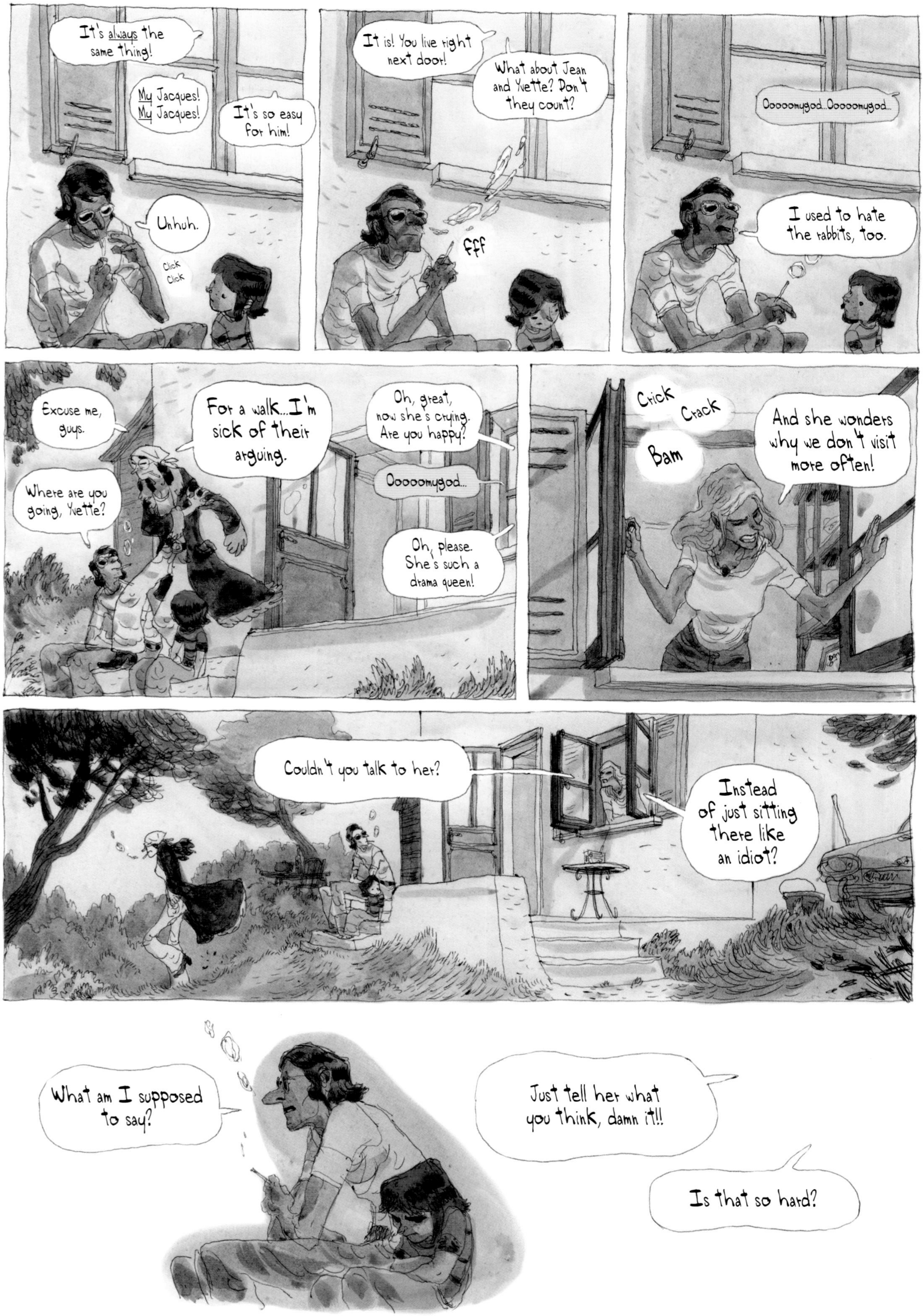
It's always the same thing!
My Jacques! My Jacques!
It's so easy for him!
Unhuh.
Click Click
It is! You live right next door!
What about Jean and Yvette? Don't they count?
fff
Ooooomygod...Ooooomygod...
I used to hate the rabbits, too.
Excuse me, guys.
For a walk...I'm sick of their arguing.
Where are you going, Yvette?
Oh, great, now she's crying. Are you happy?
Ooooomygod...
Oh, please. She's such a drama queen!
Crick
Crack
Bam
And she wonders why we don't visit more often!
Couldn't you talk to her?
Instead of just sitting there like an idiot?
What am I supposed to say?
Just tell her what you think, damn it!!
Is that so hard?

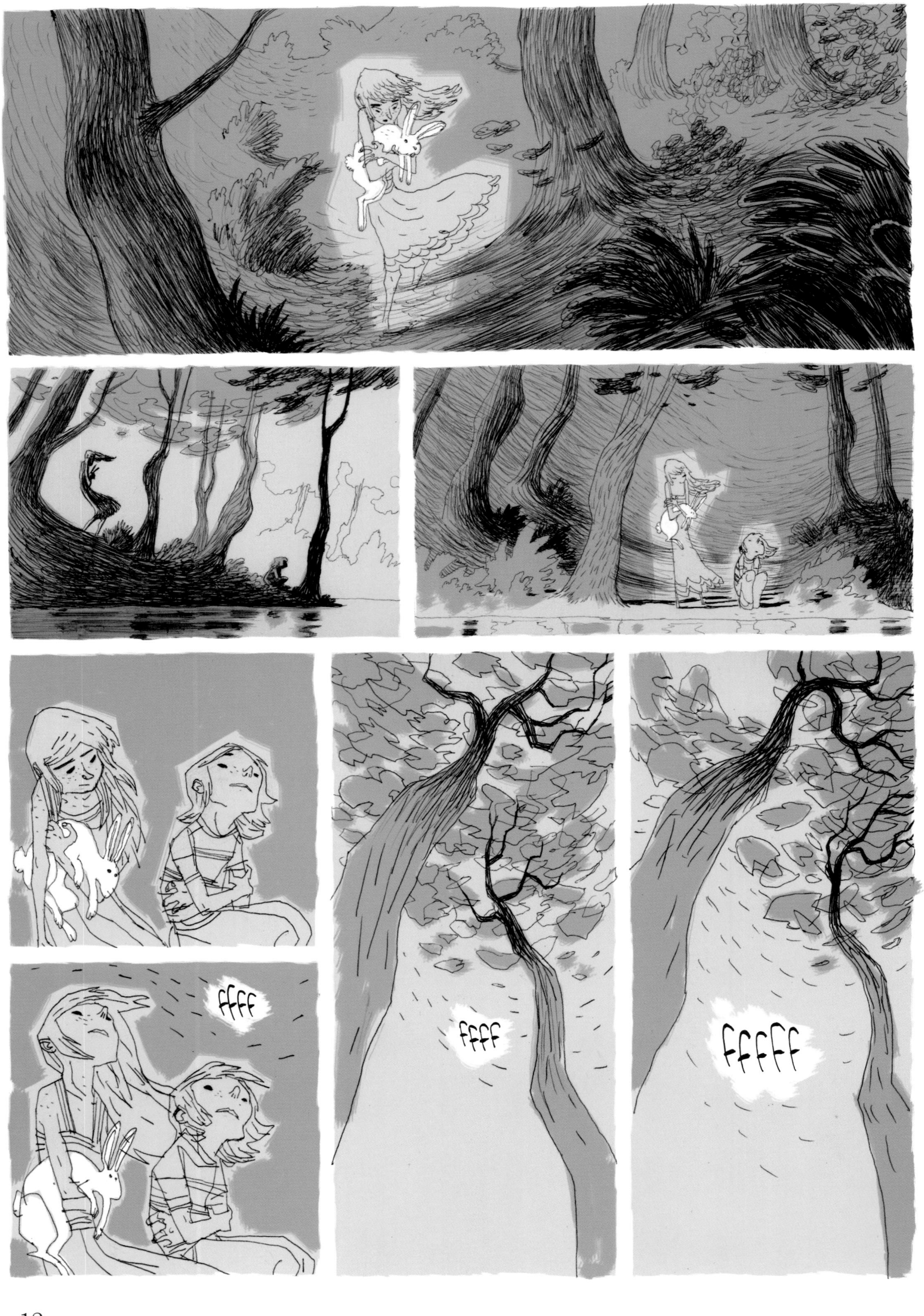
ffff
ffff
fffff

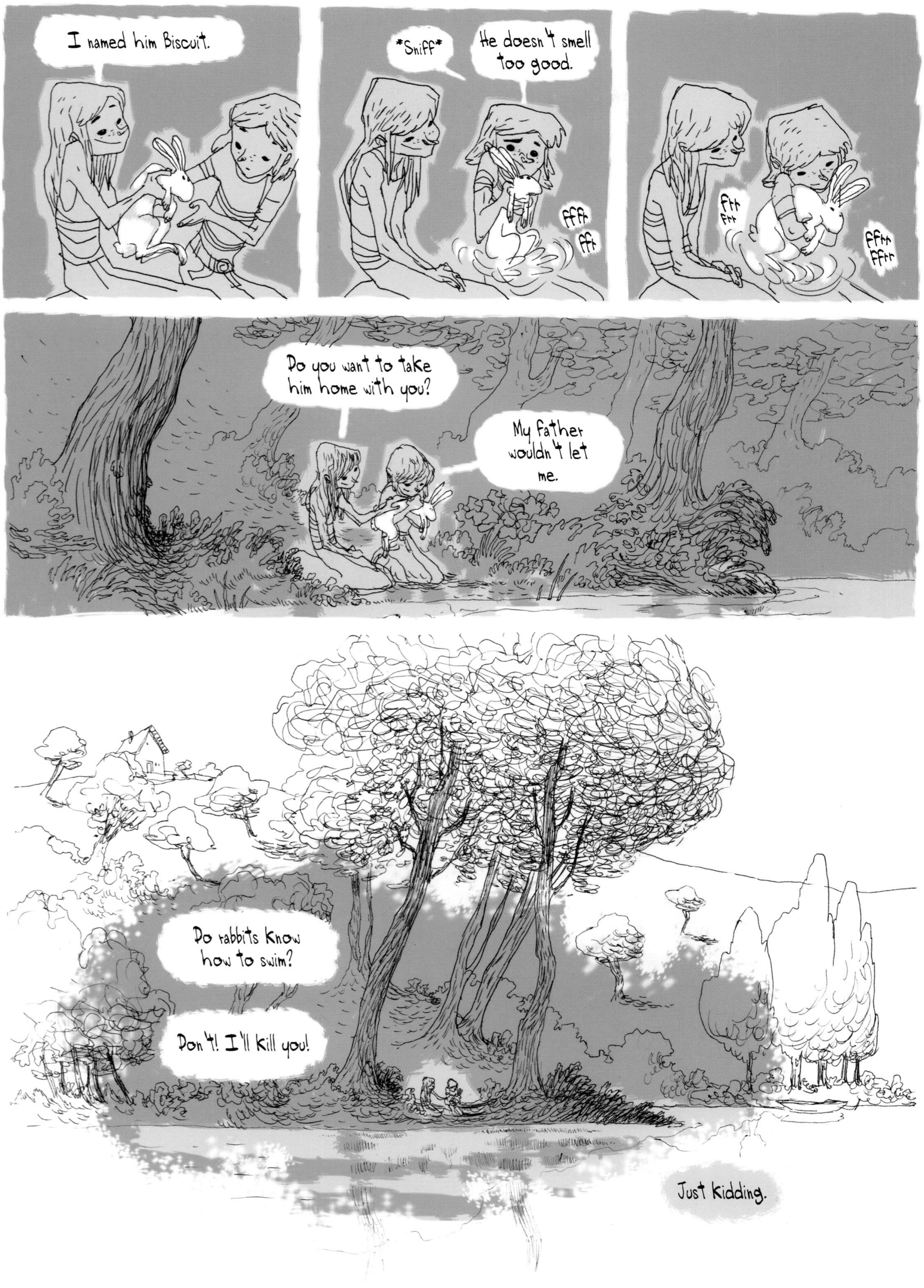
I named him Biscuit.
Sniff
He doesn't smell too good.
ffff
fff
fff
fff
ffff
ffff
Do you want to take him home with you?
My father wouldn't let me.
Do rabbits know how to swim?
Don't! I'll kill you!
Just kidding.

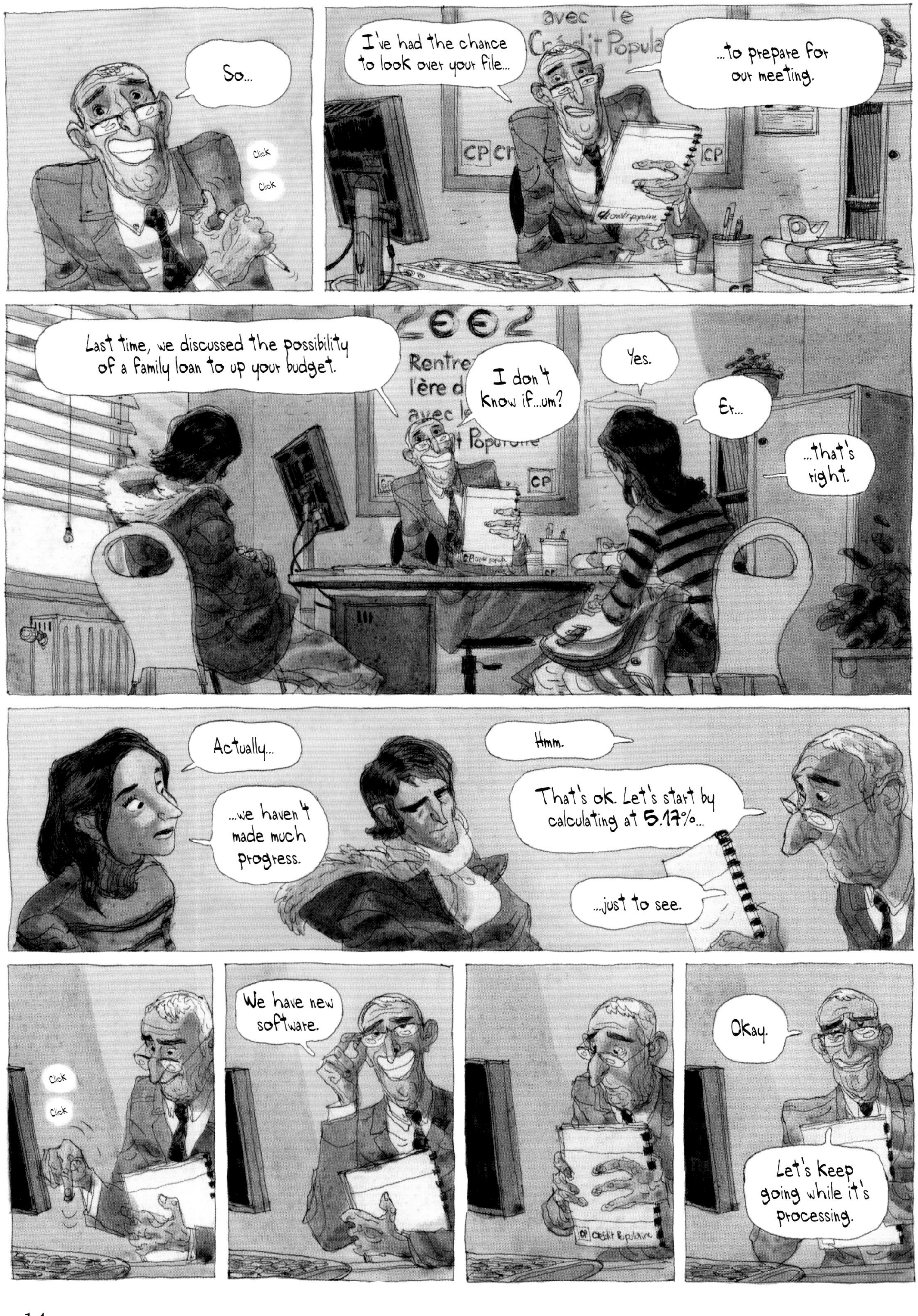
So...
Click
Click
I've had the chance to look over your file...
...to prepare for our meeting.
Last time, we discussed the possibility of a family loan to up your budget.
I don't know if...um?
Yes.
Er...
...that's right.
Actually...
...we haven't made much progress.
Hmm.
That's ok. Let's start by calculating at 5.17%...
...just to see.
Click
Click
We have new software.
Okay.
Let's keep going while it's processing.

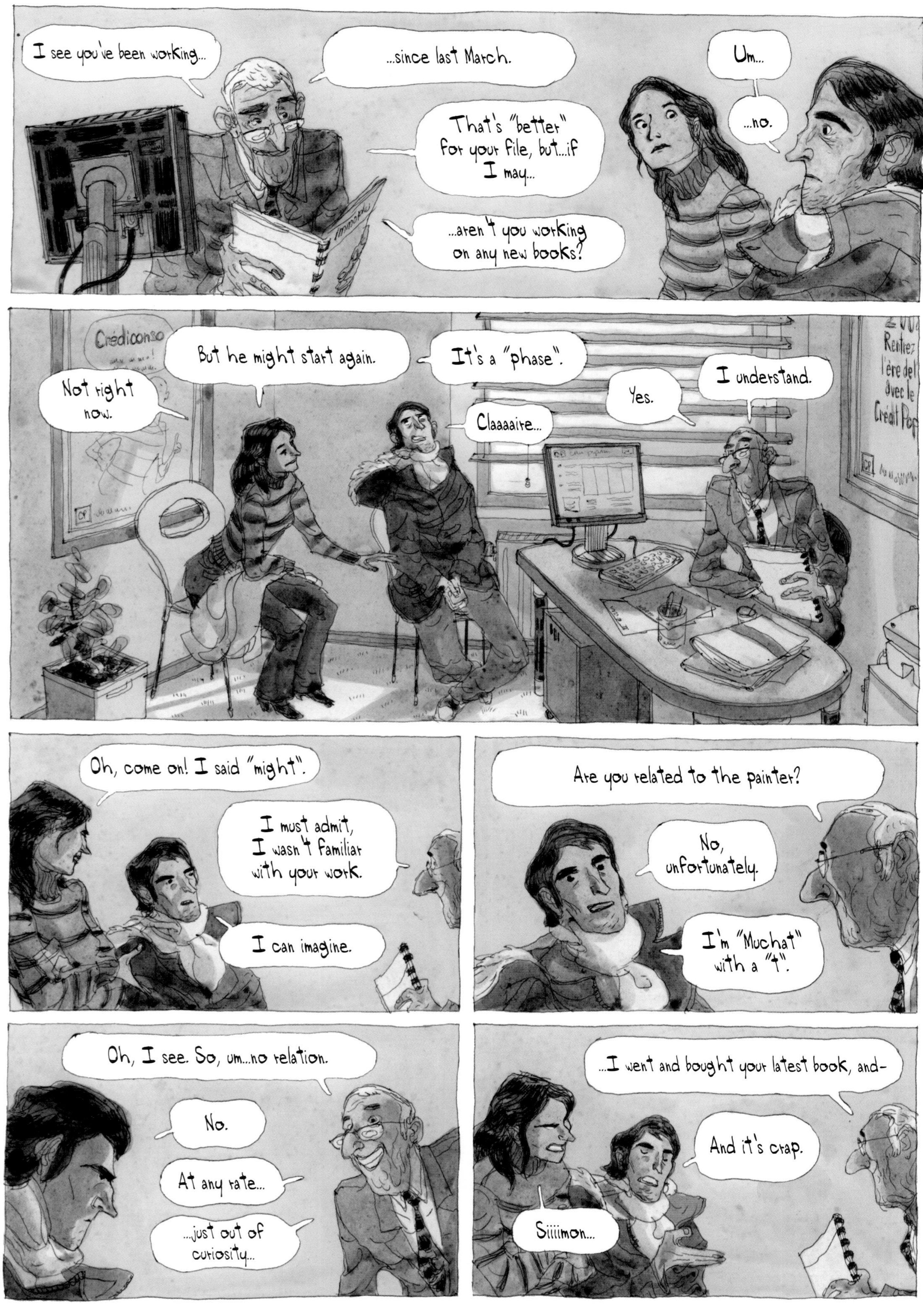
I see you've been working...
...since last March.
That's "better" for your file, but...if I may...
...aren't you working on any new books?
Um...
...no.
Crédiconso
Not right now.
But he might start again.
It's a "phase".
Claaaaire...
Yes.
I understand.
Rentrez l'ère de l' avec le Crédit Pop
Oh, come on! I said "might".
I must admit, I wasn't familiar with your work.
I can imagine.
Are you related to the painter?
No, unfortunately.
I'm "Muchat" with a "t".
Oh, I see. So, um...no relation.
No.
At any rate...
...just out of curiosity...
...I went and bought your latest book, and-
And it's crap.
Siiiimon...

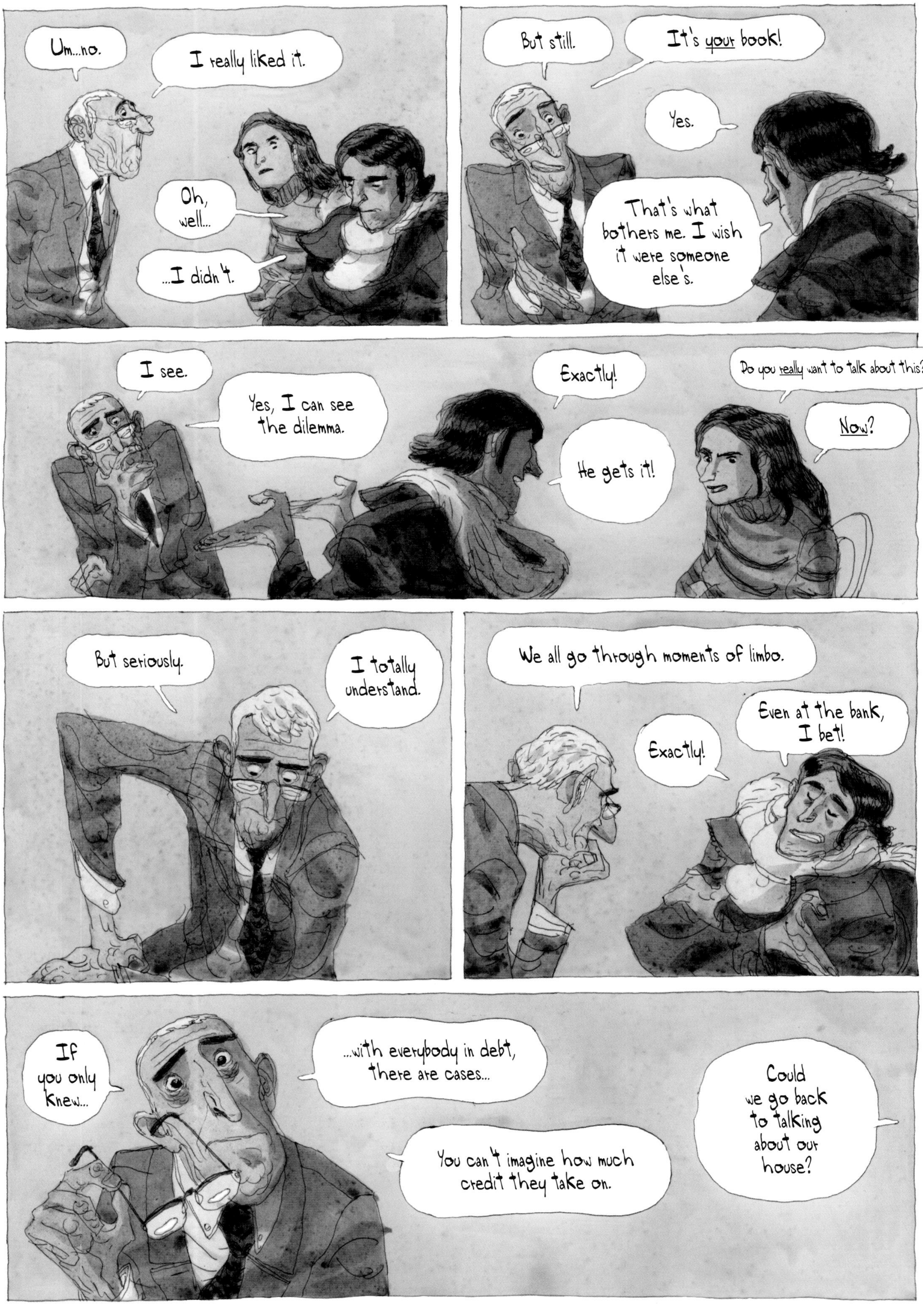
Um...no.
I really liked it.
Oh, well...
...I didn't.
But still.
It's your book!
Yes.
That's what bothers me. I wish it were someone else's.
I see.
Yes, I can see the dilemma.
Exactly!
He gets it!
Do you really want to talk about this?
Now?
But seriously.
I totally understand.
We all go through moments of limbo.
Exactly!
Even at the bank, I bet!
If you only knew...
...with everybody in debt, there are cases...
You can't imagine how much credit they take on.
Could we go back to talking about our house?

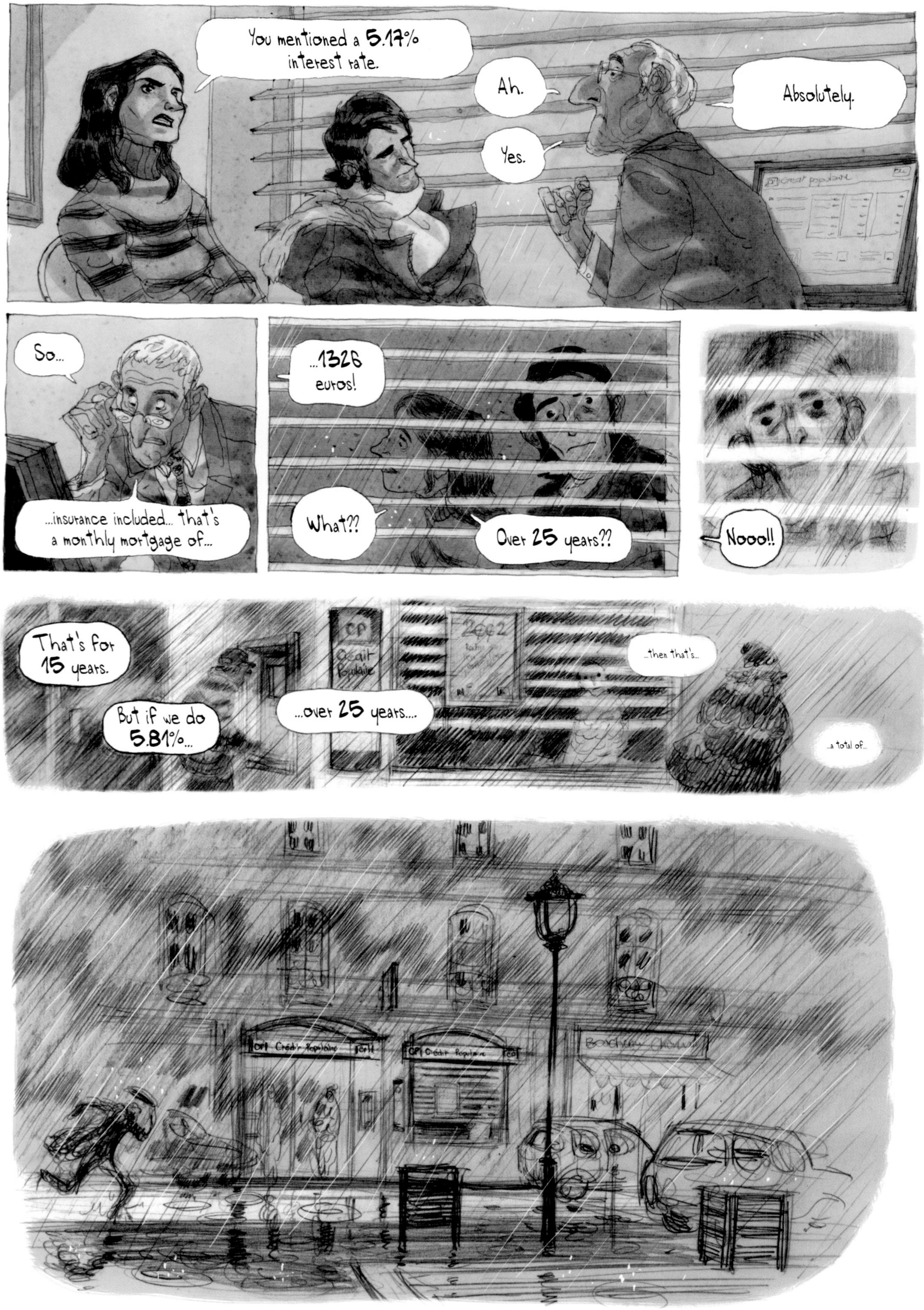
You mentioned a 5.17% interest rate.
Ah.
Yes.
Absolutely.
So...
...insurance included... that's a monthly mortgage of...
...1326 euros!
What??
Over 25 years??
Nooo!!
That's for 15 years.
But if we do 5.81%...
...over 25 years....
...then that's...
...a total of...

What you're doing is pointless.

Excuse me?

What you're doing is pointless.

Sir!

I messed up!

You "messed up"? How?

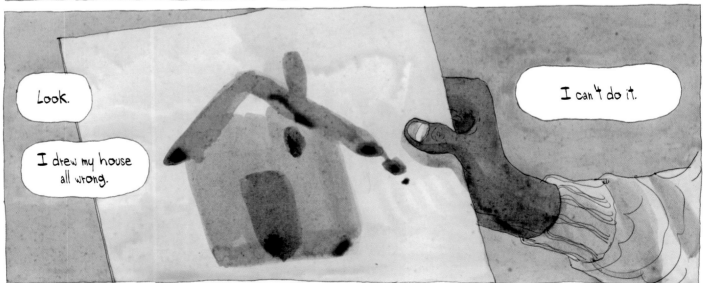

Look.

I drew my house all wrong.

I can't do it.

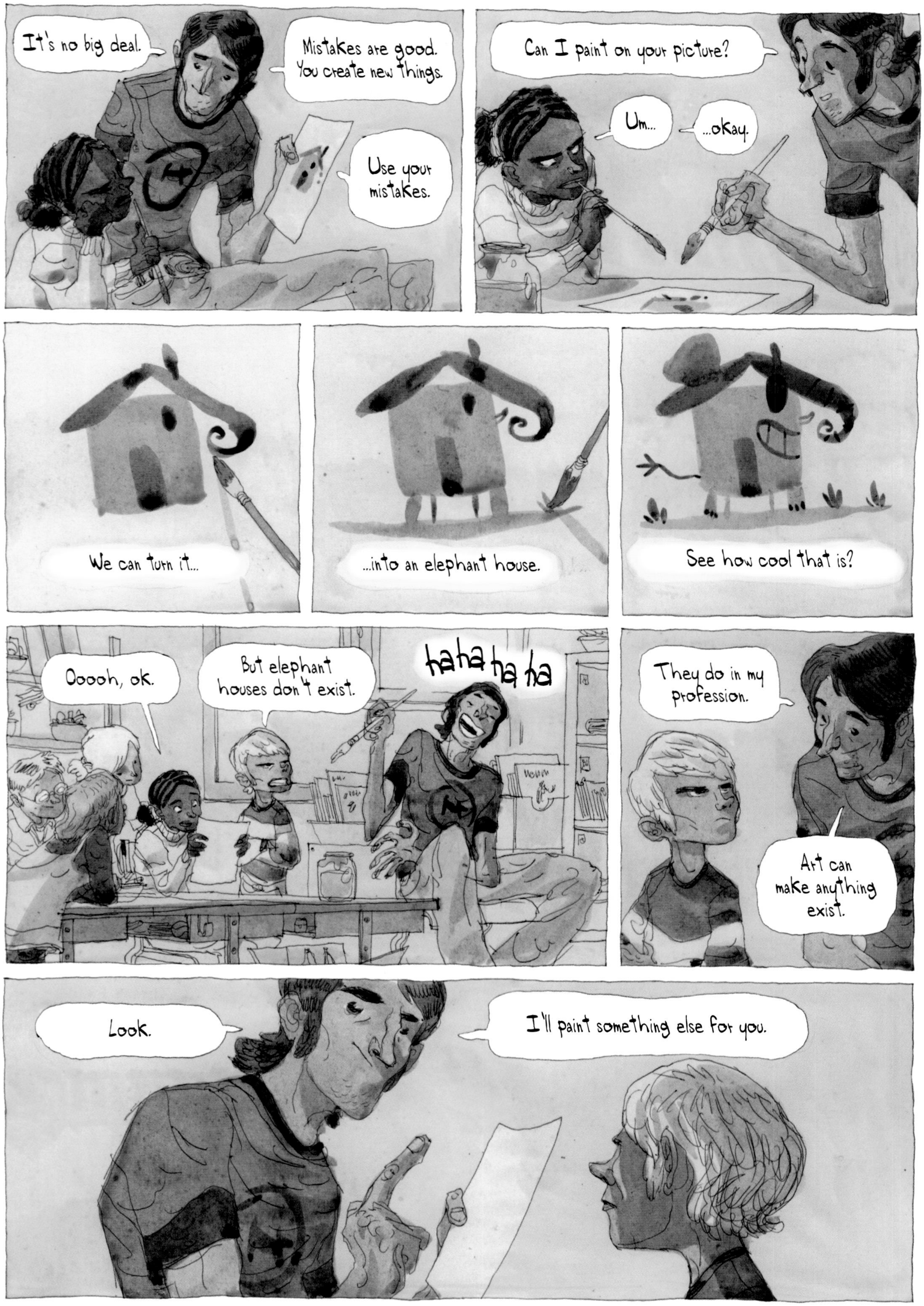
It's no big deal.
Mistakes are good. You create new things.
Use your mistakes.
Can I paint on your picture?
Um...
...okay.
We can turn it...
...into an elephant house.
See how cool that is?
Ooooh, ok.
But elephant houses don't exist.
haha ha ha
They do in my profession.
Art can make anything exist.
Look.
I'll paint something else for you.

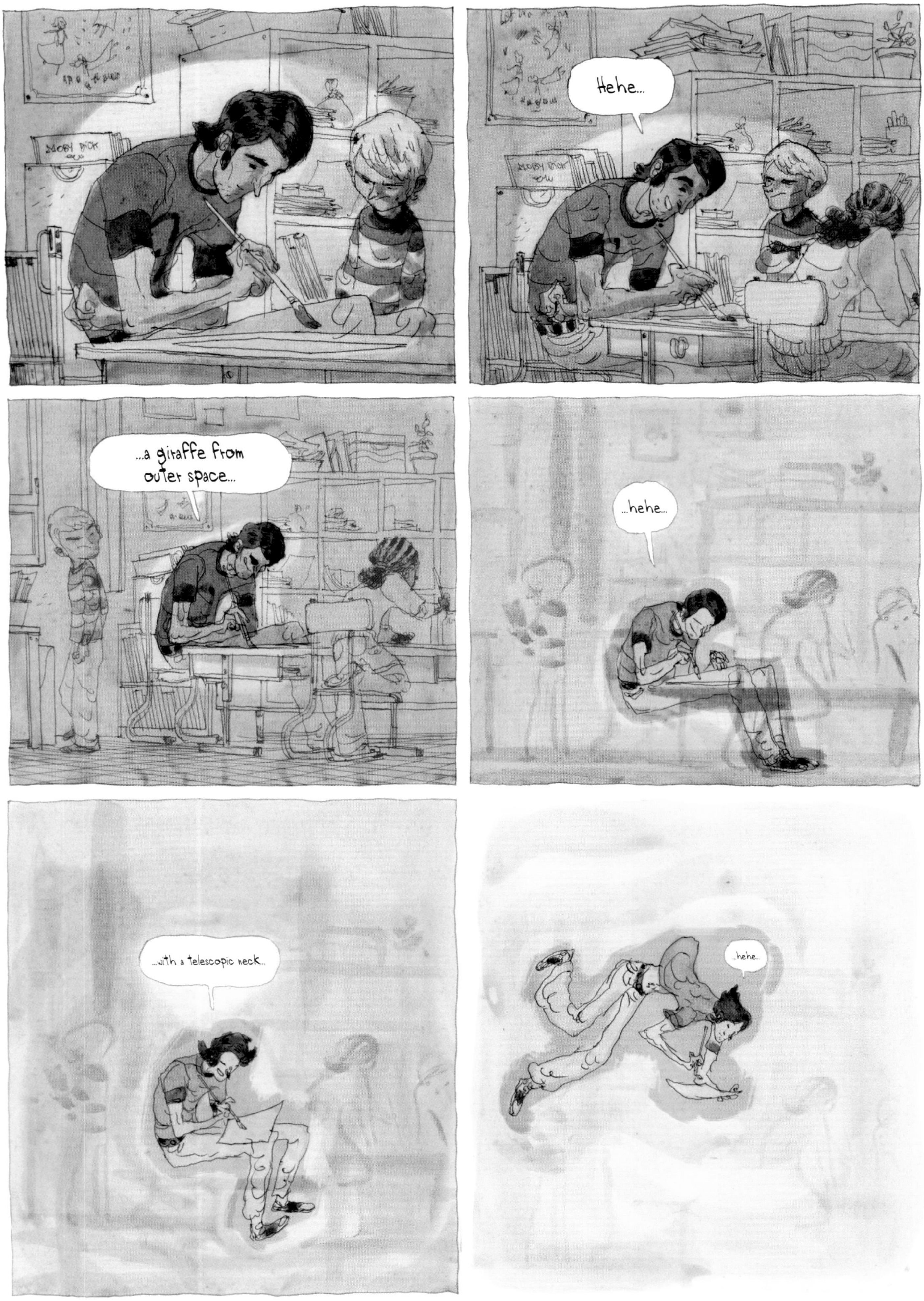
Hehe...
...a giraffe from outer space...
...hehe...
...with a telescopic neck...
...hehe...

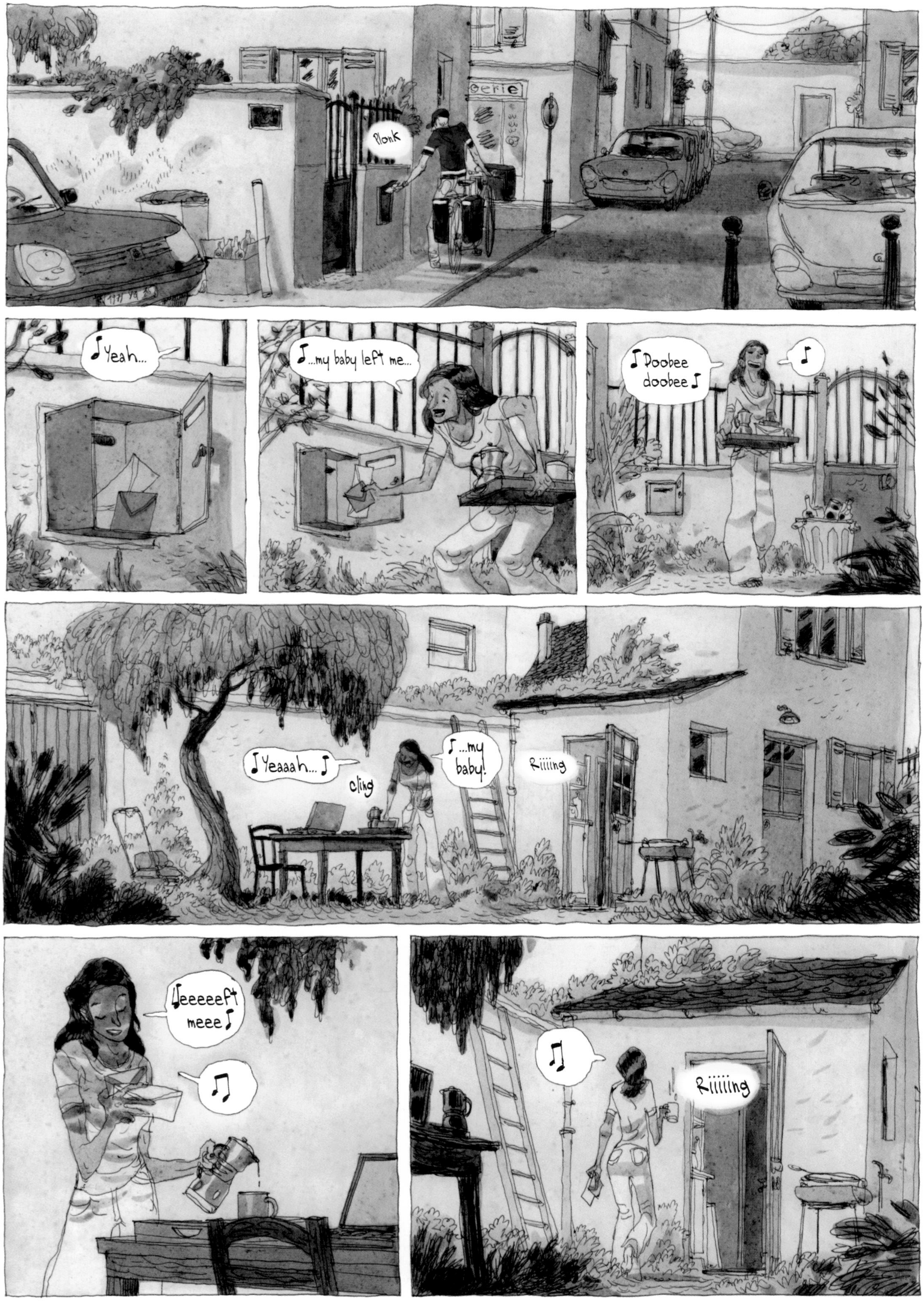
Plonk
Yeah...
...my baby left me...
Doobee doobee
Yeaaah...
cling
...my baby!
Riiiing
Leeeeeft meee
Riiiiing

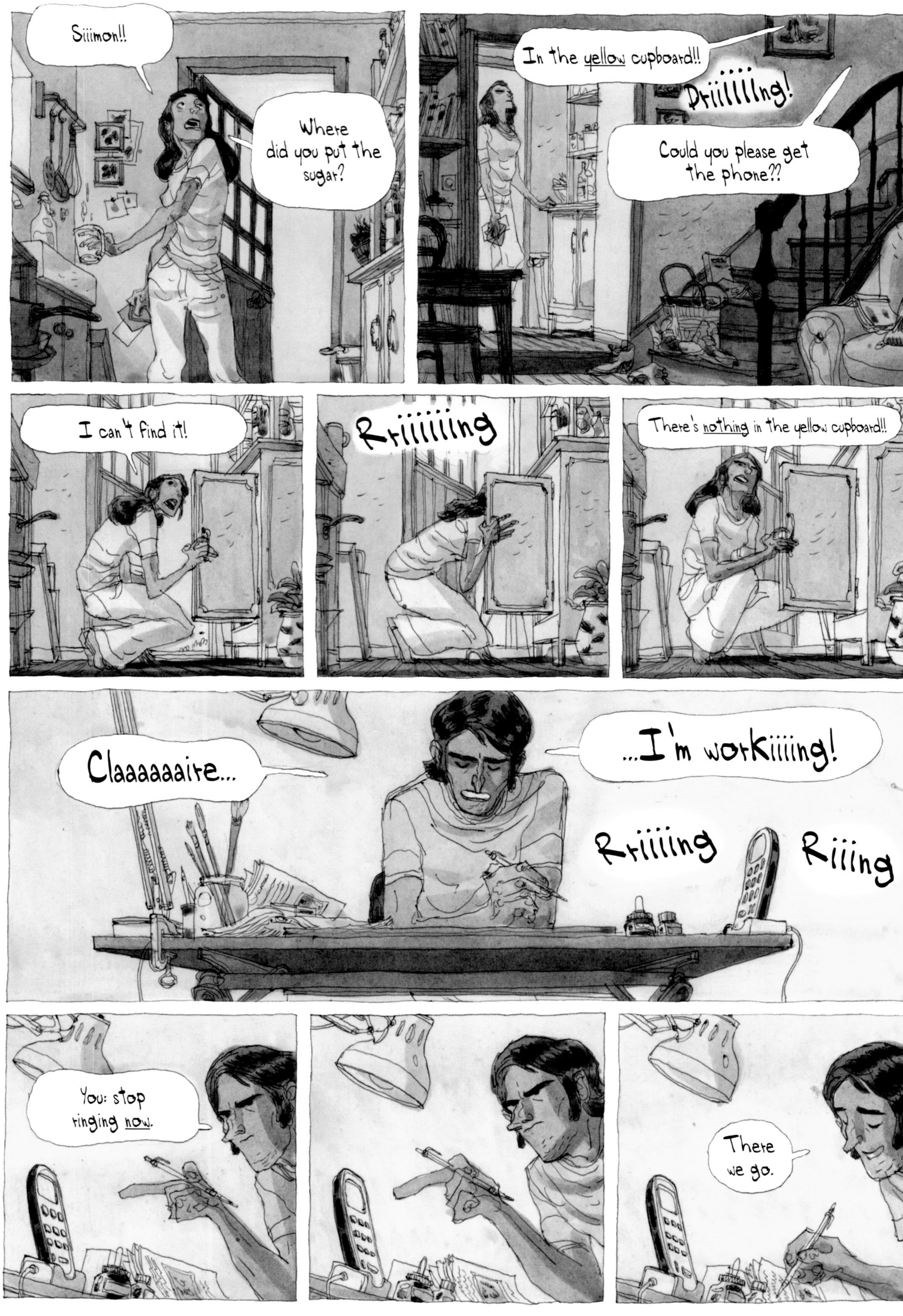
Siiimon!!
Where did you put the sugar?
In the yellow cupboard!!
....
Driilllng!
Could you please get the phone??
I can't find it!
Rriiiiiing
There's nothing in the yellow cupboard!!
Claaaaaaire...
...I'm workiiiing!
Rriiiing
Riiing
You: stop ringing now.
There we go.

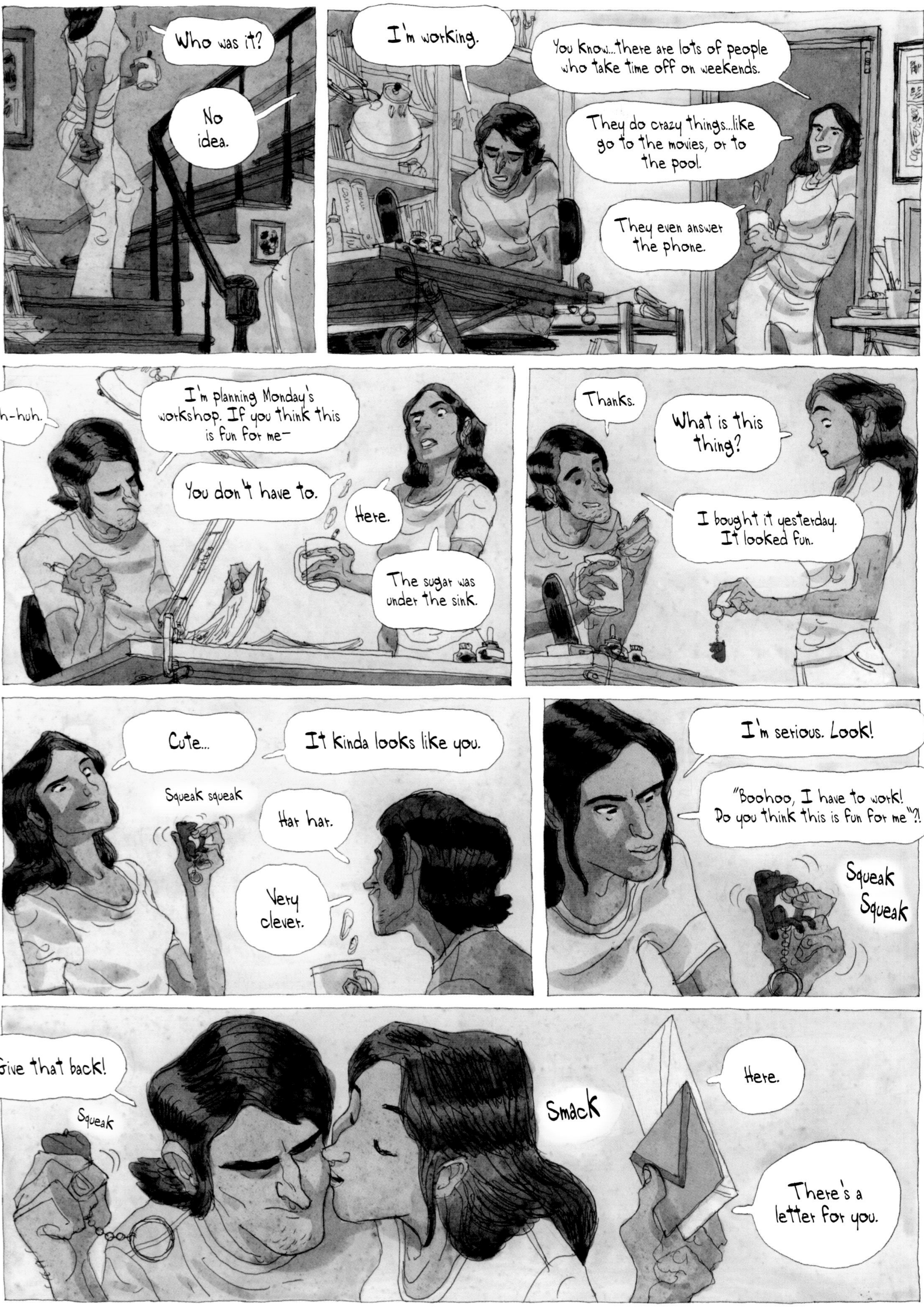
Who was it?
No idea.
I'm working.
You know...there are lots of people who take time off on weekends.
They do crazy things...like go to the movies, or to the pool.
They even answer the phone.
Uh-huh.
I'm planning Monday's workshop. If you think this is fun for me–
You don't have to.
Here.
The sugar was under the sink.
Thanks.
What is this thing?
I bought it yesterday. It looked fun.
Cute...
It kinda looks like you.
Squeak squeak
Har har.
Very clever.
I'm serious. Look!
"Boohoo, I have to work! Do you think this is fun for me"?!
Squeak Squeak
Give that back!
Squeak
Smack
Here.
There's a letter for you.

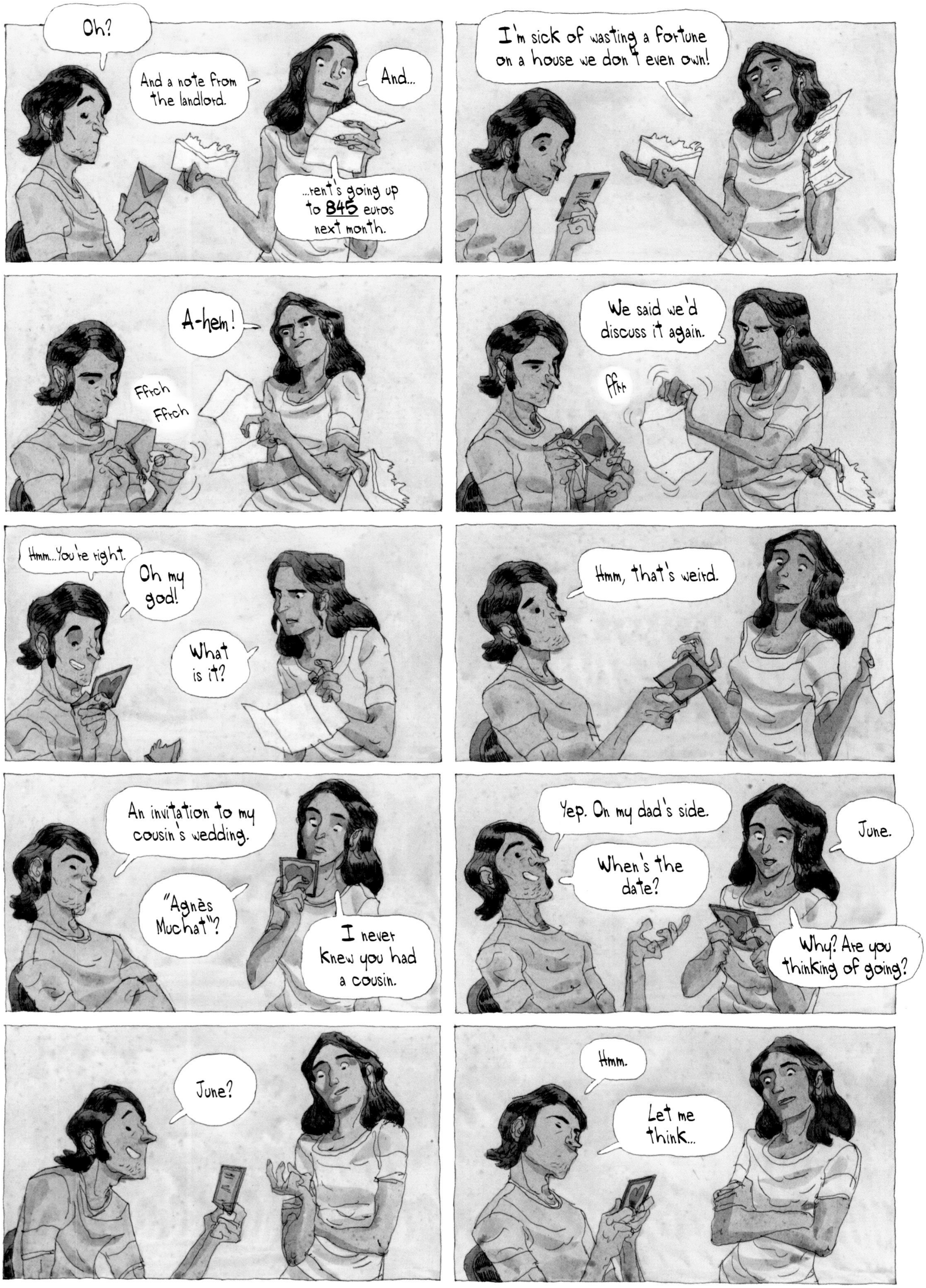
Oh?
And a note from the landlord.
And...
...rent's going up to 845 euros next month.
I'm sick of wasting a fortune on a house we don't even own!
A-hem!
Ffrch
Ffrch
We said we'd discuss it again.
ffrr
Hmm... You're right.
Oh my god!
What is it?
Hmm, that's weird.
An invitation to my cousin's wedding.
"Agnès Muchat"?
I never knew you had a cousin.
Yep. On my dad's side.
When's the date?
June.
Why? Are you thinking of going?
June?
Hmm.
Let me think...

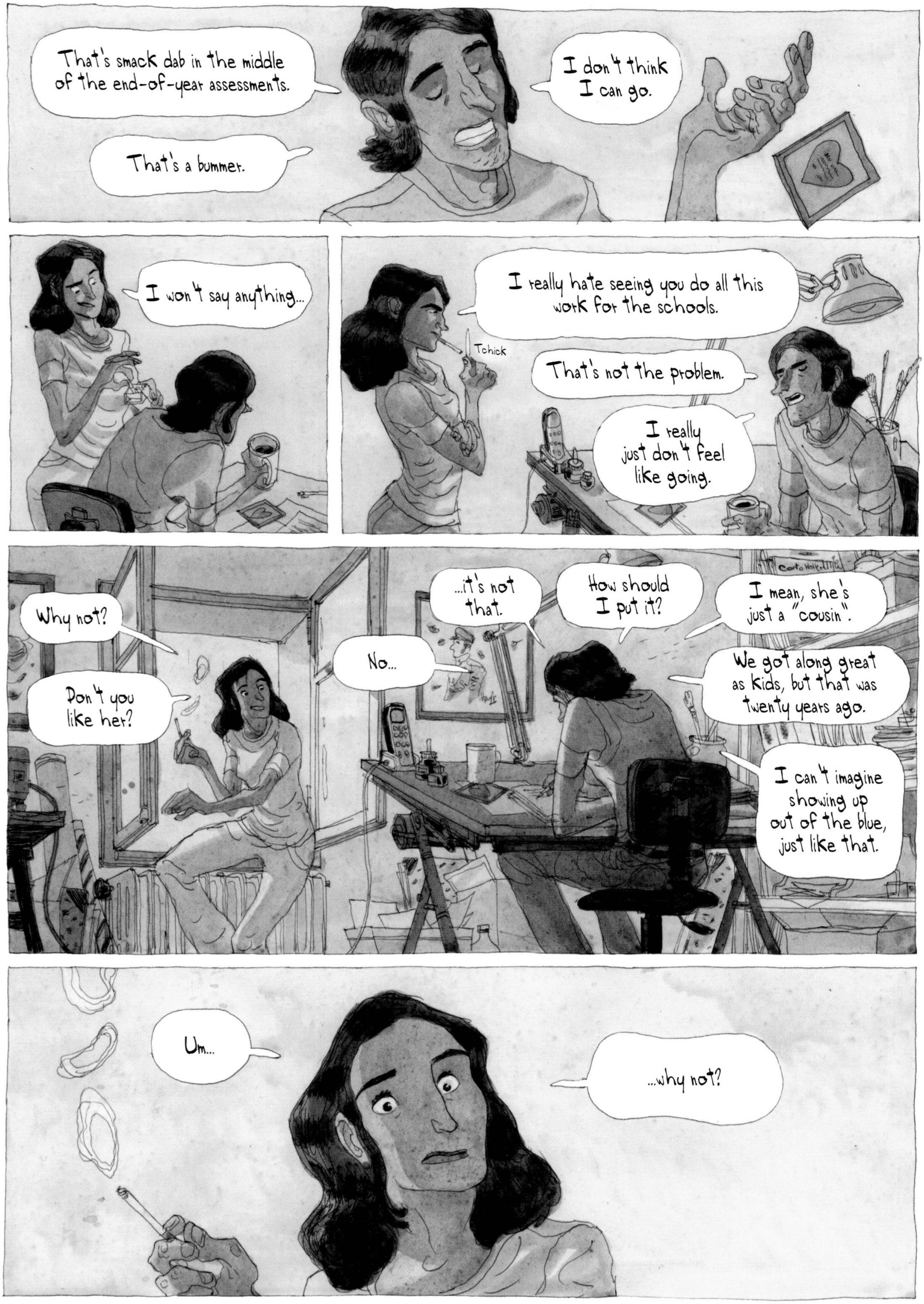
That's smack dab in the middle of the end-of-year assessments.
I don't think I can go.
That's a bummer.
I won't say anything...
I really hate seeing you do all this work for the schools.
Tchick
That's not the problem.
I really just don't feel like going.
Why not?
Don't you like her?
No...
...it's not that.
How should I put it?
I mean, she's just a "cousin".
We got along great as kids, but that was twenty years ago.
I can't imagine showing up out of the blue, just like that.
Um...
...why not?

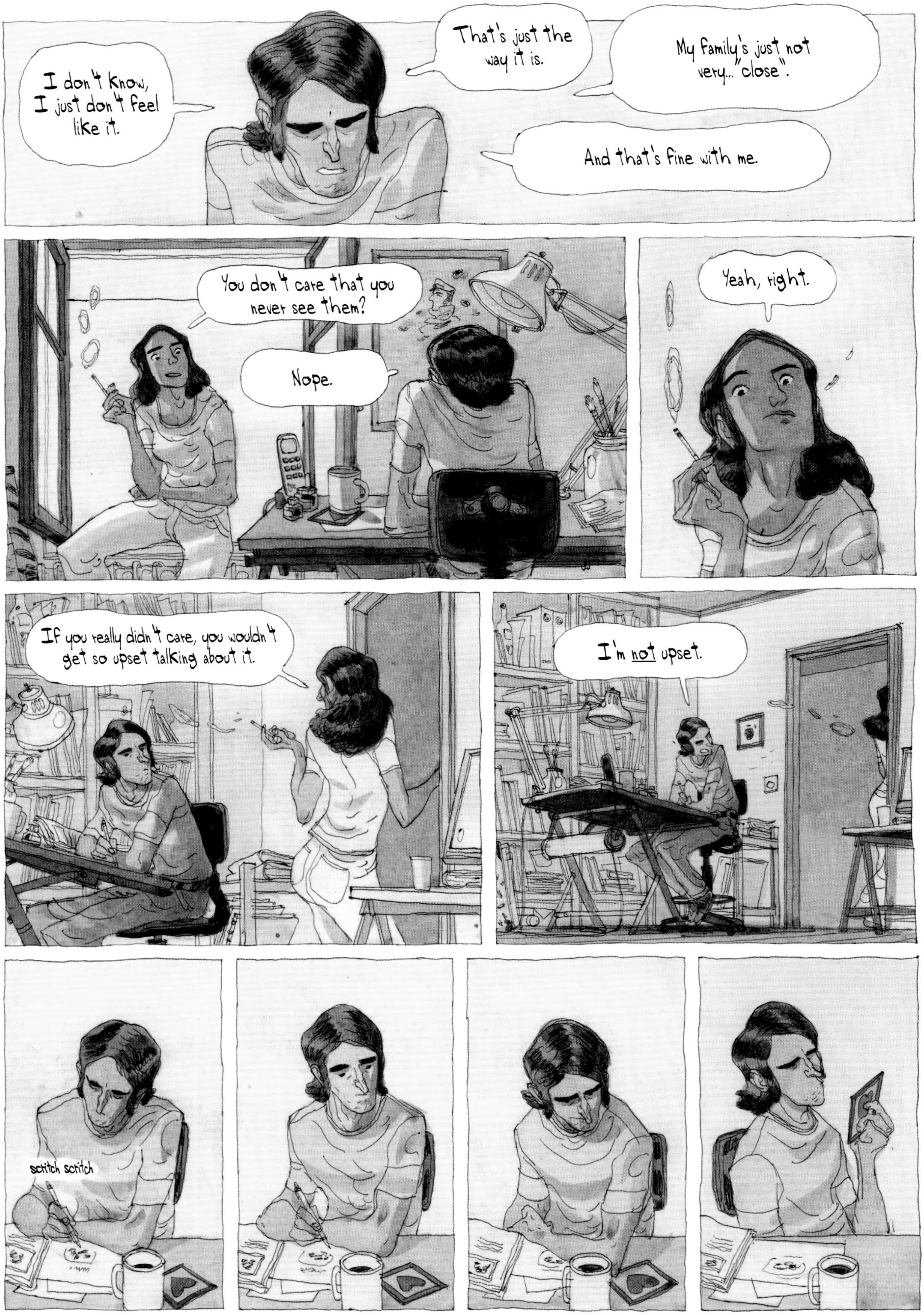
I don't know, I just don't feel like it.
That's just the way it is.
My family's just not very... "close".
And that's fine with me.
You don't care that you never see them?
Nope.
Yeah, right.
If you really didn't care, you wouldn't get so upset talking about it.
I'm not upset.
scritch scritch

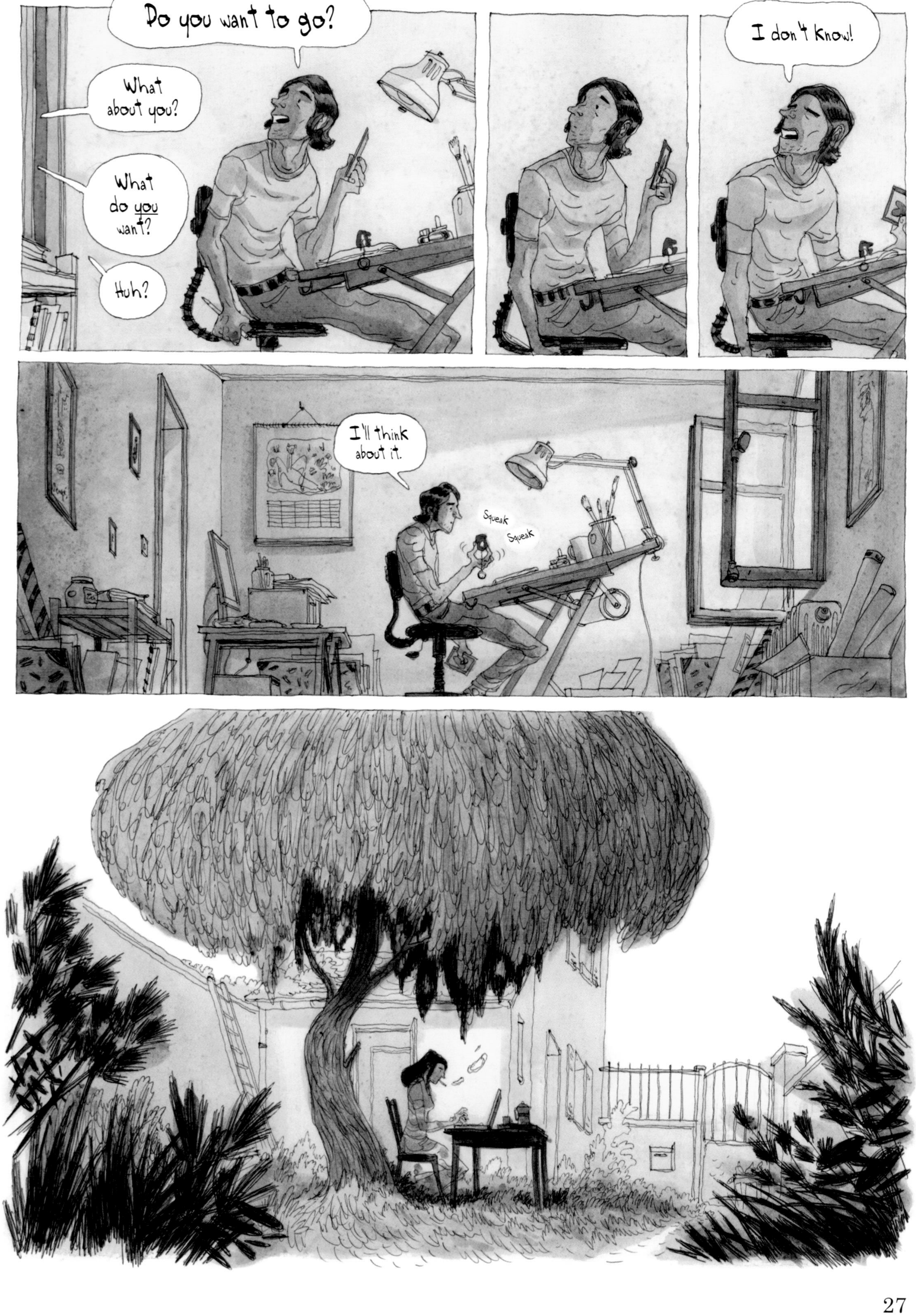

Do you want to go?
What about you?
What do you want?
Huh?
I don't know!
I'll think about it.
Squeak
Squeak

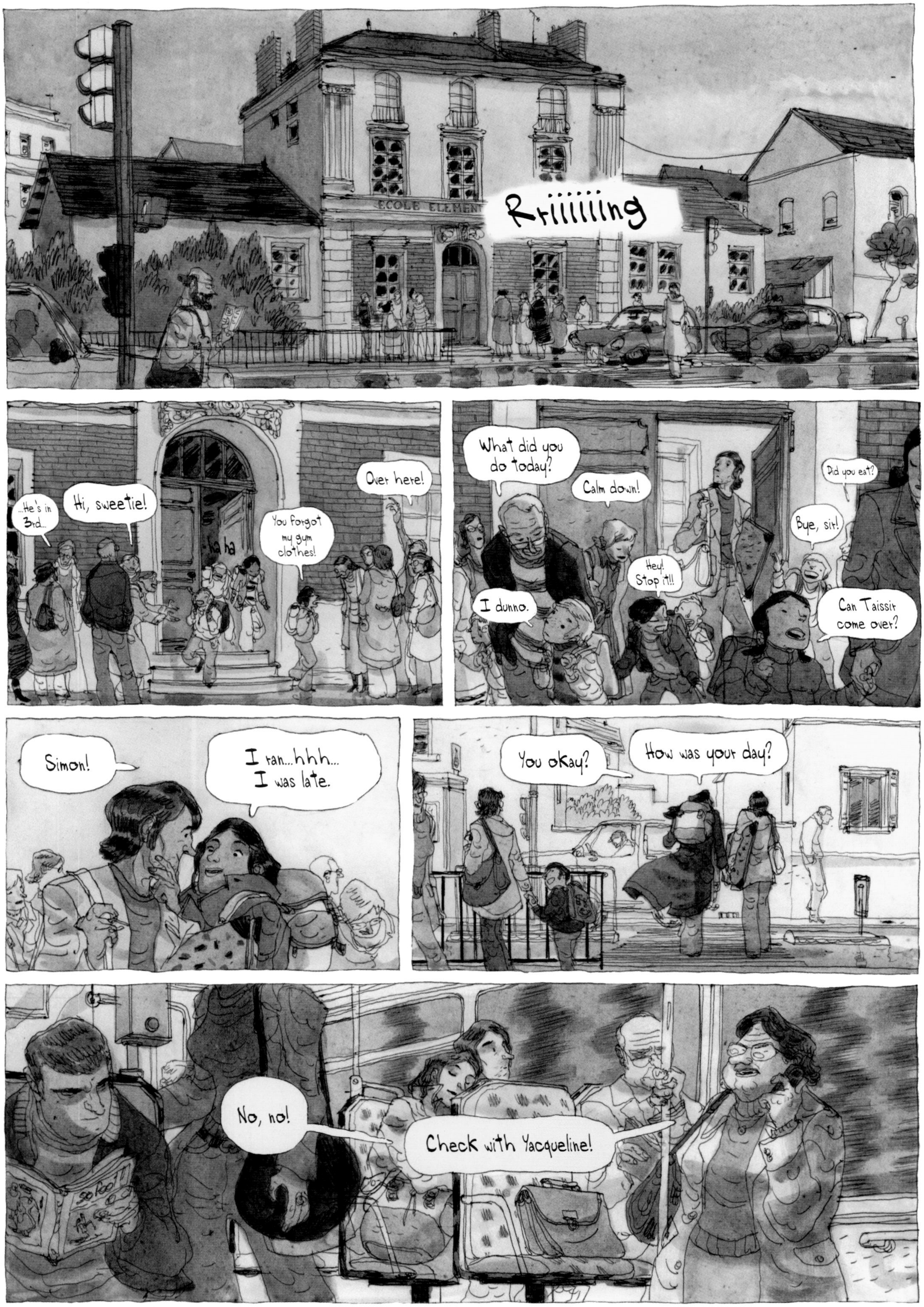
ECOLE ELEMEN
Rriiiiiiing
...He's in 3rd...
Hi, sweetie!
ha ha
You forgot my gym clothes!
Over here!
What did you do today?
Calm down!
Did you eat?
Bye, sir!
Hey! Stop it!!
I dunno.
Can Taissir come over?
Simon!
I ran...hhh... I was late.
You okay?
How was your day?
No, no!
Check with Yacqueline!

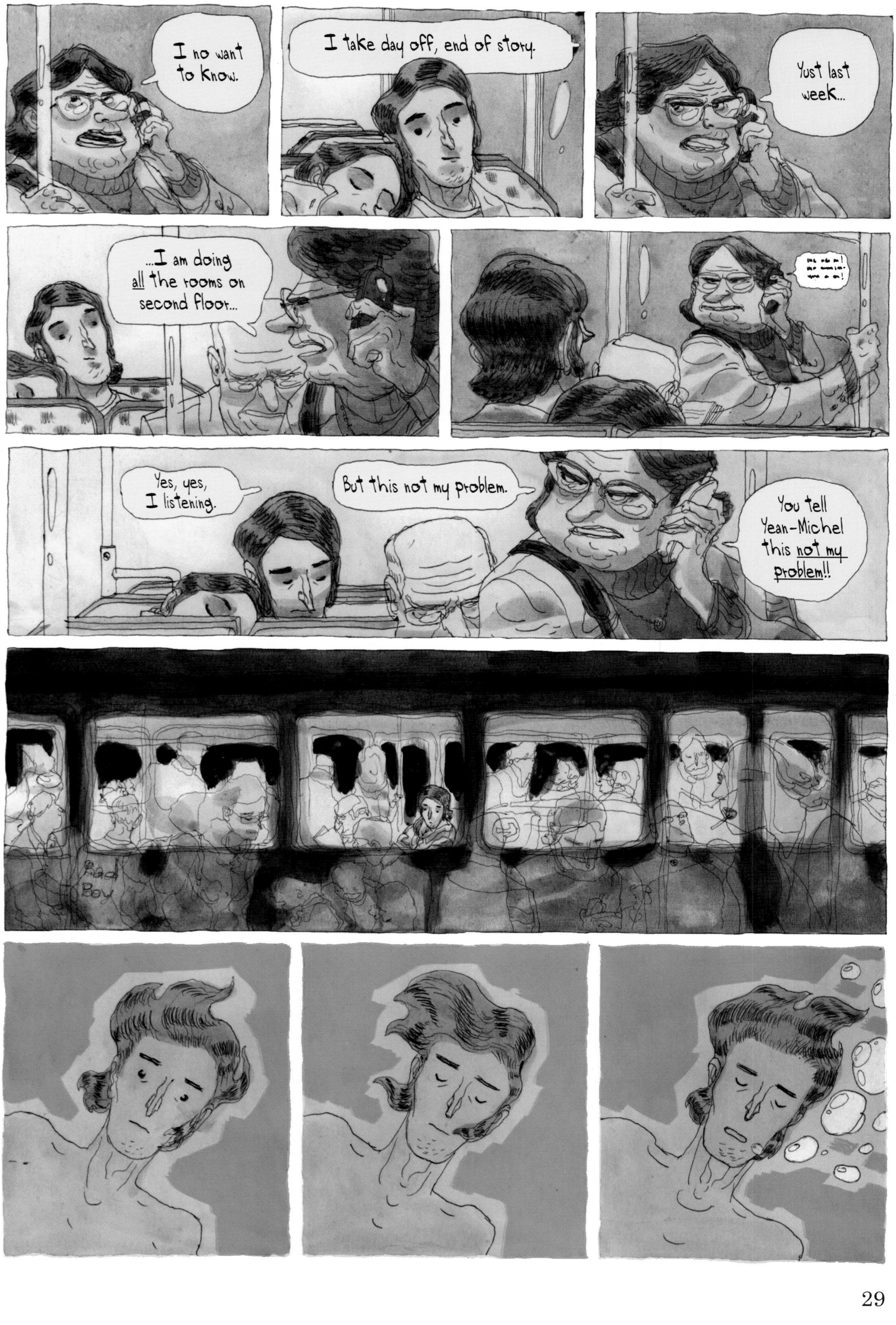
I no want to know.
I take day off, end of story.
Yust last week...
...I am doing all the rooms on second floor...
Yes, yes, I listening.
But this not my problem.
You tell Yean-Michel this not my problem!!
Bad Boy

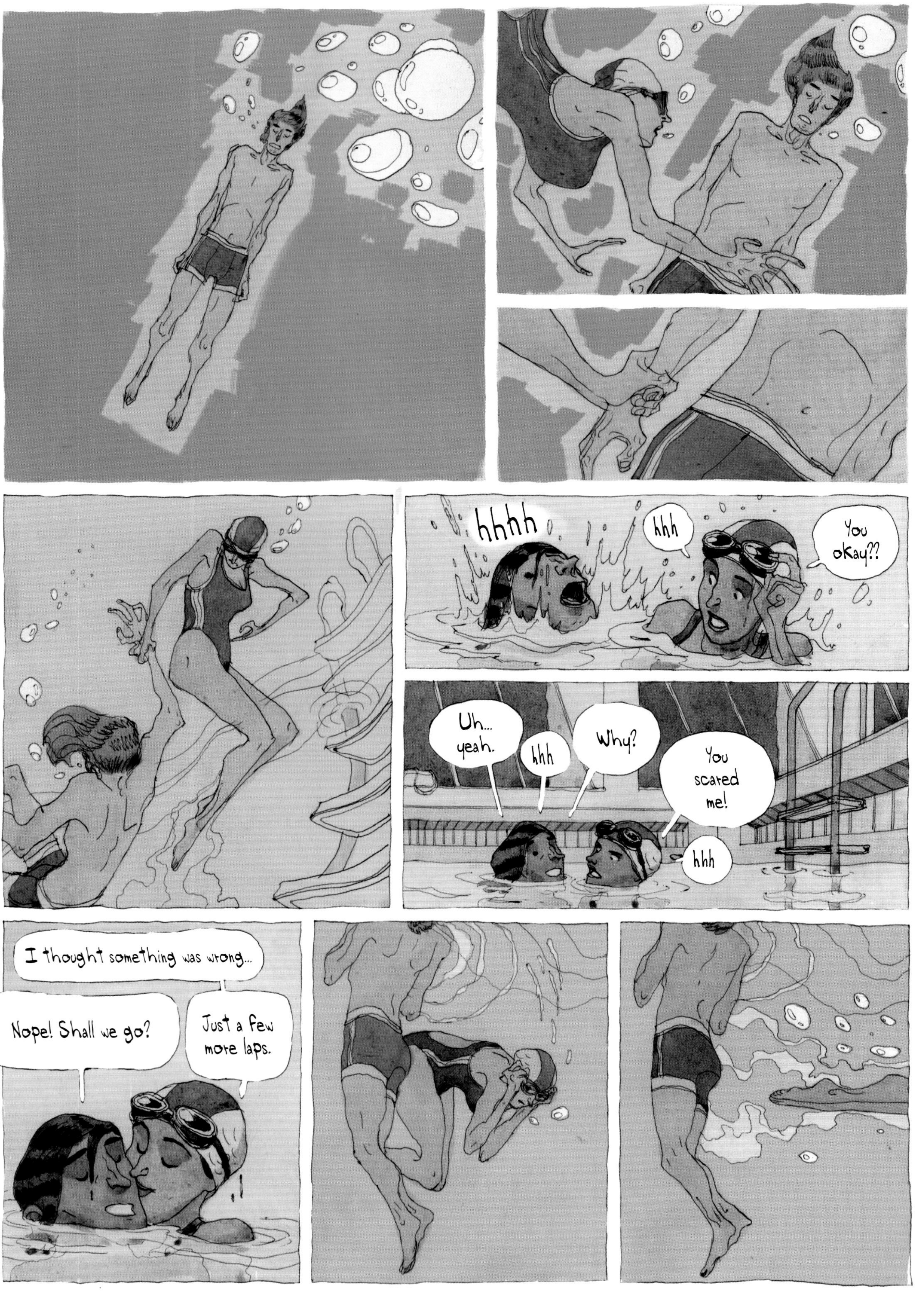
hhhh
hhh
You okay??
Uh... yeah.
hhh
Why?
You scared me!
hhh
I thought something was wrong...
Nope! Shall we go?
Just a few more laps.

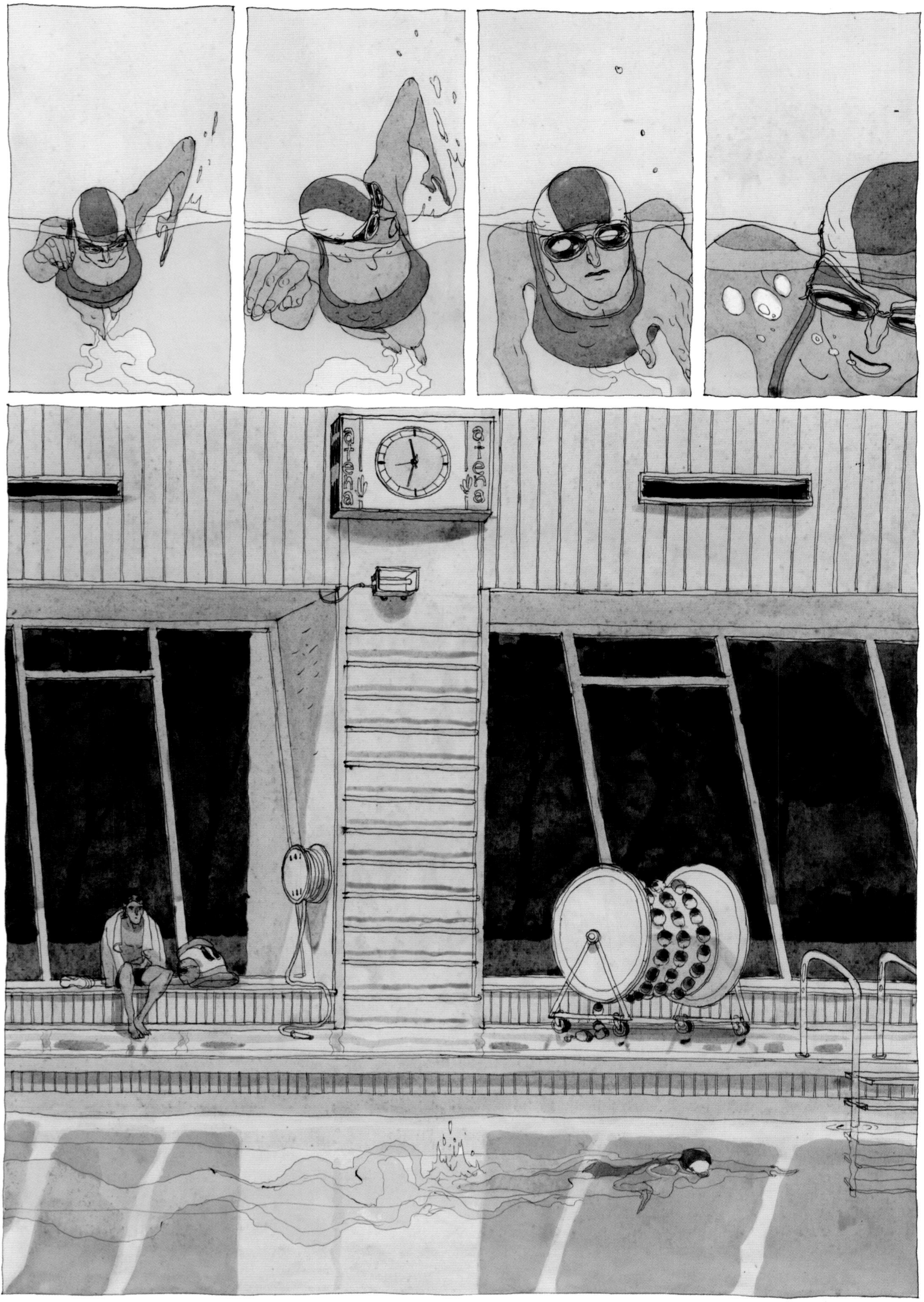
atena
atena

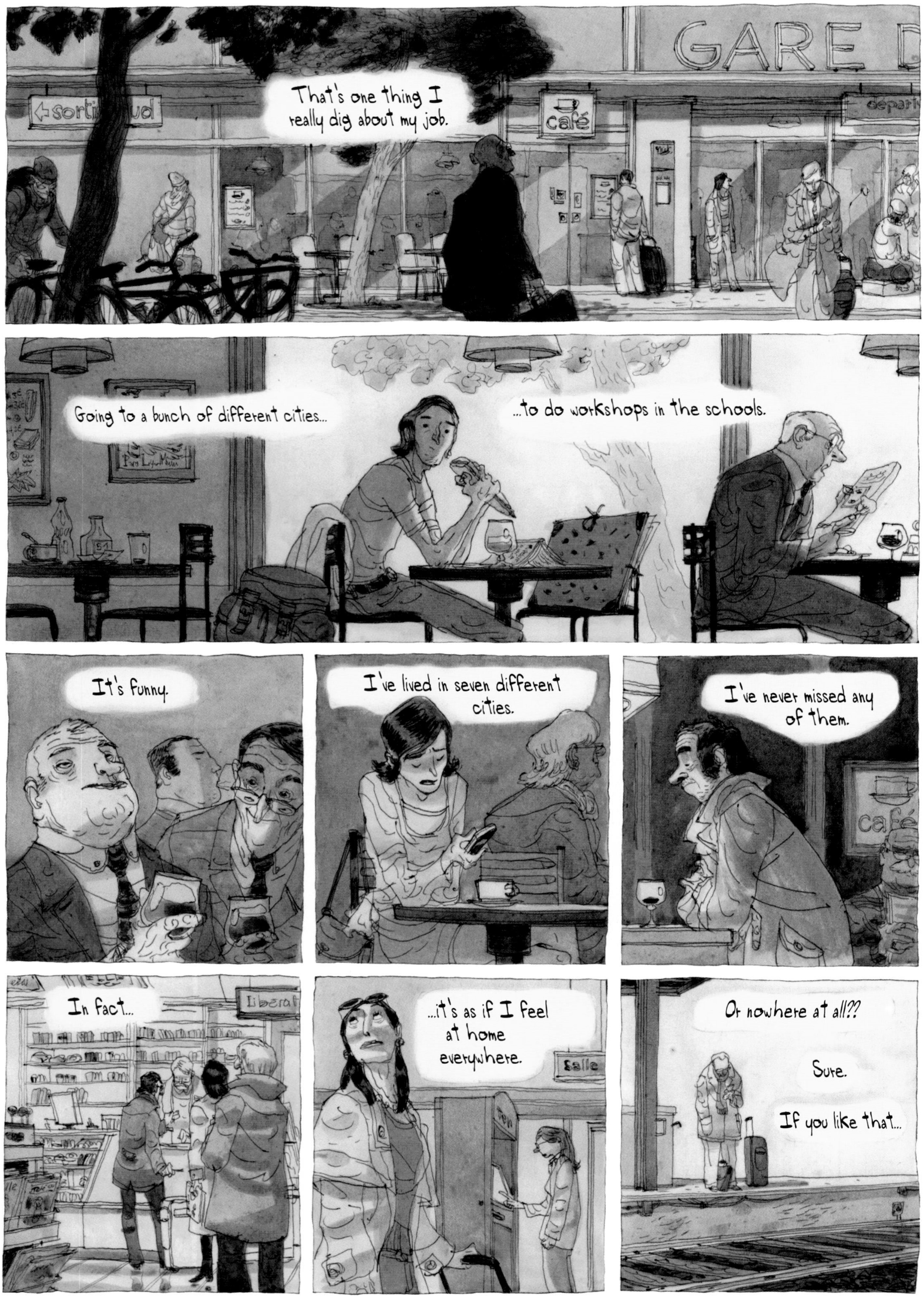
GARE D
sortie sud
café
That's one thing I really dig about my job.
Going to a bunch of different cities...
...to do workshops in the schools.
It's funny.
I've lived in seven different cities.
I've never missed any of them.
café
In fact...
Liberat
...it's as if I feel at home everywhere.
Salle
Or nowhere at all??
Sure.
If you like that...

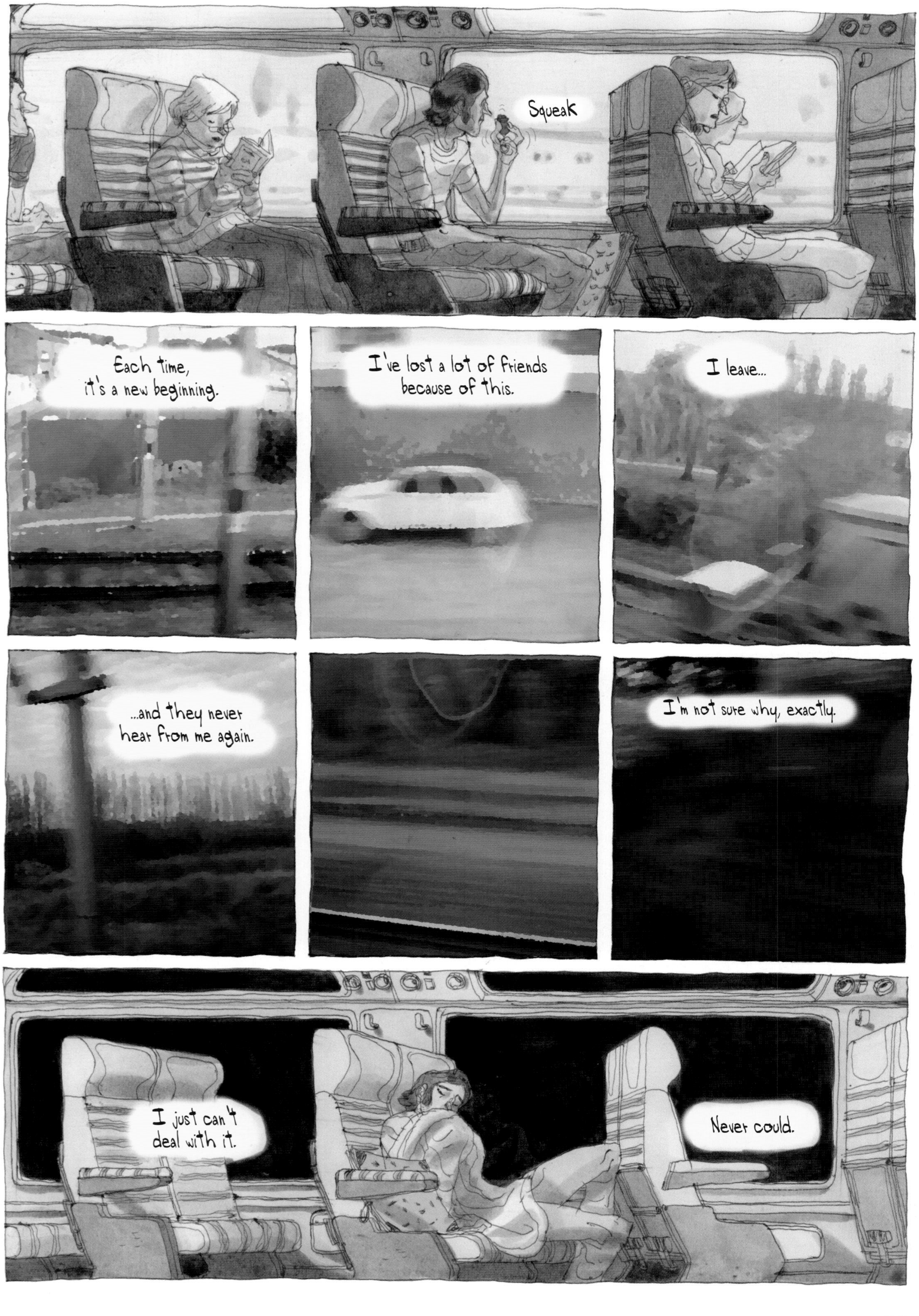
Squeak
Each time, it's a new beginning.
I've lost a lot of friends because of this.
I leave...
...and they never hear from me again.
I'm not sure why, exactly.
I just can't deal with it.
Never could.

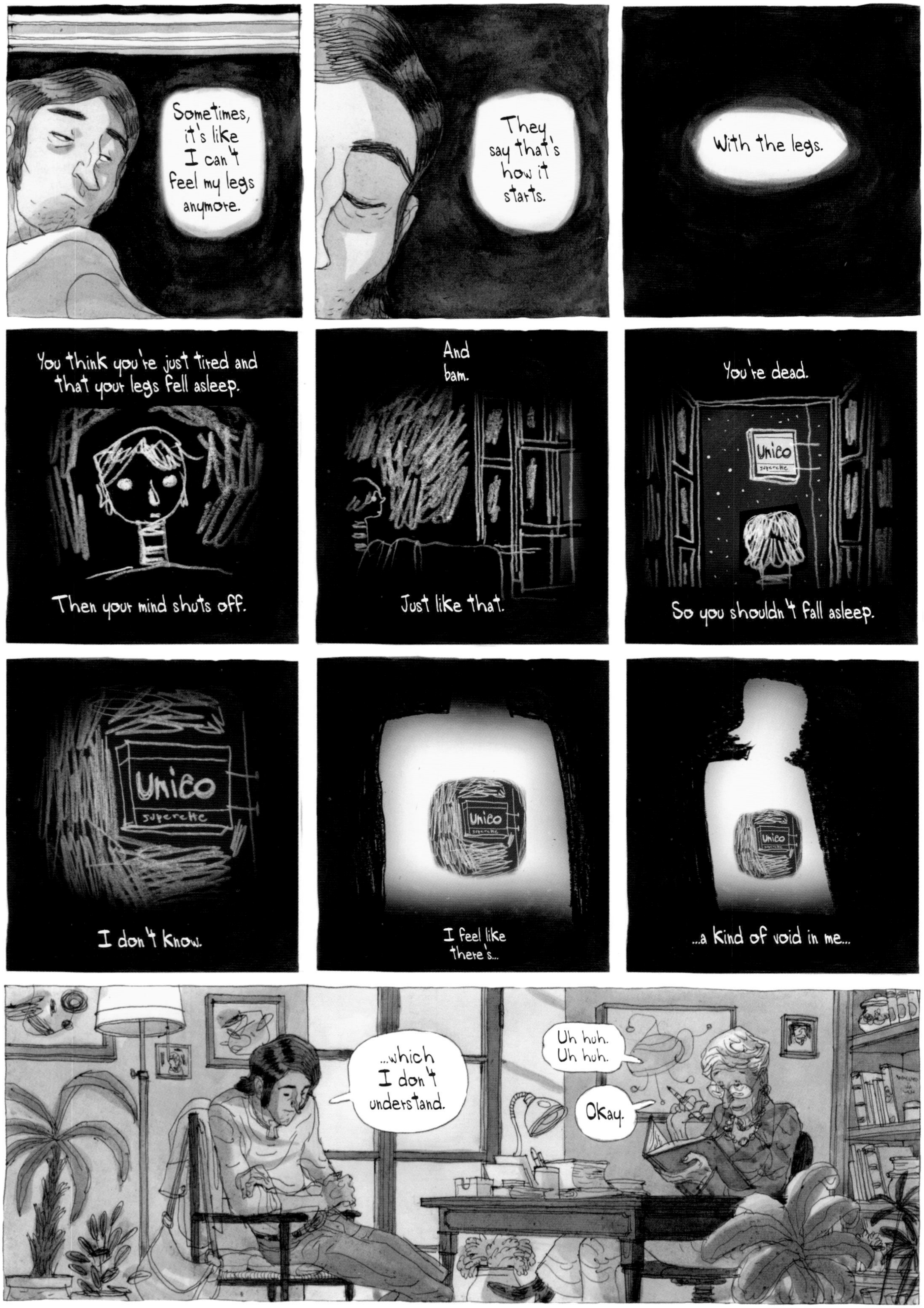
Sometimes, it's like I can't feel my legs anymore.
They say that's how it starts.
With the legs.
You think you're just tired and that your legs fell asleep.
Then your mind shuts off.
And bam.
Just like that.
You're dead.
Unico superette
So you shouldn't fall asleep.
Unico superette
I don't know.
Unico
I feel like there's...
Unico
...a kind of void in me...
...which I don't understand.
Uh huh. Uh huh.
Okay.

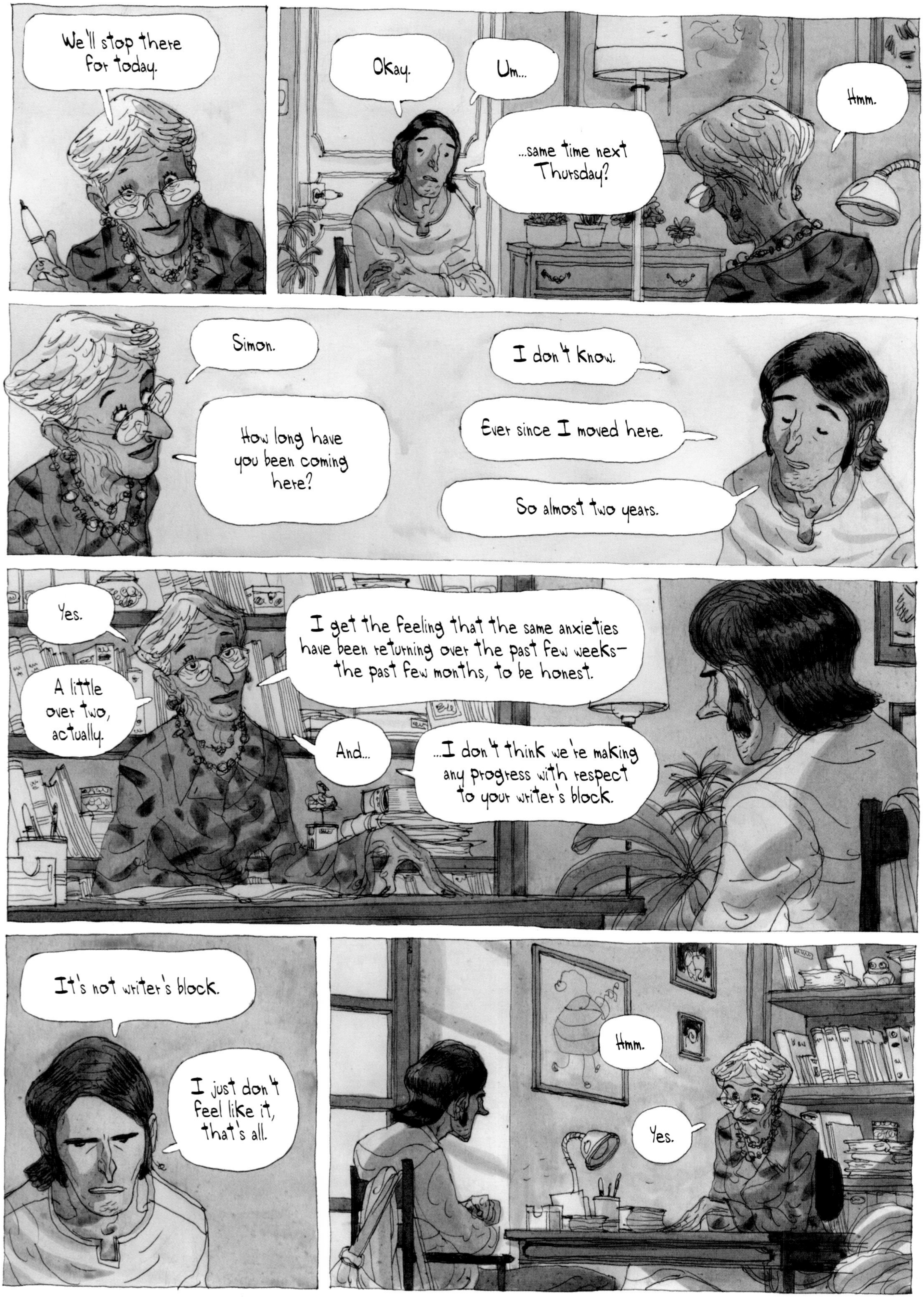
We'll stop there for today.
Okay.
Um...
...same time next Thursday?
Hmm.
Simon.
How long have you been coming here?
I don't know.
Ever since I moved here.
So almost two years.
Yes.
A little over two, actually.
I get the feeling that the same anxieties have been returning over the past few weeks—the past few months, to be honest.
And...
...I don't think we're making any progress with respect to your writer's block.
It's not writer's block.
I just don't feel like it, that's all.
Hmm.
Yes.

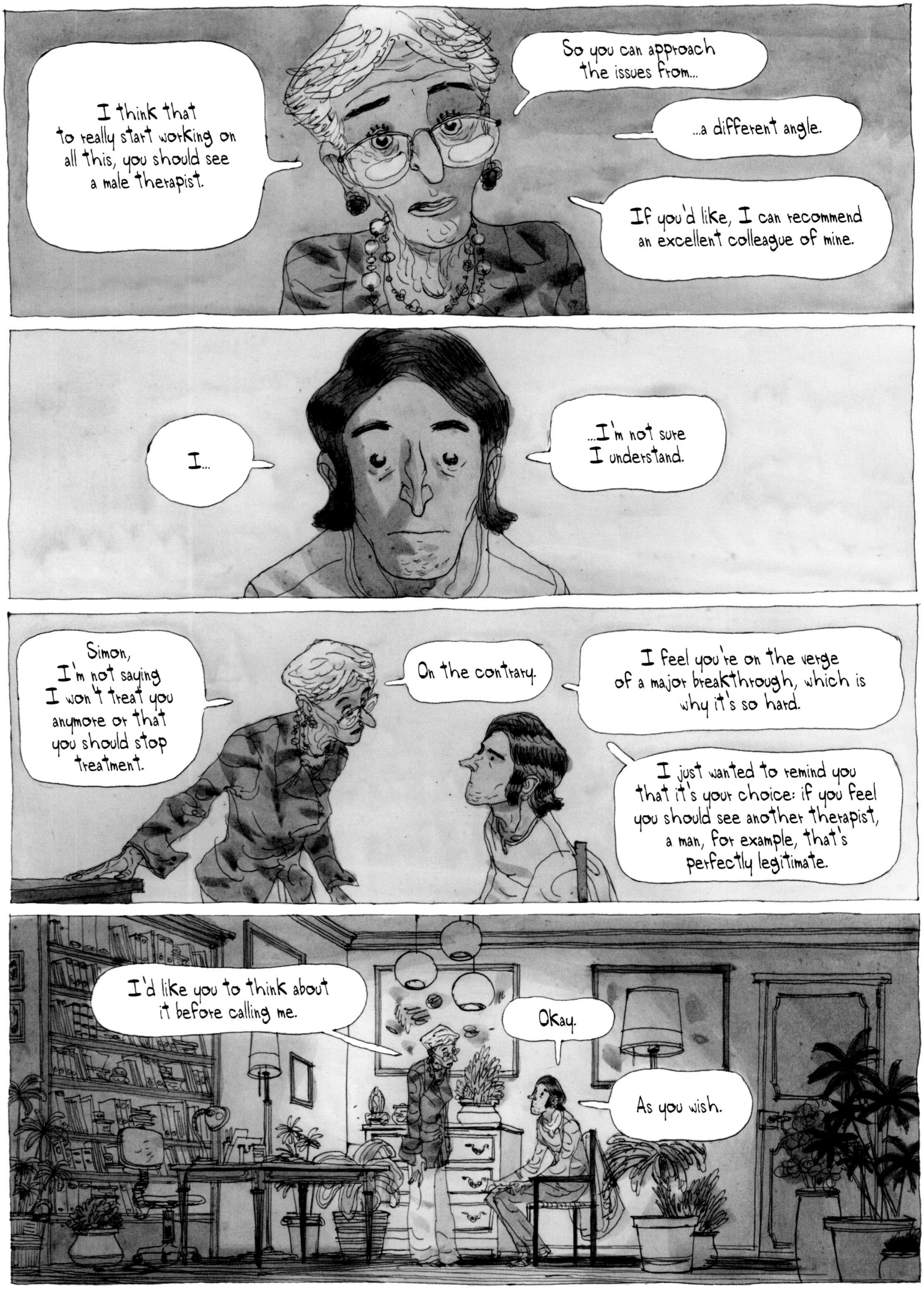
I think that to really start working on all this, you should see a male therapist.
So you can approach the issues from...
...a different angle.
If you'd like, I can recommend an excellent colleague of mine.
I...
...I'm not sure I understand.
Simon, I'm not saying I won't treat you anymore or that you should stop treatment.
On the contrary.
I feel you're on the verge of a major breakthrough, which is why it's so hard.
I just wanted to remind you that it's your choice: if you feel you should see another therapist, a man, for example, that's perfectly legitimate.
I'd like you to think about it before calling me.
Okay.
As you wish.

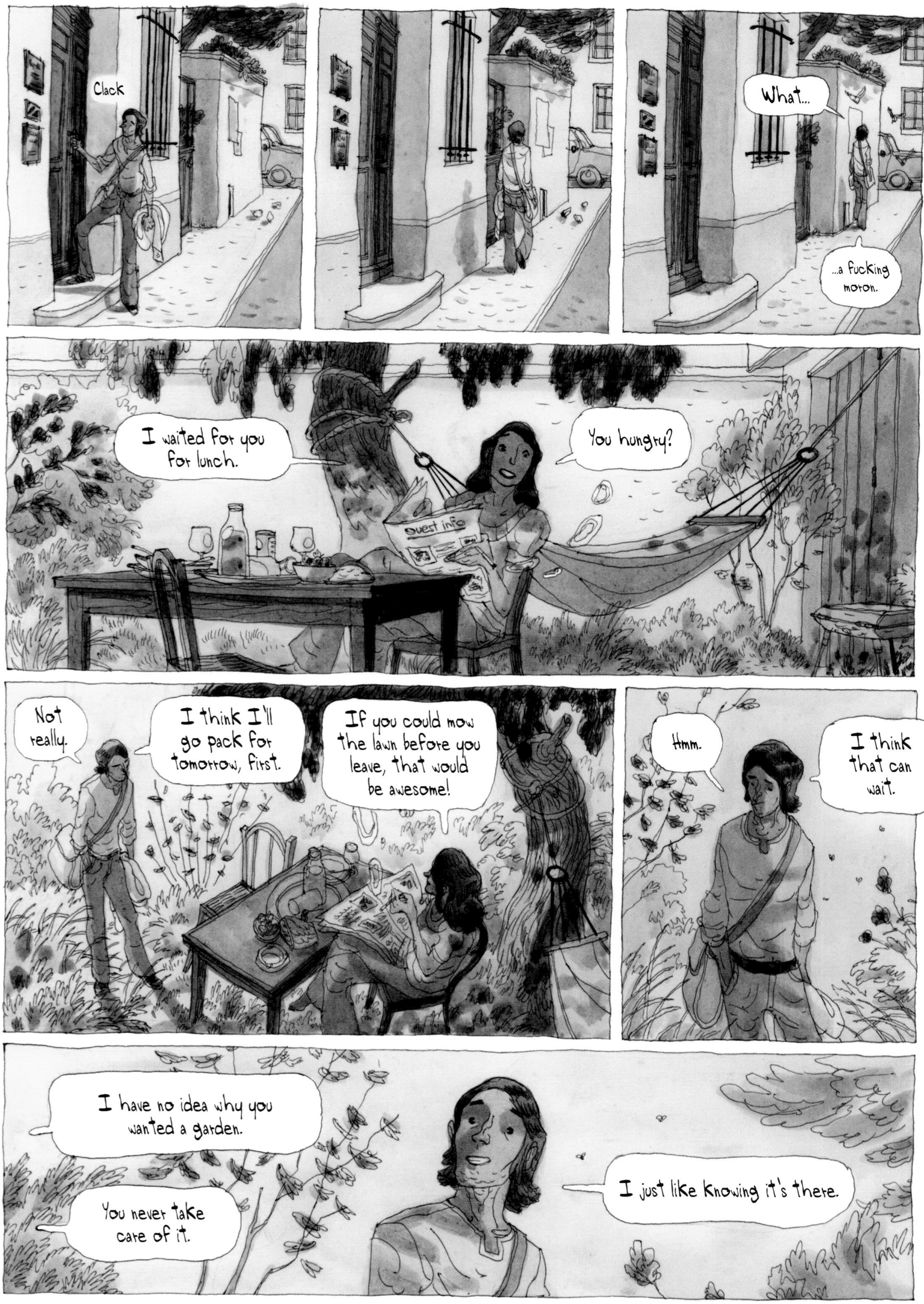
Clack
What...
...a fucking moron.
I waited for you for lunch.
You hungry?
Ouest info
Not really.
I think I'll go pack for tomorrow, first.
If you could mow the lawn before you leave, that would be awesome!
Hmm.
I think that can wait.
I have no idea why you wanted a garden.
You never take care of it.
I just like knowing it's there.

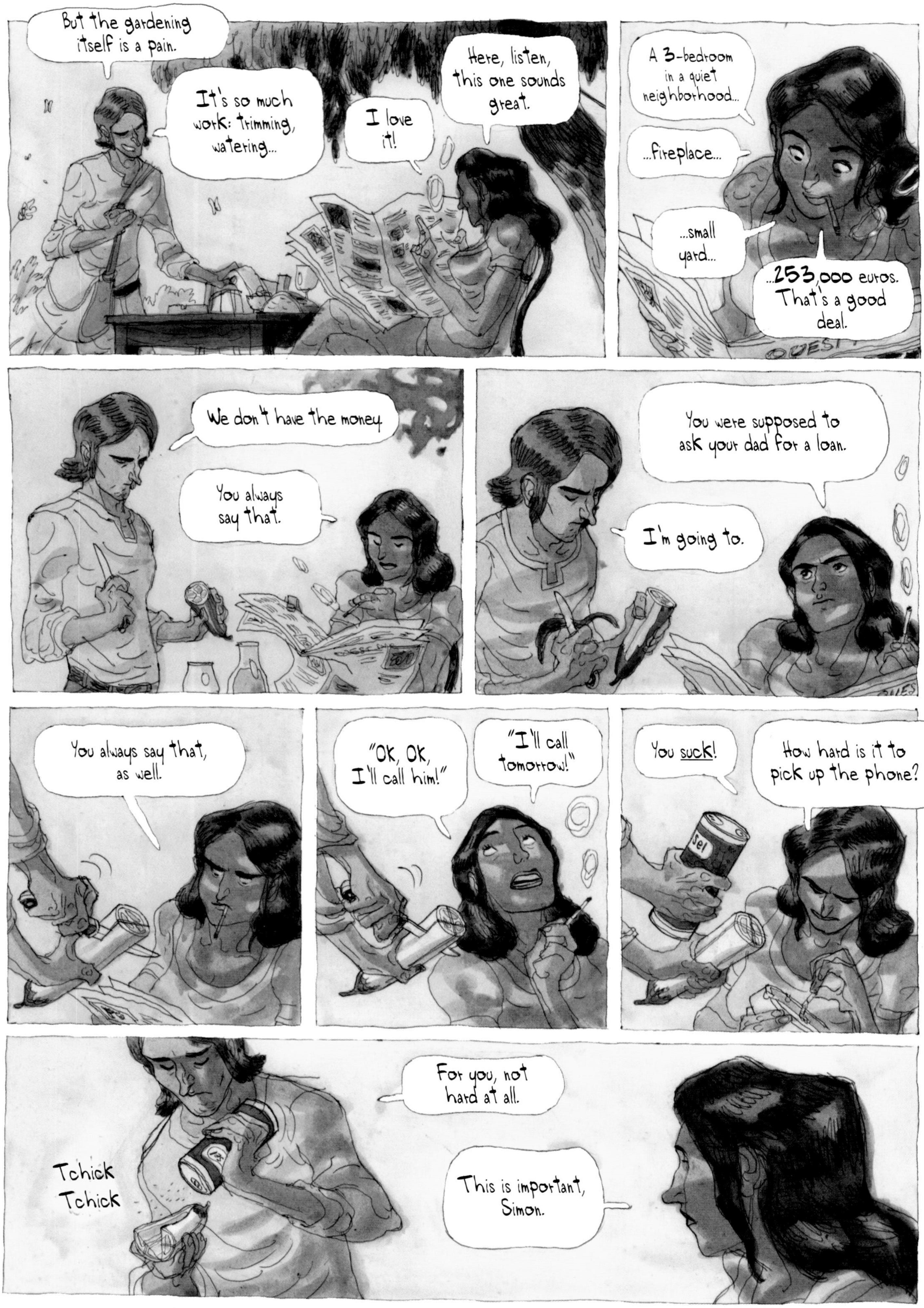
But the gardening itself is a pain.
It's so much work: trimming, watering...
I love it!
Here, listen, this one sounds great.
A 3-bedroom in a quiet neighborhood...
...fireplace...
...small yard...
...253,000 euros. That's a good deal.
We don't have the money.
You always say that.
You were supposed to ask your dad for a loan.
I'm going to.
You always say that, as well.
"OK, OK, I'll call him!"
"I'll call tomorrow!"
You suck!
How hard is it to pick up the phone?
For you, not hard at all.
Tchick Tchick
This is important, Simon.

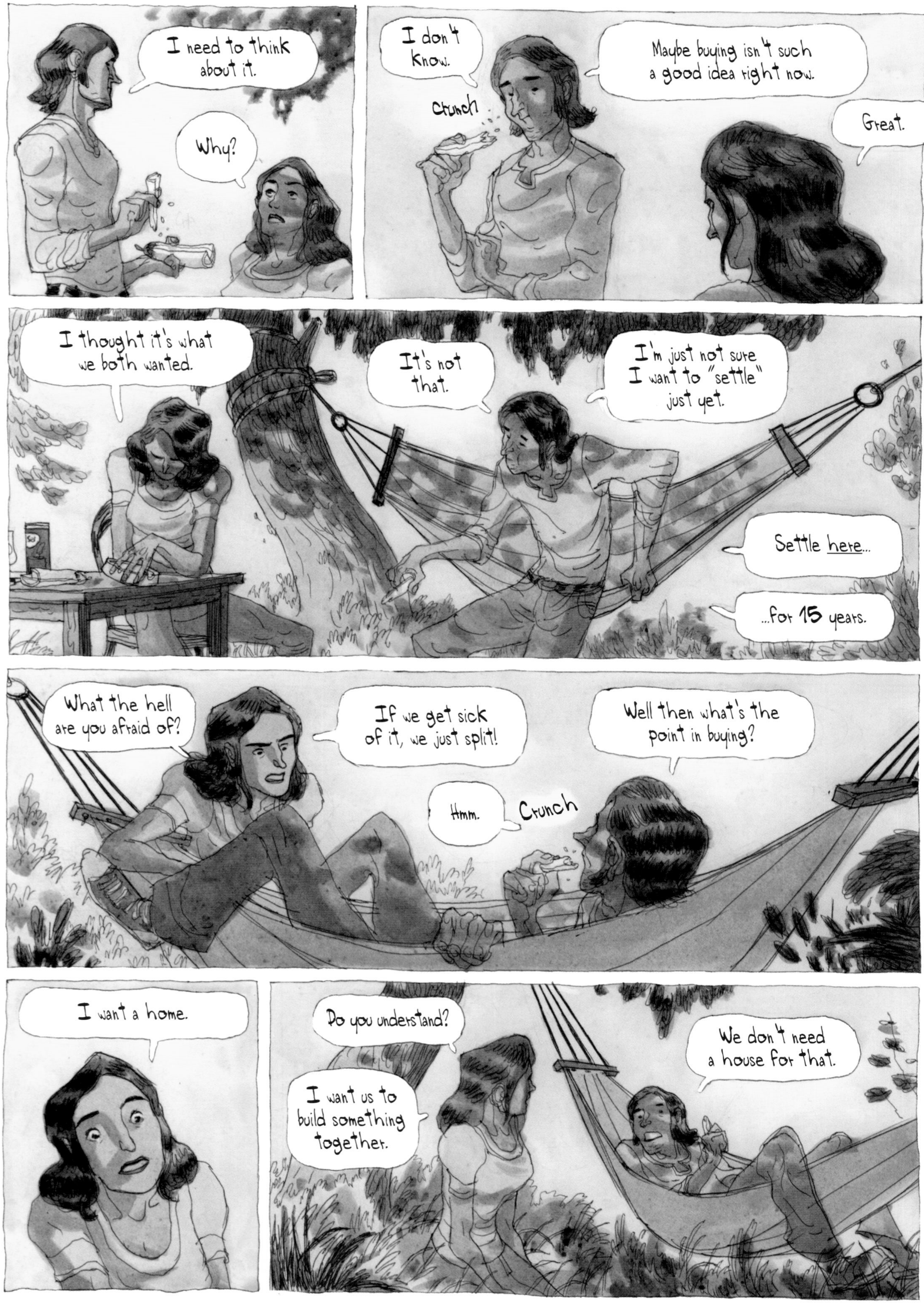
I need to think about it.
Why?
I don't know.
Crunch
Maybe buying isn't such a good idea right now.
Great.
I thought it's what we both wanted.
It's not that.
I'm just not sure I want to "settle" just yet.
Settle here...
...for 15 years.
What the hell are you afraid of?
If we get sick of it, we just split!
Well then what's the point in buying?
Hmm.
Crunch
I want a home.
Do you understand?
I want us to build something together.
We don't need a house for that.

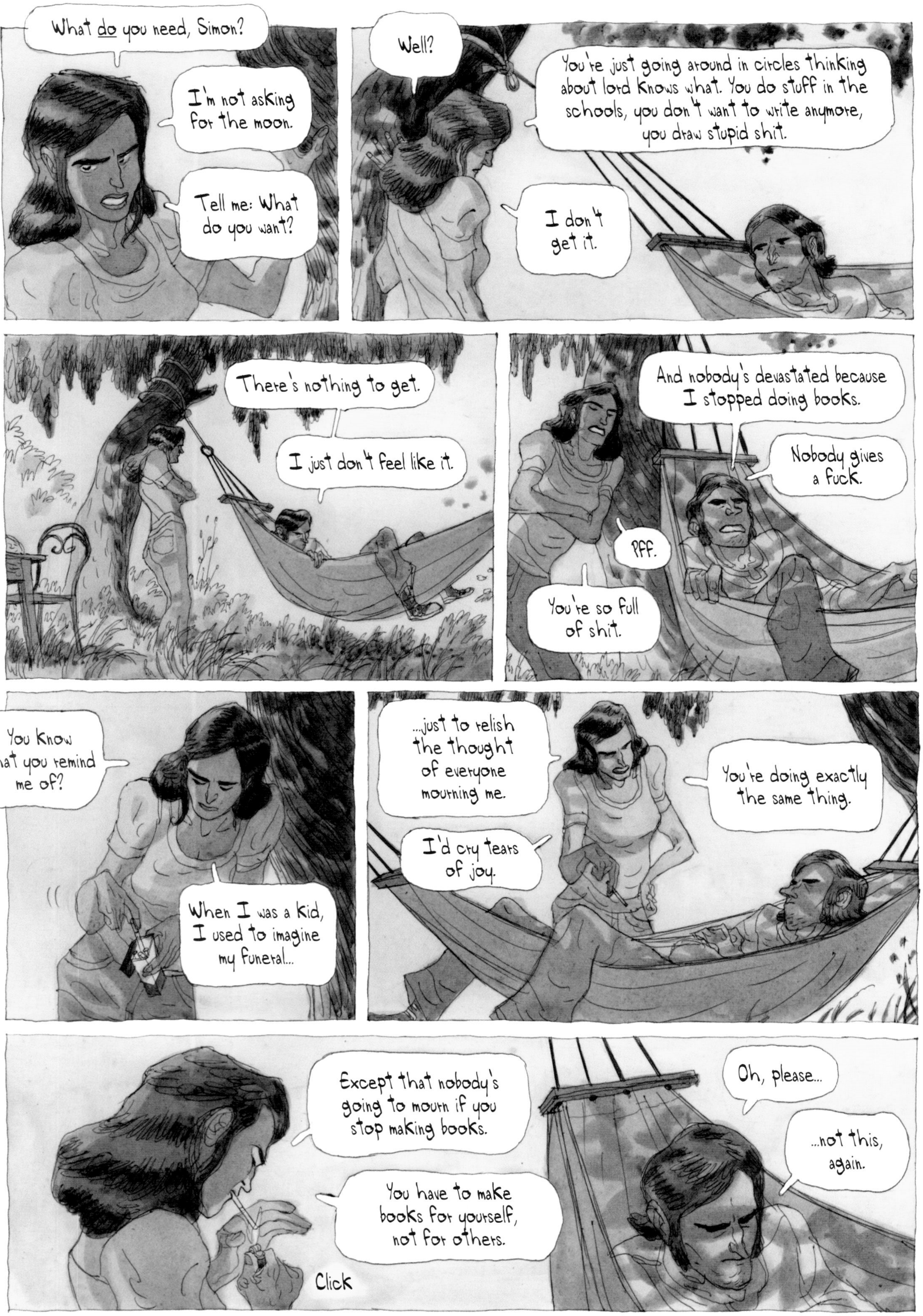

What do you need, Simon?
I'm not asking for the moon.
Tell me: What do you want?
Well?
You're just going around in circles thinking about lord knows what. You do stuff in the schools, you don't want to write anymore, you draw stupid shit.
I don't get it.
There's nothing to get.
I just don't feel like it.
And nobody's devastated because I stopped doing books.
Nobody gives a fuck.
PFF.
You're so full of shit.
You know what you remind me of?
When I was a kid, I used to imagine my funeral...
...just to relish the thought of everyone mourning me.
I'd cry tears of joy.
You're doing exactly the same thing.
Except that nobody's going to mourn if you stop making books.
You have to make books for yourself, not for others.
Click
Oh, please...
...not this, again.

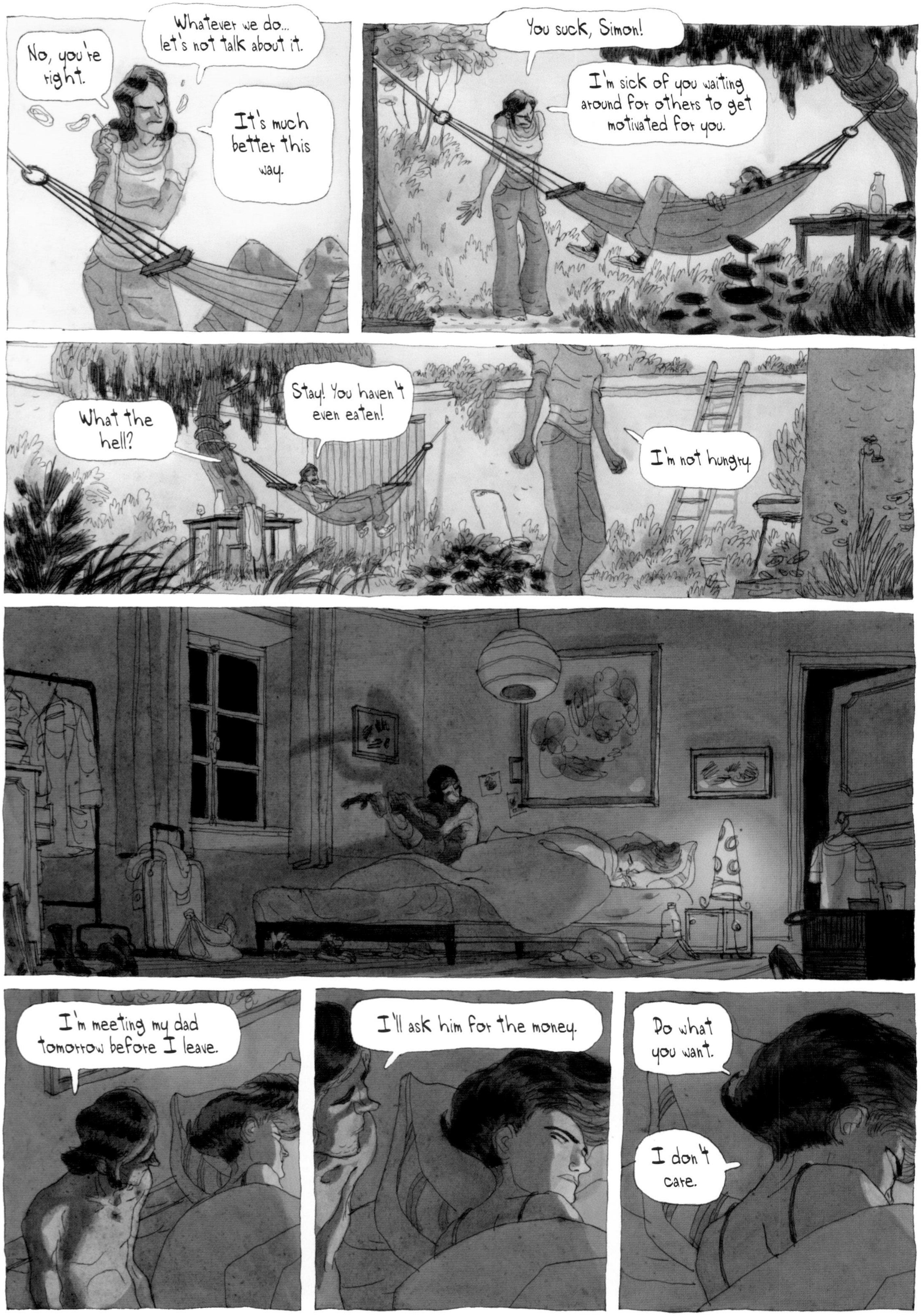
No, you're right.
Whatever we do... let's not talk about it.
It's much better this way.
You suck, Simon!
I'm sick of you waiting around for others to get motivated for you.
What the hell?
Stay! You haven't even eaten!
I'm not hungry.
I'm meeting my dad tomorrow before I leave.
I'll ask him for the money.
Do what you want.
I don't care.

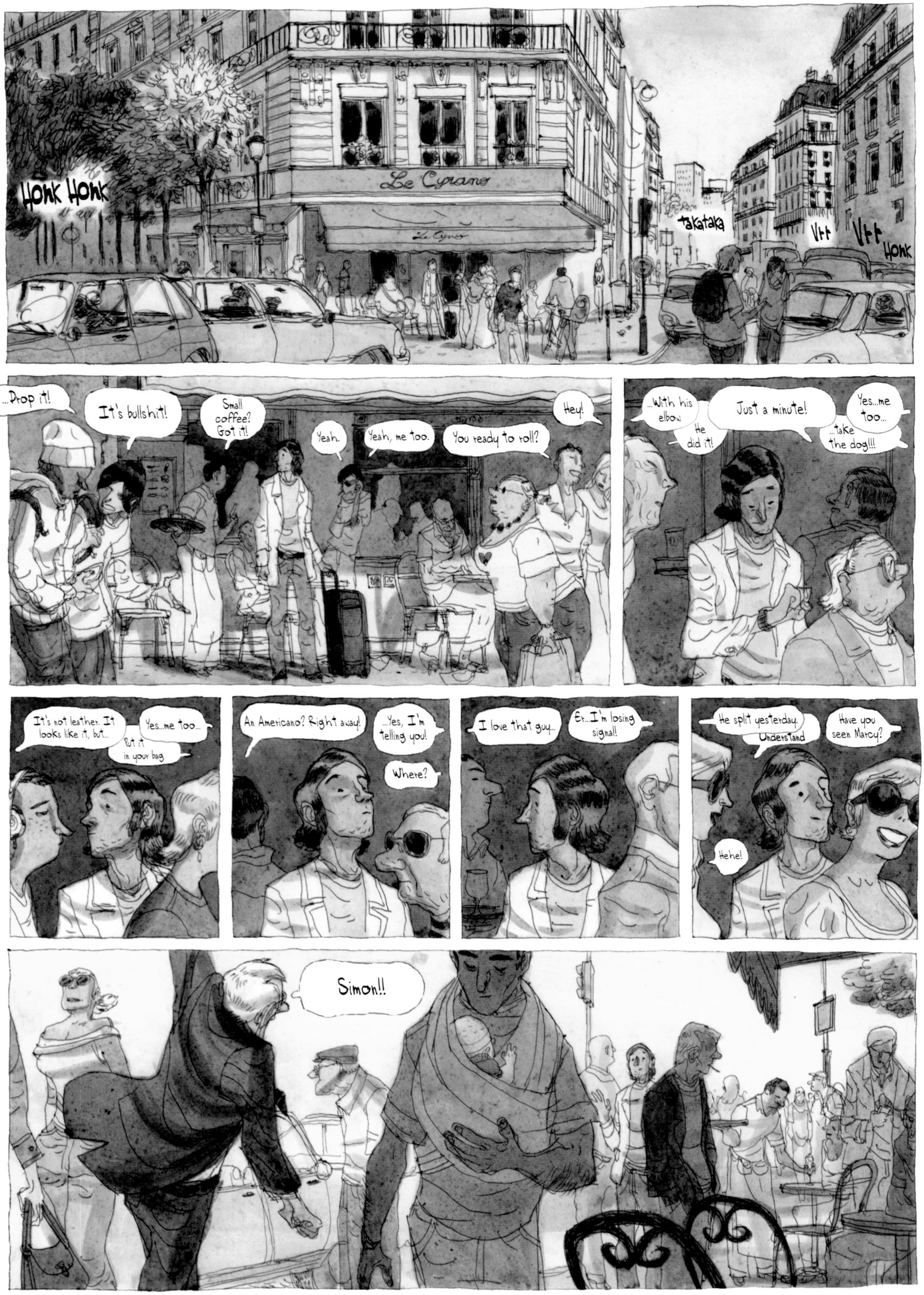
HONK HONK
Le Cyrano
Takataka
Vrr
Vrr
HONK
...Drop it!
It's bullshit!
Small coffee? Got it!
Yeah.
Yeah, me too.
You ready to roll?
Hey!
...With his elbow
He did it!
Just a minute!
Yes...me too...
...take the dog!!!
It's not leather. It looks like it, but...
Yes...me too...
Put it in your bag
An Americano? Right away!
...Yes, I'm telling you!
Where?
I love that guy...
Er...I'm losing signal!
He split yesterday.
Understand
Have you seen Marcy?
Hehe!
Simon!!

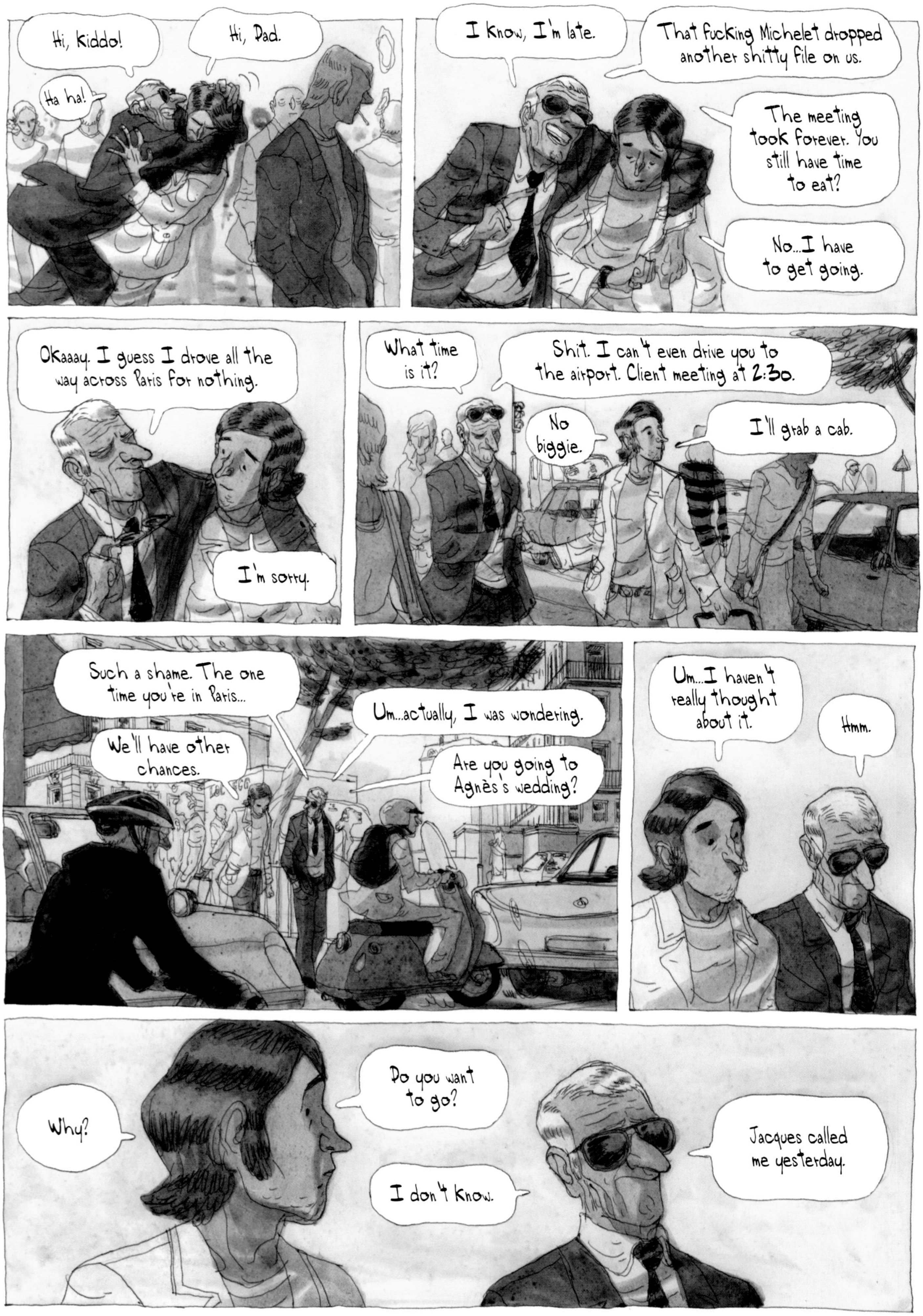
Hi, kiddo!
Ha ha!
Hi, Dad.
I know, I'm late.
That fucking Michelet dropped another shitty file on us.
The meeting took forever. You still have time to eat?
No...I have to get going.
Okaaay. I guess I drove all the way across Paris for nothing.
I'm sorry.
What time is it?
Shit. I can't even drive you to the airport. Client meeting at 2:30.
No biggie.
I'll grab a cab.
Such a shame. The one time you're in Paris...
We'll have other chances.
Um...actually, I was wondering.
Are you going to Agnès's wedding?
Um...I haven't really thought about it.
Hmm.
Why?
Jacques called me yesterday.
Do you want to go?
I don't know.

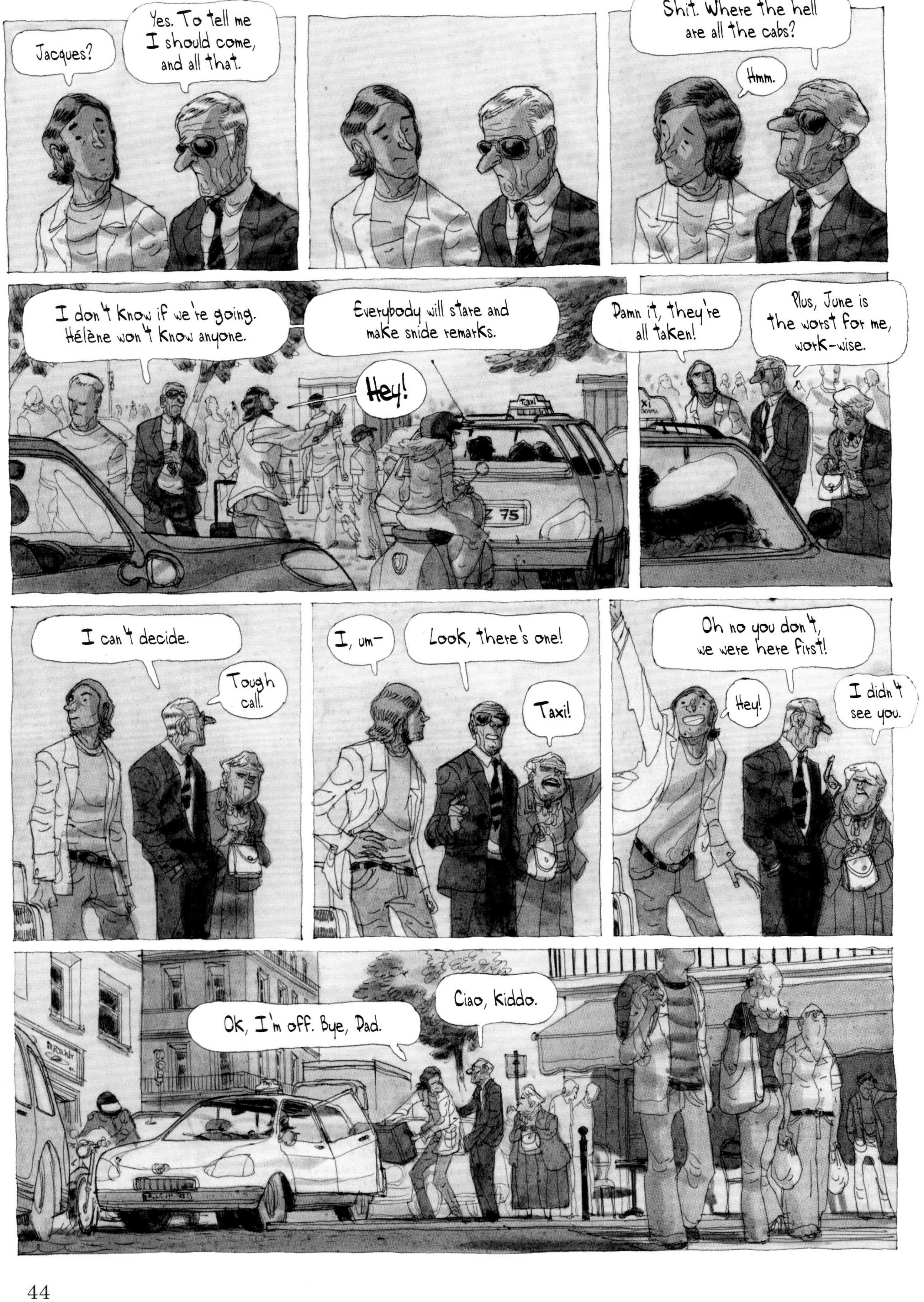
Jacques?
Yes. To tell me I should come, and all that.
Shit. Where the hell are all the cabs?
Hmm.
I don't know if we're going. Hélène won't know anyone.
Everybody will stare and make snide remarks.
Hey!
Damn it, they're all taken!
Plus, June is the worst for me, work-wise.
I can't decide.
Tough call.
I, um-
Look, there's one!
Taxi!
Oh no you don't, we were here first!
Hey!
I didn't see you.
Ok, I'm off. Bye, Dad.
Ciao, kiddo.

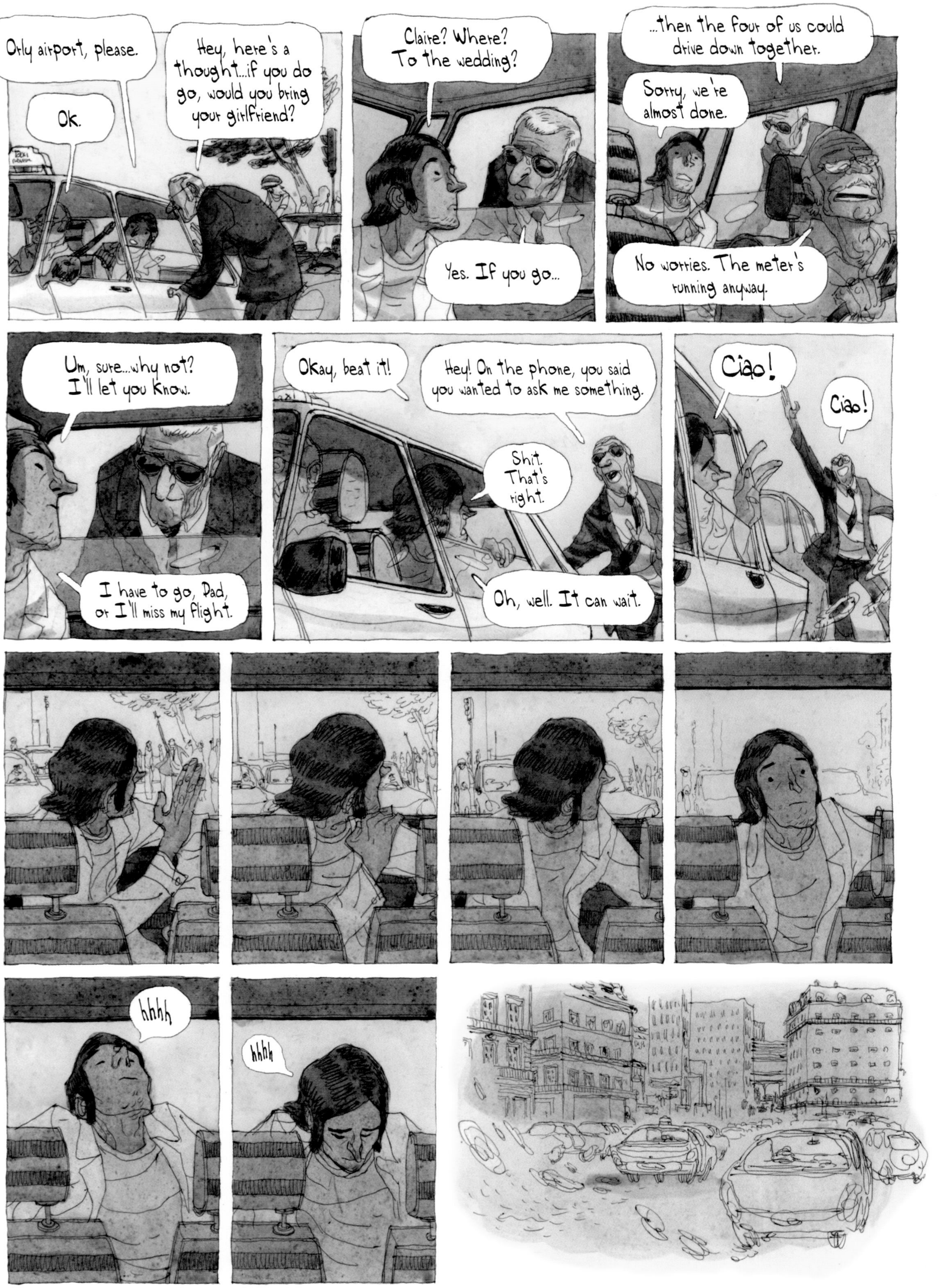
Orly airport, please.
Ok.
Hey, here's a thought...if you do go, would you bring your girlfriend?
Claire? Where? To the wedding?
Yes. If you go...
...then the four of us could drive down together.
Sorry, we're almost done.
No worries. The meter's running anyway.
Um, sure...why not? I'll let you know.
I have to go, Dad, or I'll miss my flight.
Okay, beat it!
Hey! On the phone, you said you wanted to ask me something.
Shit. That's right.
Oh, well. It can wait.
Ciao!
Ciao!
hhhh
hhhh

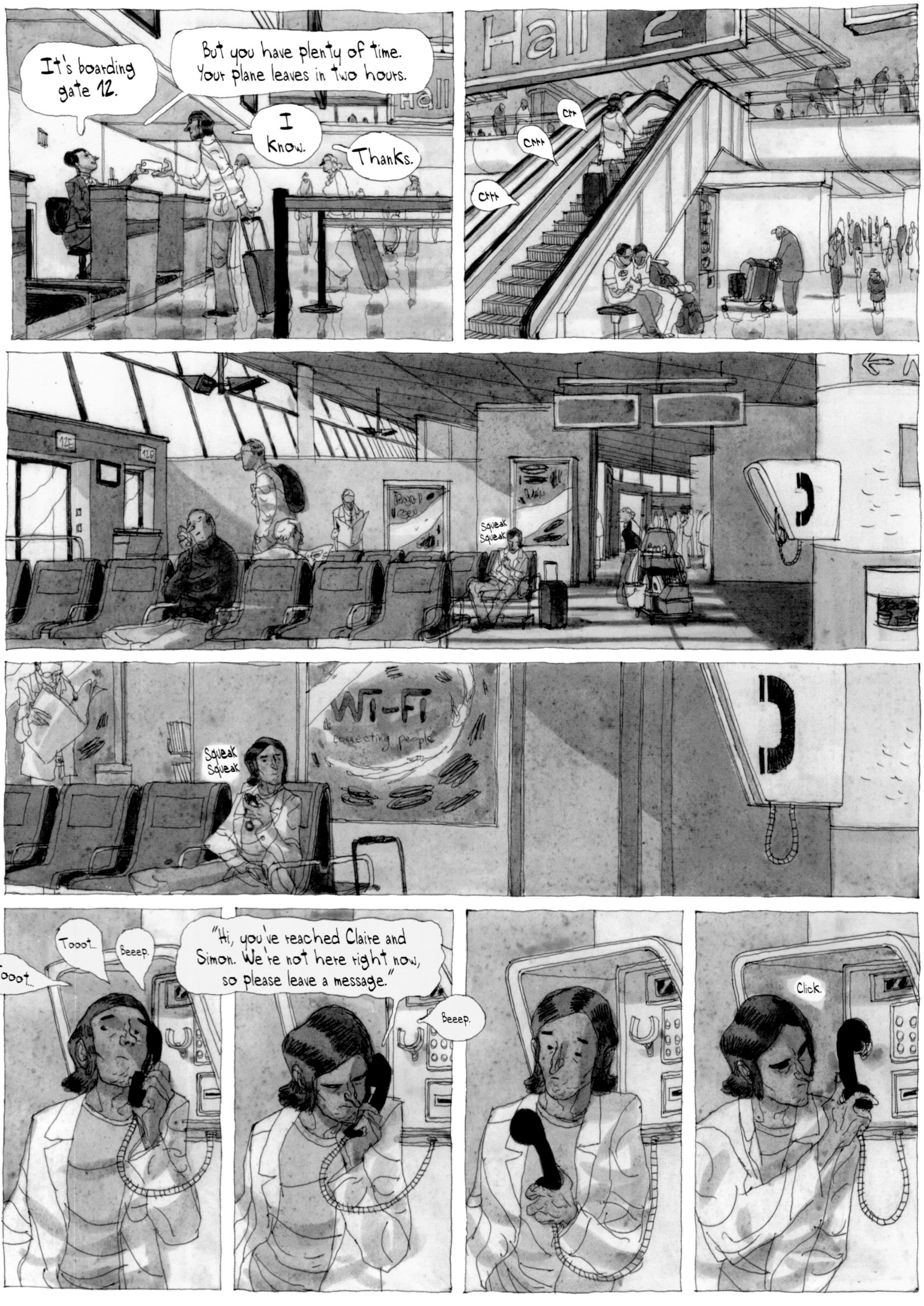
It's boarding gate 12.
But you have plenty of time. Your plane leaves in two hours.
I know.
Thanks.
Hall 2
Crr
Crrr
Crrr
Squeak Squeak
WI-FI
connecting people
Squeak Squeak
Tooot...
Tooot...
Beeep.
"Hi, you've reached Claire and Simon. We're not here right now, so please leave a message."
Beeep.
Click.

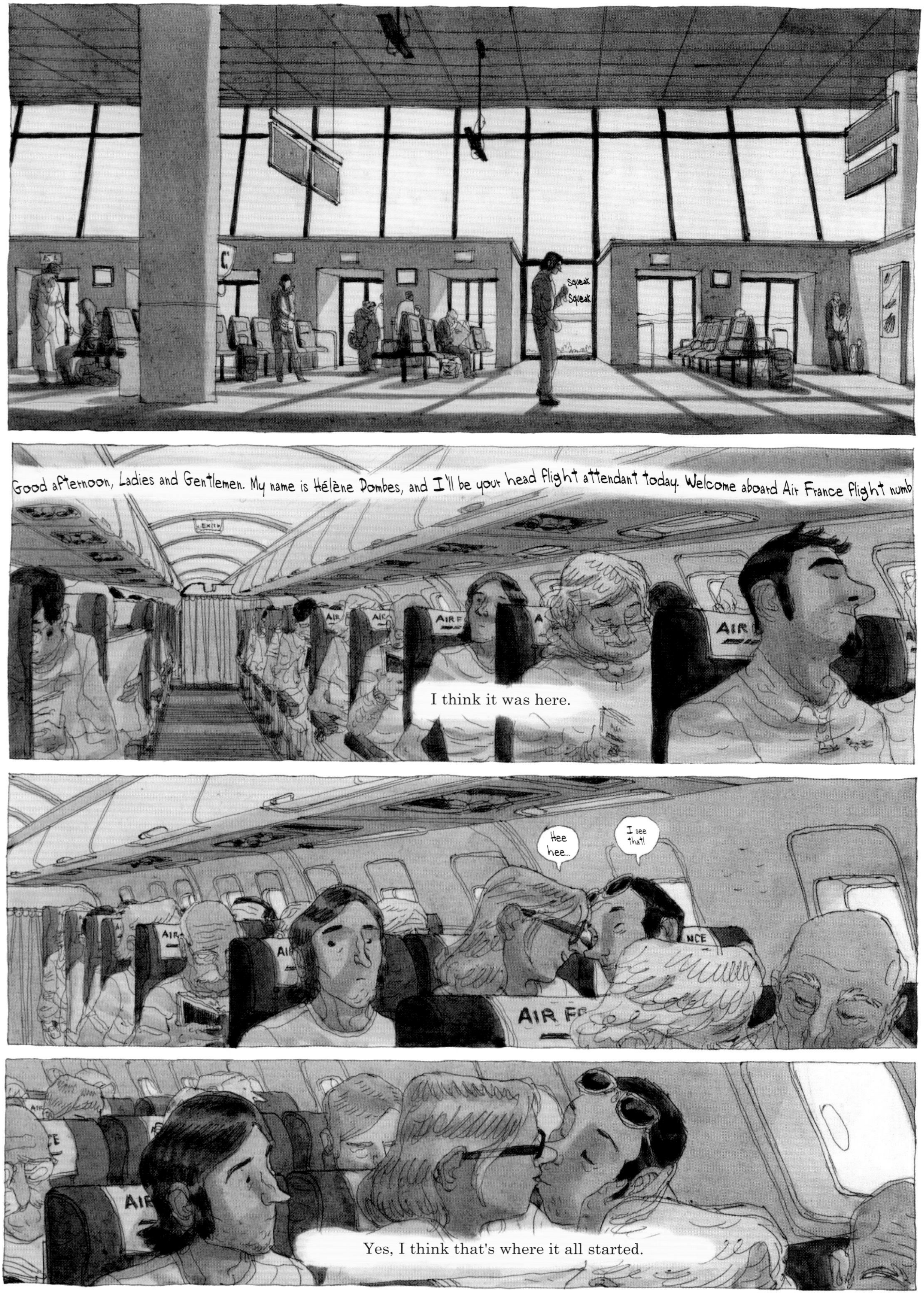

Squeak
Squeak
Good afternoon, Ladies and Gentlemen. My name is Hélène Dombes, and I'll be your head flight attendant today. Welcome aboard Air France flight numb
I think it was here.
Hee hee...
I see that!
Yes, I think that's where it all started.

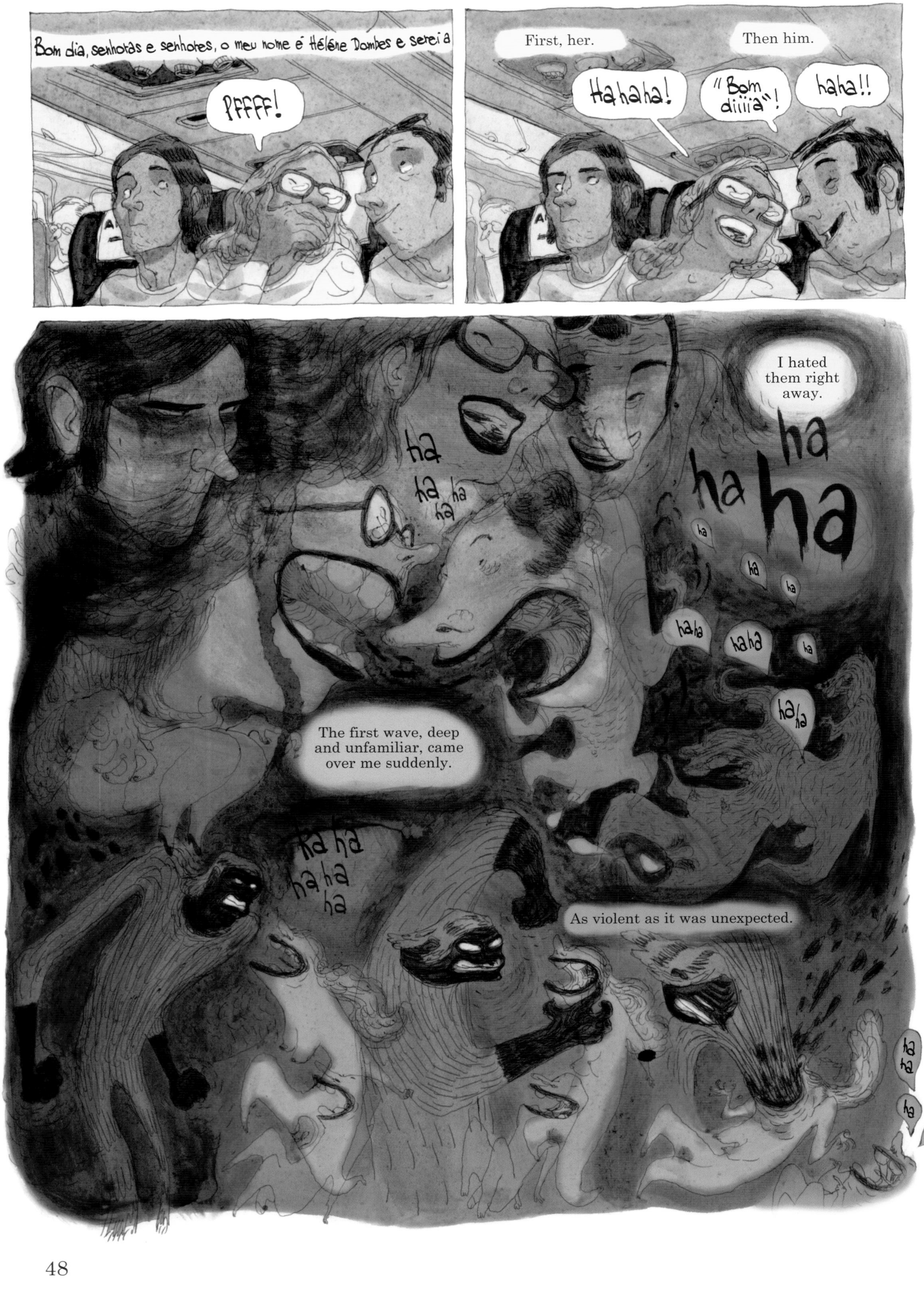

Bom dia, senhoras e senhores, o meu nome é Hélène Dombes e serei a
PFFFF!
First, her.
Then him.
Hahaha!
"Bom diiiia"!
haha!!
I hated them right away.
ha
ha ha ha
ha ha ha
ha
ha
ha
ha
haha
haha
ha
haha
The first wave, deep and unfamiliar, came over me suddenly.
ha ha ha ha ha
As violent as it was unexpected.
ha ha ha

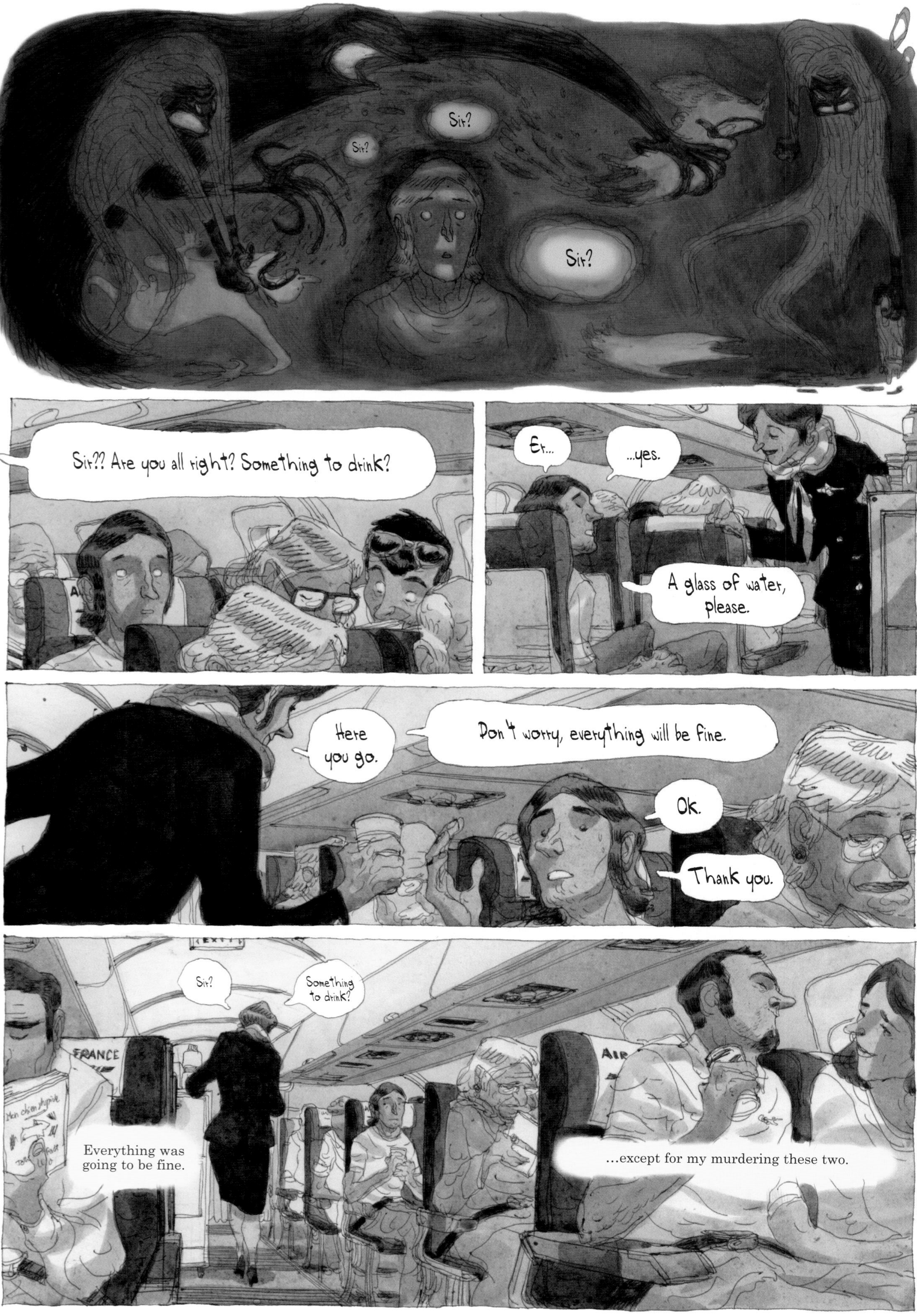
Sir?
Sir?
Sir?
Sir?? Are you all right? Something to drink?
Er...
...yes.
A glass of water, please.
Here you go.
Don't worry, everything will be fine.
Ok.
Thank you.
Sir?
Something to drink?
Everything was going to be fine.
...except for my murdering these two.

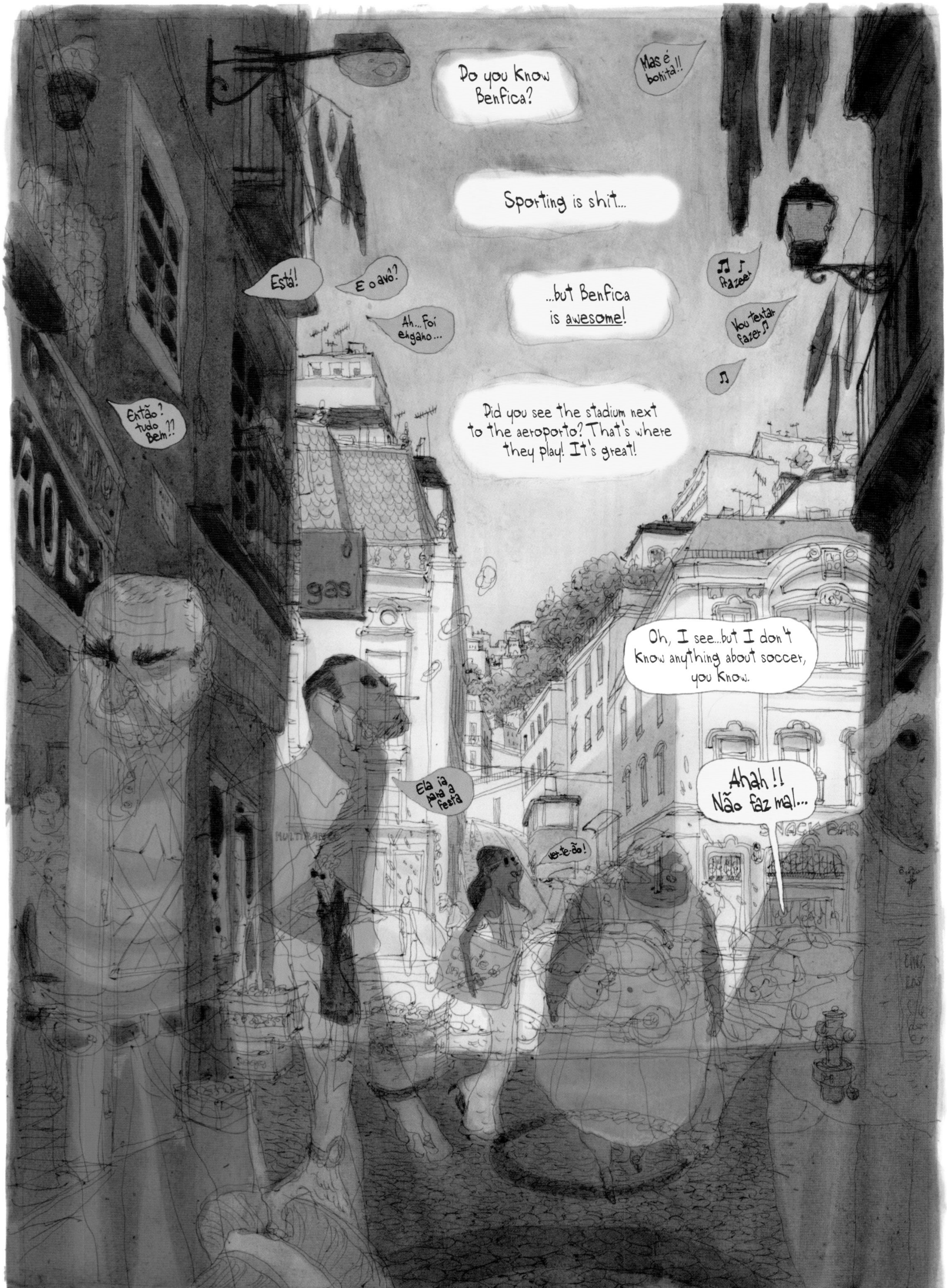

Do you know Benfica?
Mas é bonita!!
Sporting is shit...
Está!
E o avô?
Ah... Foi engano...
...but Benfica is awesome!
♫ ♪ Prazer
Vou tentar fazer ♫
♫
Então? tudo Bem??
Did you see the stadium next to the aeroporto? That's where they play! It's great!
gas
Oh, I see...but I don't know anything about soccer, you know.
Ela ia para a festa
Ahah!! Não faz mal...
ver-te-ão!
SNACK BAR

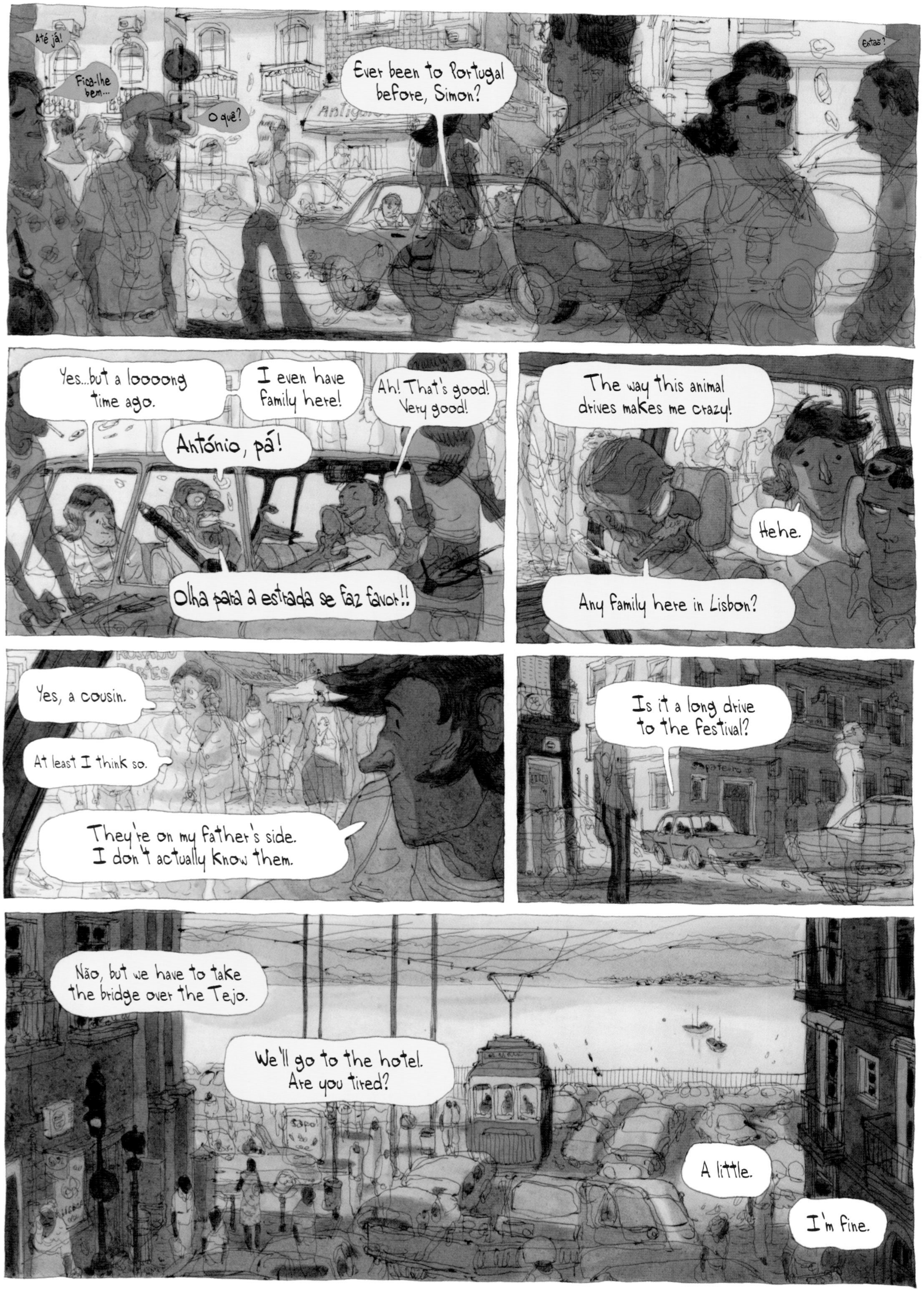

Até já!
Fica-lhe bem...
O quê?
Ever been to Portugal before, Simon?
Extas?
Yes...but a loooong time ago.
I even have family here!
Ah! That's good! Very good!
António, pá!
Olha para a estrada se faz favor!!
The way this animal drives makes me crazy!
Hehe.
Any family here in Lisbon?
Yes, a cousin.
At least I think so.
They're on my father's side. I don't actually know them.
Is it a long drive to the festival?
Não, but we have to take the bridge over the Tejo.
We'll go to the hotel. Are you tired?
A little.
I'm fine.

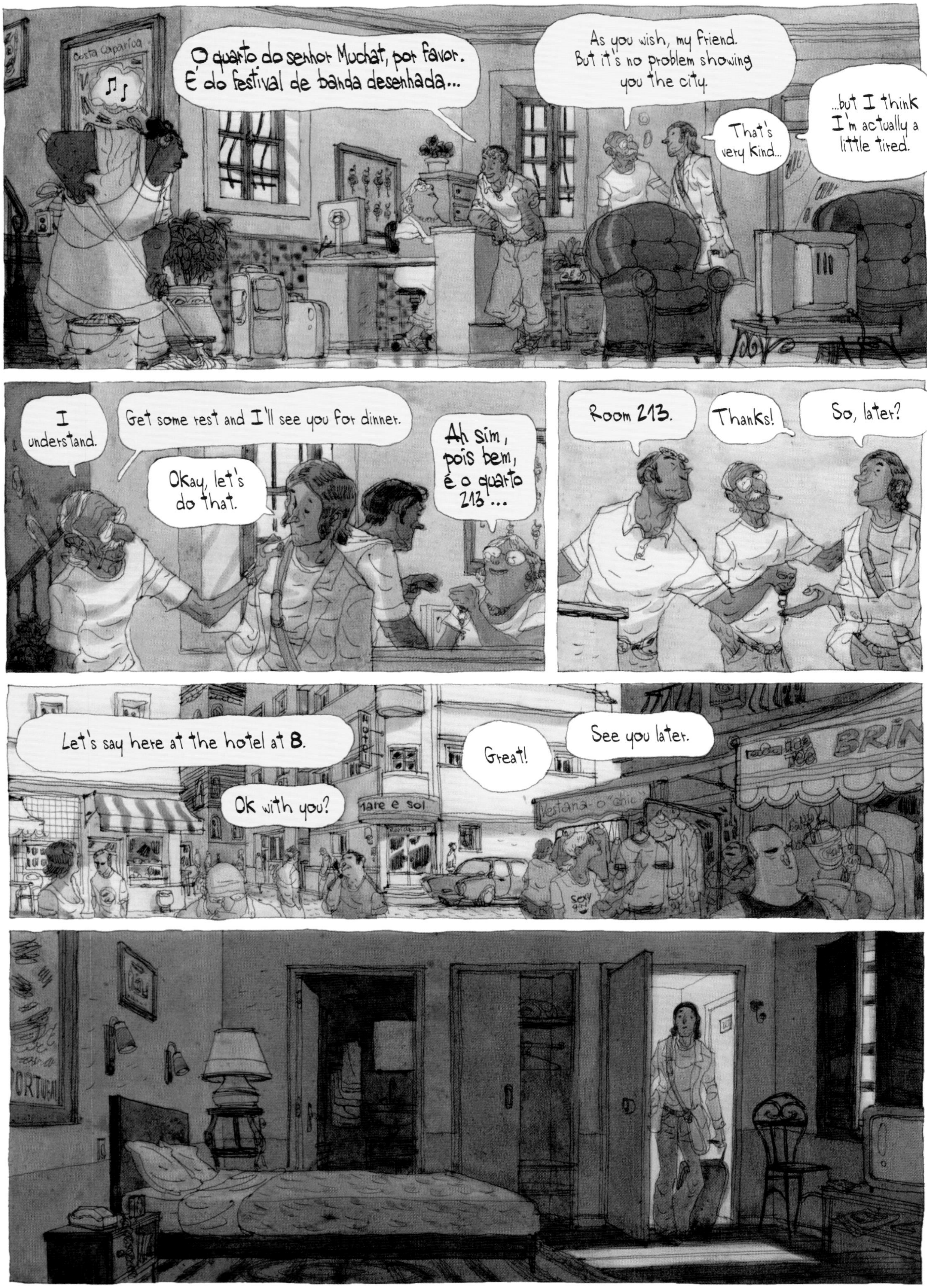

Costa Caparica
O quarto do senhor Muchat, por favor. É do festival de banda desenhada...
As you wish, my friend. But it's no problem showing you the city.
That's very kind...
...but I think I'm actually a little tired.
I understand.
Get some rest and I'll see you for dinner.
Okay, let's do that.
Ah sim, pois bem, é o quarto 213...
Room 213.
Thanks!
So, later?
Let's say here at the hotel at 8.
Ok with you?
Great!
See you later.
Mare e sol
Vestana-o "chic"
PORTUGAL

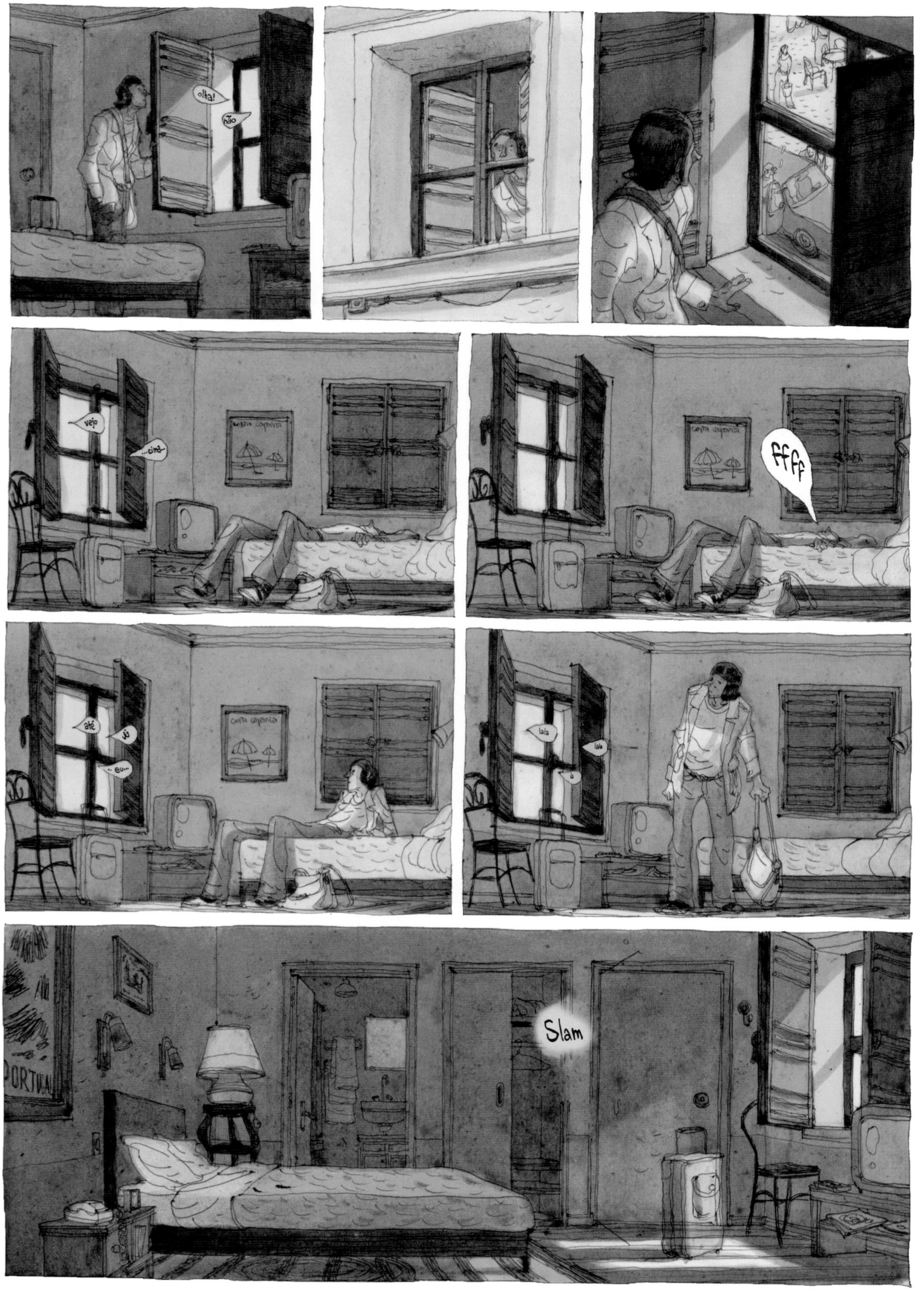
olha!
não
vejo
...cima...
ffff
até
já
...eu...
lala
lala
la
Slam

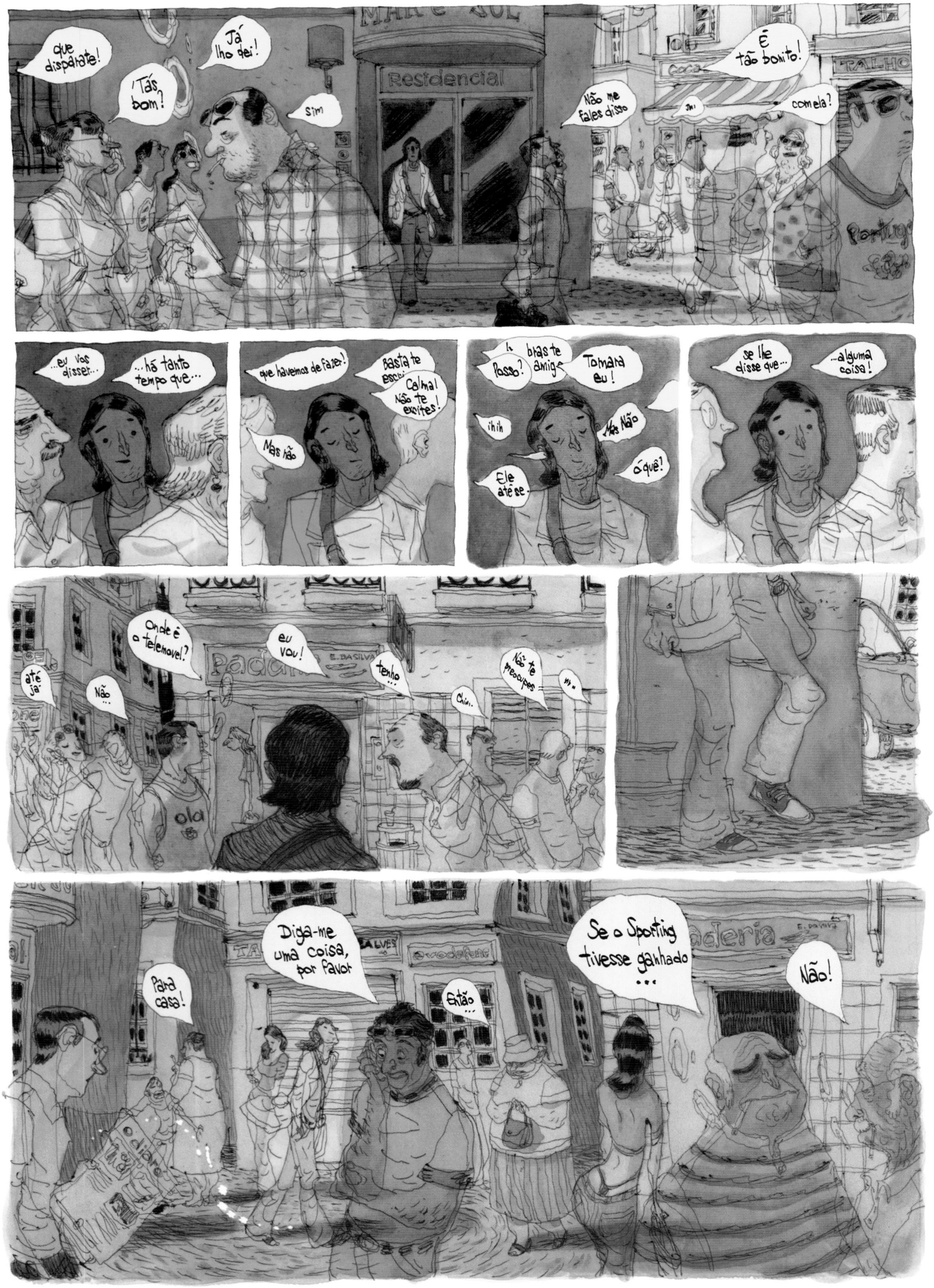
Residencial
TALHO
que disparate!
'Tás bom?
Já lho dei!
Sim
Não me fales disso
É tão bonito!
com ela?
...eu vos disse...
...há tanto tempo que...
que havemos de fazer!
Calma! Não te excites!
Mas não
Passo?
Tomara eu!
ihih
Mas Não
o quê?
Ele até se
se lhe disse que...
...alguma coisa!
até já
Onde é a telemovel?
Não...
eu vou!
tenho...
Não te preocupes
Para casa!
Diga-me uma coisa, por favor
Então...
Se o Sporting tivesse ganhado ...
Não!

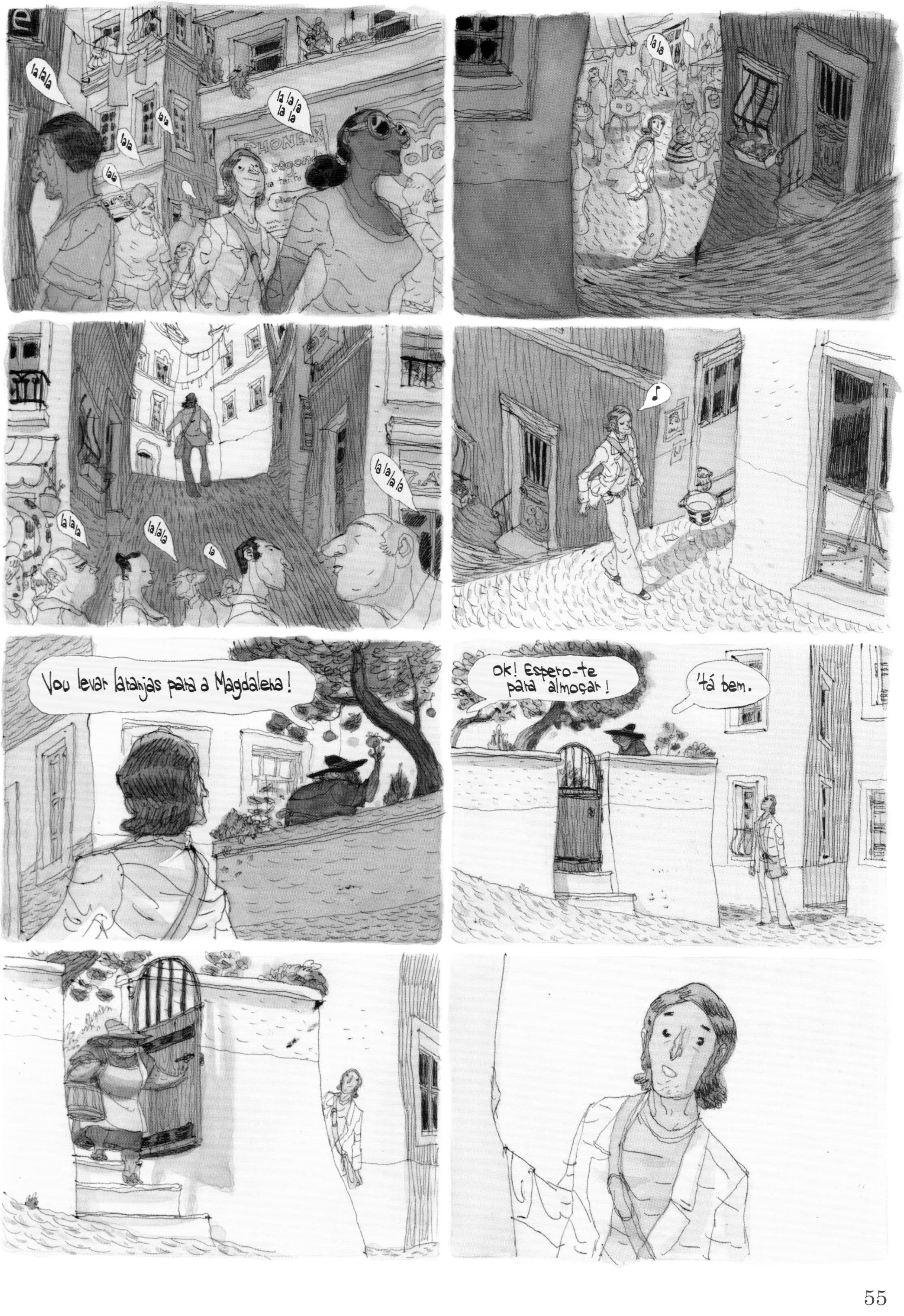
la la la
la la la
la la
la la la
la la
la la
la la
la la la la
la la la
la la la
la
Vou levar laranjas para a Magdalena!
Ok! Espero-te para almoçar!
'tá bem.

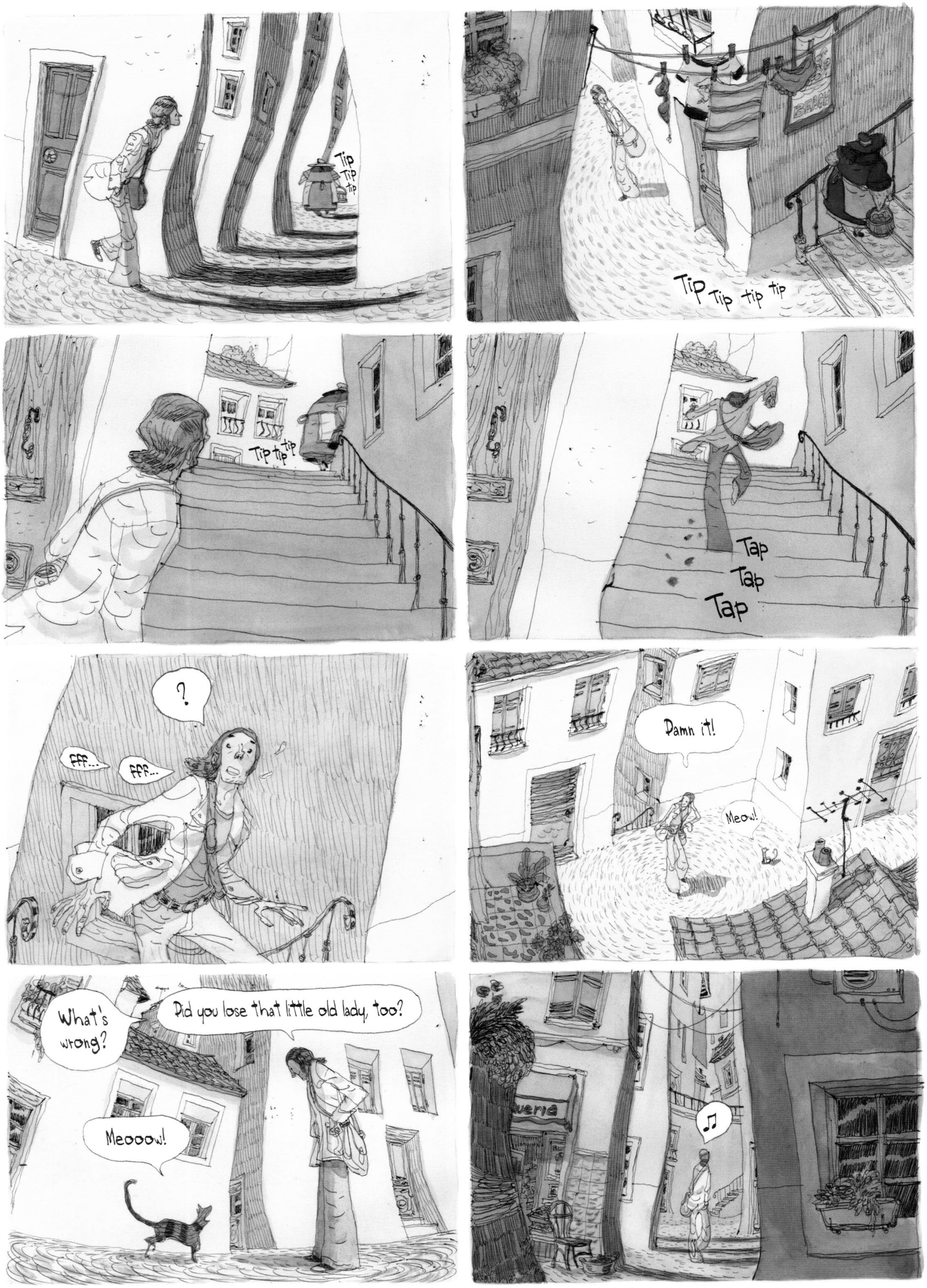
Tip
Tip
tip
Tip Tip tip tip
Tip tip tip
Tap
Tap
Tap
?
FFF...
FFF...
Damn it!
Meow!
What's wrong?
Did you lose that little old lady, too?
Meooow!
♫

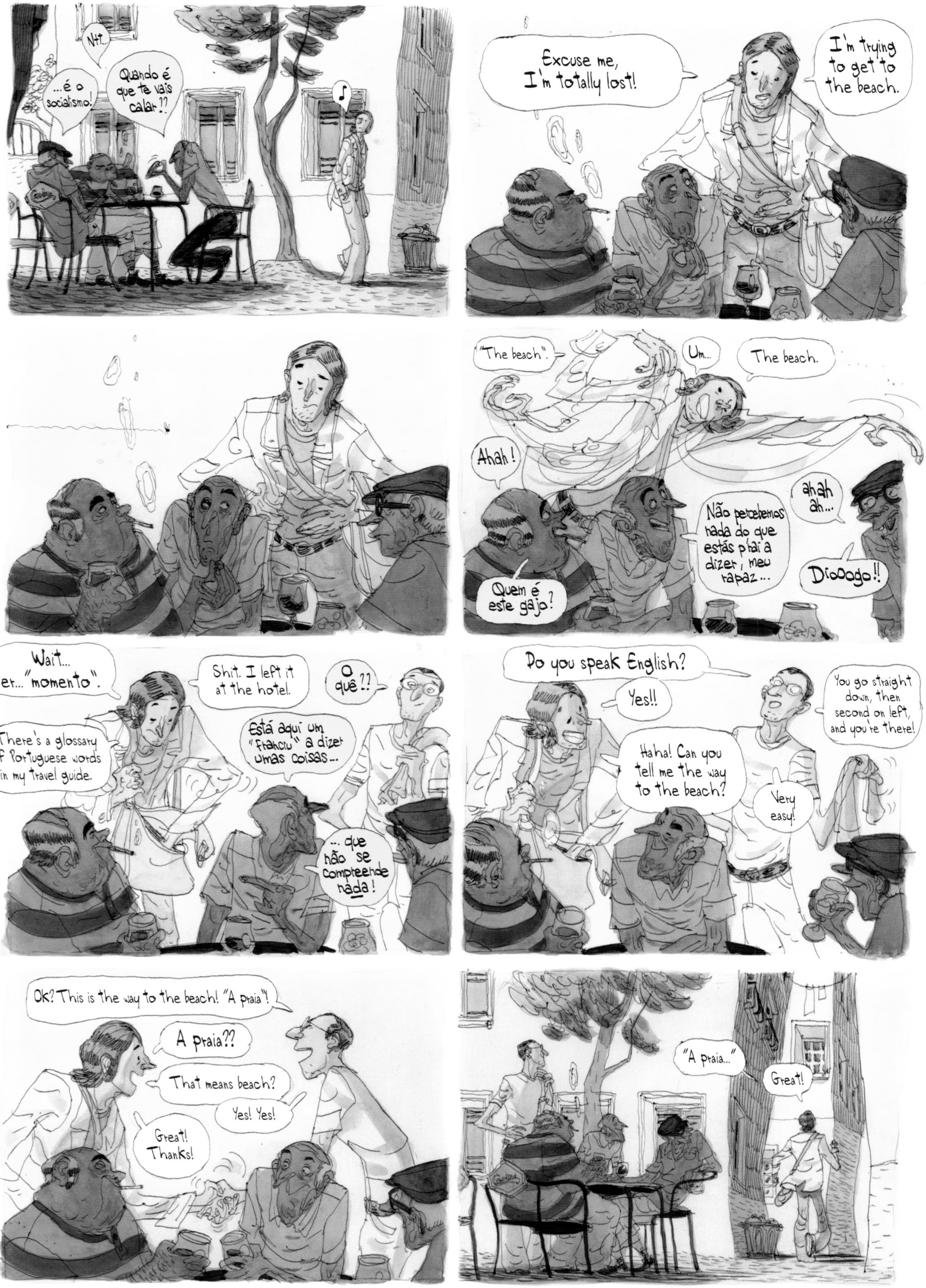
...é o socialismo!
Nt-t...
Quando é que te vais calar??
Excuse me, I'm totally lost!
I'm trying to get to the beach.
"The beach".
Um...
The beach.
Ahah!
Não percebemos nada do que estás p'rai a dizer, meu rapaz...
ahah ah...
Quem é este gajo?
Dioooogo!!
Wait... er... "momento".
Shit. I left it at the hotel.
O quê??
There's a glossary of Portuguese words in my travel guide.
Está aqui um "franciu" a dizer umas coisas...
...que não se compreende nada!
Do you speak English?
Yes!!
Haha! Can you tell me the way to the beach?
Very easy!
You go straight down, then second on left, and you're there!
Ok? This is the way to the beach! "A praia"!
A praia??
That means beach?
Yes! Yes!
Great! Thanks!
"A praia..."
Great!

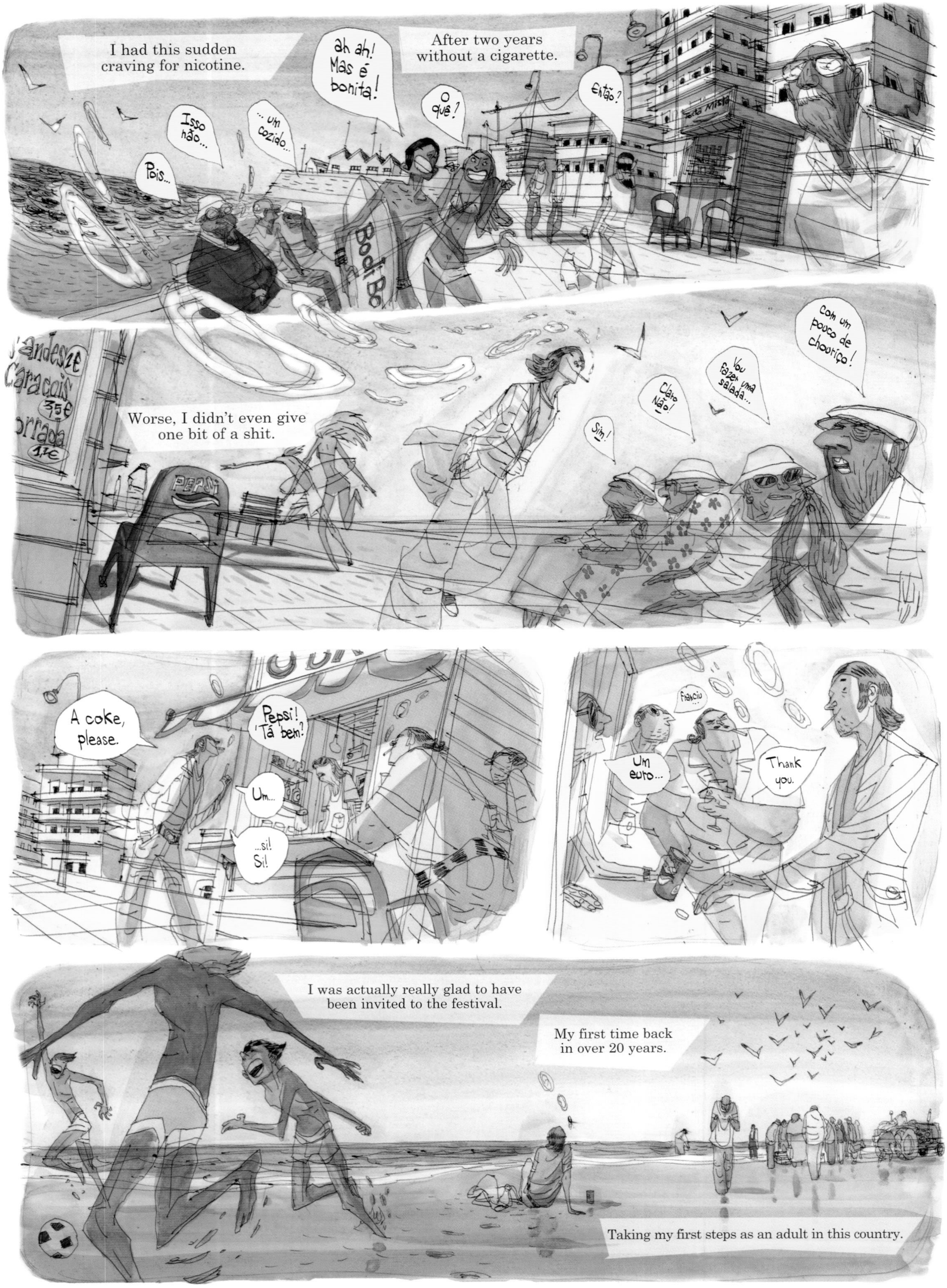

I had this sudden craving for nicotine.
ah ah! Mas é bonita!
After two years without a cigarette.
O quê?
Então?
Isso não...
...um cozido...
Pois...
Worse, I didn't even give one bit of a shit.
Sim!
Claro Não!
Vou fazer uma salada...
Com um pouco de chouriço!
A coke, please.
Pepsi! 'Tá bem?
Um...
...si! Si!
Franciu...
Um euro...
Thank you.
I was actually really glad to have been invited to the festival.
My first time back in over 20 years.
Taking my first steps as an adult in this country.

And then that wave came over me again.

Warm, friendly, and a little sad.

I suddenly felt like hugging all those people.

Like walking in the sand, among the suffocating fish.

Like listening to the mothers chat, to the children scream with fear and excitement.

It's as if I knew those fishmongers, those fishermen...

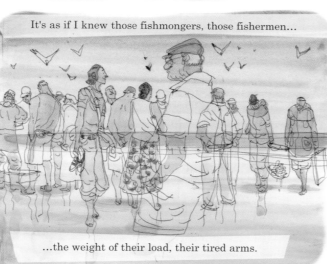

...the weight of their load, their tired arms.

My friends...

...my brothers.

Let me hug you!

I love you!!

I was fascinated and happy.

Like a total idiot.

And I was trying to figure out where that strange anger and the sweet melancholy that followed, both of which had suddenly come over me in less than 24 hours, could possibly have come from.

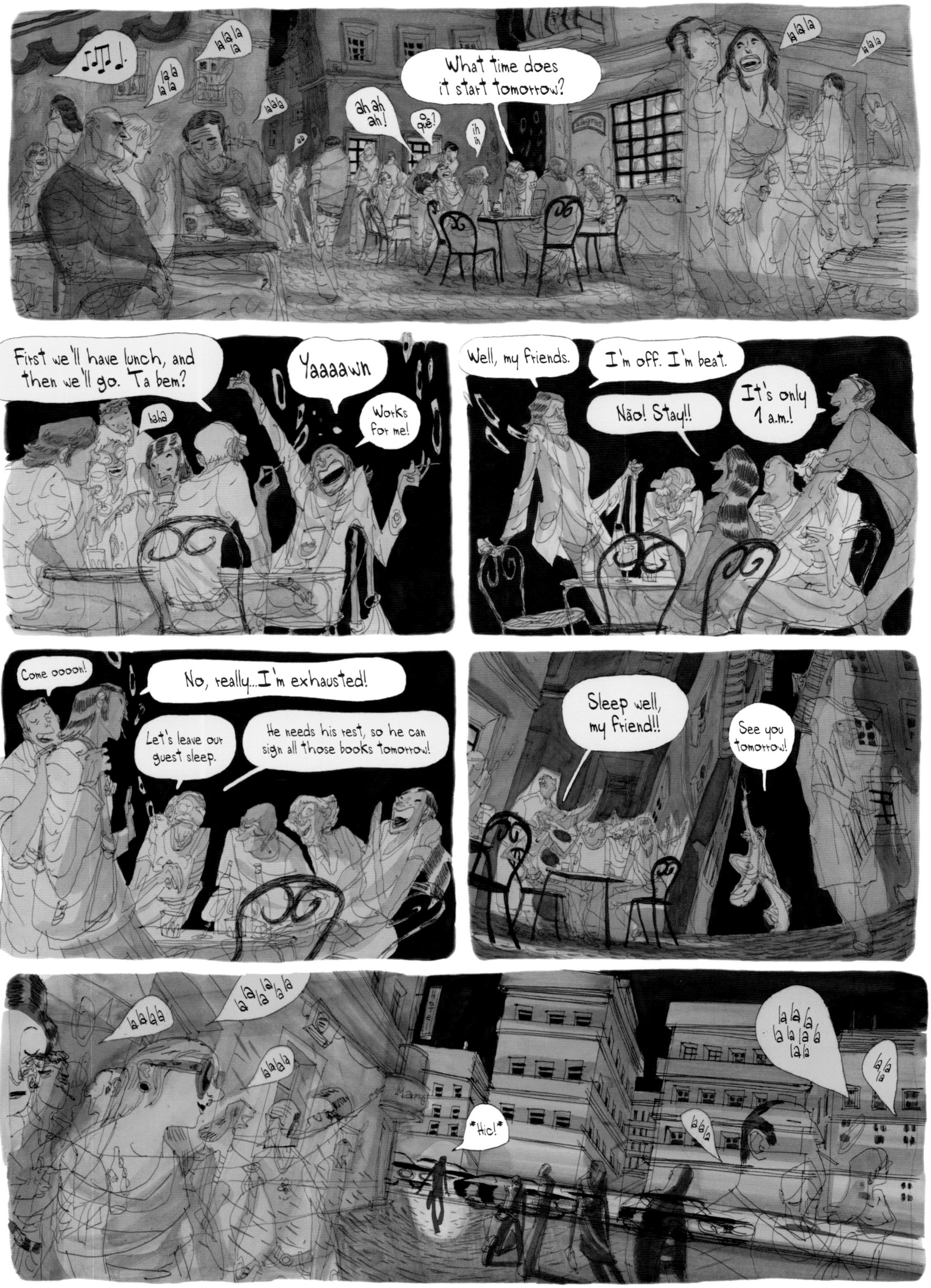
la la la
la la la
la la
la la
la la la
la
ah ah ah!
o quê?
ih ih
What time does it start tomorrow?
la la la
la la la
First we'll have lunch, and then we'll go. Ta bem?
haha
Yaaaawn
Works for me!
Well, my friends.
I'm off. I'm beat.
Não! Stay!!
It's only 1 a.m.!
Come ooooon!
No, really...I'm exhausted!
Let's leave our guest sleep.
He needs his rest, so he can sign all those books tomorrow!
Sleep well, my friend!!
See you tomorrow!
la la la
la la la la la
la la la
Hic!
la la la
la la la la la la la la la
la la la

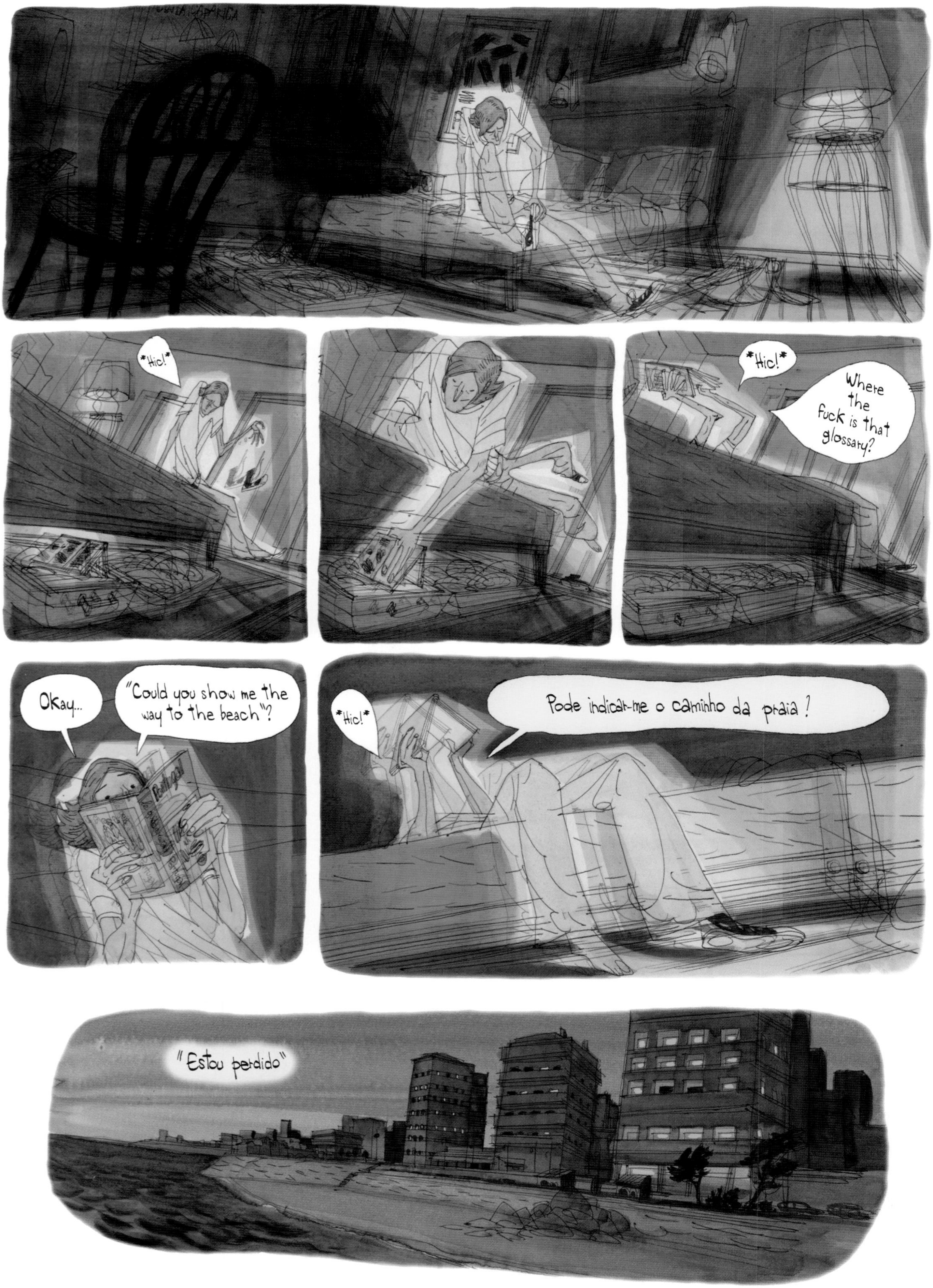
Hic!
Hic!
Where the fuck is that glossary?
Okay...
"Could you show me the way to the beach"?
Hic!
Pode indicar-me o caminho da praia?
"Estou perdido"

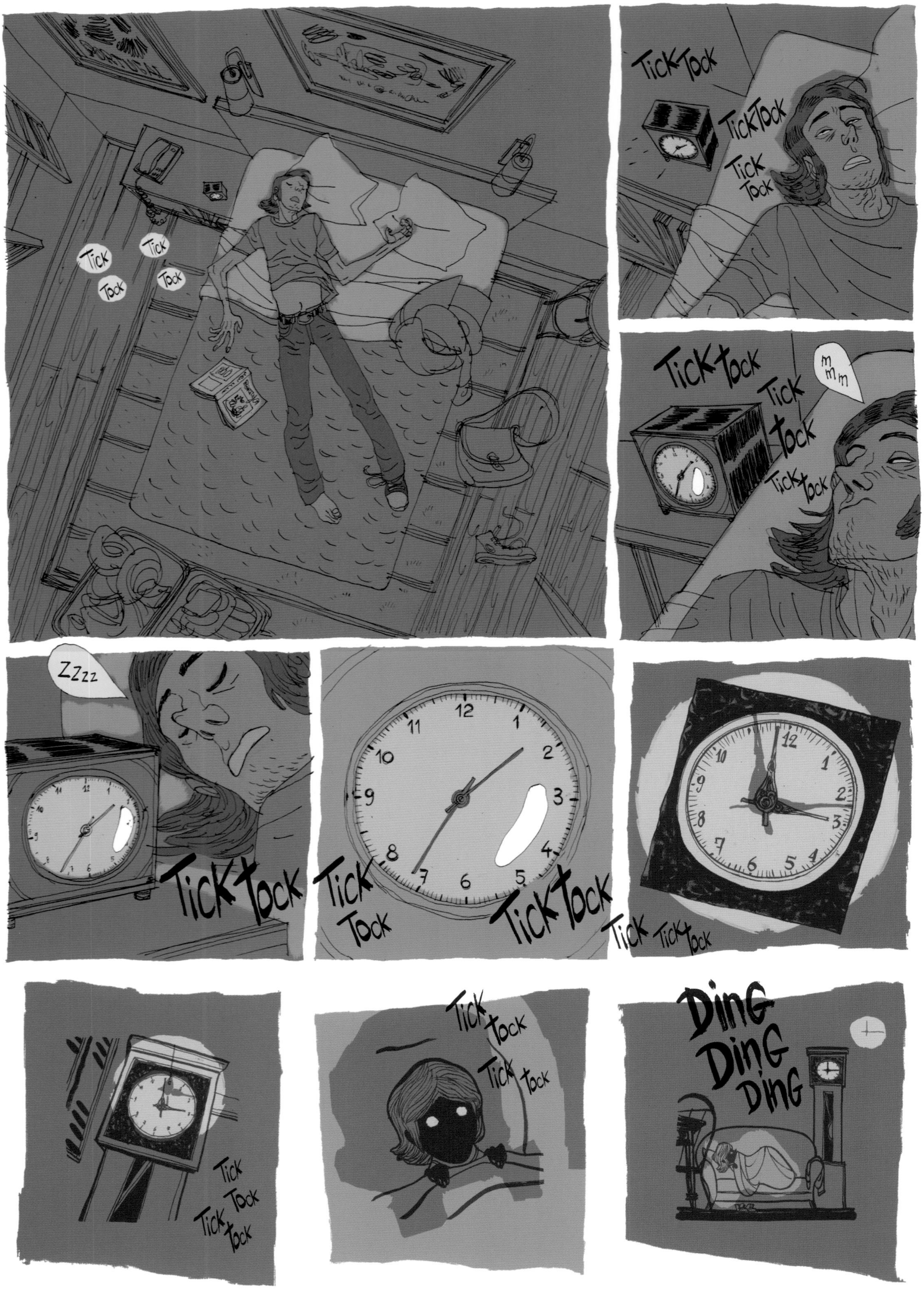
Tick
Tock
Tick
Tock
TickTock
TickTock
Tick
Tock
TickTock
mmm
Tick
Tock
TickTock
Zzzz
TickTock
Tick
Tock
TickTock
Tick
TickTock
Tick
Tock
Tick
Tock
TickTock
Tick
Tock
Ding
Ding
Ding

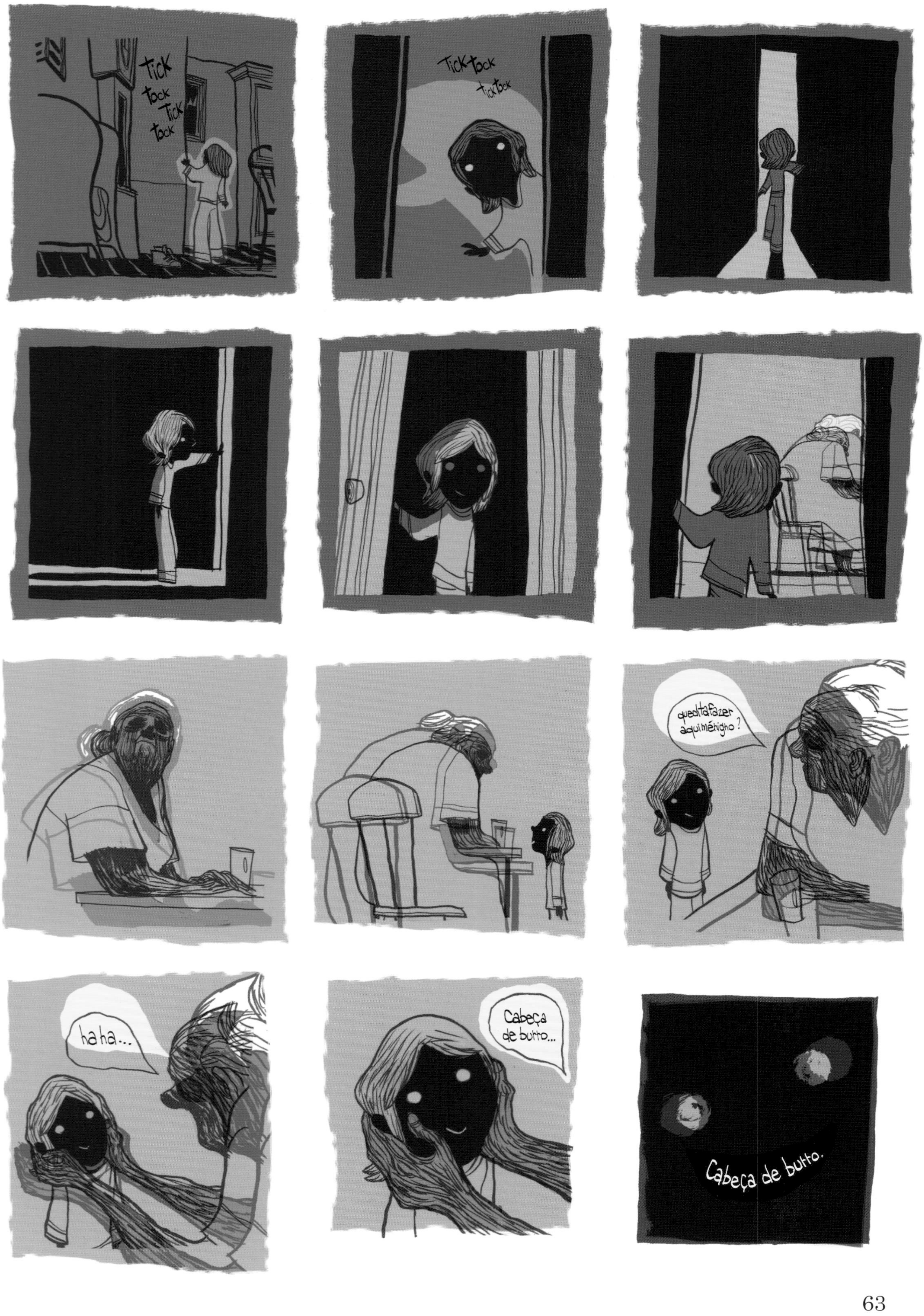

Tick tock Tick tock
Tick tock tick tock
quechtafazer aquiméhigho?
ha ha...
Cabeça de butto...
Cabeça de butto.

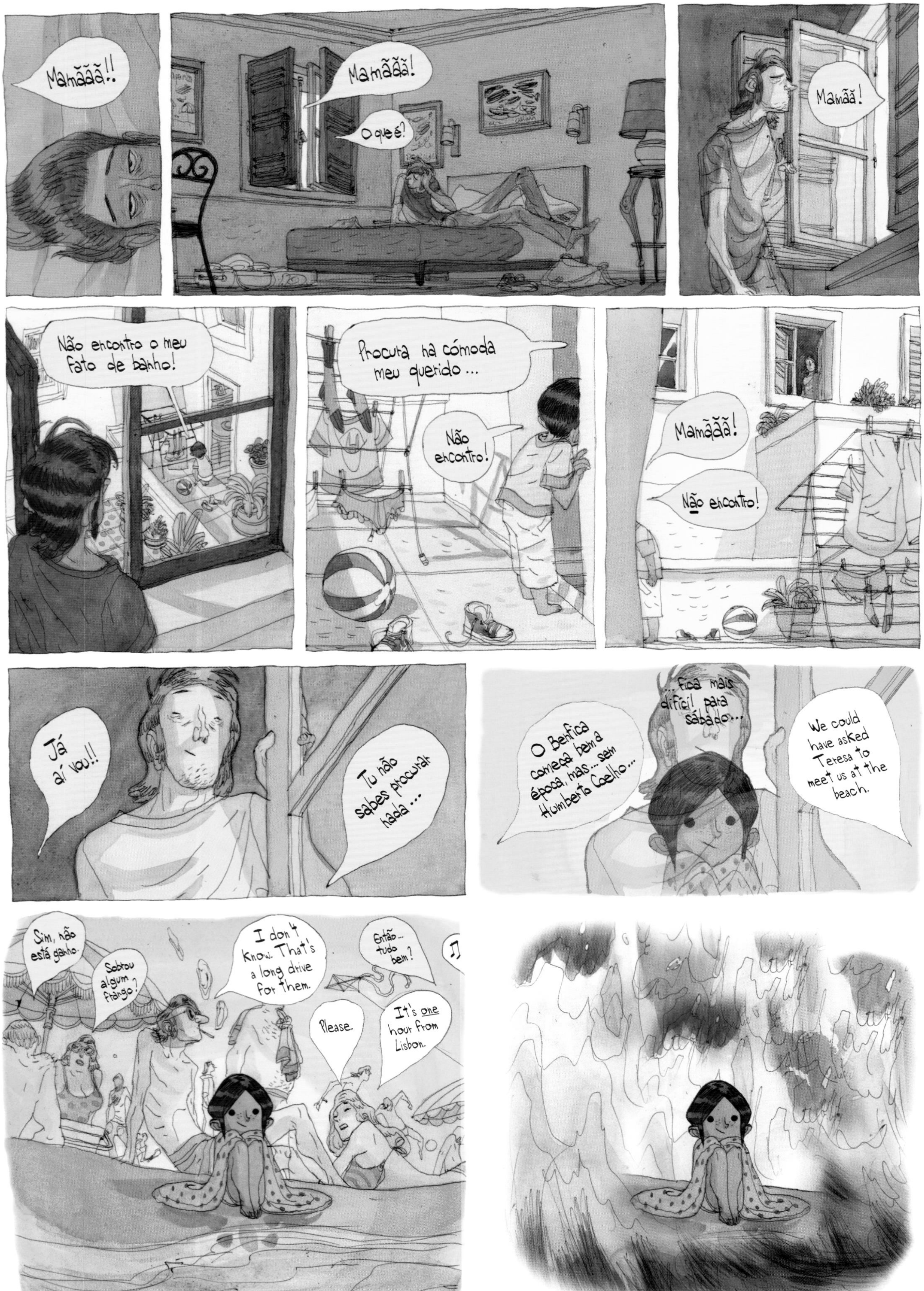
Mamããã!!
Mamããã!
O que é?
Mamãã!
Não encontro o meu fato de banho!
Procura na cómoda meu querido...
Não encontro!
Mamããã!
Não encontro!
Já aí vou!!
Tu não sabes procurar nada...
... fica mais difícil para sábado...
O Benfica começa bem a época, mas... sem Humberto Coelho...
We could have asked Teresa to meet us at the beach.
Sim, não está ganho.
Sobrou algum frango?
I don't know. That's a long drive for them.
Então... tudo bem?
Please.
It's one hour from Lisbon.

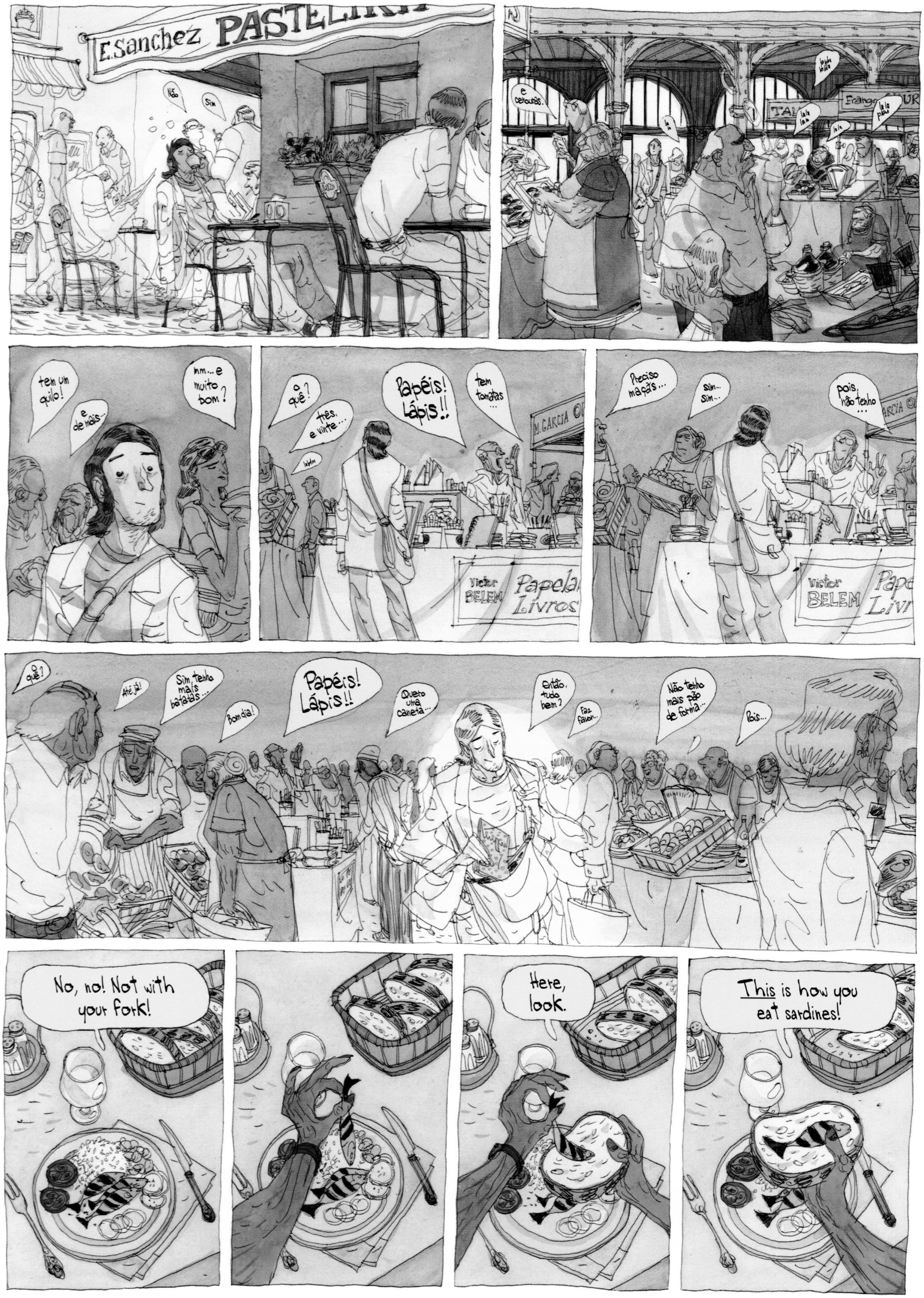
E. Sanchez PASTELARIA
Não
Sim
e cenouras.
la la
lala lala
la la
la la lala
la la plau
tem um quilo!
e de mais...
mm... e muito bom?
o quê?
três, e vinte...
Papéis! Lápis!!
tem tomatas ...
M. GARCIA
Victor BELEM Papelaria Livros
Preciso maçãs...
sim... sim...
pois, não tenho ...
o quê?
Até já!
Sim, tenho mais batatas...
Bom dia!
Papéis! Lápis!!
Quero uma caneta...
Então, tudo bem?
Faz favor...
Não tenho mais pão de forma...
Pois...
No, no! Not with your fork!
Here, look.
This is how you eat sardines!

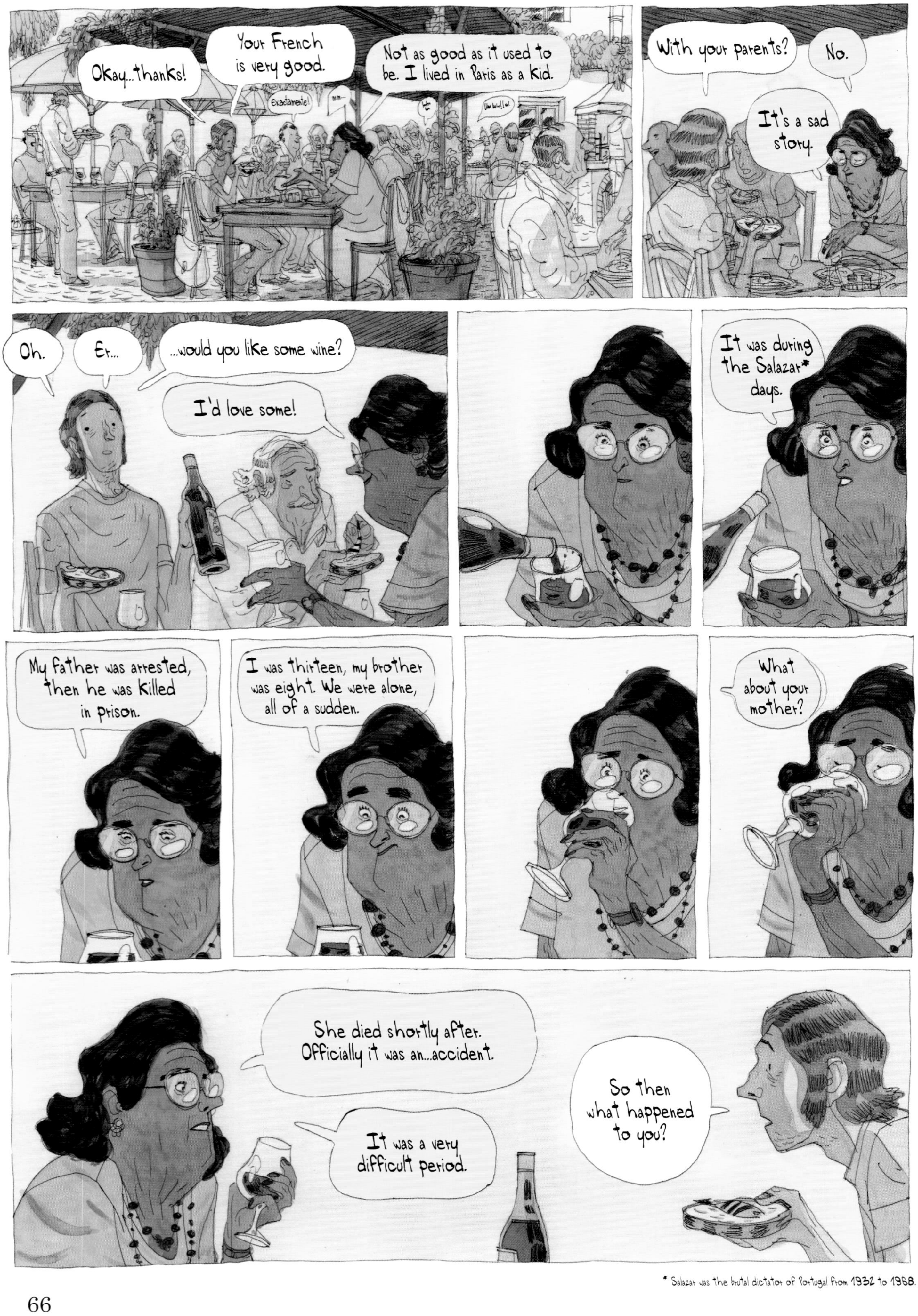
Okay...thanks!
Your French is very good.
Exactamente!
Not as good as it used to be. I lived in Paris as a kid.
With your parents?
No.
It's a sad story.
Oh.
Er...
...would you like some wine?
I'd love some!
It was during the Salazar* days.
My father was arrested, then he was killed in prison.
I was thirteen, my brother was eight. We were alone, all of a sudden.
What about your mother?
She died shortly after. Officially it was an...accident.
It was a very difficult period.
So then what happened to you?

* Salazar was the brutal dictator of Portugal from 1932 to 1968.

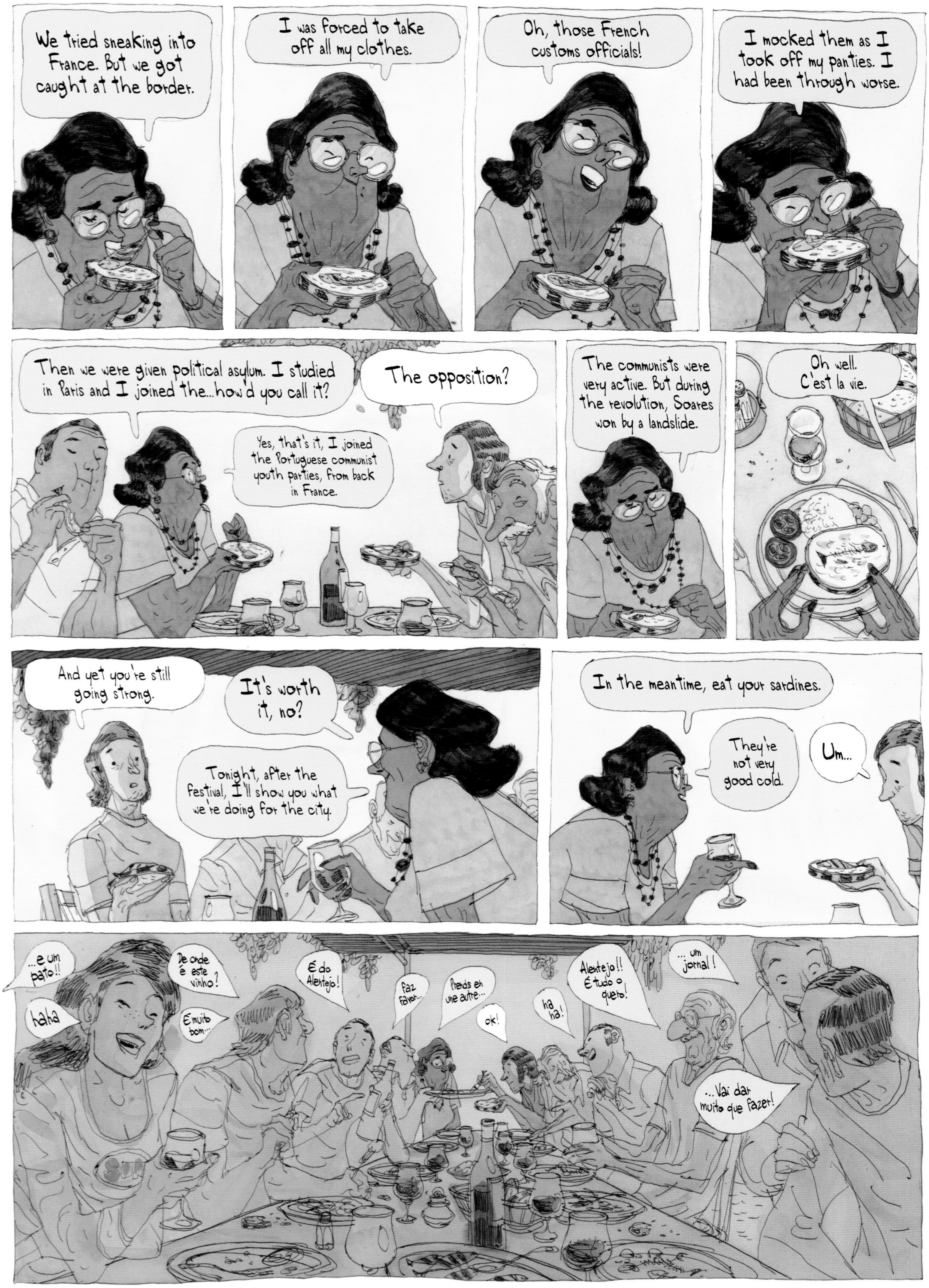
We tried sneaking into France. But we got caught at the border.
I was forced to take off all my clothes.
Oh, those French customs officials!
I mocked them as I took off my panties. I had been through worse.
Then we were given political asylum. I studied in Paris and I joined the... how'd you call it?
The opposition?
Yes, that's it, I joined the Portuguese communist youth parties, from back in France.
The communists were very active. But during the revolution, Soares won by a landslide.
Oh well. C'est la vie.
And yet you're still going strong.
It's worth it, no?
Tonight, after the festival, I'll show you what we're doing for the city.
In the meantime, eat your sardines.
They're not very good cold.
Um...
...e um pato!!
haha
De onde é este vinho?
É muito bom...
É do Alentejo!
Faz favor...
Prends en une autre...
ok!
ha ha!
Alentejo!! É tudo o quero!
... um jornal!
...Vai dar muito que fazer!

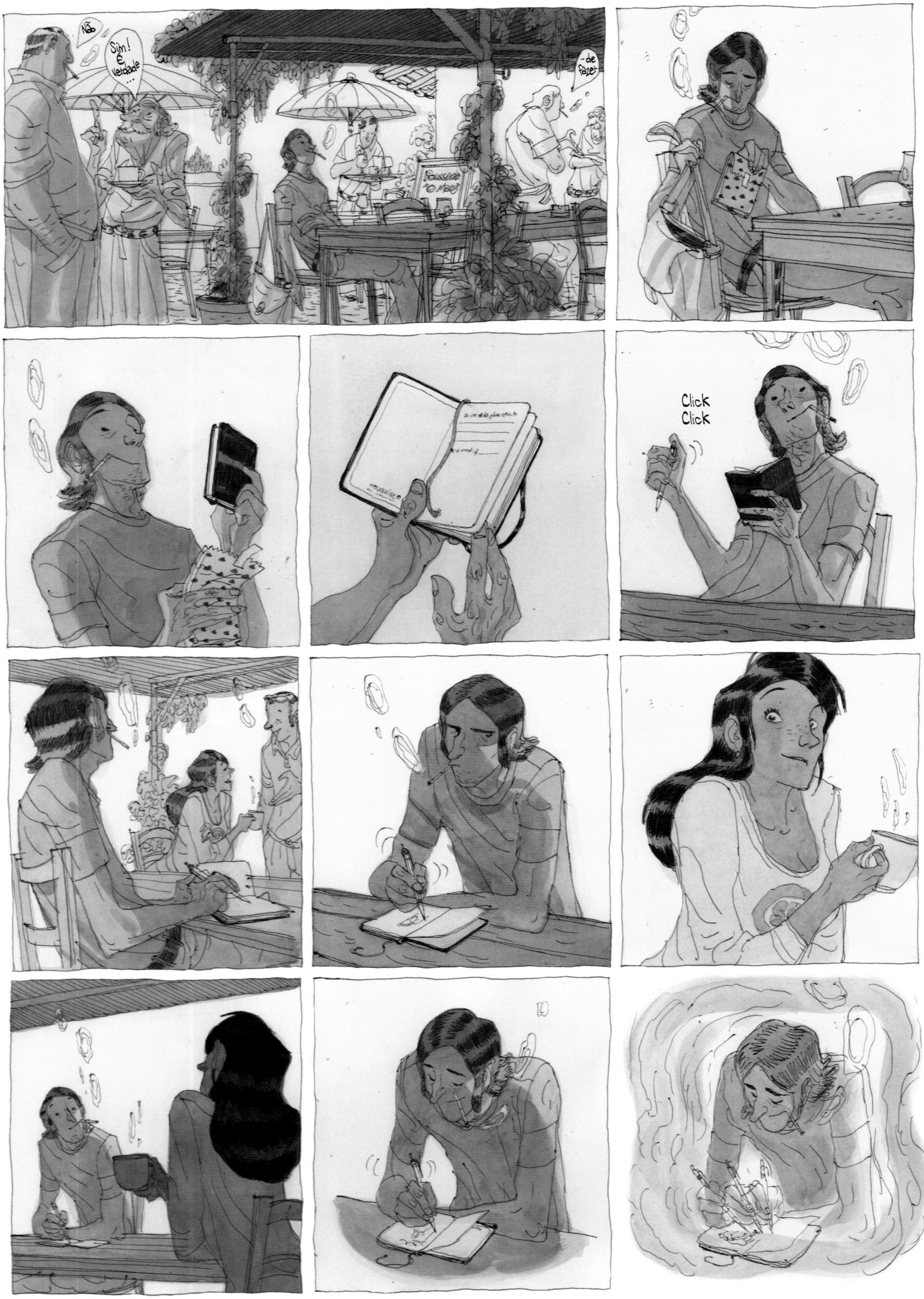
Não
Sim! É verdade ...
...de fazer
Click Click

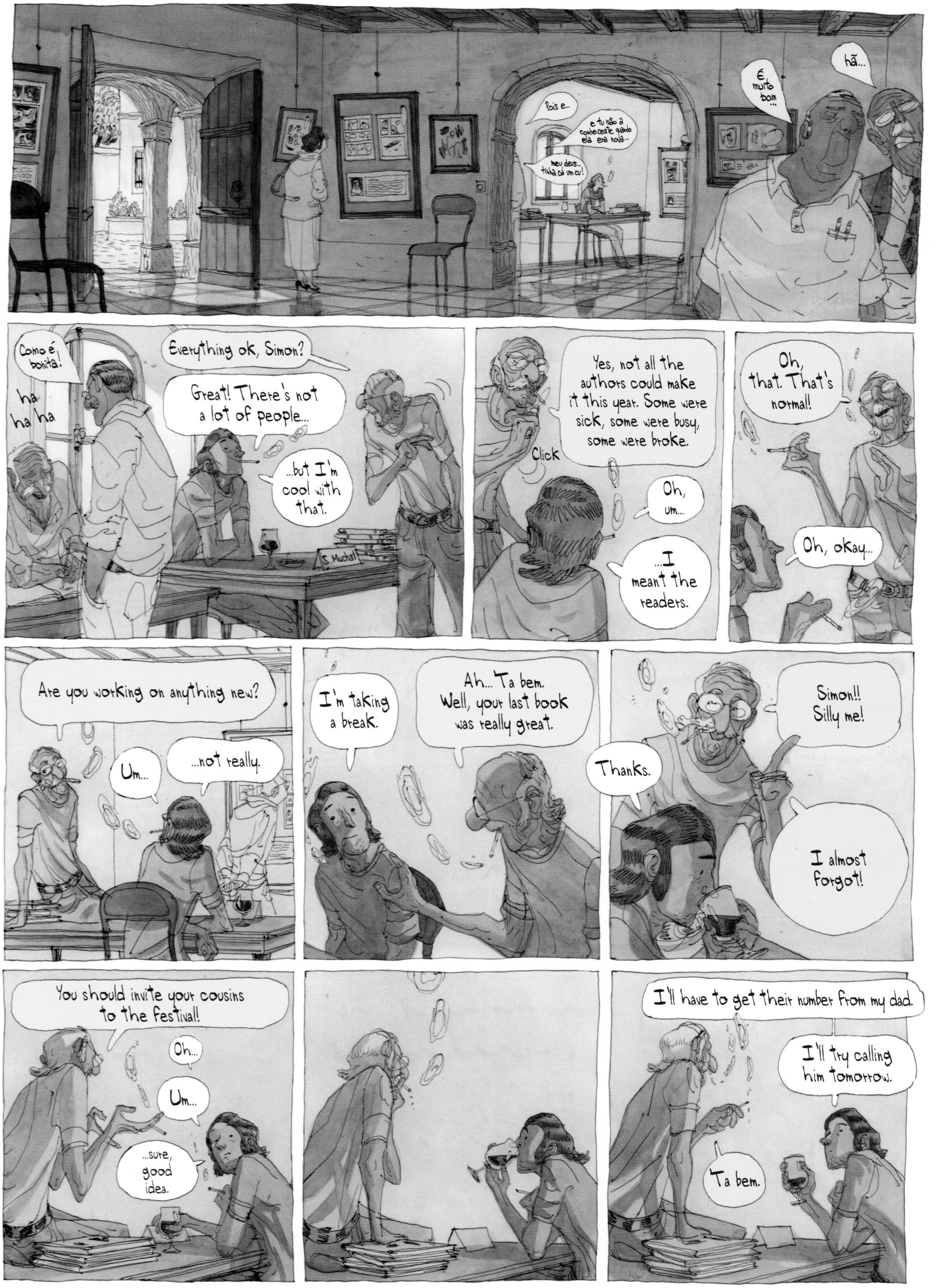
Pois e...
e tu não a conheceste quando ela era nova...
meu deus... tinha cá um cu!
É muito bom...
hã...
Como é bonita!
ha ha ha
Everything ok, Simon?
Great! There's not a lot of people...
...but I'm cool with that.
S. Muchat
Yes, not all the authors could make it this year. Some were sick, some were busy, some were broke.
Click
Oh, um...
...I meant the readers.
Oh, that. That's normal!
Oh, okay...
Are you working on anything new?
Um...
...not really.
I'm taking a break.
Ah... Ta bem. Well, your last book was really great.
Thanks.
Simon!! Silly me!
I almost forgot!
You should invite your cousins to the festival!
Oh...
Um...
...sure, good idea.
I'll have to get their number from my dad.
I'll try calling him tomorrow.
Ta bem.

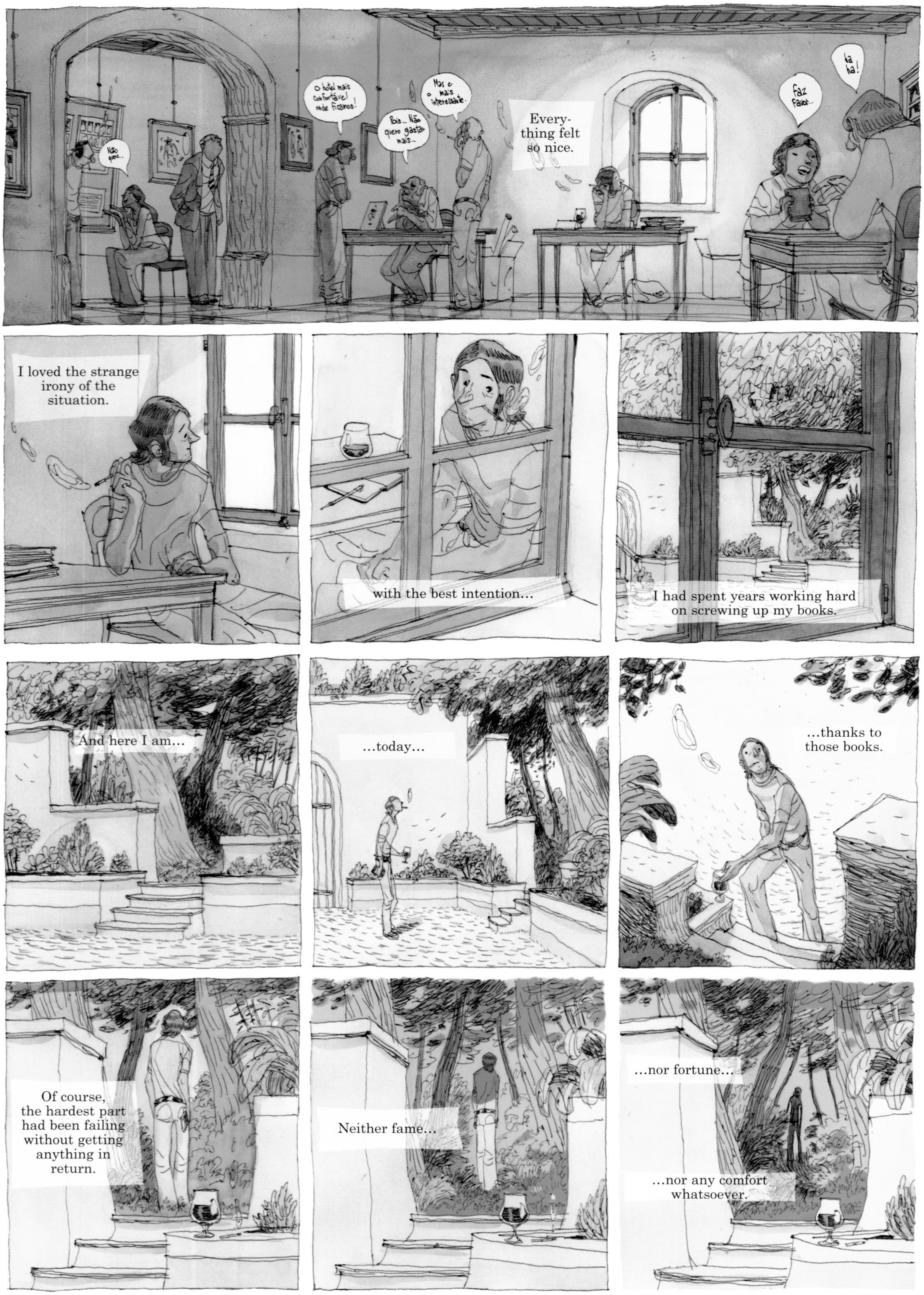
Não quero...
O hotel mais confortável onde ficamos!
Pois... Não quero gastar mais...
Mas é o mais interessante.
Every-thing felt so nice.
Faz favor...
Ha ha!
I loved the strange irony of the situation.
with the best intention...
I had spent years working hard on screwing up my books.
And here I am...
...today...
...thanks to those books.
Of course, the hardest part had been failing without getting anything in return.
Neither fame...
...nor fortune...
...nor any comfort whatsoever.

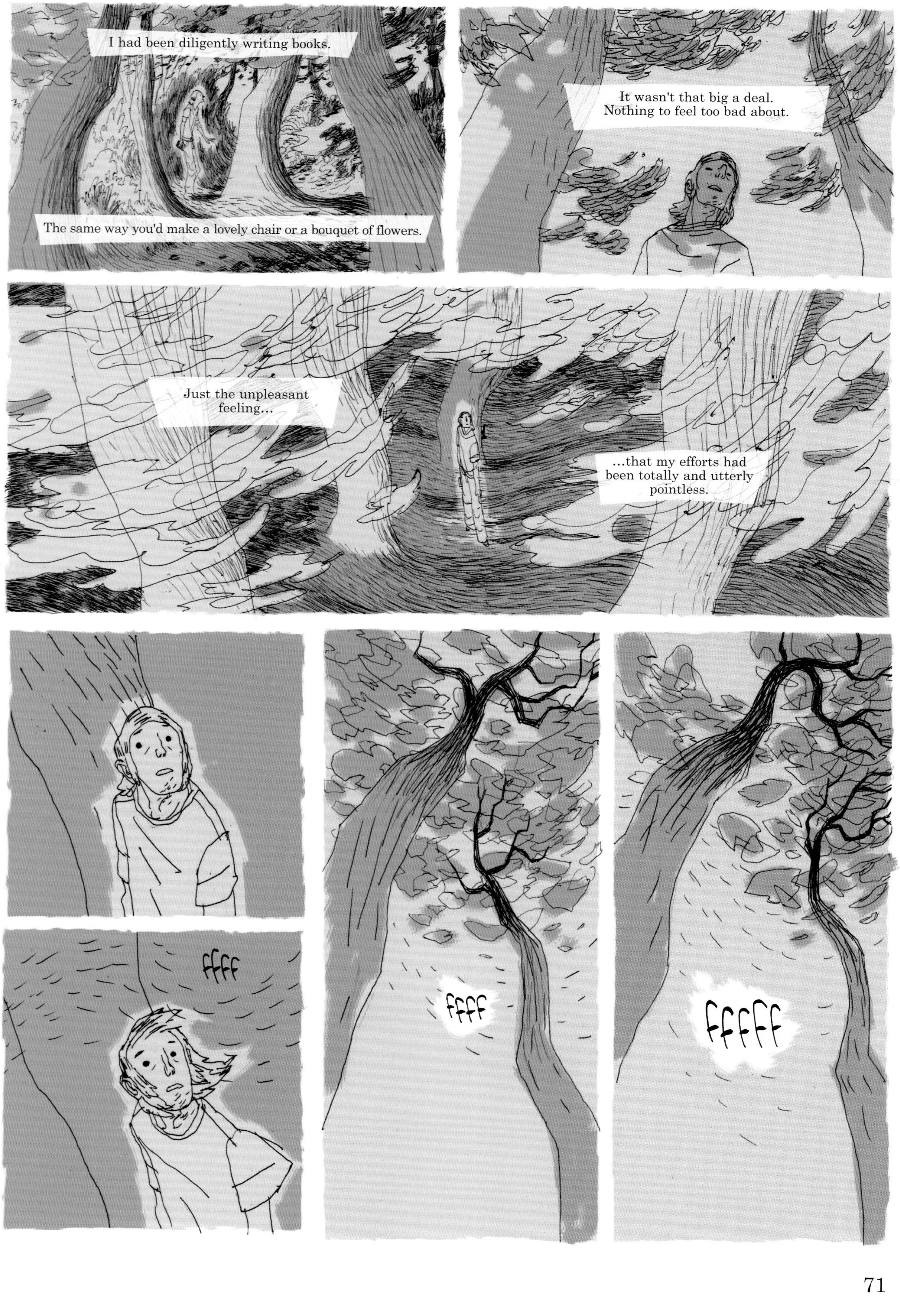
I had been diligently writing books.
The same way you'd make a lovely chair or a bouquet of flowers.
It wasn't that big a deal. Nothing to feel too bad about.
Just the unpleasant feeling...
...that my efforts had been totally and utterly pointless.
ffff
ffff
fffff

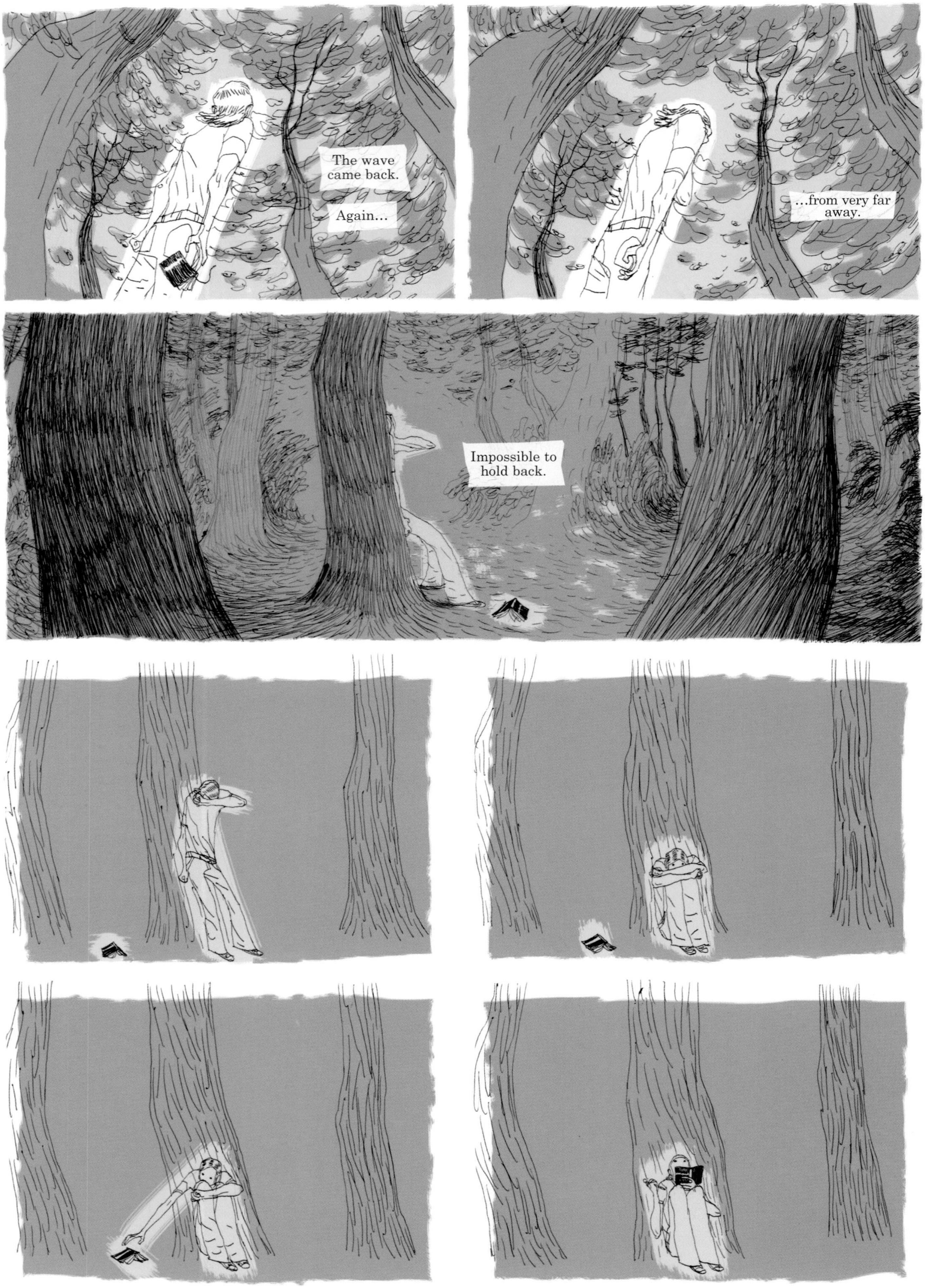
The wave came back.
Again...
...from very far away.
Impossible to hold back.

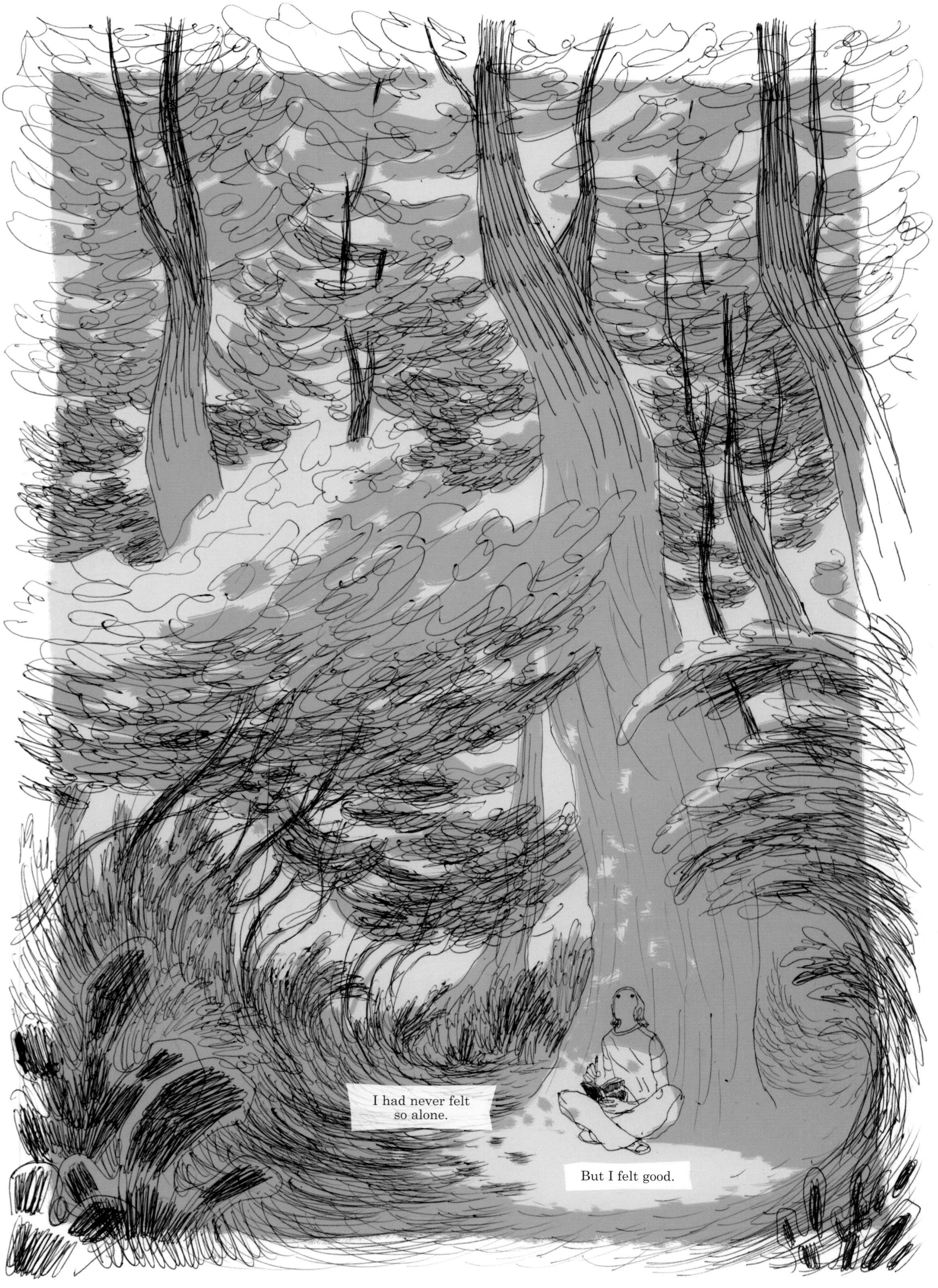
I had never felt so alone.
But I felt good.

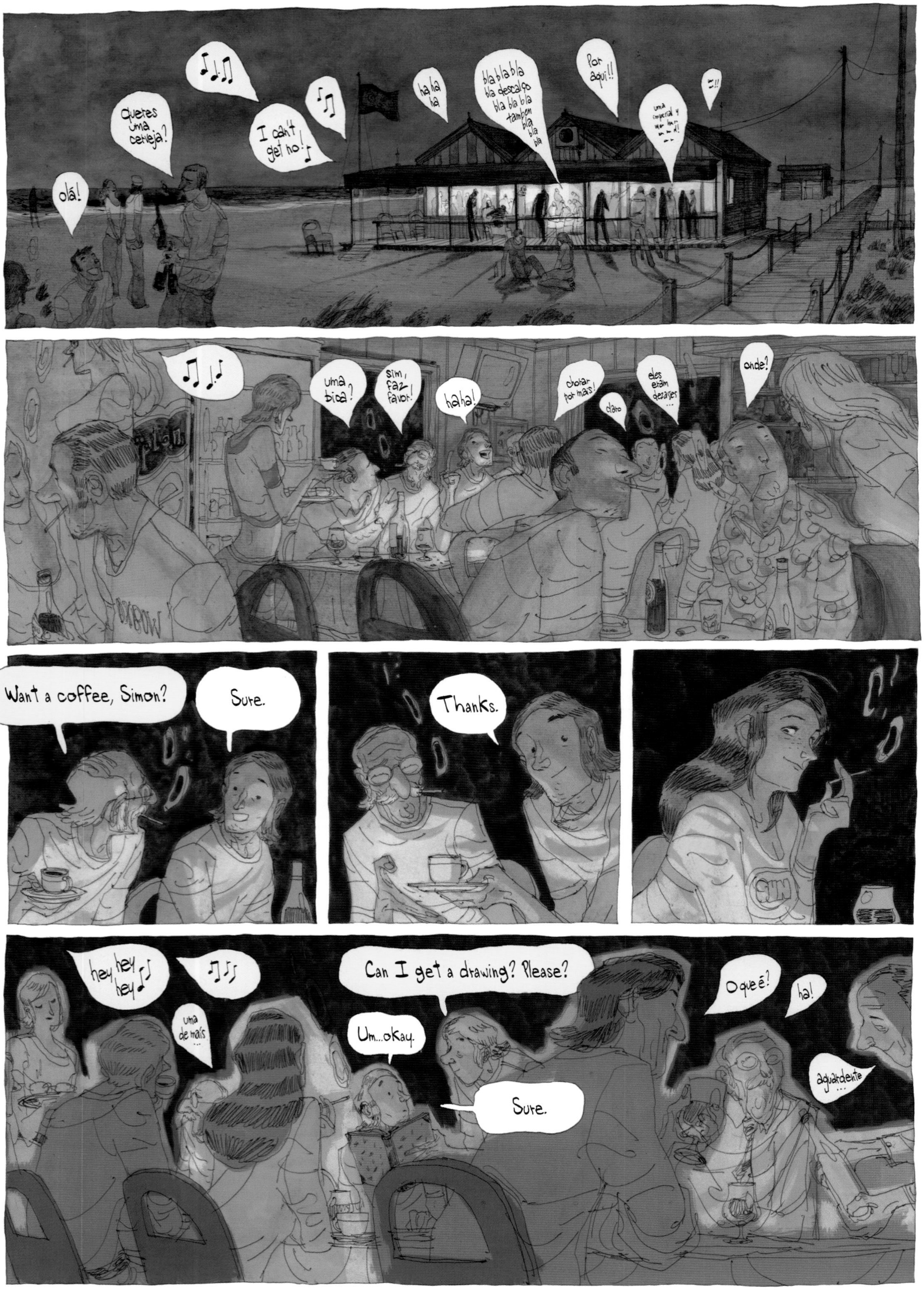
olá!
Queres uma cerveja?
I can't get no!
ha ha ha
bla bla bla bla descalço bla bla bla tambem bla bla bla
Por aqui!!
uma imperial y
uma bica?
sim, faz favor!
haha!
chorar por mais!
claro
eles eram dezasseis ...
onde?
Want a coffee, Simon?
Sure.
Thanks.
hey hey hey
uma de mais ...
Can I get a drawing? Please?
Um...okay.
Sure.
O que é?
ha!
aguardente ...

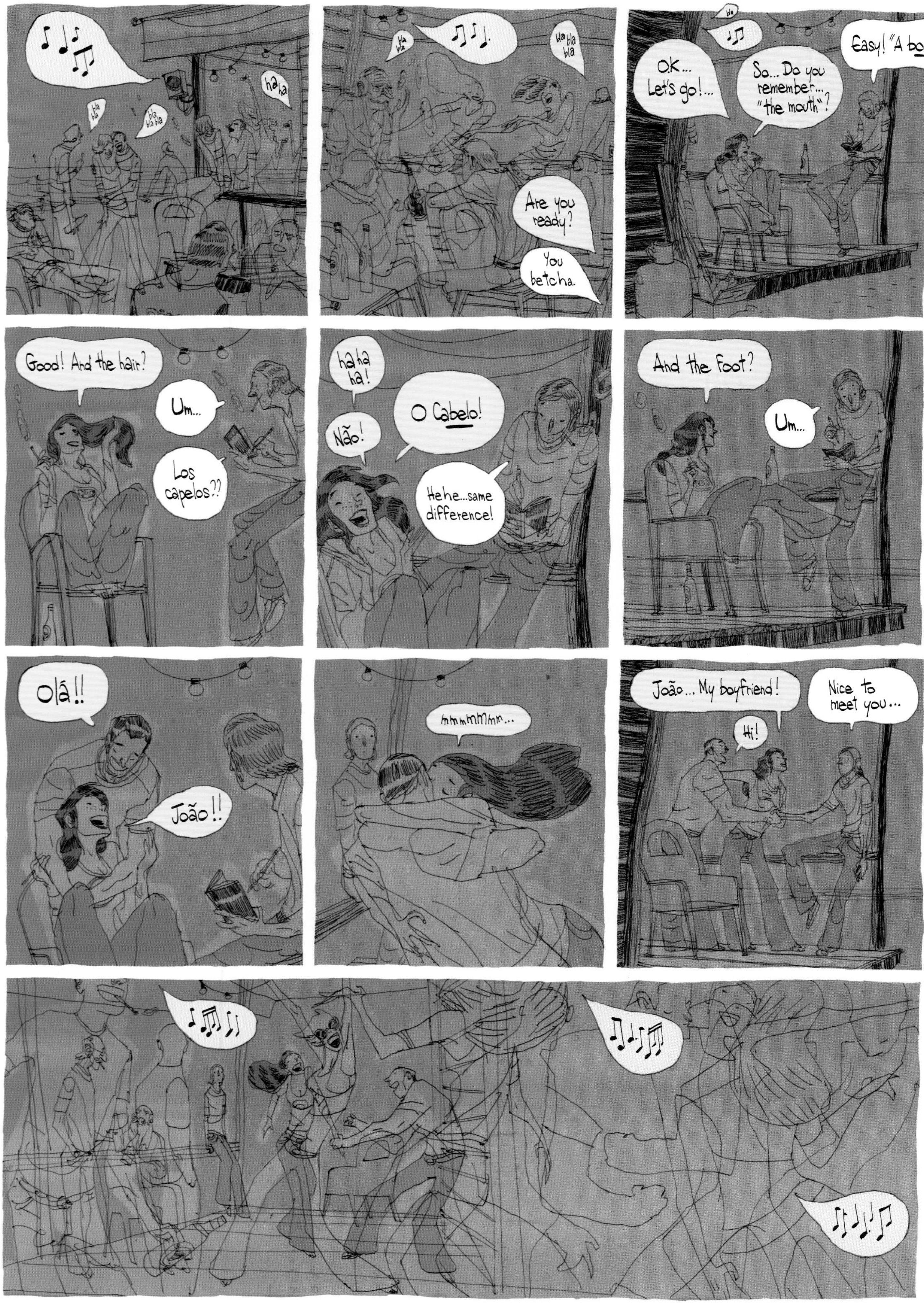
ha ha
bla bla
bla bla bla
bla bla
bla bla bla
Are you ready?
You betcha.
bla
O.K... Let's go!...
So... Do you remember... "the mouth"?
Easy! "A boca"!
Good! And the hair?
Um...
Los capelos??
ha ha ha!
Não!
O Cabelo!
Hehe...same difference!
And the foot?
Um...
Olá!!
João!!
mmmMMmm...
João... My boyfriend!
Hi!
Nice to meet you...

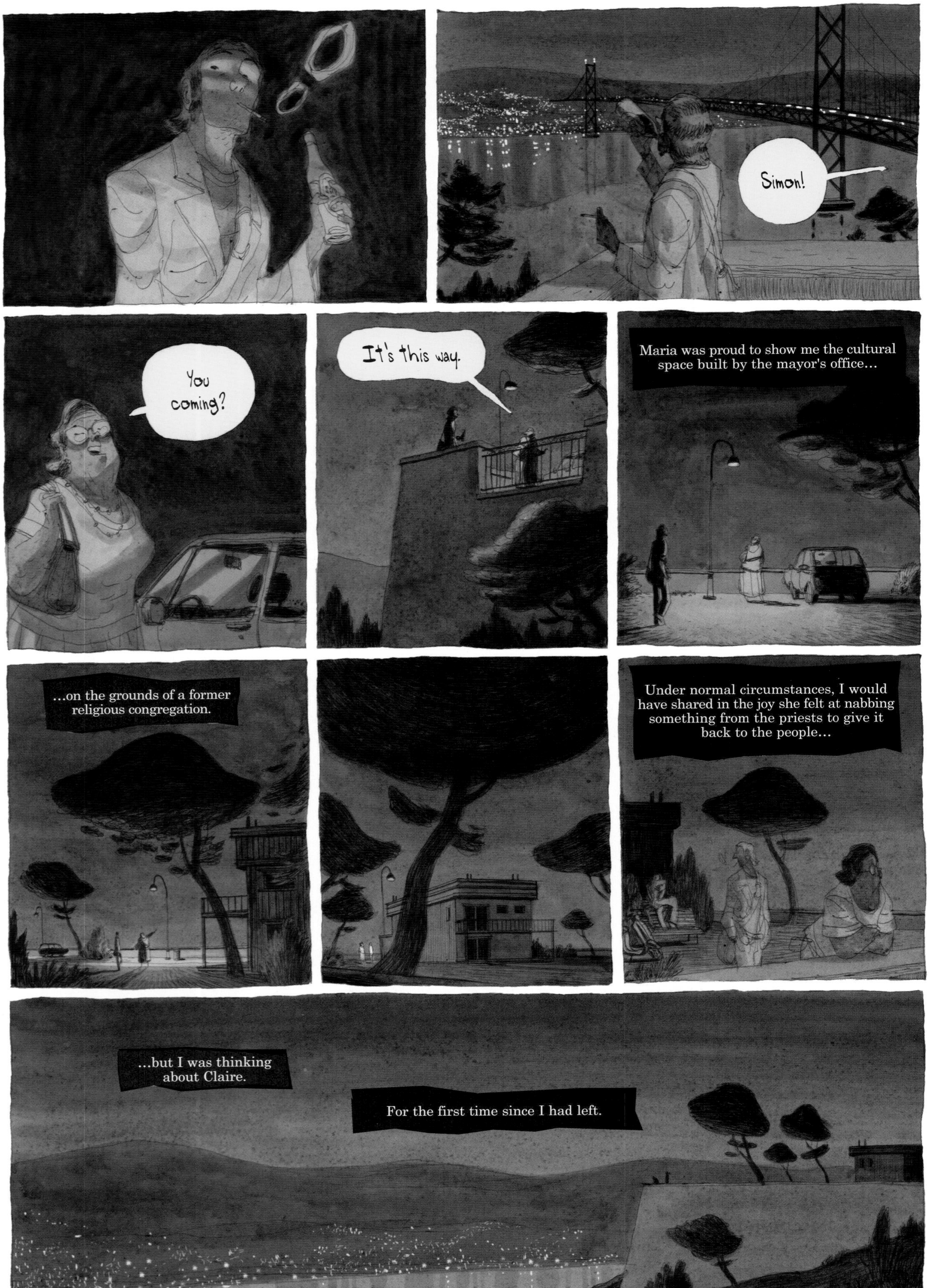
Simon!
You coming?
It's this way.
Maria was proud to show me the cultural space built by the mayor's office...
...on the grounds of a former religious congregation.
Under normal circumstances, I would have shared in the joy she felt at nabbing something from the priests to give it back to the people...
...but I was thinking about Claire.
For the first time since I had left.

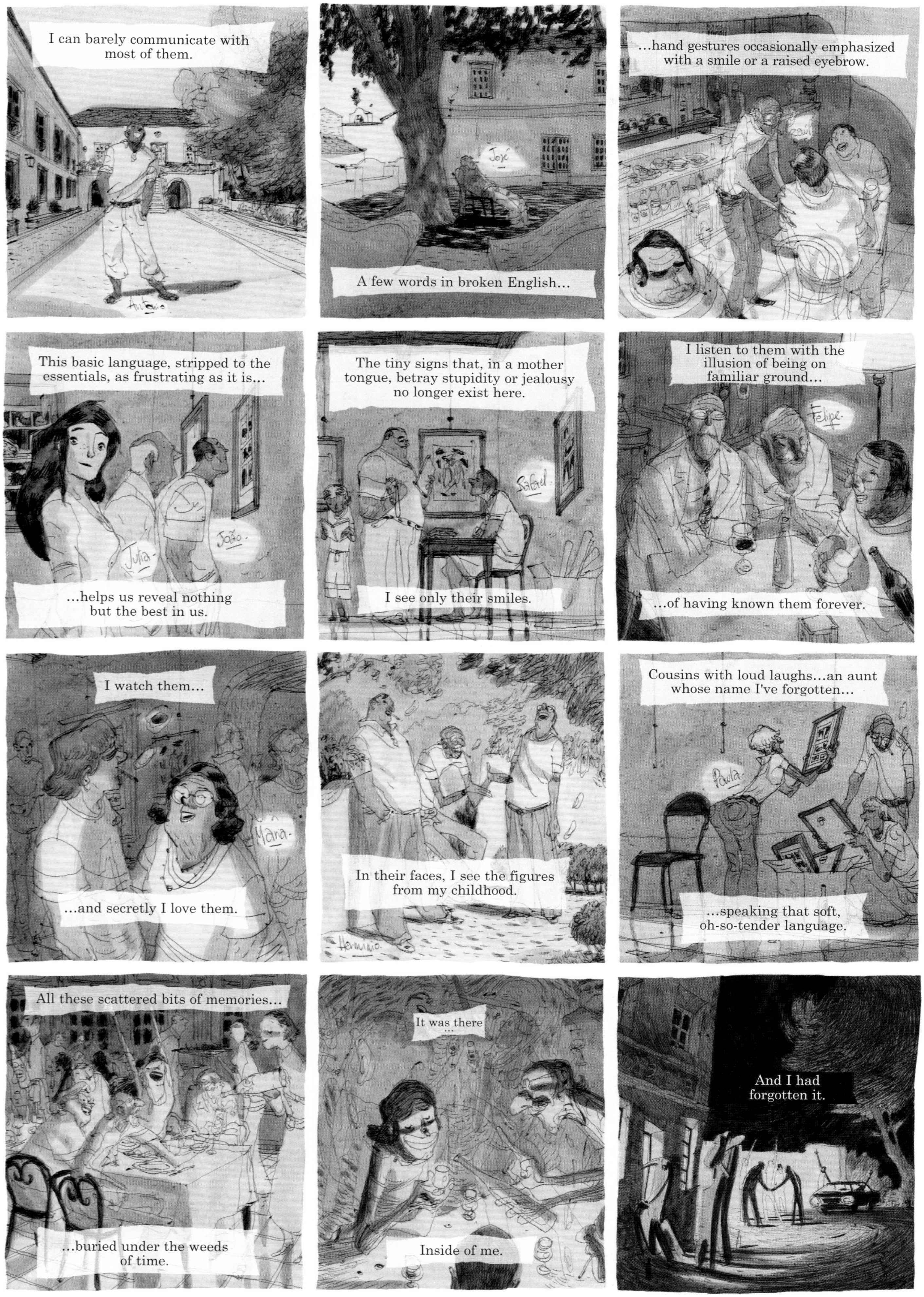

I can barely communicate with most of them.
Antonio
A few words in broken English...
José
...hand gestures occasionally emphasized with a smile or a raised eyebrow.
Raul
This basic language, stripped to the essentials, as frustrating as it is...
Julia
João
...helps us reveal nothing but the best in us.
The tiny signs that, in a mother tongue, betray stupidity or jealousy no longer exist here.
Rafael
I see only their smiles.
I listen to them with the illusion of being on familiar ground...
Felipe
...of having known them forever.
I watch them...
Maria
...and secretly I love them.
In their faces, I see the figures from my childhood.
Herminio.
Cousins with loud laughs...an aunt whose name I've forgotten...
Paula
...speaking that soft, oh-so-tender language.
All these scattered bits of memories...
...buried under the weeds of time.
It was there
...
Inside of me.
And I had forgotten it.

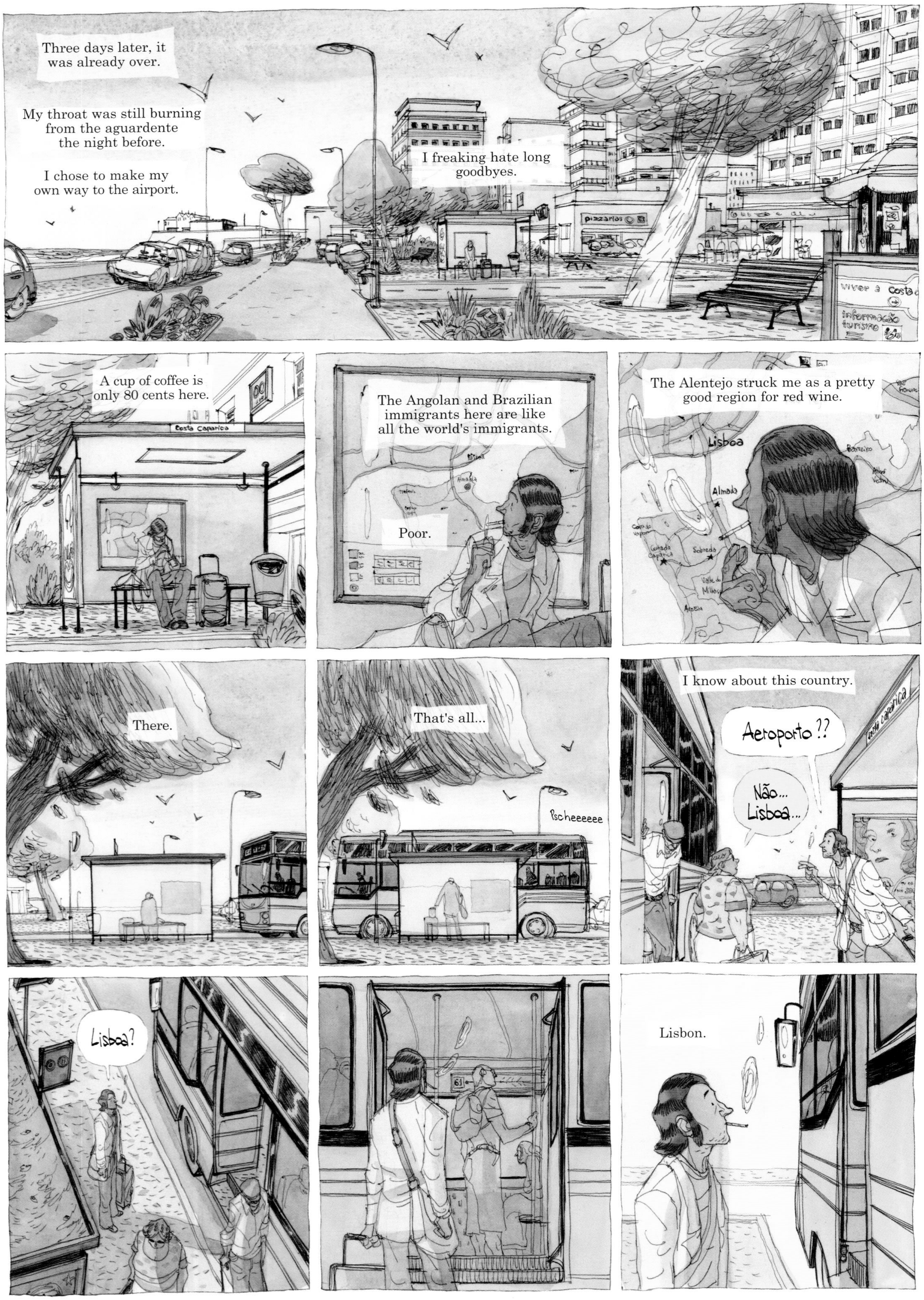

Three days later, it was already over.
My throat was still burning from the aguardente the night before.
I chose to make my own way to the airport.
I freaking hate long goodbyes.
pizzarias
viver a costa
informação turismo
A cup of coffee is only 80 cents here.
Costa Caparica
The Angolan and Brazilian immigrants here are like all the world's immigrants.
Poor.
The Alentejo struck me as a pretty good region for red wine.
Lisboa
Almada
There.
That's all...
Pscheeeeee
I know about this country.
Aeroporto ??
Não... Lisboa...
Costa Caparica
Lisboa?
61
Lisbon.

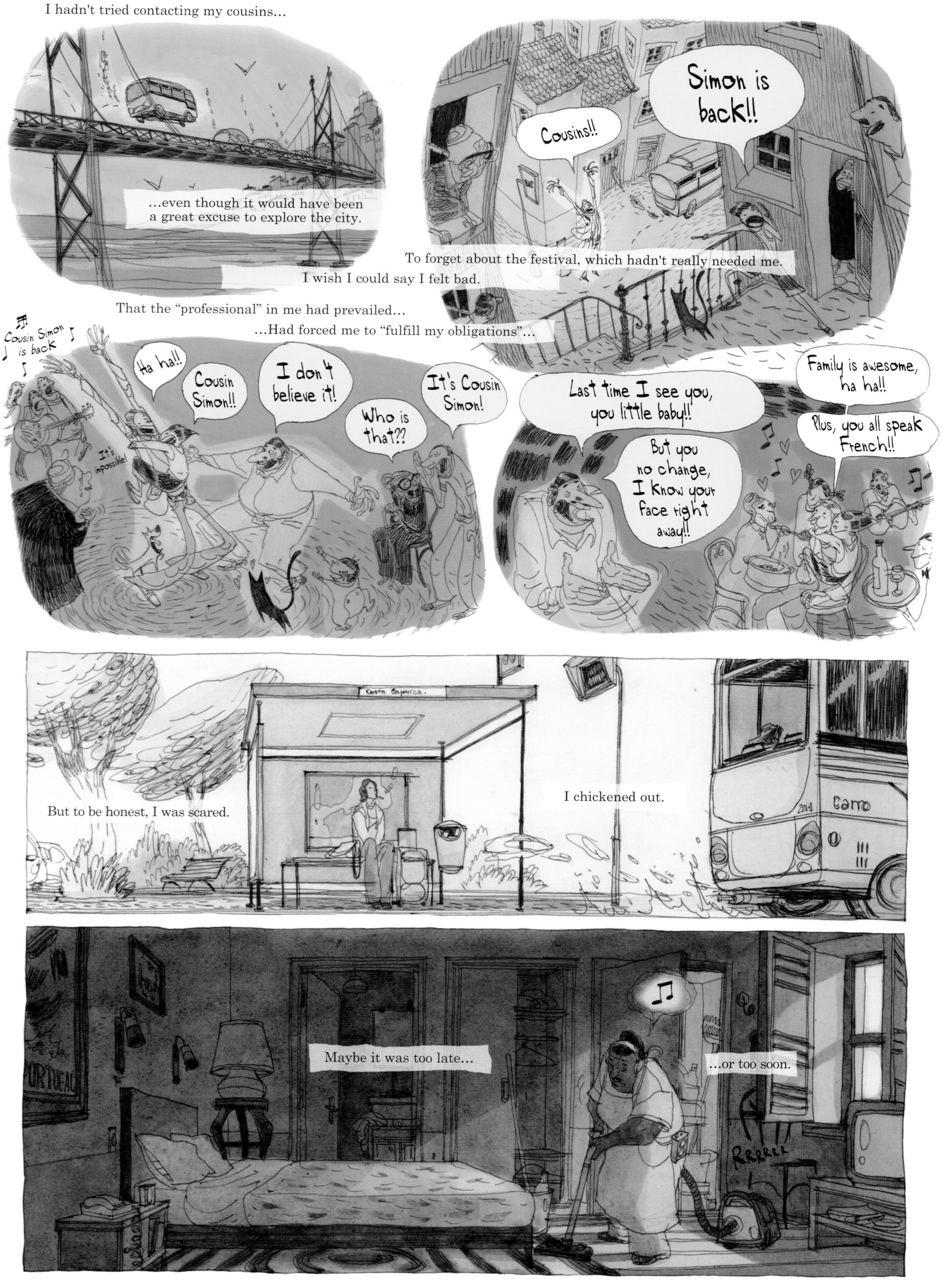
I hadn't tried contacting my cousins...
...even though it would have been a great excuse to explore the city.
To forget about the festival, which hadn't really needed me.
Cousins!!
Simon is back!!
I wish I could say I felt bad.
That the "professional" in me had prevailed...
...Had forced me to "fulfill my obligations"...
Cousin Simon is back
Ha ha!!
It's impossible!
Cousin Simon!!
I don't believe it!
Who is that??
It's Cousin Simon!
Last time I see you, you little baby!!
But you no change, I know your face right away!!
Family is awesome, ha ha!!
Plus, you all speak French!!
But to be honest, I was scared.
I chickened out.
Maybe it was too late...
...or too soon.
Rrrrrr

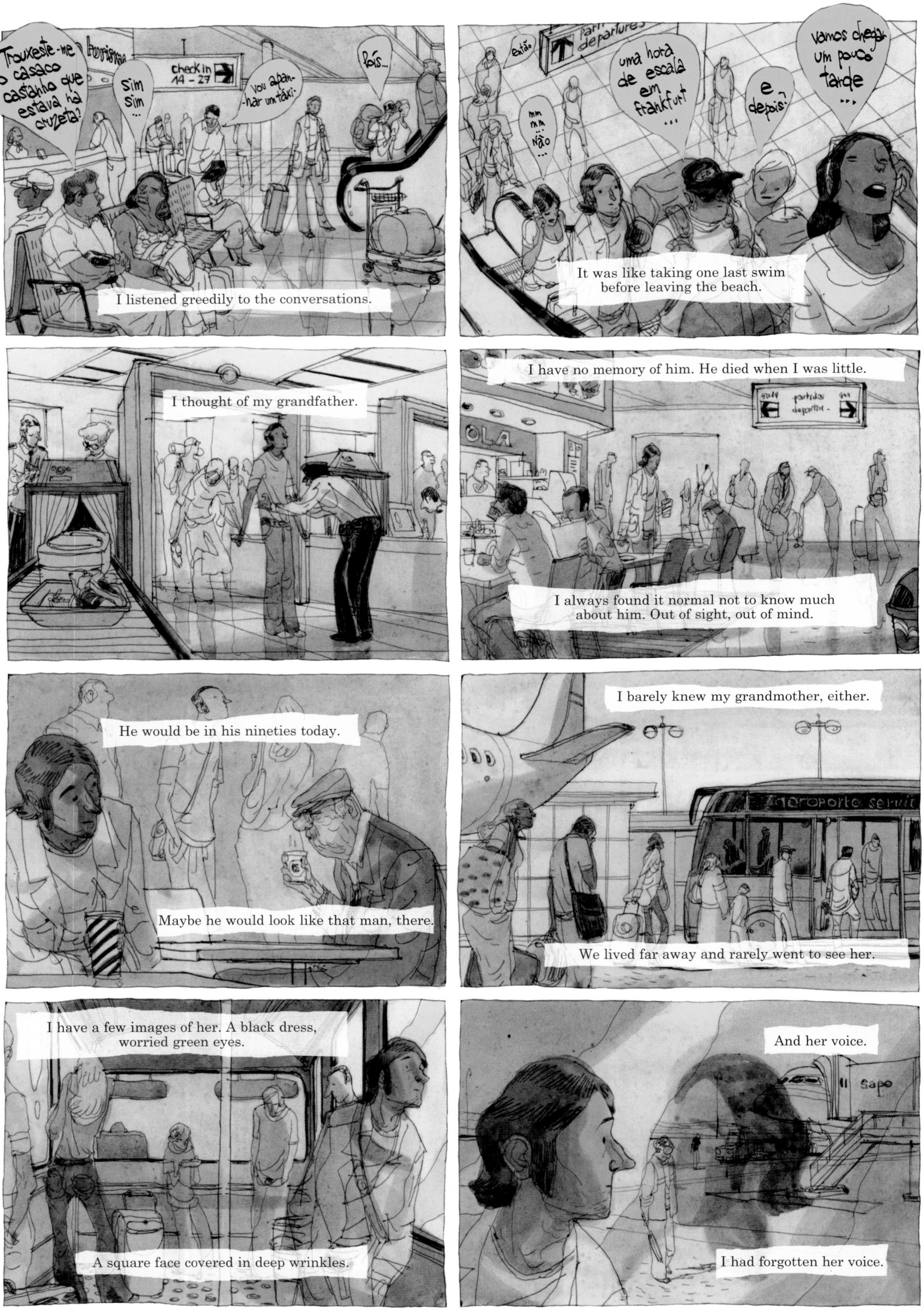
Trouxeste-me o casaco castanho que estava na cruzeta?
Sim sim ...
check in 14 - 27
Vou apanhar um táxi.
Luís...
I listened greedily to the conversations.
então
departures
mm mm ... Não ...
uma hora de escala em frankfurt ...
e depois?
Vamos chegar um pouco tarde ...
It was like taking one last swim before leaving the beach.
I thought of my grandfather.
I have no memory of him. He died when I was little.
I always found it normal not to know much about him. Out of sight, out of mind.
He would be in his nineties today.
Maybe he would look like that man, there.
I barely knew my grandmother, either.
We lived far away and rarely went to see her.
I have a few images of her. A black dress, worried green eyes.
A square face covered in deep wrinkles.
And her voice.
sapo
I had forgotten her voice.

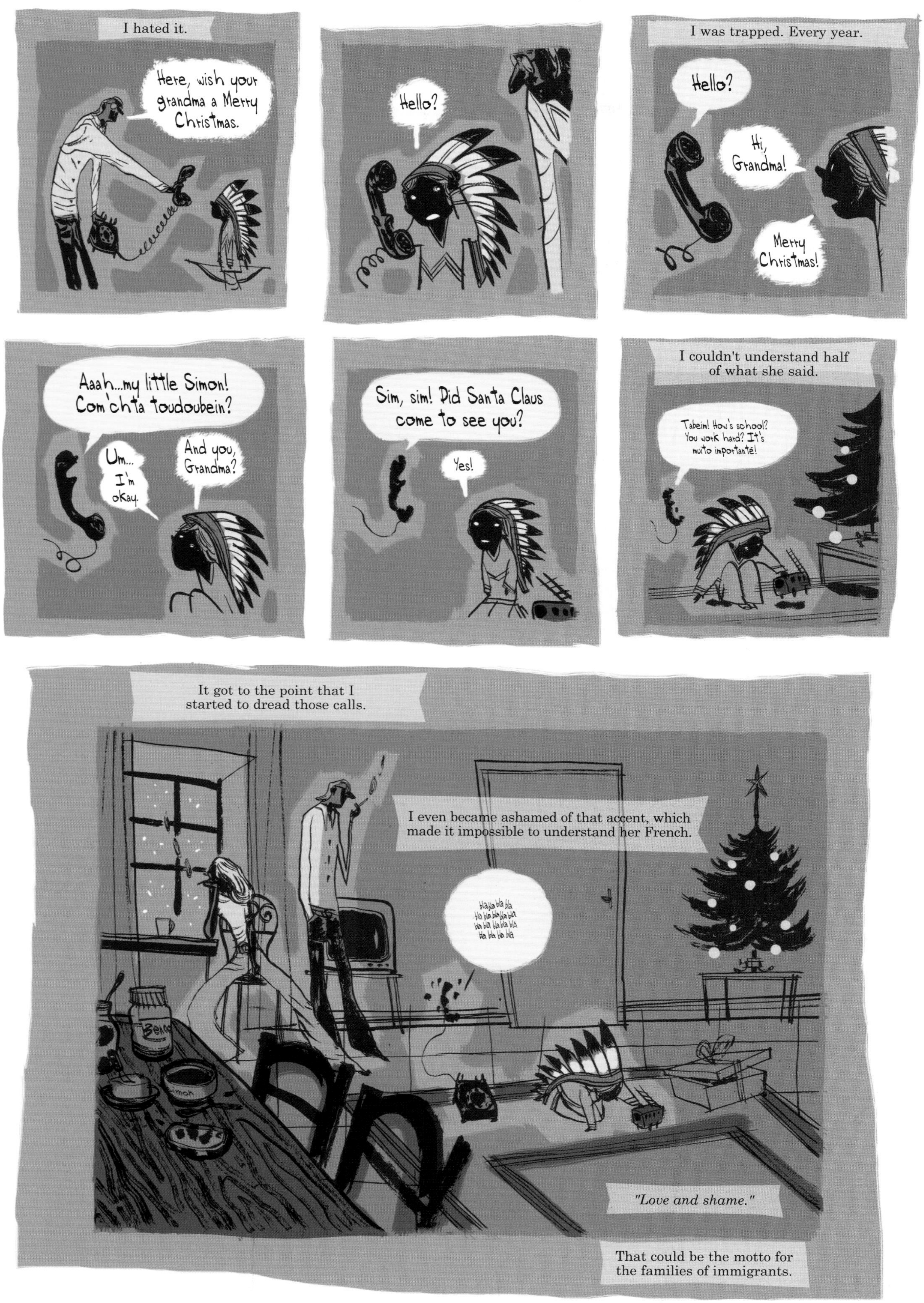
I hated it.
Here, wish your grandma a Merry Christmas.
Hello?
I was trapped. Every year.
Hello?
Hi, Grandma!
Merry Christmas!
Aaah...my little Simon! Com'ch'ta toudoubein?
Um... I'm okay.
And you, Grandma?
Sim, sim! Did Santa Claus come to see you?
Yes!
I couldn't understand half of what she said.
Tabeim! How's school? You work hard? It's muito importanté!
It got to the point that I started to dread those calls.
I even became ashamed of that accent, which made it impossible to understand her French.
bla bla bla bla bla bla bla bla bla bla bla bla bla bla bla bla bla bla
"Love and shame."
That could be the motto for the families of immigrants.

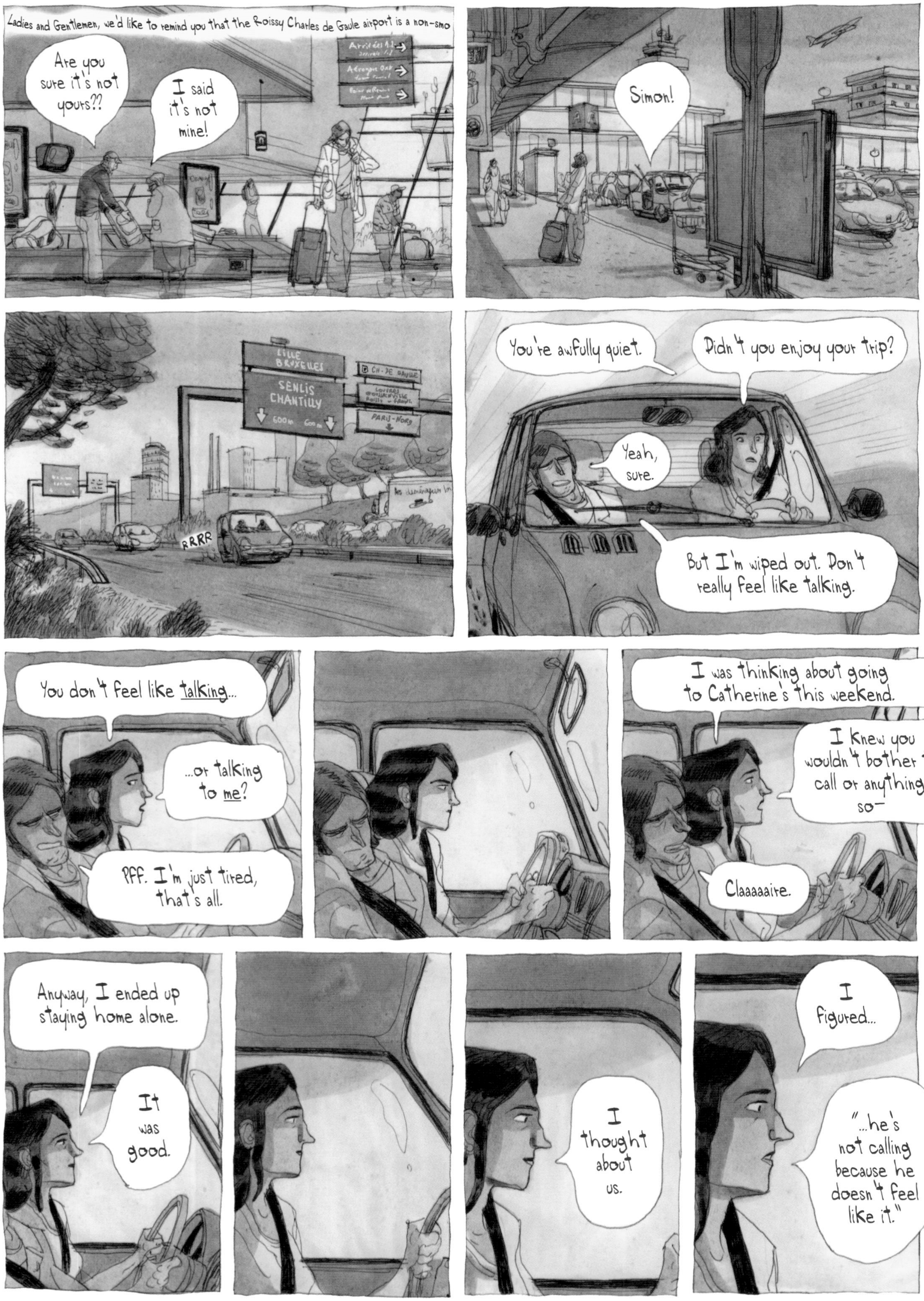
Ladies and Gentlemen, we'd like to remind you that the Roissy Charles de Gaule airport is a non-smo
Are you sure it's not yours??
I said it's not mine!
Simon!
SENLIS CHANTILLY
PARIS-NORD
RRRR
You're awfully quiet.
Didn't you enjoy your trip?
Yeah, sure.
But I'm wiped out. Don't really feel like talking.
You don't feel like talking...
...or talking to me?
Pff. I'm just tired, that's all.
I was thinking about going to Catherine's this weekend.
I knew you wouldn't bother to call or anything, so—
Claaaaaire.
Anyway, I ended up staying home alone.
It was good.
I thought about us.
I figured...
"...he's not calling because he doesn't feel like it."

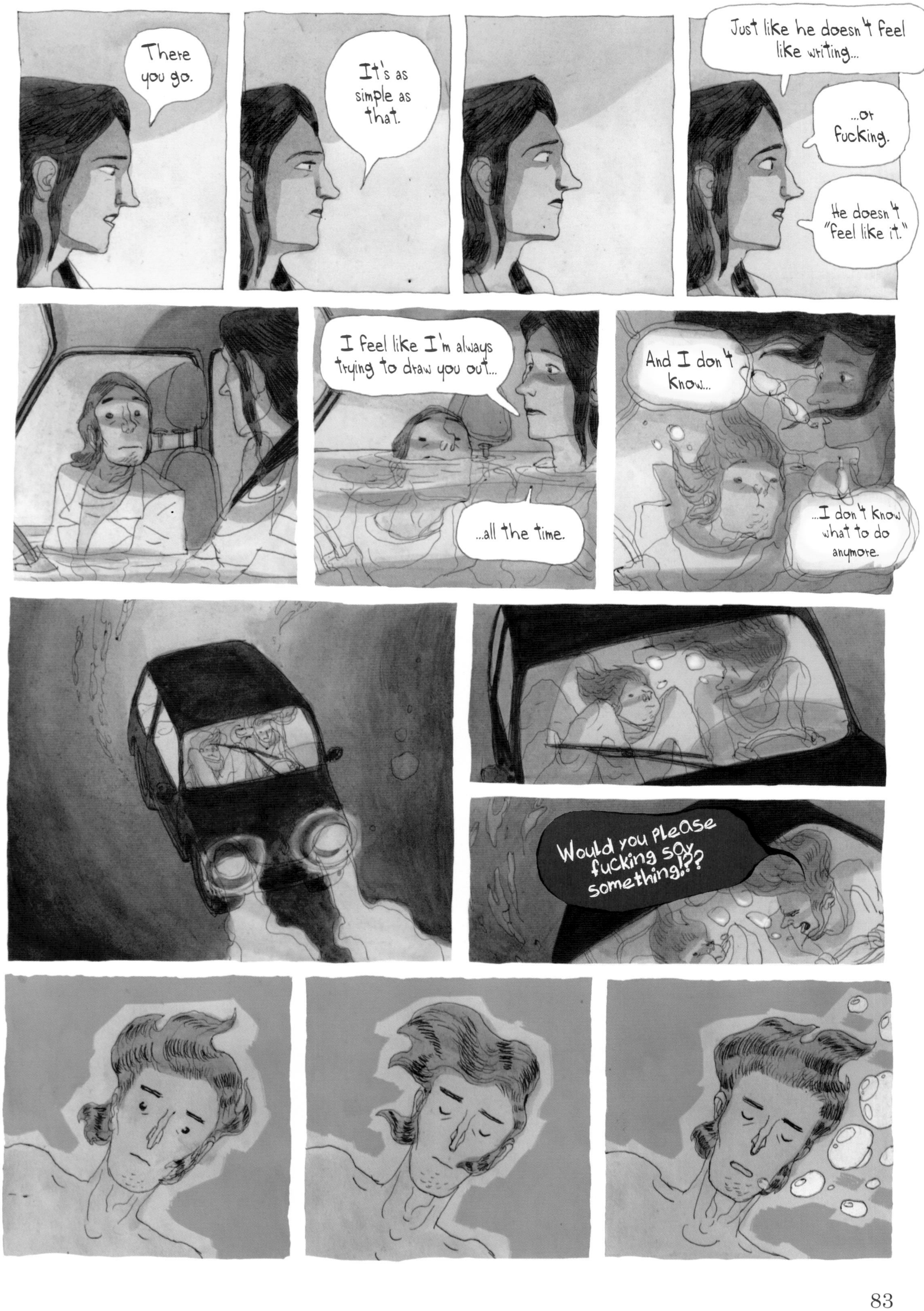
There you go.
It's as simple as that.
Just like he doesn't feel like writing...
...or fucking.
He doesn't "feel like it."
I feel like I'm always trying to draw you out...
...all the time.
And I don't know...
...I don't know what to do anymore.
Would you please fucking say something!??

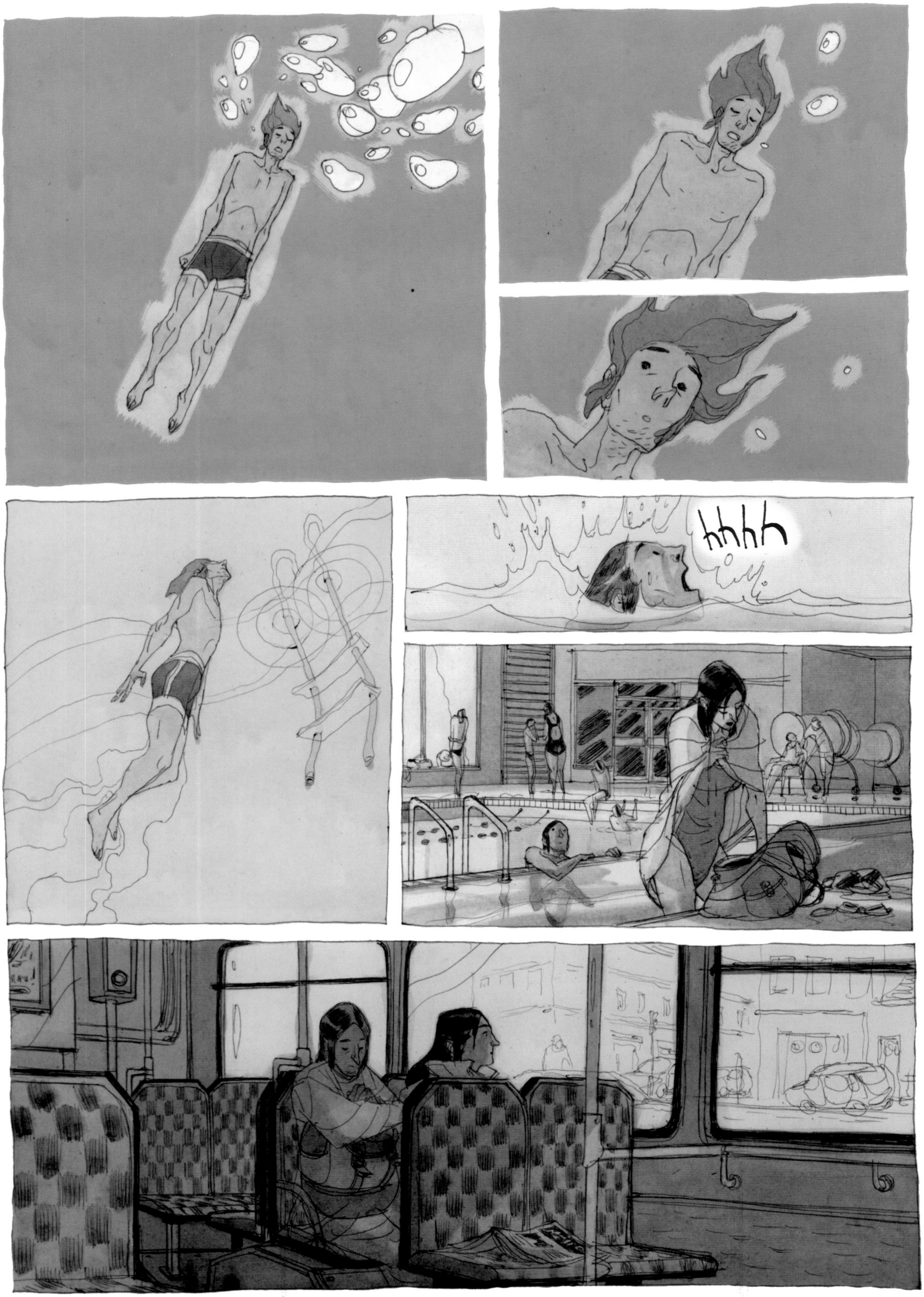
hhhh

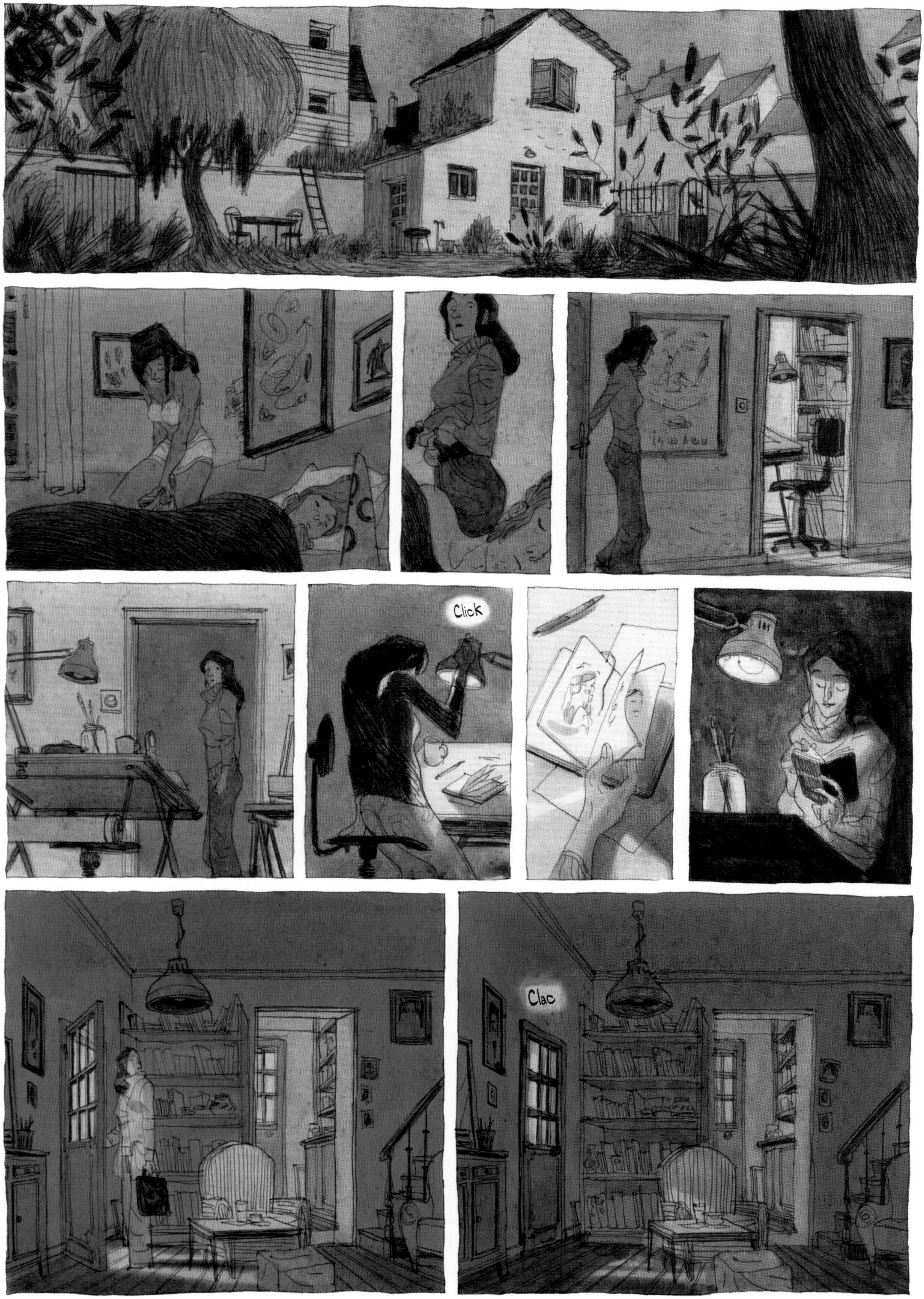
Click
Clac

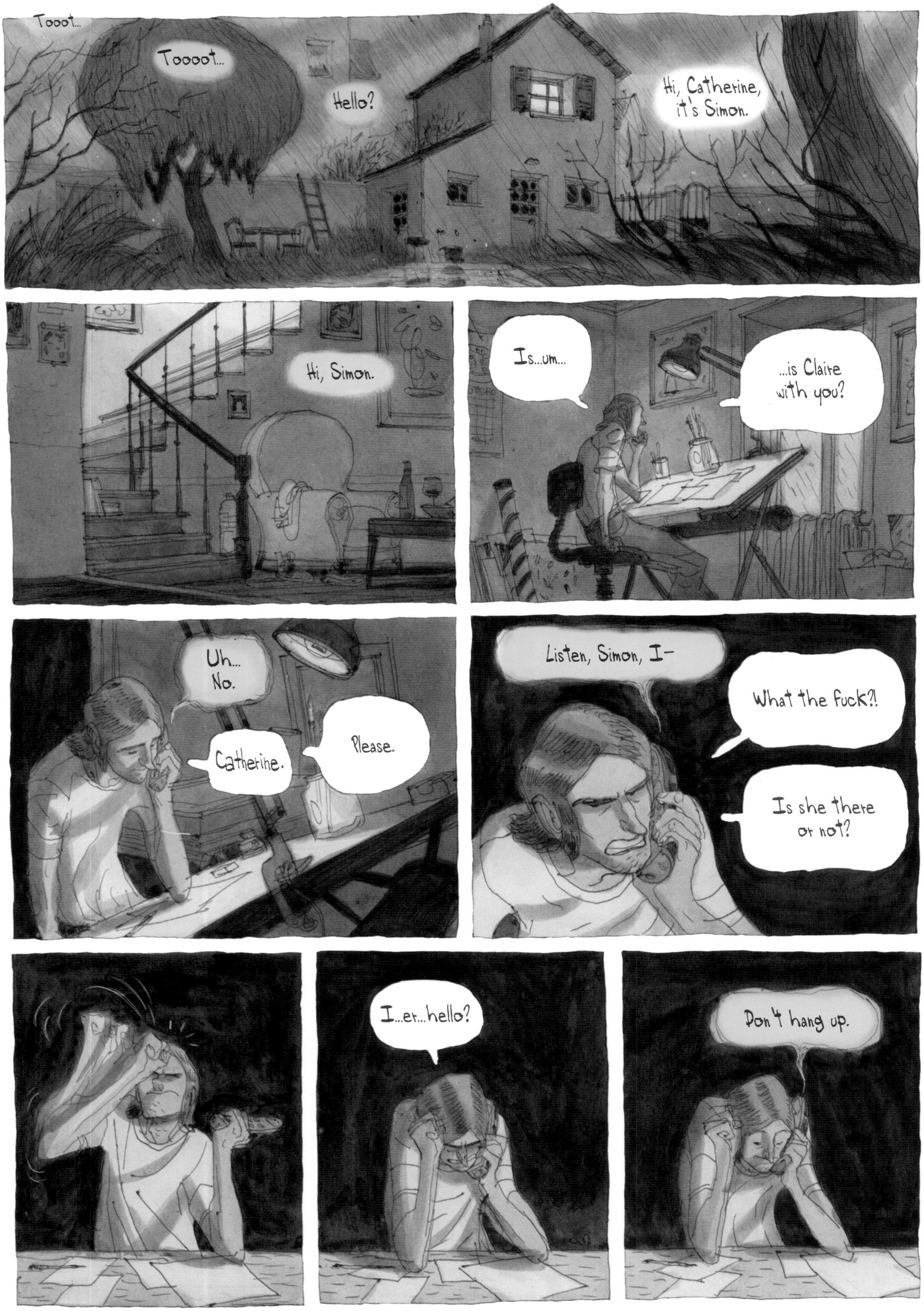
Tooot...
Toooot...
Hello?
Hi, Catherine, it's Simon.
Hi, Simon.
Is...um...
...is Claire with you?
Uh... No.
Catherine.
Please.
Listen, Simon, I-
What the fuck?!
Is she there or not?
I...er...hello?
Don't hang up.

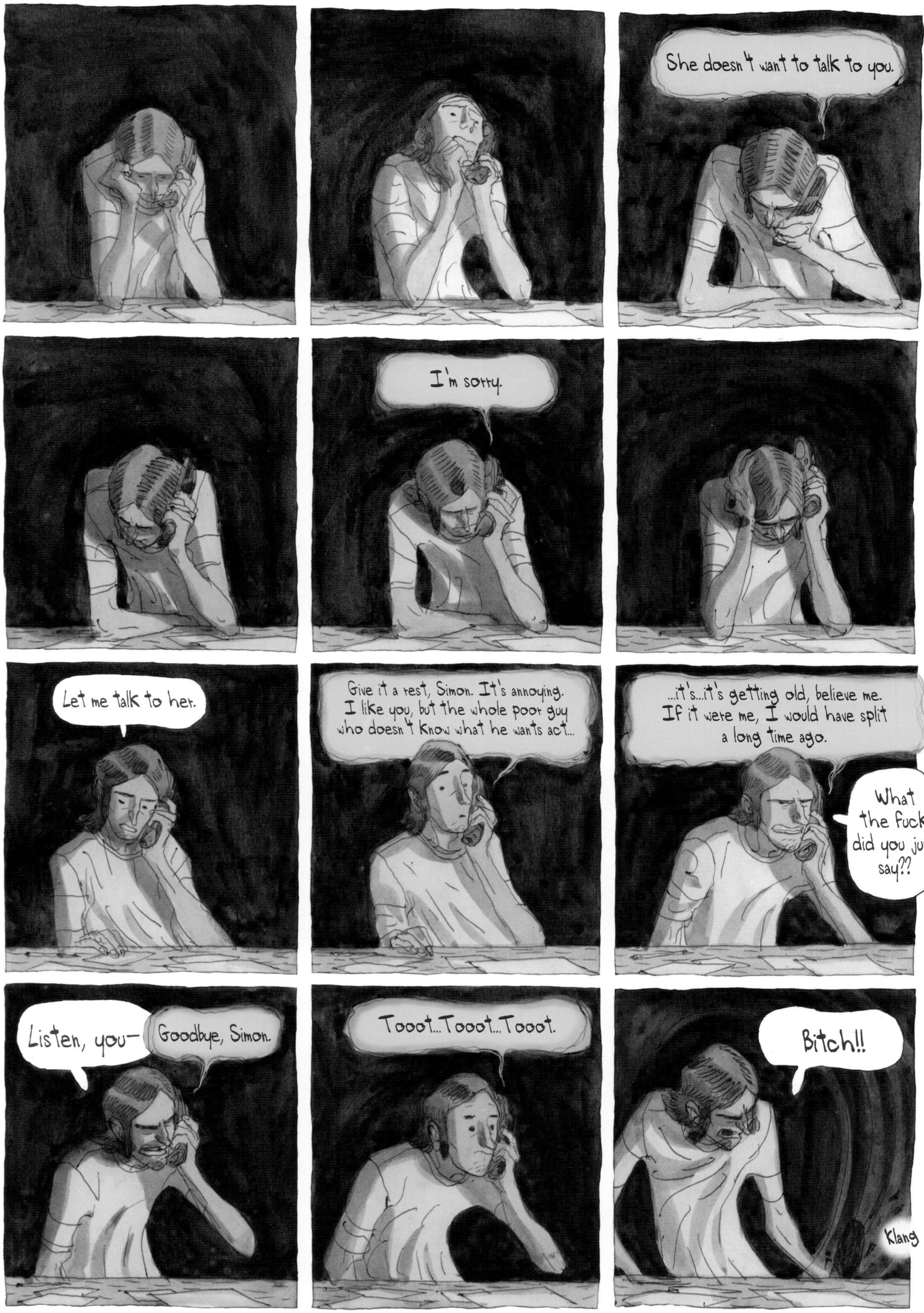
She doesn't want to talk to you.
I'm sorry.
Let me talk to her.
Give it a rest, Simon. It's annoying. I like you, but the whole poor guy who doesn't know what he wants act...
...it's...it's getting old, believe me. If it were me, I would have split a long time ago.
What the fuck did you just say??
Listen, you-
Goodbye, Simon.
Tooot...Tooot...Tooot.
Bitch!!
Klang

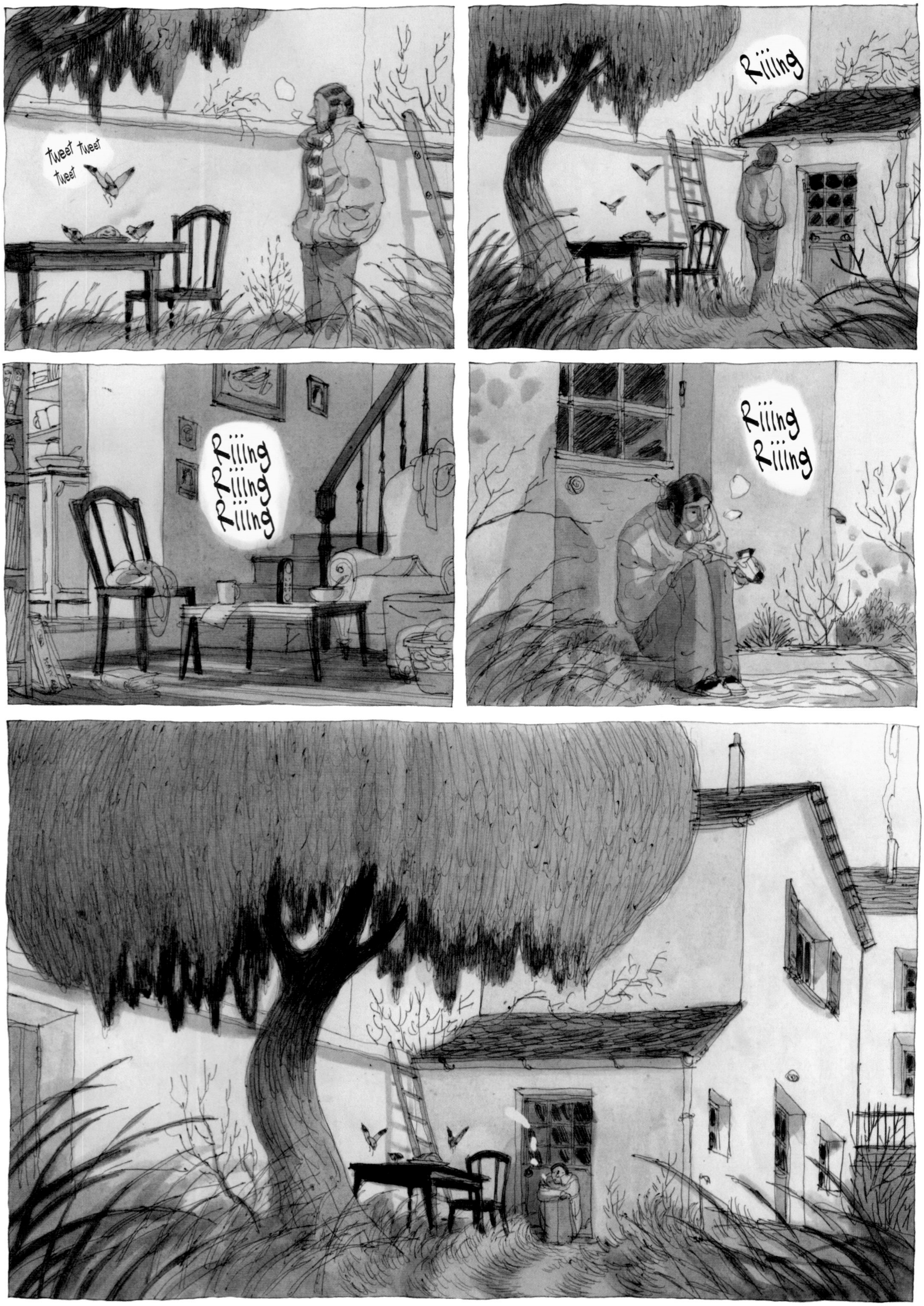
tweet tweet
tweet
Riiing
Riiing
Riiing
Riiing
Riiing
Riiing

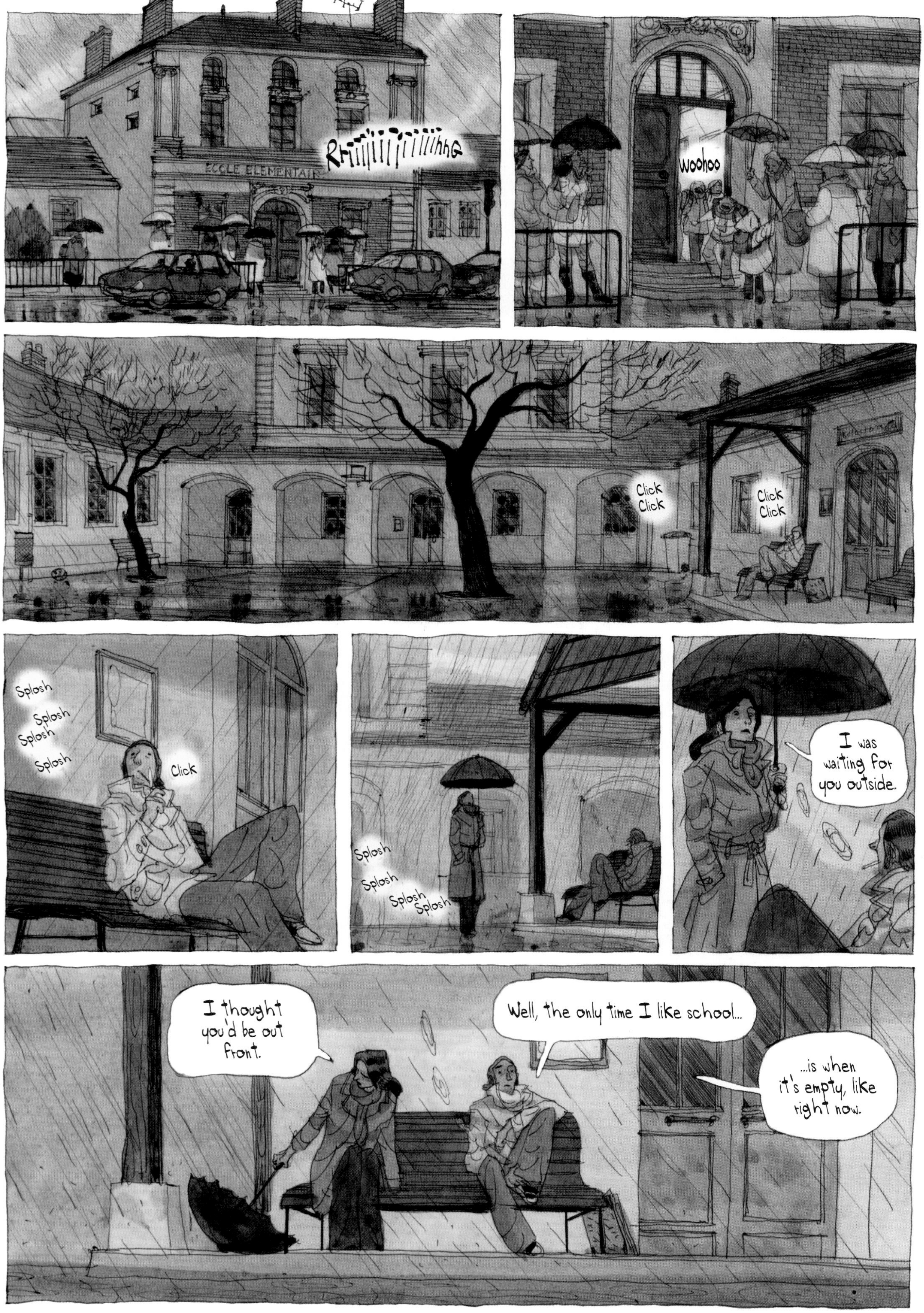
RRIIIIIIIIIIIIIIIINNG
ECOLE ELEMENTAIR
Woohoo
Click
Click
Click
Click
Splosh
Splosh
Splosh
Splosh
Click
Splosh
Splosh
Splosh
Splosh
I was waiting for you outside.
I thought you'd be out front.
Well, the only time I like school...
...is when it's empty, like right now.

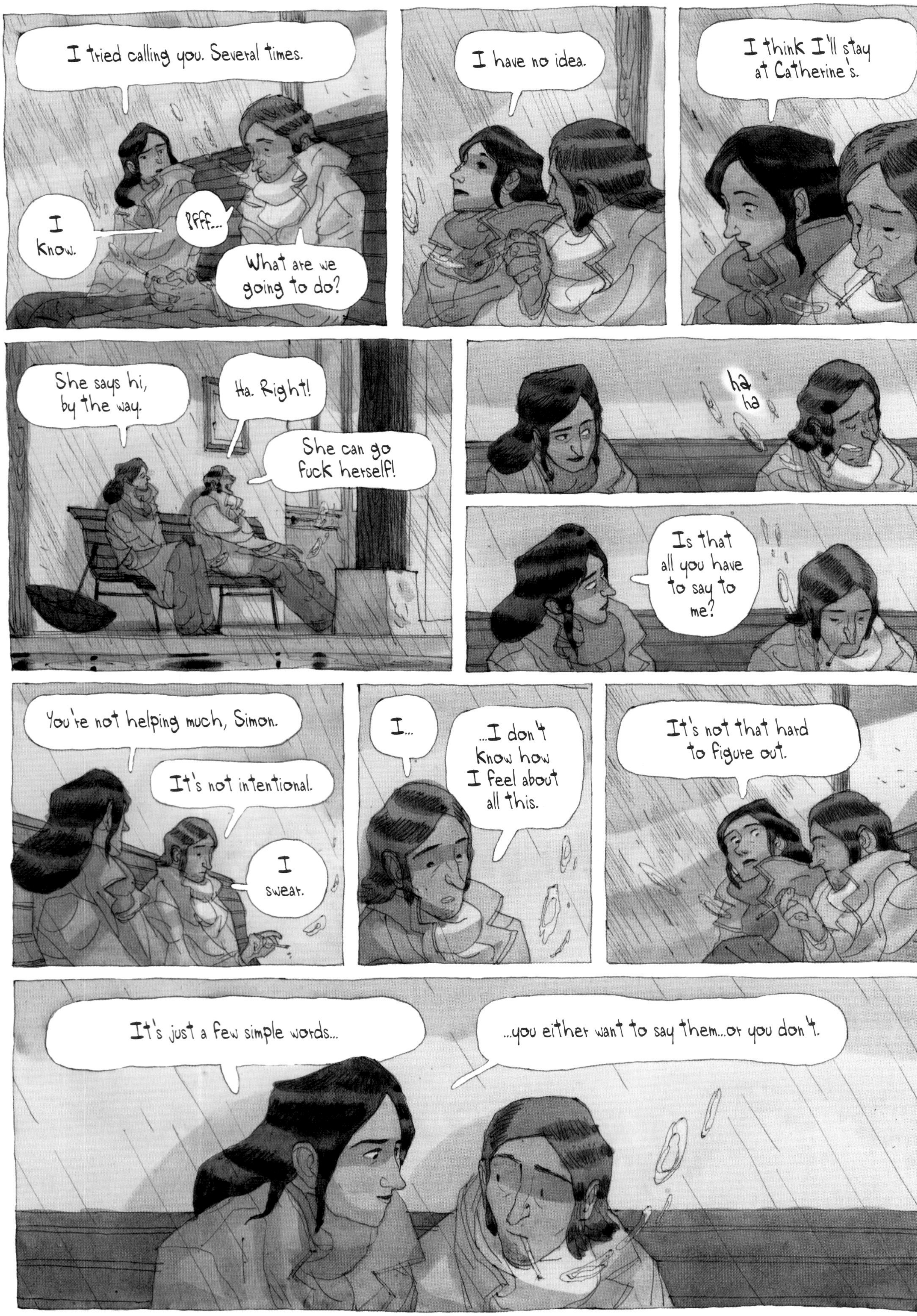
I tried calling you. Several times.
I know.
Pfff...
What are we going to do?
I have no idea.
I think I'll stay at Catherine's.
She says hi, by the way.
Ha. Right!
She can go fuck herself!
ha ha
Is that all you have to say to me?
You're not helping much, Simon.
It's not intentional.
I swear.
I...
...I don't know how I feel about all this.
It's not that hard to figure out.
It's just a few simple words...
...you either want to say them...or you don't.

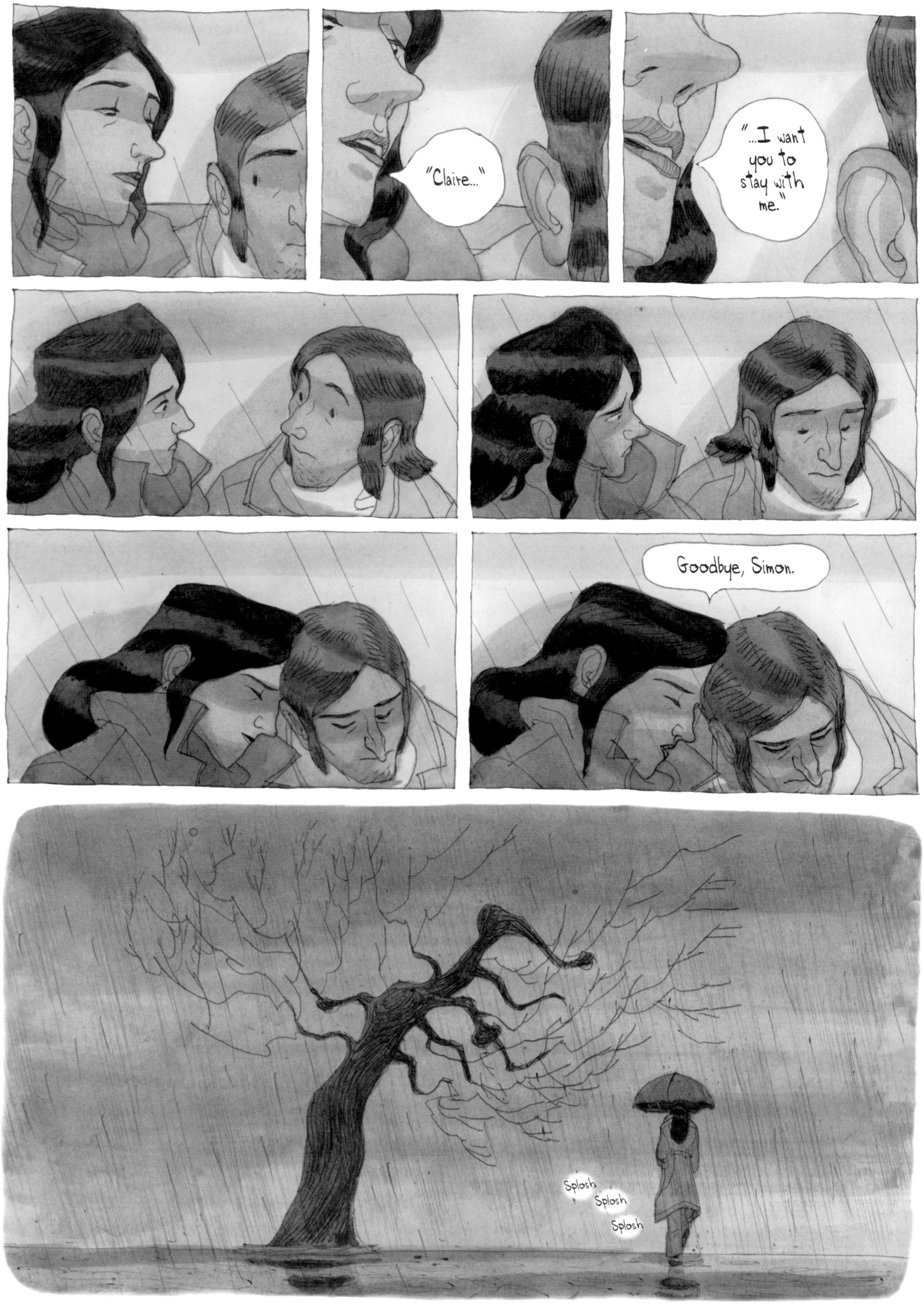
"Claire..."
"...I want you to stay with me."
Goodbye, Simon.
Splosh
Splosh
Splosh

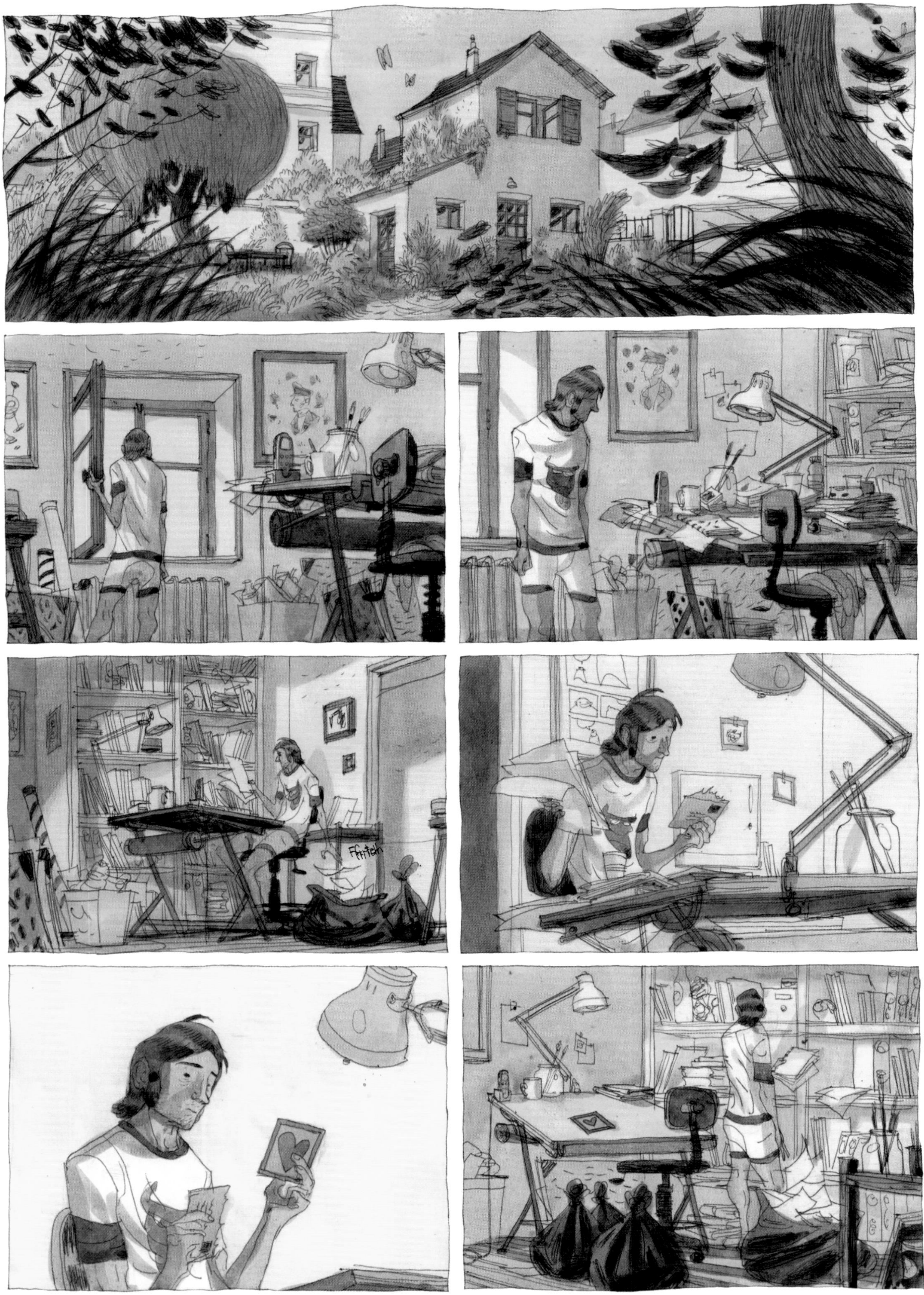
Ffrfrtch

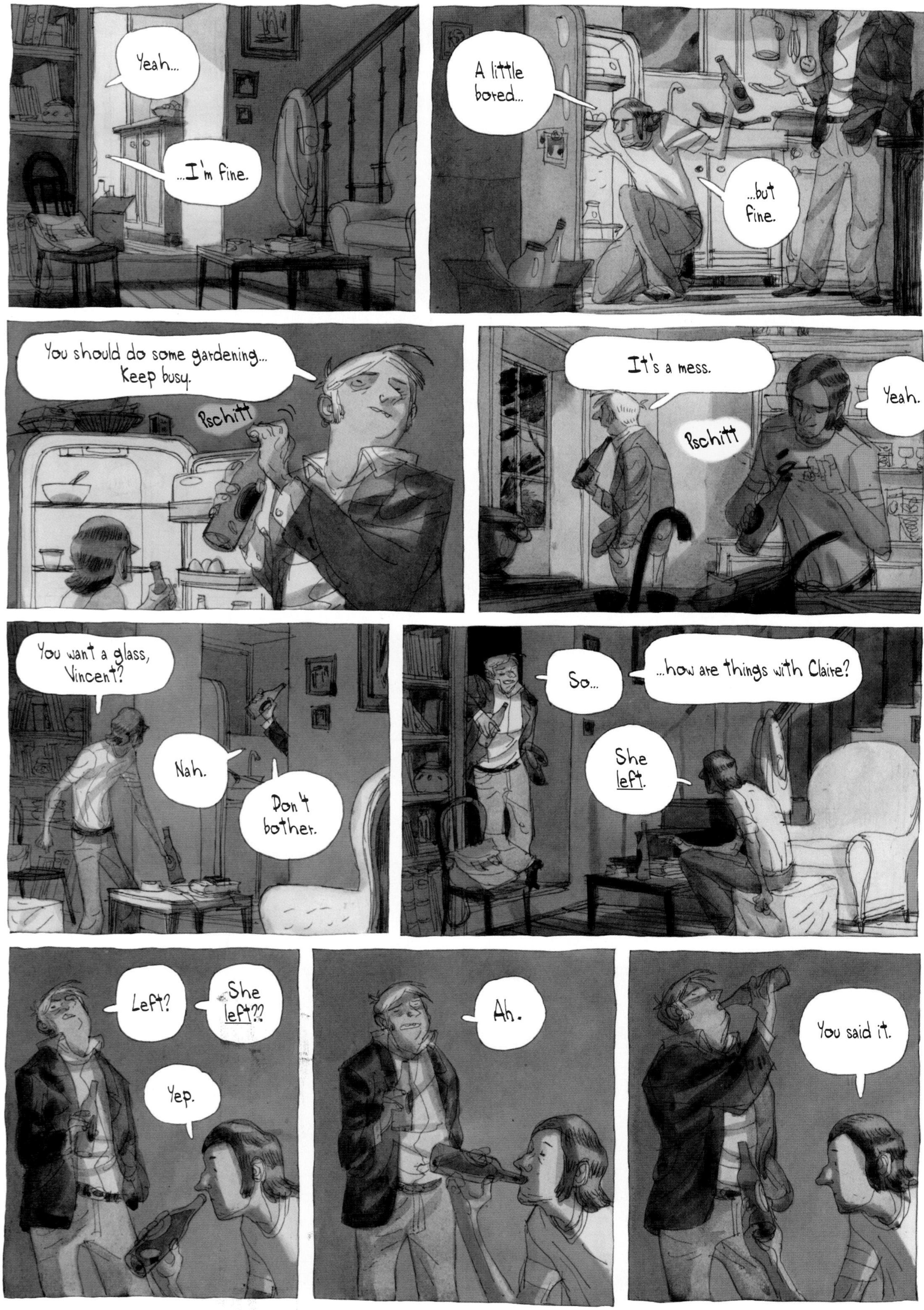
Yeah...
...I'm fine.
A little bored...
...but fine.
You should do some gardening... Keep busy.
Pschitt
It's a mess.
Pschitt
Yeah.
You want a glass, Vincent?
Nah.
Don't bother.
So...
...how are things with Claire?
She left.
Left?
She left??
Yep.
Ah.
You said it.

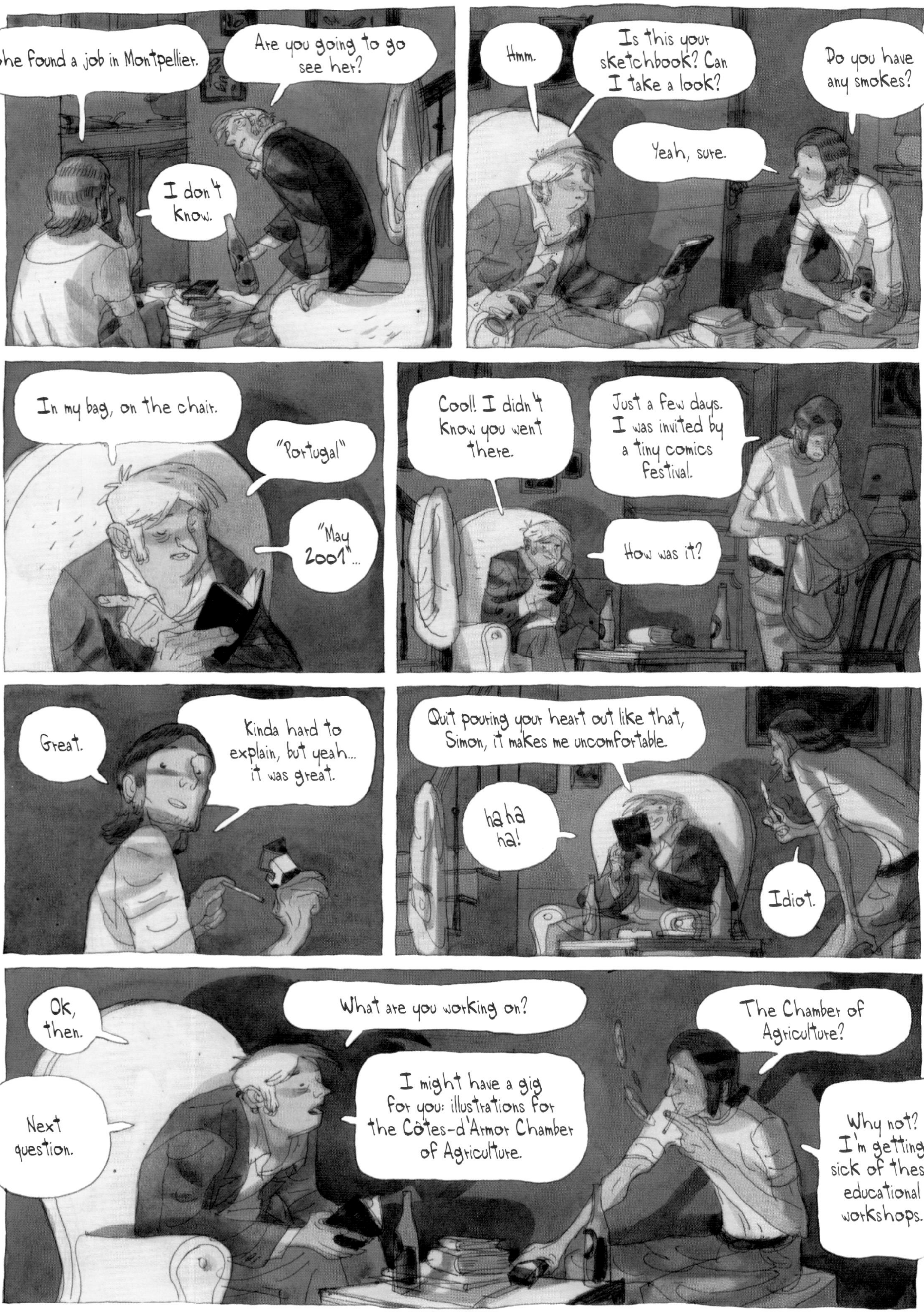
She found a job in Montpellier.
Are you going to go see her?
I don't know.
Hmm.
Is this your sketchbook? Can I take a look?
Do you have any smokes?
Yeah, sure.
In my bag, on the chair.
"Portugal"
"May 2001"...
Cool! I didn't know you went there.
Just a few days. I was invited by a tiny comics festival.
How was it?
Great.
Kinda hard to explain, but yeah... it was great.
Quit pouring your heart out like that, Simon, it makes me uncomfortable.
ha ha ha!
Idiot.
Ok, then.
What are you working on?
Next question.
I might have a gig for you: illustrations for the Côtes-d'Armor Chamber of Agriculture.
The Chamber of Agriculture?
Why not? I'm getting sick of these educational workshops.

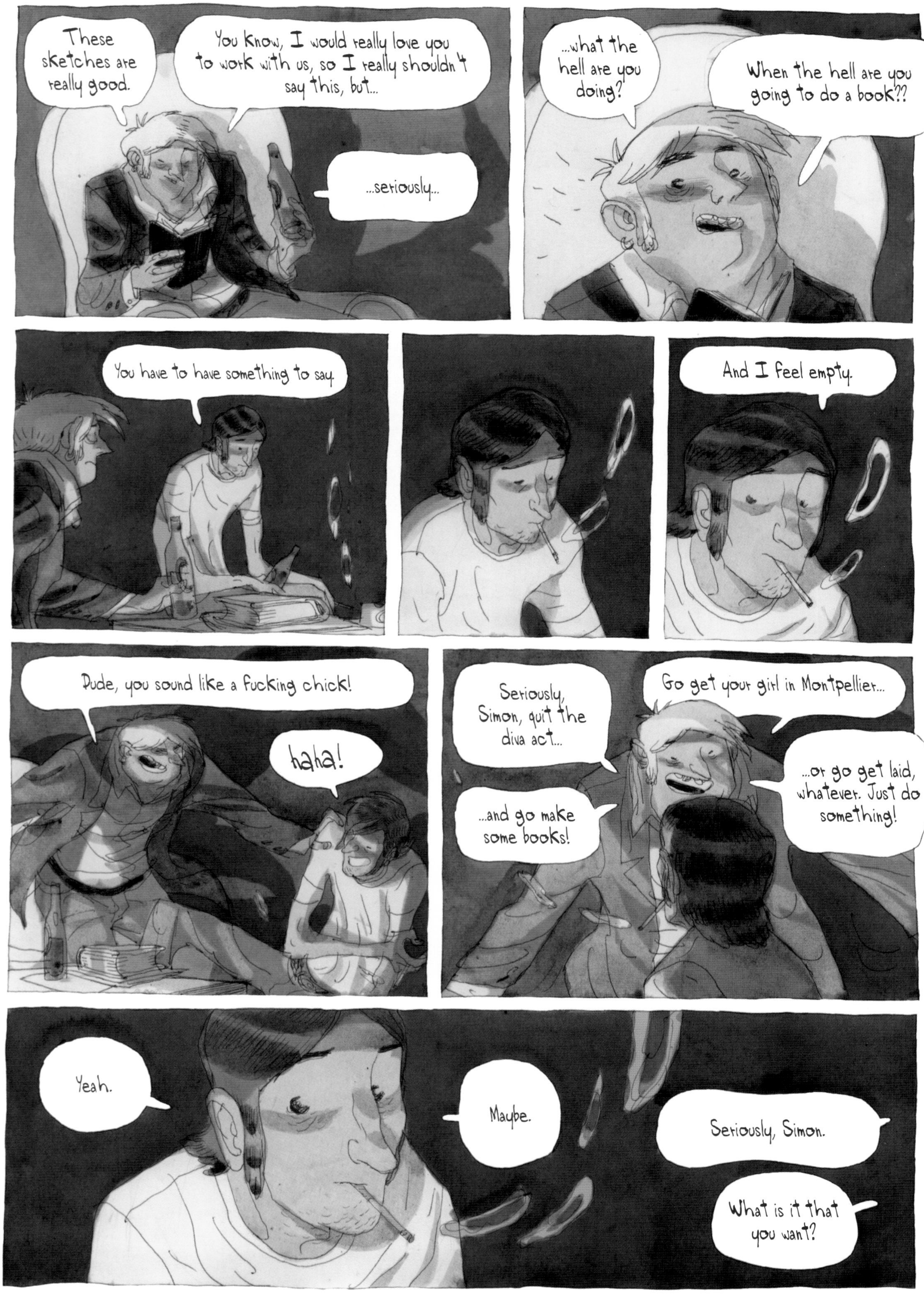
These sketches are really good.
You know, I would really love you to work with us, so I really shouldn't say this, but...
...seriously...
...what the hell are you doing?
When the hell are you going to do a book??
You have to have something to say.
And I feel empty.
Dude, you sound like a fucking chick!
haha!
Seriously, Simon, quit the diva act...
...and go make some books!
Go get your girl in Montpellier...
...or go get laid, whatever. Just do something!
Yeah.
Maybe.
Seriously, Simon.
What is it that you want?

According to Jean

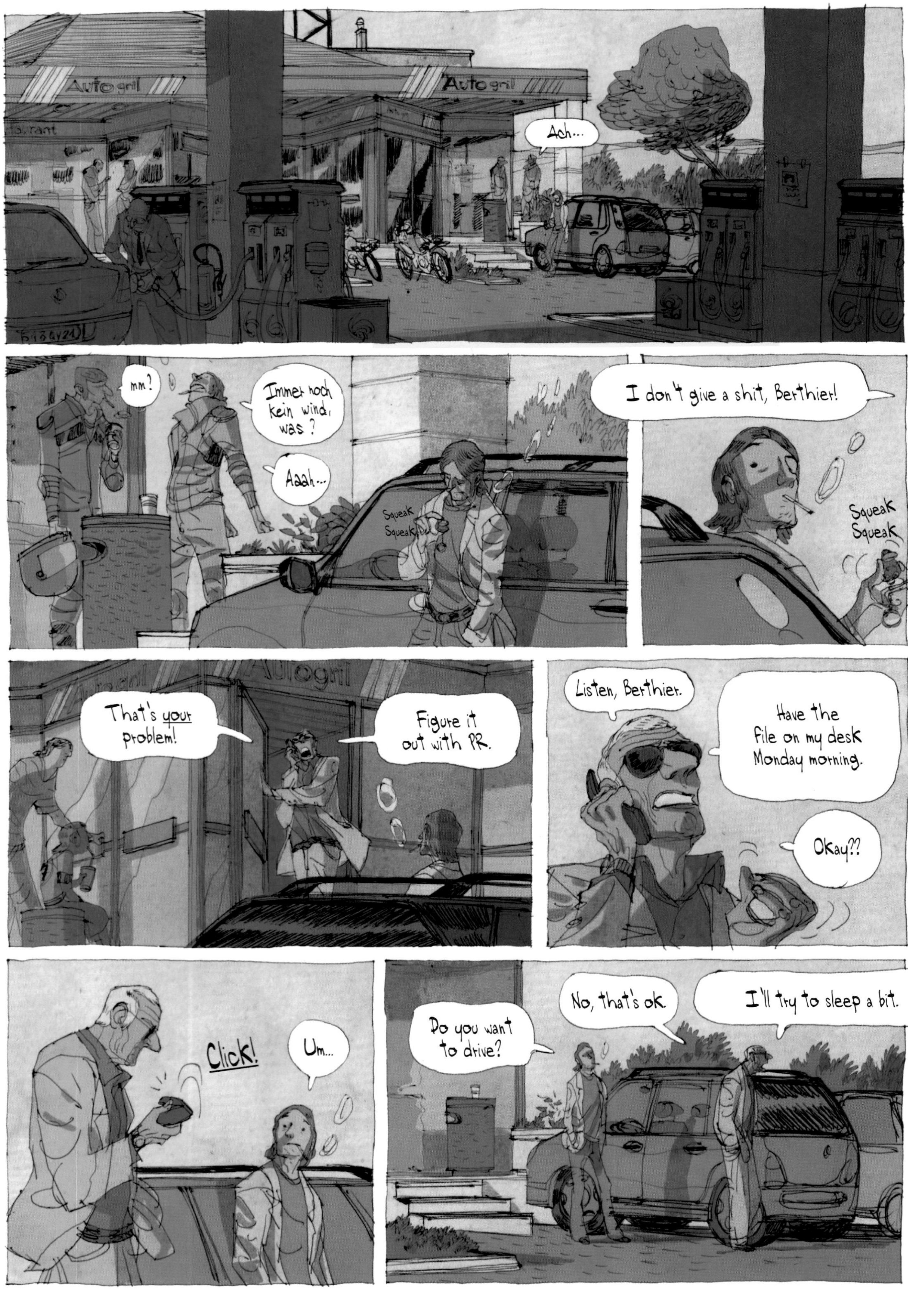
Autogril
Autogril
Ach...
mm?
Immer noch kein wind, was ?
Aaah...
Squeak Squeak
I don't give a shit, Berthier!
Squeak Squeak
Autogril
That's your problem!
Figure it out with PR.
Listen, Berthier.
Have the file on my desk Monday morning.
Okay??
Click!
Um...
Do you want to drive?
No, that's ok.
I'll try to sleep a bit.

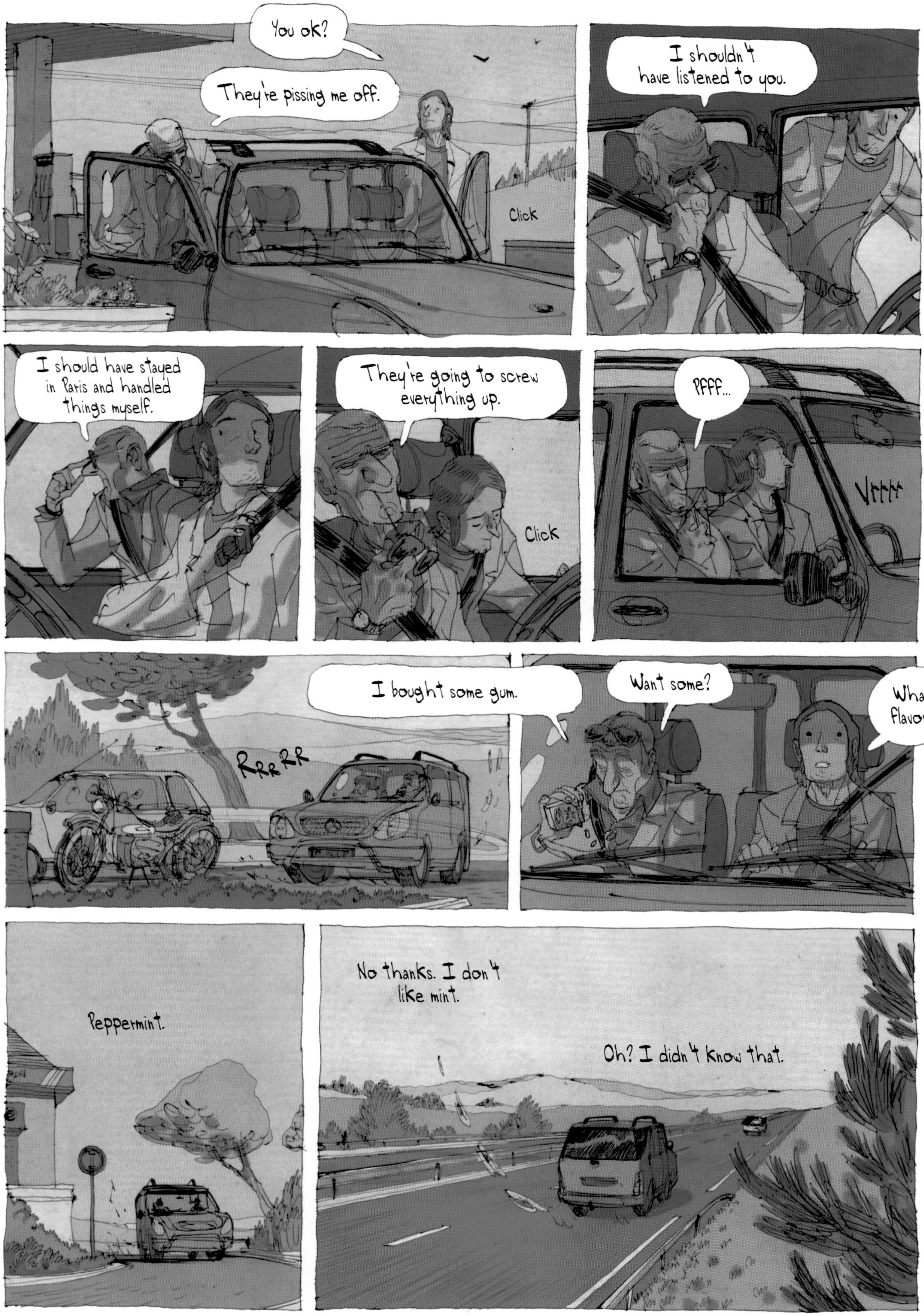
You ok?
They're pissing me off.
Click
I shouldn't have listened to you.
I should have stayed in Paris and handled things myself.
They're going to screw everything up.
Click
PFFF...
Vrrrr
RRRRR
I bought some gum.
Want some?
What flavor?
Peppermint.
No thanks. I don't like mint.
Oh? I didn't know that.

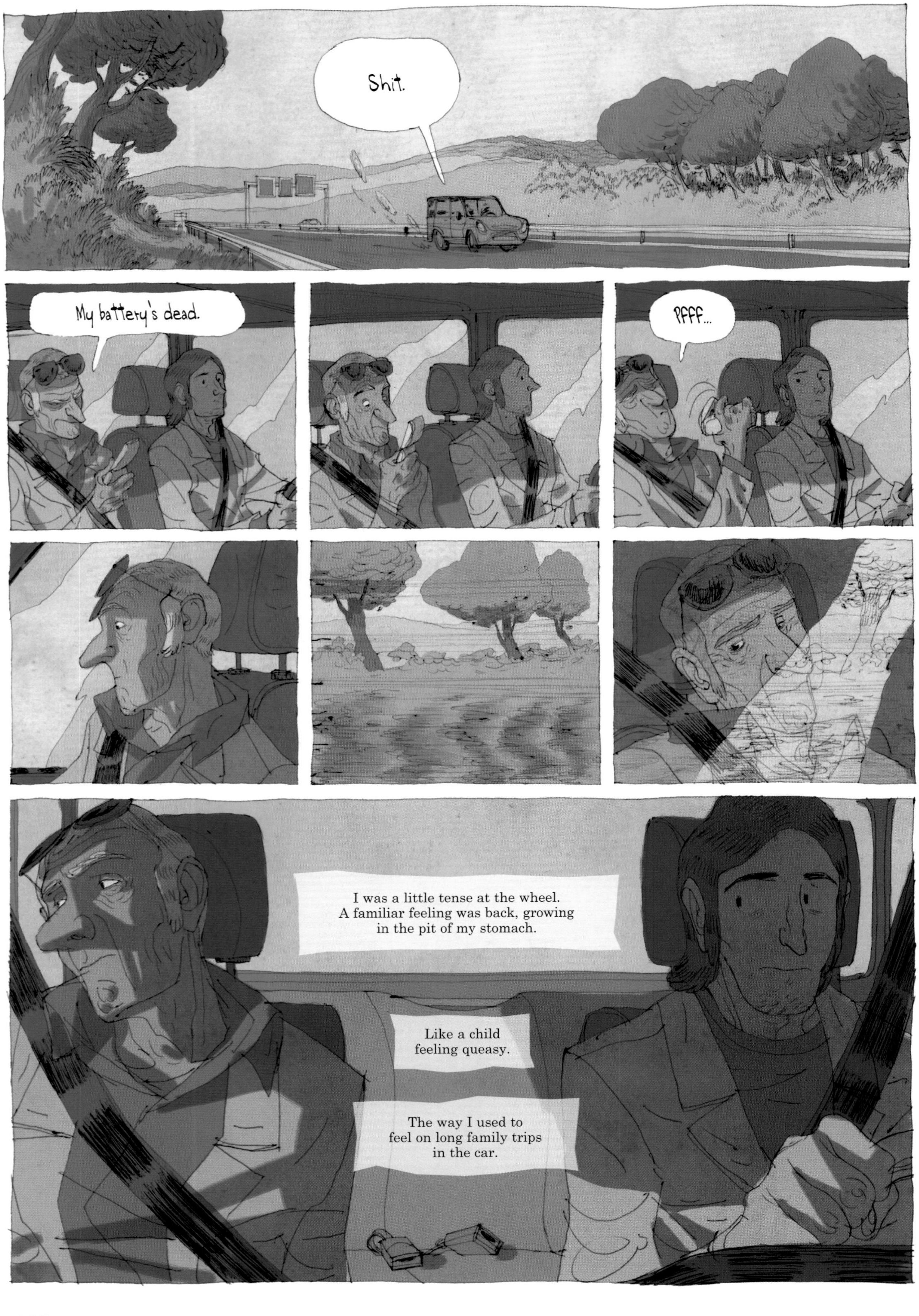
Shit.
My battery's dead.
PFFF...
I was a little tense at the wheel. A familiar feeling was back, growing in the pit of my stomach.
Like a child feeling queasy.
The way I used to feel on long family trips in the car.

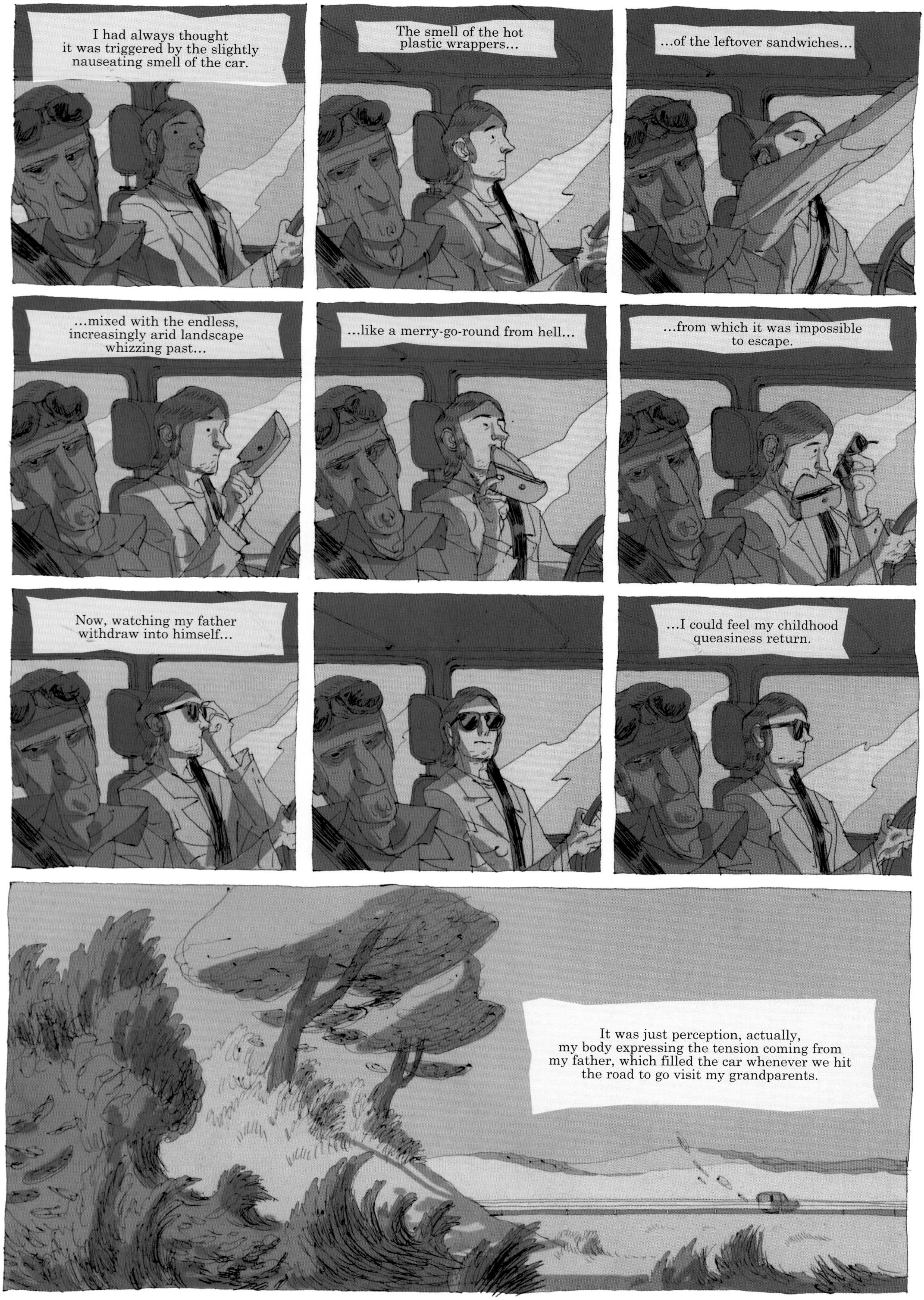
I had always thought it was triggered by the slightly nauseating smell of the car.
The smell of the hot plastic wrappers...
...of the leftover sandwiches...
...mixed with the endless, increasingly arid landscape whizzing past...
...like a merry-go-round from hell...
...from which it was impossible to escape.
Now, watching my father withdraw into himself...
...I could feel my childhood queasiness return.
It was just perception, actually, my body expressing the tension coming from my father, which filled the car whenever we hit the road to go visit my grandparents.

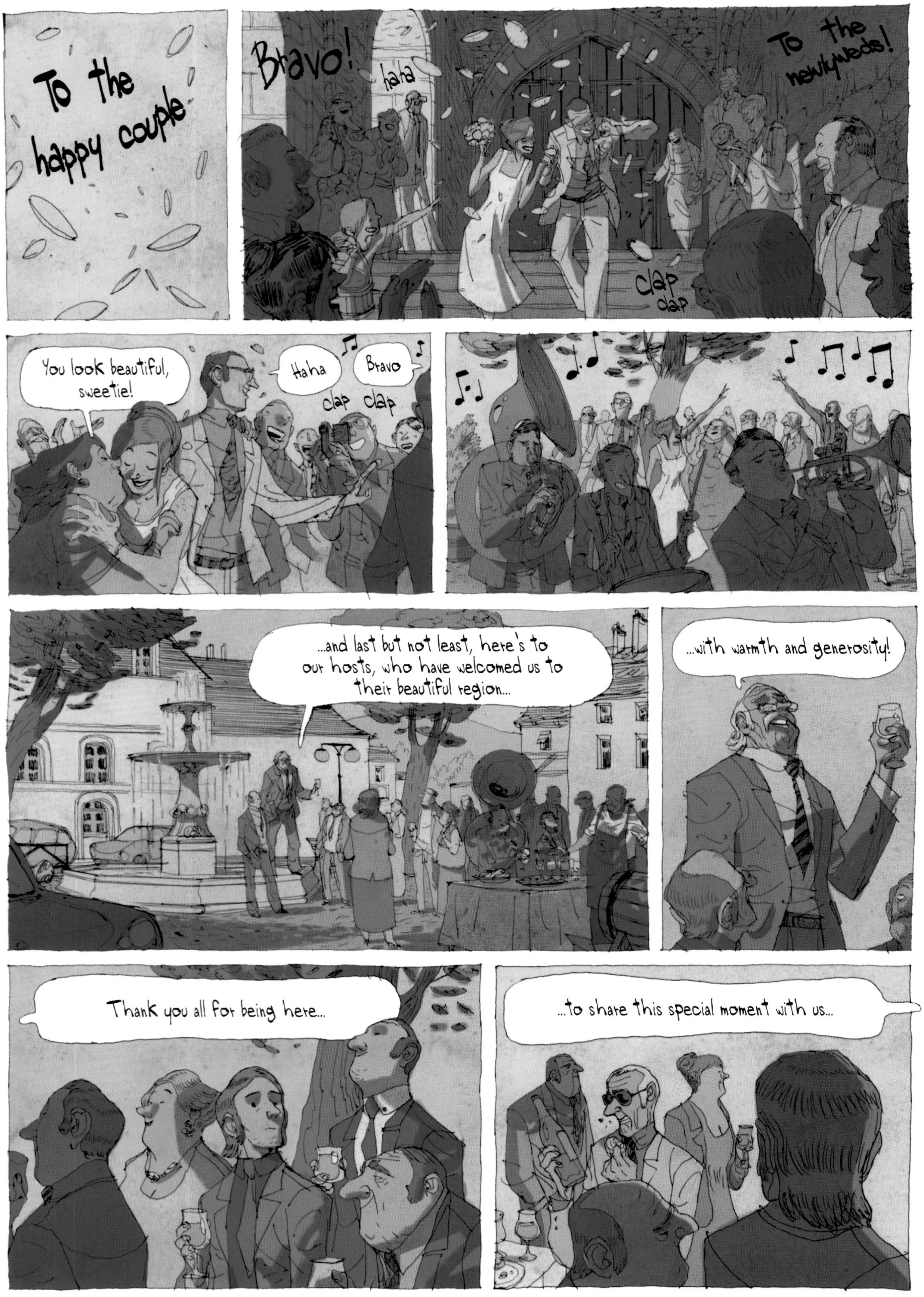
To the happy couple
Bravo!
haha
To the newlyweds!
clap
clap
You look beautiful, sweetie!
Haha
Bravo
clap clap
...and last but not least, here's to our hosts, who have welcomed us to their beautiful region...
...with warmth and generosity!
Thank you all for being here...
...to share this special moment with us...

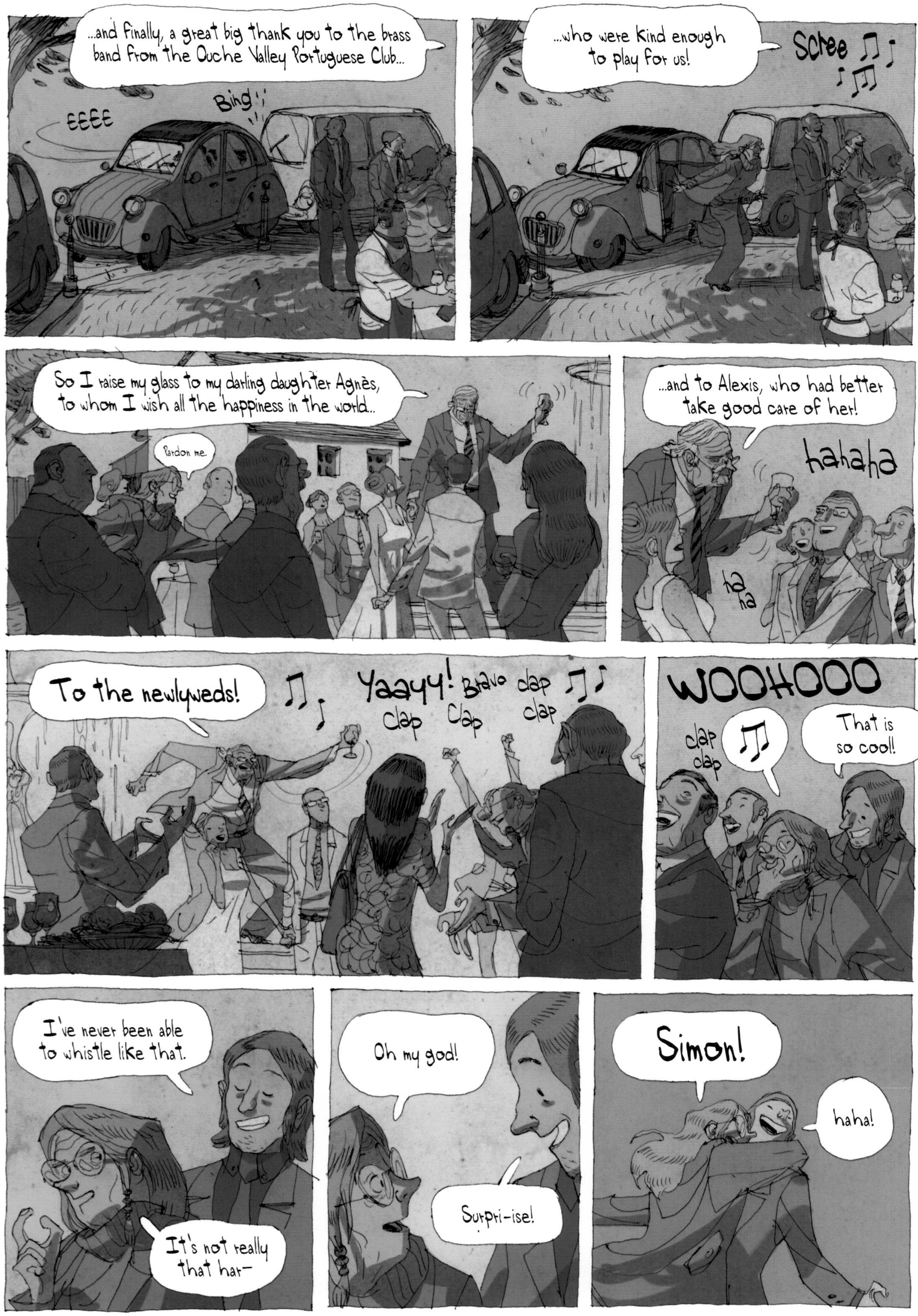
...and finally, a great big thank you to the brass band from the Ouche Valley Portuguese Club...
EEEE
Bing
...who were kind enough to play for us!
Scree
So I raise my glass to my darling daughter Agnès, to whom I wish all the happiness in the world...
Pardon me.
...and to Alexis, who had better take good care of her!
hahaha
ha ha
To the newlyweds!
Yaayy!
Bravo
clap
clap
clap
clap
WOOHOOO
clap
clap
That is so cool!
I've never been able to whistle like that.
It's not really that har–
Oh my god!
Surpri-ise!
Simon!
haha!

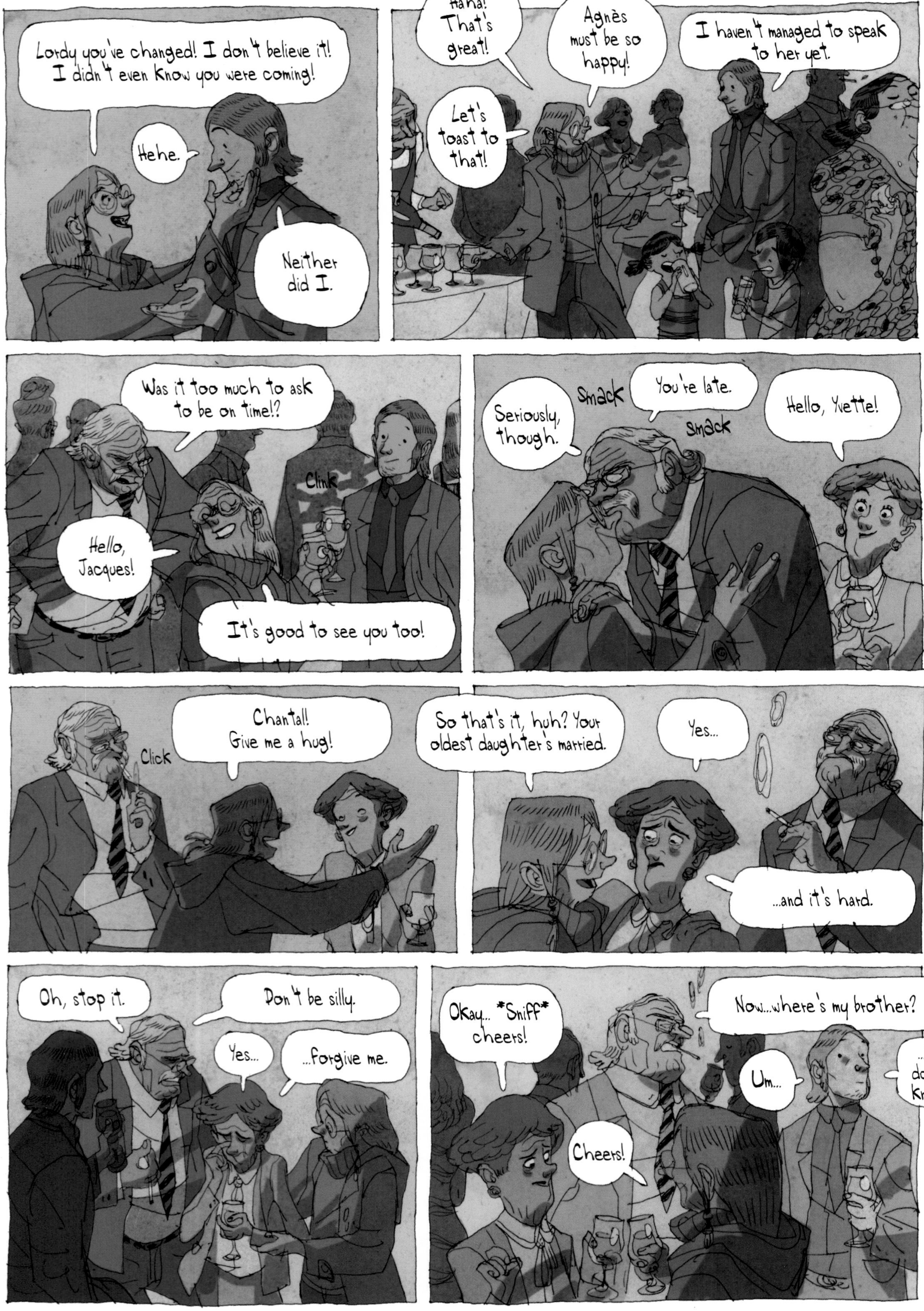
Lordy you've changed! I don't believe it! I didn't even know you were coming!
Hehe.
Neither did I.
Haha! That's great!
Agnès must be so happy!
I haven't managed to speak to her yet.
Let's toast to that!
Was it too much to ask to be on time!?
Clink
Hello, Jacques!
It's good to see you too!
Smack
You're late.
Seriously, though.
Smack
Hello, Yvette!
Chantal! Give me a hug!
Click
So that's it, huh? Your oldest daughter's married.
Yes...
...and it's hard.
Oh, stop it.
Don't be silly.
Yes...
...forgive me.
Okay... *Sniff* cheers!
Now...where's my brother?
Um...
...I don't know.
Cheers!

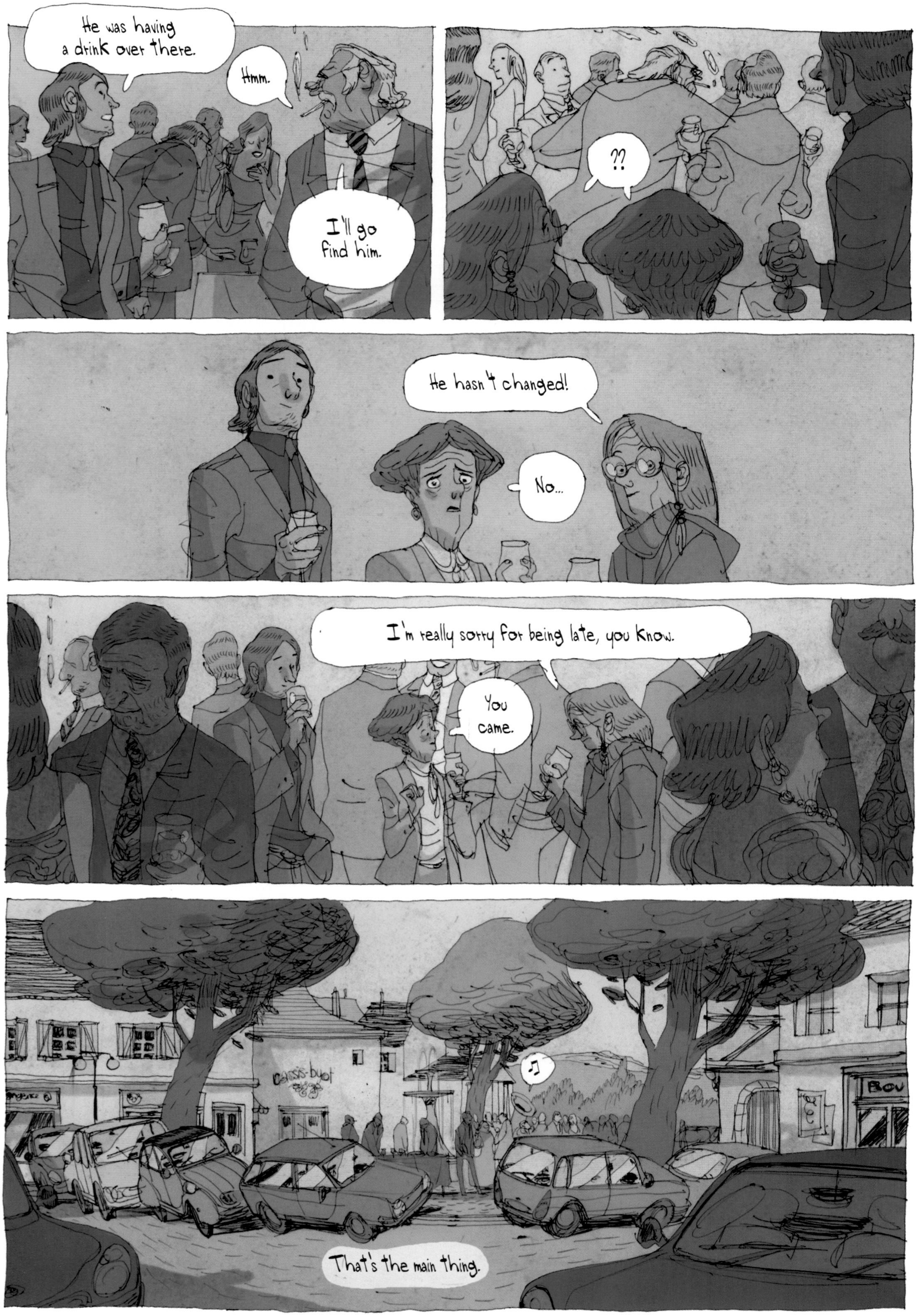
He was having a drink over there.
Hmm.
I'll go find him.
??
He hasn't changed!
No...
I'm really sorry for being late, you know.
You came.
cassis-bijot
BOU
That's the main thing.

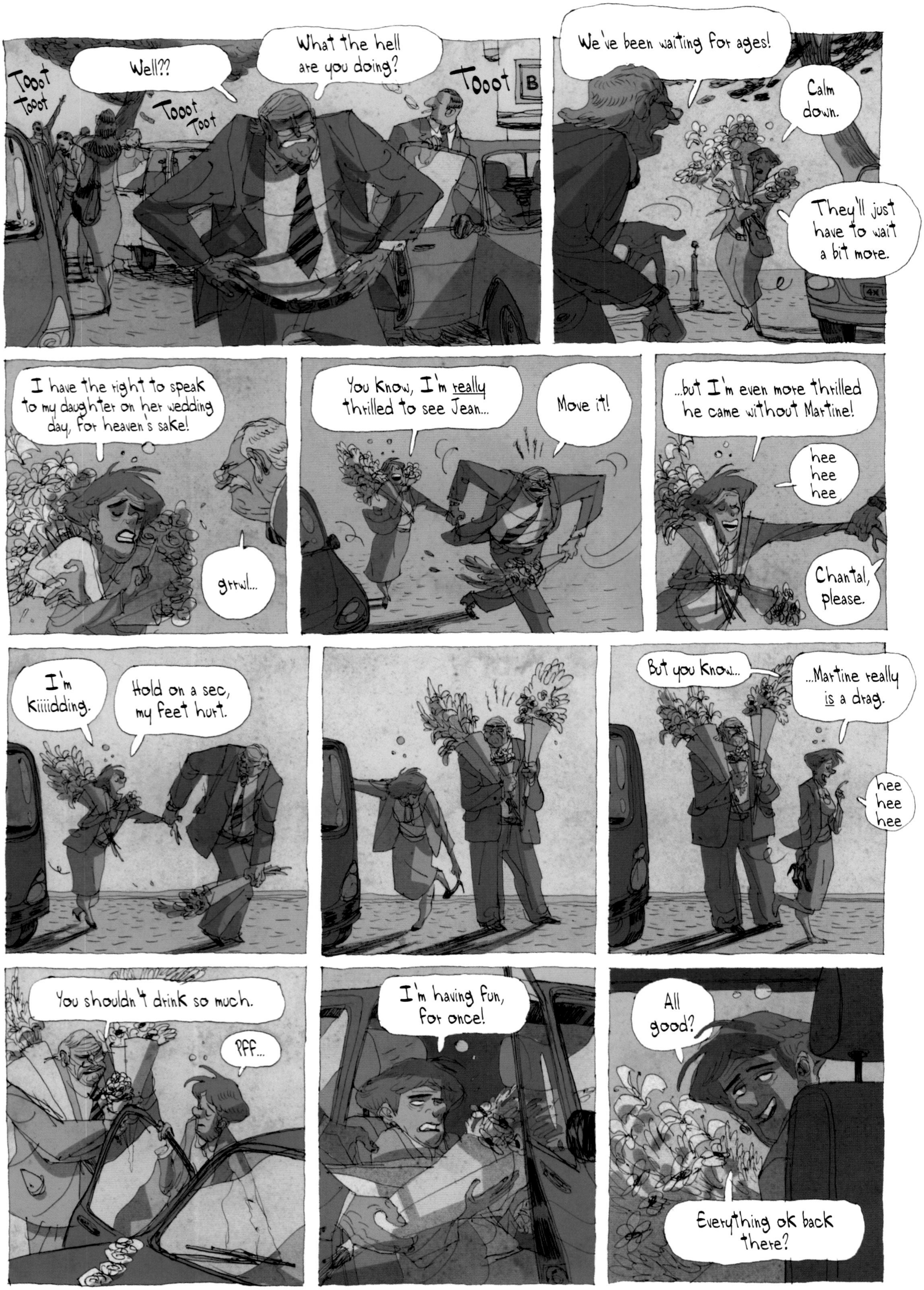

Tooot Tooot
Well??
Tooot Toot
What the hell are you doing?
Tooot
We've been waiting for ages!
Calm down.
They'll just have to wait a bit more.
I have the right to speak to my daughter on her wedding day, for heaven's sake!
grrwl...
You know, I'm really thrilled to see Jean...
Move it!
...but I'm even more thrilled he came without Martine!
hee hee hee
Chantal, please.
I'm kiiiidding.
Hold on a sec, my feet hurt.
But you know...
...Martine really is a drag.
hee hee hee
You shouldn't drink so much.
PFF...
I'm having fun, for once!
All good?
Everything ok back there?

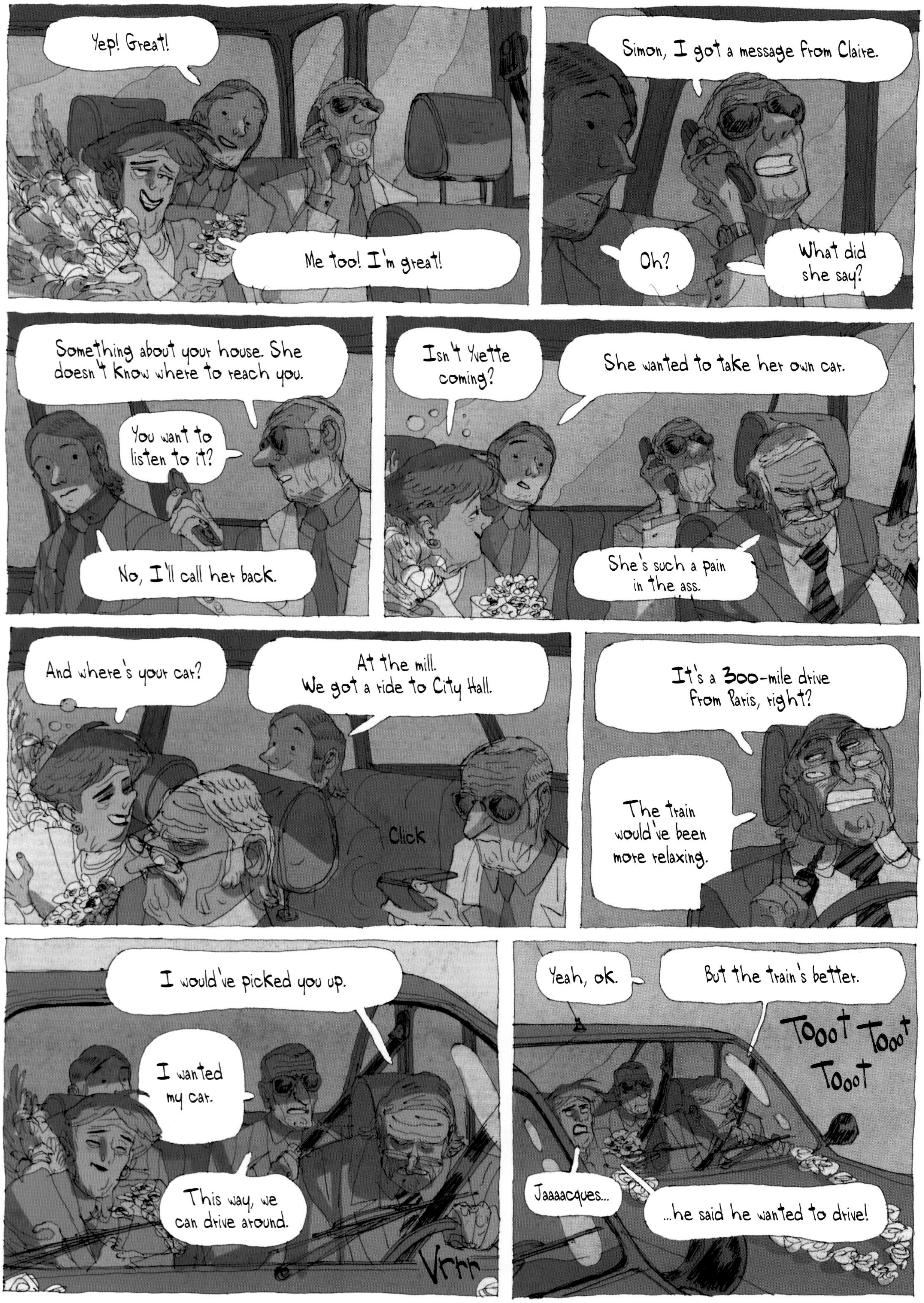
Yep! Great!
Me too! I'm great!
Simon, I got a message from Claire.
Oh?
What did she say?
Something about your house. She doesn't know where to reach you.
You want to listen to it?
No, I'll call her back.
Isn't Yvette coming?
She wanted to take her own car.
She's such a pain in the ass.
And where's your car?
At the mill. We got a ride to City Hall.
Click
It's a 300-mile drive from Paris, right?
The train would've been more relaxing.
I would've picked you up.
I wanted my car.
This way, we can drive around.
Vrrr
Yeah, ok.
But the train's better.
Tooot Tooot Tooot
Jaaaacques...
...he said he wanted to drive!

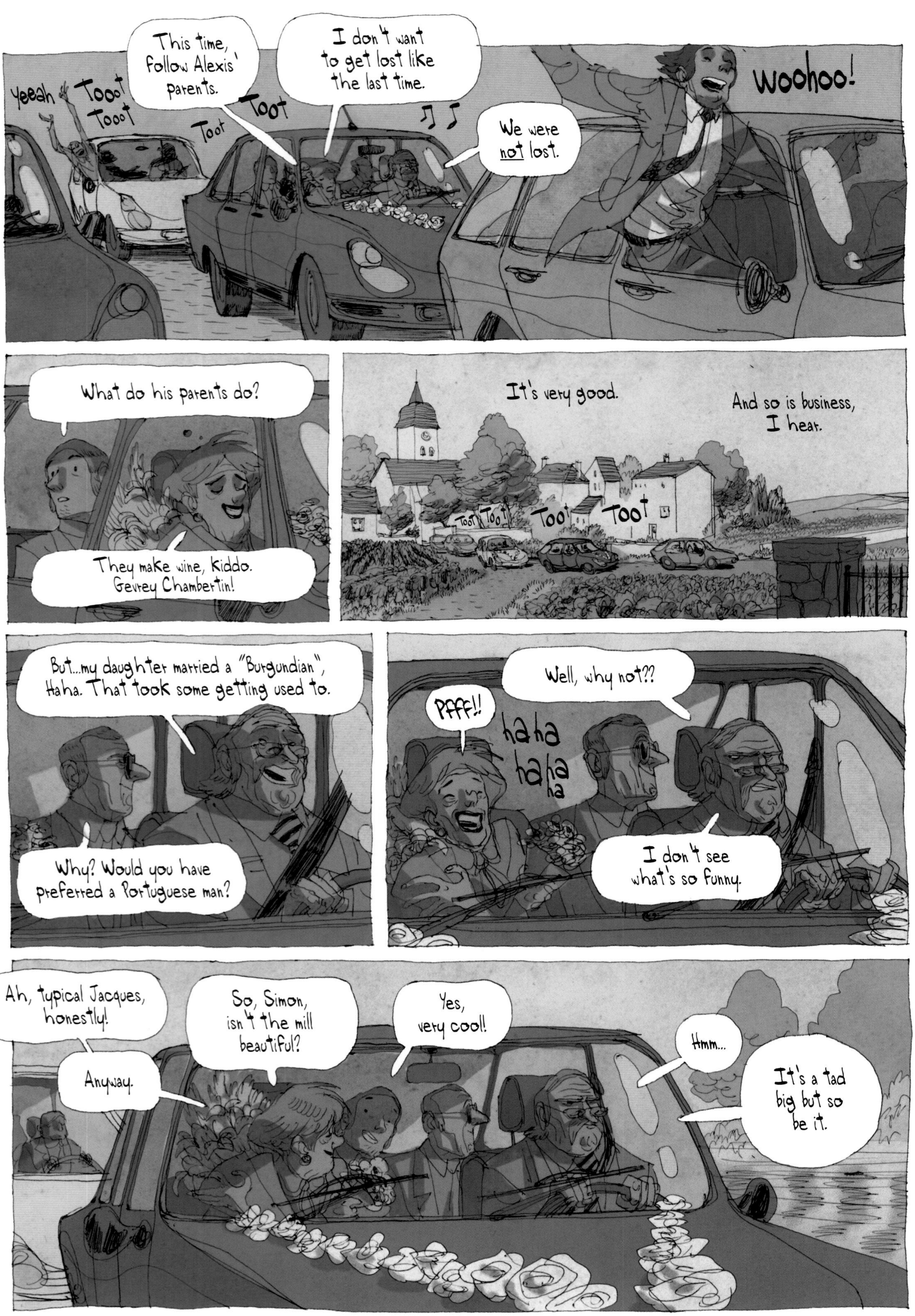
Yeeah
Tooot
Tooot
This time, follow Alexis' parents.
Toot
Toot
I don't want to get lost like the last time.
We were not lost.
woohoo!
What do his parents do?
They make wine, kiddo. Gevrey Chambertin!
It's very good.
And so is business, I hear.
Toot Toot
Toot
Toot
But...my daughter married a "Burgundian", Haha. That took some getting used to.
Why? Would you have preferred a Portuguese man?
Well, why not??
Pfff!!
haha haha ha
I don't see what's so funny.
Ah, typical Jacques, honestly!
Anyway.
So, Simon, isn't the mill beautiful?
Yes, very cool!
Hmm...
It's a tad big but so be it.

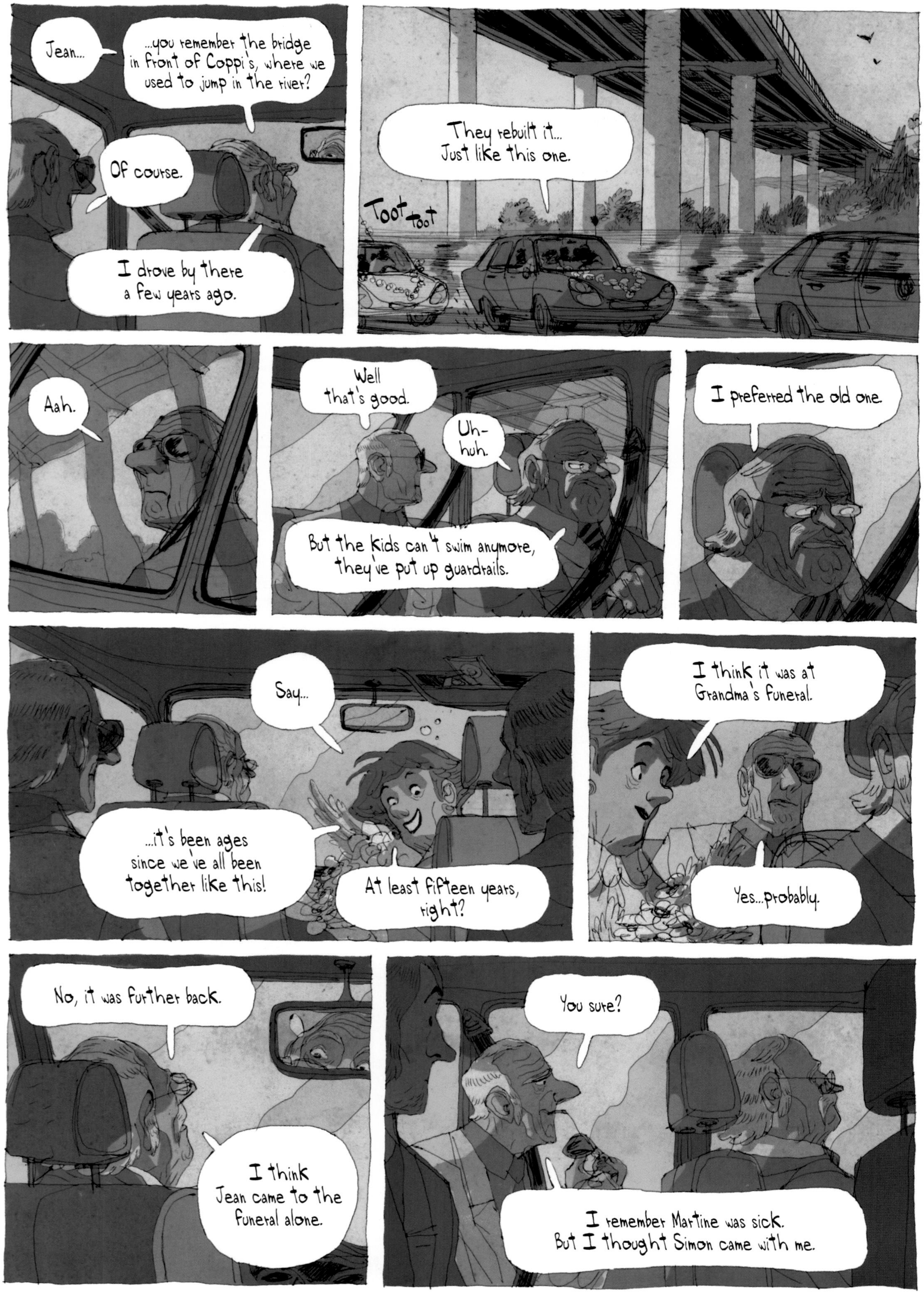
Jean...
...you remember the bridge in front of Coppi's, where we used to jump in the river?
Of course.
I drove by there a few years ago.
They rebuilt it... Just like this one.
Toot toot
Aah.
Well that's good.
Uh-huh.
But the kids can't swim anymore, they've put up guardrails.
I preferred the old one.
Say...
...it's been ages since we've all been together like this!
At least fifteen years, right?
I think it was at Grandma's funeral.
Yes...probably.
No, it was further back.
I think Jean came to the funeral alone.
You sure?
I remember Martine was sick. But I thought Simon came with me.

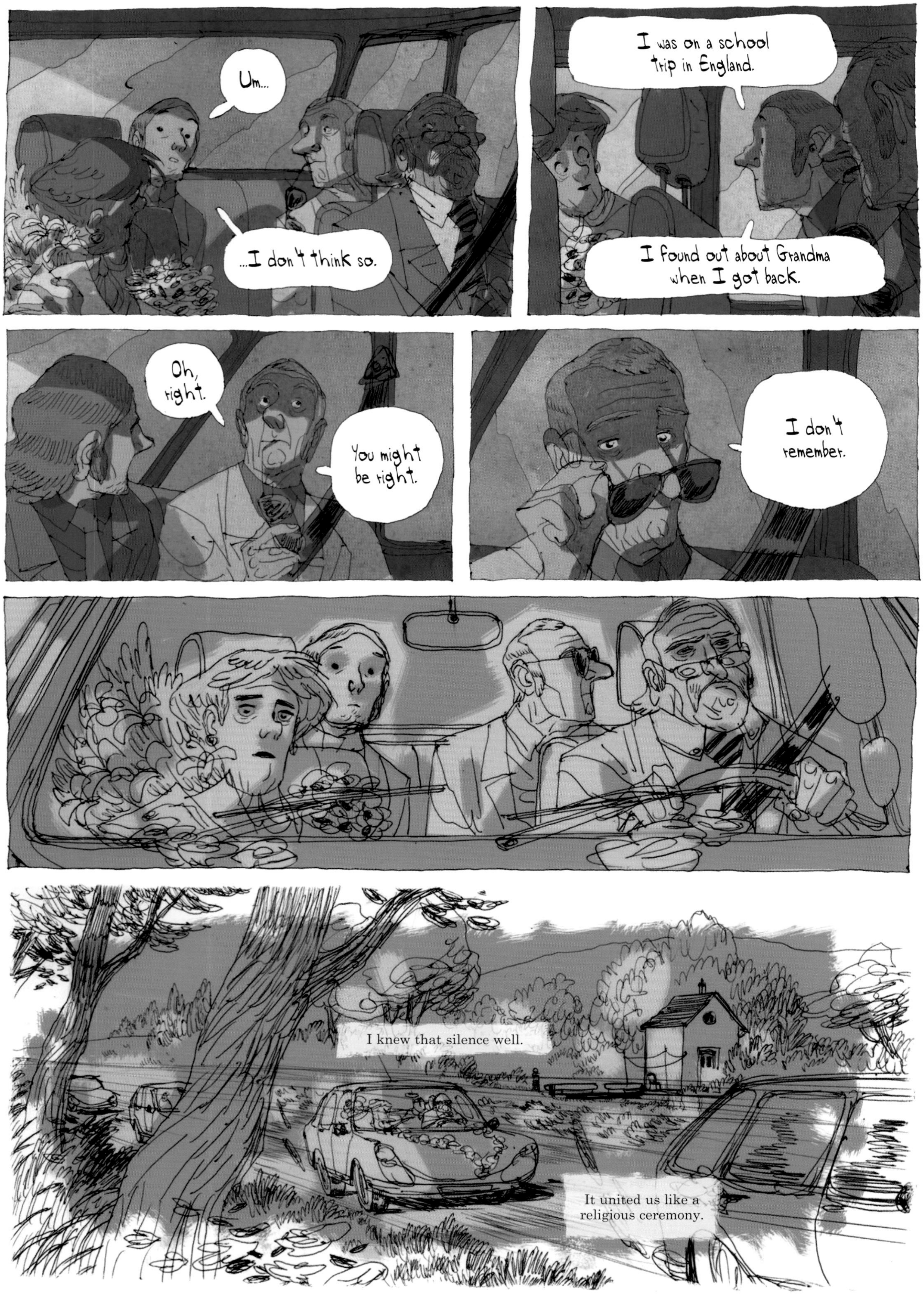
Um...
...I don't think so.
I was on a school trip in England.
I found out about Grandma when I got back.
Oh, right.
You might be right.
I don't remember.
I knew that silence well.
It united us like a religious ceremony.

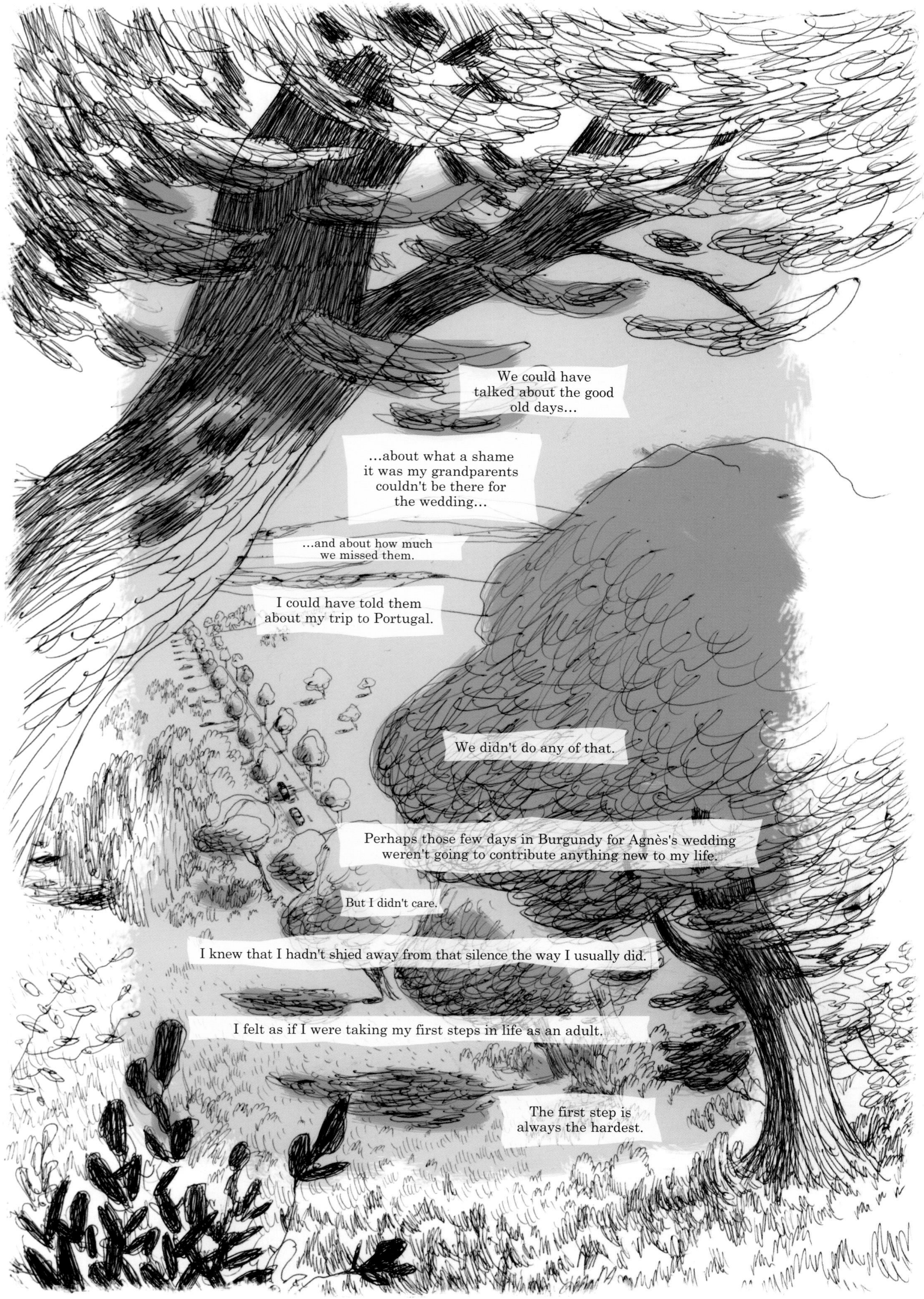
We could have talked about the good old days...
...about what a shame it was my grandparents couldn't be there for the wedding...
...and about how much we missed them.
I could have told them about my trip to Portugal.
We didn't do any of that.
Perhaps those few days in Burgundy for Agnès's wedding weren't going to contribute anything new to my life.
But I didn't care.
I knew that I hadn't shied away from that silence the way I usually did.
I felt as if I were taking my first steps in life as an adult.
The first step is always the hardest.

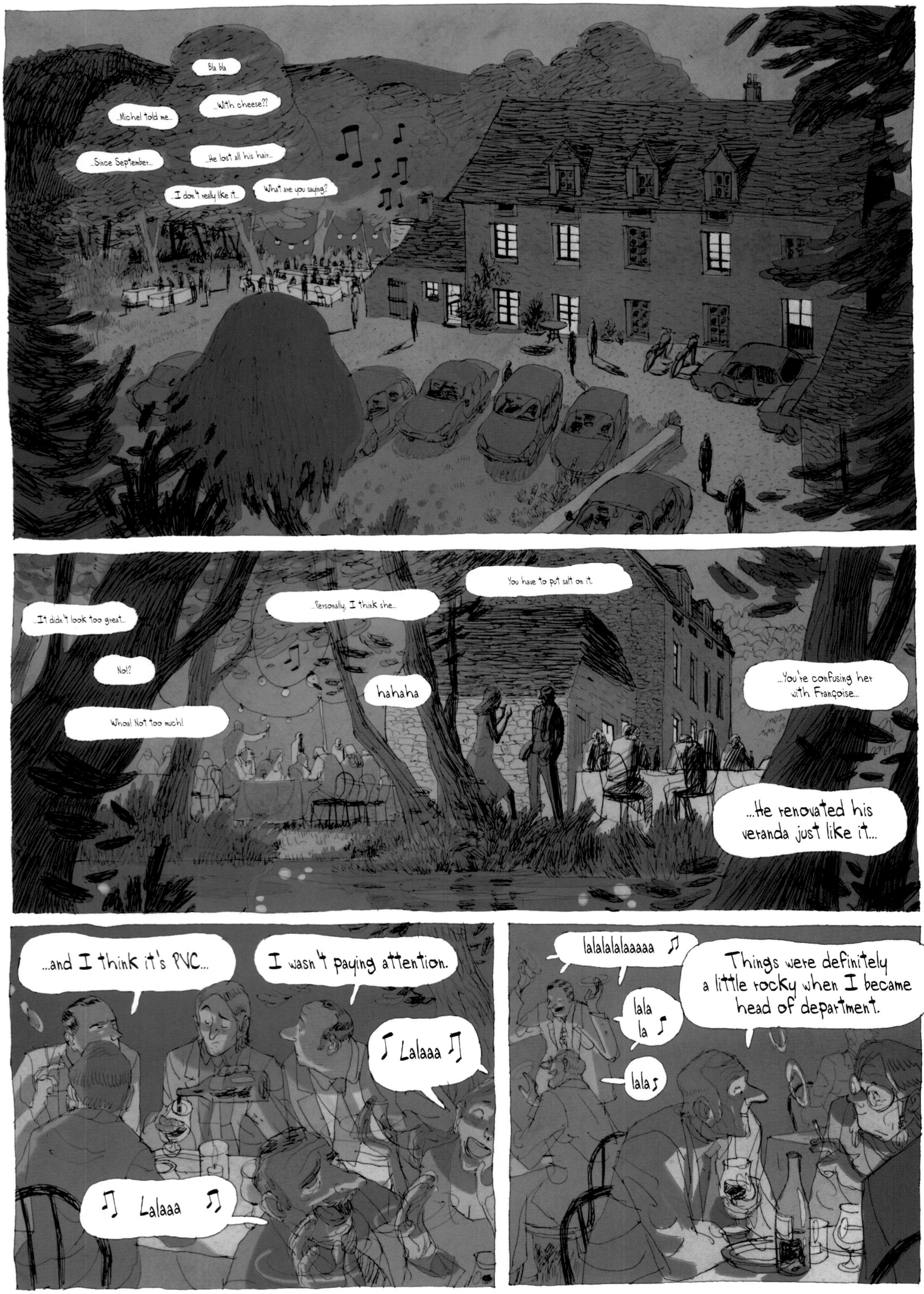

Bla bla
...Michel told me...
...With cheese??
...Since September...
...He lost all his hair...
...I don't really like it...
What are you saying?
...It didn't look too great...
...Personally, I think she...
You have to put salt on it.
No!?
hahaha
...You're confusing her with Françoise...
Whoa! Not too much!
...He renovated his veranda just like it...
...and I think it's PVC...
I wasn't paying attention.
Lalaaa
Lalaaa
lalalalalaaaaa
lala la
lala
Things were definitely a little rocky when I became head of department.

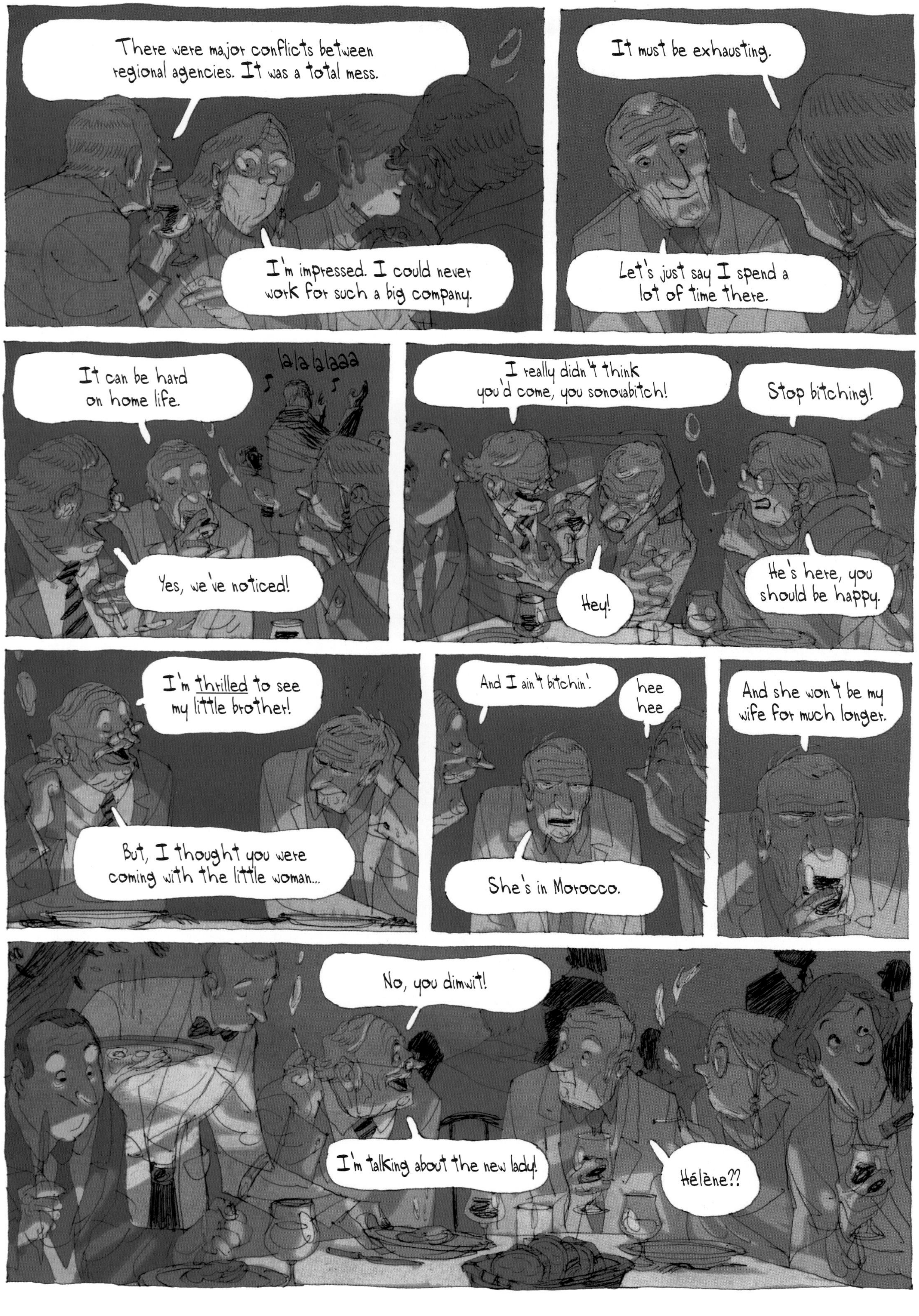
There were major conflicts between regional agencies. It was a total mess.
I'm impressed. I could never work for such a big company.
It must be exhausting.
Let's just say I spend a lot of time there.
It can be hard on home life.
lalalalaaa
Yes, we've noticed!
I really didn't think you'd come, you sonovabitch!
Hey!
Stop bitching!
He's here, you should be happy.
I'm thrilled to see my little brother!
But, I thought you were coming with the little woman...
And I ain't bitchin'.
hee hee
She's in Morocco.
And she won't be my wife for much longer.
No, you dimwit!
I'm talking about the new lady!
Hélène??

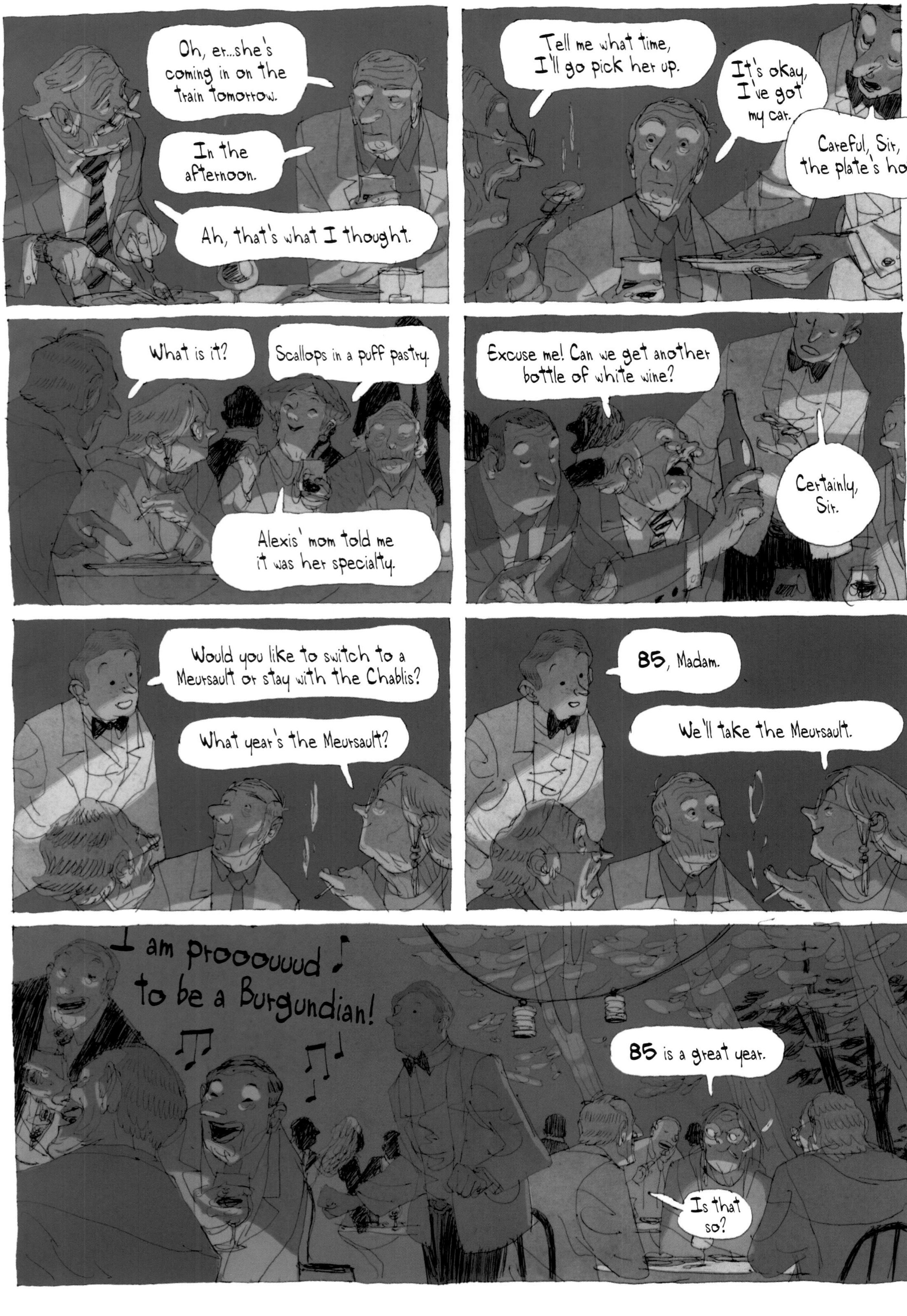
Oh, er...she's coming in on the train tomorrow.
In the afternoon.
Ah, that's what I thought.
Tell me what time, I'll go pick her up.
It's okay, I've got my car.
Careful, Sir, the plate's hot.
What is it?
Scallops in a puff pastry.
Alexis' mom told me it was her specialty.
Excuse me! Can we get another bottle of white wine?
Certainly, Sir.
Would you like to switch to a Meursault or stay with the Chablis?
What year's the Meursault?
85, Madam.
We'll take the Meursault.
I am proooouuud to be a Burgundian!
85 is a great year.
Is that so?

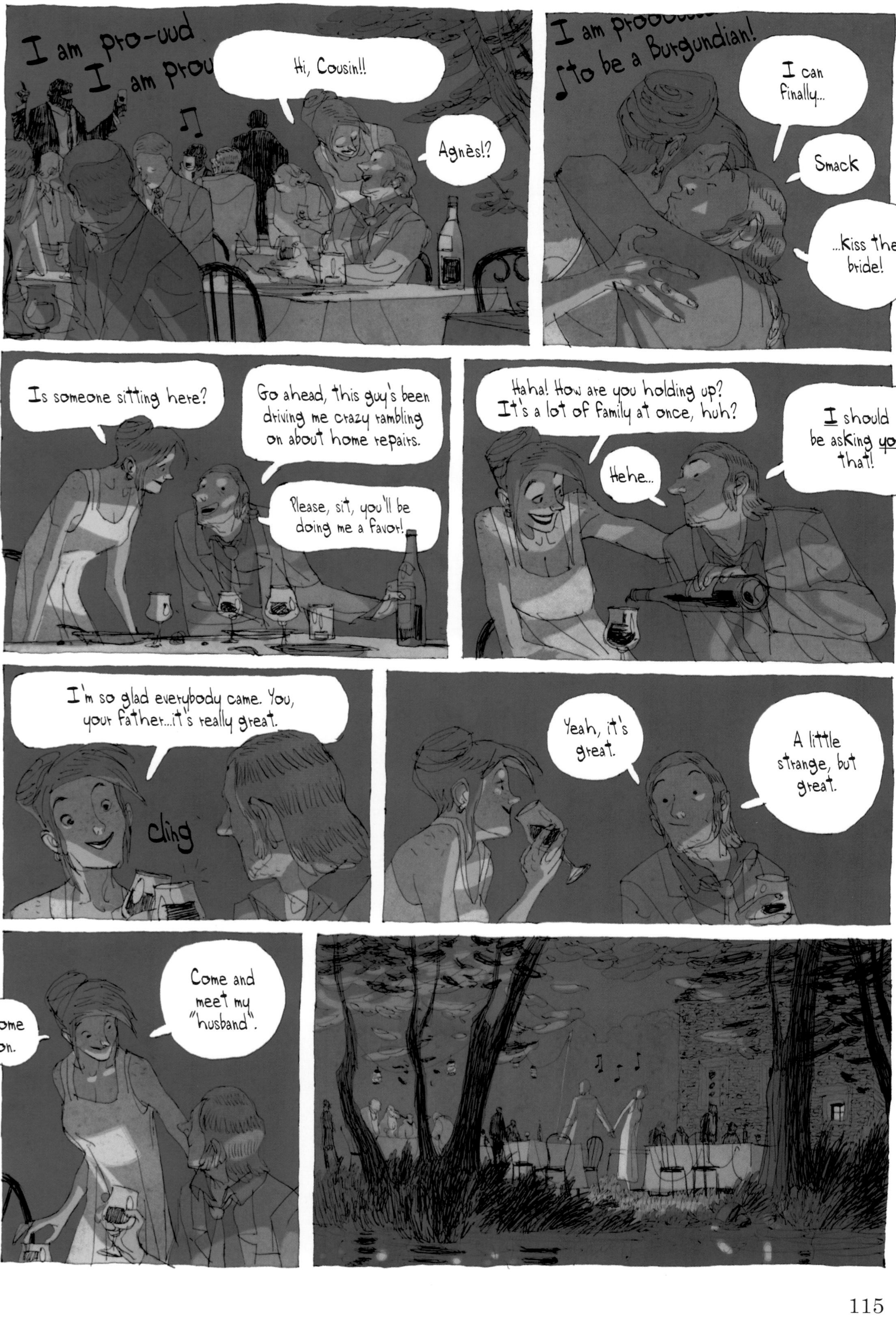
I am pro-uud
I am prou
Hi, Cousin!!
Agnès!?
I am proo
to be a Burgundian!
I can finally...
Smack
...kiss the bride!
Is someone sitting here?
Go ahead, this guy's been driving me crazy rambling on about home repairs.
Please, sit, you'll be doing me a favor!
Haha! How are you holding up? It's a lot of family at once, huh?
Hehe...
I should be asking you that!
I'm so glad everybody came. You, your father...it's really great.
cling
Yeah, it's great.
A little strange, but great.
Come on.
Come and meet my "husband".

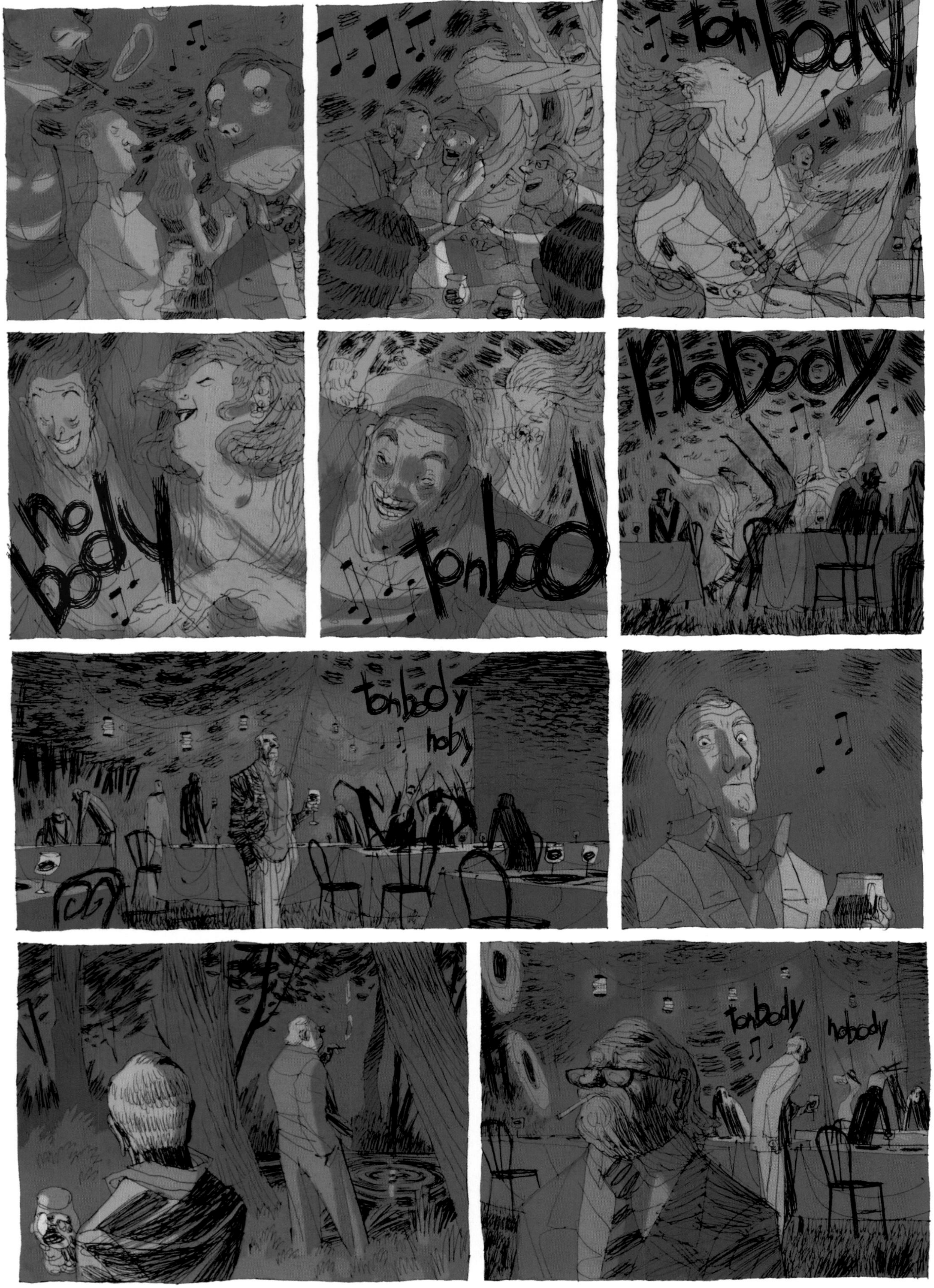
tonbody
nobody
tonbod
nobody
tonbody
noby
tonbody
nobody

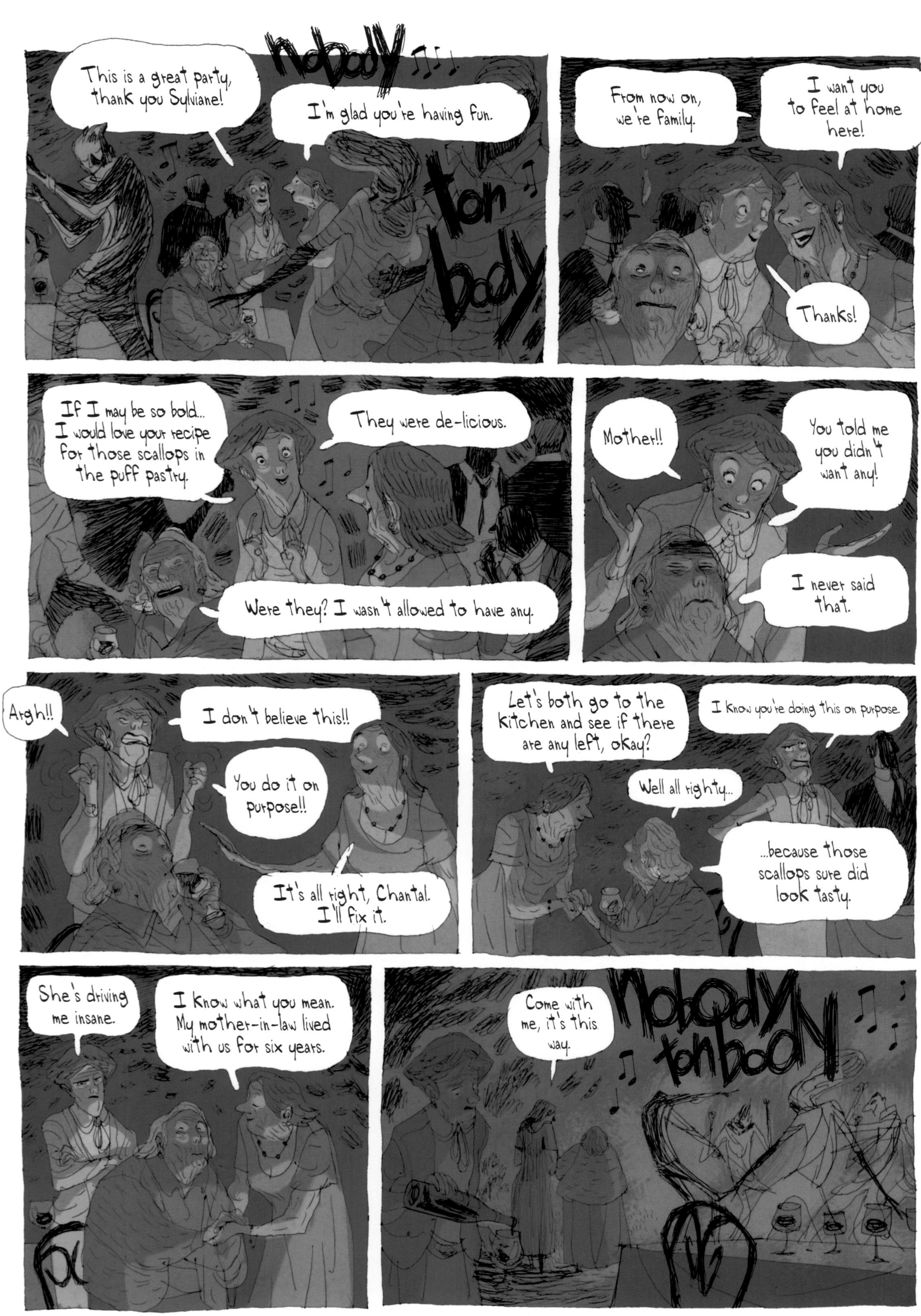
This is a great party, thank you Sylviane!
nobody
I'm glad you're having fun.
ton body
From now on, we're family.
I want you to feel at home here!
Thanks!
If I may be so bold... I would love your recipe for those scallops in the puff pastry.
They were de-licious.
Were they? I wasn't allowed to have any.
Mother!!
You told me you didn't want any!
I never said that.
Argh!!
I don't believe this!!
You do it on purpose!!
It's all right, Chantal. I'll fix it.
Let's both go to the kitchen and see if there are any left, okay?
I know you're doing this on purpose.
Well all righty...
...because those scallops sure did look tasty.
She's driving me insane.
I know what you mean. My mother-in-law lived with us for six years.
Come with me, it's this way.
nobody ton body

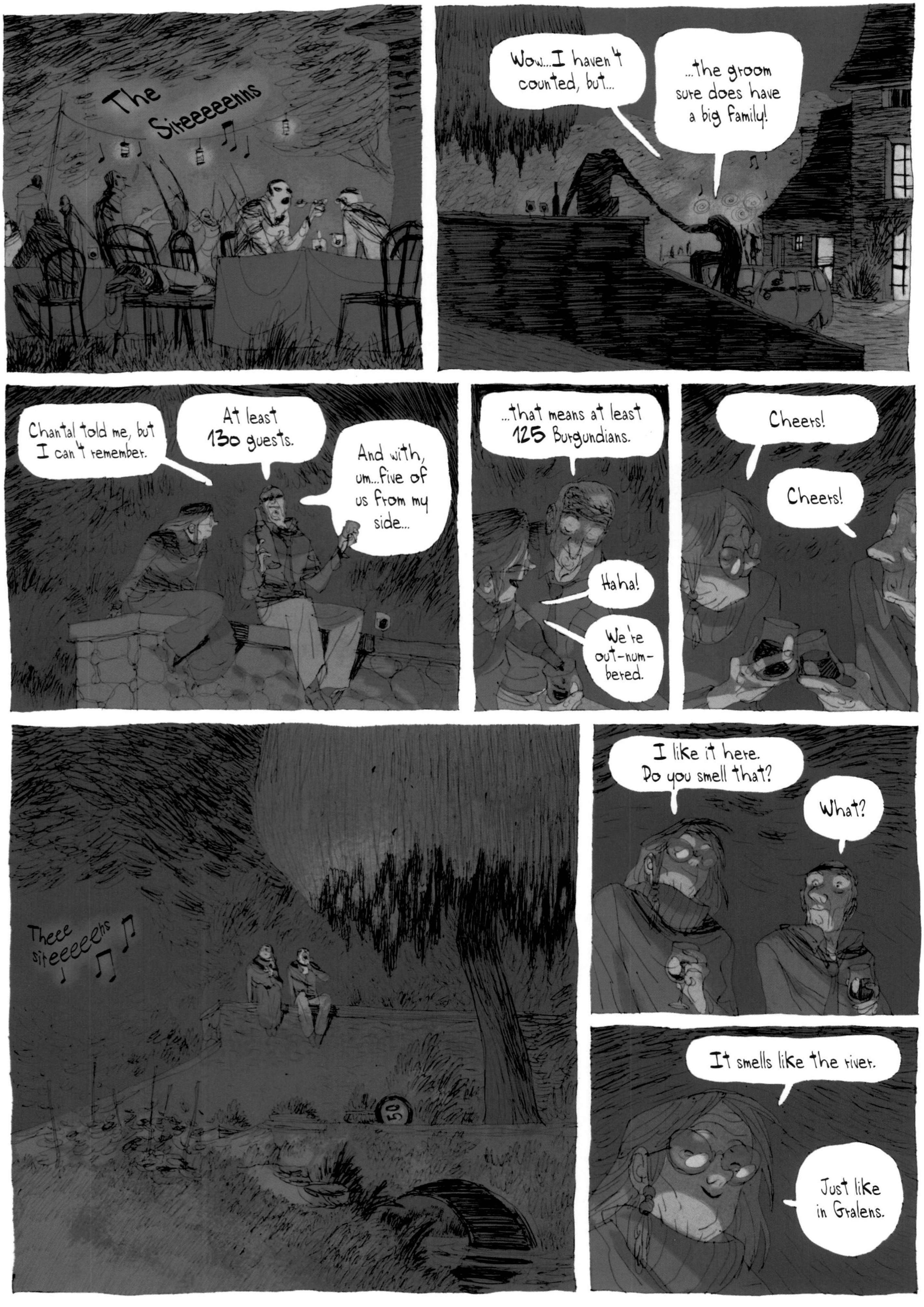
The Sireeeeenns
Wow...I haven't counted, but...
...the groom sure does have a big family!
Chantal told me, but I can't remember.
At least 130 guests.
And with, um...five of us from my side...
...that means at least 125 Burgundians.
Haha!
We're out-numbered.
Cheers!
Cheers!
Theee sireeeeens
I like it here. Do you smell that?
What?
It smells like the river.
Just like in Gralens.

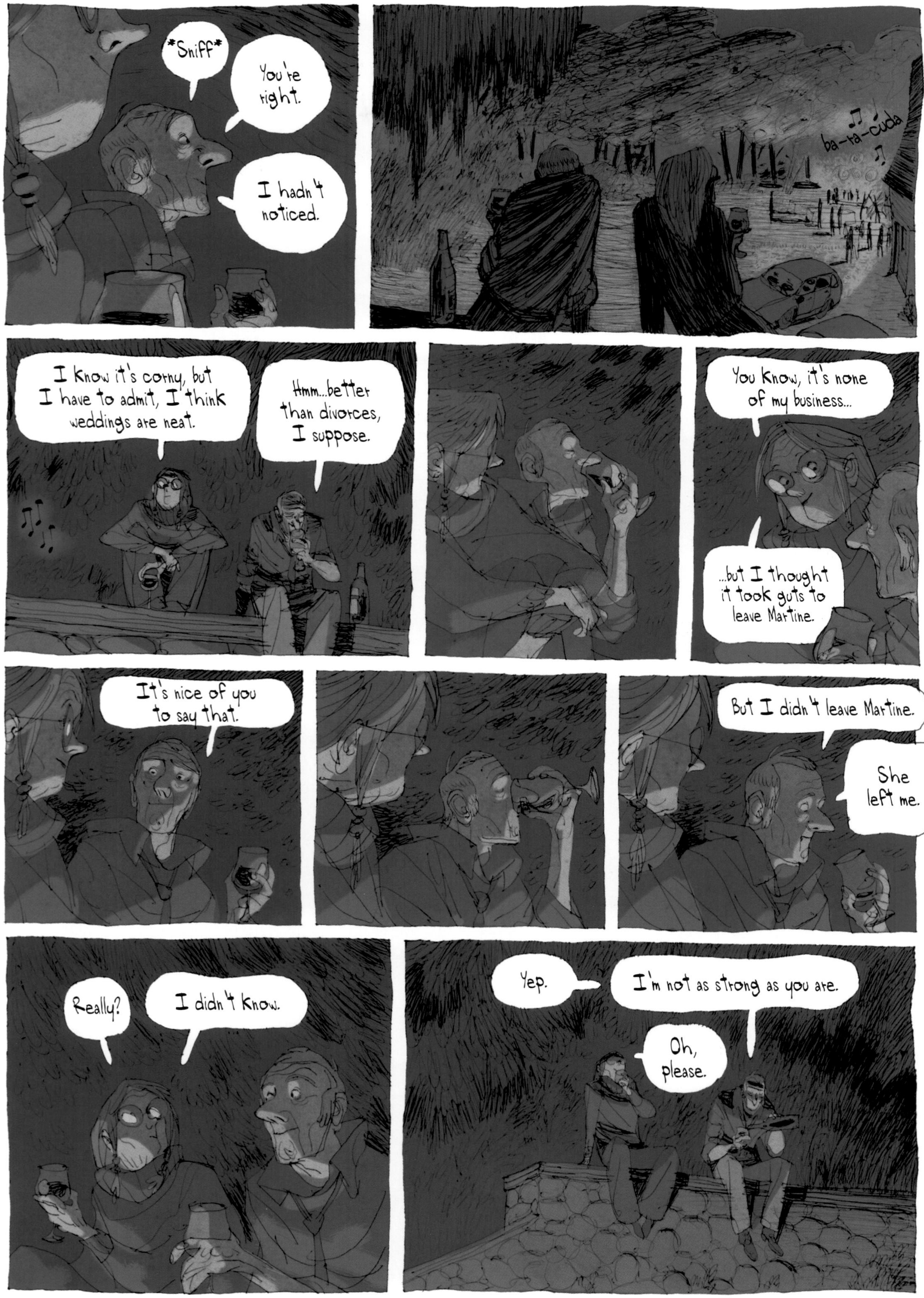
Sniff
You're right.
I hadn't noticed.
ba-ra-cuda
I know it's corny, but I have to admit, I think weddings are neat.
Hmm...better than divorces, I suppose.
You know, it's none of my business...
...but I thought it took guts to leave Martine.
It's nice of you to say that.
But I didn't leave Martine.
She left me.
Really?
I didn't know.
Yep.
I'm not as strong as you are.
Oh, please.

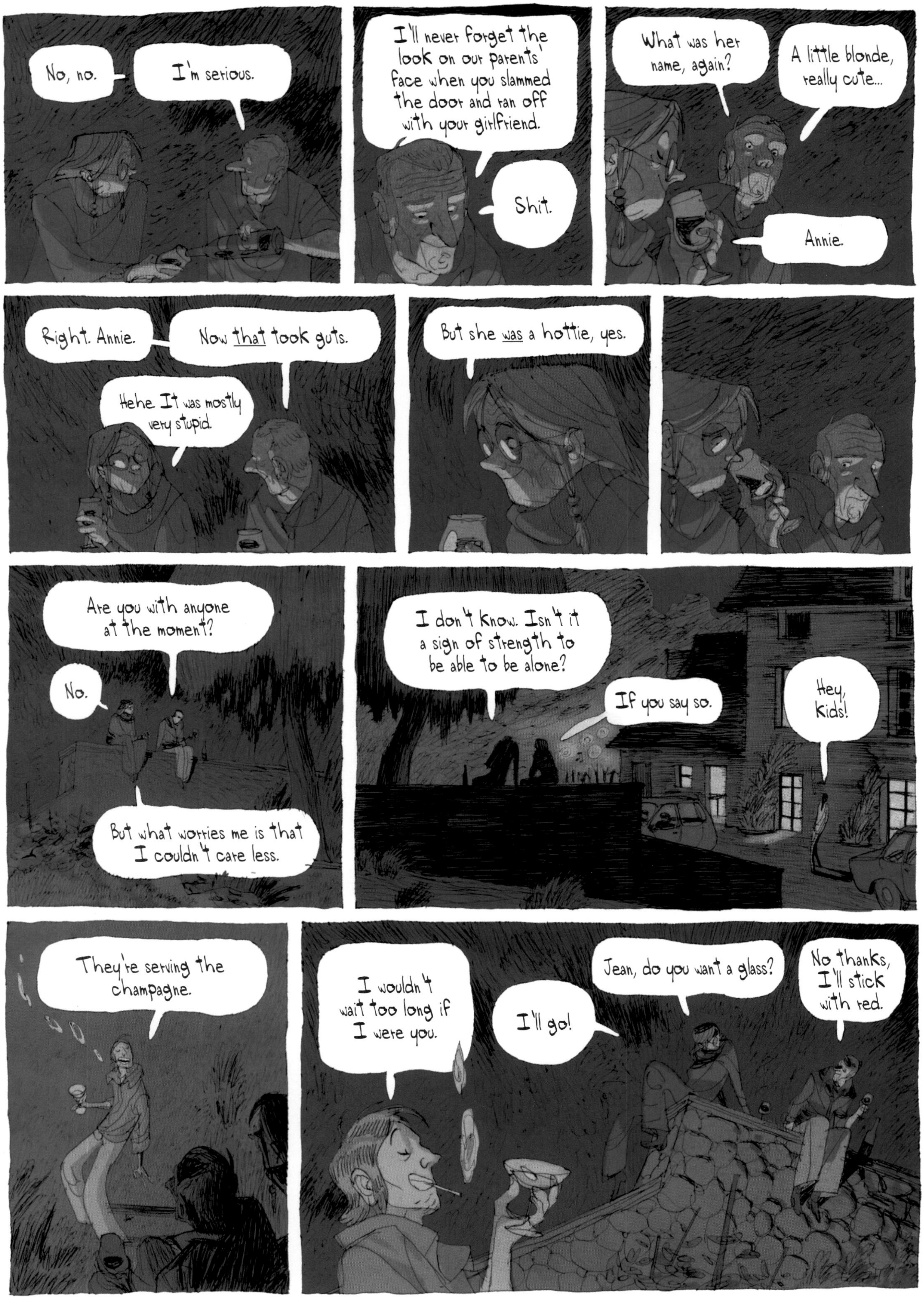
No, no.
I'm serious.
I'll never forget the look on our parents' face when you slammed the door and ran off with your girlfriend.
Shit.
What was her name, again?
A little blonde, really cute...
Annie.
Right. Annie.
Now that took guts.
Hehe. It was mostly very stupid.
But she was a hottie, yes.
Are you with anyone at the moment?
No.
But what worries me is that I couldn't care less.
I don't know. Isn't it a sign of strength to be able to be alone?
If you say so.
Hey, kids!
They're serving the champagne.
I wouldn't wait too long if I were you.
I'll go!
Jean, do you want a glass?
No thanks, I'll stick with red.

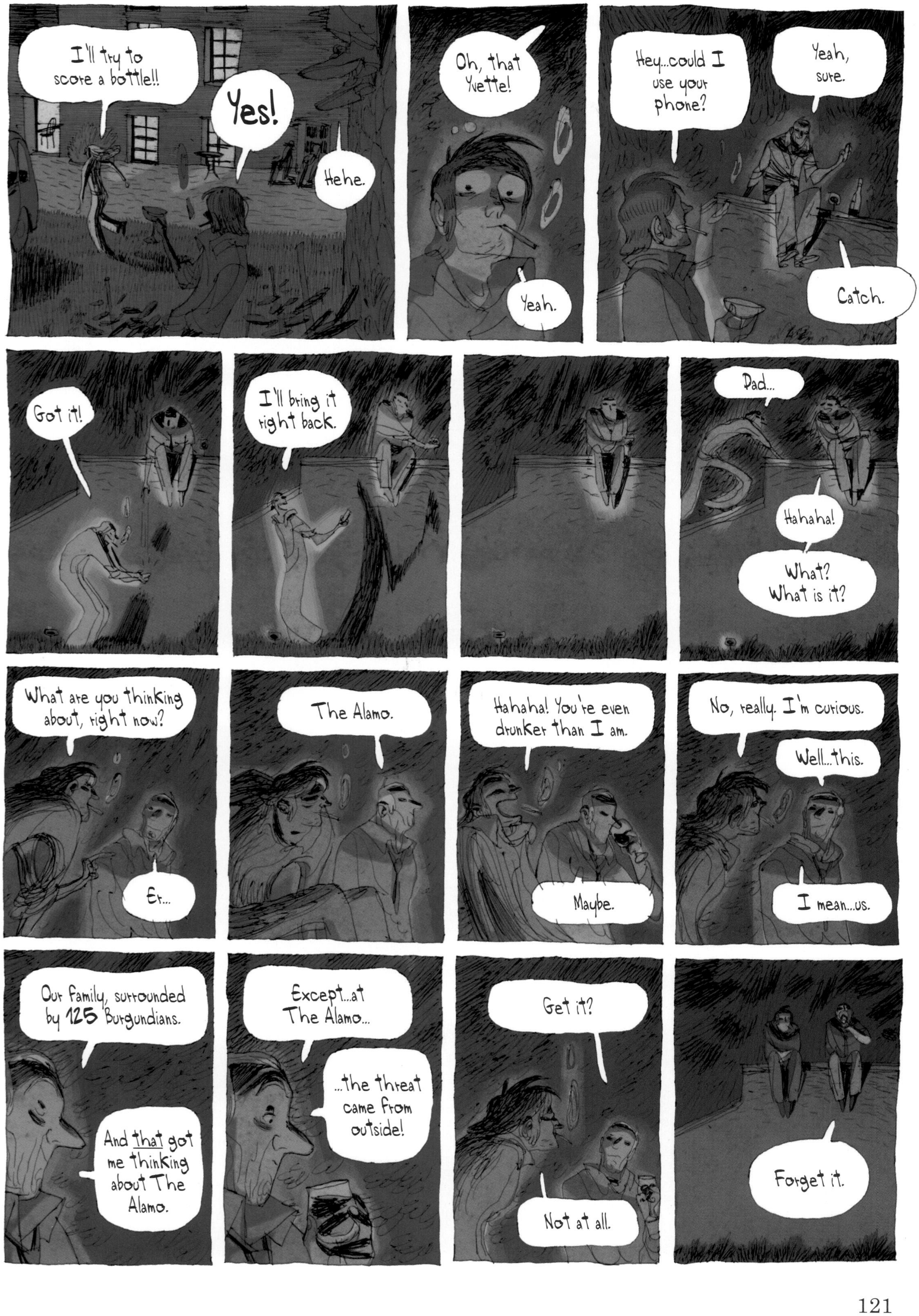
I'll try to score a bottle!!
Yes!
Hehe.
Oh, that Yvette!
Yeah.
Hey...could I use your phone?
Yeah, sure.
Catch.
Got it!
I'll bring it right back.
Dad...
Hahaha!
What? What is it?
What are you thinking about, right now?
Er...
The Alamo.
Hahaha! You're even drunker than I am.
Maybe.
No, really. I'm curious.
Well...this.
I mean...us.
Our family, surrounded by 125 Burgundians.
And that got me thinking about The Alamo.
Except...at The Alamo...
...the threat came from outside!
Get it?
Not at all.
Forget it.

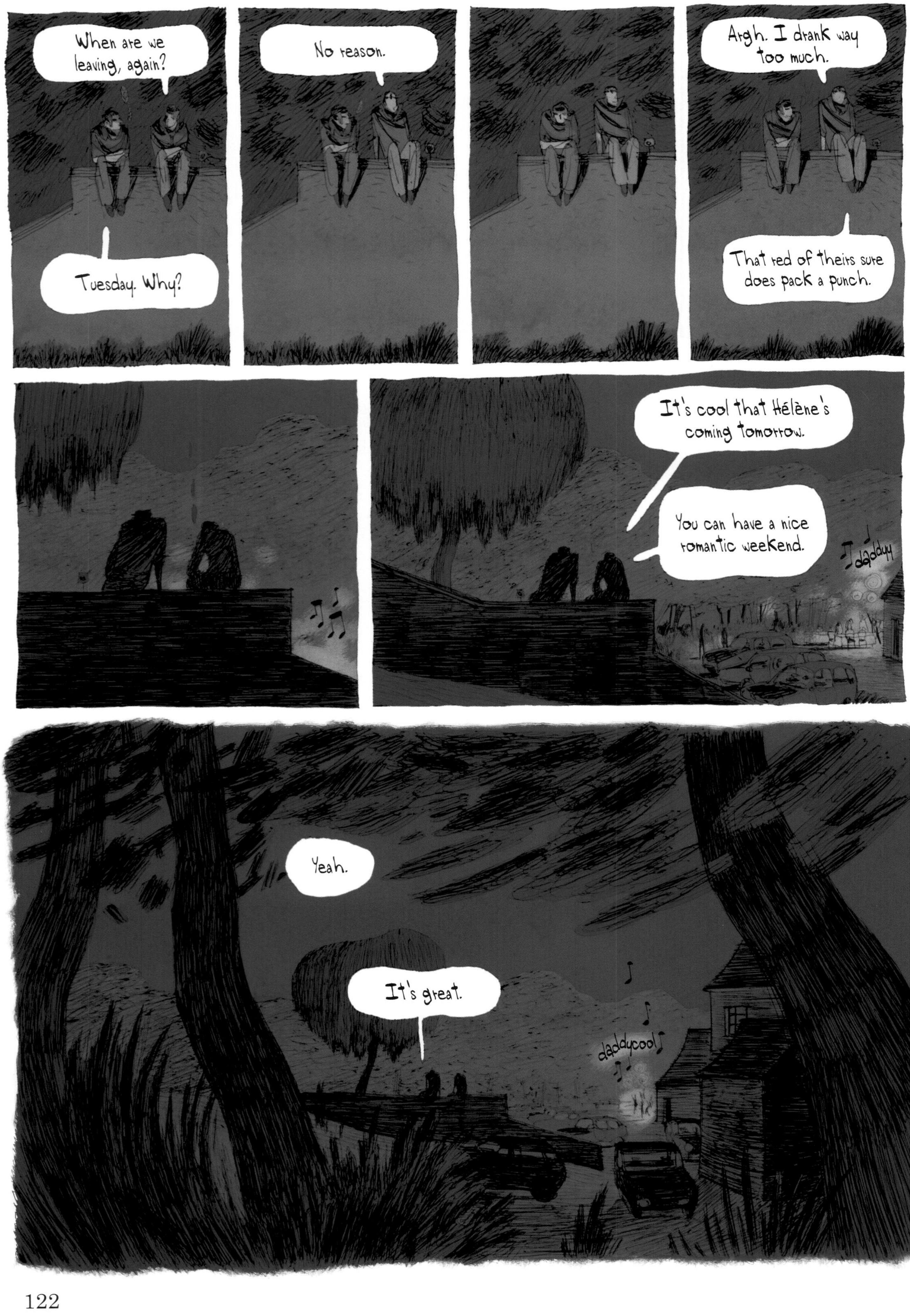
When are we leaving, again?
Tuesday. Why?
No reason.
Argh. I drank way too much.
That red of theirs sure does pack a punch.
It's cool that Hélène's coming tomorrow.
You can have a nice romantic weekend.
daddyy
Yeah.
It's great.
daddycool

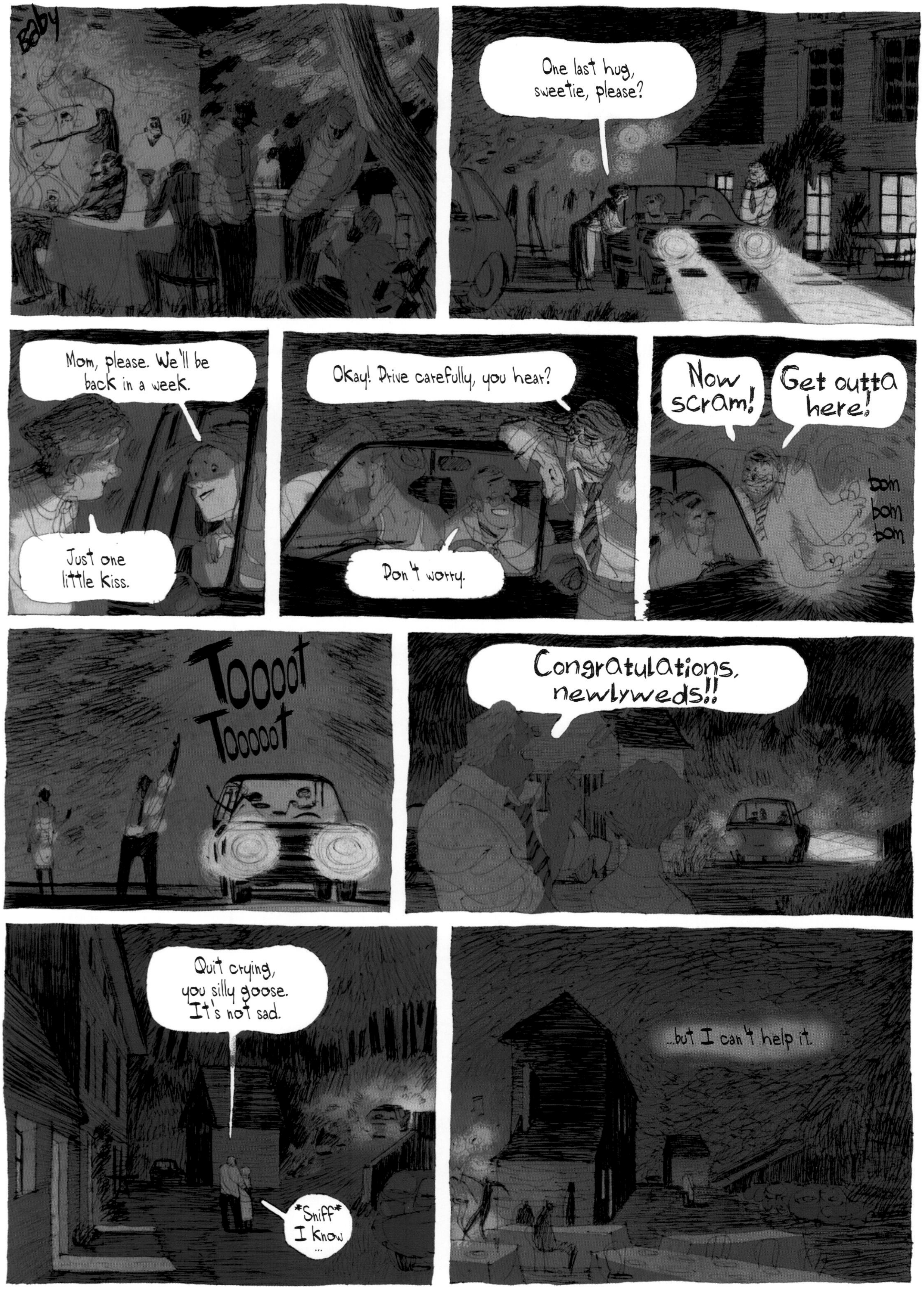

Baby
One last hug, sweetie, please?
Mom, please. We'll be back in a week.
Just one little kiss.
Okay! Drive carefully, you hear?
Don't worry.
Now scram!
Get outta here!
bom bom bom
Toooot
Tooooot
Congratulations, newlyweds!!
Quit crying, you silly goose. It's not sad.
Sniff I know ...
...but I can't help it.

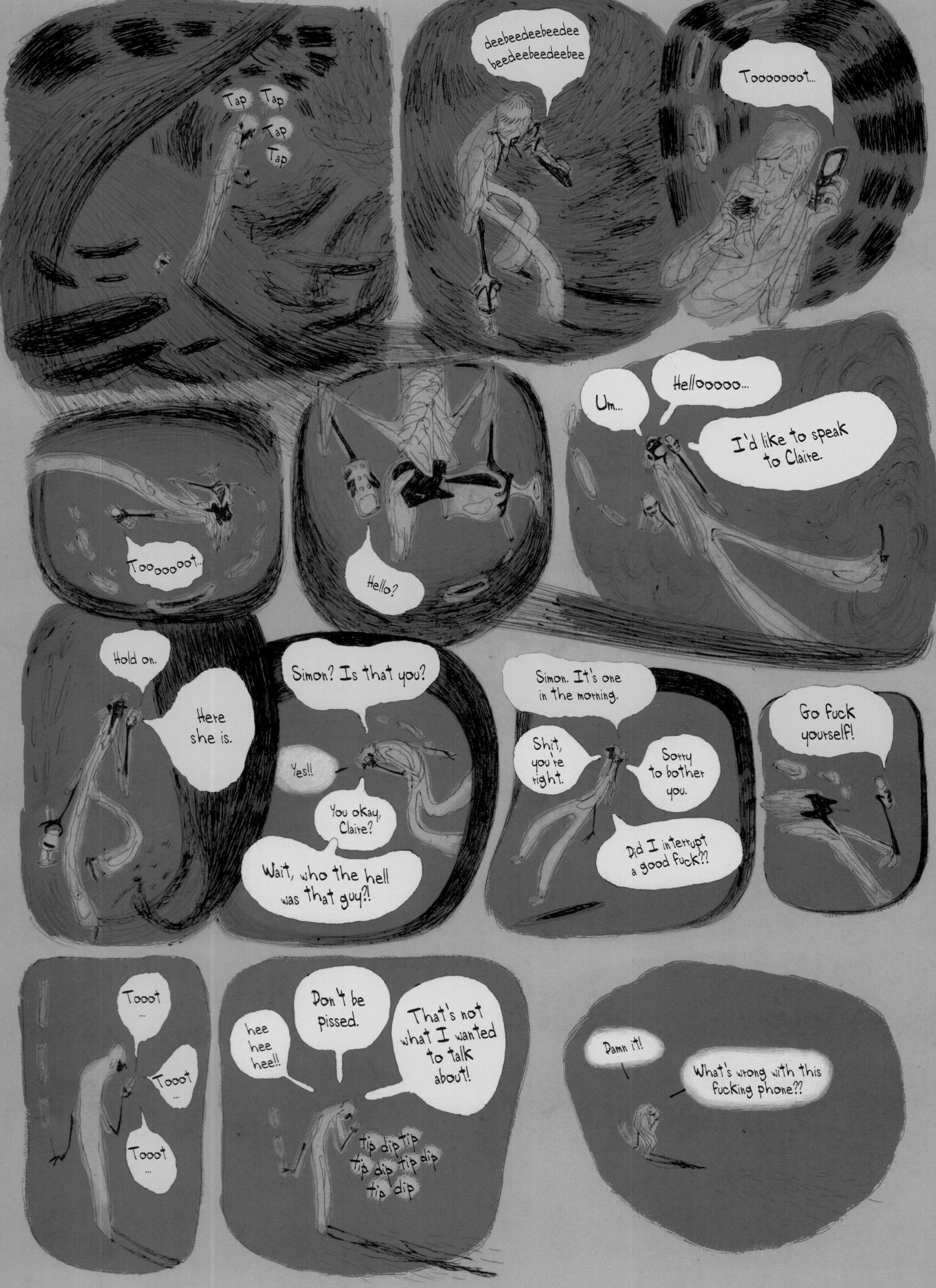

Tap
Tap
Tap
Tap
deebeedeebeedee beedeebeedeebee
Toooooooot...
Tooooooot...
Hello?
Um...
Hellooooo...
I'd like to speak to Claire.
Hold on.
Here she is.
Simon? Is that you?
Yes!!
You okay, Claire?
Wait, who the hell was that guy?!
Simon. It's one in the morning.
Shit, you're right.
Sorry to bother you.
Did I interrupt a good fuck??
Go fuck yourself!
Tooot ...
Tooot ...
Tooot ...
hee hee hee!!
Don't be pissed.
That's not what I wanted to talk about!
tip dip tip tip dip tip dip tip dip
Damn it!
What's wrong with this fucking phone??

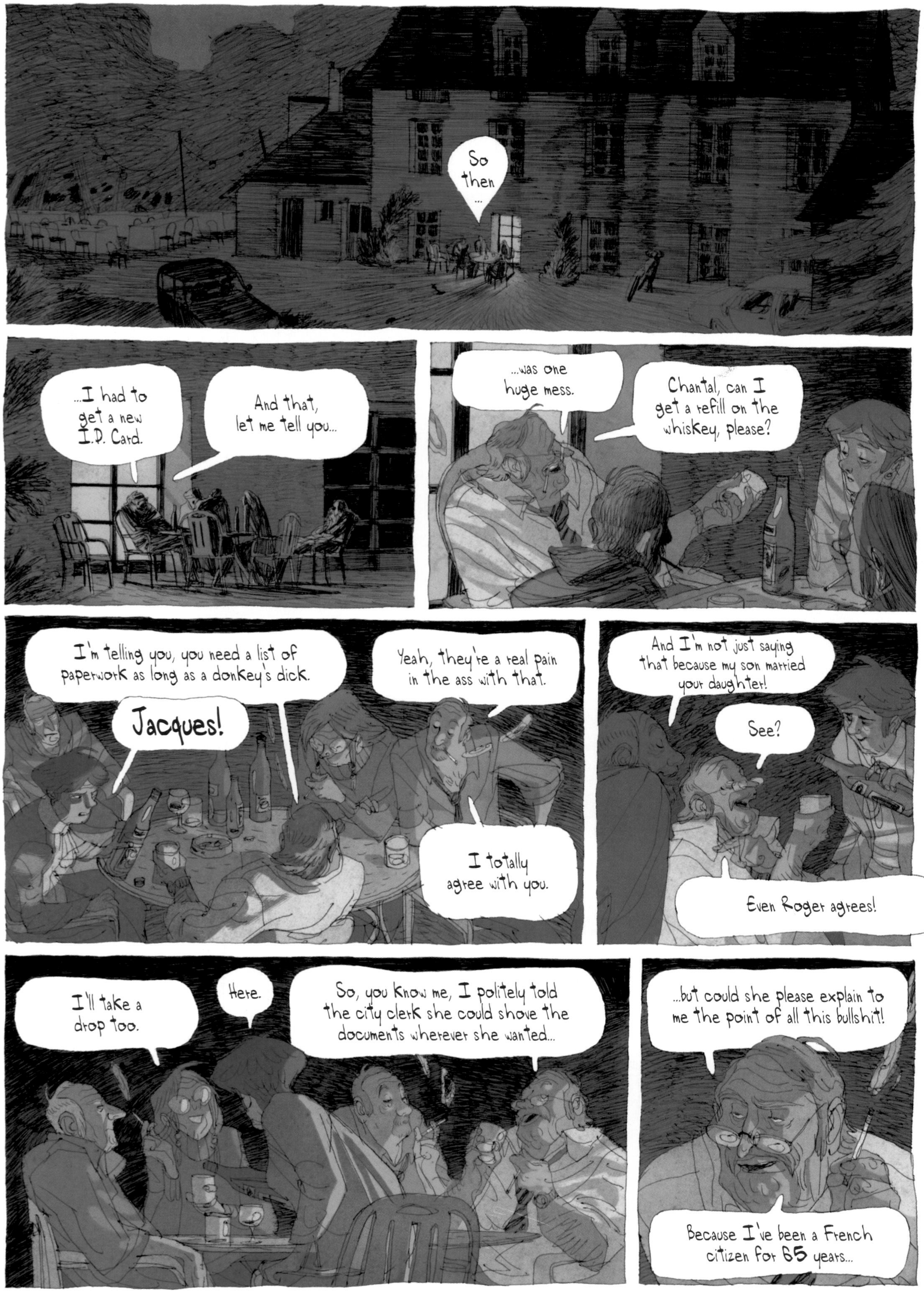
So then ...
...I had to get a new I.D. Card.
And that, let me tell you...
...was one huge mess.
Chantal, can I get a refill on the whiskey, please?
I'm telling you, you need a list of paperwork as long as a donkey's dick.
Jacques!
Yeah, they're a real pain in the ass with that.
I totally agree with you.
And I'm not just saying that because my son married your daughter!
See?
Even Roger agrees!
I'll take a drop too.
Here.
So, you know me, I politely told the city clerk she could shove the documents wherever she wanted...
...but could she please explain to me the point of all this bullshit!
Because I've been a French citizen for 65 years...

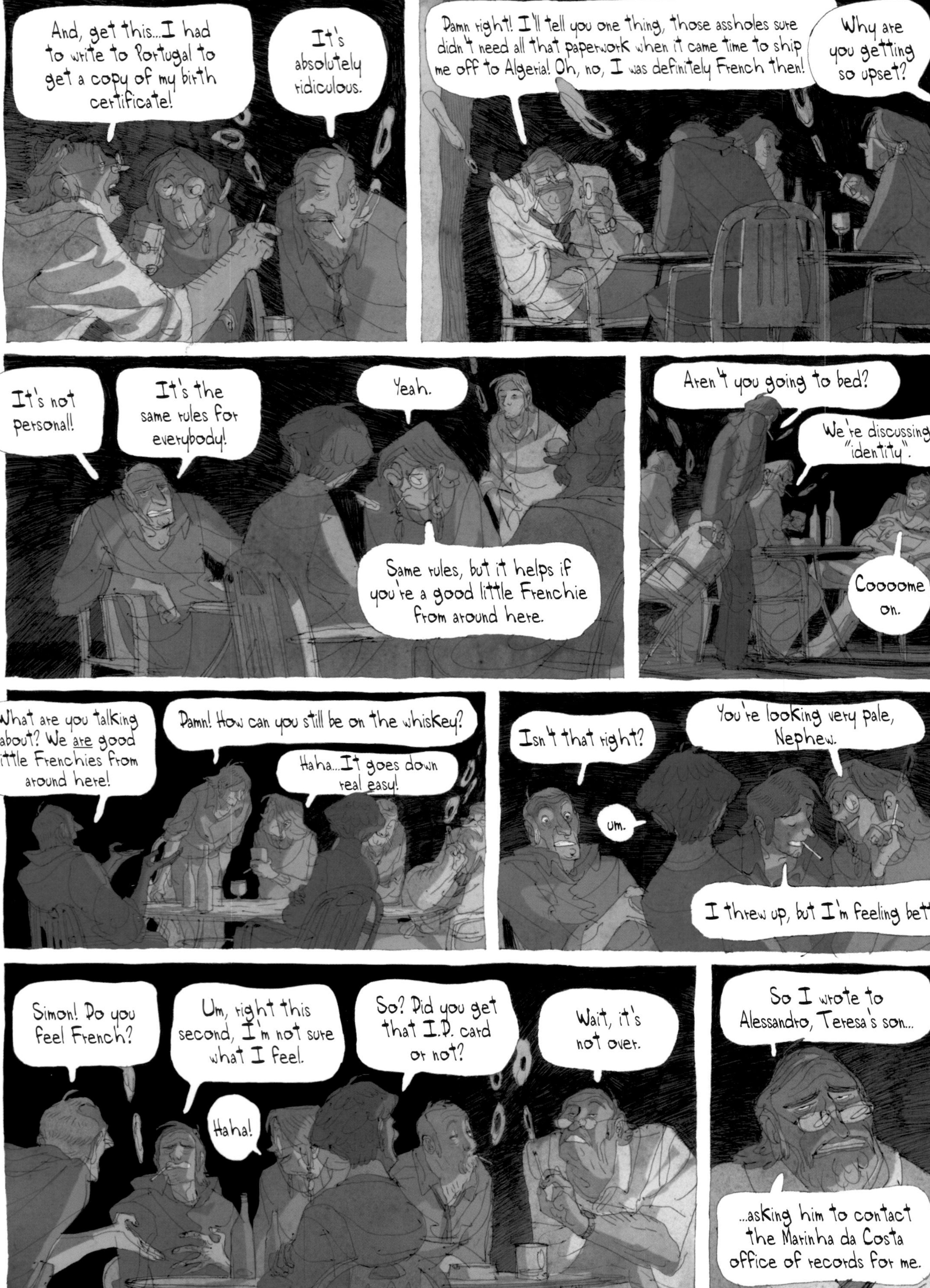
And, get this...I had to write to Portugal to get a copy of my birth certificate!
It's absolutely ridiculous.
Damn right! I'll tell you one thing, those assholes sure didn't need all that paperwork when it came time to ship me off to Algeria! Oh, no, I was definitely French then!
Why are you getting so upset?
It's not personal!
It's the same rules for everybody!
Yeah.
Same rules, but it helps if you're a good little Frenchie from around here.
Aren't you going to bed?
We're discussing "identity".
Coooome on.
What are you talking about? We are good little Frenchies from around here!
Damn! How can you still be on the whiskey?
Haha...It goes down real easy!
Isn't that right?
Um.
You're looking very pale, Nephew.
I threw up, but I'm feeling better.
Simon! Do you feel French?
Um, right this second, I'm not sure what I feel.
Haha!
So? Did you get that I.D. card or not?
Wait, it's not over.
So I wrote to Alessandro, Teresa's son...
...asking him to contact the Marinha da Costa office of records for me.

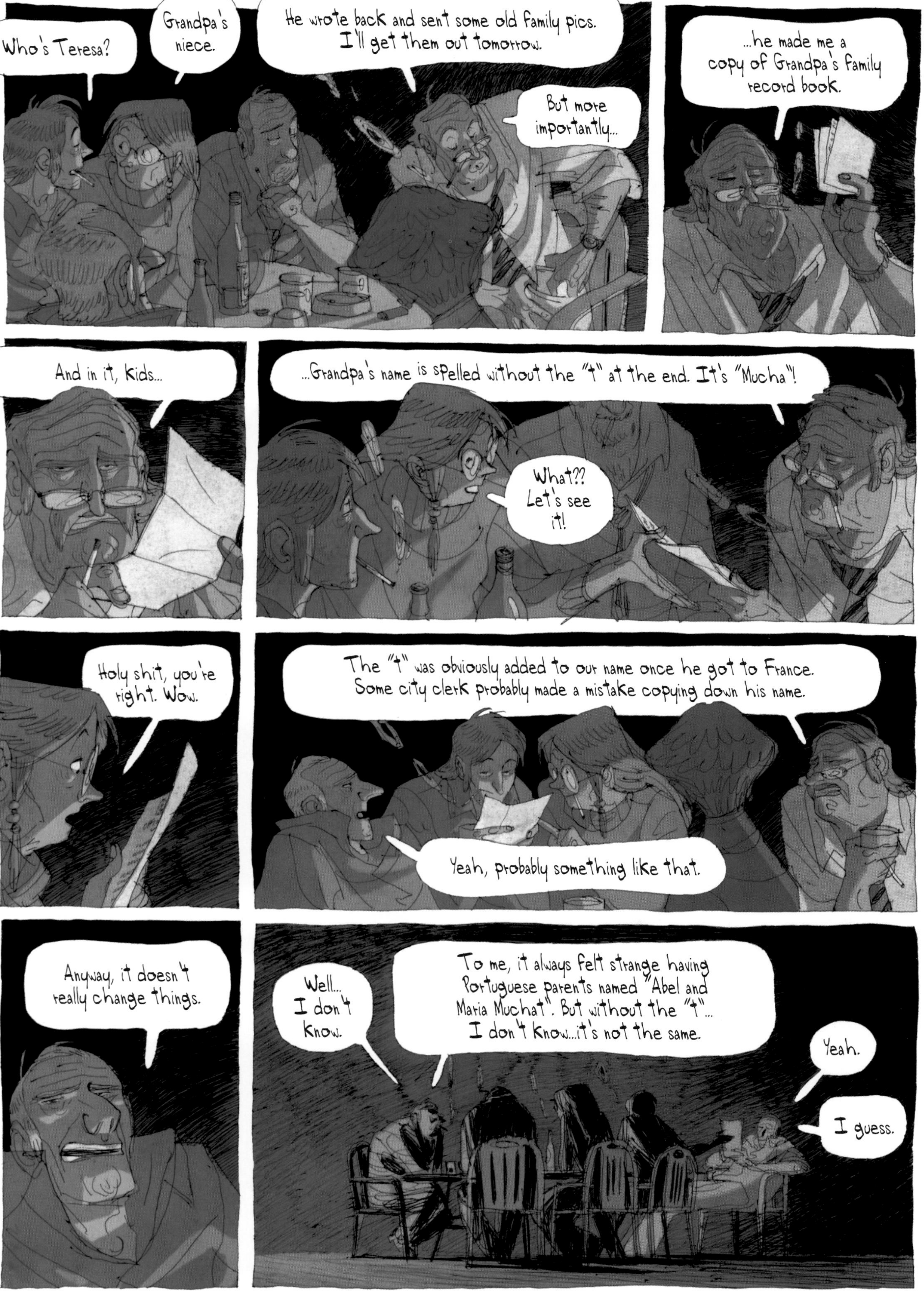

Who's Teresa?
Grandpa's niece.
He wrote back and sent some old family pics. I'll get them out tomorrow.
But more importantly...
...he made me a copy of Grandpa's family record book.
And in it, kids...
...Grandpa's name is spelled without the "t" at the end. It's "Mucha"!
What?? Let's see it!
Holy shit, you're right. Wow.
The "t" was obviously added to our name once he got to France. Some city clerk probably made a mistake copying down his name.
Yeah, probably something like that.
Anyway, it doesn't really change things.
Well... I don't know.
To me, it always felt strange having Portuguese parents named "Abel and Maria Muchat". But without the "t"... I don't know...it's not the same.
Yeah.
I guess.

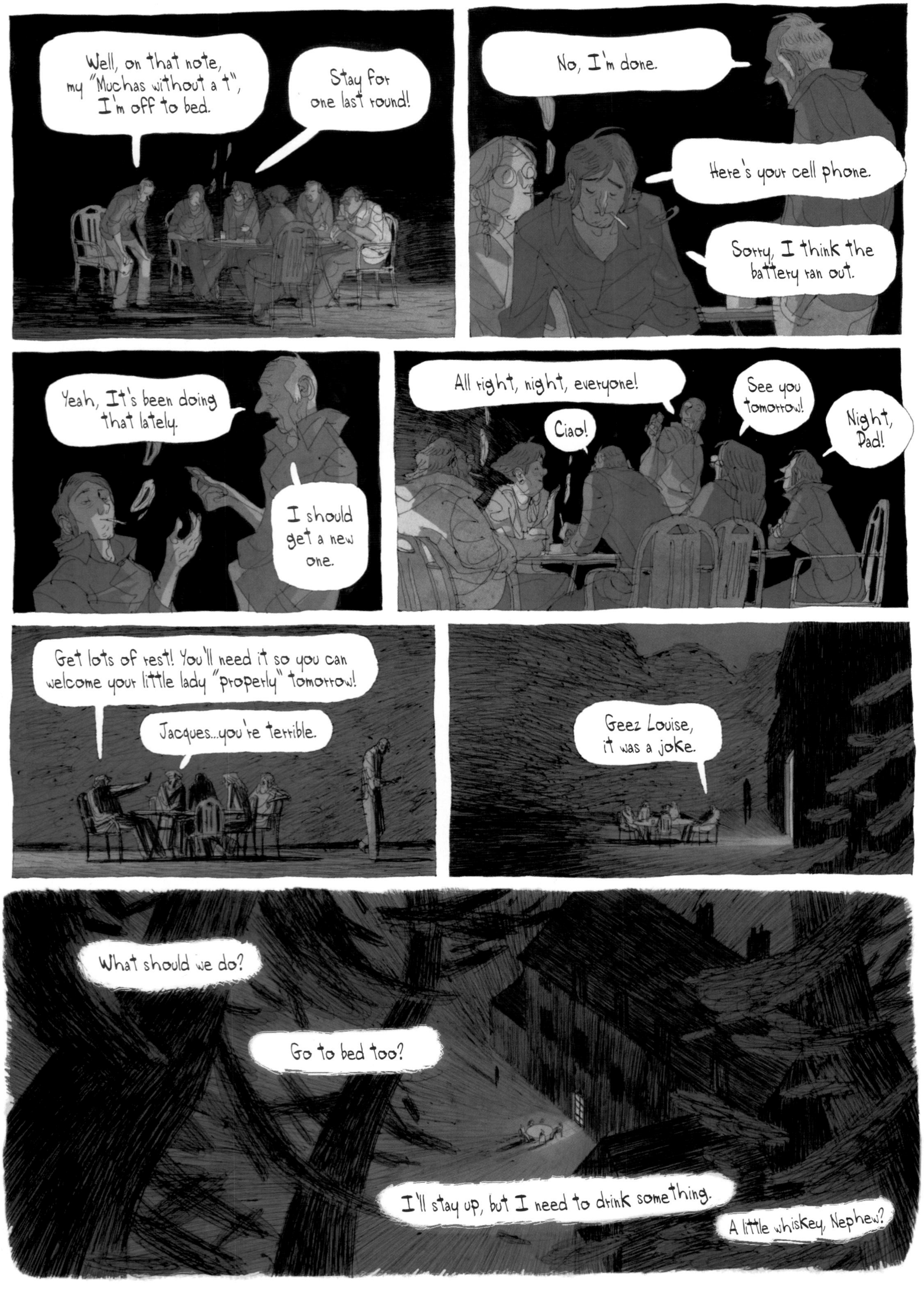
Well, on that note, my "Muchas without a t", I'm off to bed.
Stay for one last round!
No, I'm done.
Here's your cell phone.
Sorry, I think the battery ran out.
Yeah, It's been doing that lately.
I should get a new one.
All right, night, everyone!
Ciao!
See you tomorrow!
Night, Dad!
Get lots of rest! You'll need it so you can welcome your little lady "properly" tomorrow!
Jacques...you're terrible.
Geez Louise, it was a joke.
What should we do?
Go to bed too?
I'll stay up, but I need to drink something.
A little whiskey, Nephew?

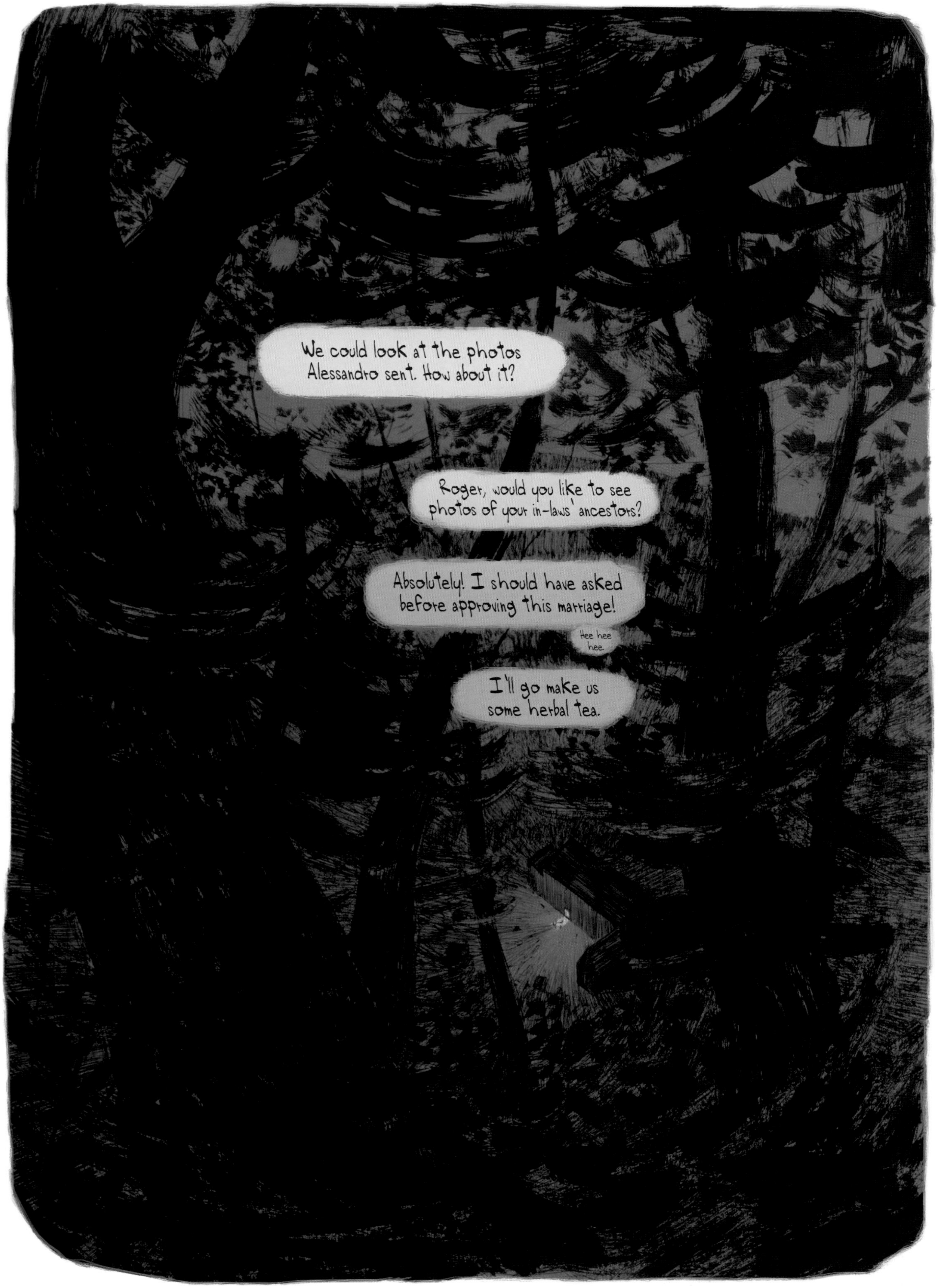
We could look at the photos Alessandro sent. How about it?
Roger, would you like to see photos of your in-laws' ancestors?
Absolutely! I should have asked before approving this marriage!
Hee hee hee.
I'll go make us some herbal tea.

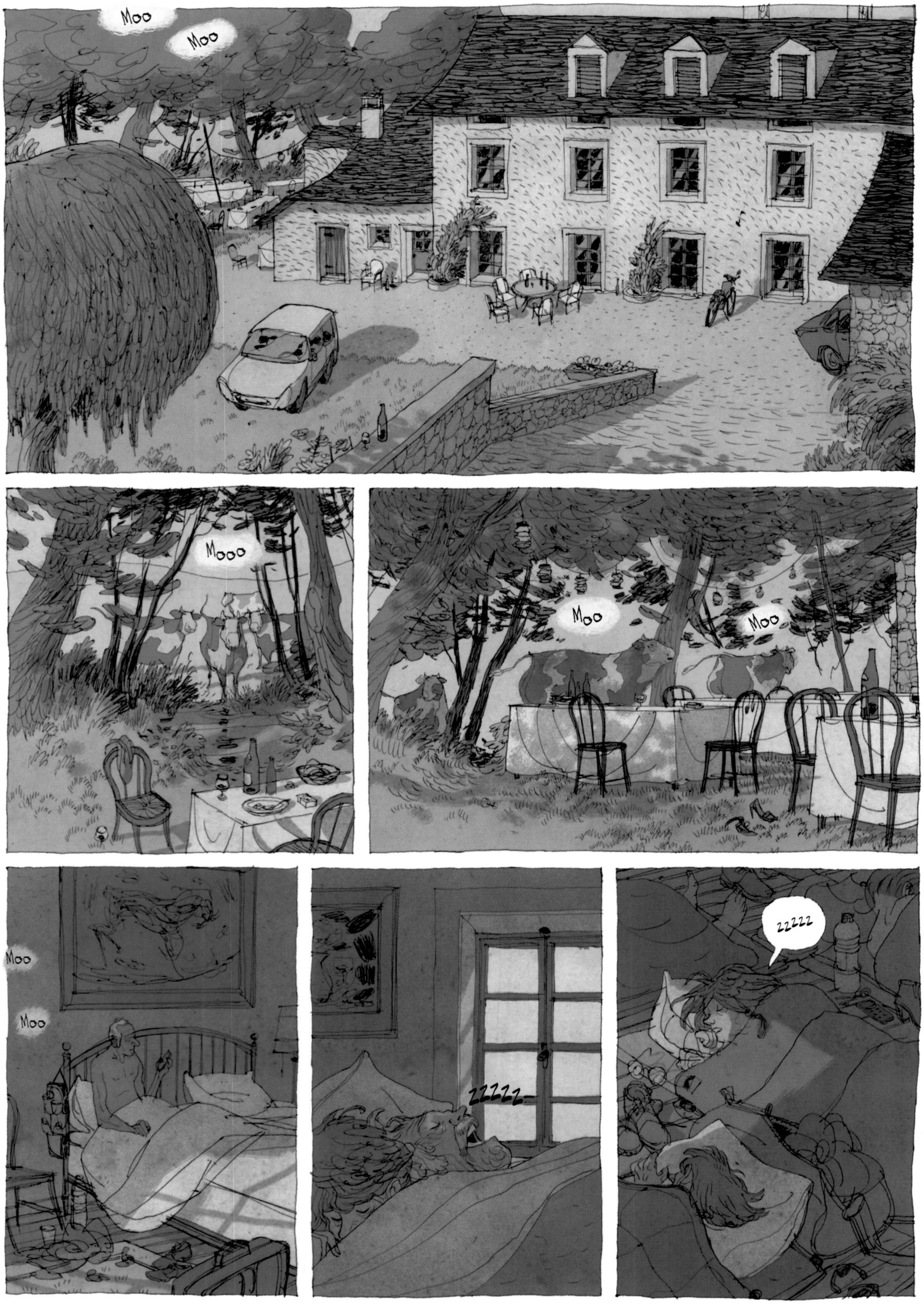
Moo
Moo
Mooo
Moo
Moo
Moo
Moo
ZZZZZ
ZZZZZ

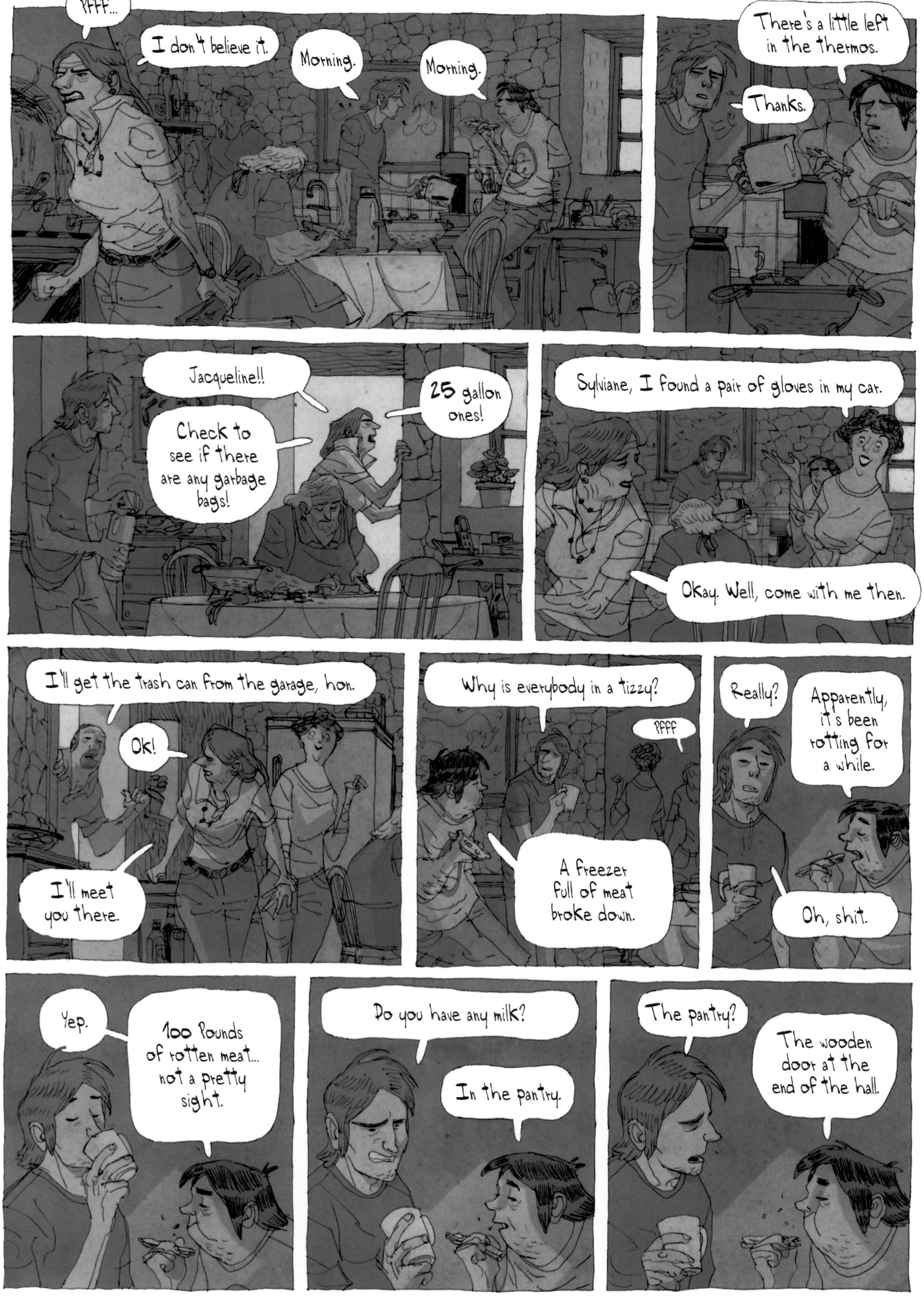
PFFF...
I don't believe it.
Morning.
Morning.
There's a little left in the thermos.
Thanks.
Jacqueline!!
Check to see if there are any garbage bags!
25 gallon ones!
Sylviane, I found a pair of gloves in my car.
Okay. Well, come with me then.
I'll get the trash can from the garage, hon.
Ok!
I'll meet you there.
Why is everybody in a tizzy?
PFFF
A freezer full of meat broke down.
Really?
Apparently, it's been rotting for a while.
Oh, shit.
Yep.
100 Pounds of rotten meat... not a pretty sight.
Do you have any milk?
In the pantry.
The pantry?
The wooden door at the end of the hall.

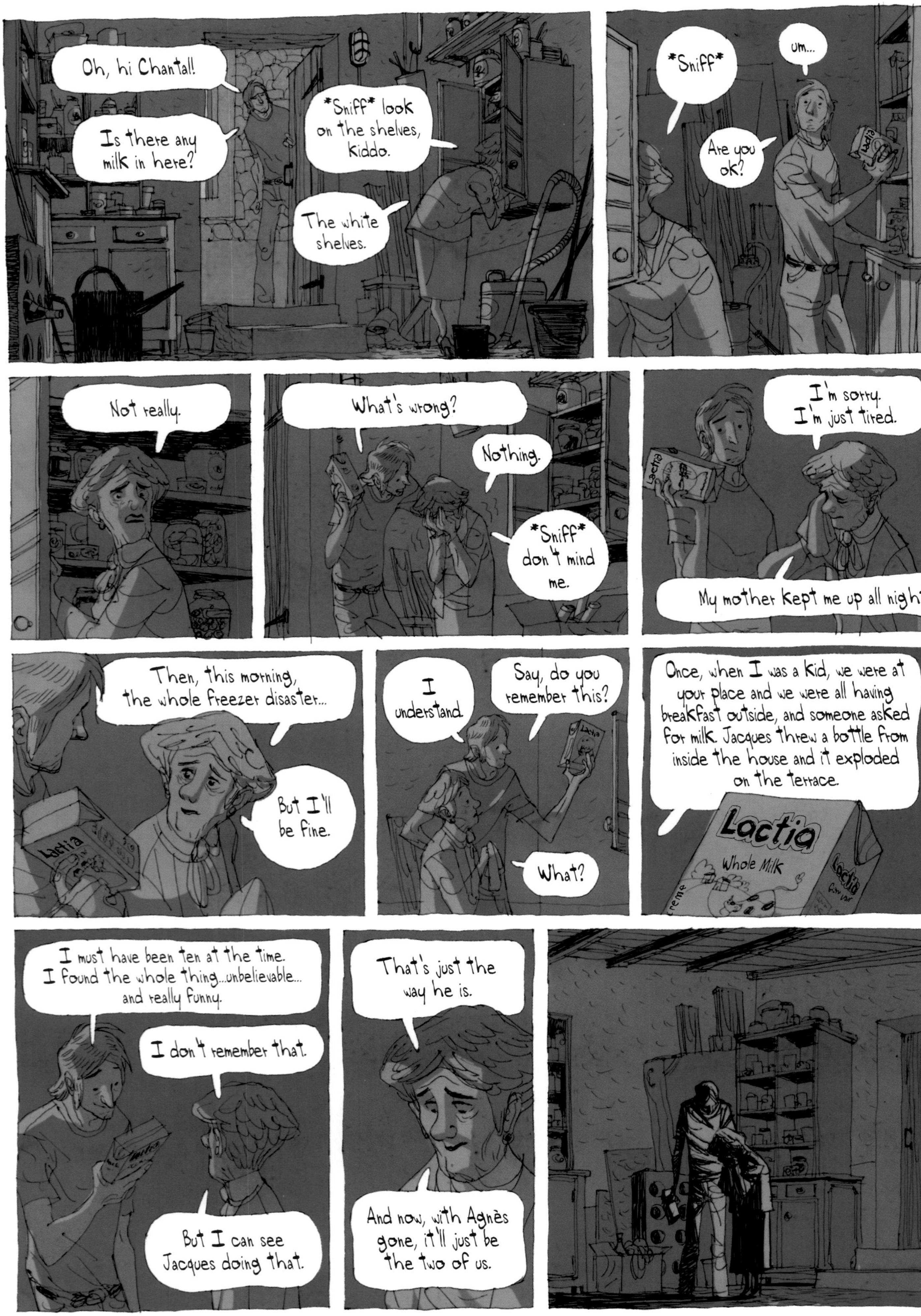
Oh, hi Chantal!
Is there any milk in here?
Sniff look on the shelves, kiddo.
The white shelves.
Sniff
um...
Are you ok?
Not really.
What's wrong?
Nothing.
Sniff don't mind me.
I'm sorry. I'm just tired.
My mother kept me up all night.
Then, this morning, the whole freezer disaster...
But I'll be fine.
I understand.
Say, do you remember this?
What?
Once, when I was a kid, we were at your place and we were all having breakfast outside, and someone asked for milk. Jacques threw a bottle from inside the house and it exploded on the terrace.
Lactia
Whole Milk
I must have been ten at the time. I found the whole thing...unbelievable... and really funny.
I don't remember that.
But I can see Jacques doing that.
That's just the way he is.
And now, with Agnès gone, it'll just be the two of us.

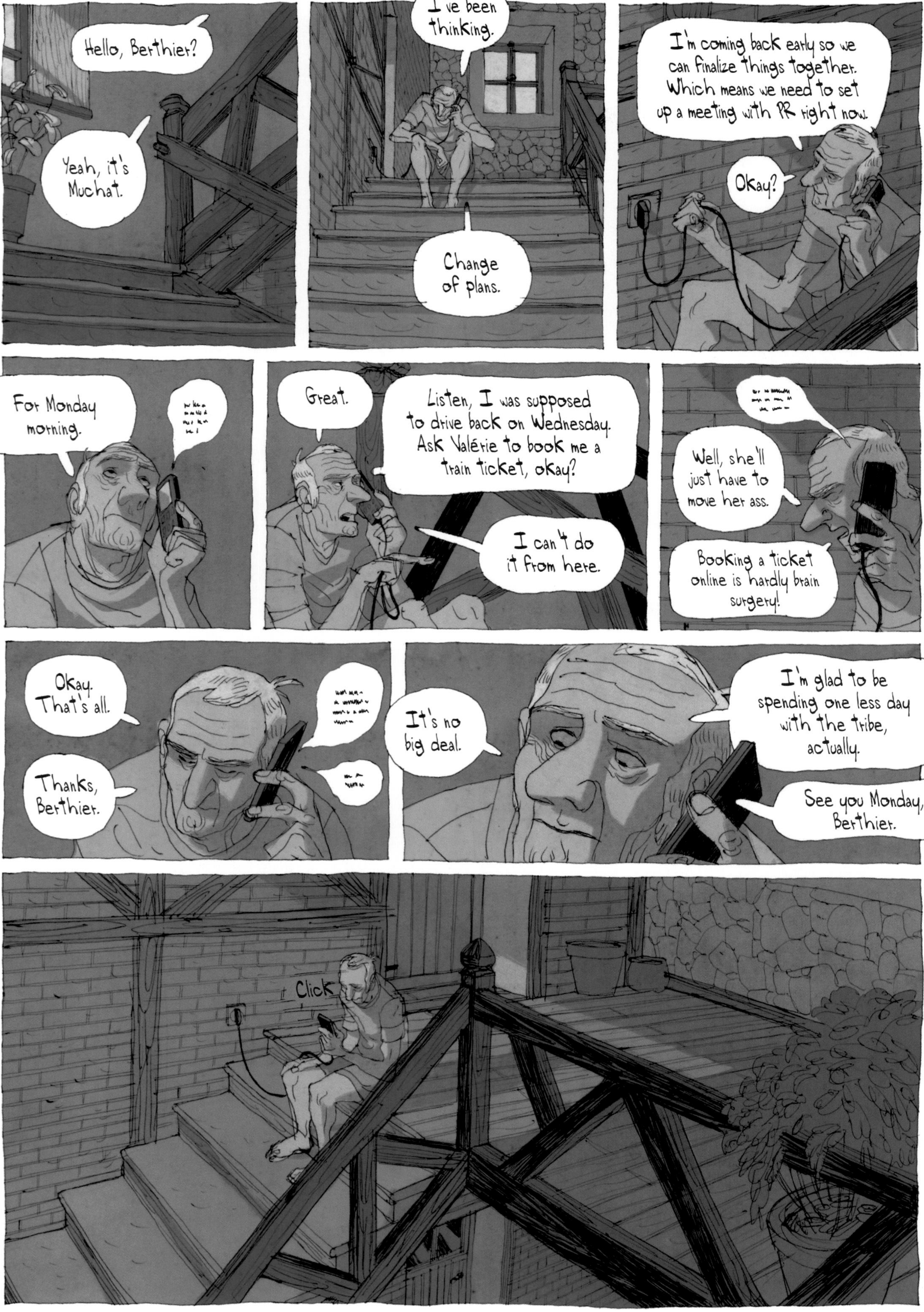
Hello, Berthier?
Yeah, it's Muchat.
I've been thinking.
Change of plans.
I'm coming back early so we can finalize things together. Which means we need to set up a meeting with PR right now.
Okay?
For Monday morning.
Great.
Listen, I was supposed to drive back on Wednesday. Ask Valérie to book me a train ticket, okay?
I can't do it from here.
Well, she'll just have to move her ass.
Booking a ticket online is hardly brain surgery!
Okay. That's all.
Thanks, Berthier.
It's no big deal.
I'm glad to be spending one less day with the tribe, actually.
See you Monday, Berthier.
Click

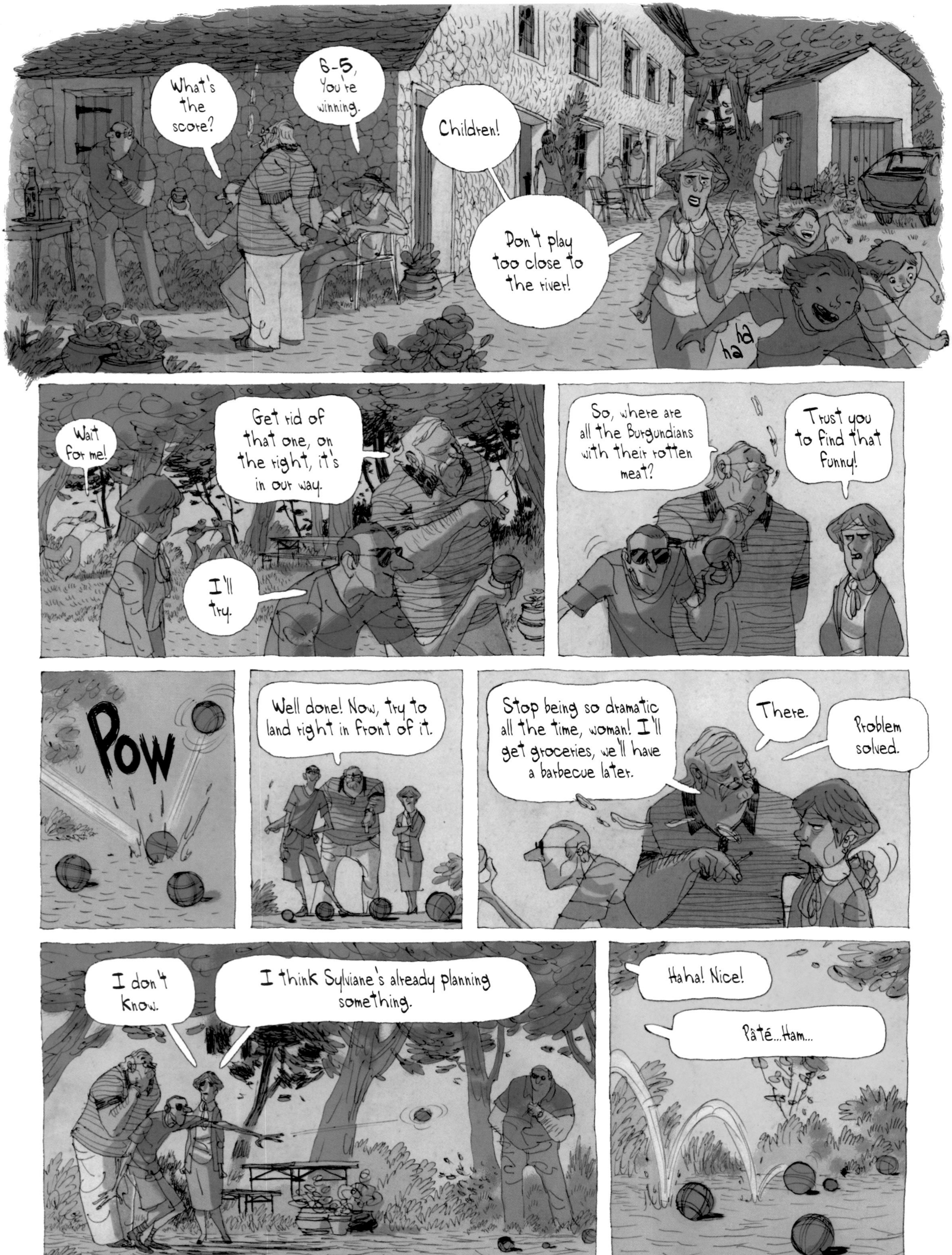
What's the score?
6-5, You're winning.
Children!
Don't play too close to the river!
ha ha
Wait for me!
Get rid of that one, on the right, it's in our way.
I'll try.
So, where are all the Burgundians with their rotten meat?
Trust you to find that funny!
POW
Well done! Now, try to land right in front of it.
Stop being so dramatic all the time, woman! I'll get groceries, we'll have a barbecue later.
There.
Problem solved.
I don't know.
I think Sylviane's already planning something.
Haha! Nice!
Pâté...Ham...

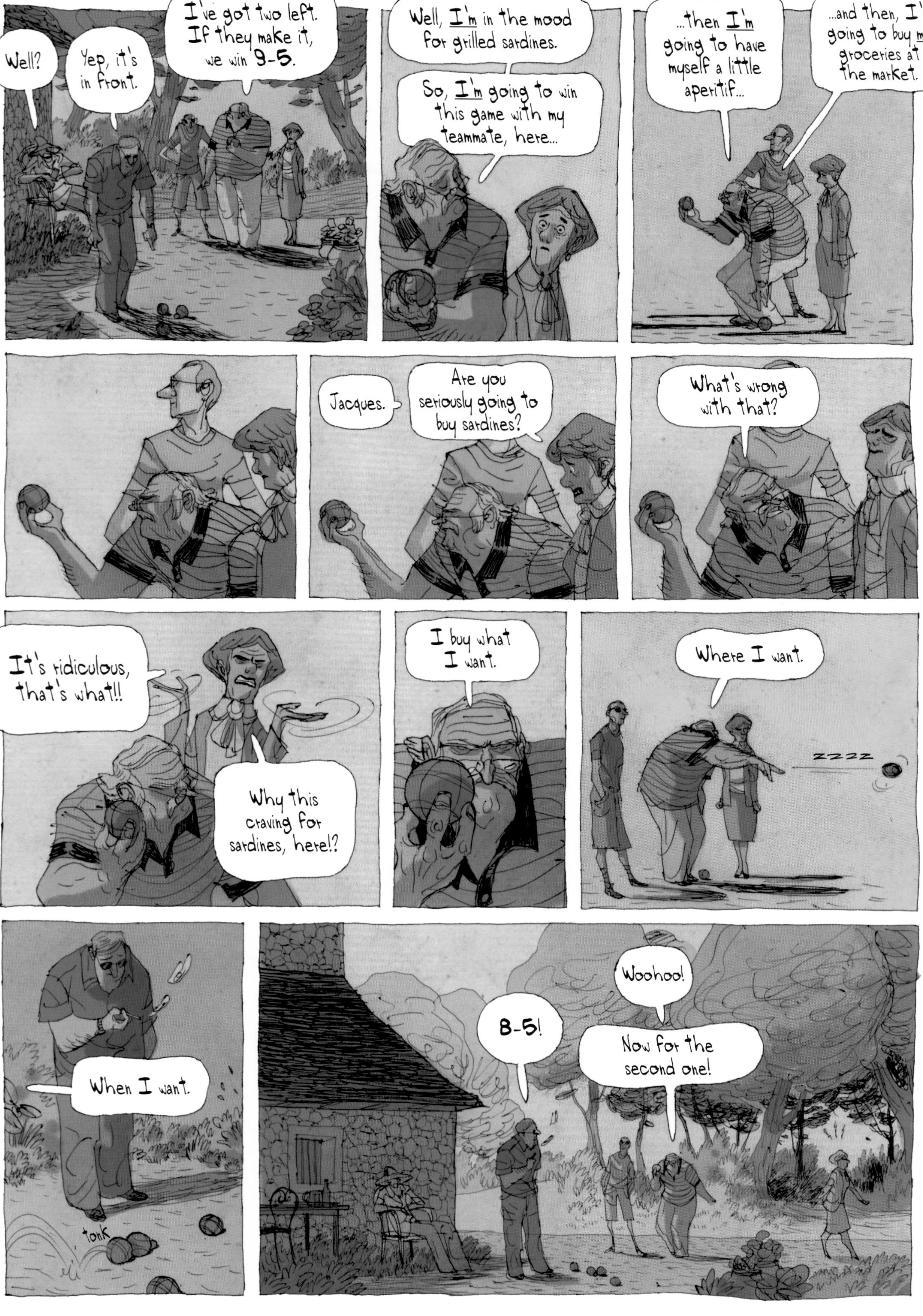
Well?
Yep, it's in front.
I've got two left. If they make it, we win 9-5.
Well, I'm in the mood for grilled sardines.
So, I'm going to win this game with my teammate, here...
...then I'm going to have myself a little aperitif...
...and then, I'm going to buy my groceries at the market.
Jacques.
Are you seriously going to buy sardines?
What's wrong with that?
It's ridiculous, that's what!!
Why this craving for sardines, here!?
I buy what I want.
Where I want.
zzzz
When I want.
tonk
8-5!
Woohoo!
Now for the second one!

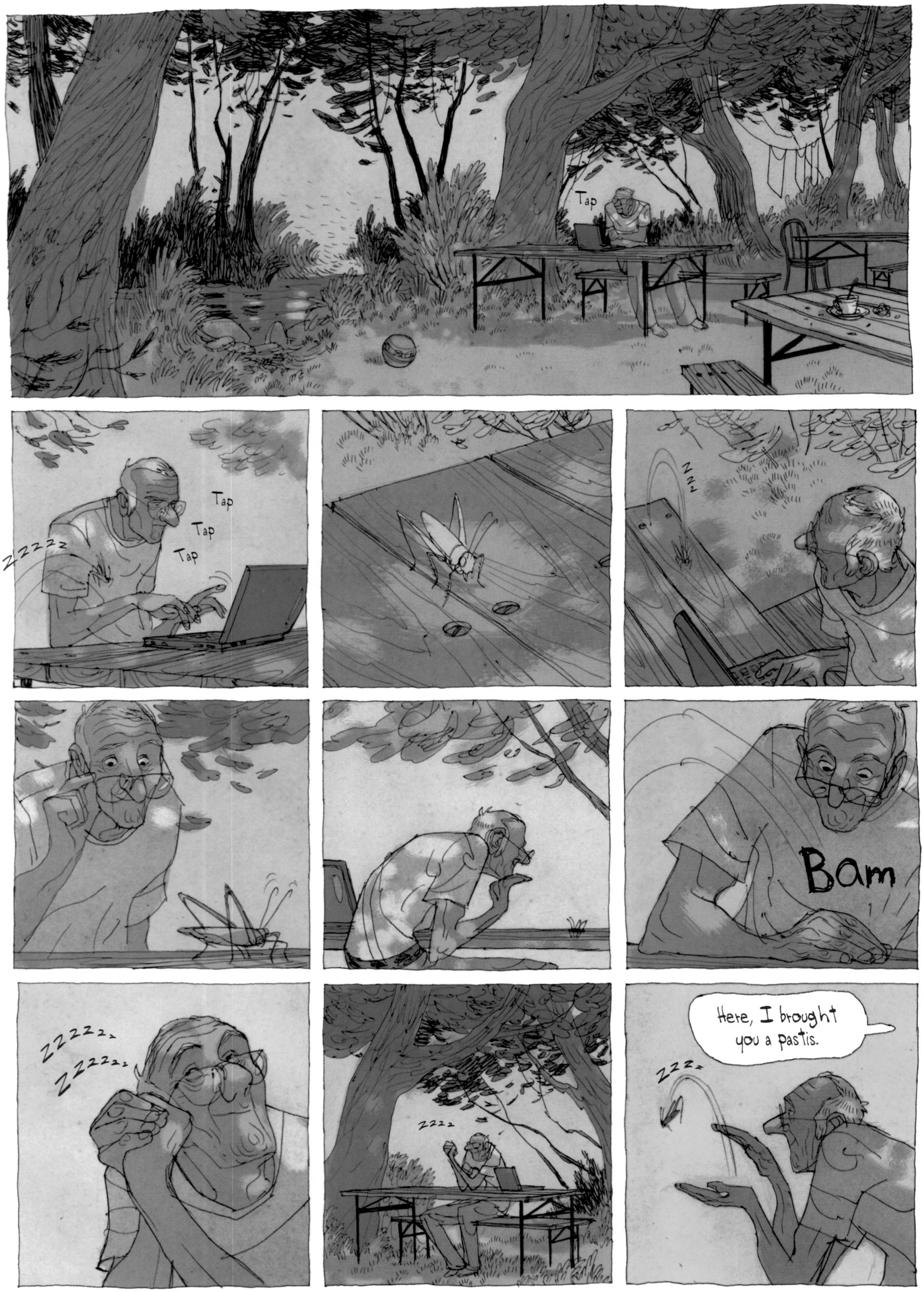
Tap
Tap
Tap
Tap
ZZZZZ
ZZZ
Bam
ZZZZZZ
ZZZZZZ
ZZZZ
Here, I brought you a pastis.
ZZZZ

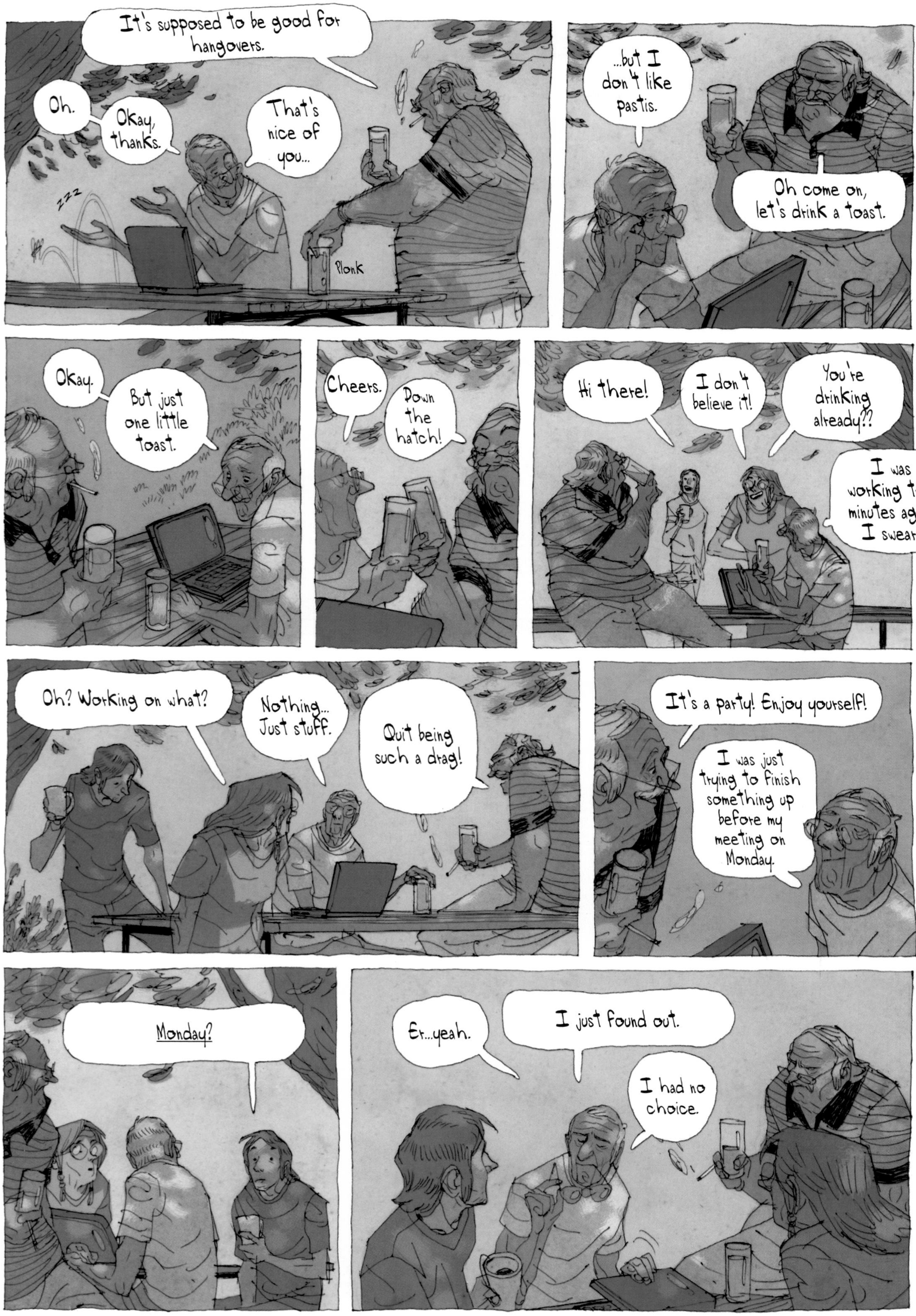
It's supposed to be good for hangovers.
Oh.
Okay, thanks.
That's nice of you...
zzz
Plonk
...but I don't like pastis.
Oh come on, let's drink a toast.
Okay.
But just one little toast.
Cheers.
Down the hatch!
Hi there!
I don't believe it!
You're drinking already??
I was working two minutes ago, I swear.
Oh? Working on what?
Nothing... Just stuff.
Quit being such a drag!
It's a party! Enjoy yourself!
I was just trying to finish something up before my meeting on Monday.
Monday?
Er...yeah.
I just found out.
I had no choice.

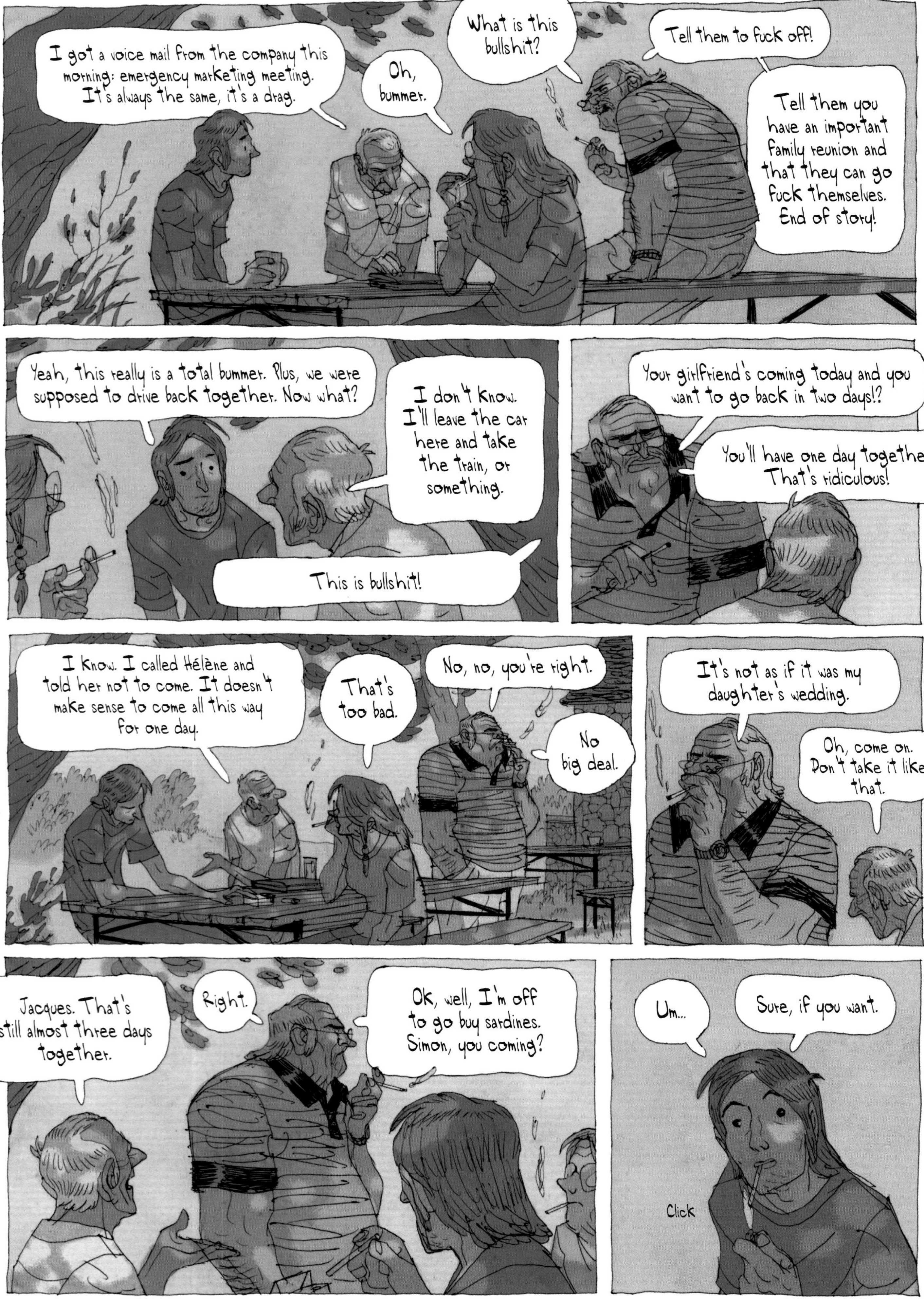
I got a voice mail from the company this morning: emergency marketing meeting. It's always the same, it's a drag.
Oh, bummer.
What is this bullshit?
Tell them to fuck off!
Tell them you have an important family reunion and that they can go fuck themselves. End of story!
Yeah, this really is a total bummer. Plus, we were supposed to drive back together. Now what?
I don't know. I'll leave the car here and take the train, or something.
This is bullshit!
Your girlfriend's coming today and you want to go back in two days!?
You'll have one day together. That's ridiculous!
I know. I called Hélène and told her not to come. It doesn't make sense to come all this way for one day.
That's too bad.
No, no, you're right.
No big deal.
It's not as if it was my daughter's wedding.
Oh, come on. Don't take it like that.
Jacques. That's still almost three days together.
Right.
Ok, well, I'm off to go buy sardines. Simon, you coming?
Um...
Sure, if you want.
Click

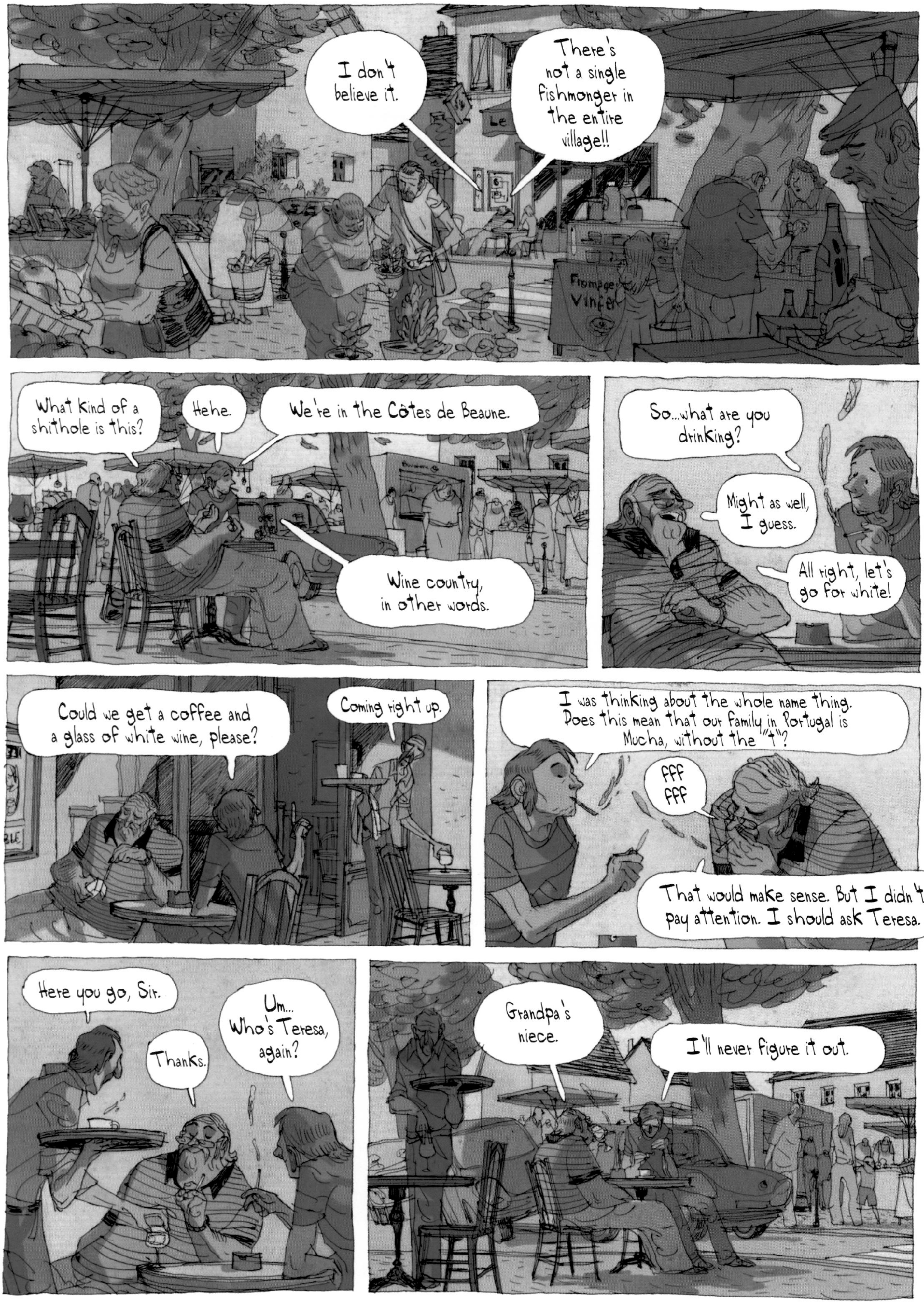

I don't believe it.
There's not a single fishmonger in the entire village!!
Le
Fromager Vinfer
What kind of a shithole is this?
Hehe.
We're in the Côtes de Beaune.
Wine country, in other words.
So...what are you drinking?
Might as well, I guess.
All right, let's go for white!
Could we get a coffee and a glass of white wine, please?
Coming right up.
I was thinking about the whole name thing. Does this mean that our family in Portugal is Mucha, without the "t"?
fff fff
That would make sense. But I didn't pay attention. I should ask Teresa.
Here you go, Sir.
Thanks.
Um... Who's Teresa, again?
Grandpa's niece.
I'll never figure it out.

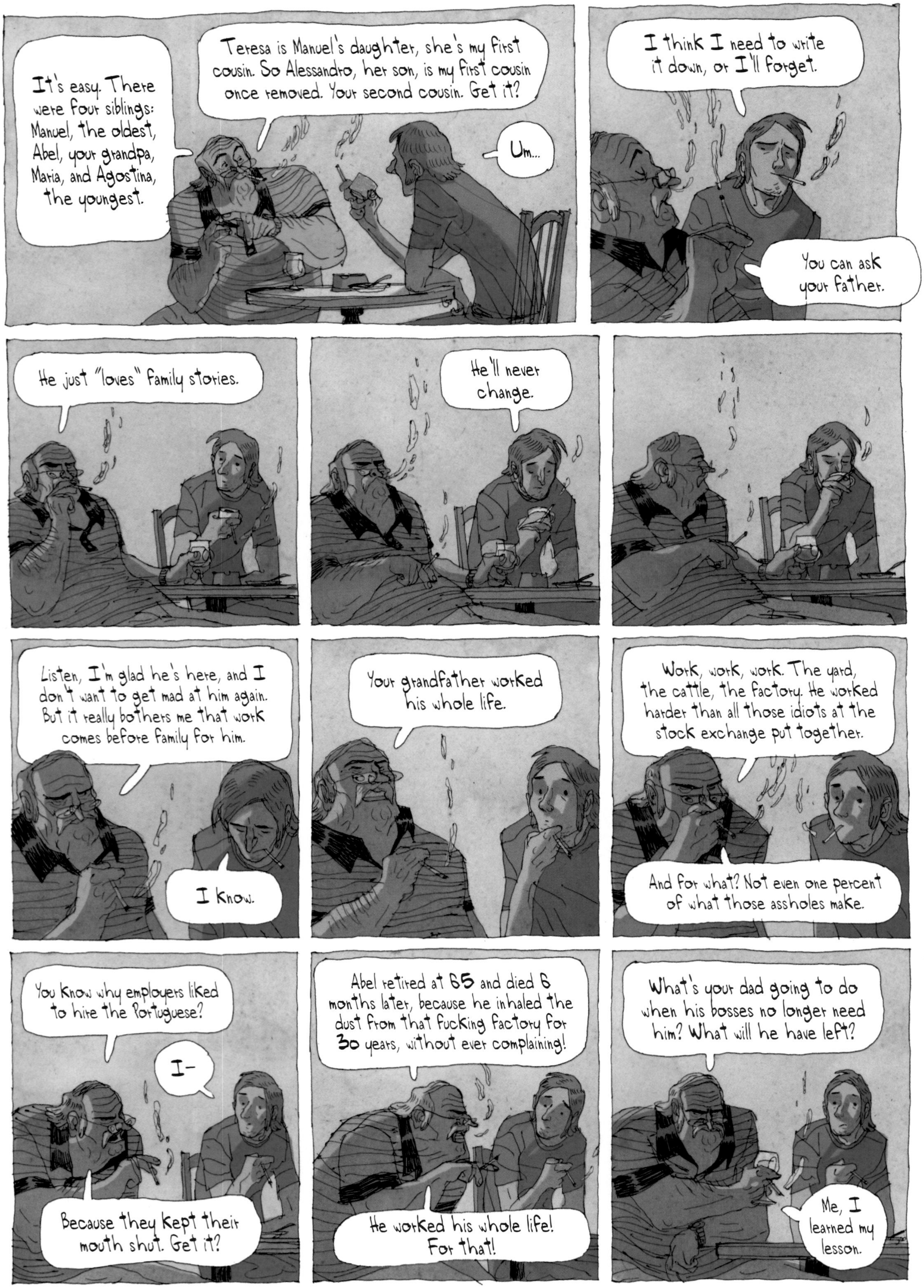
It's easy. There were four siblings: Manuel, the oldest, Abel, your grandpa, Maria, and Agostina, the youngest.
Teresa is Manuel's daughter, she's my first cousin. So Alessandro, her son, is my first cousin once removed. Your second cousin. Get it?
Um...
I think I need to write it down, or I'll forget.
You can ask your father.
He just "loves" family stories.
He'll never change.
Listen, I'm glad he's here, and I don't want to get mad at him again. But it really bothers me that work comes before family for him.
I know.
Your grandfather worked his whole life.
Work, work, work. The yard, the cattle, the factory. He worked harder than all those idiots at the stock exchange put together.
And for what? Not even one percent of what those assholes make.
You know why employers liked to hire the Portuguese?
I-
Because they kept their mouth shut. Get it?
Abel retired at 65 and died 6 months later, because he inhaled the dust from that fucking factory for 30 years, without ever complaining!
He worked his whole life! For that!
What's your dad going to do when his bosses no longer need him? What will he have left?
Me, I learned my lesson.

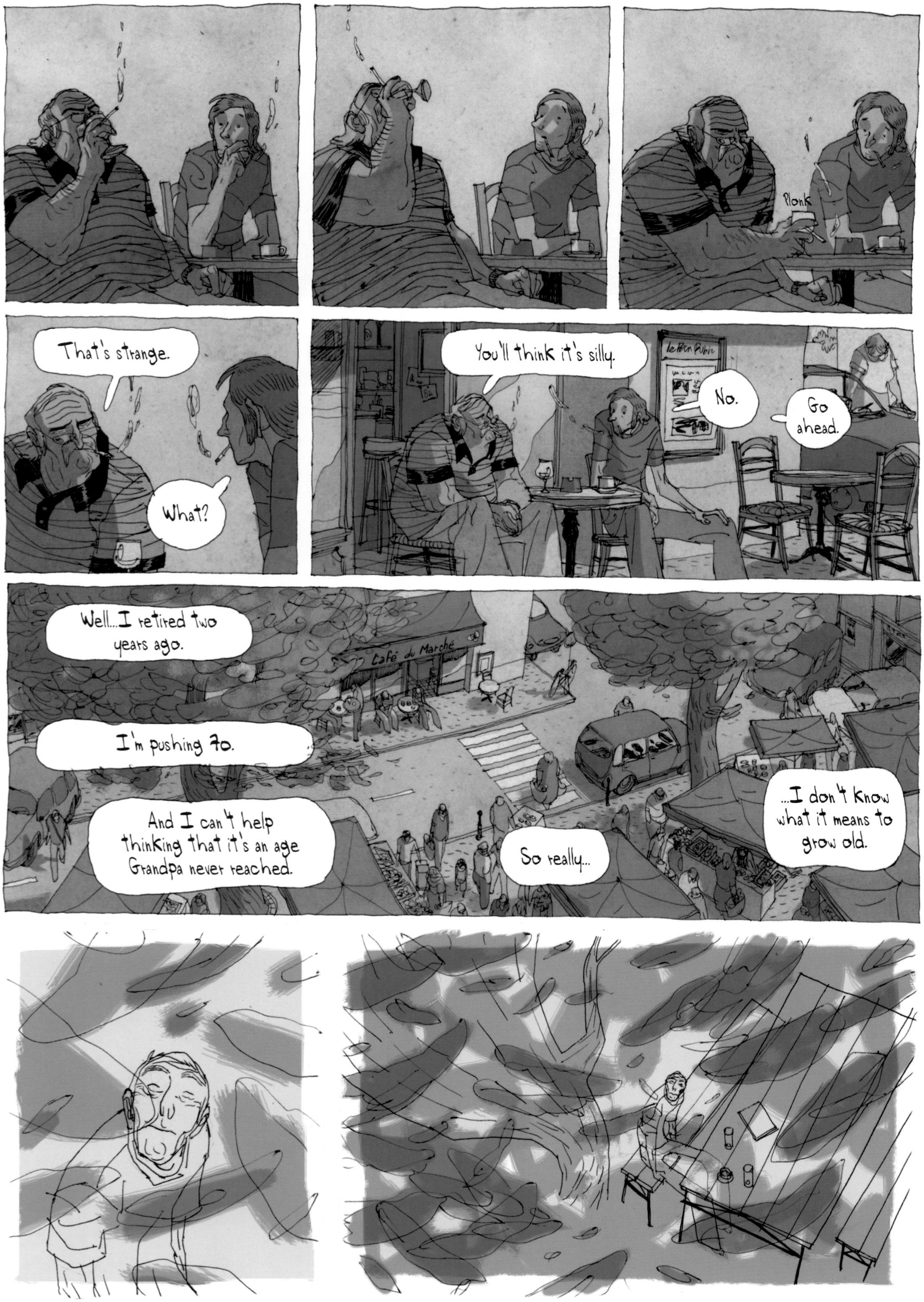
Plonk
That's strange.
What?
You'll think it's silly.
No.
Go ahead.
Well...I retired two years ago.
Café du Marché
I'm pushing 70.
And I can't help thinking that it's an age Grandpa never reached.
So really...
...I don't know what it means to grow old.

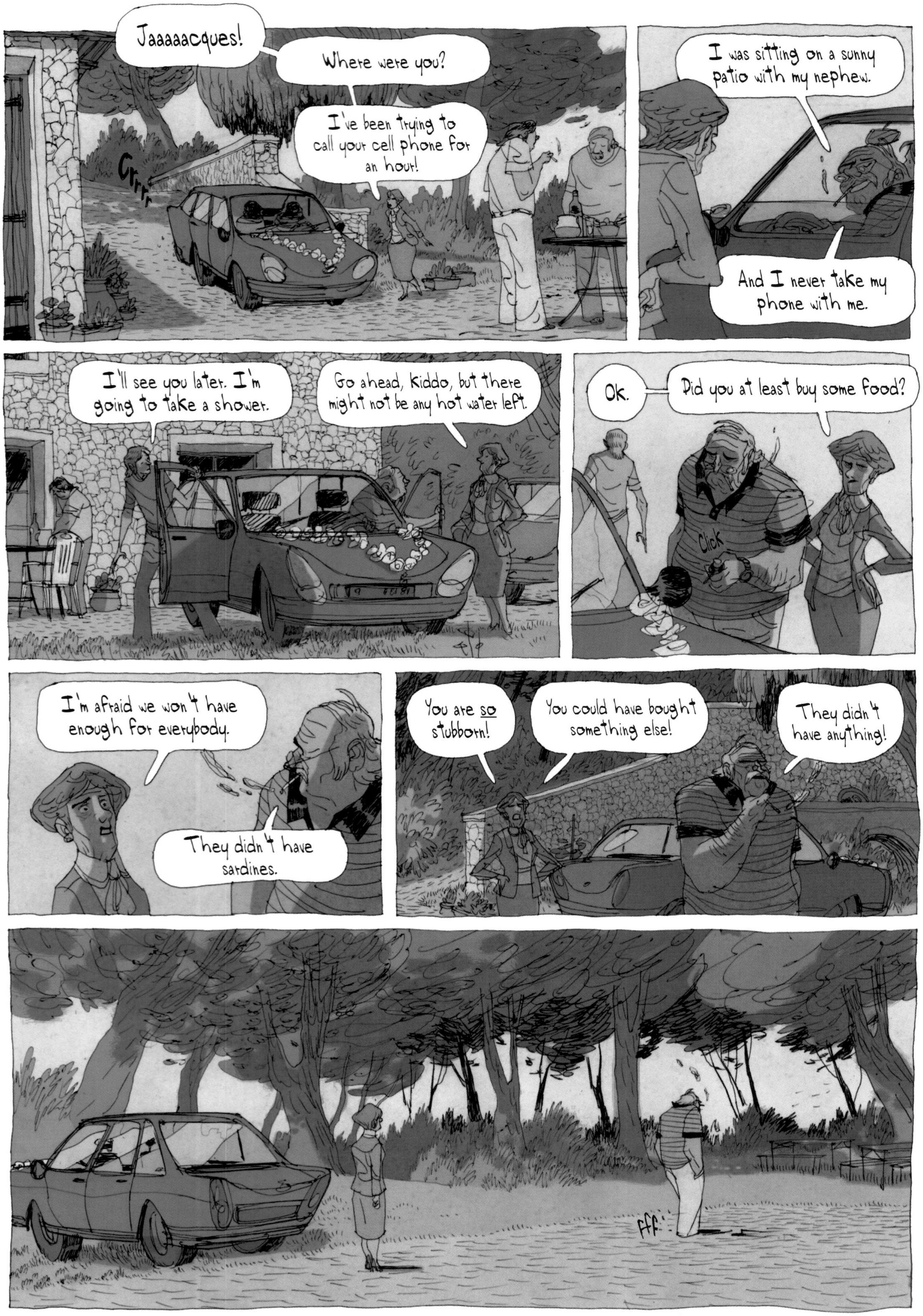
Jaaaaacques!
Where were you?
I've been trying to call your cell phone for an hour!
Crrrr
I was sitting on a sunny patio with my nephew.
And I never take my phone with me.
I'll see you later. I'm going to take a shower.
Go ahead, kiddo, but there might not be any hot water left.
Ok.
Did you at least buy some food?
Click
I'm afraid we won't have enough for everybody.
They didn't have sardines.
You are so stubborn!
You could have bought something else!
They didn't have anything!
fff

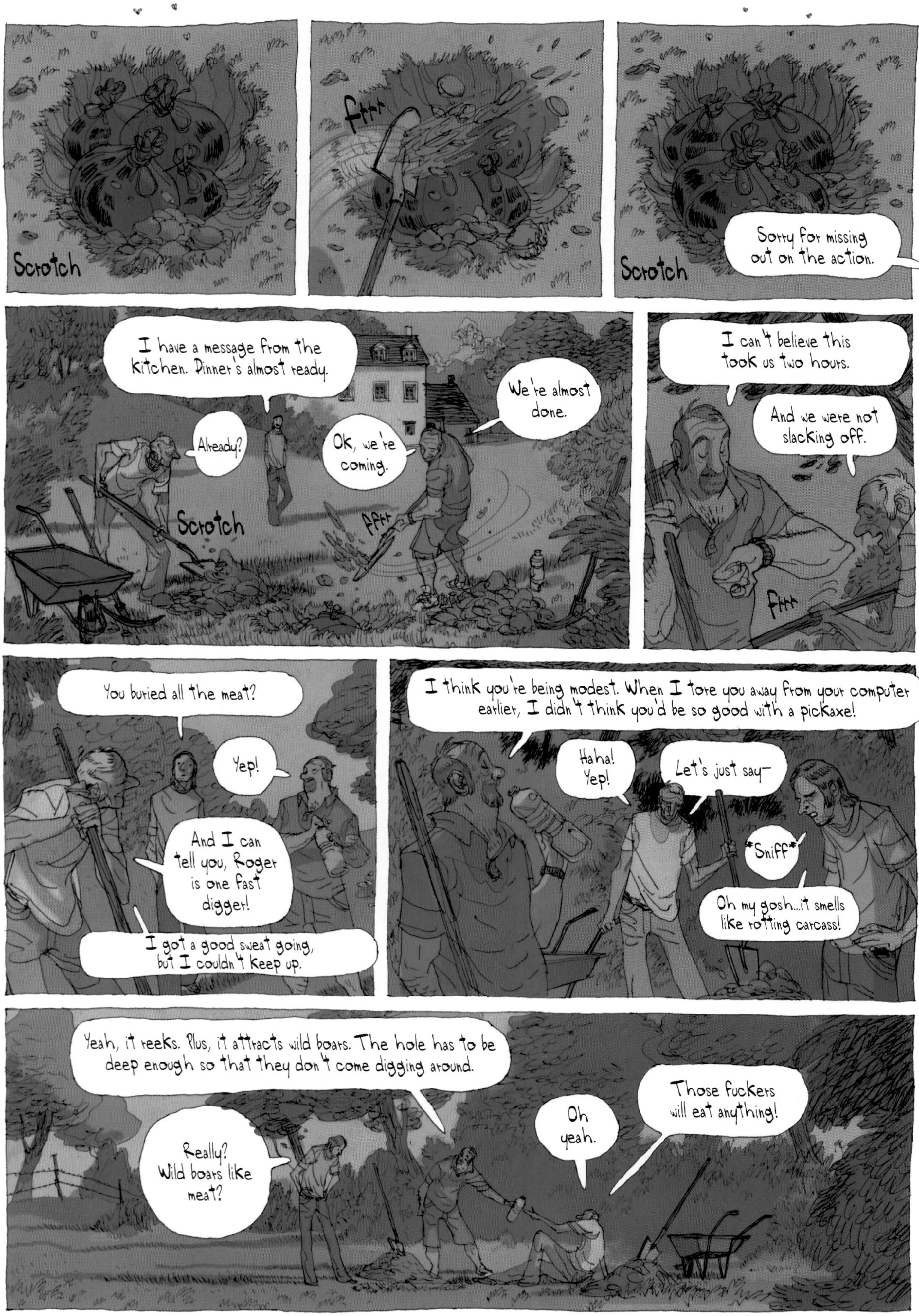
Scrotch
fffr
Scrotch
Sorry for missing out on the action.
I have a message from the kitchen. Dinner's almost ready.
Already?
Ok, we're coming.
We're almost done.
Scrotch
fffr
I can't believe this took us two hours.
And we were not slacking off.
fffr
You buried all the meat?
Yep!
And I can tell you, Roger is one fast digger!
I got a good sweat going, but I couldn't keep up.
I think you're being modest. When I tore you away from your computer earlier, I didn't think you'd be so good with a pickaxe!
Haha! Yep!
Let's just say–
Sniff
Oh my gosh...it smells like rotting carcass!
Yeah, it reeks. Plus, it attracts wild boars. The hole has to be deep enough so that they don't come digging around.
Really? Wild boars like meat?
Oh yeah.
Those fuckers will eat anything!

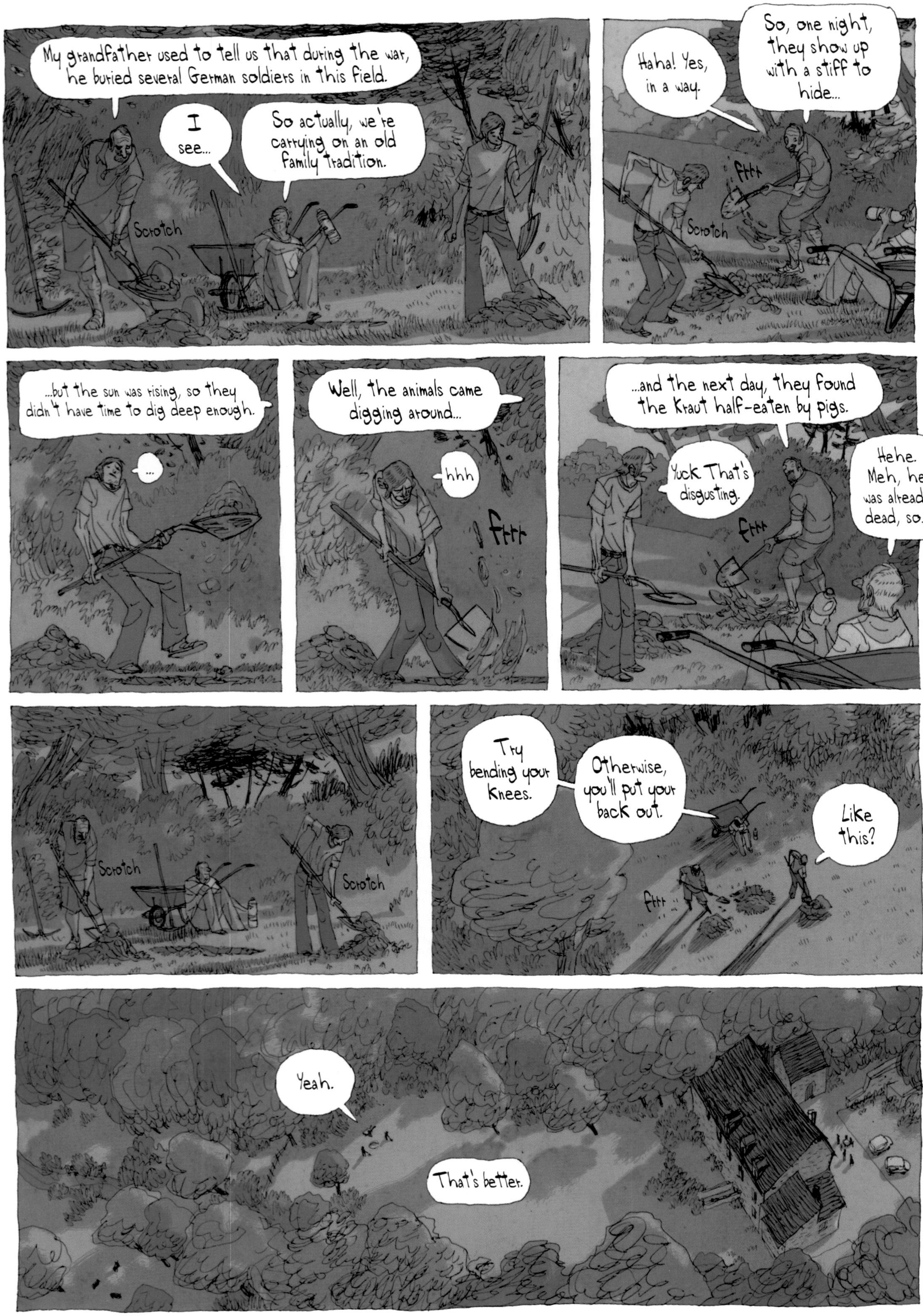
My grandfather used to tell us that during the war, he buried several German soldiers in this field.
I see...
So actually, we're carrying on an old family tradition.
Scrotch
Haha! Yes, in a way.
So, one night, they show up with a stiff to hide...
Frrr
Scrotch
...but the sun was rising, so they didn't have time to dig deep enough.
...
Well, the animals came digging around...
hhh
Frrr
...and the next day, they found the Kraut half-eaten by pigs.
Yuck. That's disgusting.
Hehe. Meh, he was already dead, so...
Frrr
Scrotch
Scrotch
Try bending your knees.
Otherwise, you'll put your back out.
Like this?
Frrr
Yeah.
That's better.

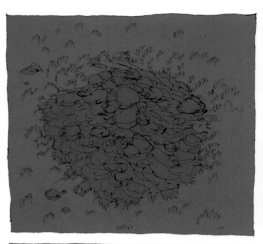

You okay, Dad?

Yeah... Glad we got that done.

Drinks are on me. I think we've earned it!

Don't mind if I do...I am beat!

Haha

Hell, yeah. So am I.

Click

Gling Gling Gling

Thanks again for helping out. I'm sorry I kept you from your work, but it would've taken me all night on my own!

No, it's okay.

I shouldn't even have brought my laptop. I'm supposed to be enjoying my weekend!

I know what that's like.

Vineyards are the same. Always something to do.

Was there a vineyard at Grandma and Grandpa's?

Yes, but it didn't belong to us. It belonged to the landlord.

Did you live on a farm?

Not really. My parents grew vegetables to make ends meet.

That brought back memories, digging that freaking hole.

Did you work in the garden too?

Gling Gling

Are you kidding?

That's all we ever did!

Me...

...Yvette...

...Jacques, when he was still at home. We were all roped in!

145

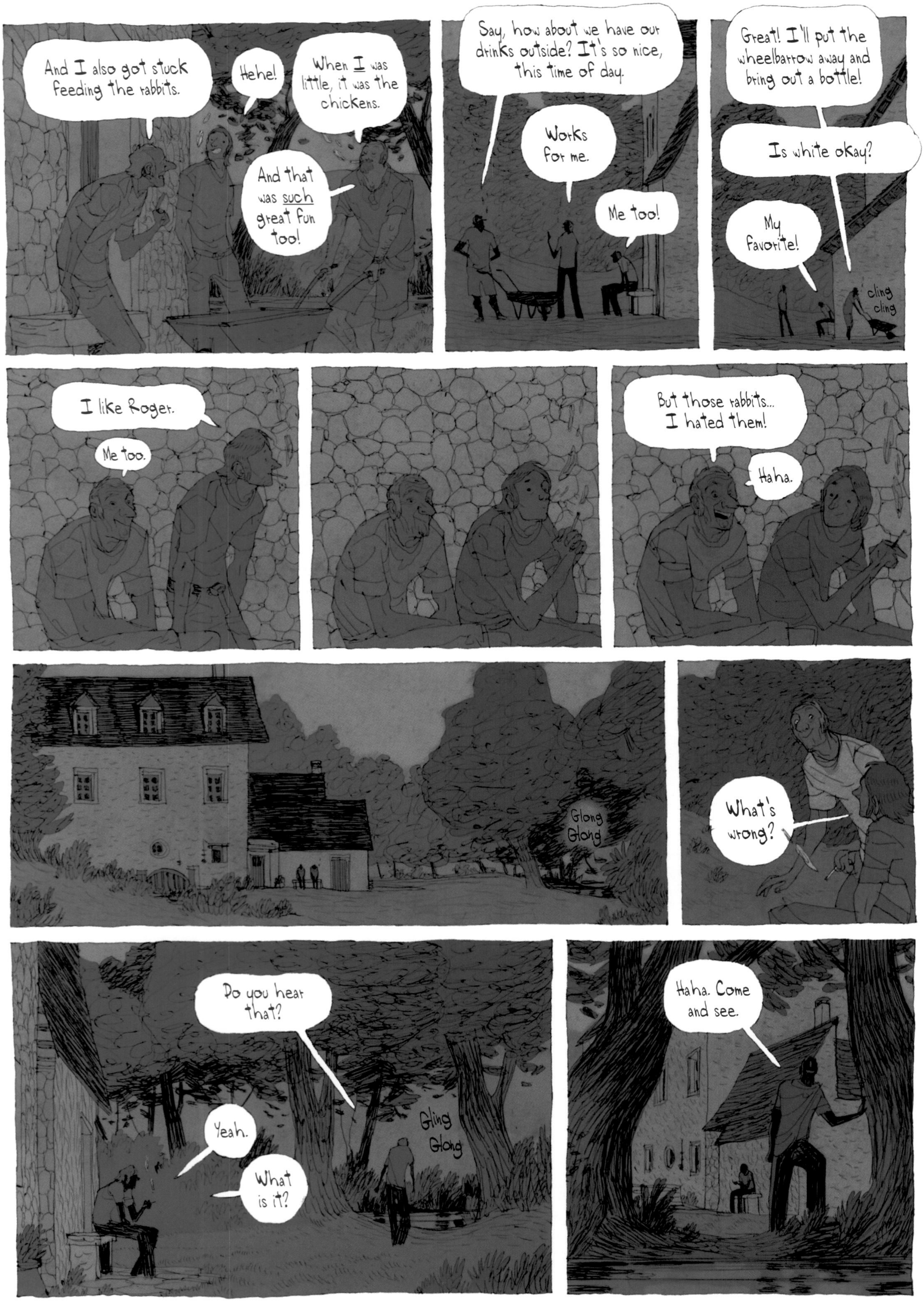
And I also got stuck feeding the rabbits.
Hehe!
When I was little, it was the chickens.
And that was such great fun too!
Say, how about we have our drinks outside? It's so nice, this time of day.
Works for me.
Me too!
Great! I'll put the wheelbarrow away and bring out a bottle!
Is white okay?
My favorite!
cling cling
I like Roger.
Me too.
But those rabbits... I hated them!
Haha.
Glong Glong
What's wrong?
Do you hear that?
Yeah.
What is it?
Gling Glong
Haha. Come and see.

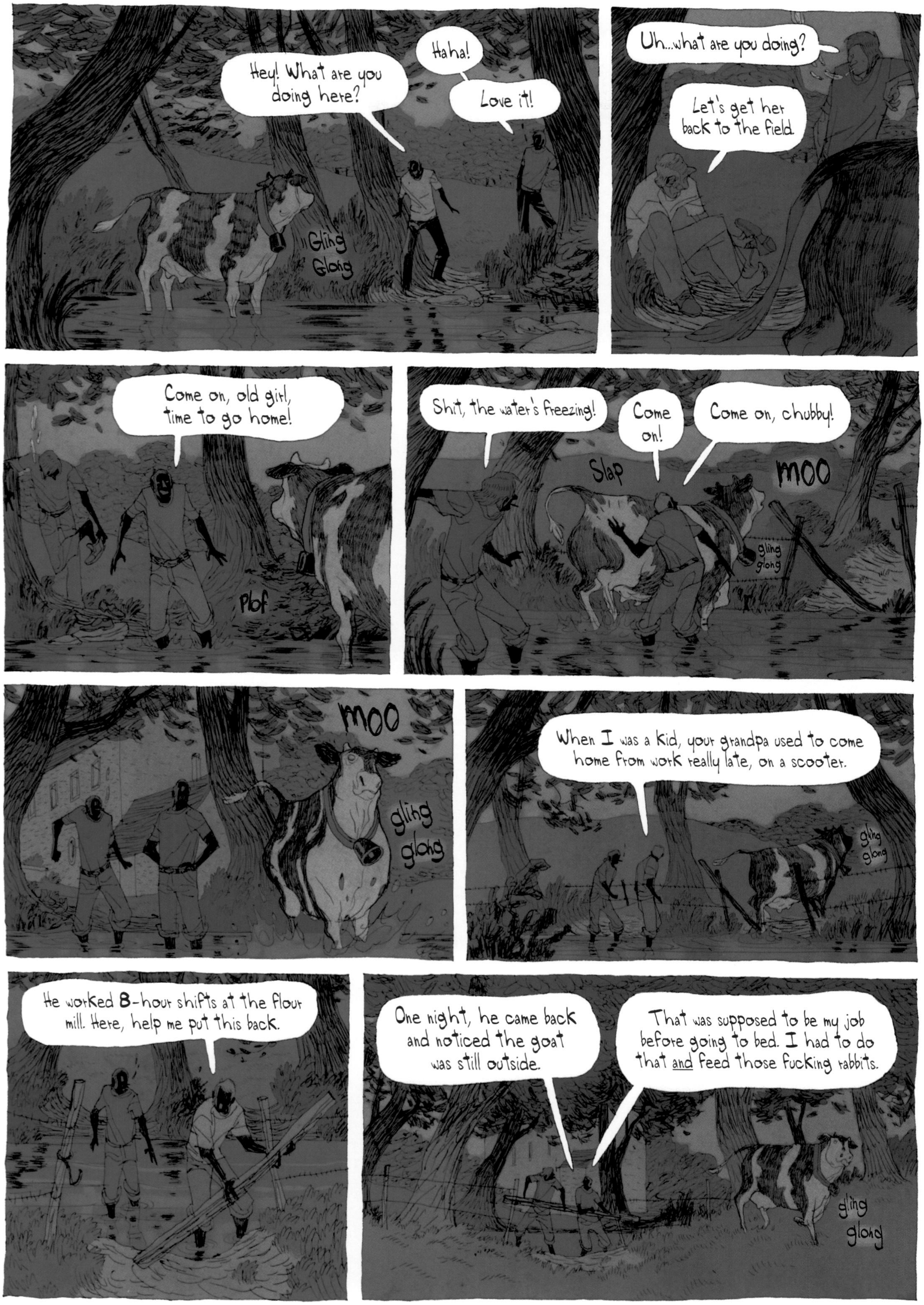
Hey! What are you doing here?
Haha!
Love it!
Gling Glong
Uh...what are you doing?
Let's get her back to the field.
Come on, old girl, time to go home!
Plof
Shit, the water's freezing!
Come on!
Come on, chubby!
Slap
MOO
gling glong
MOO
gling glong
When I was a kid, your grandpa used to come home from work really late, on a scooter.
gling glong
He worked 8-hour shifts at the flour mill. Here, help me put this back.
One night, he came back and noticed the goat was still outside.
That was supposed to be my job before going to bed. I had to do that and feed those fucking rabbits.
gling glong

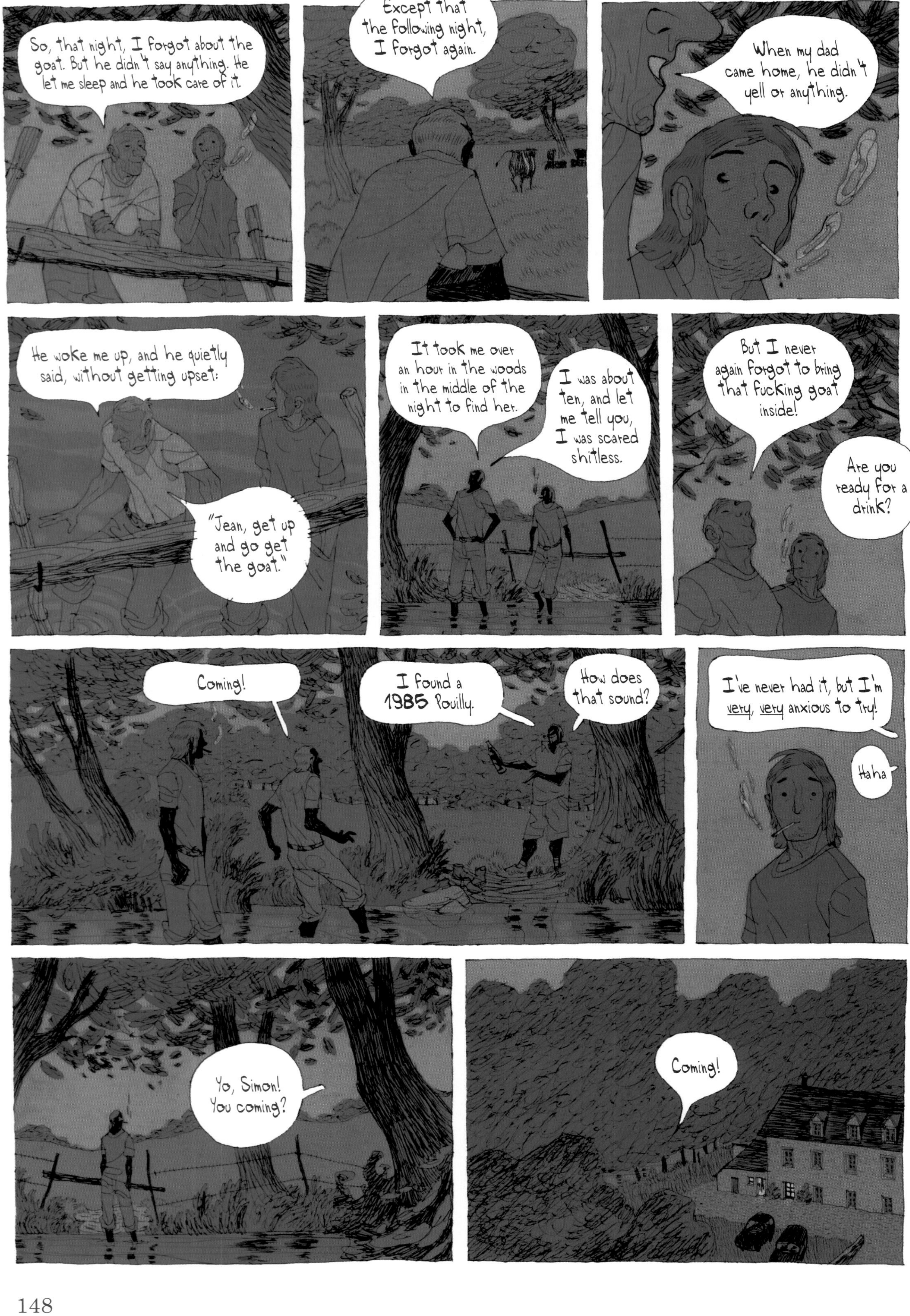
So, that night, I forgot about the goat. But he didn't say anything. He let me sleep and he took care of it.
Except that the following night, I forgot again.
When my dad came home, he didn't yell or anything.
He woke me up, and he quietly said, without getting upset:
"Jean, get up and go get the goat."
It took me over an hour in the woods in the middle of the night to find her.
I was about ten, and let me tell you, I was scared shitless.
But I never again forgot to bring that fucking goat inside!
Are you ready for a drink?
Coming!
I found a 1985 Pouilly.
How does that sound?
I've never had it, but I'm very, very anxious to try!
Haha
Yo, Simon! You coming?
Coming!

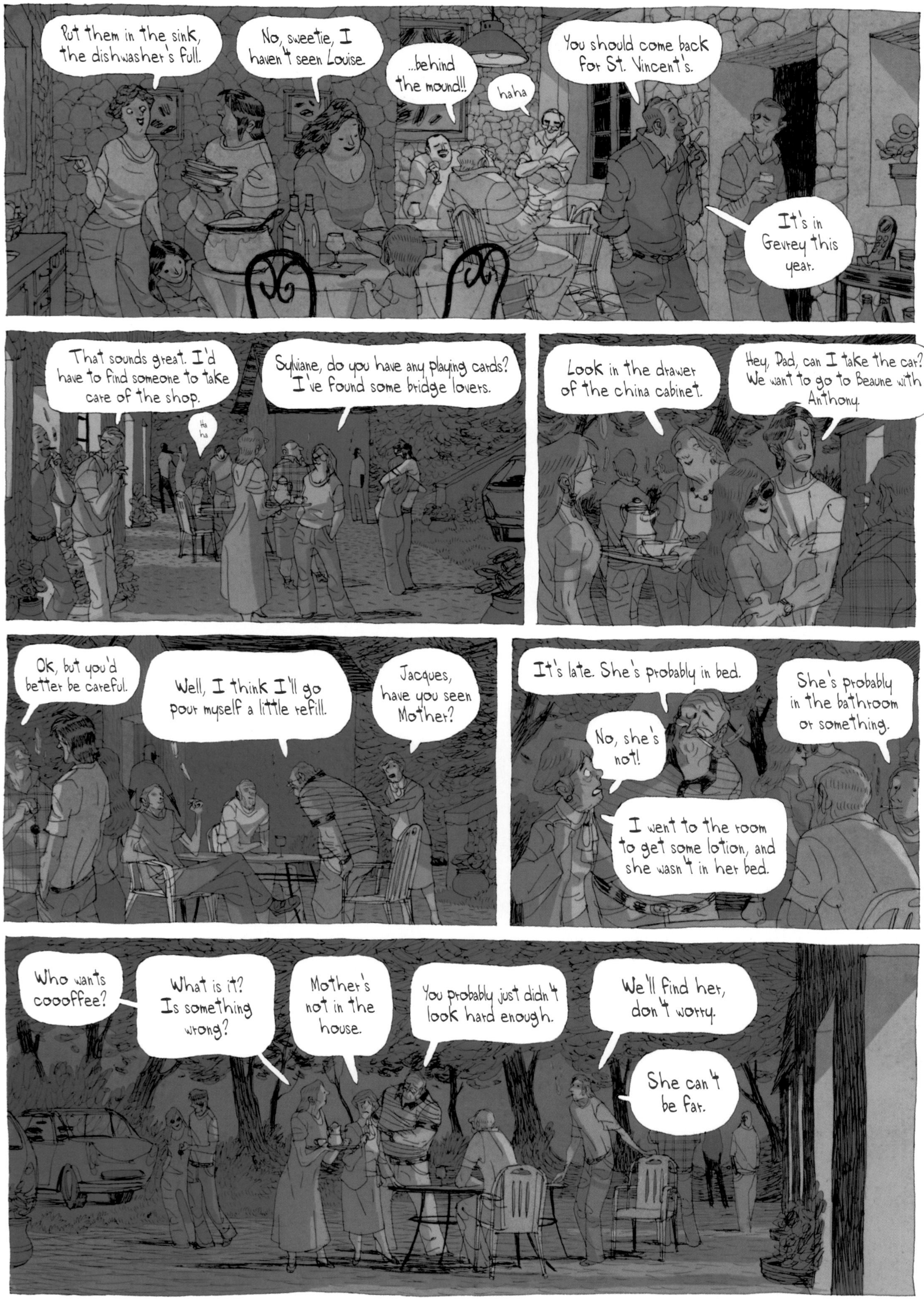

Put them in the sink, the dishwasher's full.
No, sweetie, I haven't seen Louise.
...behind the mound!!
haha
You should come back for St. Vincent's.
It's in Gevrey this year.
That sounds great. I'd have to find someone to take care of the shop.
Ha ha
Sylviane, do you have any playing cards? I've found some bridge lovers.
Look in the drawer of the china cabinet.
Hey, Dad, can I take the car? We want to go to Beaune with Anthony.
Ok, but you'd better be careful.
Well, I think I'll go pour myself a little refill.
Jacques, have you seen Mother?
It's late. She's probably in bed.
She's probably in the bathroom or something.
No, she's not!
I went to the room to get some lotion, and she wasn't in her bed.
Who wants coooffee?
What is it? Is something wrong?
Mother's not in the house.
You probably just didn't look hard enough.
We'll find her, don't worry.
She can't be far.

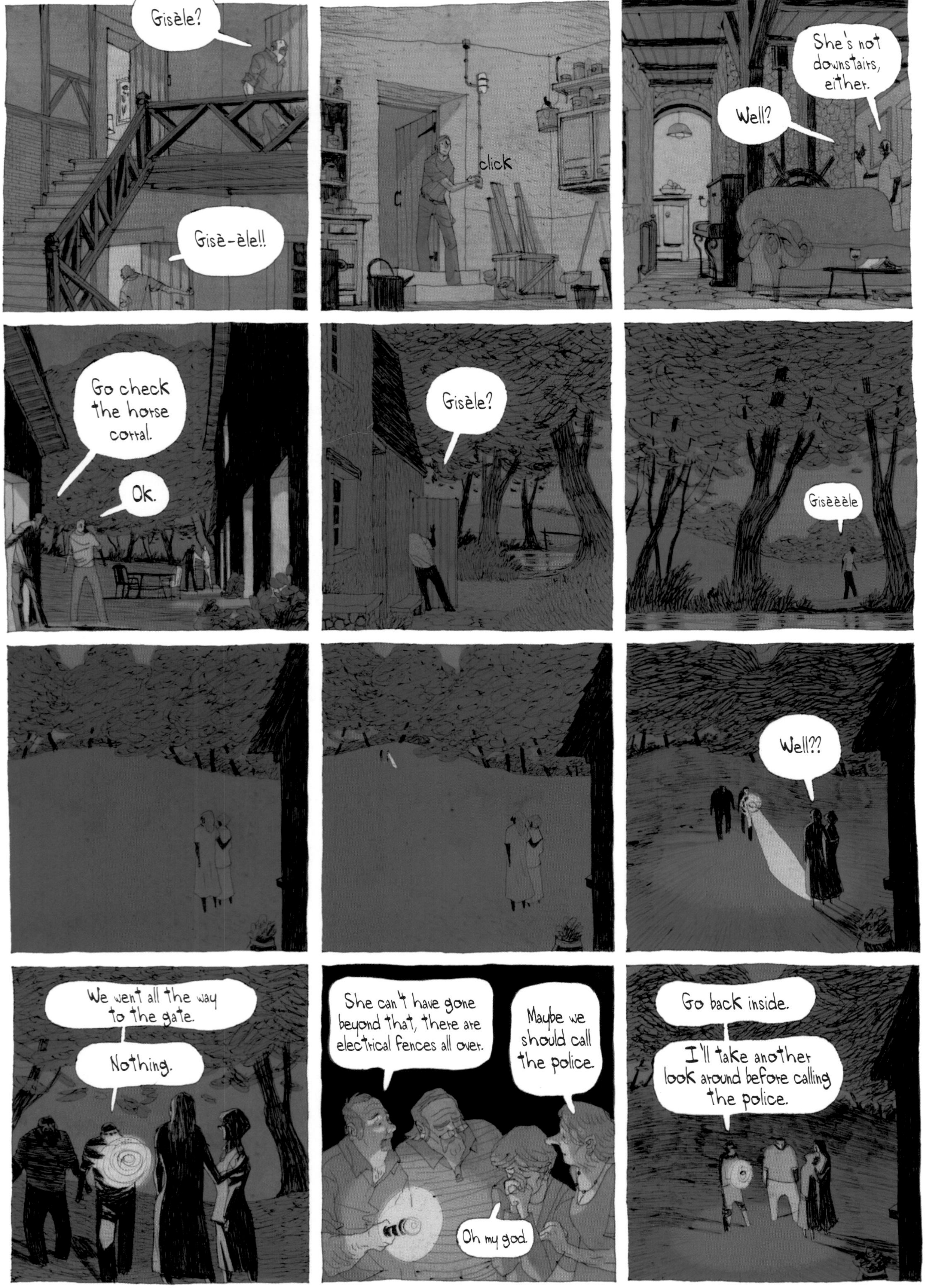
Gisèle?
Gisè-èle!!
click
Well?
She's not downstairs, either.
Go check the horse corral.
Ok.
Gisèle?
Gisèèèle
Well??
We went all the way to the gate.
Nothing.
She can't have gone beyond that, there are electrical fences all over.
Maybe we should call the police.
Oh my god.
Go back inside.
I'll take another look around before calling the police.

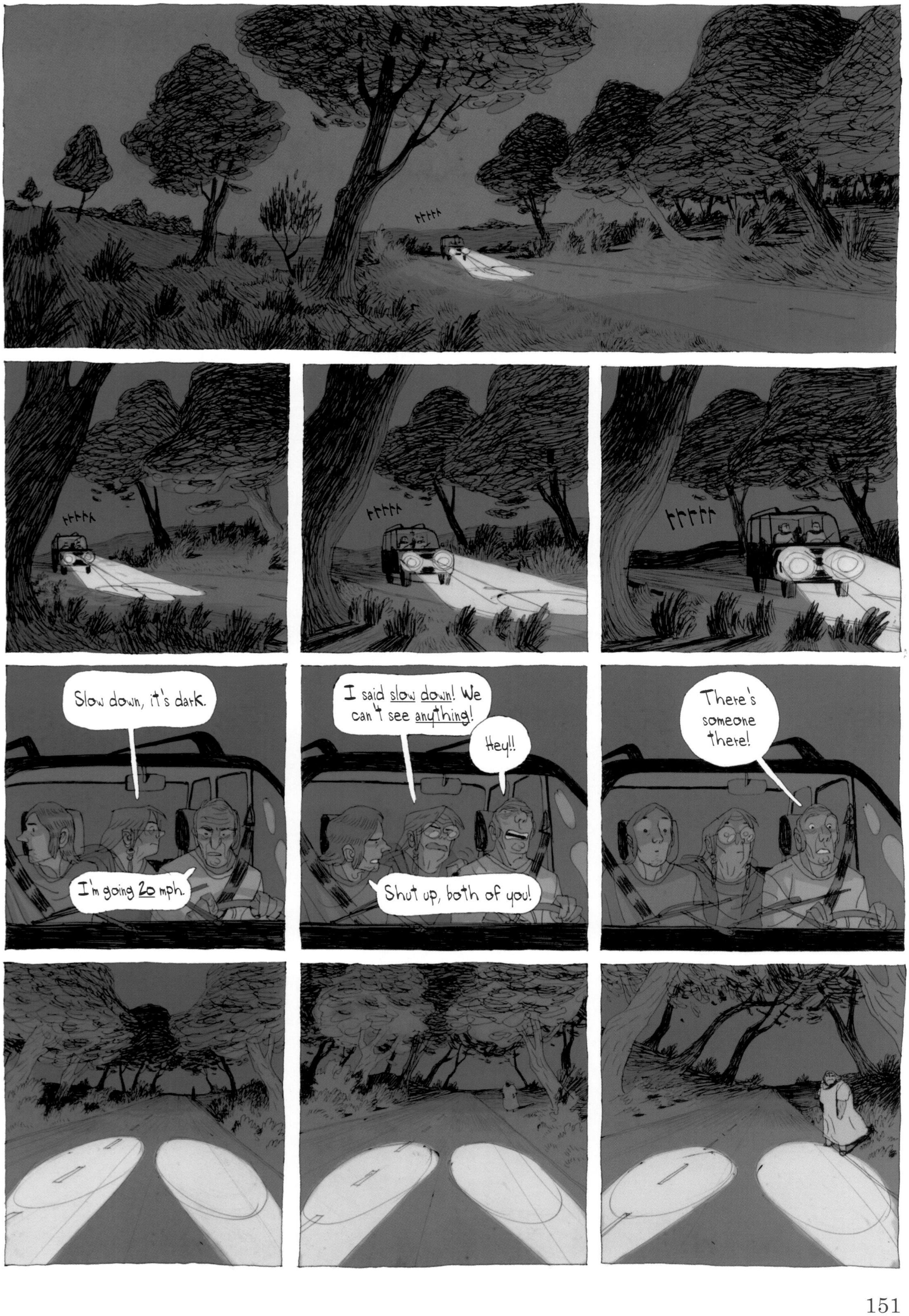
rrrrr
rrrrr
rrrrr
rrrrr
Slow down, it's dark.
I'm going 20 mph.
I said slow down! We can't see anything!
Hey!!
Shut up, both of you!
There's someone there!

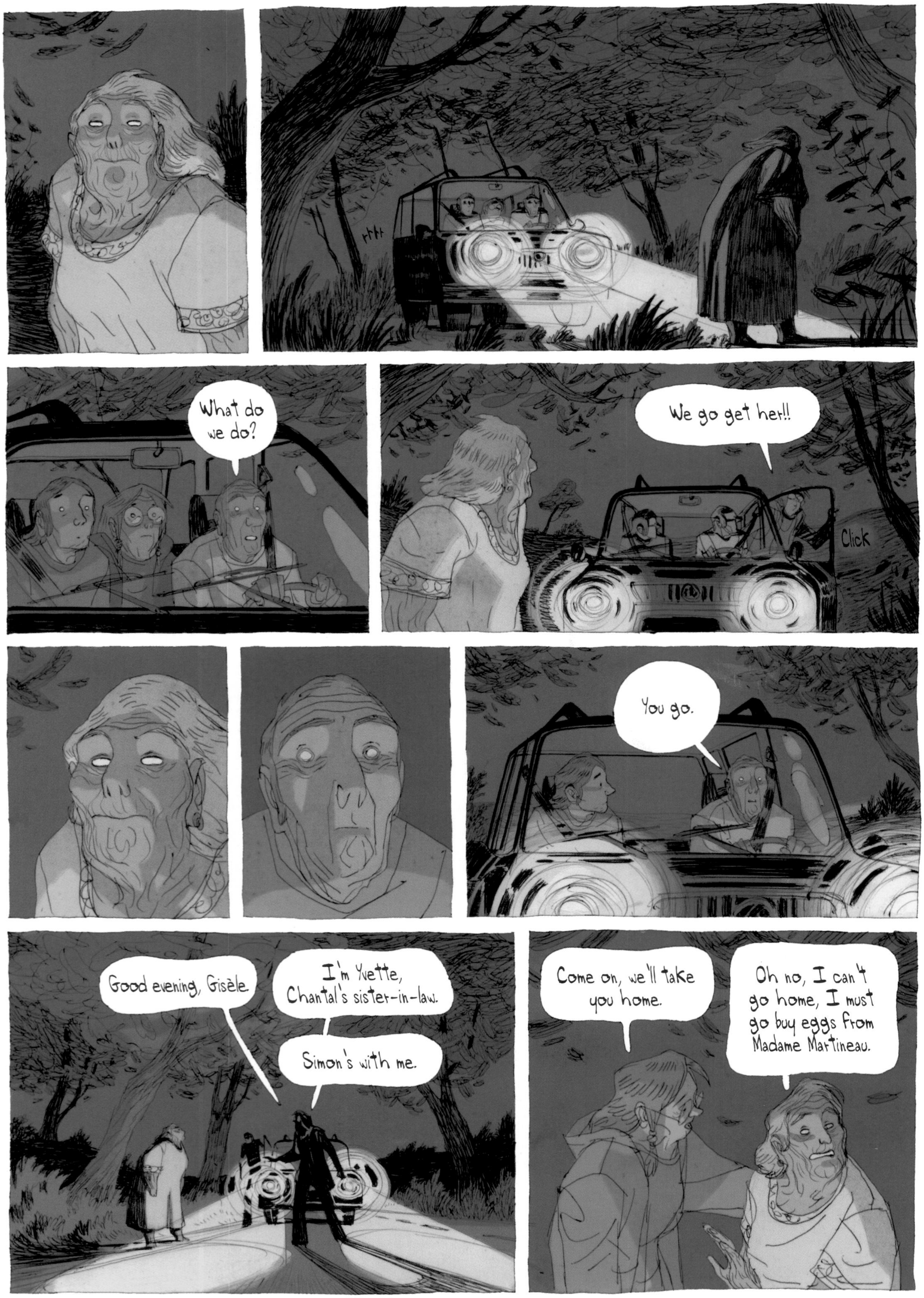
rrrr
What do we do?
We go get her!!
Click
You go.
Good evening, Gisèle.
I'm Yvette, Chantal's sister-in-law.
Simon's with me.
Come on, we'll take you home.
Oh no, I can't go home, I must go buy eggs from Madame Martineau.

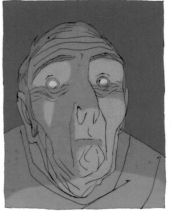

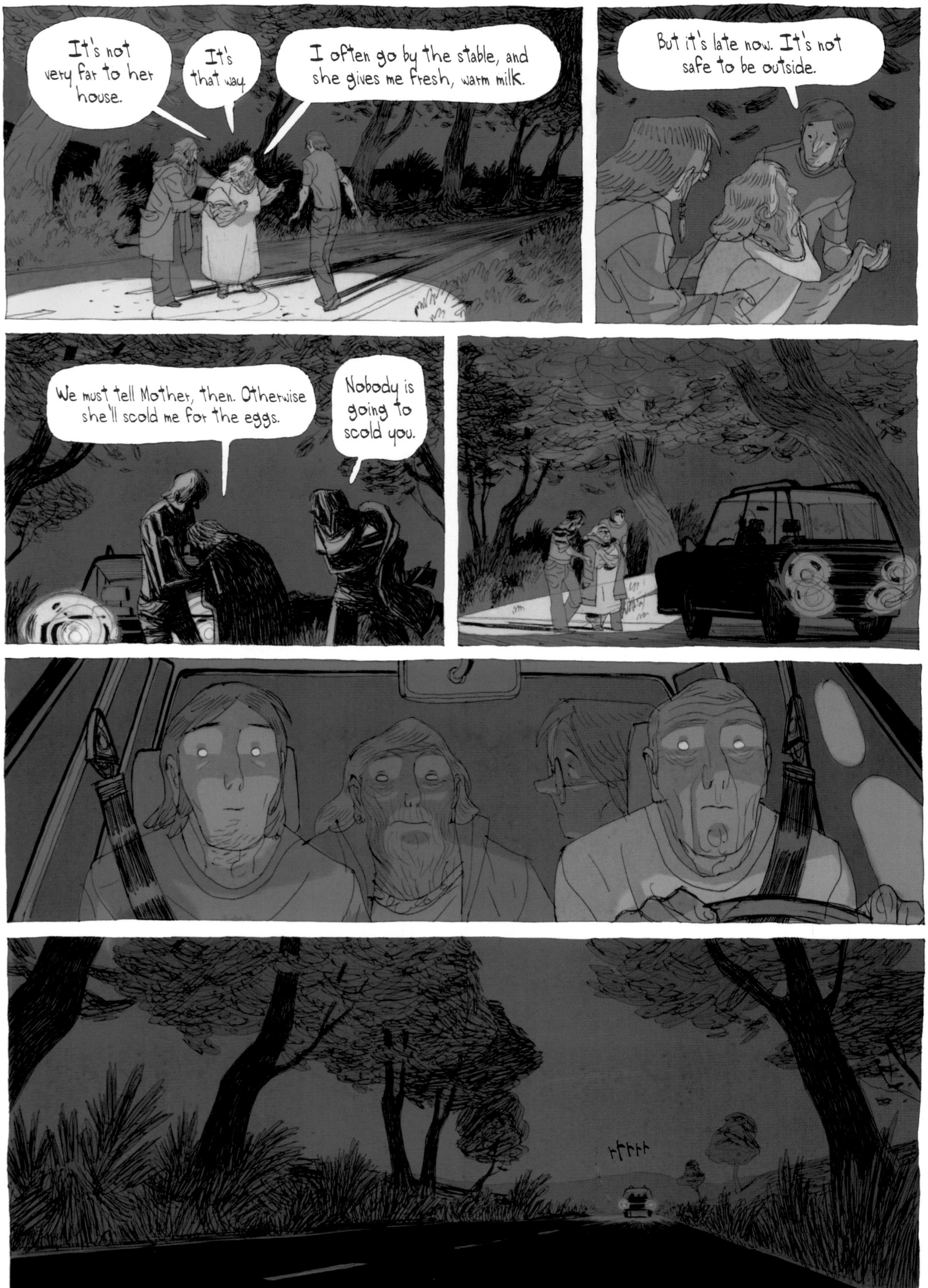

It's not very far to her house.
It's that way.
I often go by the stable, and she gives me fresh, warm milk.
But it's late now. It's not safe to be outside.
We must tell Mother, then. Otherwise she'll scold me for the eggs.
Nobody is going to scold you.

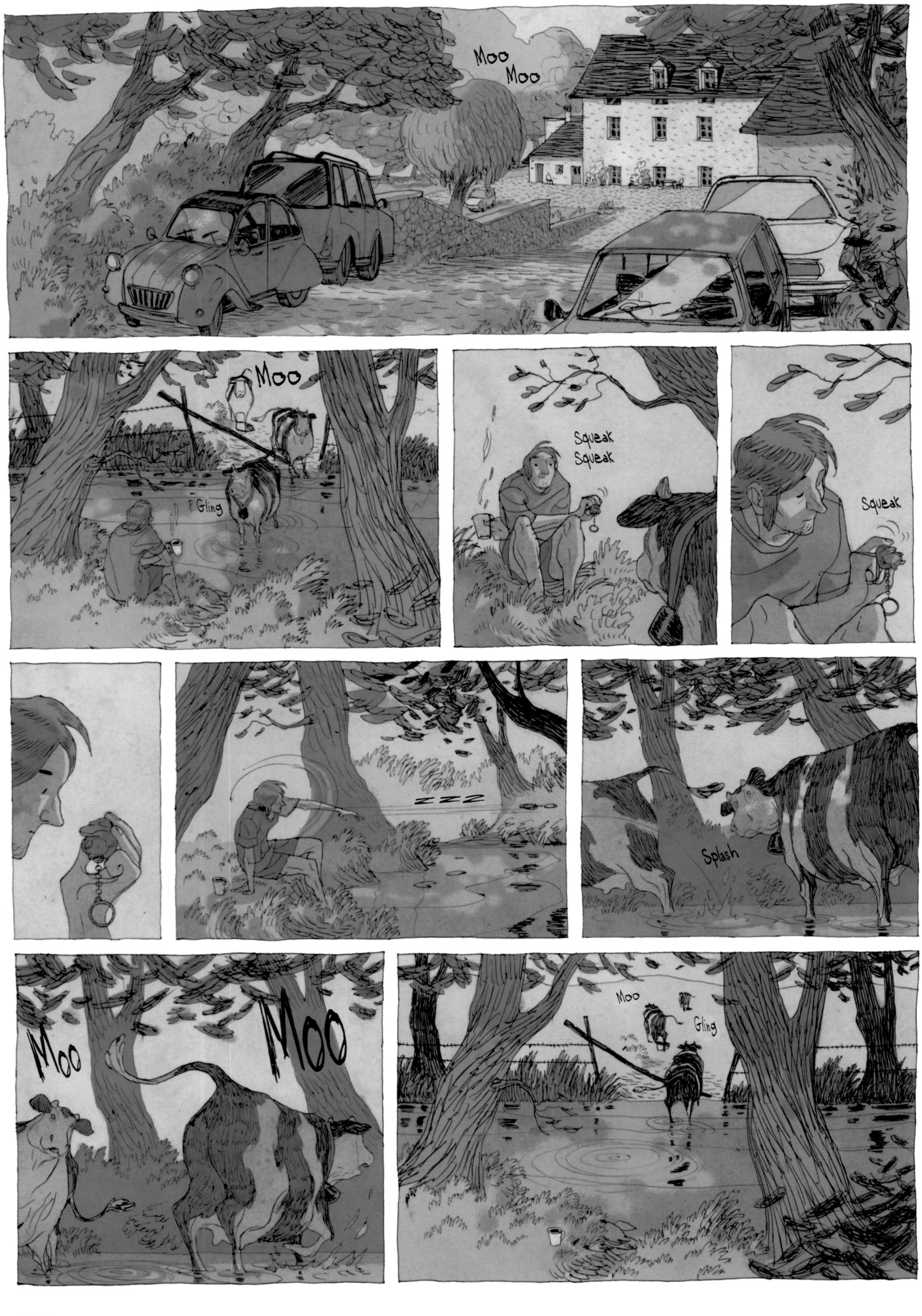
Moo
Moo
Moo
Gling
Squeak
Squeak
Squeak
ZZZ
Splash
Moo
Moo
Moo
Gling

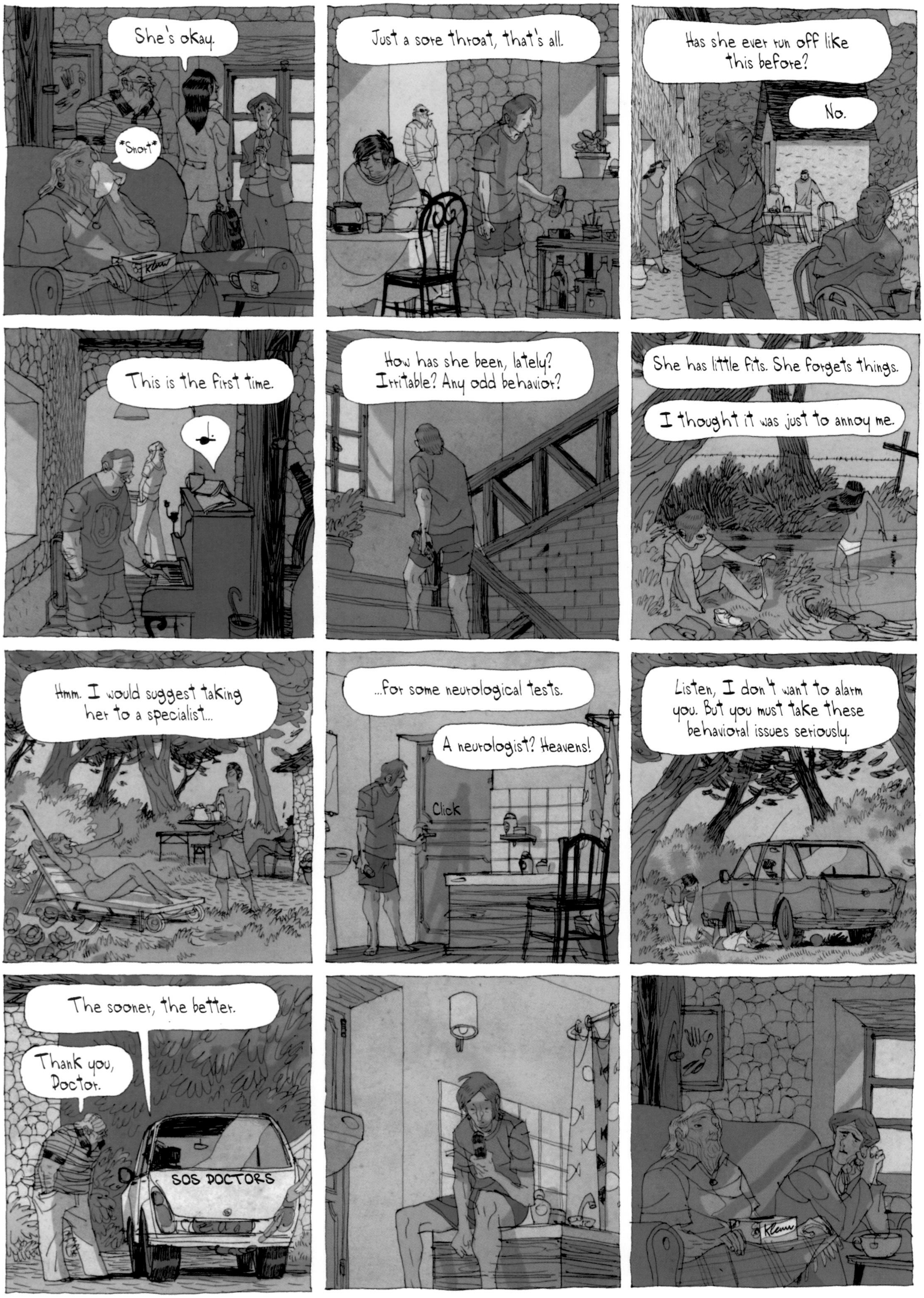
She's okay.
Snort
Just a sore throat, that's all.
Has she ever run off like this before?
No.
This is the first time.
How has she been, lately? Irritable? Any odd behavior?
She has little fits. She forgets things.
I thought it was just to annoy me.
Hmm. I would suggest taking her to a specialist...
...for some neurological tests.
A neurologist? Heavens!
Click
Listen, I don't want to alarm you. But you must take these behavioral issues seriously.
The sooner, the better.
Thank you, Doctor.
SOS DOCTORS

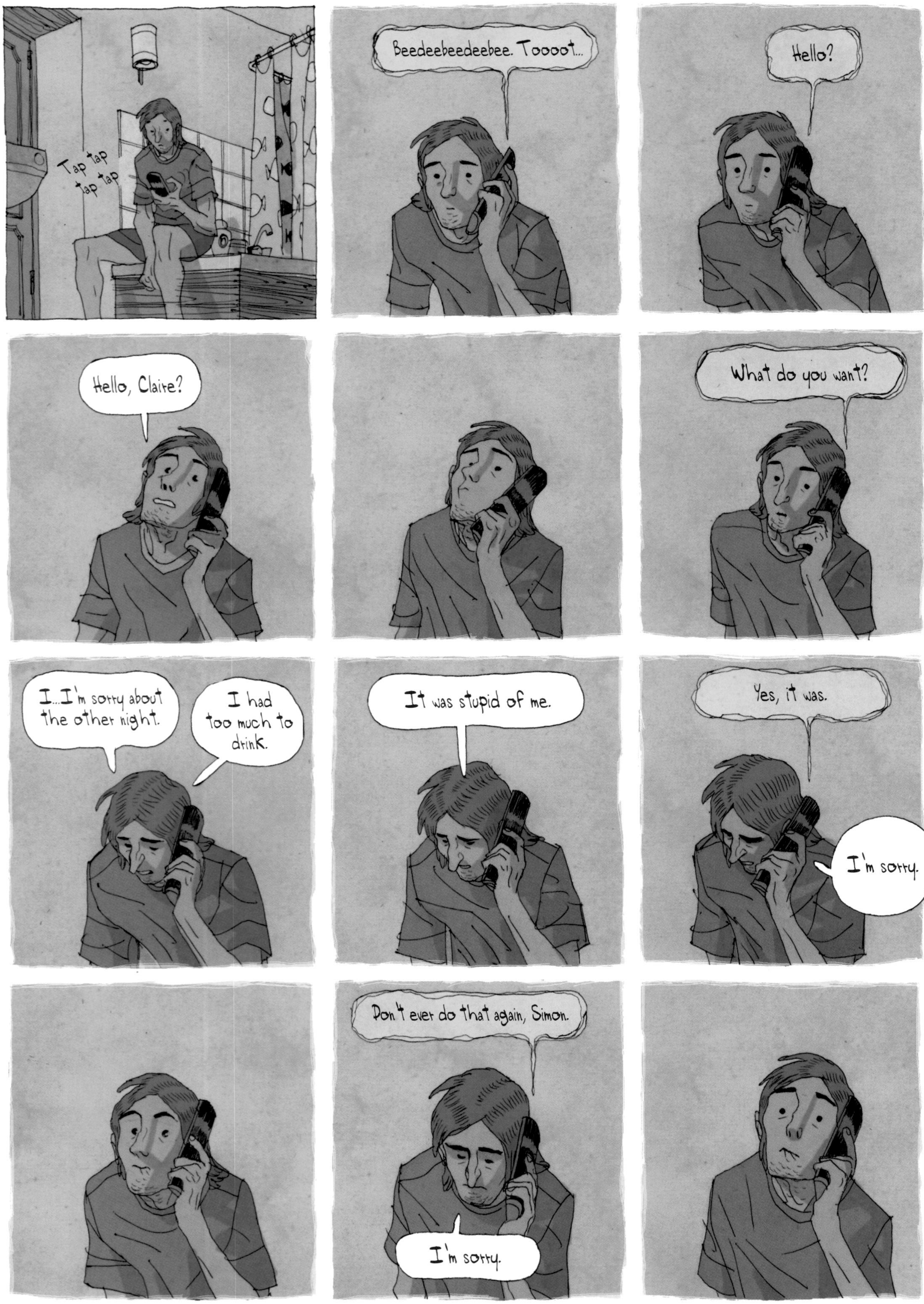
Tap tap
tap tap
Beedeebeedeebee. Toooot...
Hello?
Hello, Claire?
What do you want?
I...I'm sorry about the other night.
I had too much to drink.
It was stupid of me.
Yes, it was.
I'm sorry.
Don't ever do that again, Simon.
I'm sorry.

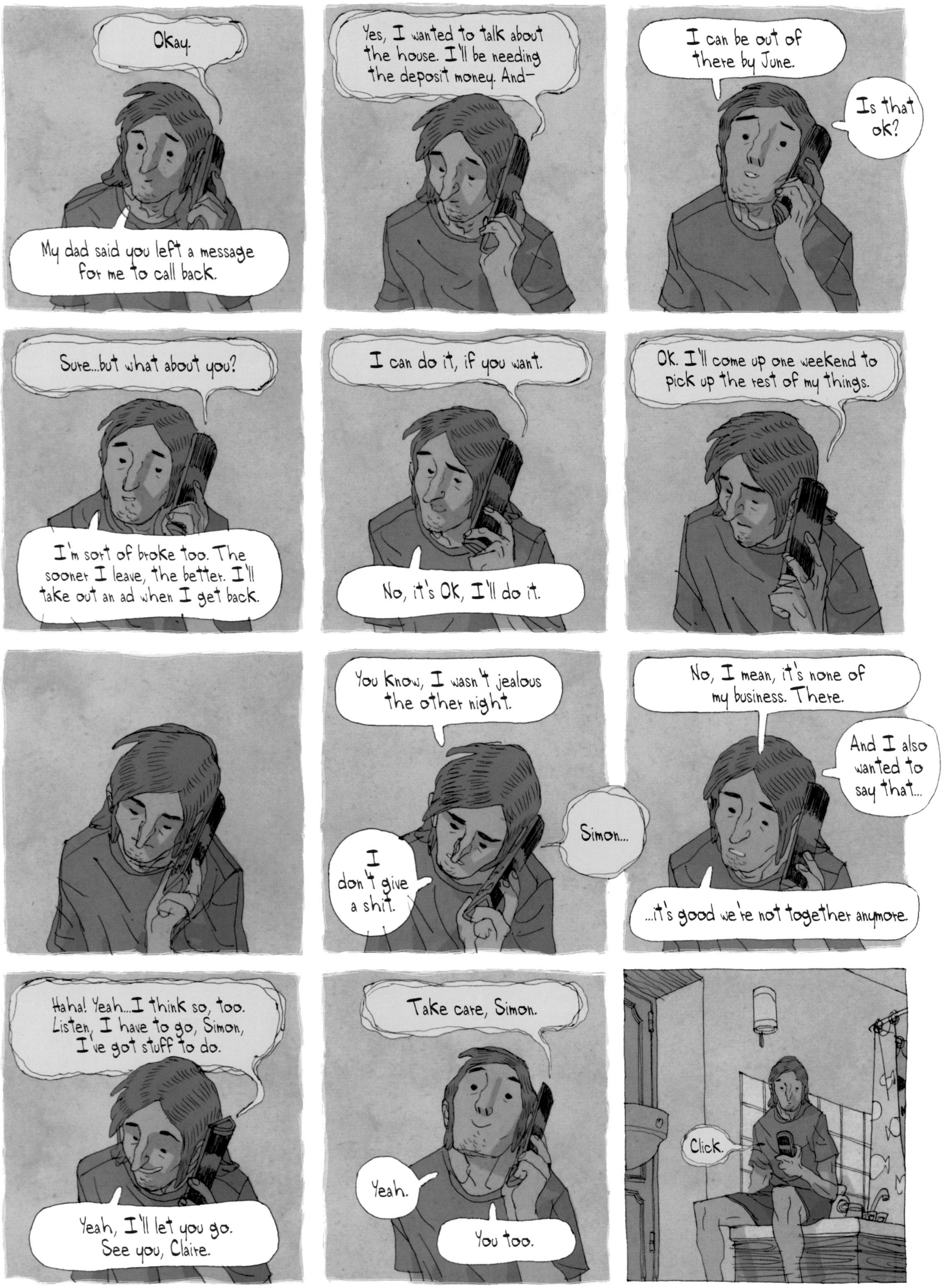

Okay.
My dad said you left a message for me to call back.
Yes, I wanted to talk about the house. I'll be needing the deposit money. And—
I can be out of there by June.
Is that ok?
Sure...but what about you?
I'm sort of broke too. The sooner I leave, the better. I'll take out an ad when I get back.
I can do it, if you want.
No, it's OK, I'll do it.
OK. I'll come up one weekend to pick up the rest of my things.
You know, I wasn't jealous the other night.
I don't give a shit.
Simon...
No, I mean, it's none of my business. There.
And I also wanted to say that...
...it's good we're not together anymore.
Haha! Yeah...I think so, too. Listen, I have to go, Simon, I've got stuff to do.
Yeah, I'll let you go. See you, Claire.
Take care, Simon.
Yeah.
You too.
Click.

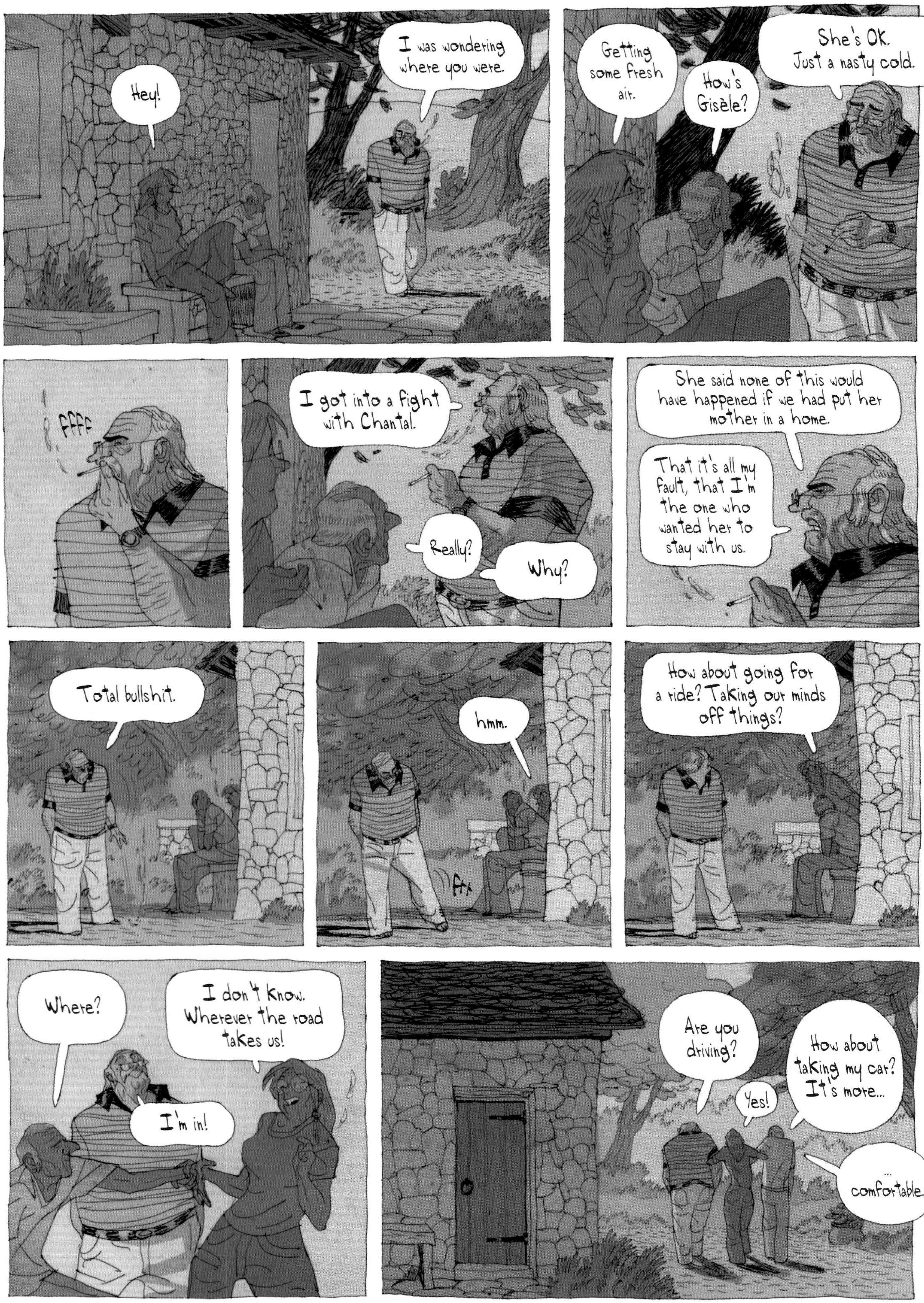
Hey!
I was wondering where you were.
Getting some fresh air.
How's Gisèle?
She's OK. Just a nasty cold.
FFFF
I got into a fight with Chantal.
Really?
Why?
She said none of this would have happened if we had put her mother in a home.
That it's all my fault, that I'm the one who wanted her to stay with us.
Total bullshit.
hmm.
ftt
How about going for a ride? Taking our minds off things?
Where?
I don't know. Wherever the road takes us!
I'm in!
Are you driving?
Yes!
How about taking my car? It's more...
... comfortable.

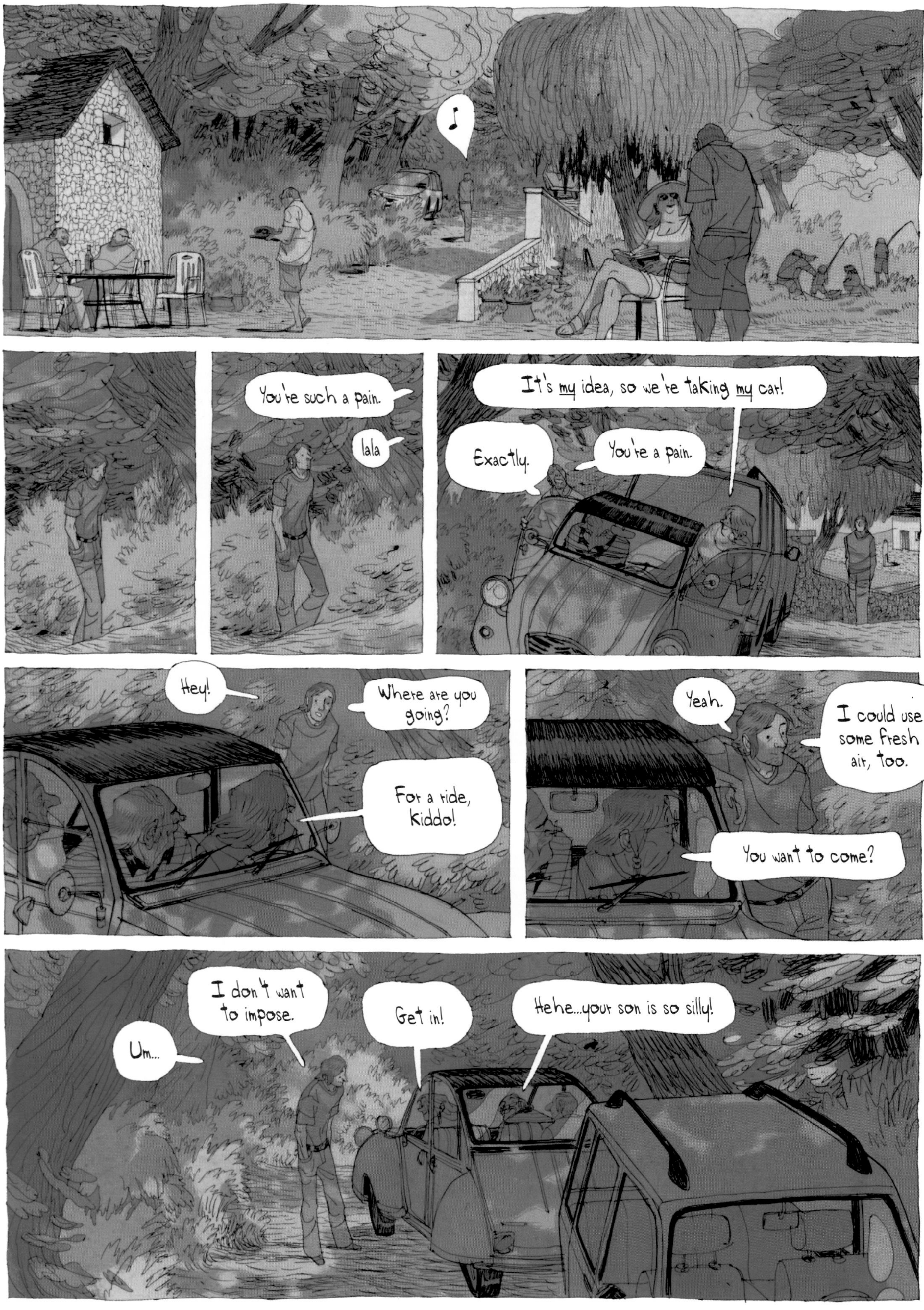
You're such a pain.
lala
It's my idea, so we're taking my car!
Exactly.
You're a pain.
Hey!
Where are you going?
For a ride, kiddo!
Yeah.
I could use some fresh air, too.
You want to come?
Um...
I don't want to impose.
Get in!
Hehe...your son is so silly!

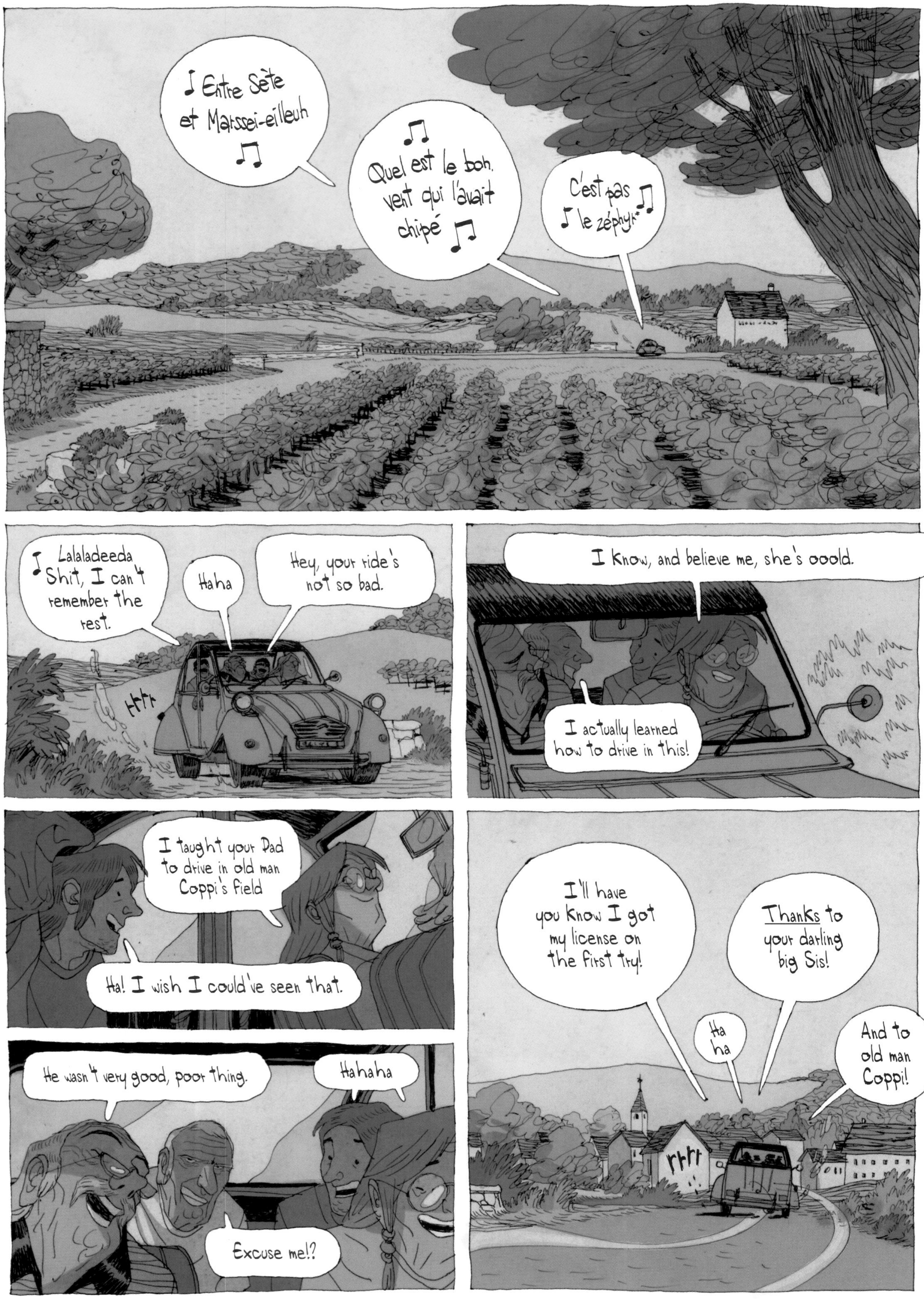
Entre Sète et Marssei-eilleuh
Quel est le bon vent qui l'avait chipé
C'est pas le zéphyr*
Lalaladeeda Shit, I can't remember the rest.
Haha
Hey, your ride's not so bad.
rrrr
I know, and believe me, she's ooold.
I actually learned how to drive in this!
I taught your Dad to drive in old man Coppi's field
Ha! I wish I could've seen that.
He wasn't very good, poor thing.
Hahaha
Excuse me!?
I'll have you know I got my license on the first try!
Thanks to your darling big Sis!
Ha ha
And to old man Coppi!
rrrr

*"Le Chapeau de Mireille" by Georges Brassens. 'Between Sète and Marseille, what was that wind that took him, not the zephyr'.

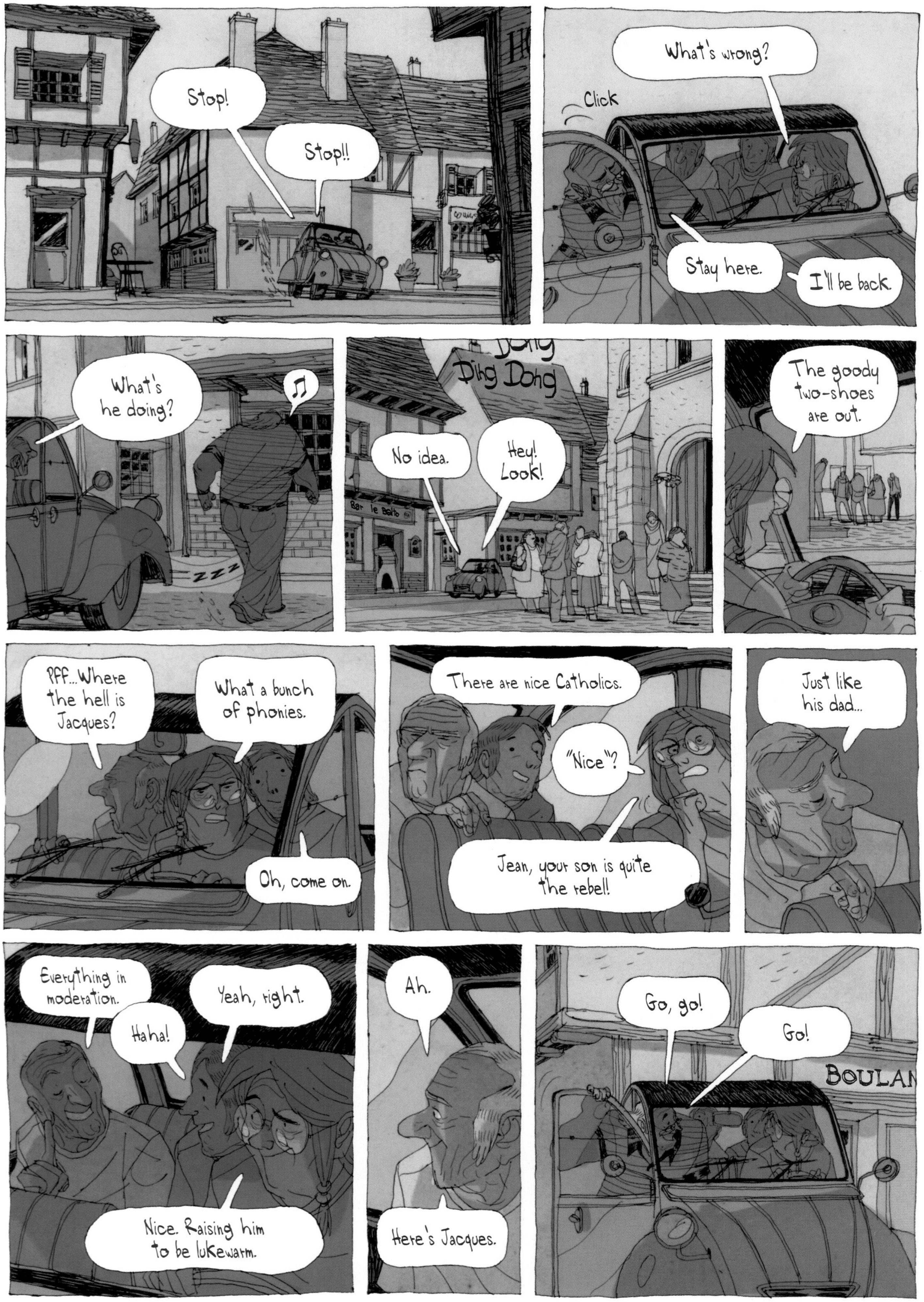
Stop!
Stop!!
What's wrong?
Click
Stay here.
I'll be back.
What's he doing?
♫
ZZZ
Dong
Ding Dong
Bar le Bistro
No idea.
Hey! Look!
The goody two-shoes are out.
PFF... Where the hell is Jacques?
What a bunch of phonies.
Oh, come on.
There are nice Catholics.
"Nice"?
Jean, your son is quite the rebel!
Just like his dad...
Everything in moderation.
Haha!
Yeah, right.
Nice. Raising him to be lukewarm.
Ah.
Here's Jacques.
Go, go!
Go!
BOULAN

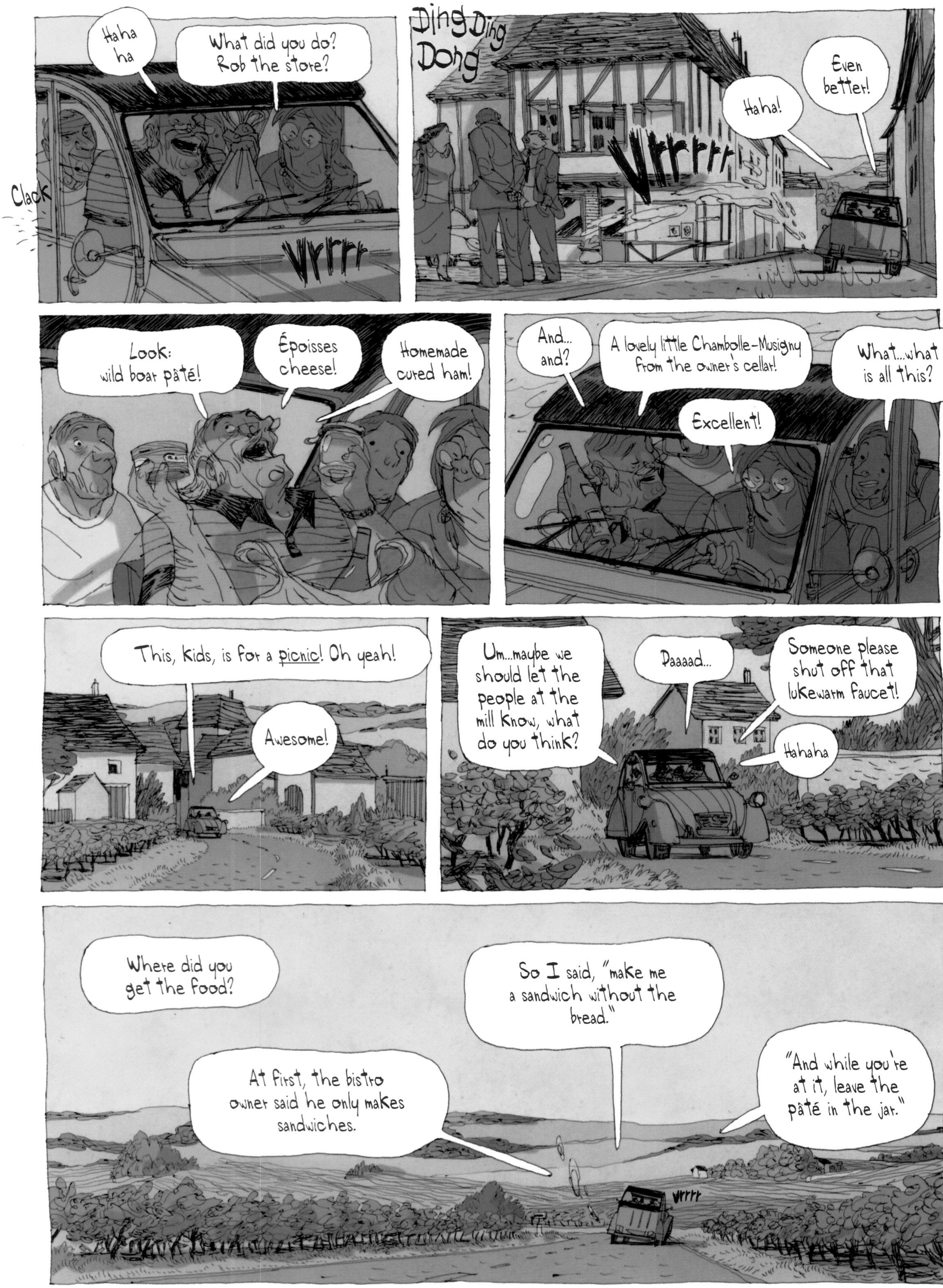
Haha ha
What did you do? Rob the store?
Clack
Vrrrr
Ding Ding Dong
Vrrrrr
Haha!
Even better!
Look: wild boar pâté!
Époisses cheese!
Homemade cured ham!
And... and?
A lovely little Chambolle-Musigny from the owner's cellar!
What...what is all this?
Excellent!
This, kids, is for a picnic! Oh yeah!
Awesome!
Um...maybe we should let the people at the mill know, what do you think?
Daaaad...
Someone please shut off that lukewarm faucet!
Hahaha
Where did you get the food?
At first, the bistro owner said he only makes sandwiches.
So I said, "make me a sandwich without the bread."
"And while you're at it, leave the pâté in the jar."
Vrrrr

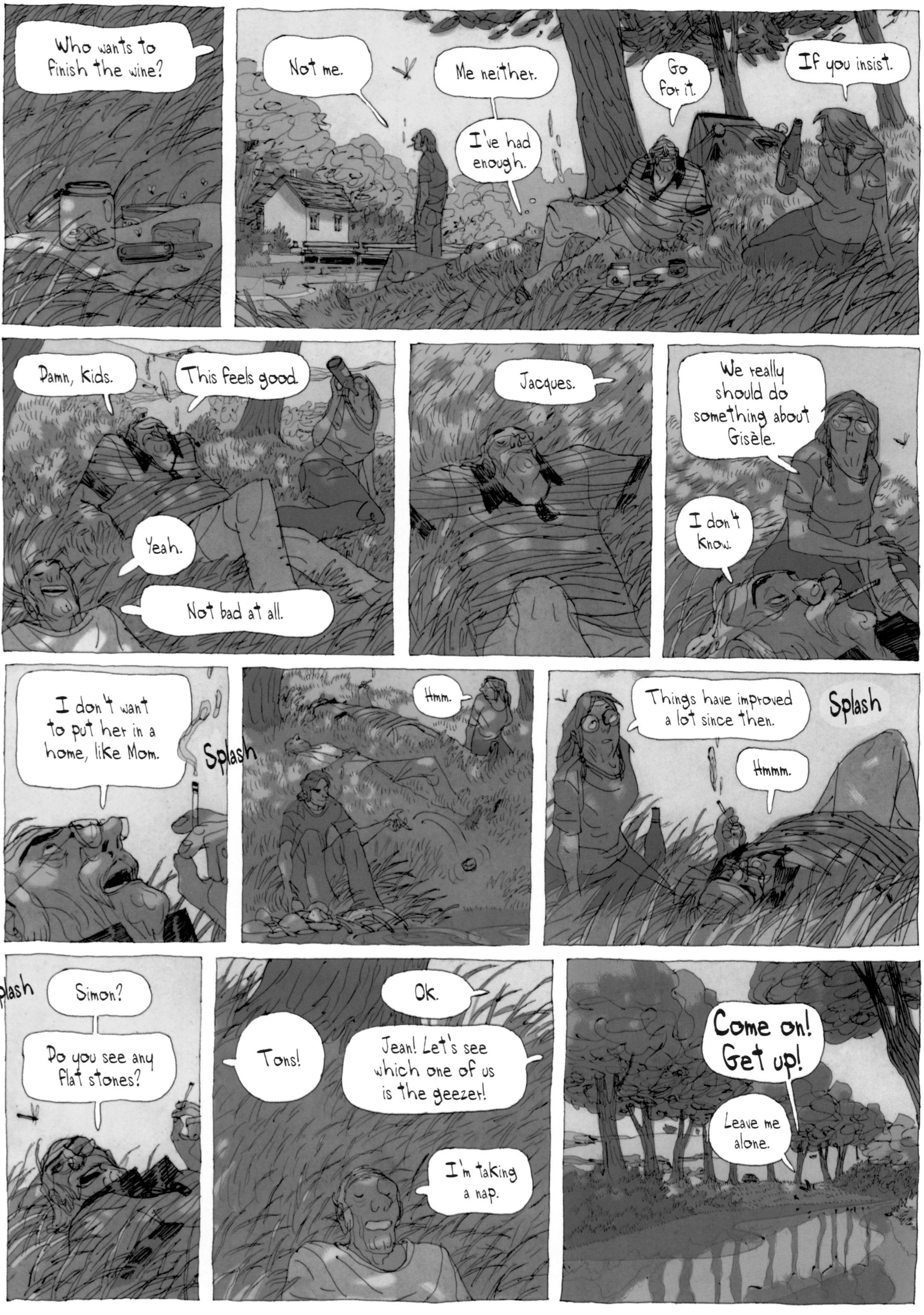
Who wants to finish the wine?
Not me.
Me neither.
I've had enough.
Go for it.
If you insist.
Damn, kids.
This feels good.
Yeah.
Not bad at all.
Jacques.
We really should do something about Gisèle.
I don't know.
I don't want to put her in a home, like Mom.
Splash
Hmm.
Things have improved a lot since then.
Splash
Hmmm.
Splash
Simon?
Do you see any flat stones?
Tons!
Ok.
Jean! Let's see which one of us is the geezer!
I'm taking a nap.
Come on! Get up!
Leave me alone.

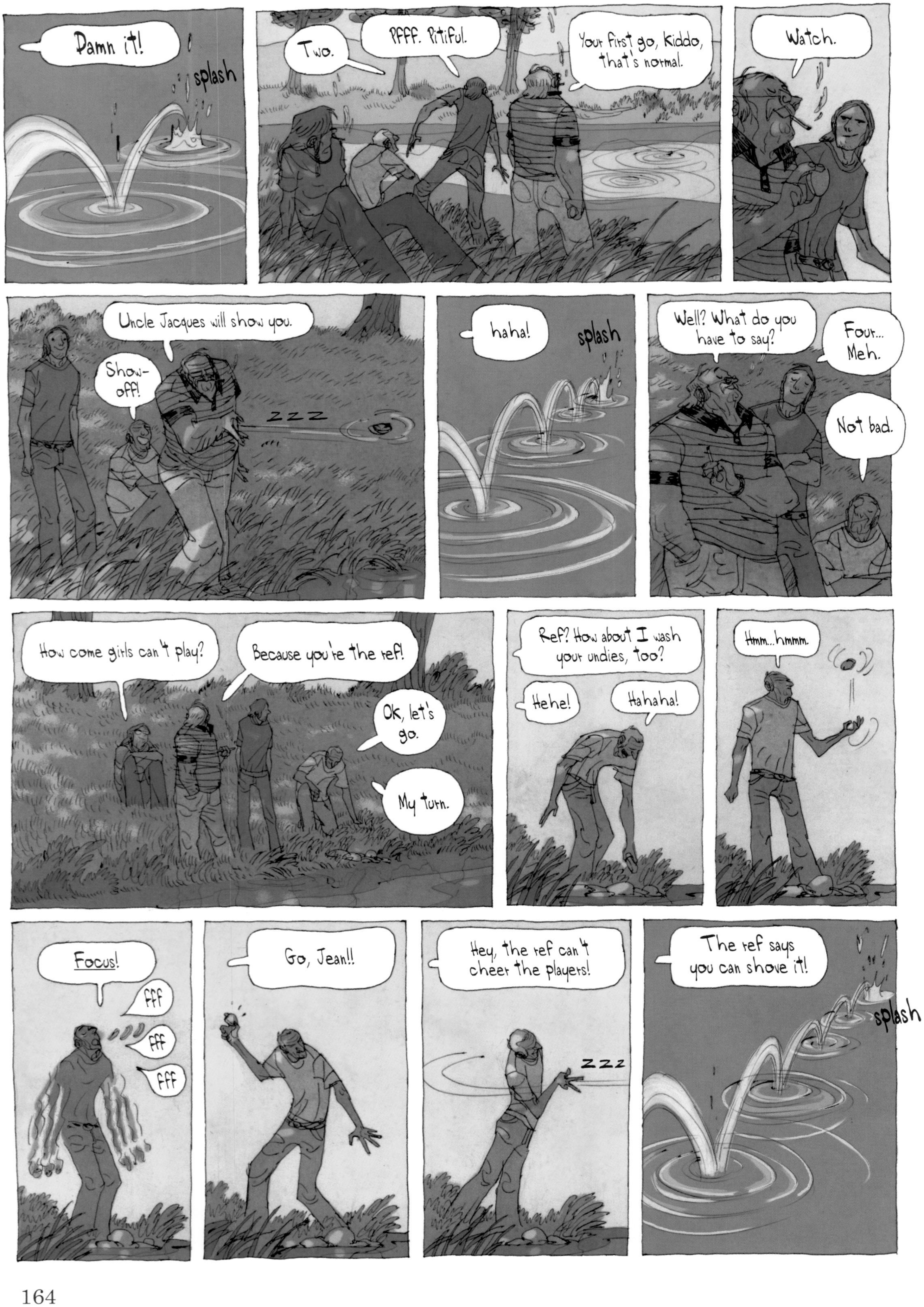
Damn it!
splash
Two.
PFFF. Pitiful.
Your first go, kiddo, that's normal.
Watch.
Uncle Jacques will show you.
Show-off!
zzz
haha!
splash
Well? What do you have to say?
Four... Meh.
Not bad.
How come girls can't play?
Because you're the ref!
Ok, let's go.
My turn.
Ref? How about I wash your undies, too?
Hehe!
Hahaha!
Hmm...hmmm.
Focus!
fff
fff
fff
Go, Jean!!
Hey, the ref can't cheer the players!
zzz
The ref says you can shove it!
splash

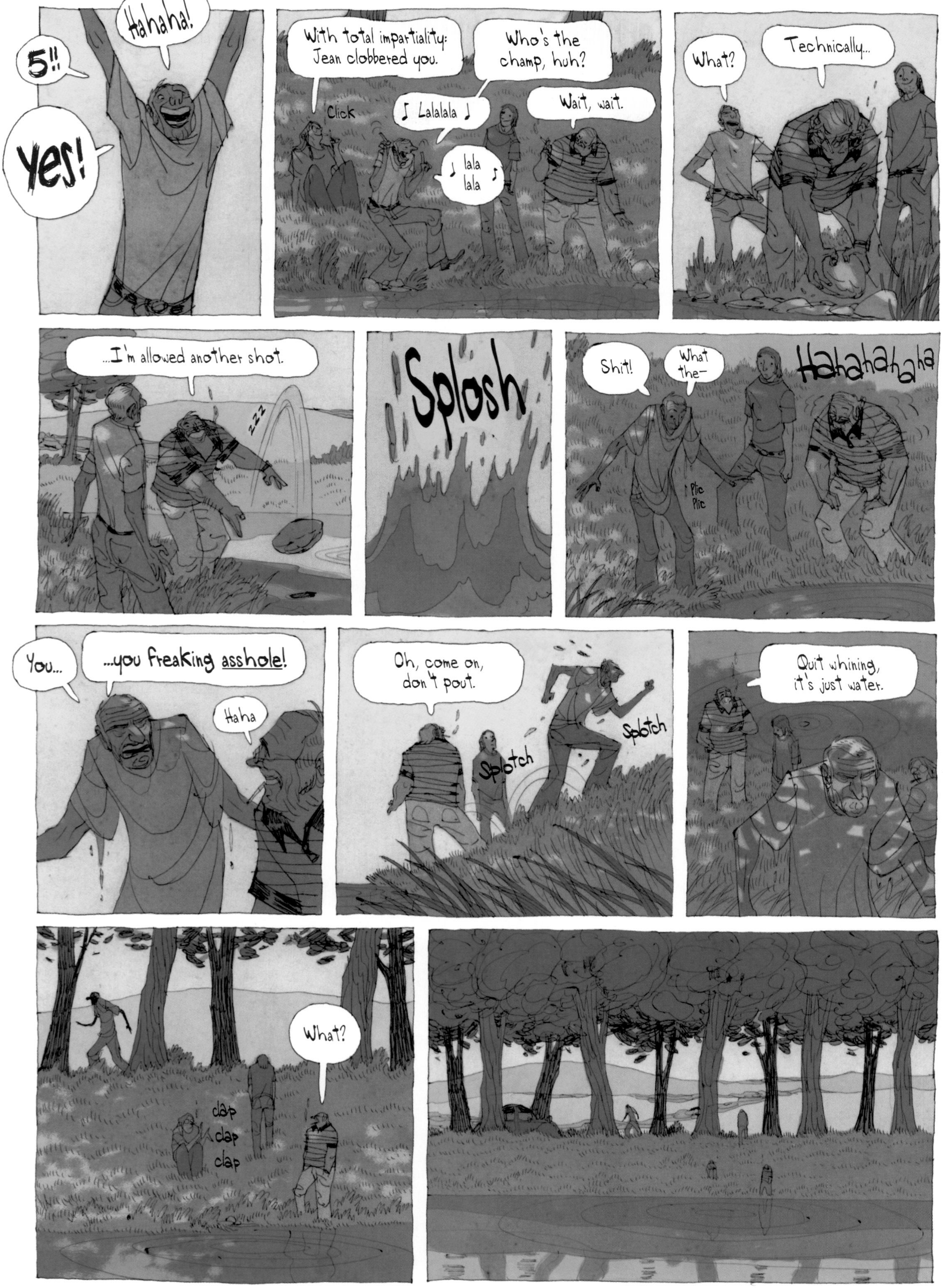
5!!
Yes!
Hahaha!
With total impartiality: Jean clobbered you.
Click
Who's the champ, huh?
♩ Lalalala ♩
♩ lala lala ♪
Wait, wait.
What?
Technically...
...I'm allowed another shot.
zzz
Splosh
Shit!
What the-
Hahahahahaha
Plic Plic
You...
...you freaking asshole!
Haha
Oh, come on, don't pout.
Splotch
Splotch
Quit whining, it's just water.
What?
clap clap clap

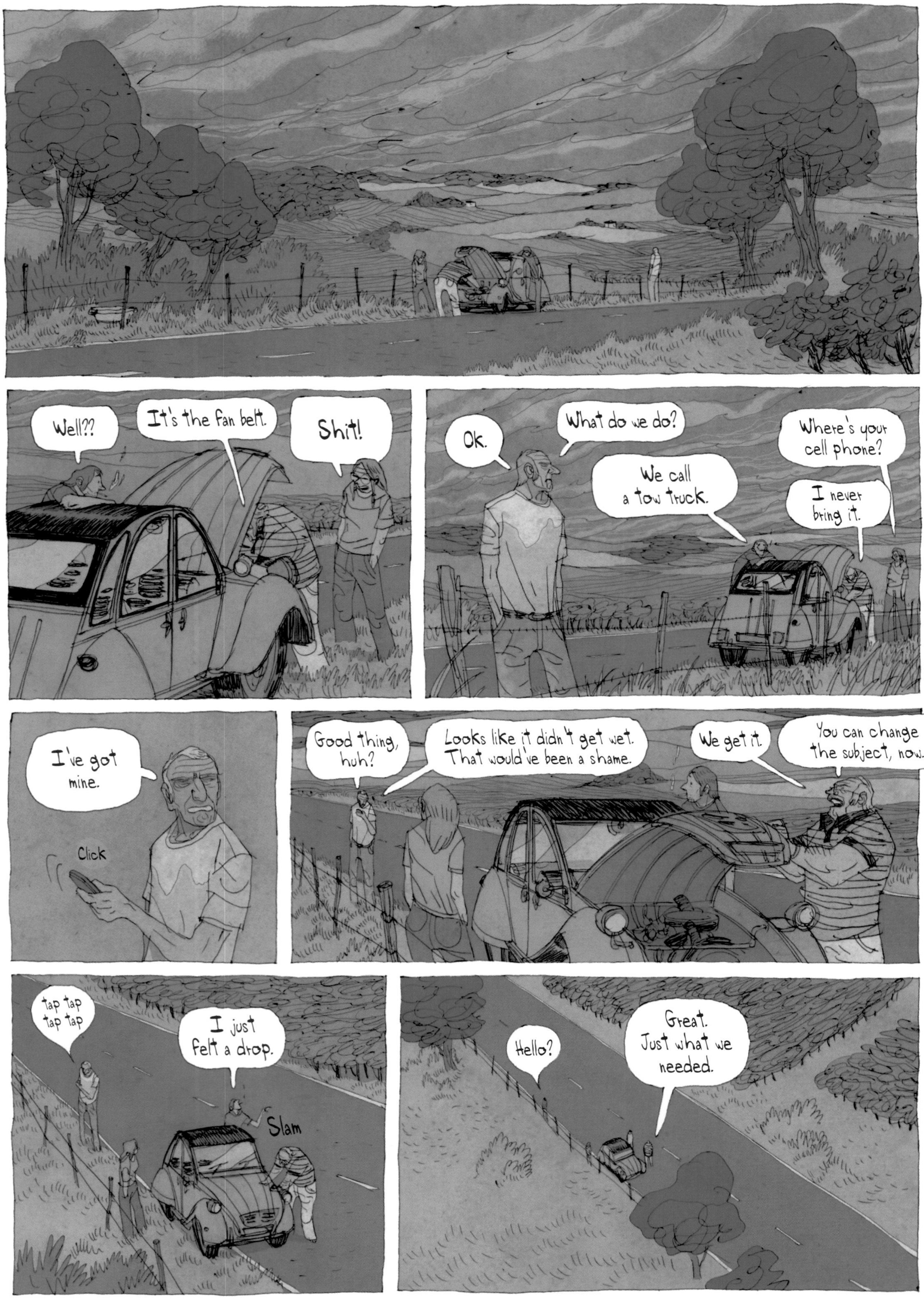
Well??
It's the fan belt.
Shit!
Ok.
What do we do?
We call a tow truck.
Where's your cell phone?
I never bring it.
I've got mine.
Click
Good thing, huh?
Looks like it didn't get wet. That would've been a shame.
We get it.
You can change the subject, now.
tap tap tap tap
I just felt a drop.
Slam
Hello?
Great. Just what we needed.

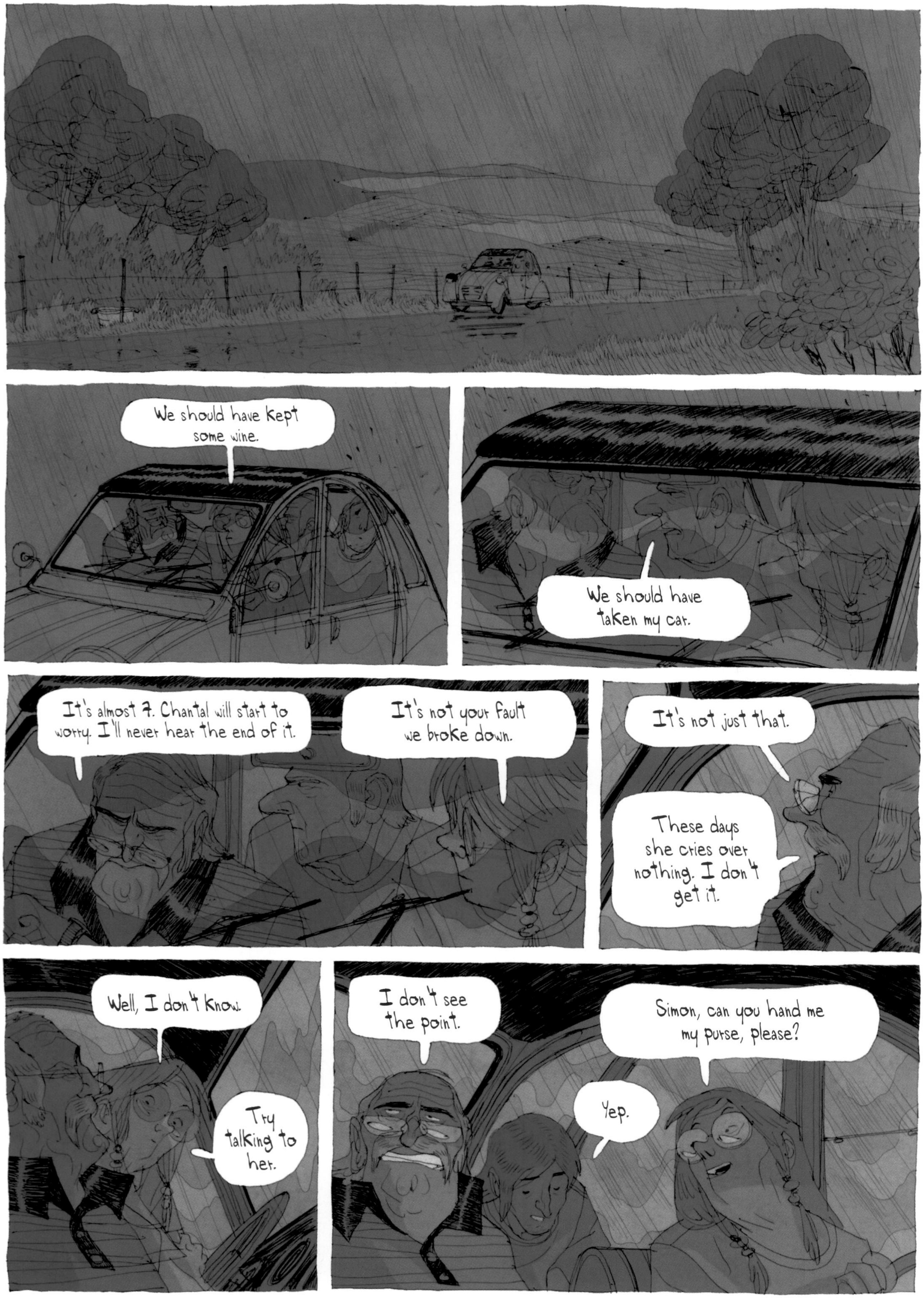
We should have kept some wine.
We should have taken my car.
It's almost 7. Chantal will start to worry. I'll never hear the end of it.
It's not your fault we broke down.
It's not just that.
These days she cries over nothing. I don't get it.
Well, I don't know.
Try talking to her.
I don't see the point.
Simon, can you hand me my purse, please?
Yep.

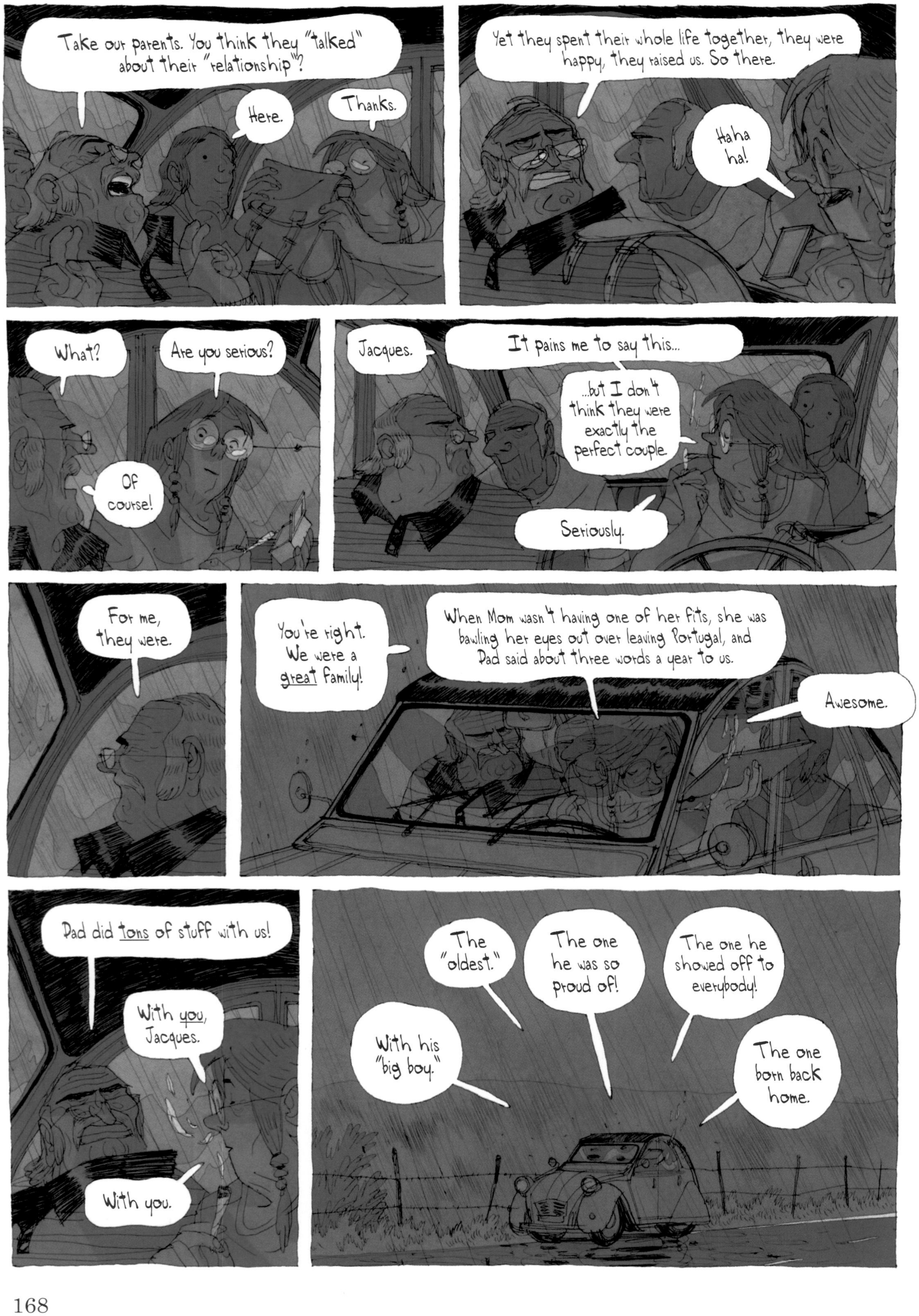
Take our parents. You think they "talked" about their "relationship"?
Here.
Thanks.
Yet they spent their whole life together, they were happy, they raised us. So there.
Haha ha!
What?
Are you serious?
Of course!
Jacques.
It pains me to say this...
...but I don't think they were exactly the perfect couple.
Seriously.
For me, they were.
You're right. We were a great family!
When Mom wasn't having one of her fits, she was bawling her eyes out over leaving Portugal, and Dad said about three words a year to us.
Awesome.
Dad did tons of stuff with us!
With you, Jacques.
With you.
With his "big boy."
The "oldest."
The one he was so proud of!
The one he showed off to everybody!
The one born back home.

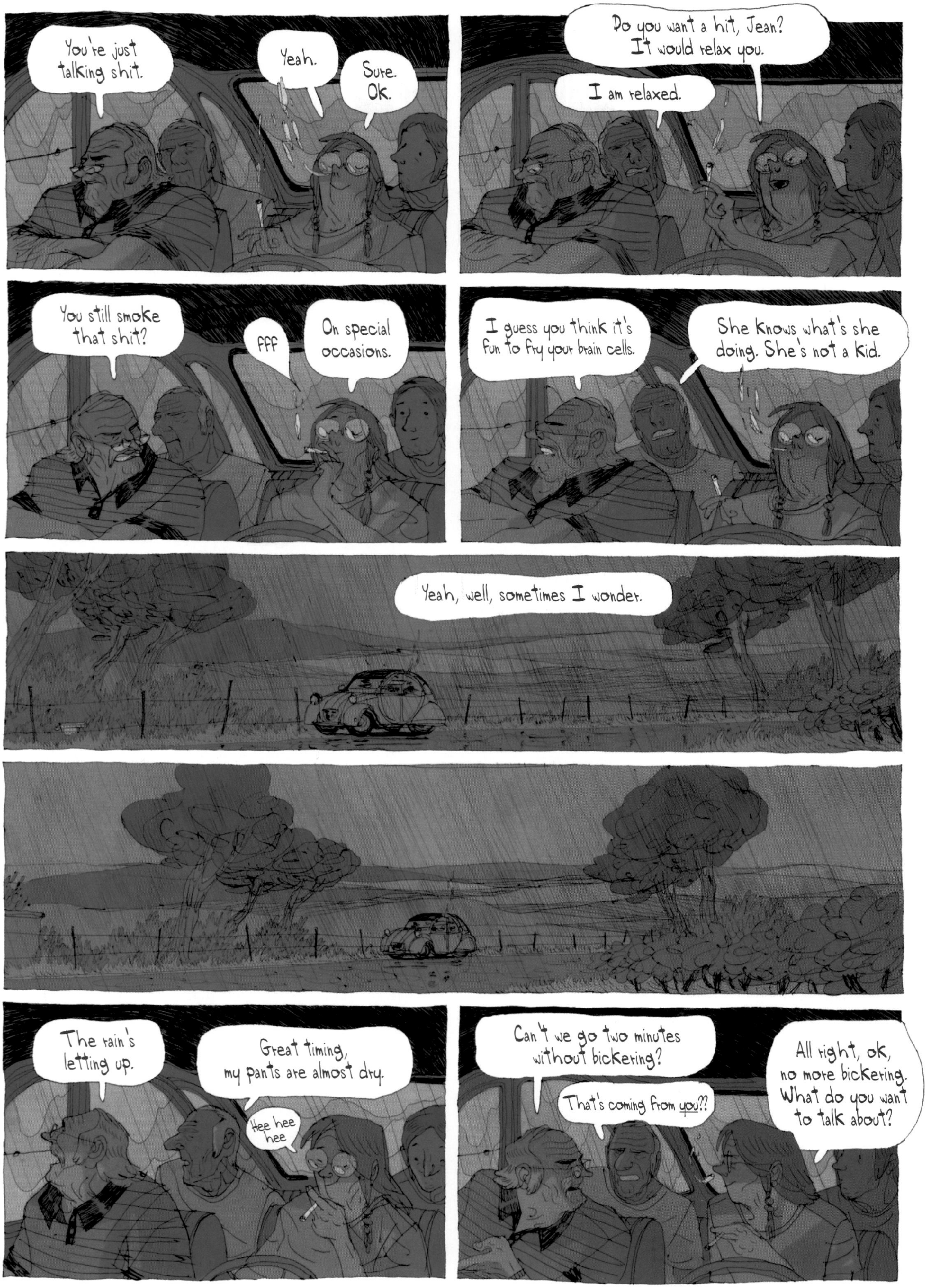

You're just talking shit.
Yeah.
Sure. Ok.
Do you want a hit, Jean? It would relax you.
I am relaxed.
You still smoke that shit?
fff
On special occasions.
I guess you think it's fun to fry your brain cells.
She knows what's she doing. She's not a kid.
Yeah, well, sometimes I wonder.
The rain's letting up.
Great timing, my pants are almost dry.
Hee hee hee
Can't we go two minutes without bickering?
That's coming from you??
All right, ok, no more bickering. What do you want to talk about?

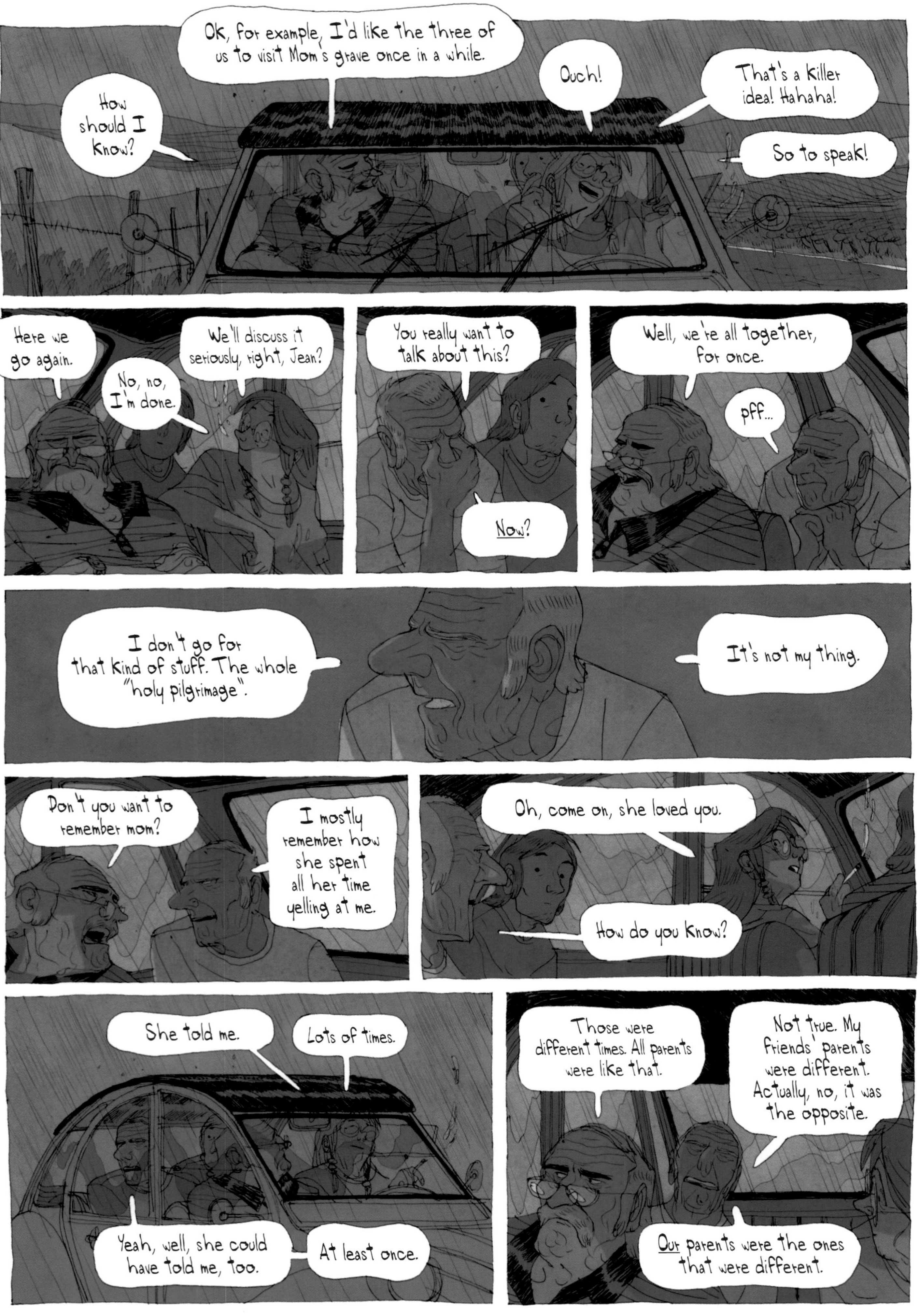
How should I know?
Ok, for example, I'd like the three of us to visit Mom's grave once in a while.
Ouch!
That's a killer idea! Hahaha!
So to speak!
Here we go again.
We'll discuss it seriously, right, Jean?
No, no, I'm done.
You really want to talk about this?
Now?
Well, we're all together, for once.
pff...
I don't go for that kind of stuff. The whole "holy pilgrimage".
It's not my thing.
Don't you want to remember mom?
I mostly remember how she spent all her time yelling at me.
Oh, come on, she loved you.
How do you know?
She told me.
Lots of times.
Yeah, well, she could have told me, too.
At least once.
Those were different times. All parents were like that.
Not true. My friends' parents were different. Actually, no, it was the opposite.
Our parents were the ones that were different.

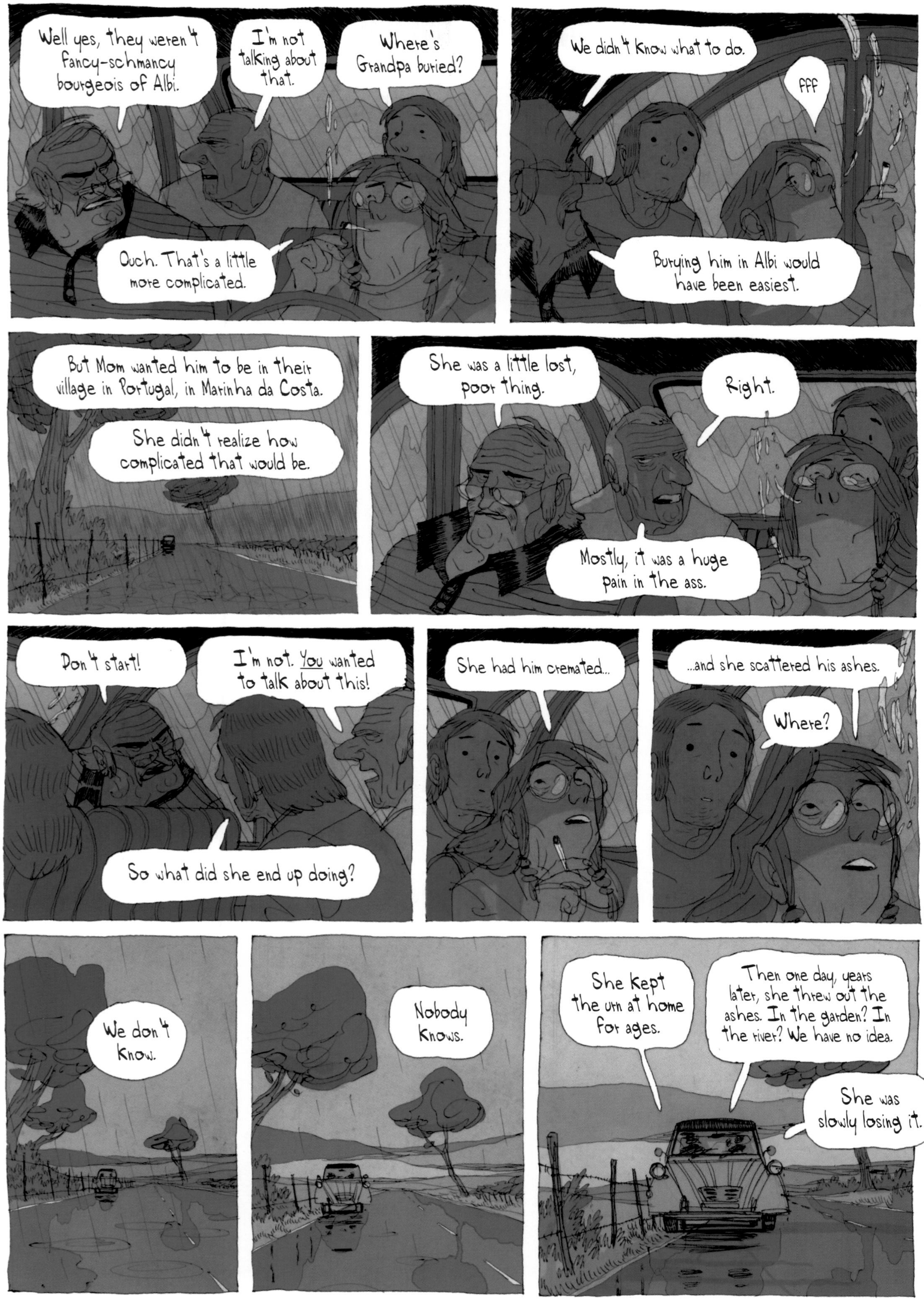
Well yes, they weren't fancy-schmancy bourgeois of Albi.
I'm not talking about that.
Where's Grandpa buried?
Ouch. That's a little more complicated.
We didn't know what to do.
fff
Burying him in Albi would have been easiest.
But Mom wanted him to be in their village in Portugal, in Marinha da Costa.
She didn't realize how complicated that would be.
She was a little lost, poor thing.
Right.
Mostly, it was a huge pain in the ass.
Don't start!
I'm not. You wanted to talk about this!
So what did she end up doing?
She had him cremated...
...and she scattered his ashes.
Where?
We don't know.
Nobody knows.
She kept the urn at home for ages.
Then one day, years later, she threw out the ashes. In the garden? In the river? We have no idea.
She was slowly losing it.

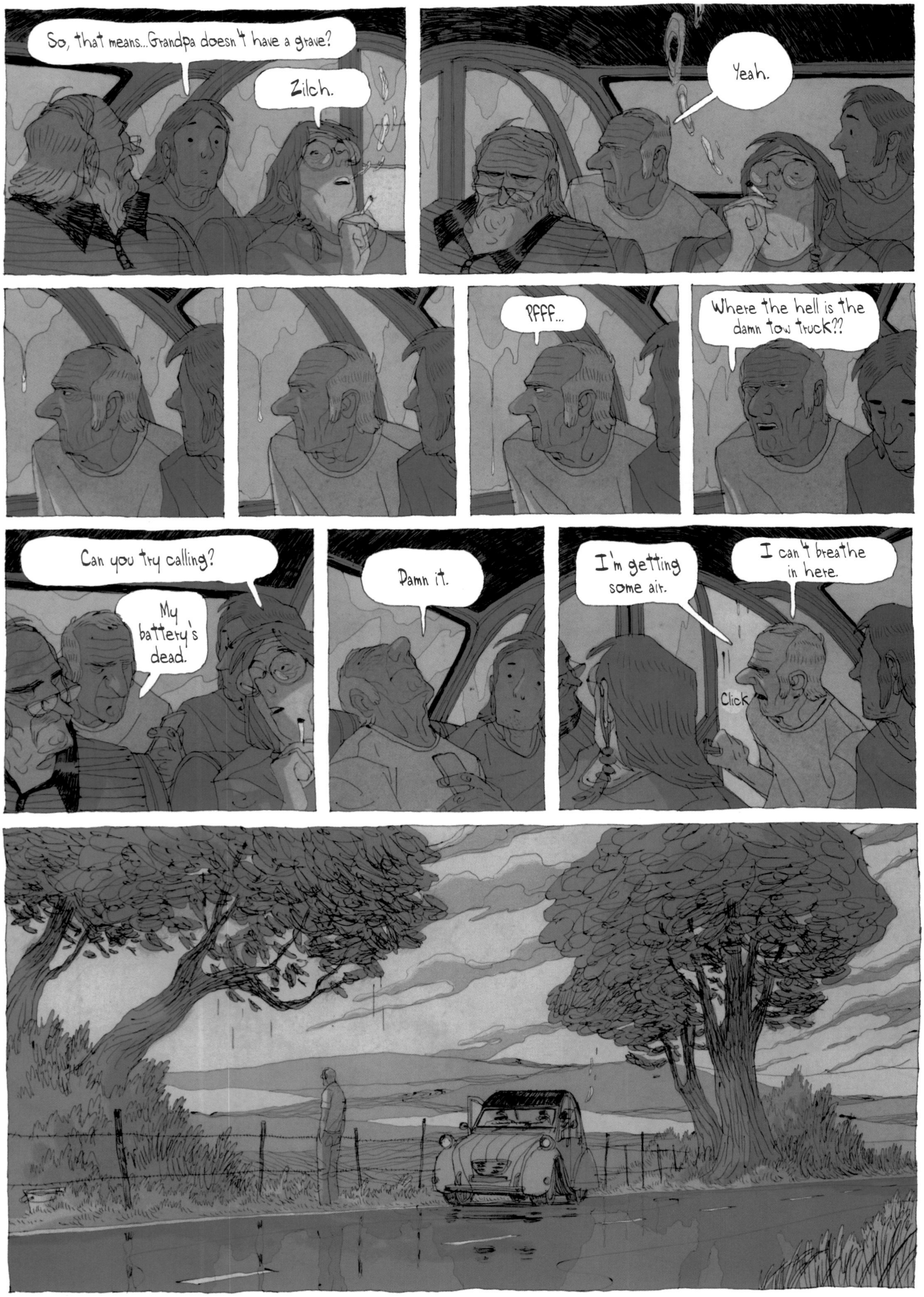

So, that means... Grandpa doesn't have a grave?
Zilch.
Yeah.
PFFF...
Where the hell is the damn tow truck??
Can you try calling?
My battery's dead.
Damn it.
I'm getting some air.
I can't breathe in here.
Click

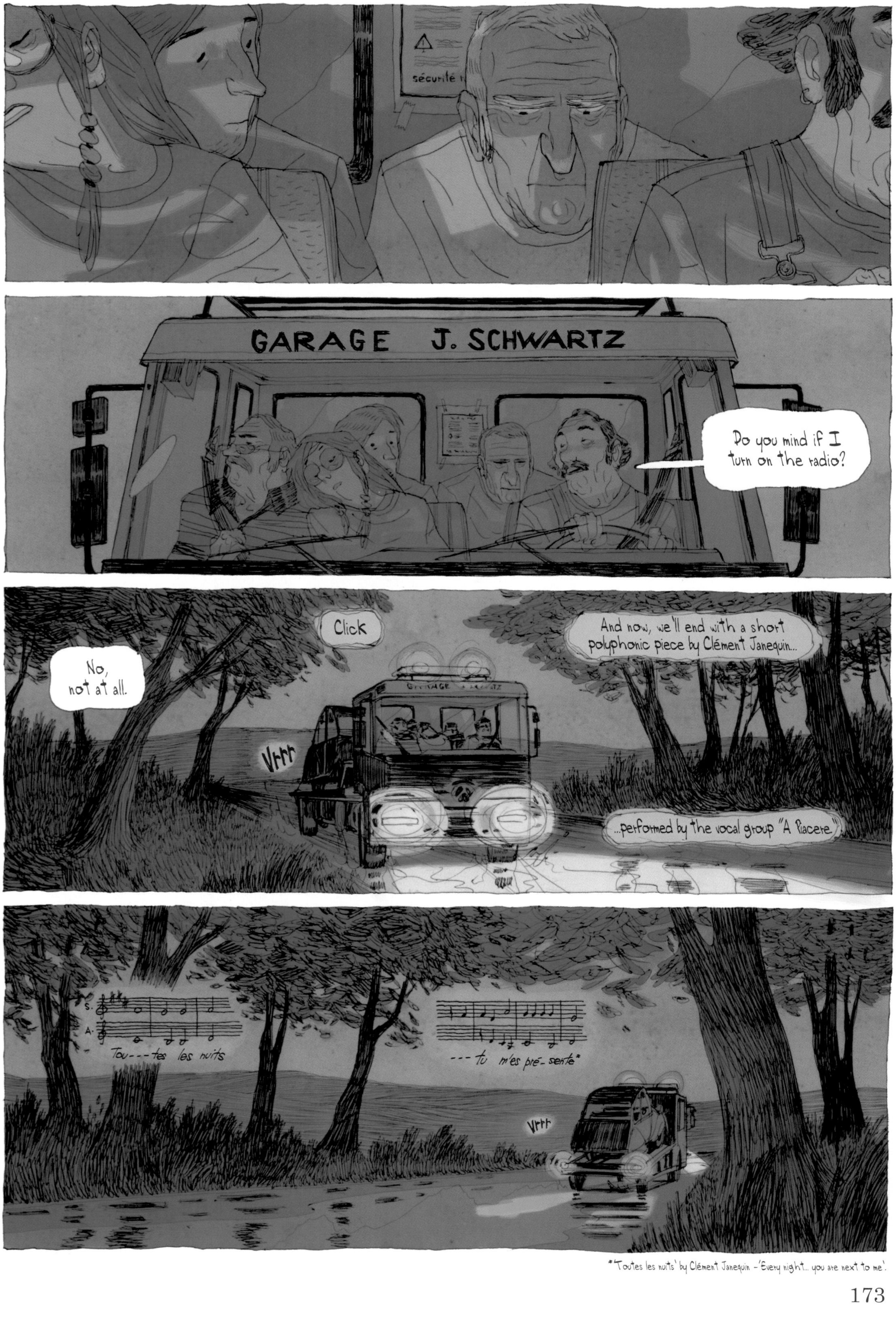
sécurité
GARAGE J. SCHWARTZ
Do you mind if I turn on the radio?
No, not at all.
Click
And now, we'll end with a short polyphonic piece by Clément Janequin...
Vrrr
...performed by the vocal group "A Piacere."
S.
A.
Tou---tes les nuits
---tu m'es pré-sente*
Vrrr

*'Toutes les nuits' by Clément Janequin – 'Every night... you are next to me'.

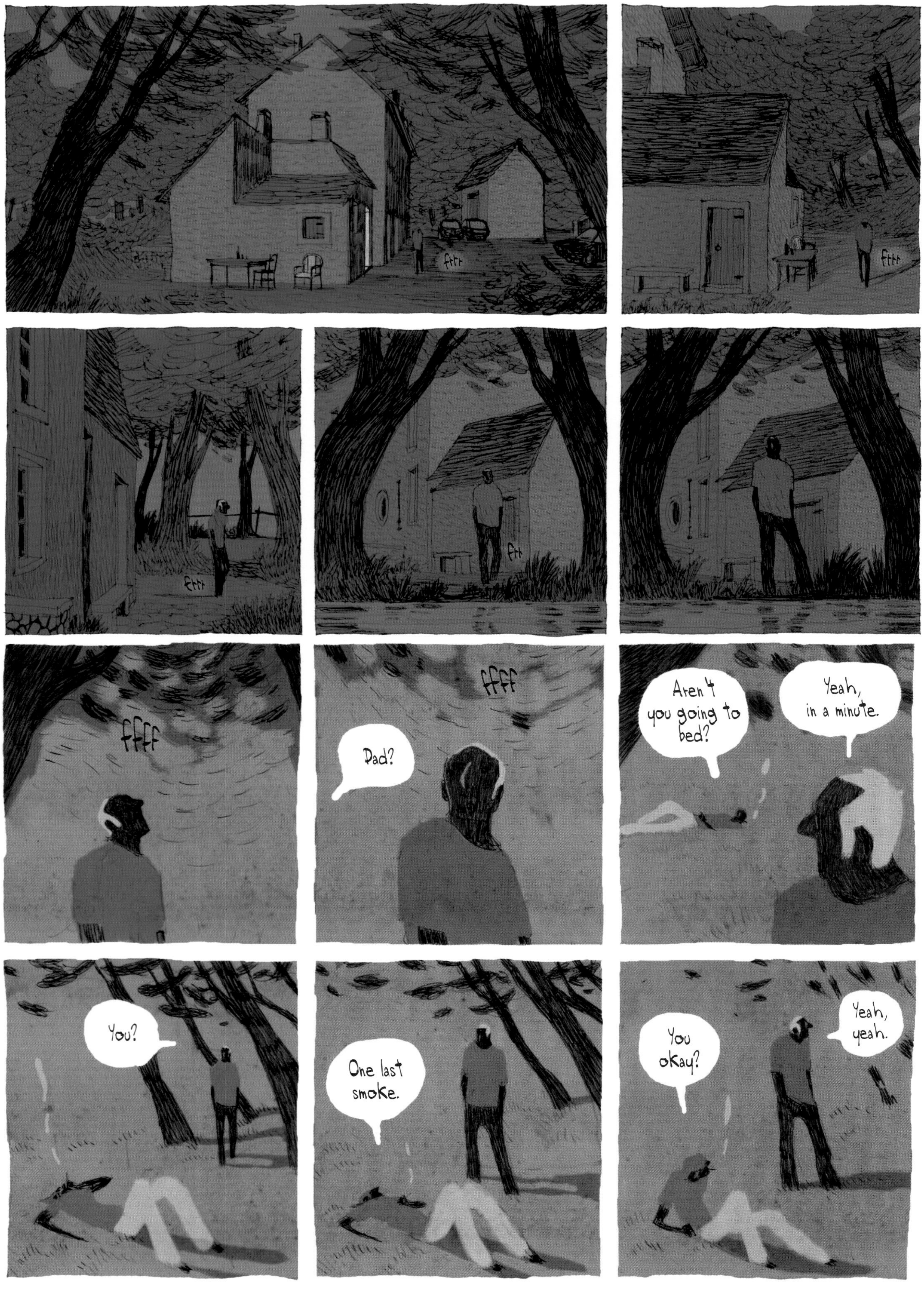
fffr
ffff
ffff
fff
ffff
ffff
Dad?
Aren't you going to bed?
Yeah, in a minute.
You?
One last smoke.
You okay?
Yeah, yeah.

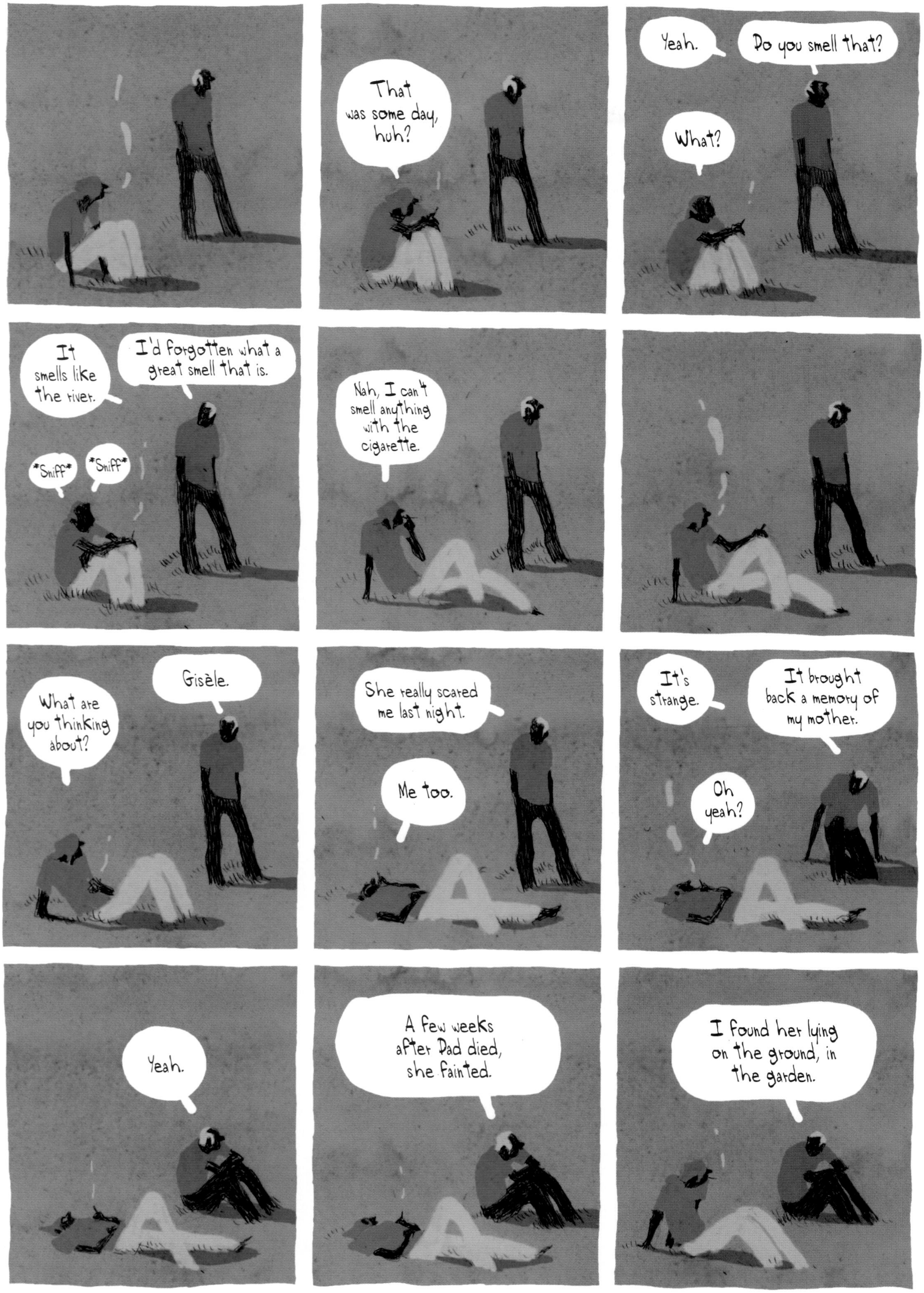
That was some day, huh?
Yeah.
Do you smell that?
What?
It smells like the river.
I'd forgotten what a great smell that is.
Sniff
Sniff
Nah, I can't smell anything with the cigarette.
What are you thinking about?
Gisèle.
She really scared me last night.
Me too.
It's strange.
It brought back a memory of my mother.
Oh yeah?
Yeah.
A few weeks after Dad died, she fainted.
I found her lying on the ground, in the garden.

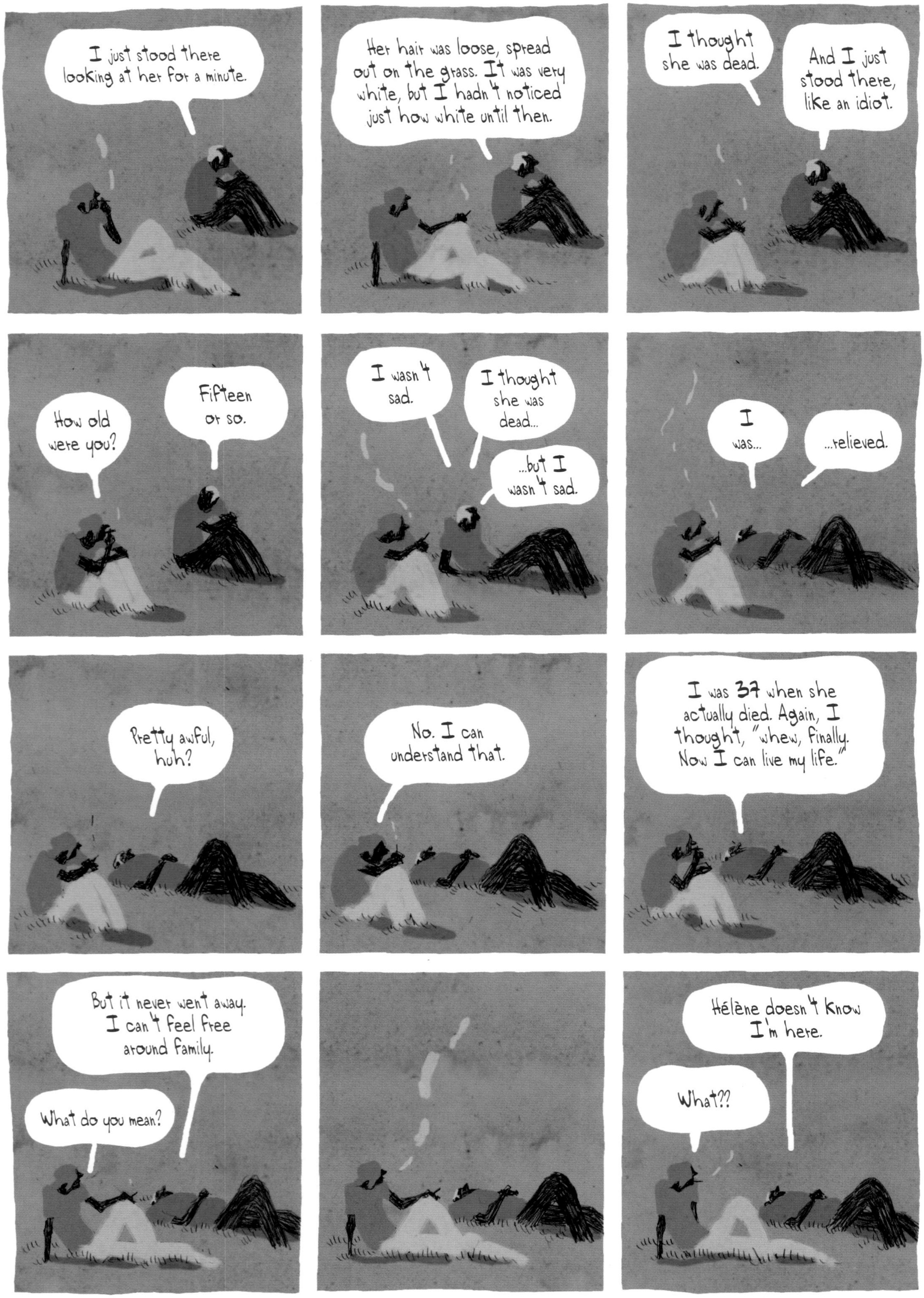
I just stood there looking at her for a minute.
Her hair was loose, spread out on the grass. It was very white, but I hadn't noticed just how white until then.
I thought she was dead.
And I just stood there, like an idiot.
How old were you?
Fifteen or so.
I wasn't sad.
I thought she was dead...
...but I wasn't sad.
I was...
...relieved.
Pretty awful, huh?
No. I can understand that.
I was 37 when she actually died. Again, I thought, "whew, finally. Now I can live my life."
But it never went away. I can't feel free around family.
What do you mean?
Hélène doesn't know I'm here.
What??

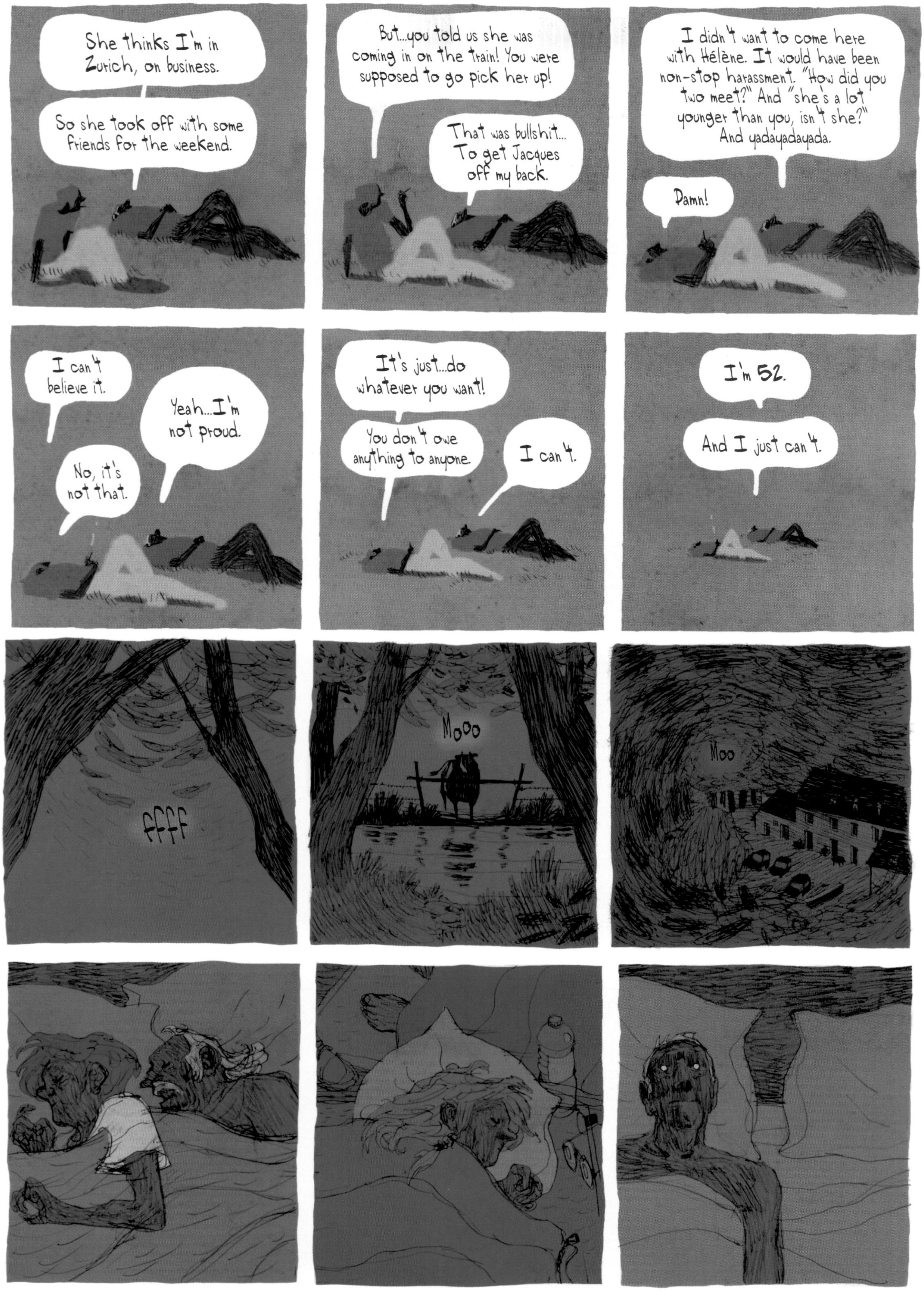
She thinks I'm in Zurich, on business.
So she took off with some friends for the weekend.
But...you told us she was coming in on the train! You were supposed to go pick her up!
That was bullshit... To get Jacques off my back.
I didn't want to come here with Hélène. It would have been non-stop harassment. "How did you two meet?" And "she's a lot younger than you, isn't she?" And yadayadayada.
Damn!
I can't believe it.
Yeah...I'm not proud.
No, it's not that.
It's just...do whatever you want!
You don't owe anything to anyone.
I can't.
I'm 52.
And I just can't.
ffff
Mooo
Moo

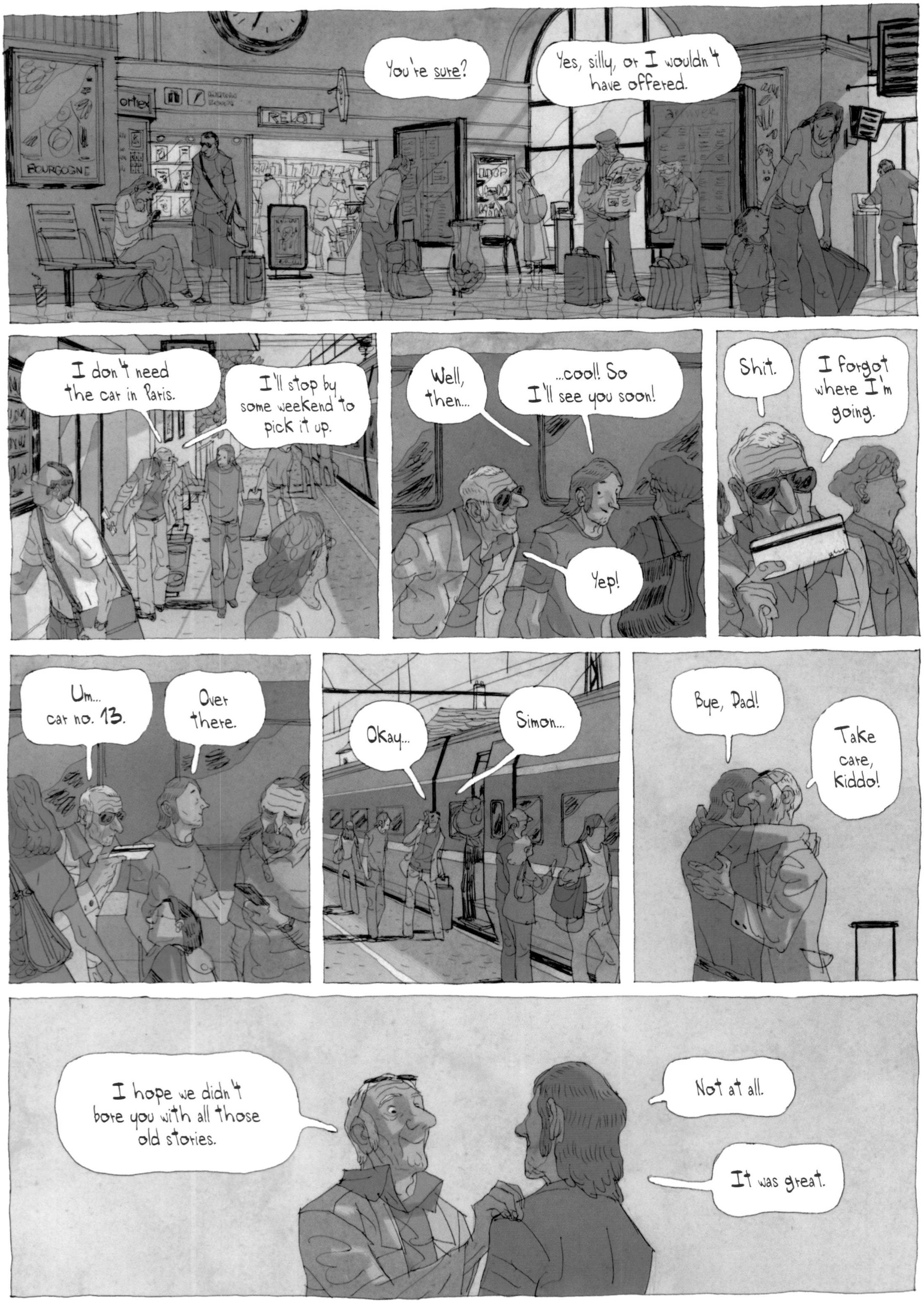
You're sure?
Yes, silly, or I wouldn't have offered.
I don't need the car in Paris.
I'll stop by some weekend to pick it up.
Well, then...
...cool! So I'll see you soon!
Yep!
Shit.
I forgot where I'm going.
Um... car no. 13.
Over there.
Okay...
Simon...
Bye, Dad!
Take care, kiddo!
I hope we didn't bore you with all those old stories.
Not at all.
It was great.

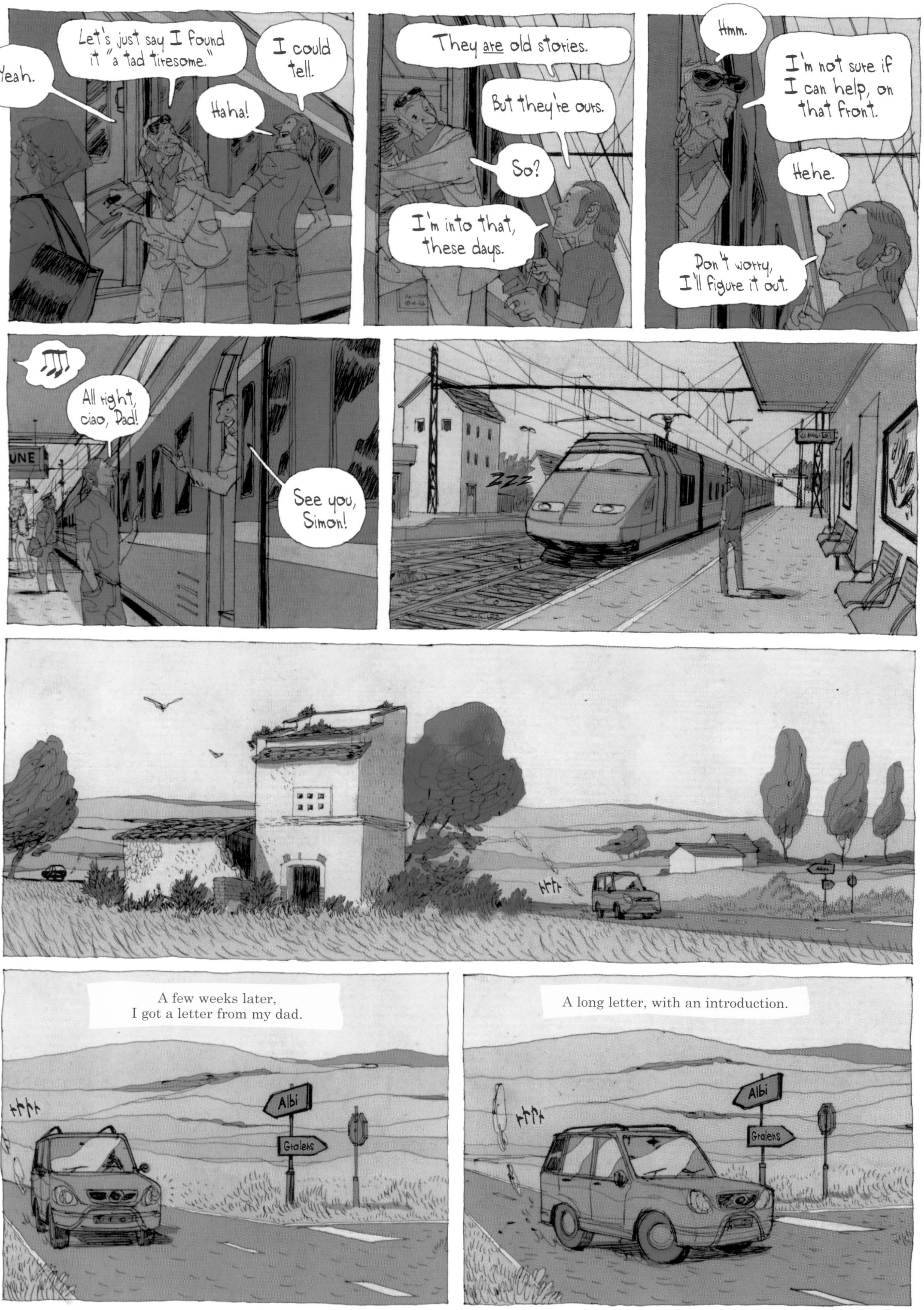
Yeah.
Let's just say I found it "a tad tiresome."
Haha!
I could tell.
They are old stories.
But they're ours.
So?
I'm into that, these days.
Hmm.
I'm not sure if I can help, on that front.
Hehe.
Don't worry, I'll figure it out.
All right, ciao, Dad!
See you, Simon!
ZZZ
A few weeks later,
I got a letter from my dad.
Albi
Graulhet
A long letter, with an introduction.
Albi
Graulhet

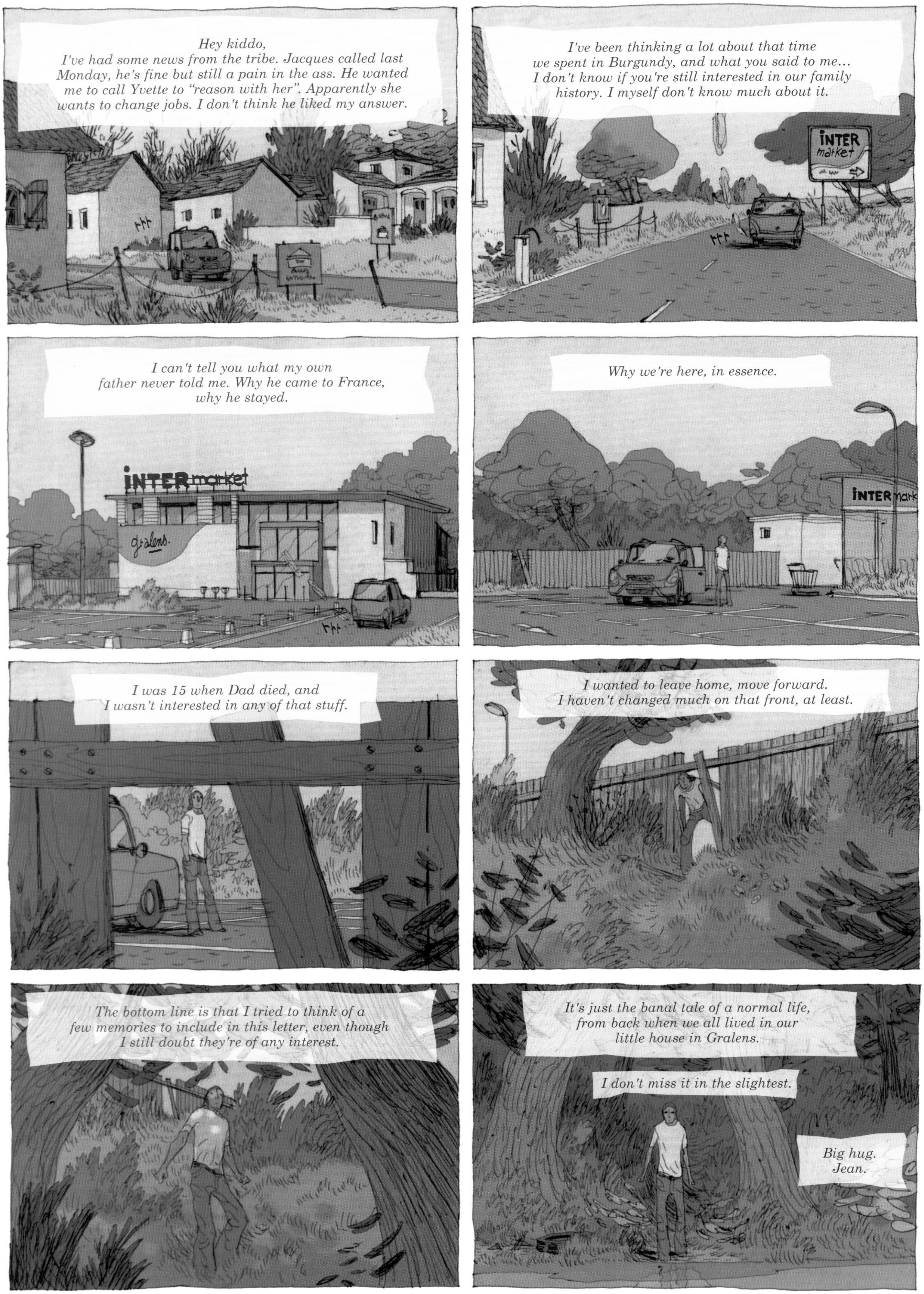
Hey kiddo,
I've had some news from the tribe. Jacques called last Monday, he's fine but still a pain in the ass. He wanted me to call Yvette to "reason with her". Apparently she wants to change jobs. I don't think he liked my answer.
I've been thinking a lot about that time we spent in Burgundy, and what you said to me… I don't know if you're still interested in our family history. I myself don't know much about it.
INTER market
I can't tell you what my own father never told me. Why he came to France, why he stayed.
INTERmarket
Gralens.
Why we're here, in essence.
INTER
I was 15 when Dad died, and I wasn't interested in any of that stuff.
I wanted to leave home, move forward. I haven't changed much on that front, at least.
The bottom line is that I tried to think of a few memories to include in this letter, even though I still doubt they're of any interest.
It's just the banal tale of a normal life, from back when we all lived in our little house in Gralens.
I don't miss it in the slightest.
Big hug.
Jean.

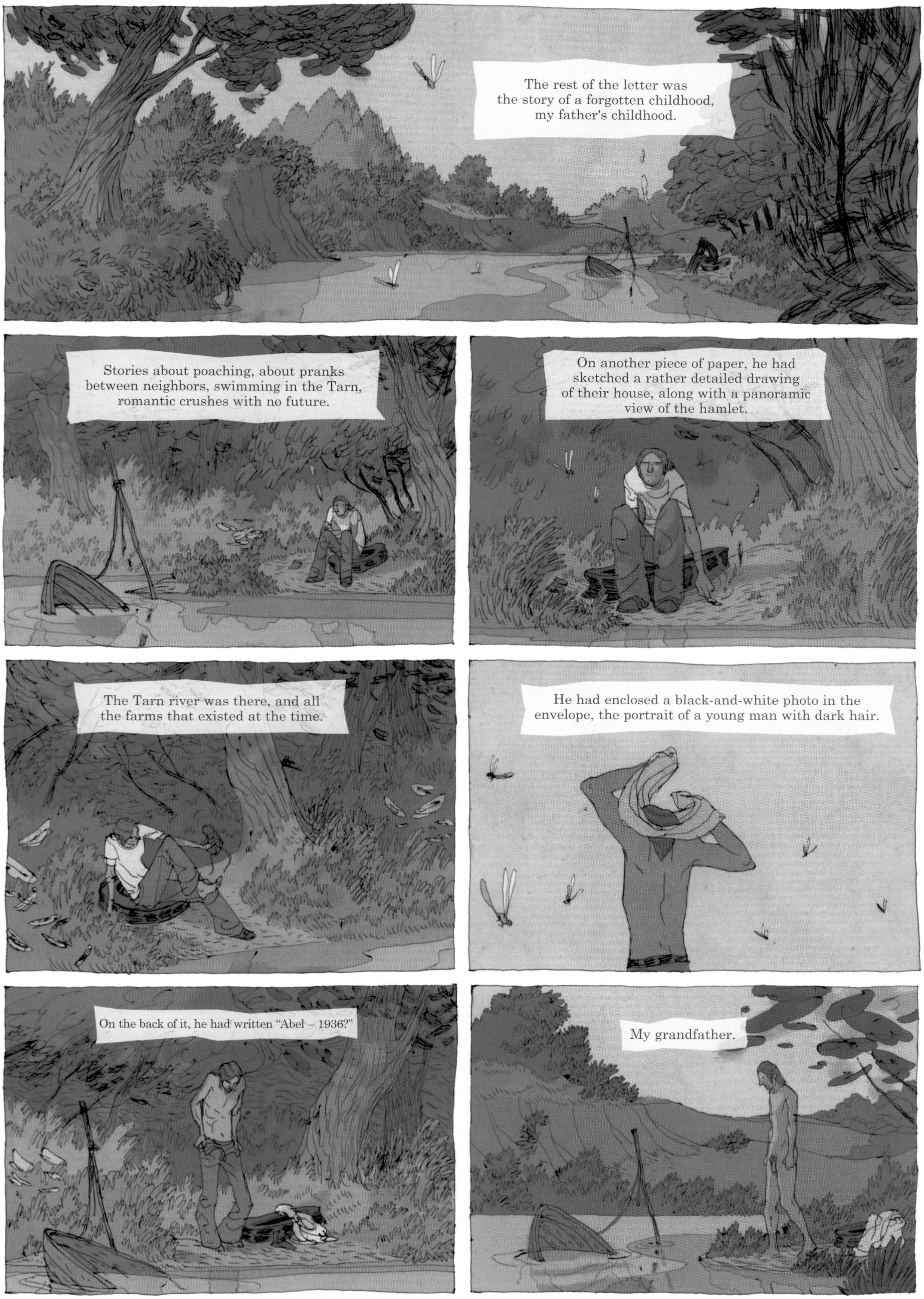
The rest of the letter was the story of a forgotten childhood, my father's childhood.
Stories about poaching, about pranks between neighbors, swimming in the Tarn, romantic crushes with no future.
On another piece of paper, he had sketched a rather detailed drawing of their house, along with a panoramic view of the hamlet.
The Tarn river was there, and all the farms that existed at the time.
He had enclosed a black-and-white photo in the envelope, the portrait of a young man with dark hair.
On the back of it, he had written "Abel – 1936?"
My grandfather.

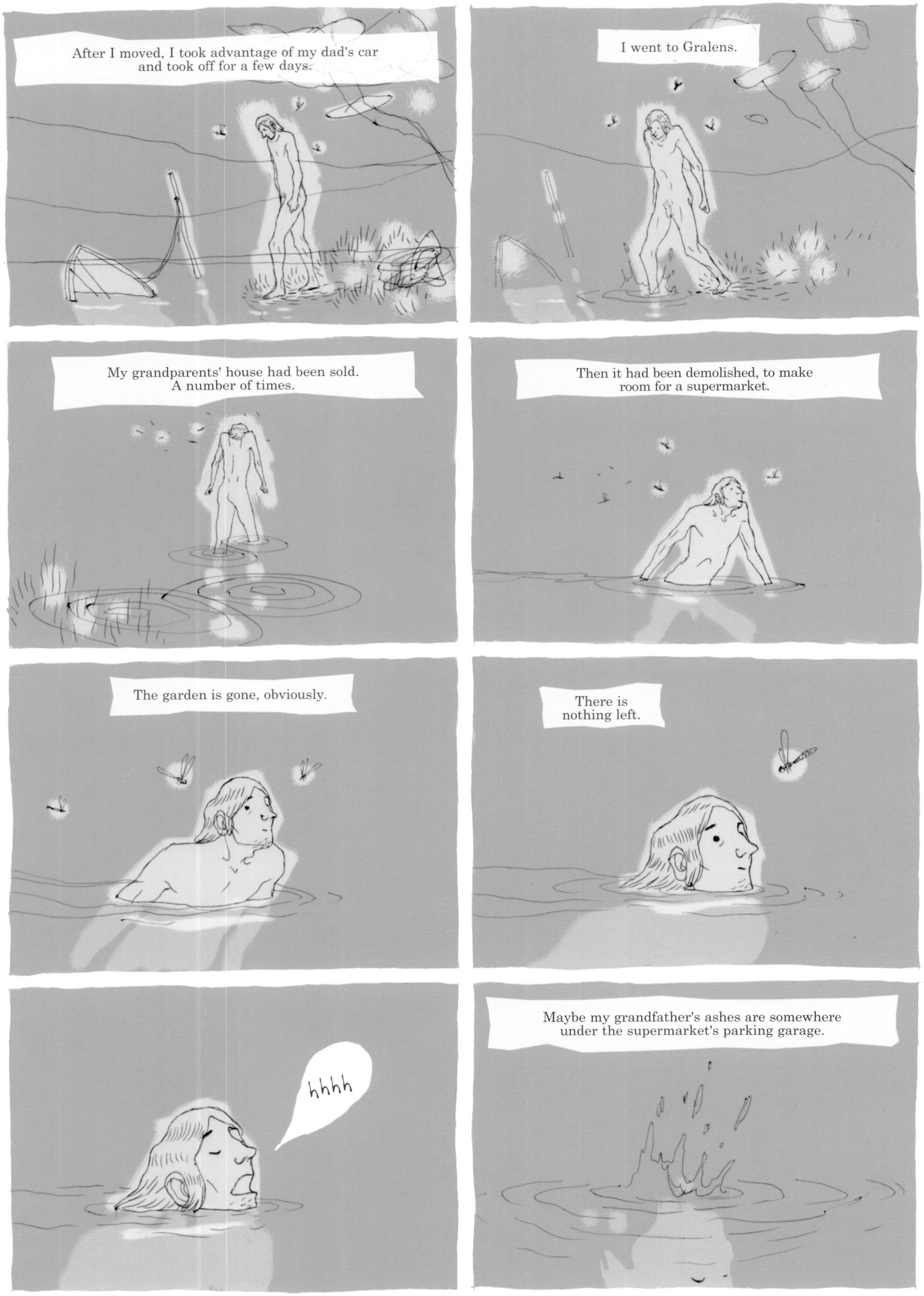
After I moved, I took advantage of my dad's car and took off for a few days.
I went to Gralens.
My grandparents' house had been sold. A number of times.
Then it had been demolished, to make room for a supermarket.
The garden is gone, obviously.
There is nothing left.
hhhh
Maybe my grandfather's ashes are somewhere under the supermarket's parking garage.

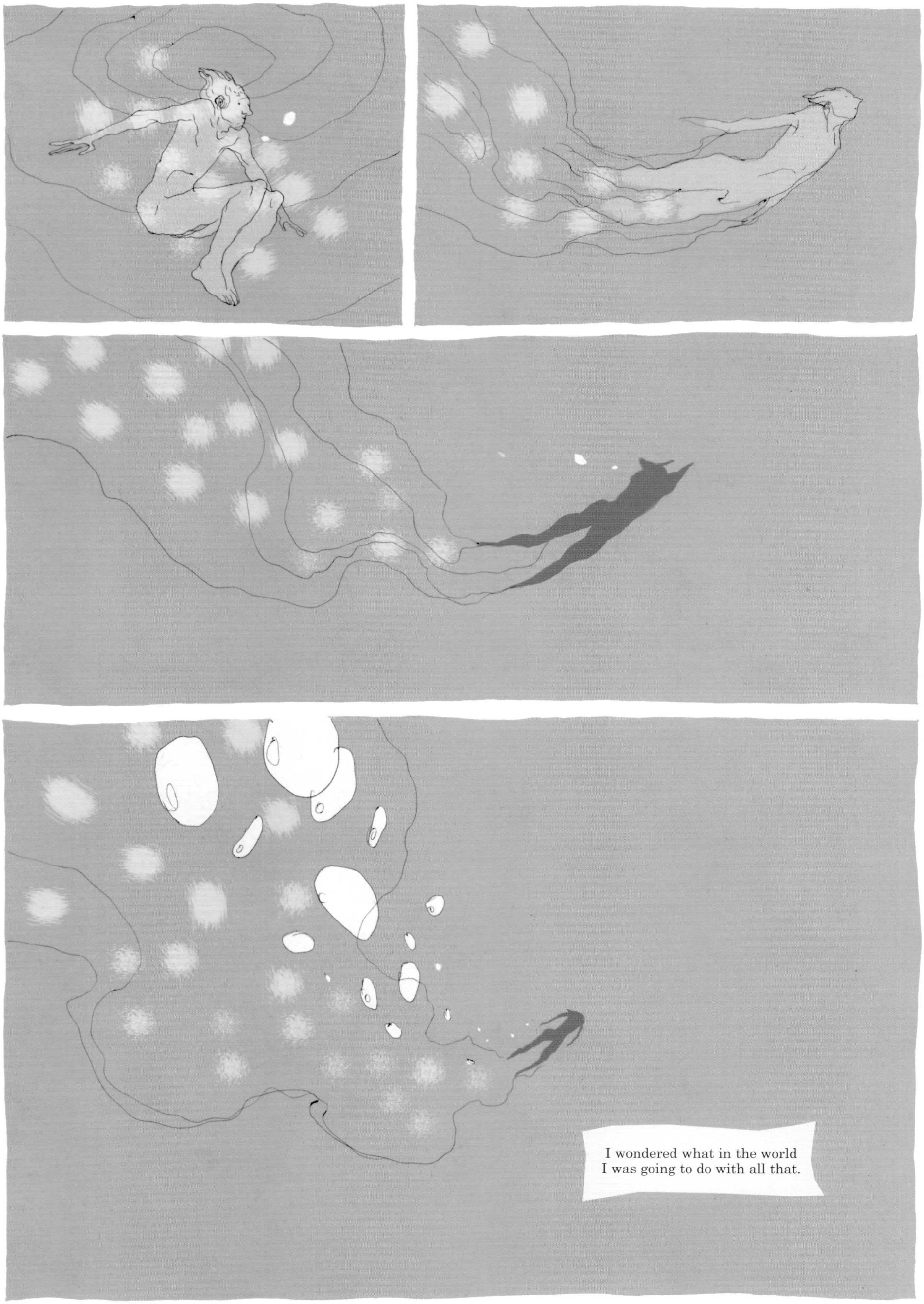
I wondered what in the world I was going to do with all that.

According to Abel

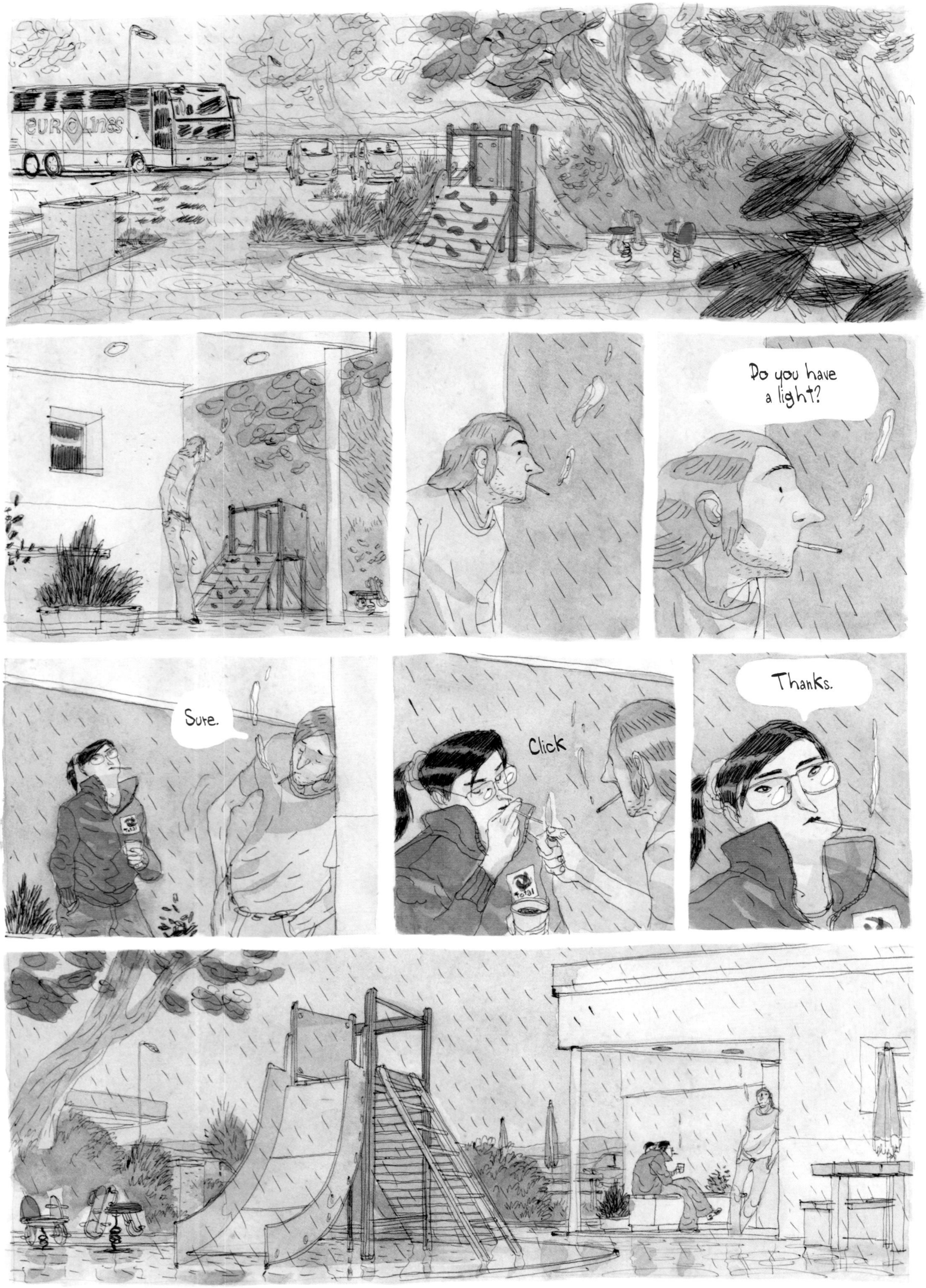
eurolines
Do you have a light?
Sure.
Click
Thanks.

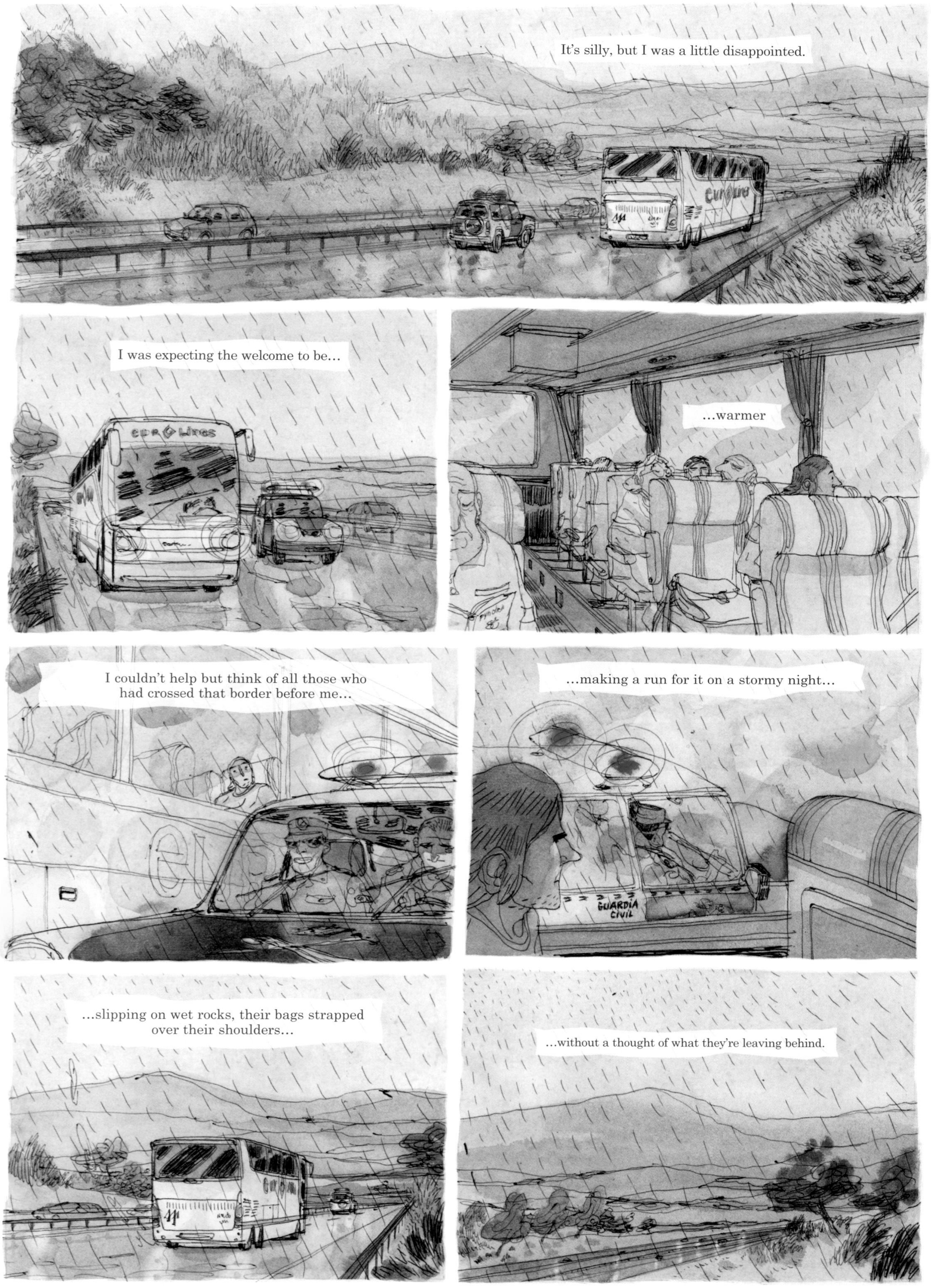
It's silly, but I was a little disappointed.
I was expecting the welcome to be...
...warmer
I couldn't help but think of all those who had crossed that border before me...
...making a run for it on a stormy night...
GUARDIA CIVIL
...slipping on wet rocks, their bags strapped over their shoulders...
...without a thought of what they're leaving behind.

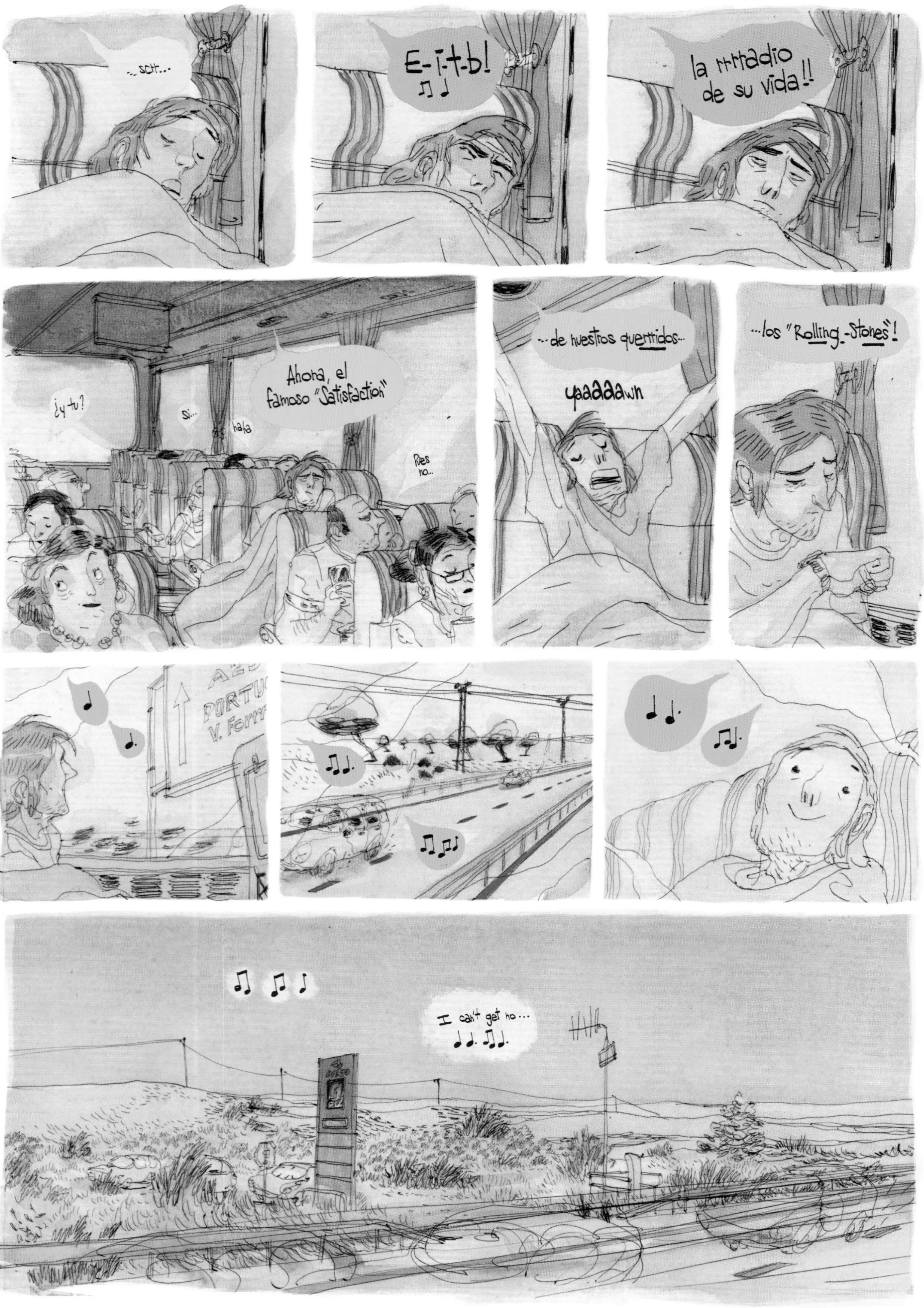
...scrr...
E-i-t-b!
la rrrradio de su vida!!
¿y tu?
si...
haha
Ahora, el famoso "Satisfaction"
Pues no...
...de nuestros querridos...
yaaaaawn
...los "Rolling-Stones"!
I can't get no...

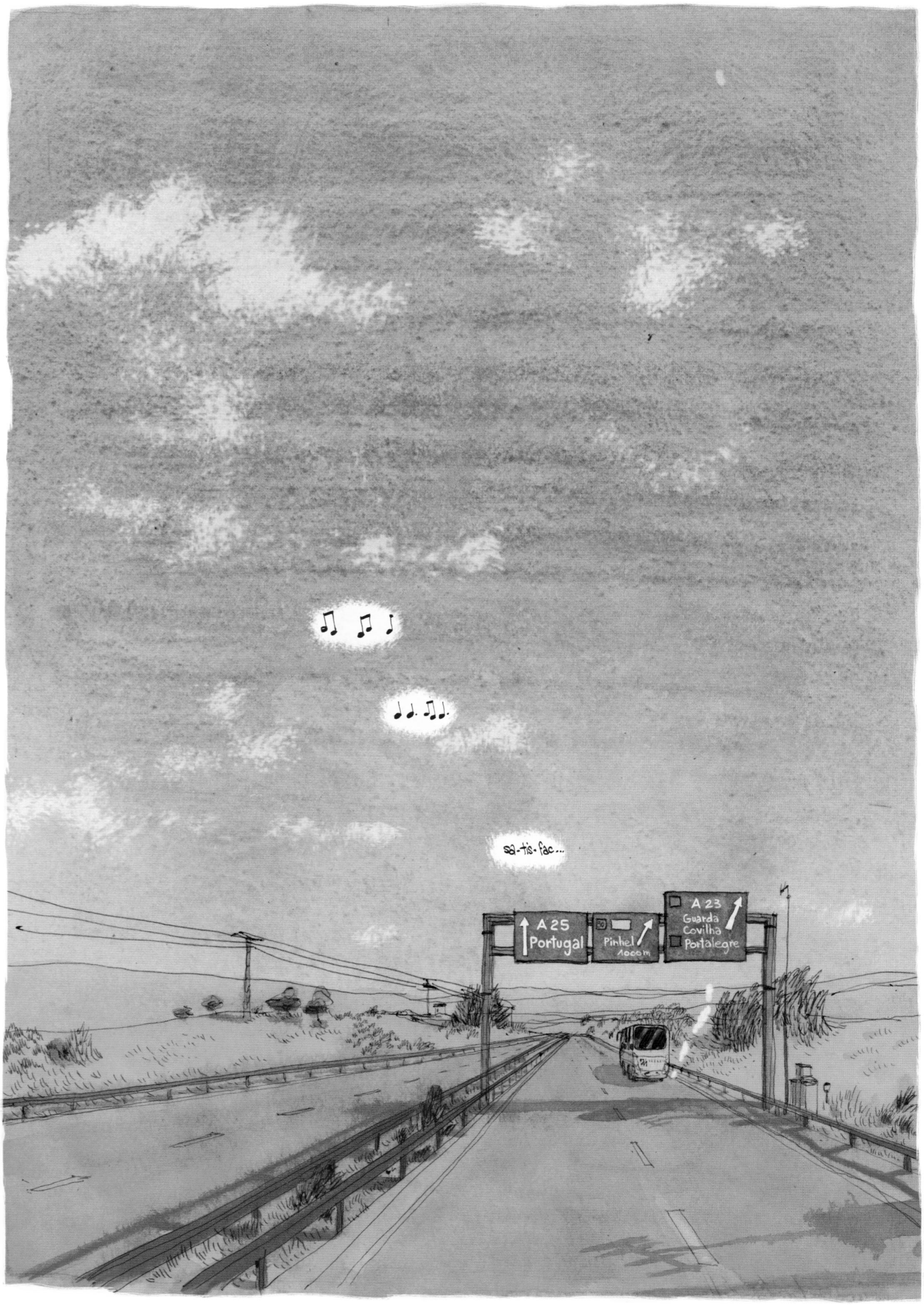
sa-tis-fac...
A 25
Portugal
Pinhel
1000 m
A 23
Guarda
Covilha
Portalegre

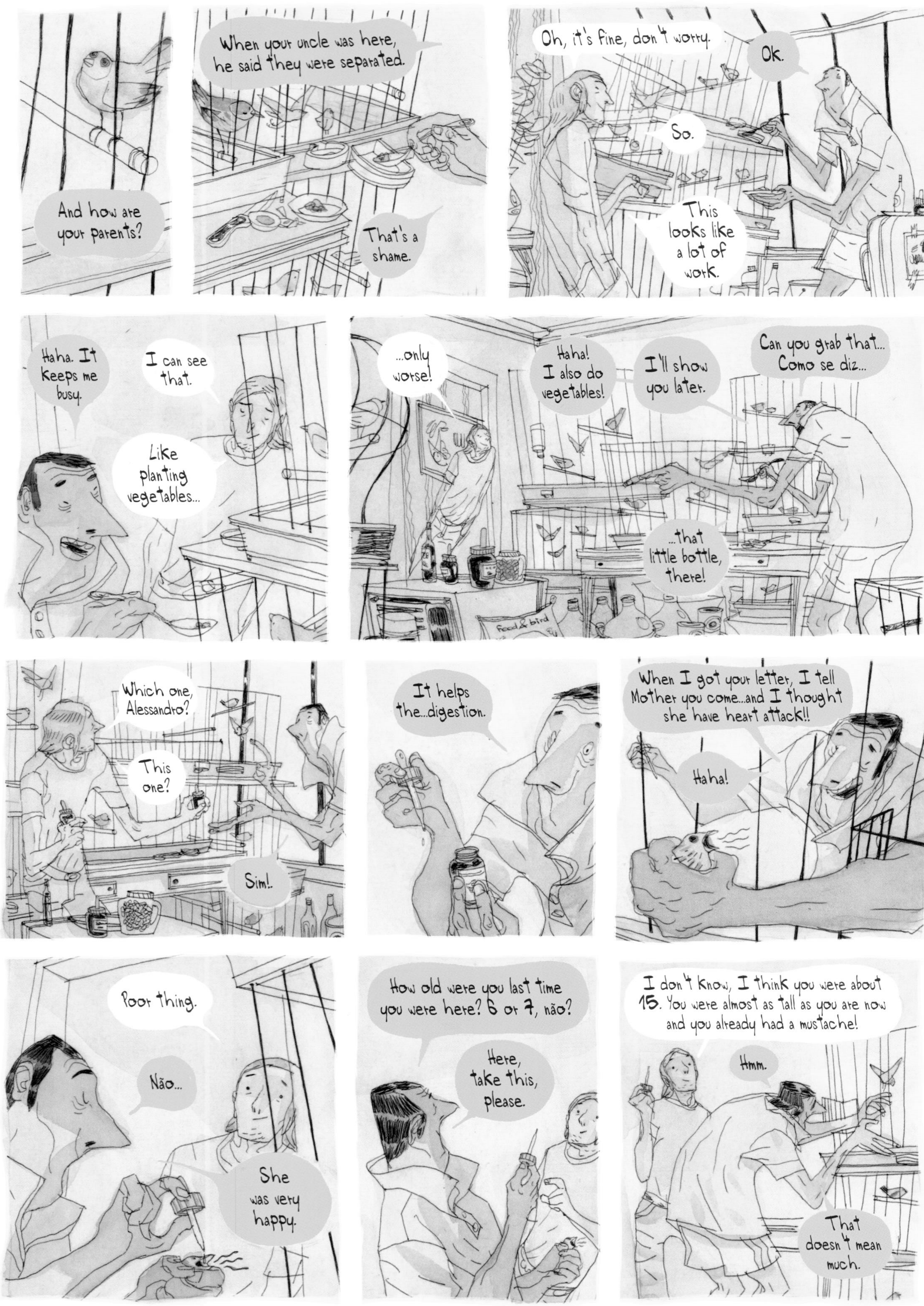
And how are your parents?
When your uncle was here, he said they were separated.
That's a shame.
Oh, it's fine, don't worry.
Ok.
So.
This looks like a lot of work.
Haha. It keeps me busy.
I can see that.
Like planting vegetables...
...only worse!
Haha! I also do vegetables!
I'll show you later.
Can you grab that... Como se diz...
...that little bottle, there!
Which one, Alessandro?
This one?
Sim!.
It helps the...digestion.
When I got your letter, I tell Mother you come...and I thought she have heart attack!!
Haha!
Poor thing.
Não...
She was very happy.
How old were you last time you were here? 6 or 7, não?
Here, take this, please.
I don't know, I think you were about 15. You were almost as tall as you are now and you already had a mustache!
Hmm.
That doesn't mean much.

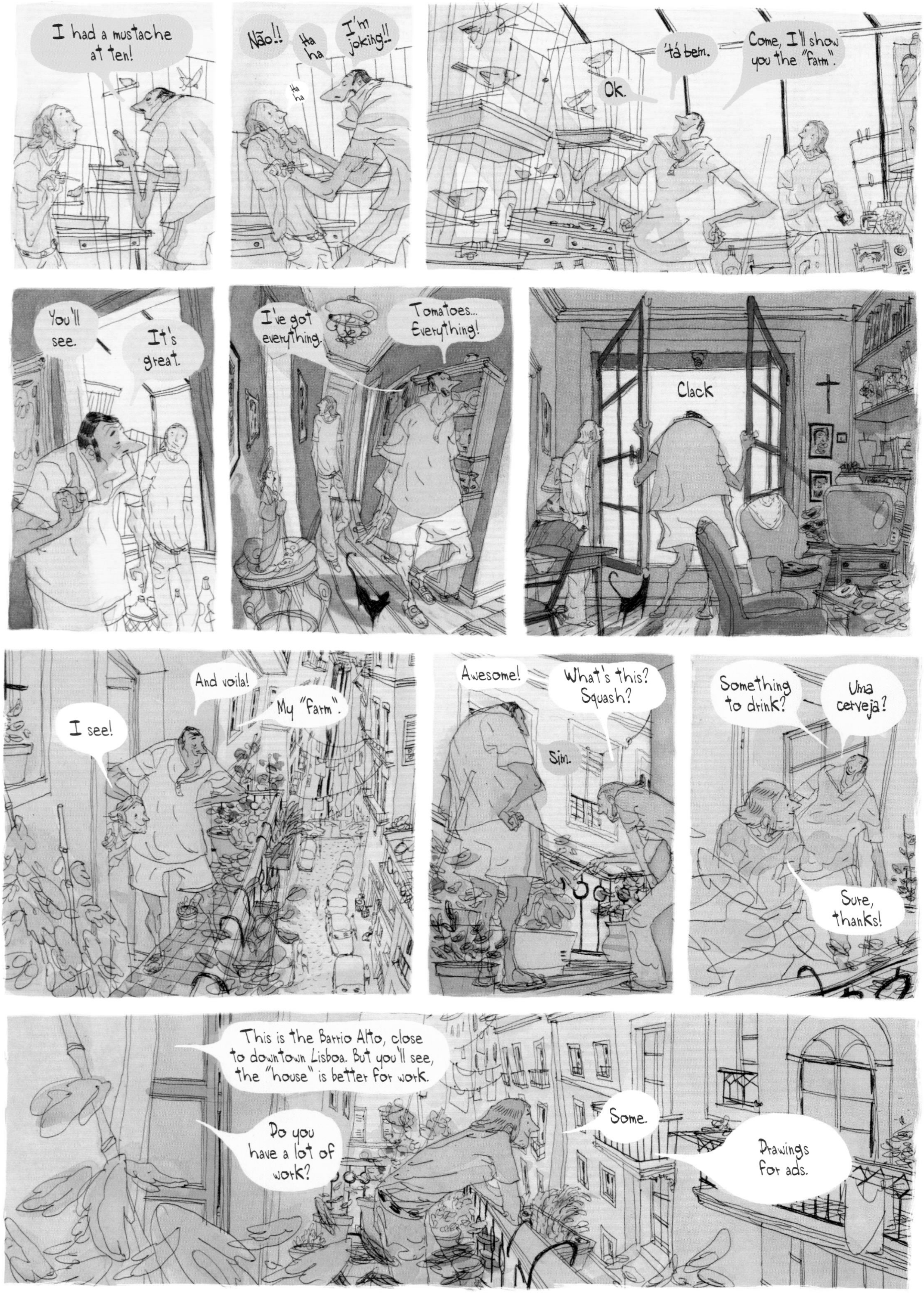
I had a mustache at ten!
Não!!
Ha ha
I'm joking!!
Ha ha
Ok.
'tá bem.
Come, I'll show you the "farm".
You'll see.
It's great.
I've got everything.
Tomatoes... Everything!
Clack
And voila!
My "farm".
I see!
Awesome!
What's this? Squash?
Sim.
Something to drink?
Uma cerveja?
Sure, thanks!
This is the Barrio Alto, close to downtown Lisboa. But you'll see, the "house" is better for work.
Do you have a lot of work?
Some.
Drawings for ads.

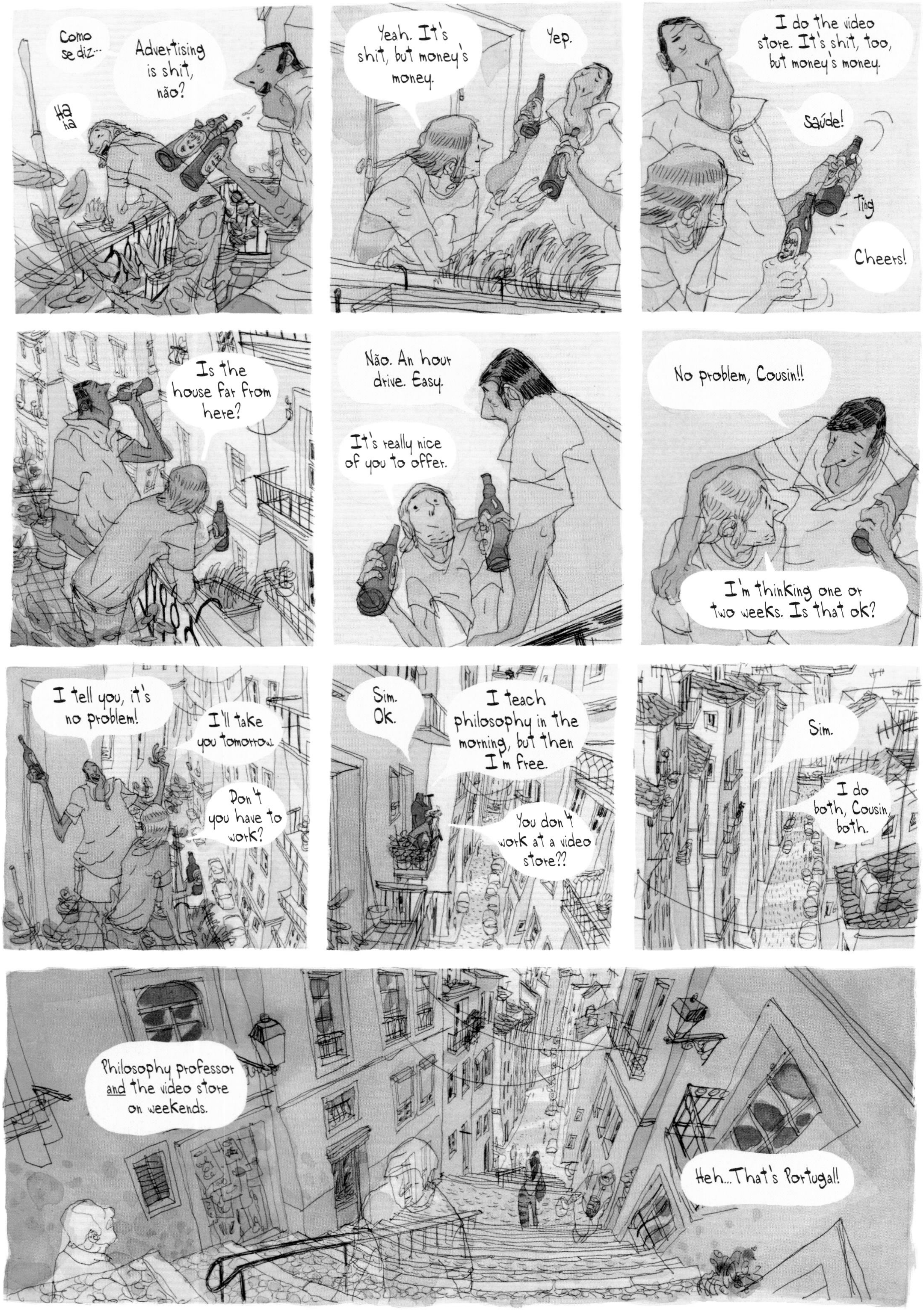

Como se diz...
Advertising is shit, não?
Ha ha
Yeah. It's shit, but money's money.
Yep.
I do the video store. It's shit, too, but money's money.
Saúde!
Ting
Cheers!
Is the house far from here?
Não. An hour drive. Easy.
It's really nice of you to offer.
No problem, Cousin!!
I'm thinking one or two weeks. Is that ok?
I tell you, it's no problem!
I'll take you tomorrow.
Don't you have to work?
Sim. Ok.
I teach philosophy in the morning, but then I'm free.
You don't work at a video store??
Sim.
I do both, Cousin, both.
Philosophy professor and the video store on weekends.
Heh...That's Portugal!

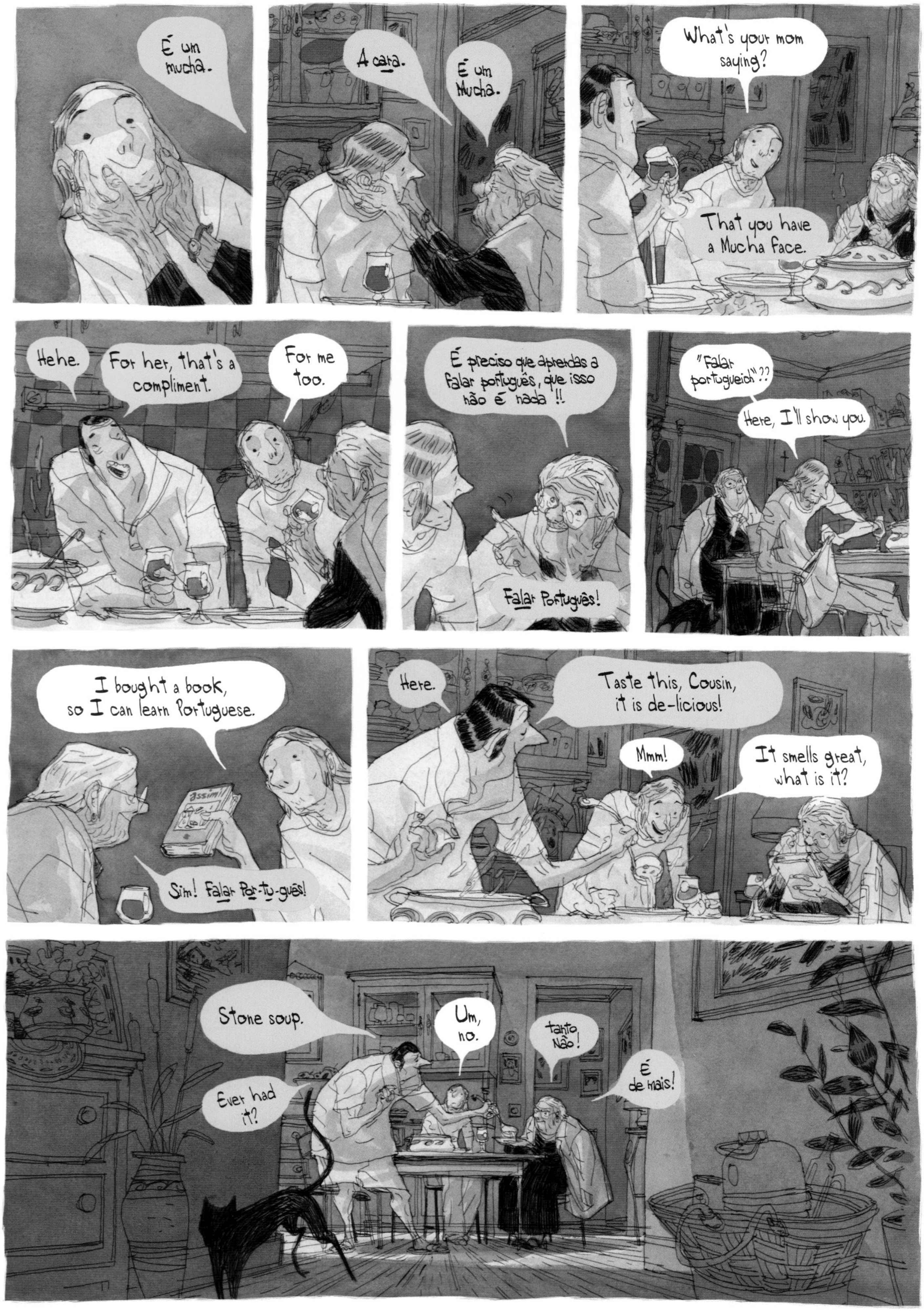
É um mucha.
A cara.
É um Mucha.
What's your mom saying?
That you have a Mucha face.
Hehe.
For her, that's a compliment.
For me too.
É preciso que aprendas a falar português, que isso não é nada !!
Falar Português!
"Falar portugueich"??
Here, I'll show you.
I bought a book, so I can learn Portuguese.
Sim! Falar Por-tu-guês!
Here.
Taste this, Cousin, it is de-licious!
Mmm!
It smells great, what is it?
Stone soup.
Ever had it?
Um, no.
tanto Não!
É de mais!

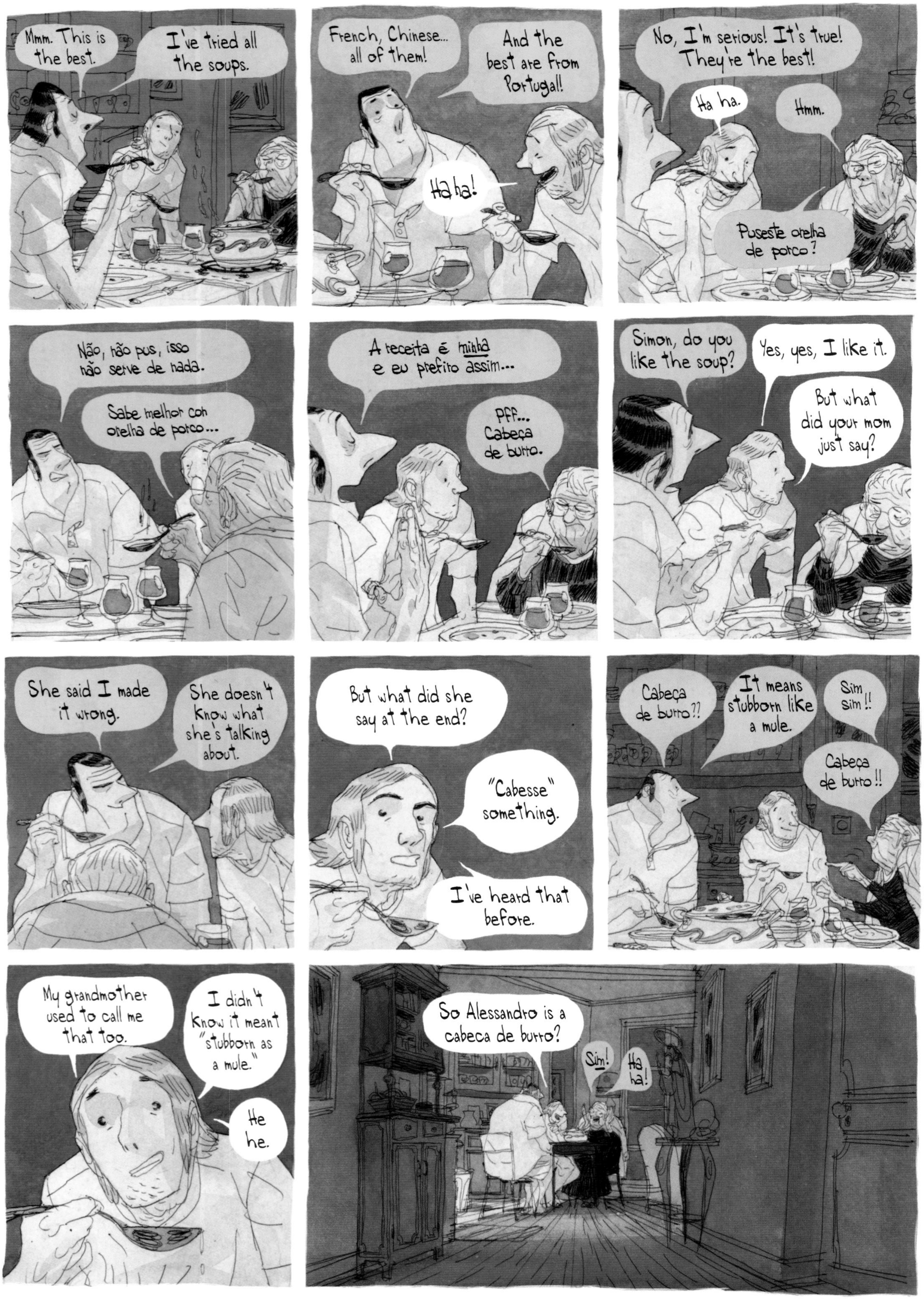
Mmm. This is the best.
I've tried all the soups.
French, Chinese... all of them!
And the best are from Portugal!
Ha ha!
No, I'm serious! It's true! They're the best!
Ha ha.
Hmm.
Puseste orelha de porco?
Não, não pus, isso não serve de nada.
Sabe melhor con orelha de porco...
A receita é minha e eu prefiro assim...
Pff... Cabeça de burro.
Simon, do you like the soup?
Yes, yes, I like it.
But what did your mom just say?
She said I made it wrong.
She doesn't know what she's talking about.
But what did she say at the end?
"Cabesse" something.
I've heard that before.
Cabeça de burro??
It means stubborn like a mule.
Sim sim!!
Cabeça de burro!!
My grandmother used to call me that too.
I didn't know it meant "stubborn as a mule."
He he.
So Alessandro is a cabeca de burro?
Sim!
Ha ha!

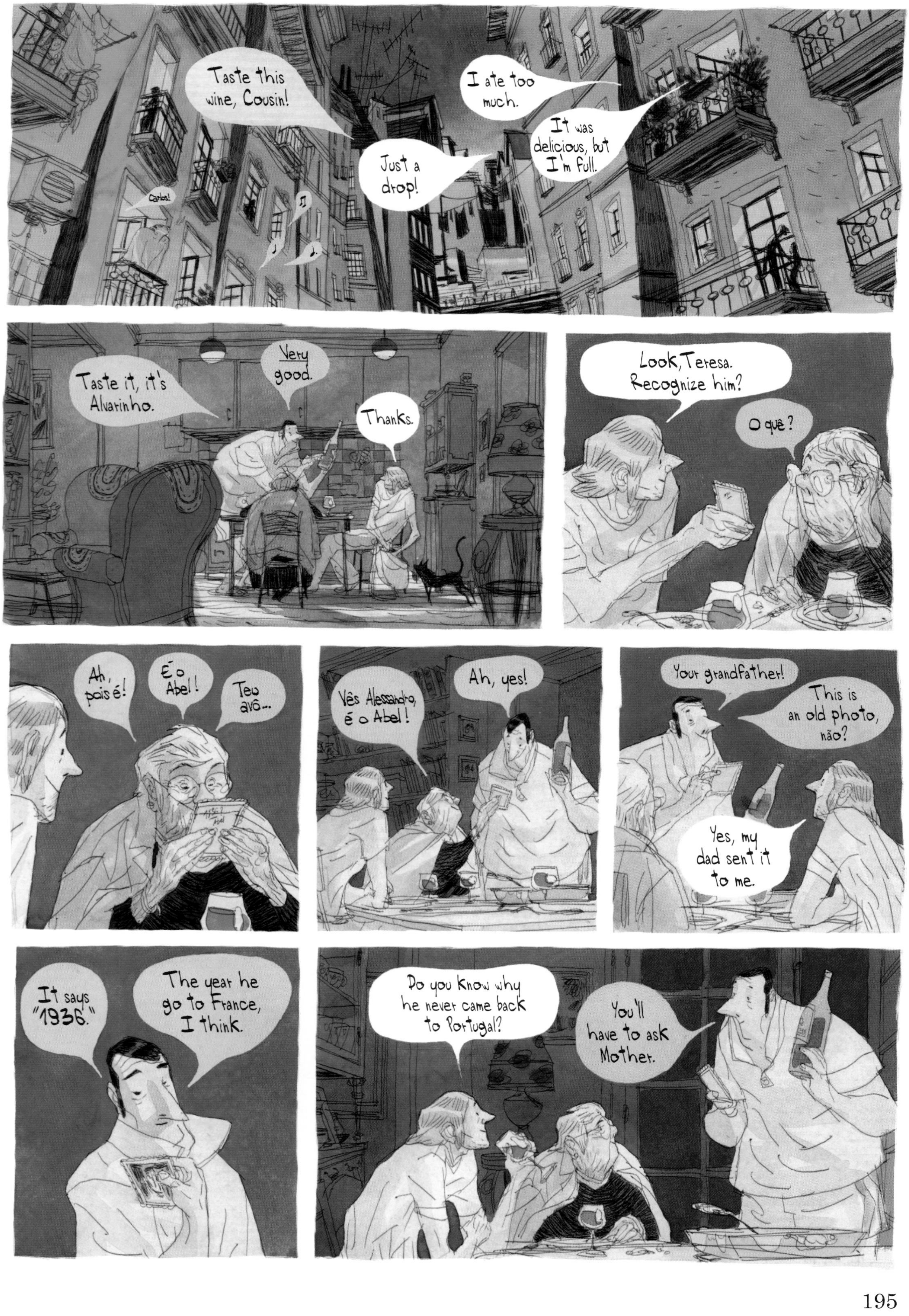
Taste this wine, Cousin!
Just a drop!
I ate too much.
It was delicious, but I'm full.
Carlos!
Taste it, it's Alvarinho.
Very good.
Thanks.
Look, Teresa. Recognize him?
O quê?
Ah, pois é!
É o Abel!
Teu avô...
Vês Alessandro, é o Abel!
Ah, yes!
Your grandfather!
This is an old photo, não?
Yes, my dad sent it to me.
It says "1936."
The year he go to France, I think.
Do you know why he never came back to Portugal?
You'll have to ask Mother.

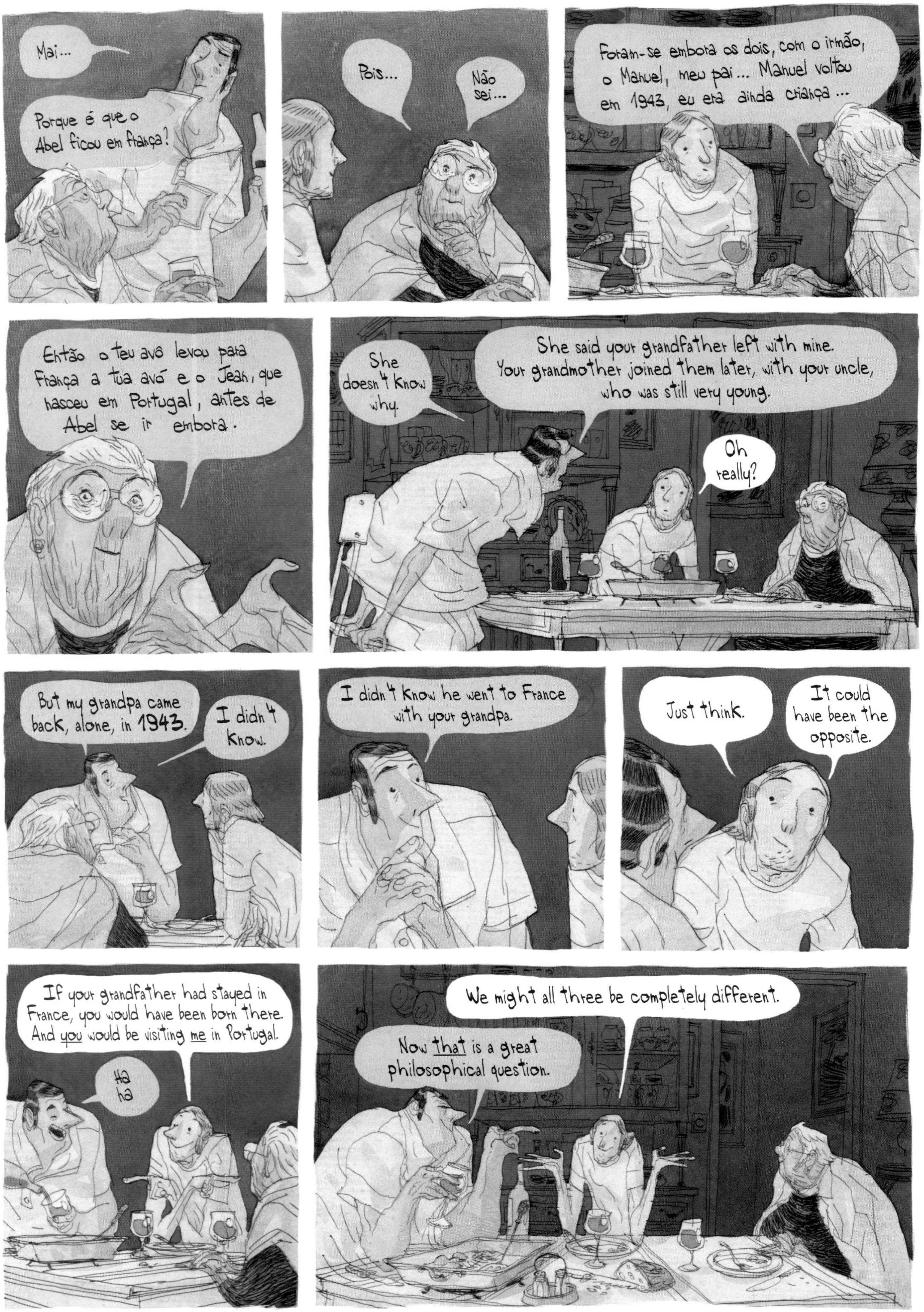

Mai...
Porque é que o Abel ficou em frança?
Pois...
Não sei...
Foram-se embora os dois, com o irmão, o Manuel, meu pai... Manuel voltou em 1943, eu era ainda criança...
Então o teu avô levou para França a tua avó e o Jean, que nasceu em Portugal, antes de Abel se ir embora.
She doesn't know why.
She said your grandfather left with mine. Your grandmother joined them later, with your uncle, who was still very young.
Oh really?
But my grandpa came back, alone, in 1943.
I didn't know.
I didn't know he went to France with your grandpa.
Just think.
It could have been the opposite.
If your grandfather had stayed in France, you would have been born there. And you would be visiting me in Portugal.
Ha ha
We might all three be completely different.
Now that is a great philosophical question.

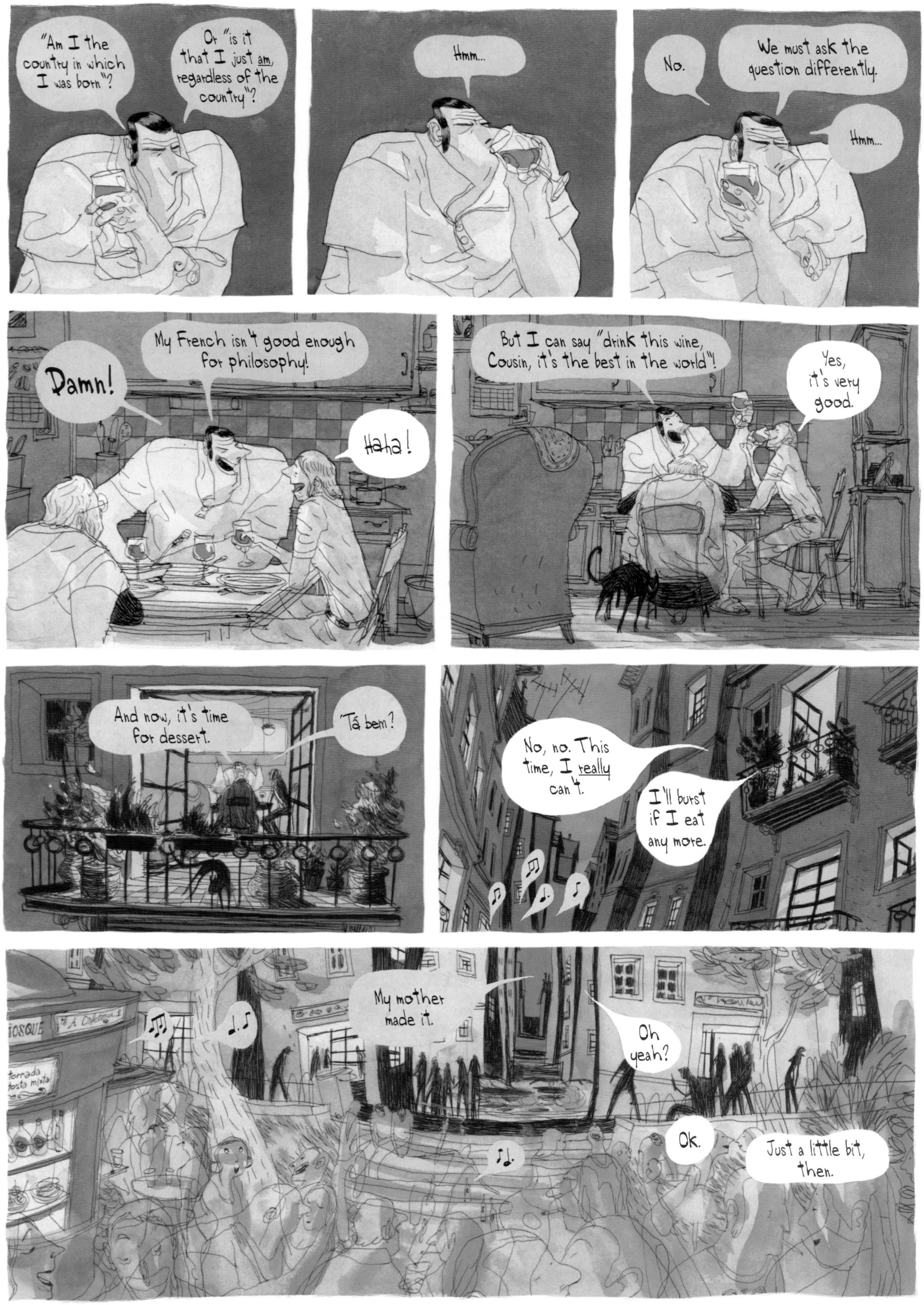
"Am I the country in which I was born"?
Or "is it that I just am, regardless of the country"?
Hmm...
No.
We must ask the question differently.
Hmm...
Damn!
My French isn't good enough for philosophy!
Haha!
But I can say "drink this wine, Cousin, it's the best in the world"!
Yes, it's very good.
And now, it's time for dessert.
'Tá bem?
No, no. This time, I really can't.
I'll burst if I eat any more.
QUIOSQUE
torrada tosta mixta
My mother made it.
Oh yeah?
Ok.
Just a little bit, then.

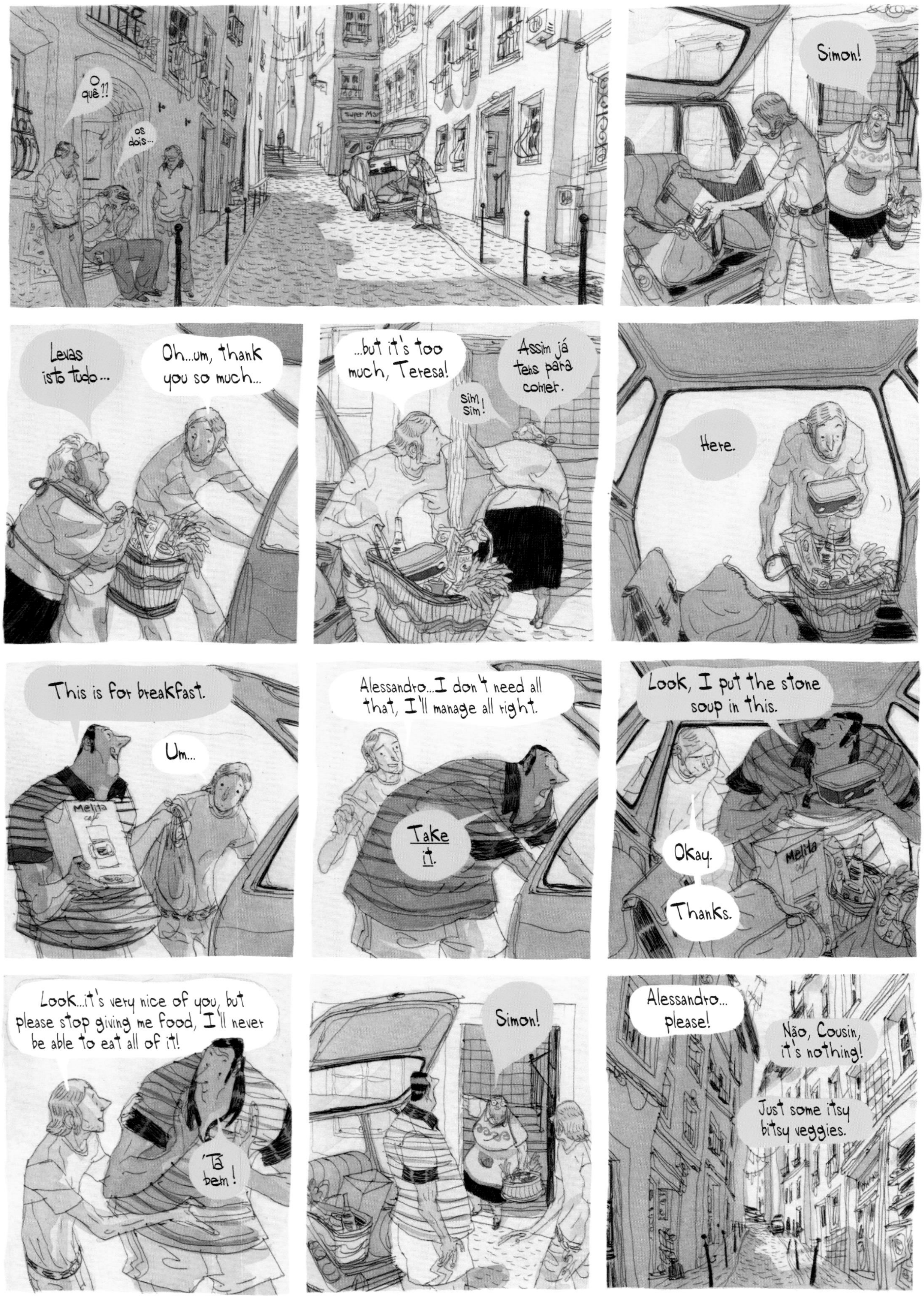
O quê?!
os dois...
Simon!
Levas isto tudo...
Oh...um, thank you so much...
...but it's too much, Teresa!
Assim já tens para comer.
Sim sim!
Here.
This is for breakfast.
Um...
Alessandro...I don't need all that, I'll manage all right.
Take it.
Look, I put the stone soup in this.
Okay.
Thanks.
Look...it's very nice of you, but please stop giving me food, I'll never be able to eat all of it!
'Tá bem!
Simon!
Alessandro... please!
Não, Cousin, it's nothing!
Just some itsy bitsy veggies.

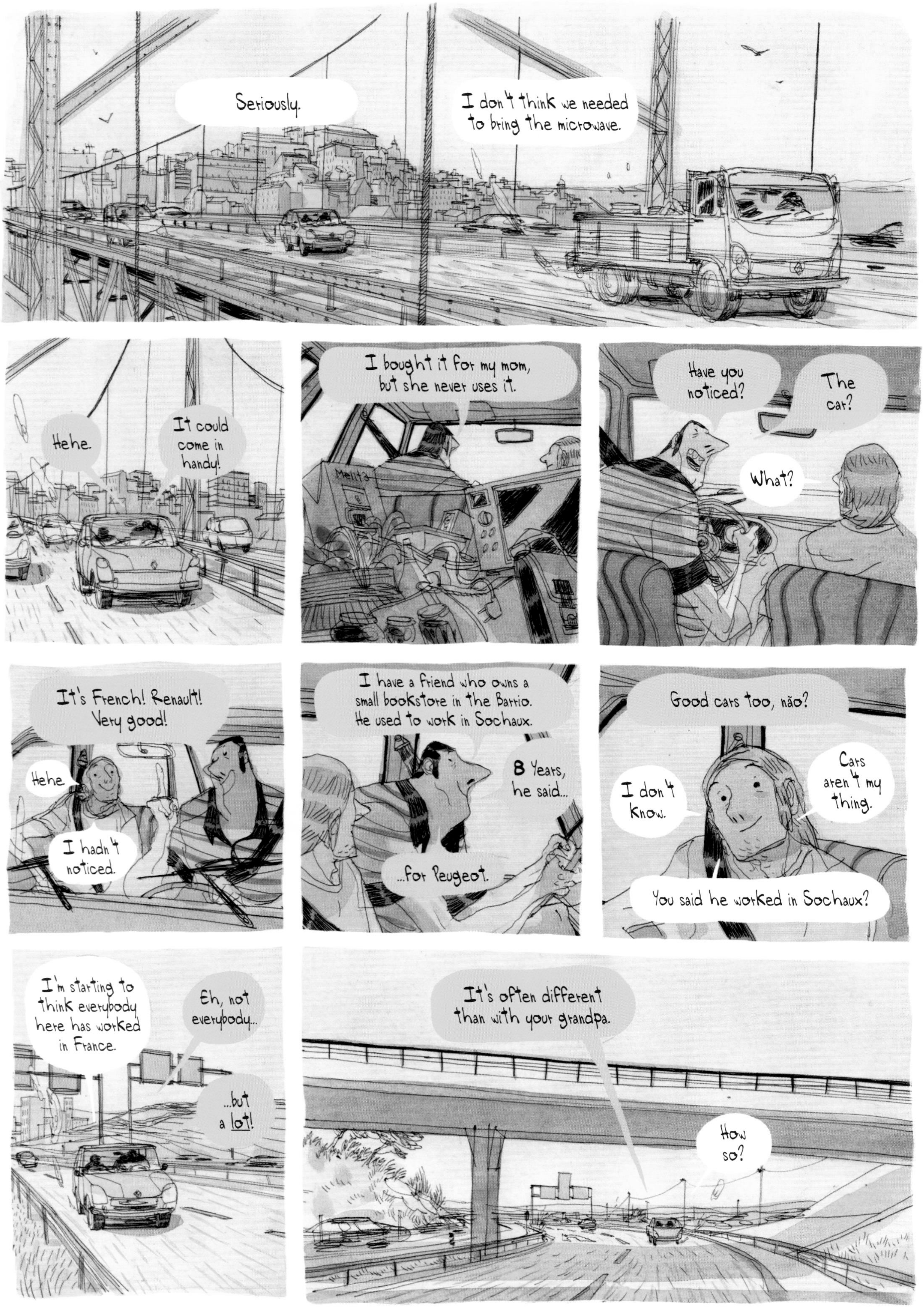
Seriously.
I don't think we needed to bring the microwave.
Hehe.
It could come in handy!
I bought it for my mom, but she never uses it.
Have you noticed?
The car?
What?
It's French! Renault! Very good!
Hehe.
I hadn't noticed.
I have a friend who owns a small bookstore in the Barrio. He used to work in Sochaux.
8 Years, he said...
...for Peugeot.
Good cars too, não?
I don't know.
Cars aren't my thing.
You said he worked in Sochaux?
I'm starting to think everybody here has worked in France.
Eh, not everybody...
...but a lot!
It's often different than with your grandpa.
How so?

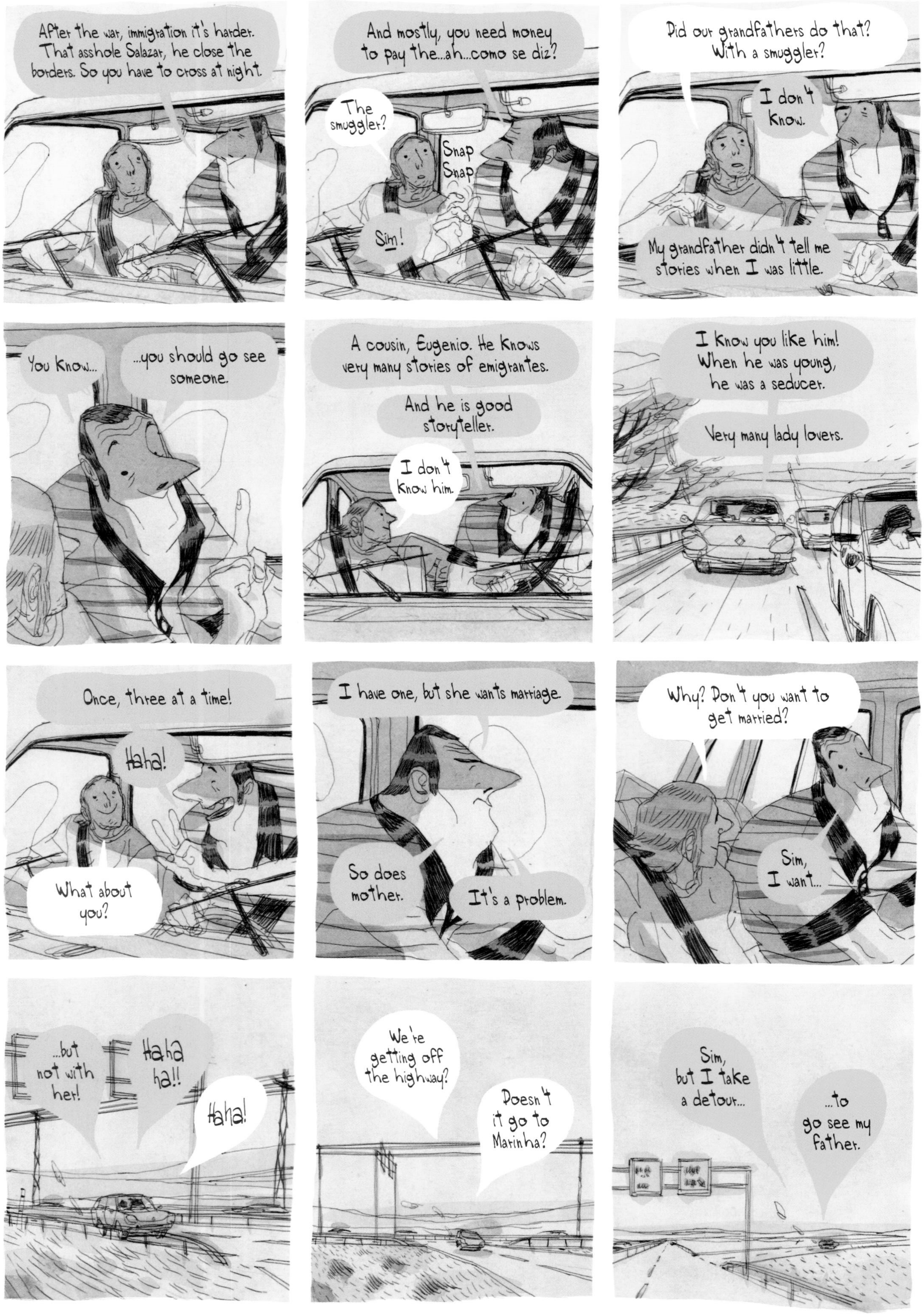
After the war, immigration it's harder. That asshole Salazar, he close the borders. So you have to cross at night.
And mostly, you need money to pay the...ah...como se diz?
The smuggler?
Snap Snap
Sim!
Did our grandfathers do that? With a smuggler?
I don't know.
My grandfather didn't tell me stories when I was little.
You know...
...you should go see someone.
A cousin, Eugenio. He knows very many stories of emigrantes.
And he is good storyteller.
I don't know him.
I know you like him! When he was young, he was a seducer.
Very many lady lovers.
Once, three at a time!
Haha!
What about you?
I have one, but she wants marriage.
So does mother.
It's a problem.
Why? Don't you want to get married?
Sim, I want...
...but not with her!
Haha ha!!
Haha!
We're getting off the highway?
Doesn't it go to Marinha?
Sim, but I take a detour...
...to go see my father.

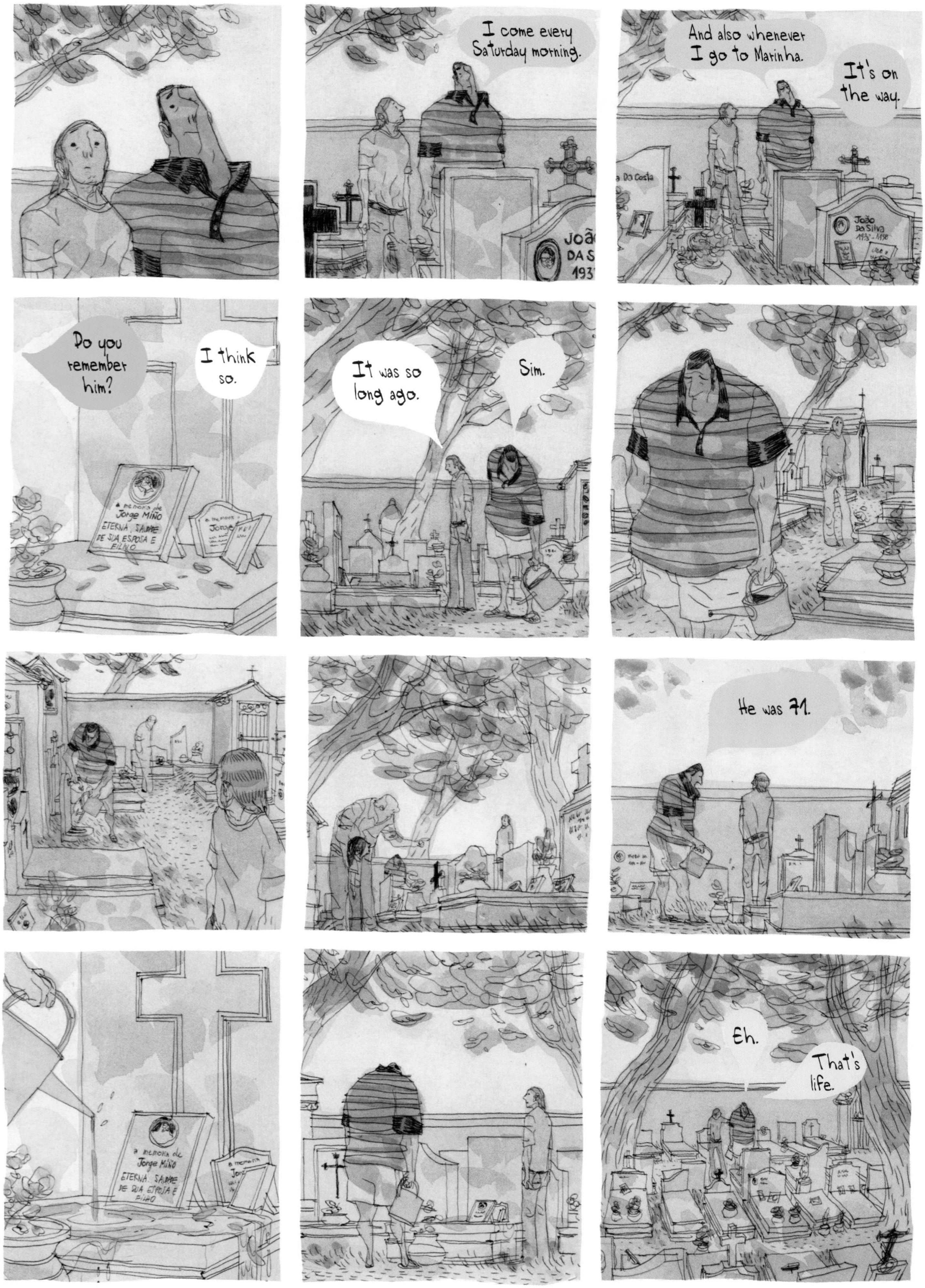
I come every Saturday morning.
And also whenever I go to Marinha.
It's on the way.
Do you remember him?
I think so.
It was so long ago.
Sim.
He was 71.
Eh.
That's life.

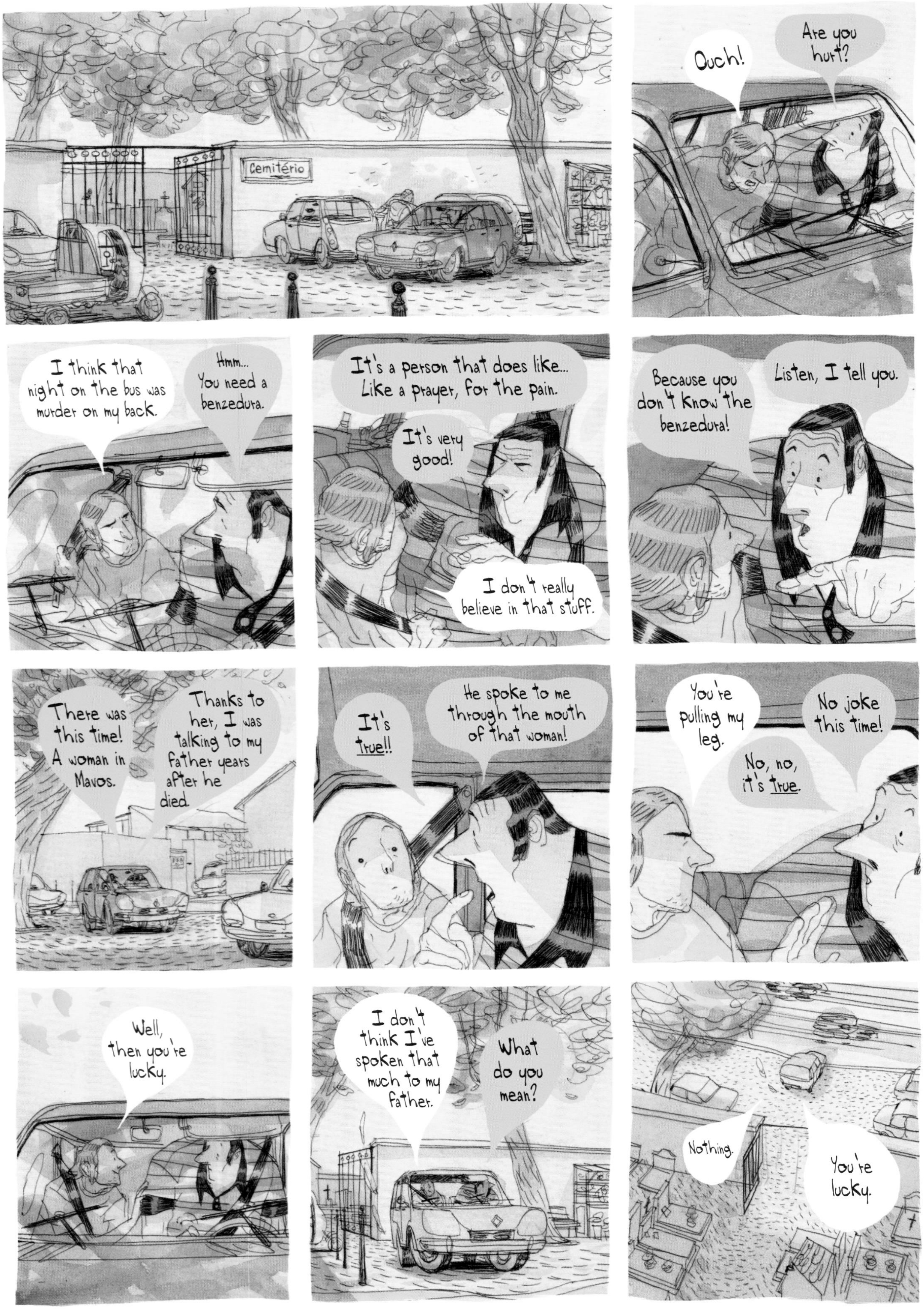
Cemitério
Ouch!
Are you hurt?
I think that night on the bus was murder on my back.
Hmm... You need a benzedura.
It's a person that does like... Like a prayer, for the pain.
It's very good!
I don't really believe in that stuff.
Because you don't know the benzedura!
Listen, I tell you.
There was this time! A woman in Mavos.
Thanks to her, I was talking to my father years after he died.
It's true!!
He spoke to me through the mouth of that woman!
You're pulling my leg.
No joke this time!
No, no, it's true.
Well, then you're lucky.
I don't think I've spoken that much to my father.
What do you mean?
Nothing.
You're lucky.

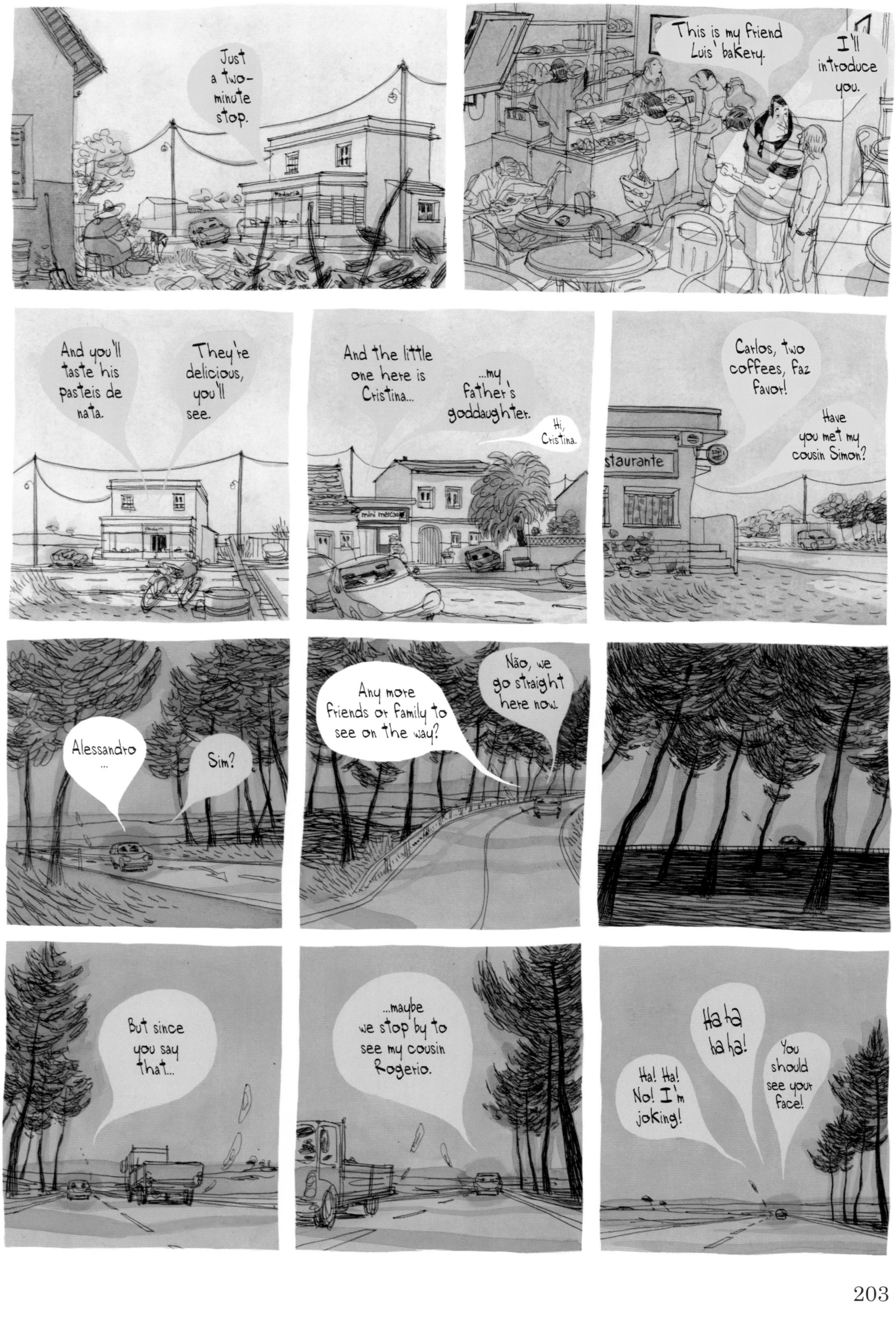
Just a two-minute stop.
This is my friend Luis' bakery.
I'll introduce you.
And you'll taste his pasteis de nata.
They're delicious, you'll see.
And the little one here is Cristina...
...my father's goddaughter.
Hi, Cristina.
Carlos, two coffees, faz favor!
Have you met my cousin Simon?
staurante
Alessandro ...
Sim?
Any more friends or family to see on the way?
Não, we go straight here now.
But since you say that...
...maybe we stop by to see my cousin Rogerio.
Ha ha ha ha!
Ha! Ha! No! I'm joking!
You should see your face!

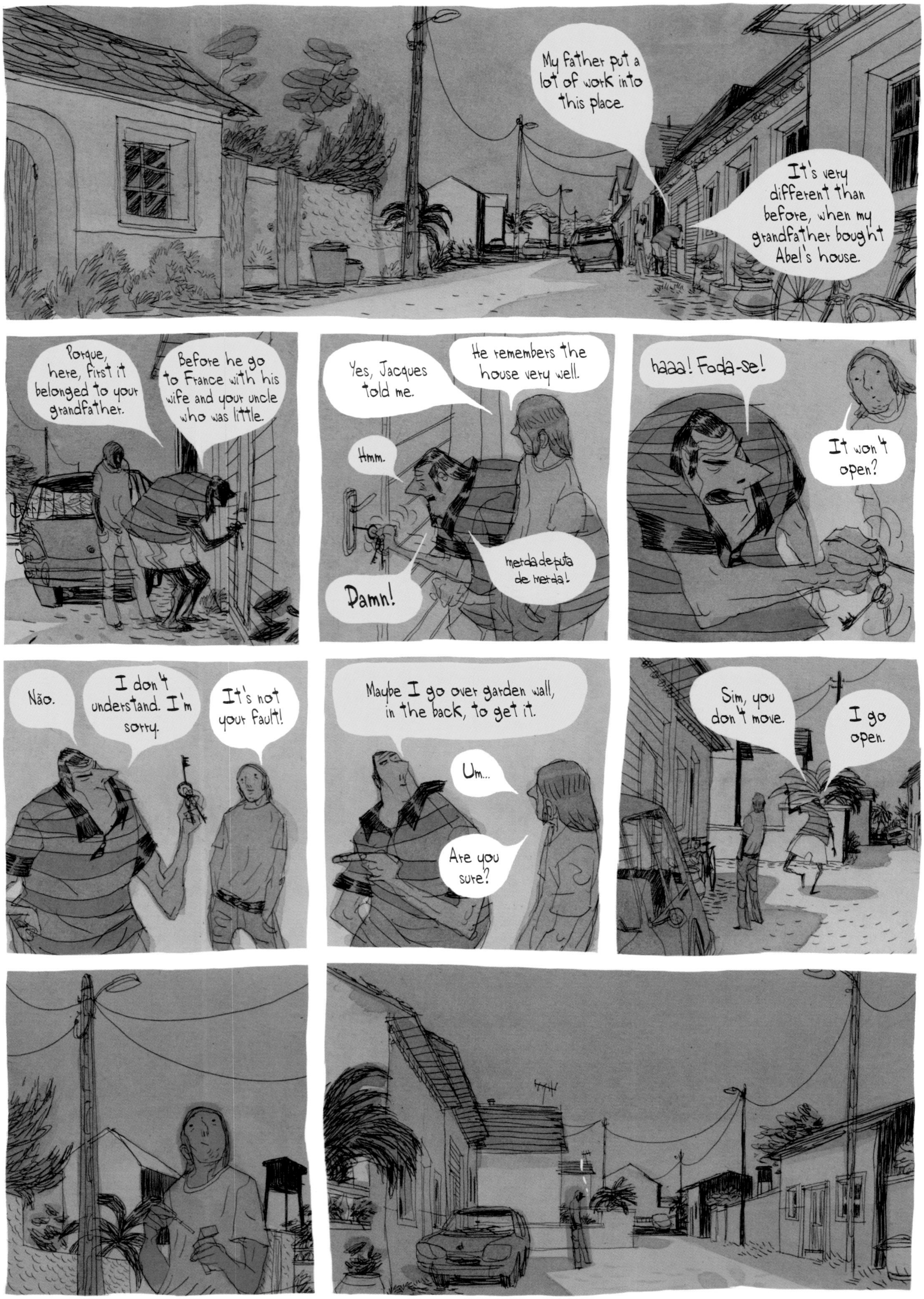
My father put a lot of work into this place.
It's very different than before, when my grandfather bought Abel's house.
Porque, here, first it belonged to your grandfather.
Before he go to France with his wife and your uncle who was little.
Yes, Jacques told me.
He remembers the house very well.
Hmm.
Damn!
merda de puta de merda!
haaa! Foda-se!
It won't open?
Não.
I don't understand. I'm sorry.
It's not your fault!
Maybe I go over garden wall, in the back, to get it.
Um...
Are you sure?
Sim, you don't move.
I go open.

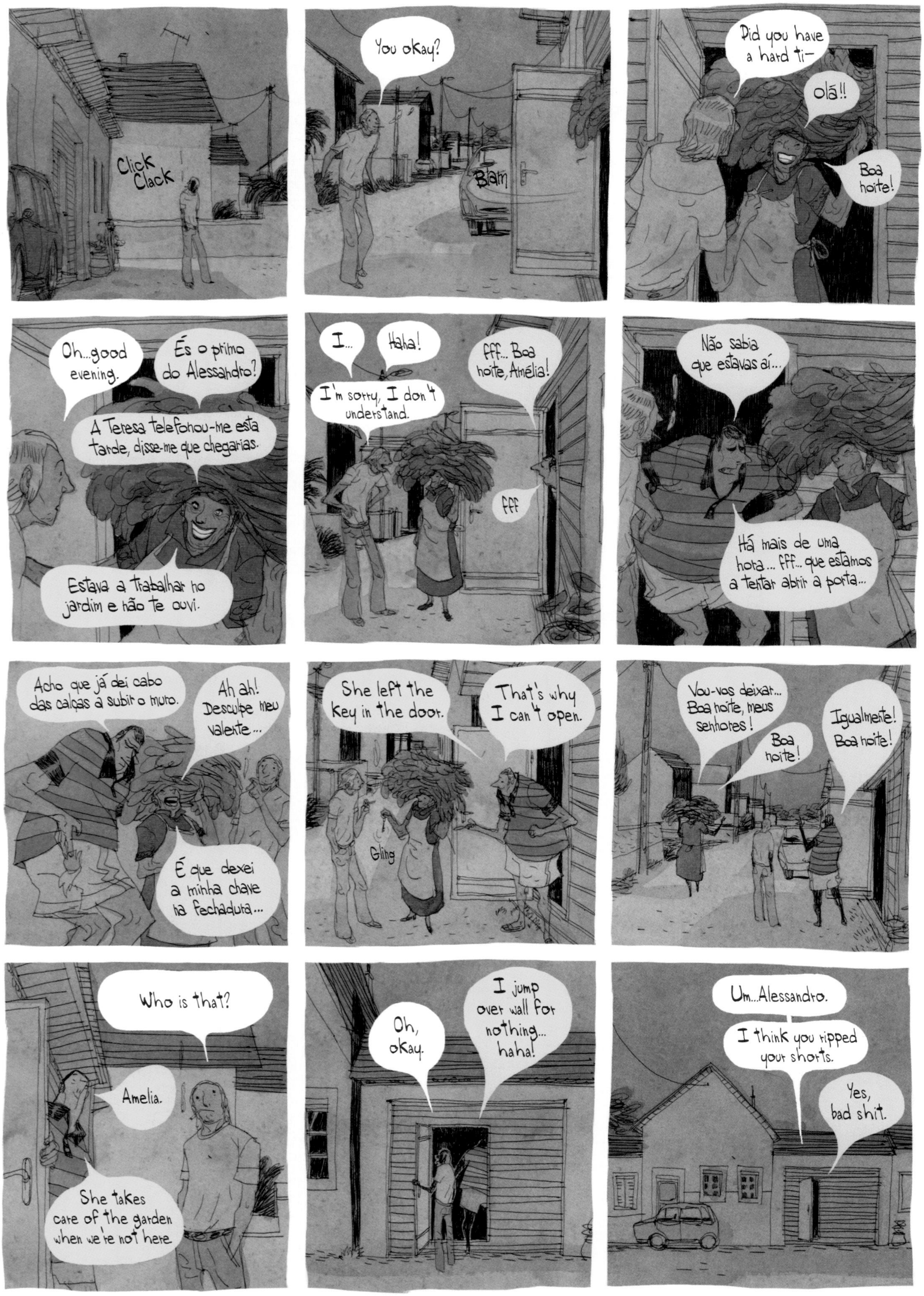

Click
Clack
You okay?
Blam
Did you have a hard ti–
Olá!!
Boa noite!
Oh...good evening.
És o primo do Alessandro?
A Teresa telefonou-me esta tarde, disse-me que chegarias.
Estava a trabalhar no jardim e não te ouvi.
I...
Haha!
I'm sorry, I don't understand.
fff... Boa noite, Amélia!
fff
Não sabia que estavas aí...
Há mais de uma hora... fff... que estamos a tentar abrir a porta...
Acho que já dei cabo das calças a subir o muro.
Ah ah! Desculpe meu valente...
É que dexei a minha chave na fechadura...
She left the key in the door.
That's why I can't open.
Gling
Vou-vos deixar... Boa noite, meus senhores!
Boa noite!
Igualmente! Boa noite!
Who is that?
Amelia.
She takes care of the garden when we're not here.
Oh, okay.
I jump over wall for nothing... haha!
Um...Alessandro.
I think you ripped your shorts.
Yes, bad shit.

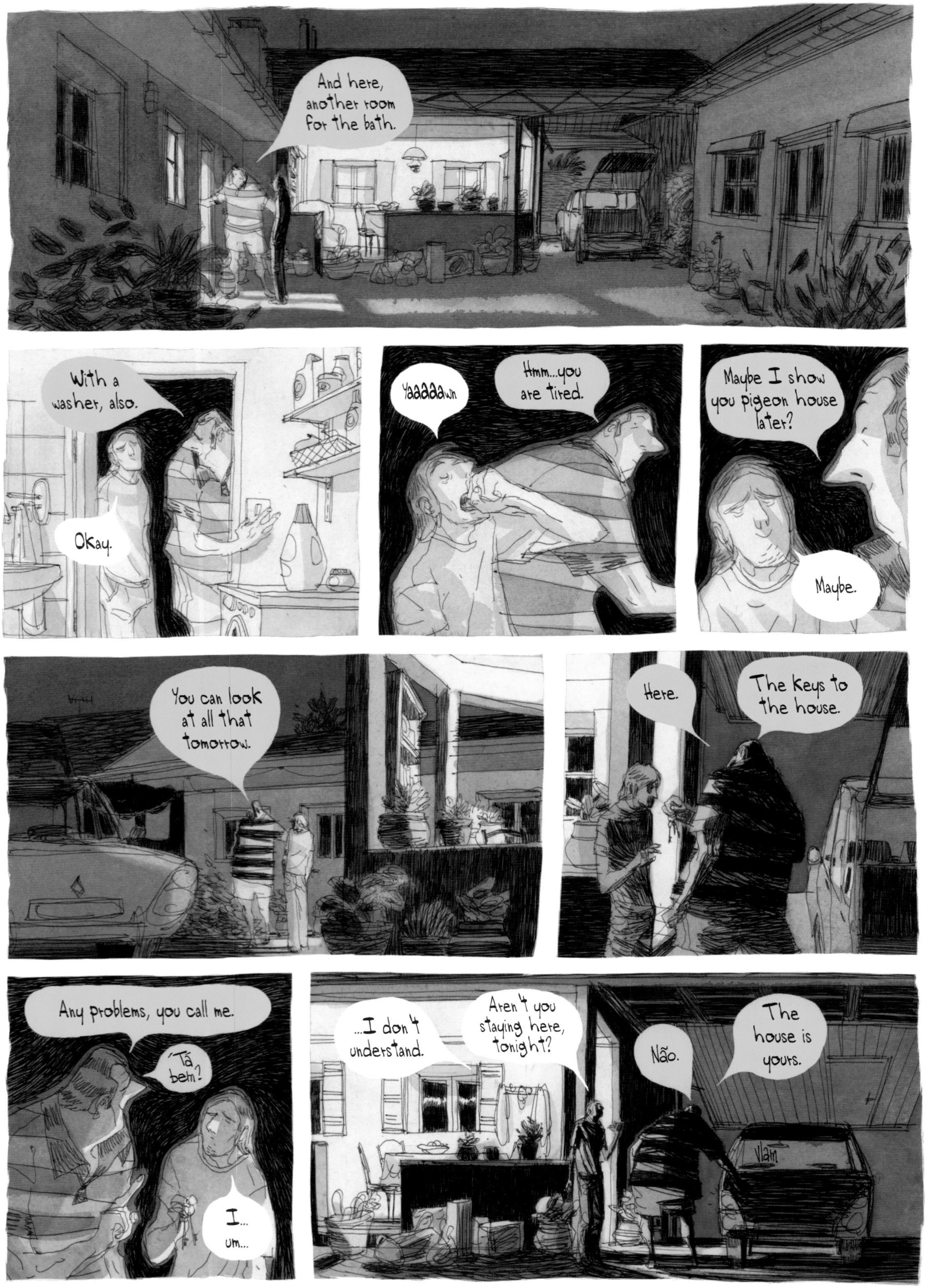
And here, another room for the bath.
With a washer, also.
Okay.
Yaaaaawn
Hmm...you are tired.
Maybe I show you pigeon house later?
Maybe.
You can look at all that tomorrow.
Here.
The keys to the house.
Any problems, you call me.
'Tá bem?
I... um...
Aren't you staying here, tonight?
...I don't understand.
Não.
The house is yours.
vlam

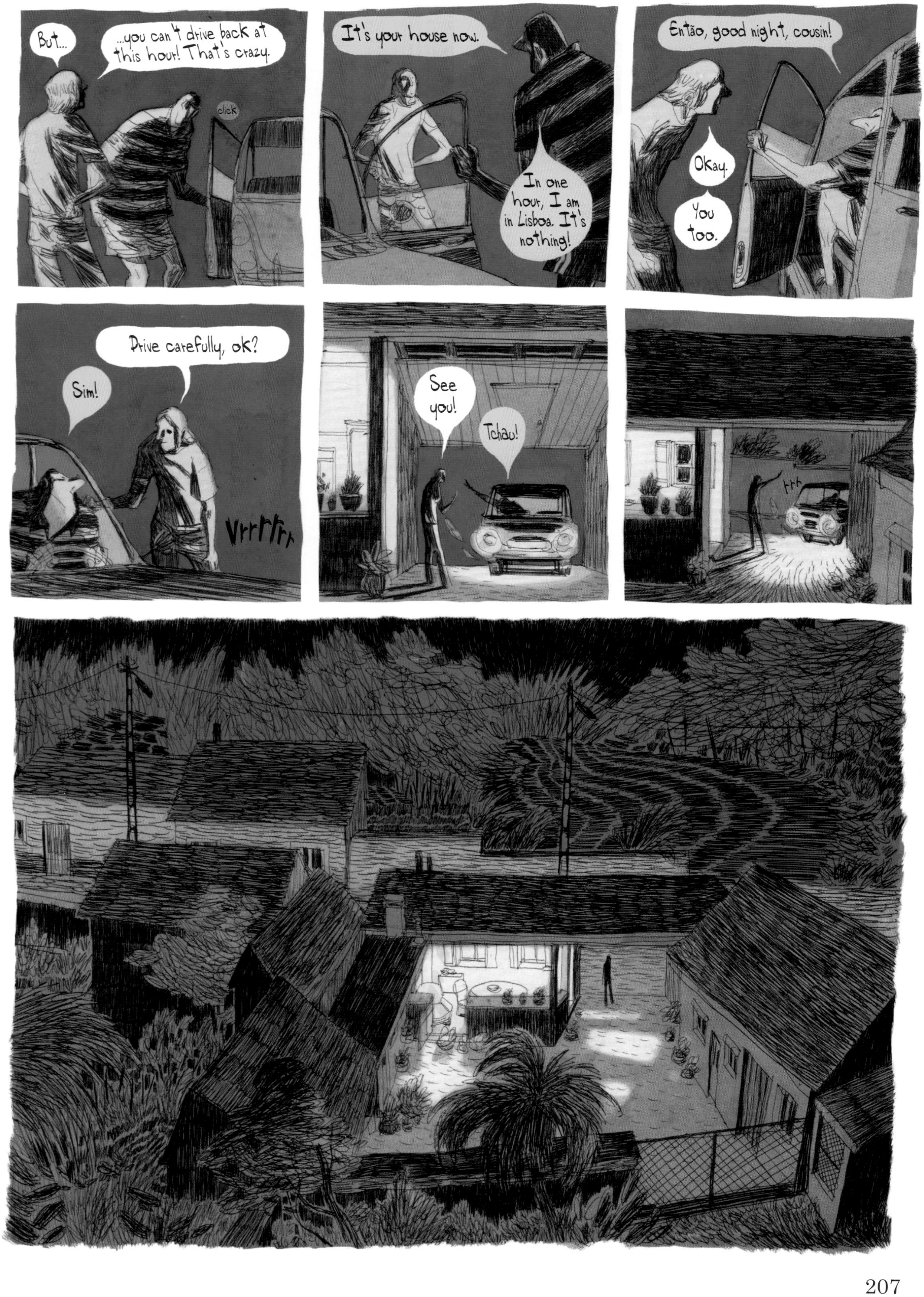
But...
...you can't drive back at this hour! That's crazy.
click
It's your house now.
In one hour, I am in Lisboa. It's nothing!
Então, good night, cousin!
Okay.
You too.
Drive carefully, ok?
Sim!
Vrrrrr
See you!
Tchau!

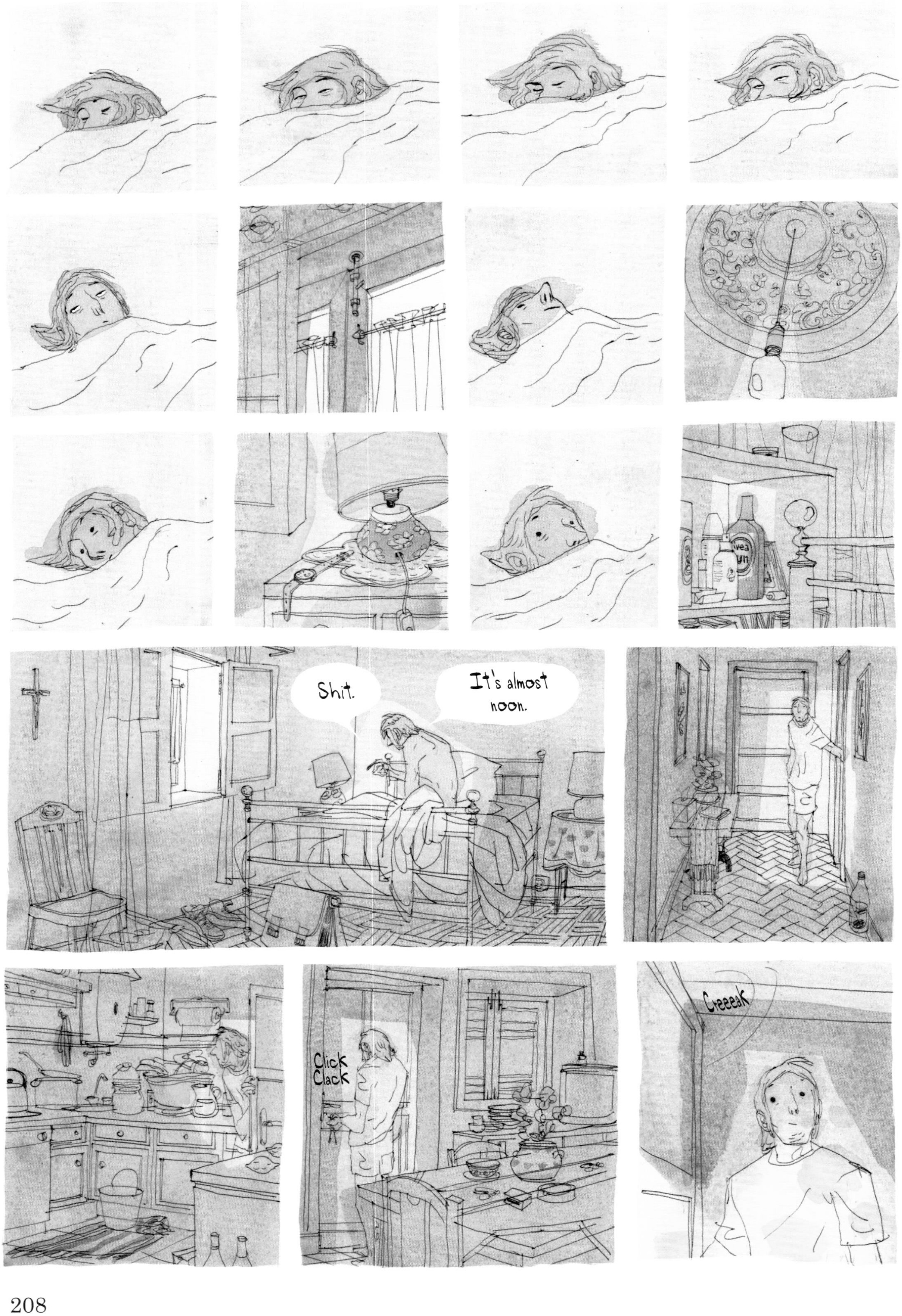
Shit.
It's almost noon.
Click Clack
Creeeak

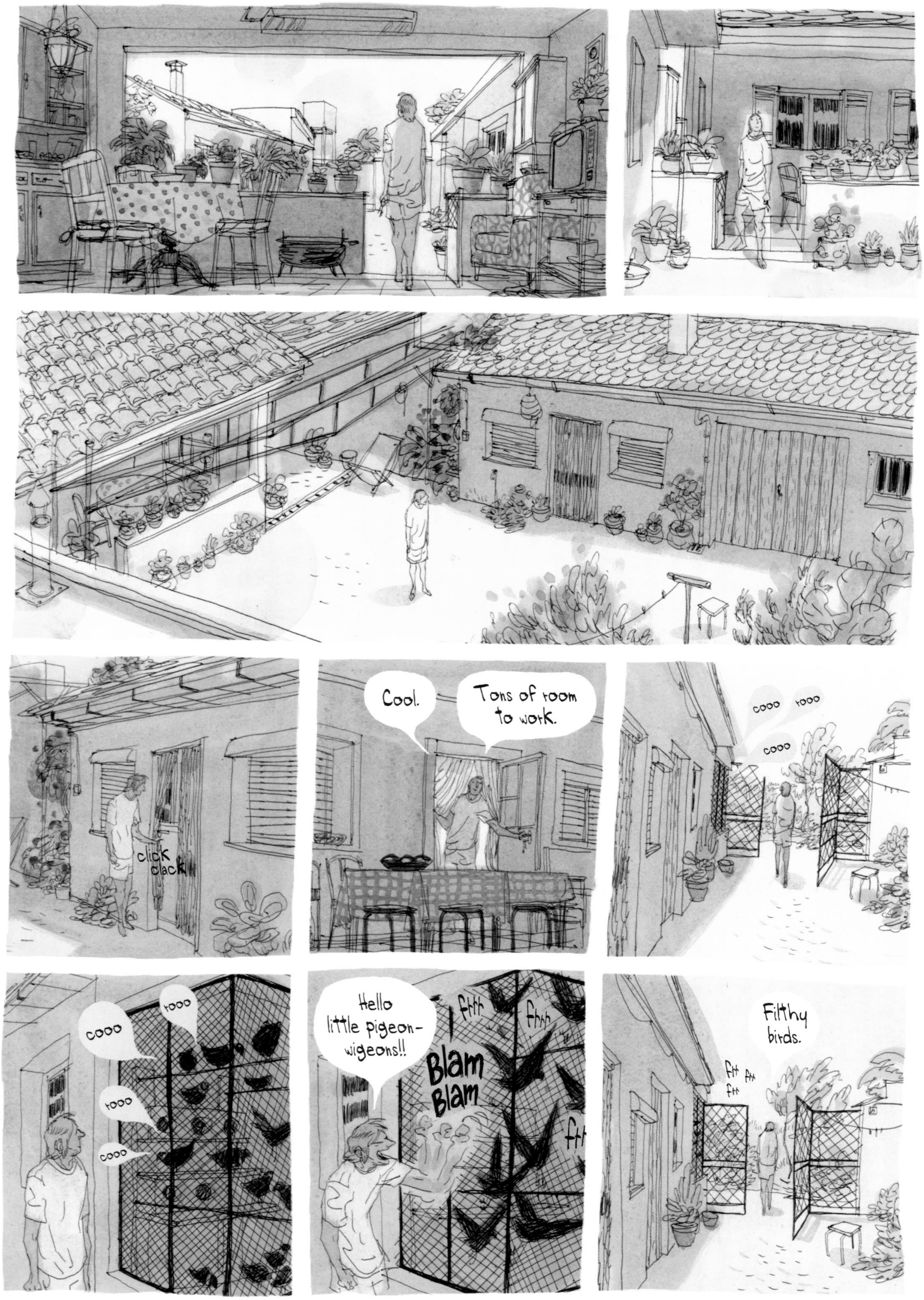
click
clack
Cool.
Tons of room to work.
cooo
rooo
cooo
cooo
rooo
rooo
cooo
Hello little pigeon-wigeons!!
frrr
frrr
Blam
Blam
frrr
Filthy birds.
frr
frr
frr

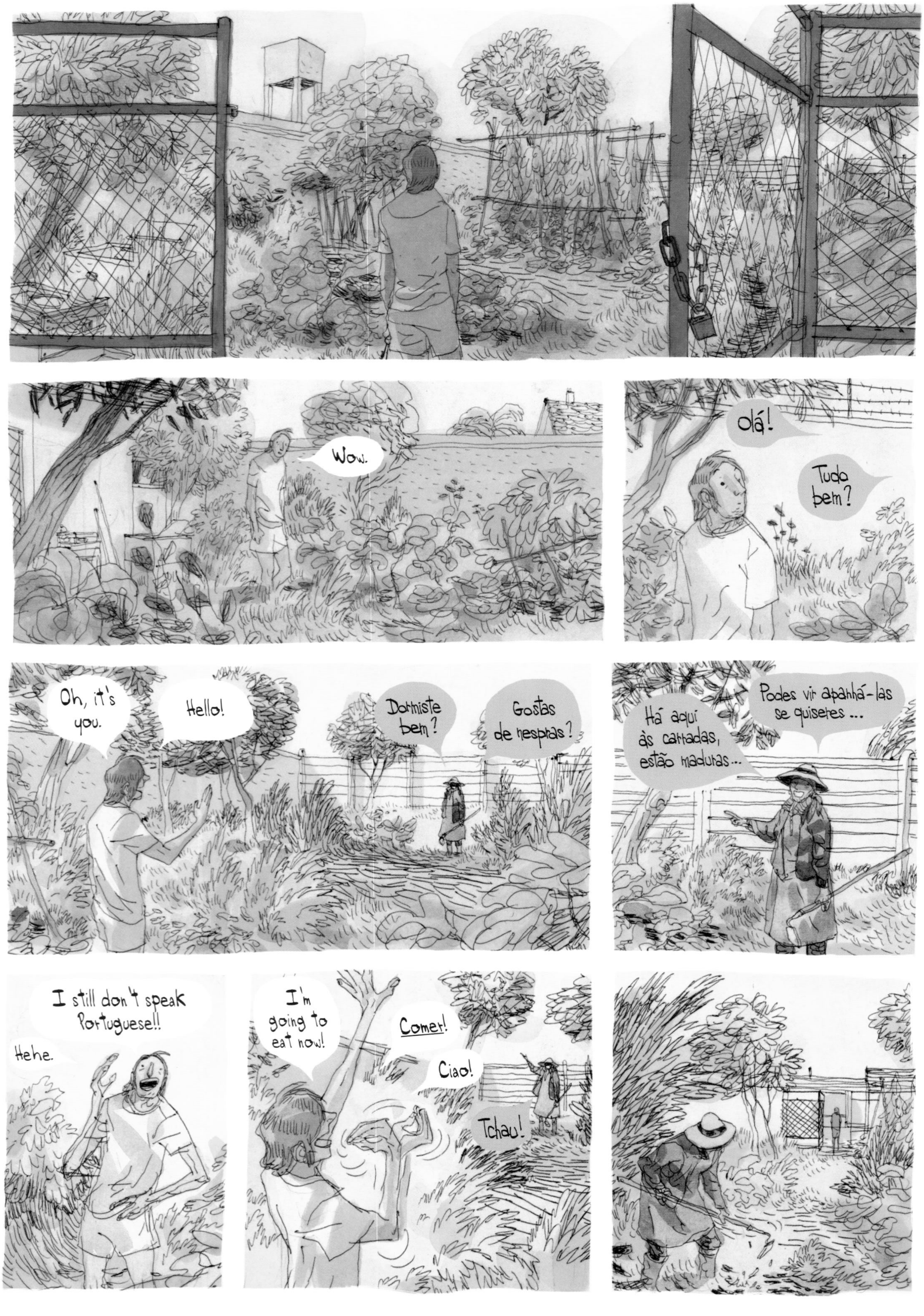
Wow.
Olá!
Tudo bem?
Oh, it's you.
Hello!
Dormiste bem?
Gostas de nespras?
Há aqui às carradas, estão maduras...
Podes vir apanhá-las se quiseres...
I still don't speak Portuguese!!
Hehe.
I'm going to eat now!
Comer!
Ciao!
Tchau!

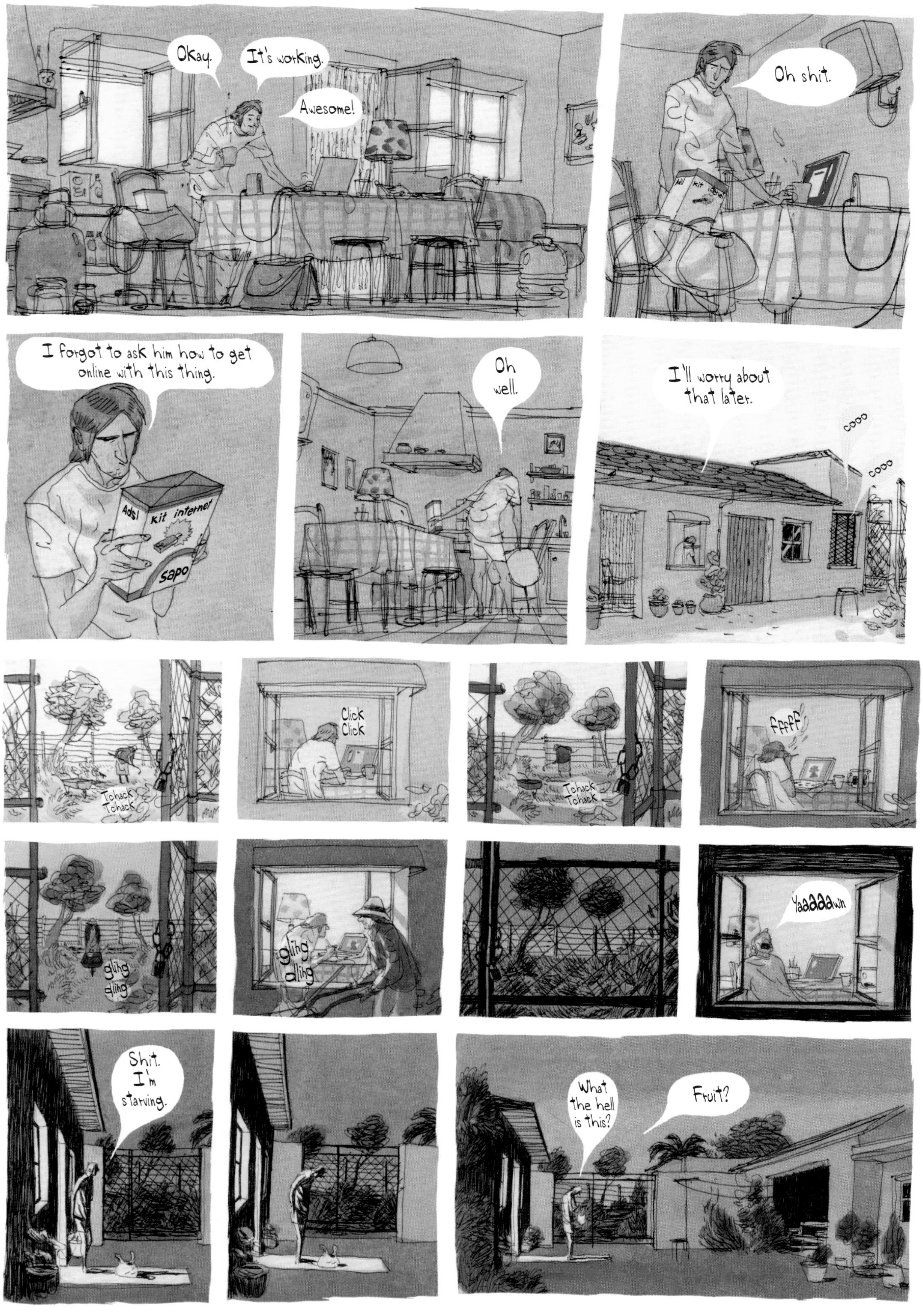
Okay.
It's working.
Awesome!
Oh shit.
I forgot to ask him how to get online with this thing.
Adsl kit internet sapo
Oh well.
I'll worry about that later.
oooo
oooo
Tchack Tchack
Click Click
Tchack Tchack
ffff
gling gling
gling gling
Yaaaaawn
Shit. I'm starving.
What the hell is this?
Fruit?

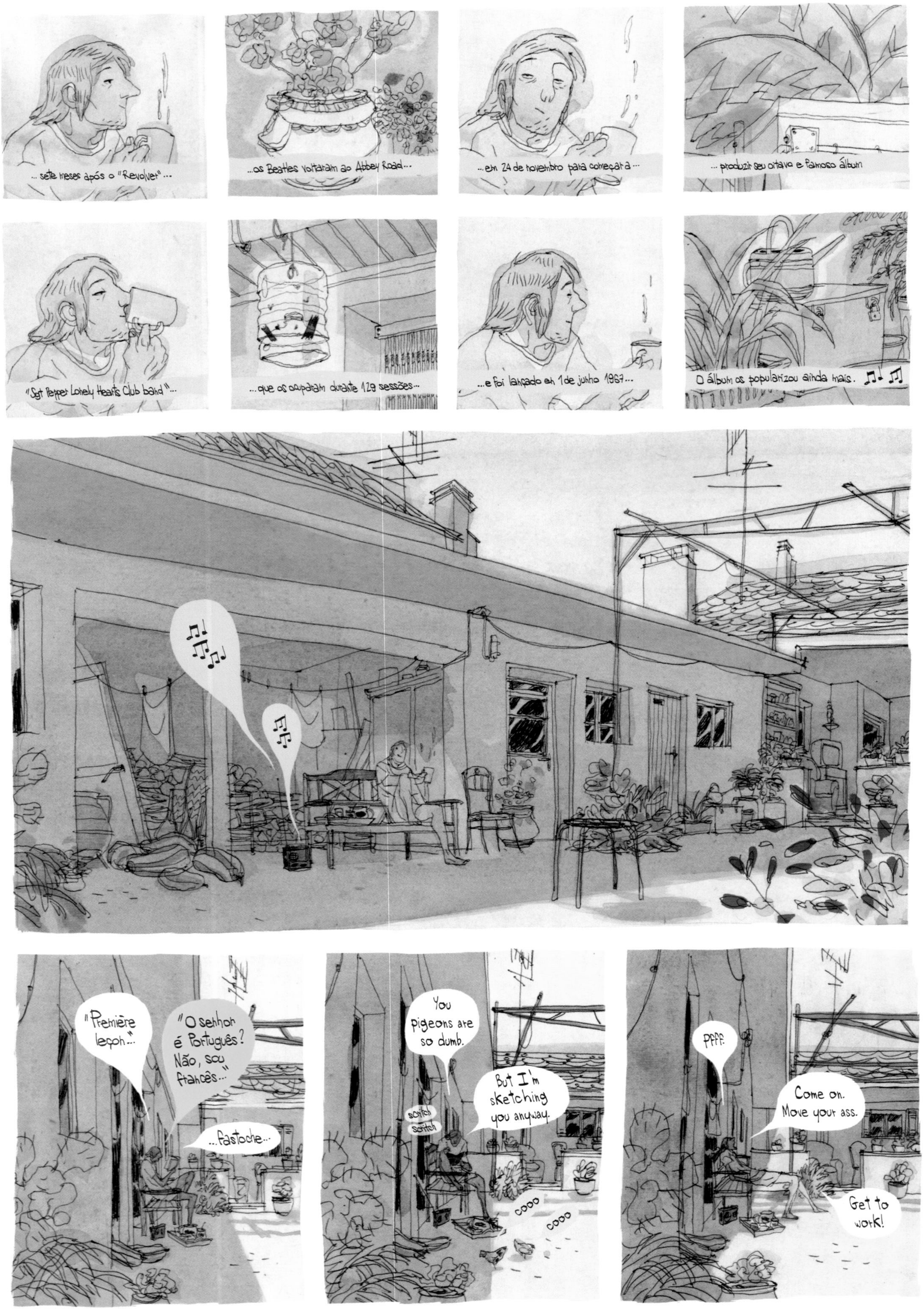
... sete meses após o "Revolver"...
...os Beatles voltaram ao Abbey Road...
...em 24 de novembro para começar a ...
... produzir seu oitavo e famoso álbum
"Sgt Pepper Lonely Hearts Club band"...
...que os ocuparam durante 129 sessões...
...e foi lançado em 1 de junho 1967...
O álbum os popularizou ainda mais.
"Première leçon"...
"O senhor é Português? Não, sou francês..."
...fastoche...
You pigeons are so dumb.
scritch scritch
But I'm sketching you anyway.
cooo
cooo
Pfff.
Come on. Move your ass.
Get to work!

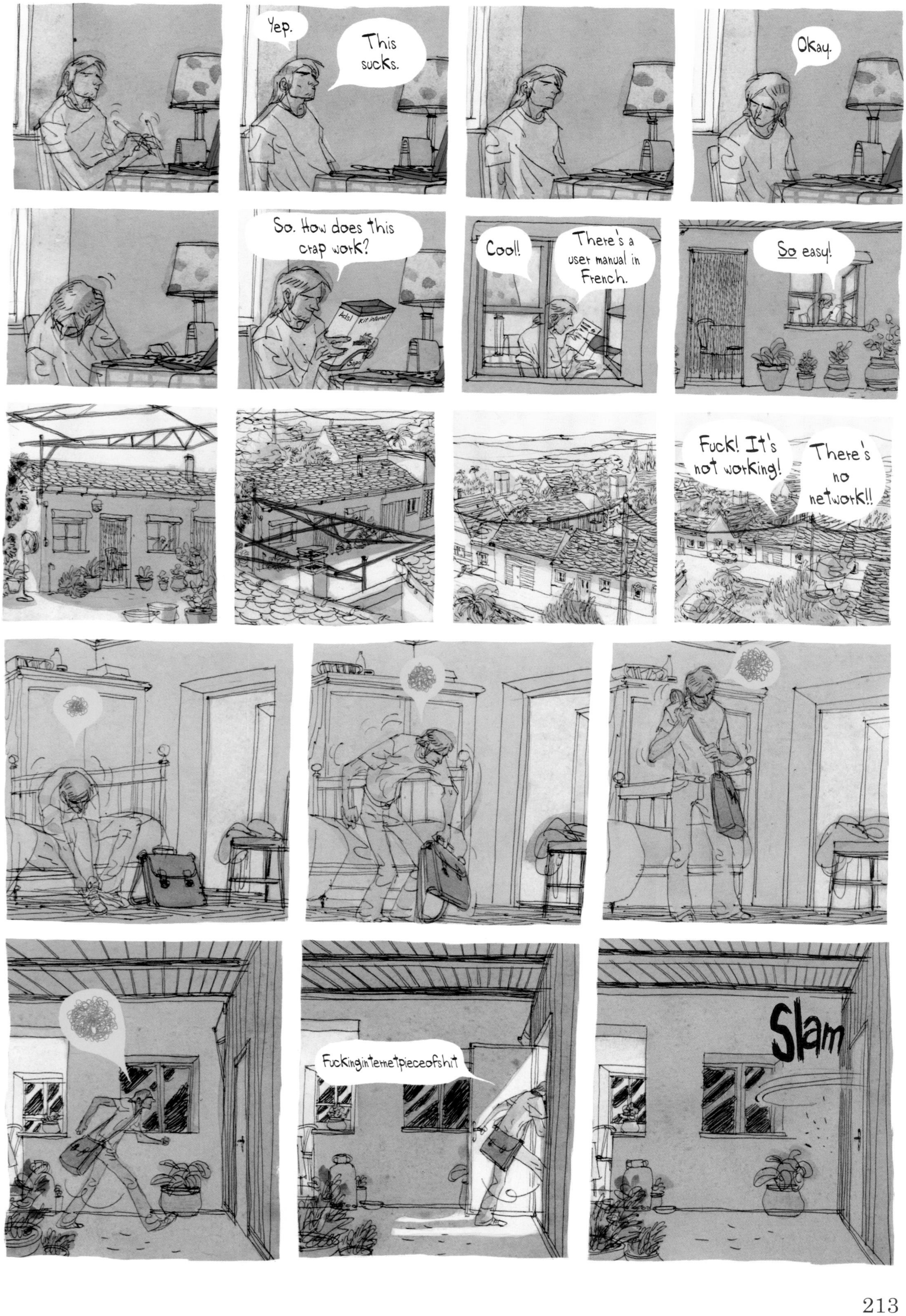
Yep.
This sucks.
Okay.
So. How does this crap work?
Cool!
There's a user manual in French.
So easy!
Fuck! It's not working!
There's no network!!
Fuckinginternetpieceofshit
Slam

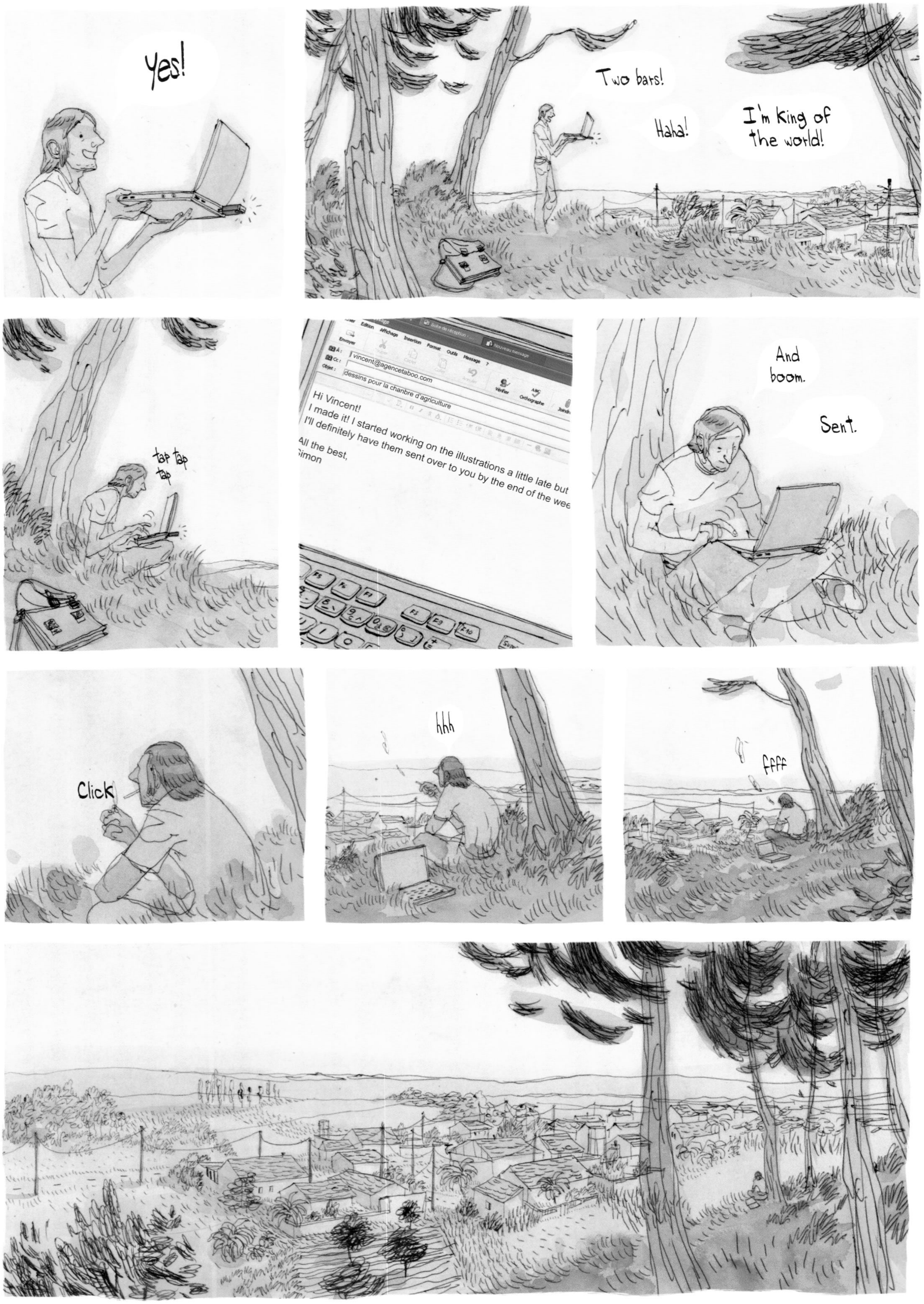
Yes!
Two bars!
Haha!
I'm King of the world!
tap tap tap
vincent@agencetaboo.com
dessins pour la chanbre d'agriculture
Hi Vincent!
I made it! I started working on the illustrations a little late but
I'll definitely have them sent over to you by the end of the wee
All the best,
Simon
And boom.
Sent.
Click
hhh
ffff

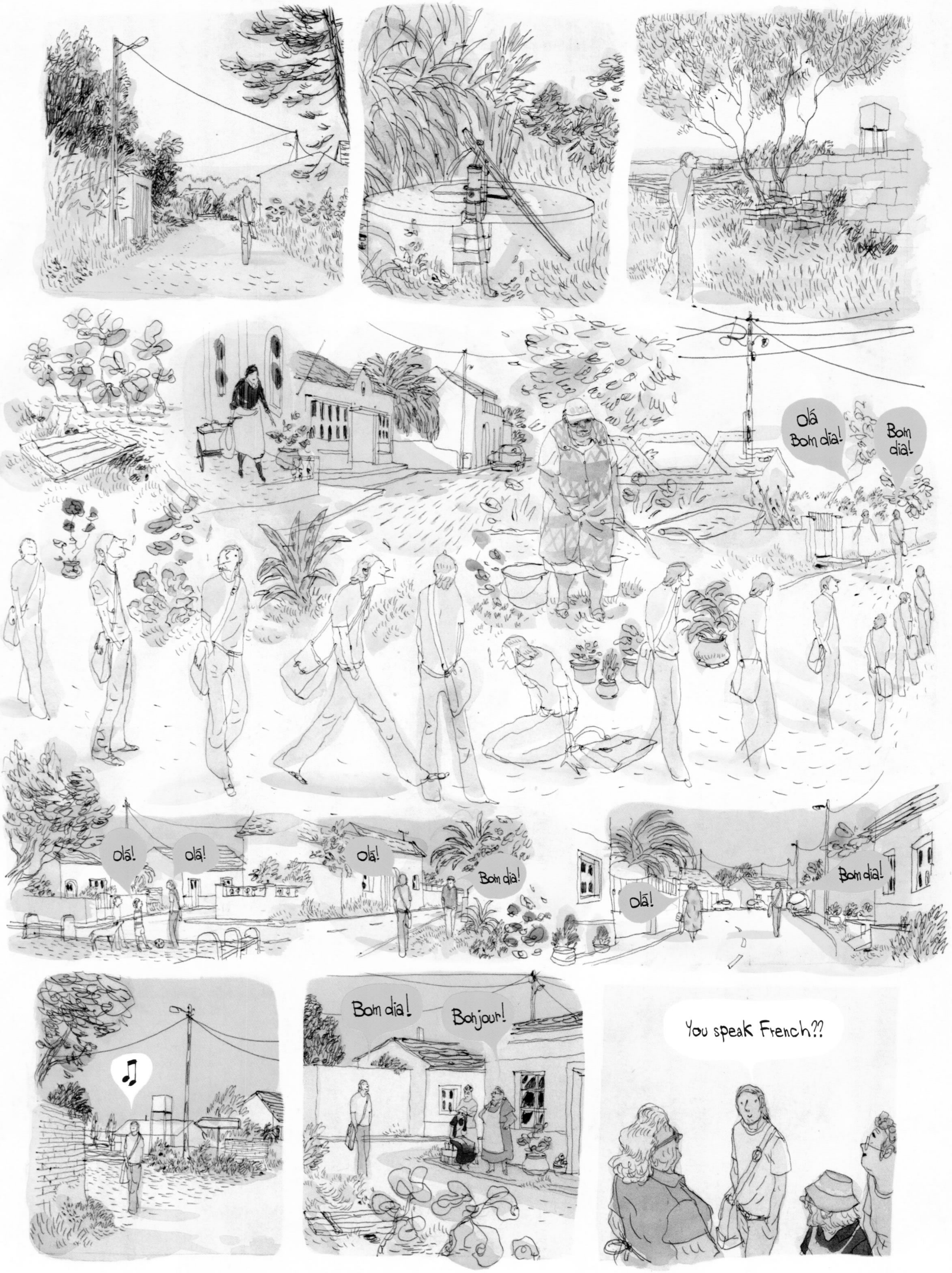
Olá
Bom dia!
Bom dia!
Olá!
Olá!
Olá!
Bom dia!
Olá!
Bom dia!
♫
Bom dia!
Bonjour!
You speak French??

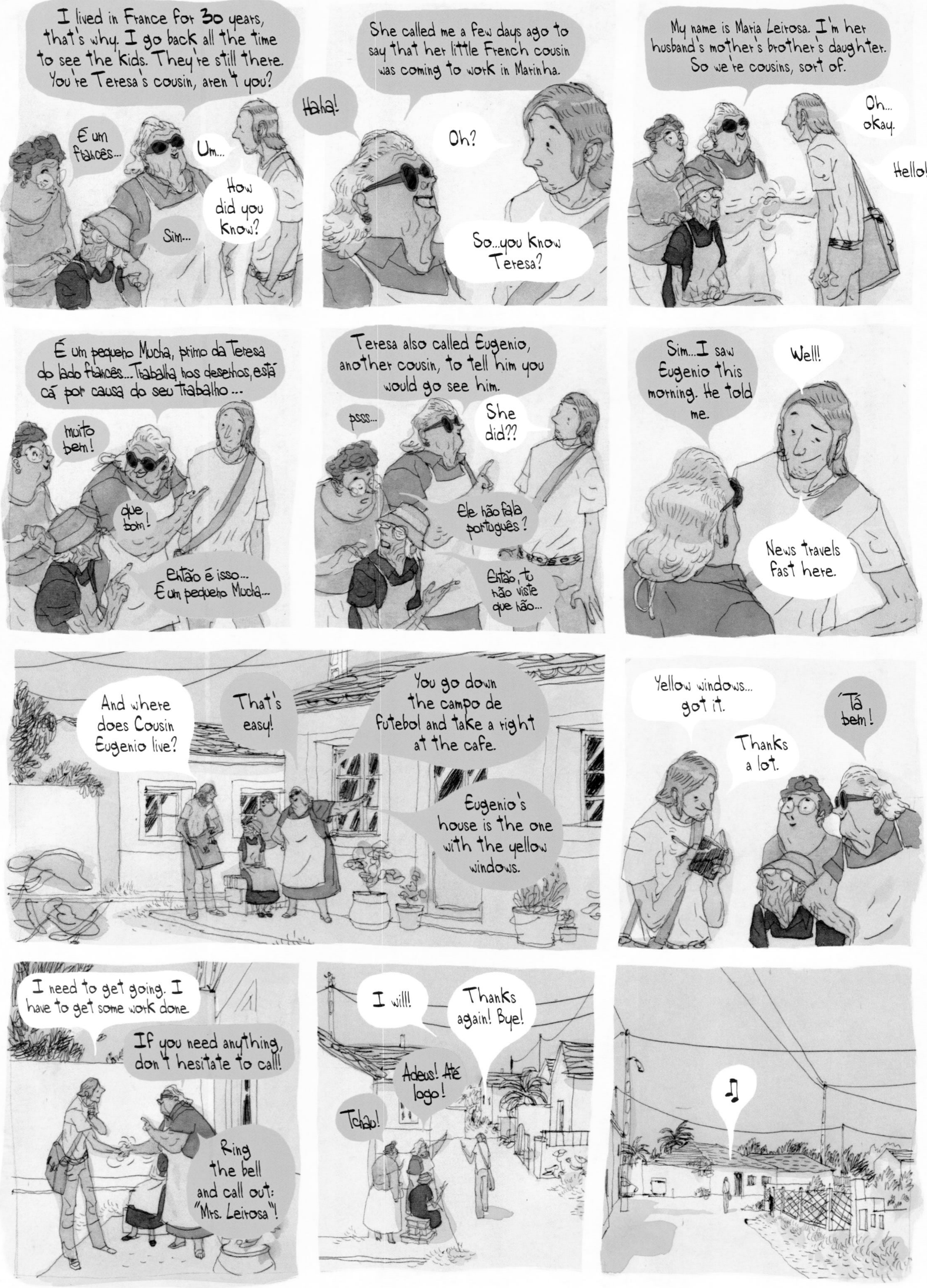
I lived in France for 30 years, that's why. I go back all the time to see the kids. They're still there. You're Teresa's cousin, aren't you?
É um francês...
Um...
How did you know?
Sim...
Haha!
She called me a few days ago to say that her little French cousin was coming to work in Marinha.
Oh?
So...you know Teresa?
My name is Maria Leirosa. I'm her husband's mother's brother's daughter. So we're cousins, sort of.
Oh... okay.
Hello!
É um pequeno Mucha, primo da Teresa do lado francês... Trabalha nos desenhos, está cá por causa do seu trabalho...
muito bem!
que bom!
Então é isso... É um pequeno Mucha...
Teresa also called Eugenio, another cousin, to tell him you would go see him.
psss...
She did??
Ele não fala português?
Então, tu não viste que não...
Sim...I saw Eugenio this morning. He told me.
Well!
News travels fast here.
And where does Cousin Eugenio live?
That's easy!
You go down the campo de futebol and take a right at the cafe.
Eugenio's house is the one with the yellow windows.
Yellow windows... got it.
Thanks a lot.
Tá bem!
I need to get going. I have to get some work done.
If you need anything, don't hesitate to call!
Ring the bell and call out: "Mrs. Leirosa"!
I will!
Thanks again! Bye!
Adeus! Até logo!
Tchau!
♫

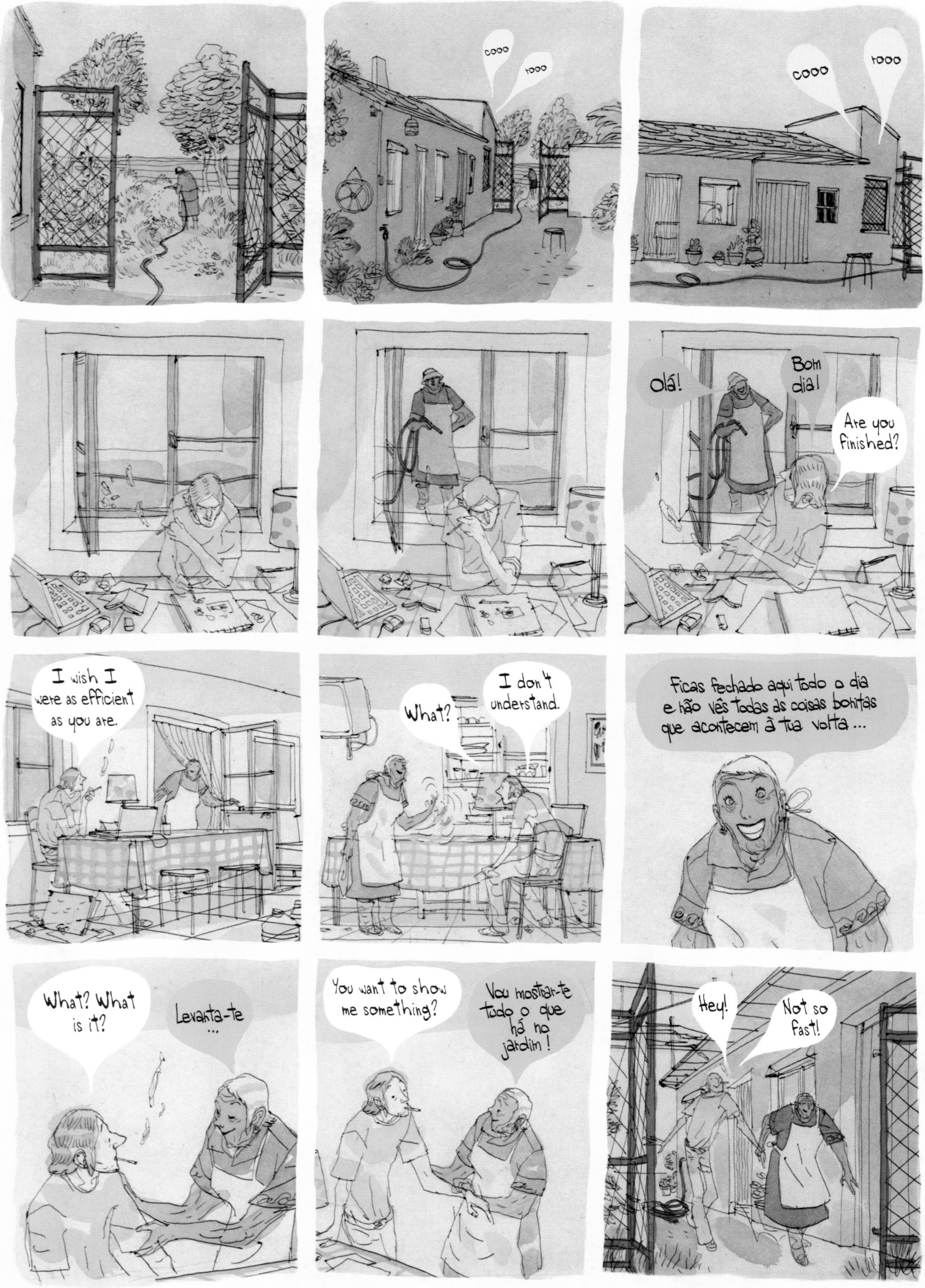
cooo
tooo
cooo
tooo
Olá!
Bom dia!
Are you finished?
I wish I were as efficient as you are.
What?
I don't understand.
Ficas fechado aqui todo o dia e não vês todas as coisas bonitas que acontecem à tua volta ...
What? What is it?
Levanta-te ...
You want to show me something?
Vou mostrar-te tudo o que há no jardim!
Hey!
Not so fast!

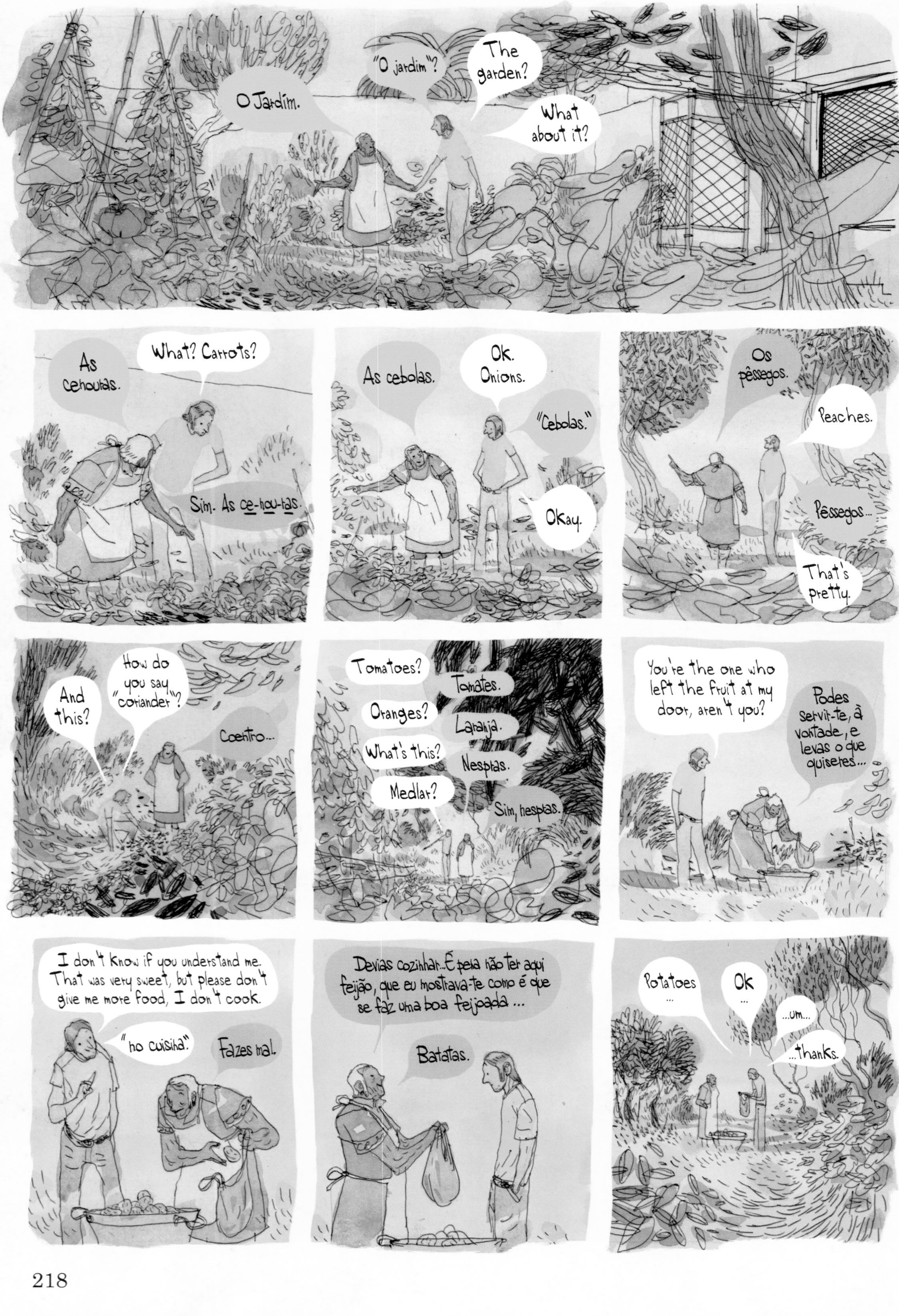
O Jardim.
"O jardim"?
The garden?
What about it?
As cenouras.
What? Carrots?
Sim. As ce-nou-ras.
As cebolas.
Ok. Onions.
"Cebolas."
Okay.
Os pêssegos.
Peaches.
Pêssegos...
That's pretty.
And this?
How do you say "coriander"?
Coentro...
Tomatoes?
Tomates.
Oranges?
Laranja.
What's this?
Nespras.
Medlar?
Sim, nespras.
You're the one who left the fruit at my door, aren't you?
Podes servir-te, à vontade, e levas o que quiseres...
I don't know if you understand me. That was very sweet, but please don't give me more food, I don't cook.
"no cuisina."
Fazes mal.
Devias cozinhar... É pena não ter aqui feijão, que eu mostrava-te como é que se faz uma boa feijoada ...
Batatas.
Potatoes ...
Ok ...
...um...
...thanks.

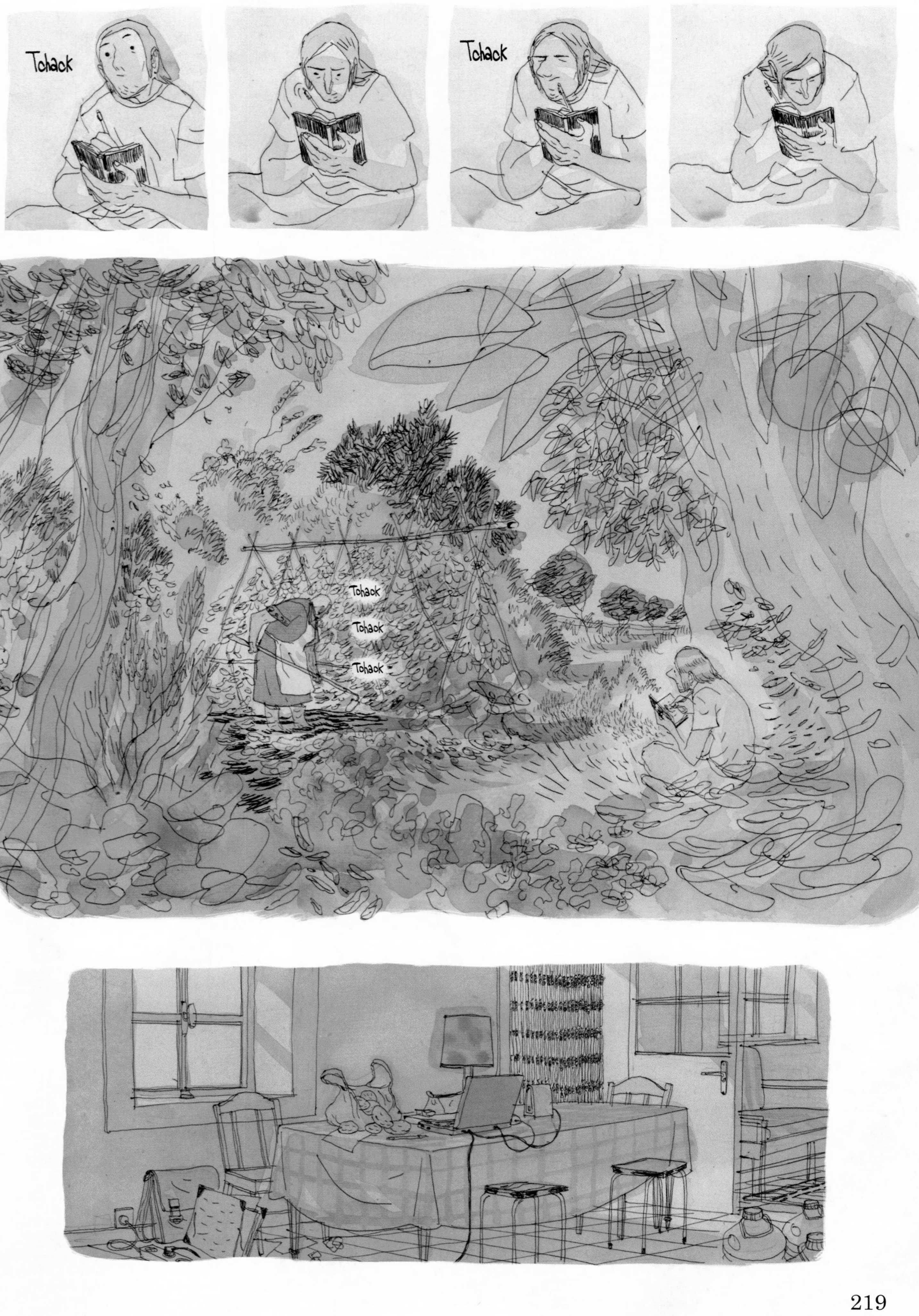
Tchack
Tchack
Tchack
Tchack
Tchack

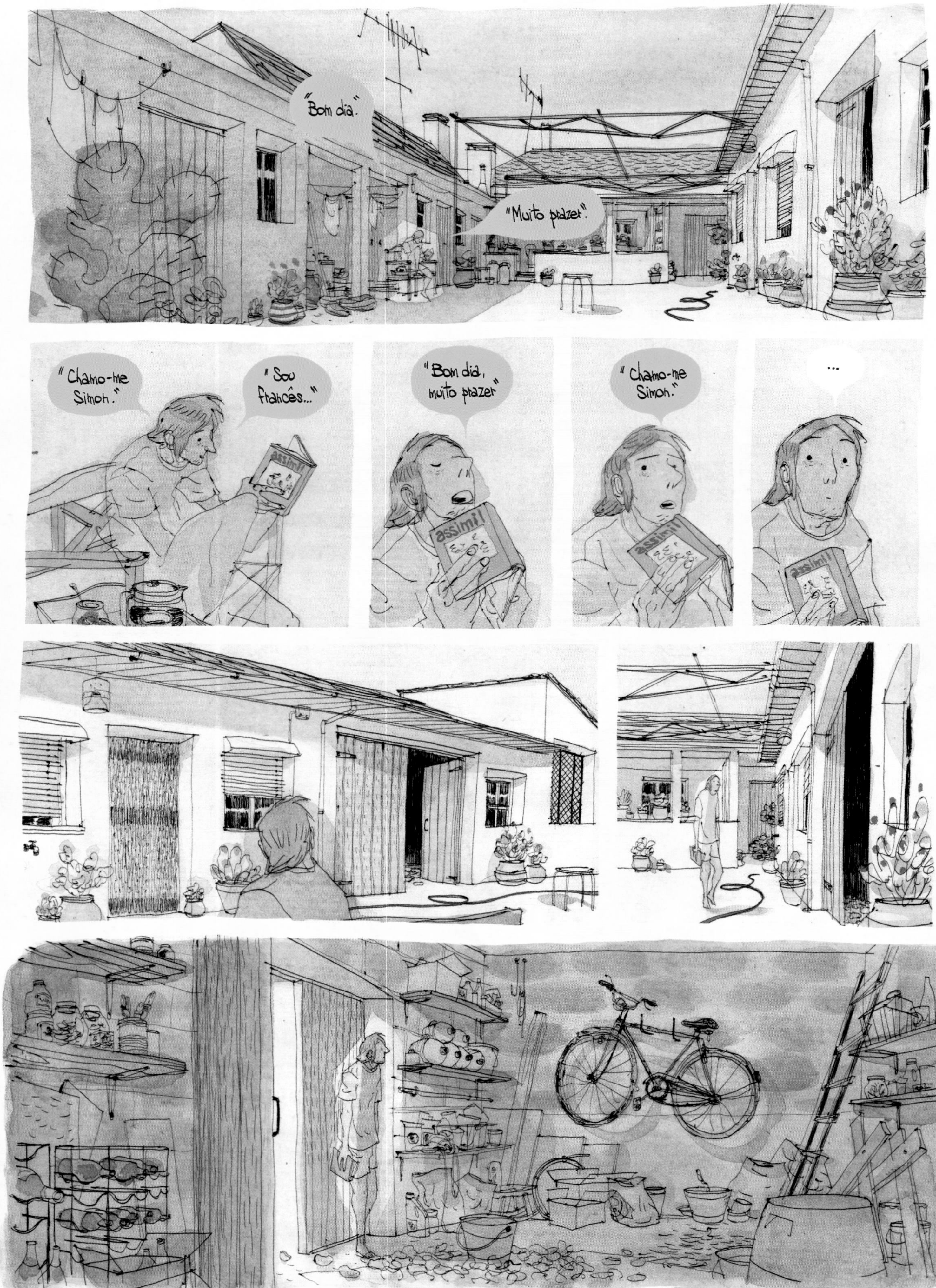
"Bom dia."
"Muito prazer."
"Chamo-me Simon."
"Sou francês..."
assimil
"Bom dia, muito prazer"
assimil
"Chamo-me Simon."
assimil
...
assimil

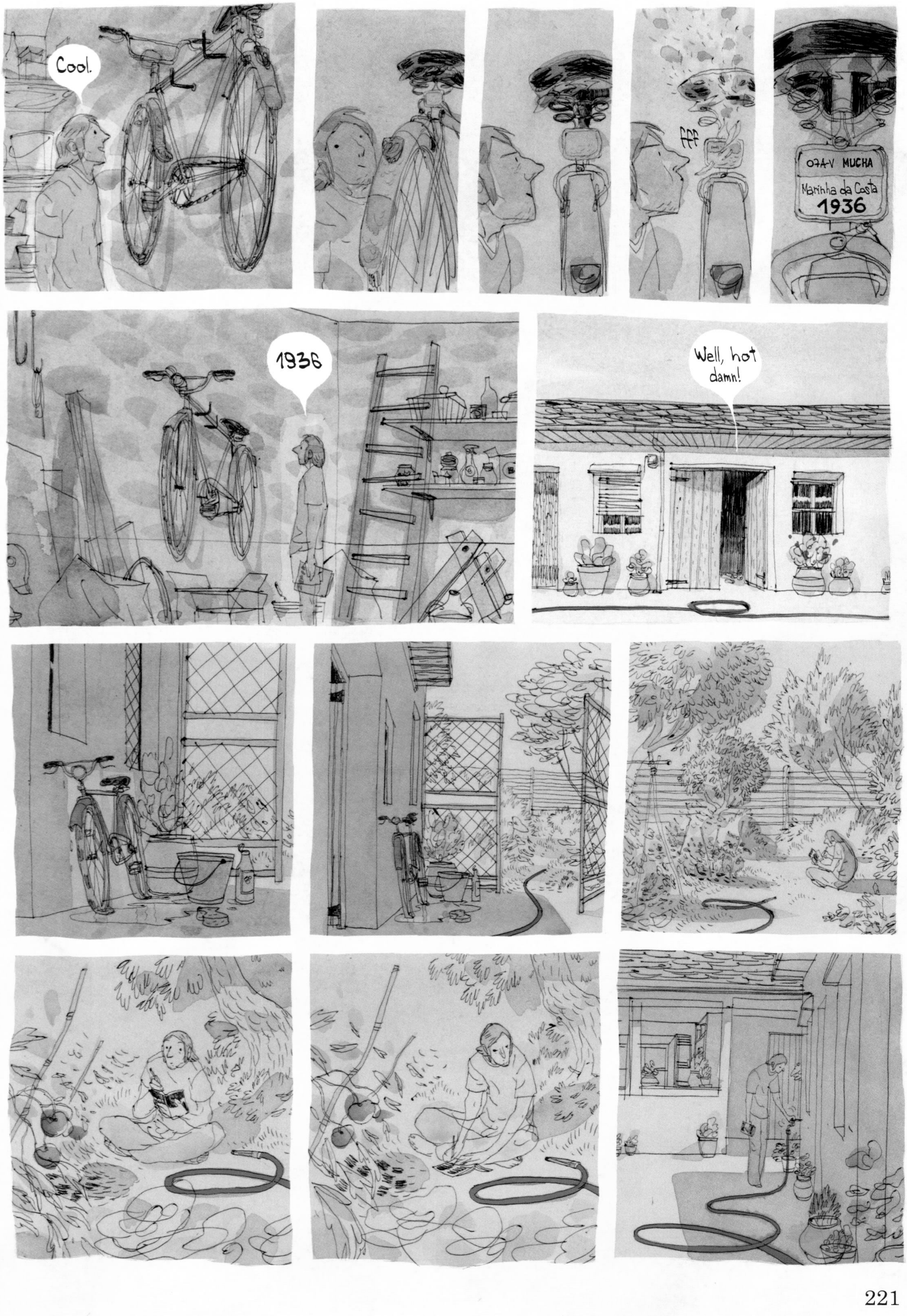
Cool.
fff
07A-V MUCHA
Marinha da Costa
1936
1936
Well, hot damn!

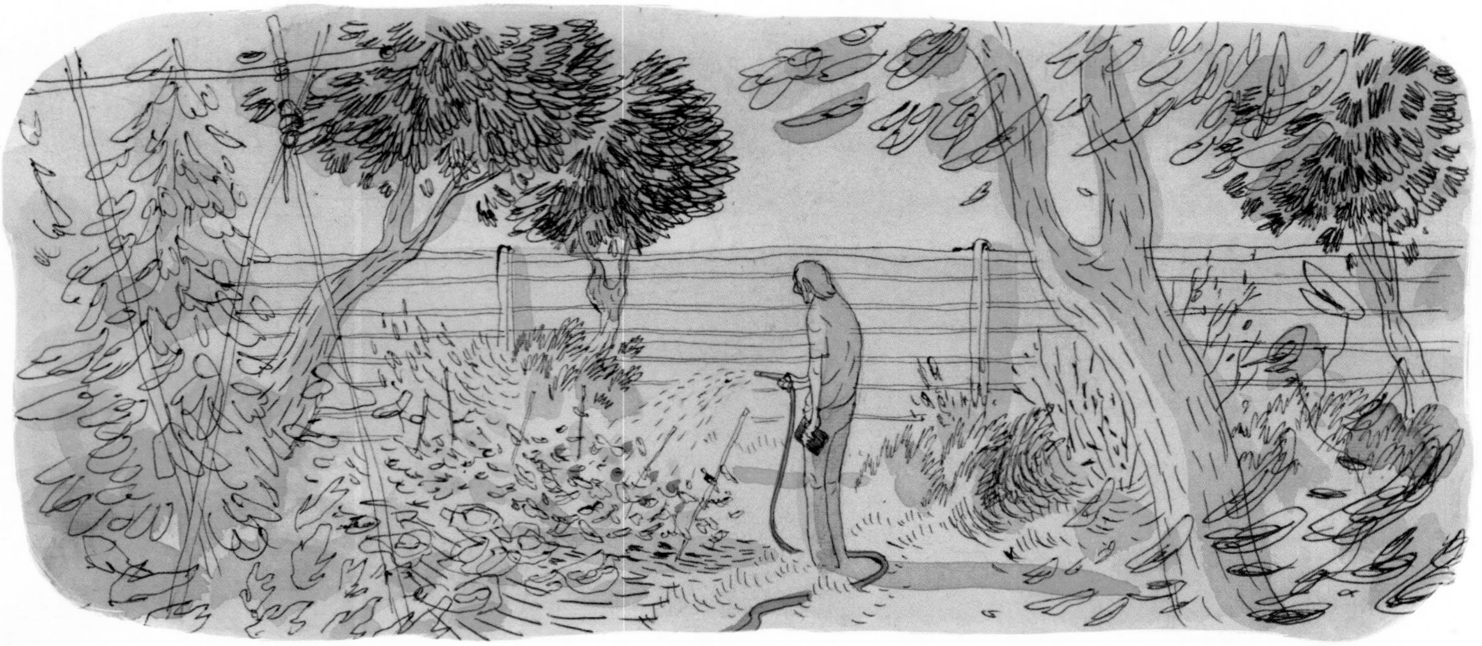

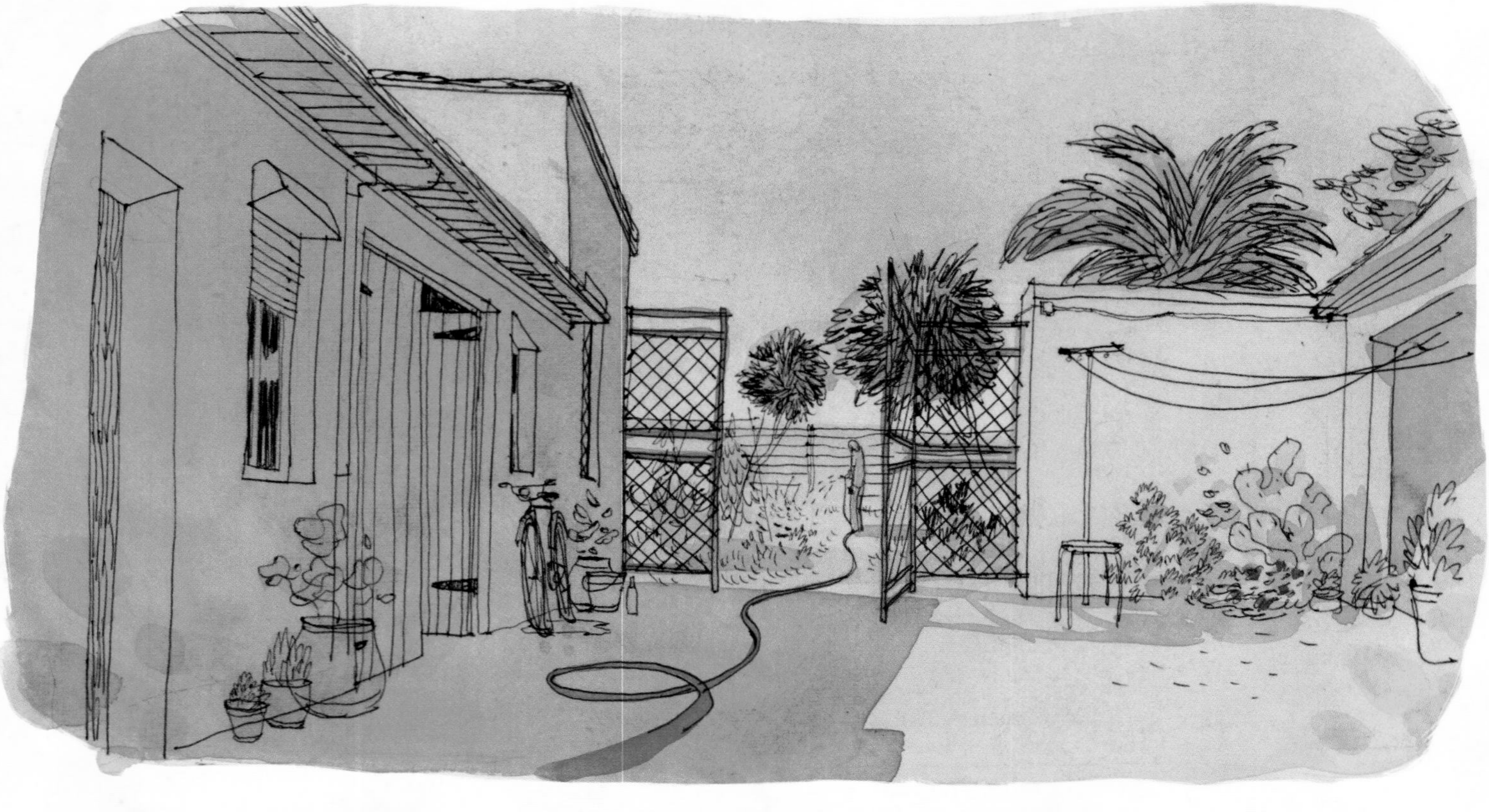

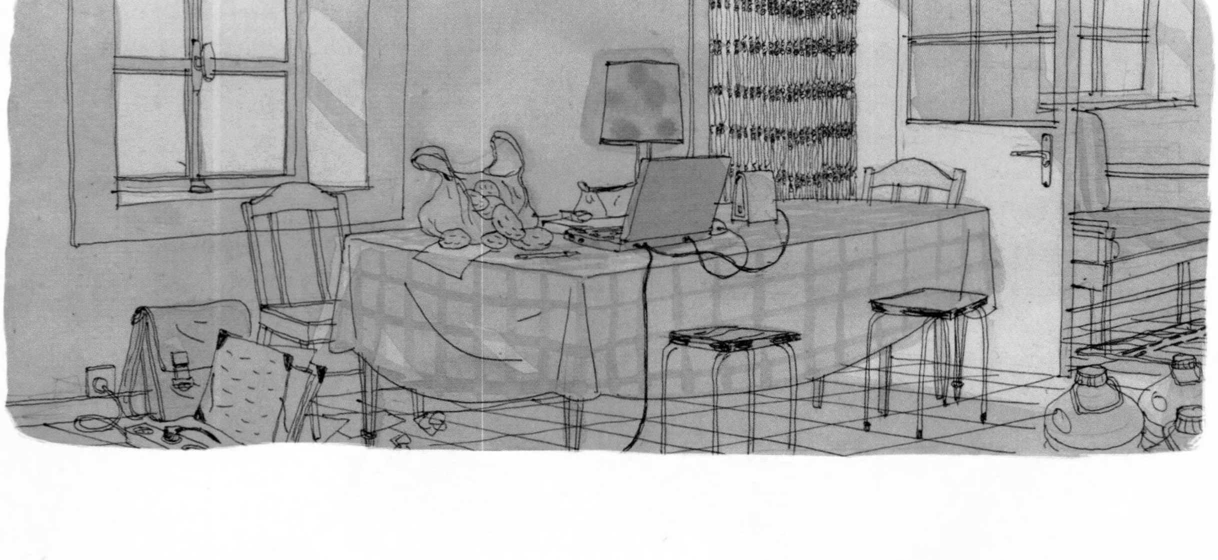

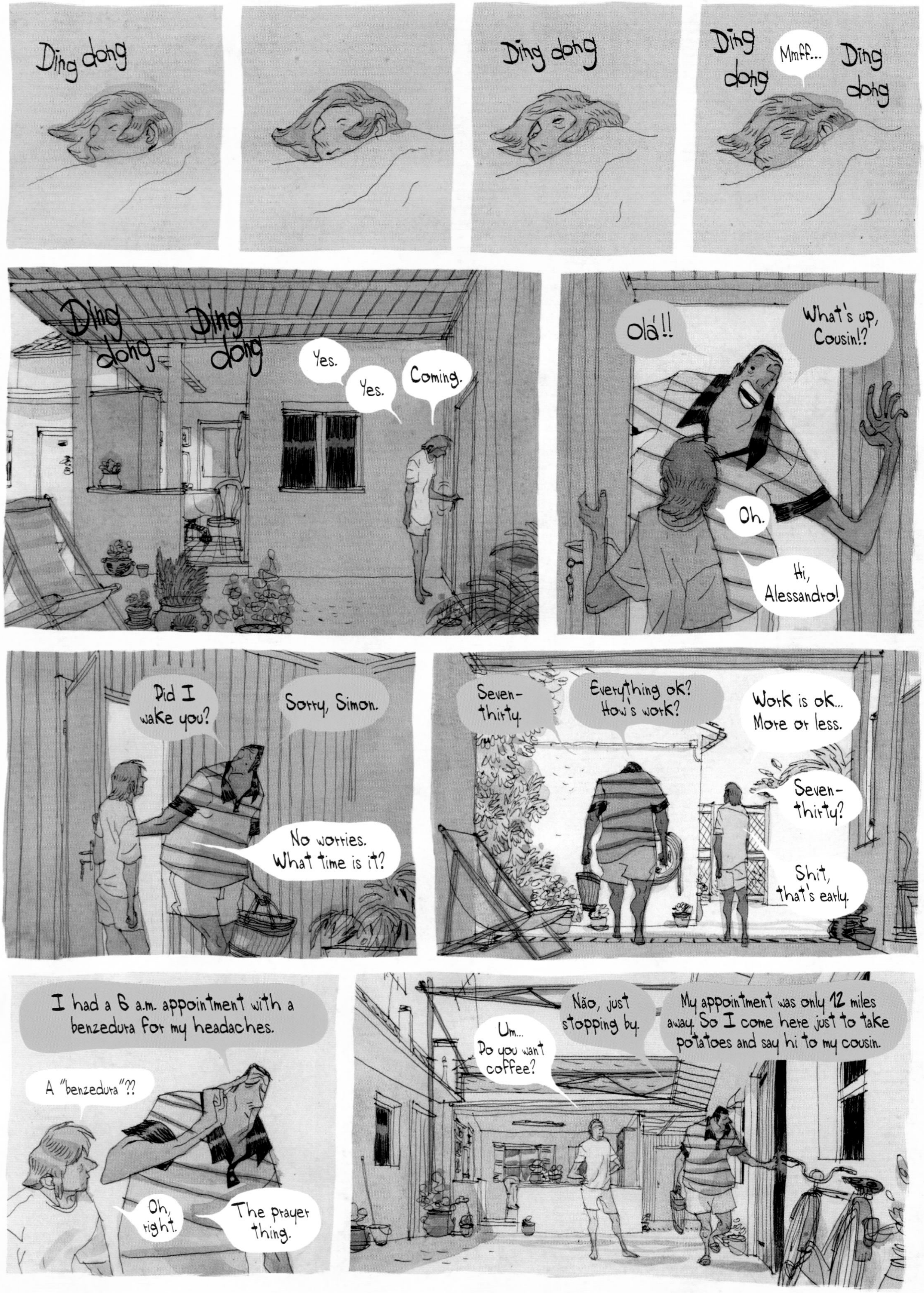
Ding dong
Ding dong
Ding dong
Mmff...
Ding dong
Ding dong
Ding dong
Yes.
Yes.
Coming.
Olá!!
What's up, Cousin!?
Oh.
Hi, Alessandro!
Did I wake you?
Sorry, Simon.
No worries. What time is it?
Seven-thirty.
Everything ok? How's work?
Work is ok... More or less.
Seven-thirty?
Shit, that's early.
I had a 6 a.m. appointment with a benzedura for my headaches.
A "benzedura"??
Oh, right.
The prayer thing.
Um... Do you want coffee?
Não, just stopping by.
My appointment was only 12 miles away. So I come here just to take potatoes and say hi to my cousin.

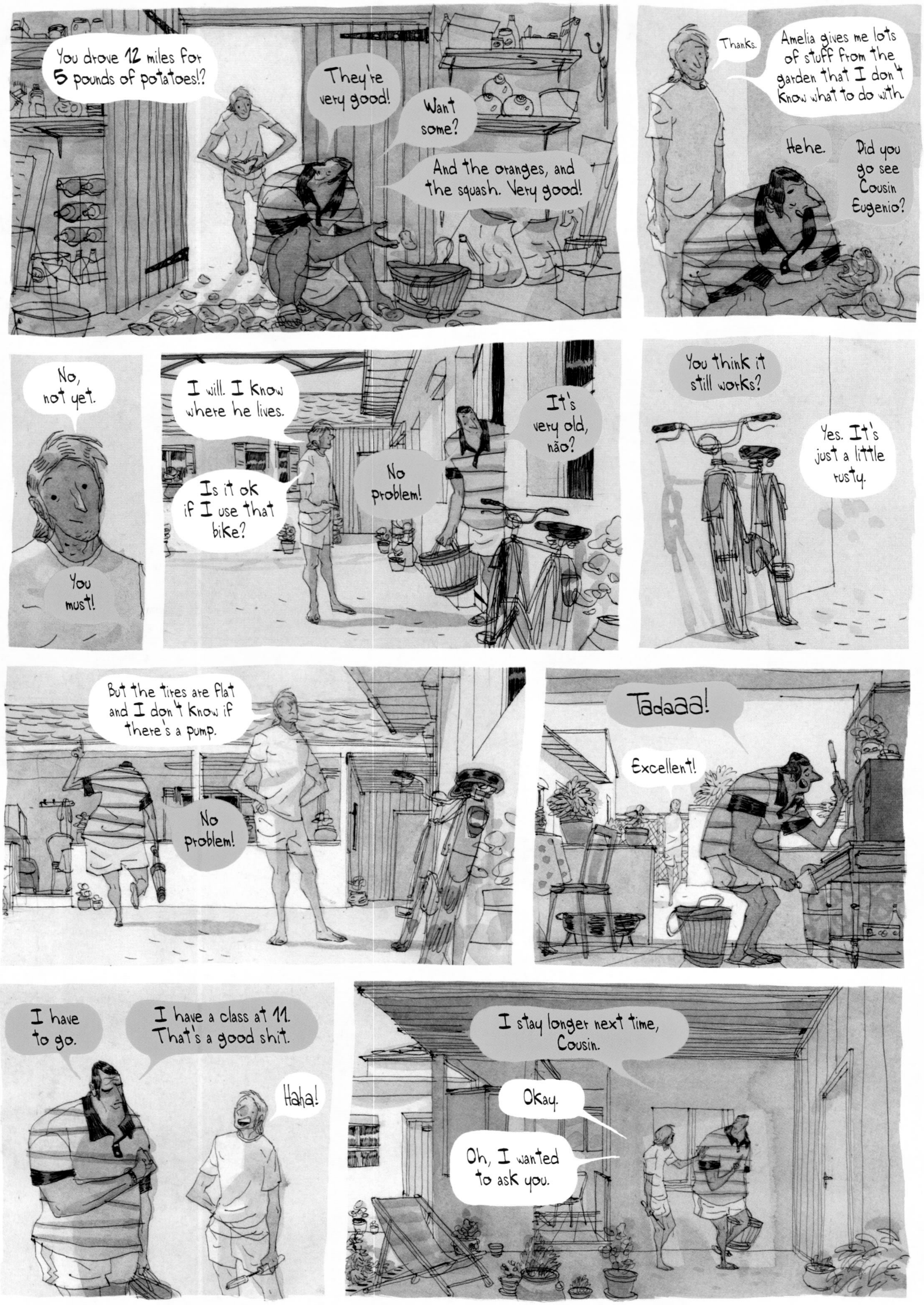

You drove 12 miles for 5 pounds of potatoes!?
They're very good!
Want some?
And the oranges, and the squash. Very good!
Thanks.
Amelia gives me lots of stuff from the garden that I don't know what to do with.
Hehe.
Did you go see Cousin Eugenio?
No, not yet.
You must!
I will. I know where he lives.
Is it ok if I use that bike?
No problem!
It's very old, não?
You think it still works?
Yes. It's just a little rusty.
But the tires are flat and I don't know if there's a pump.
No problem!
Tadaaa!
Excellent!
I have to go.
I have a class at 11. That's a good shit.
Haha!
I stay longer next time, Cousin.
Okay.
Oh, I wanted to ask you.

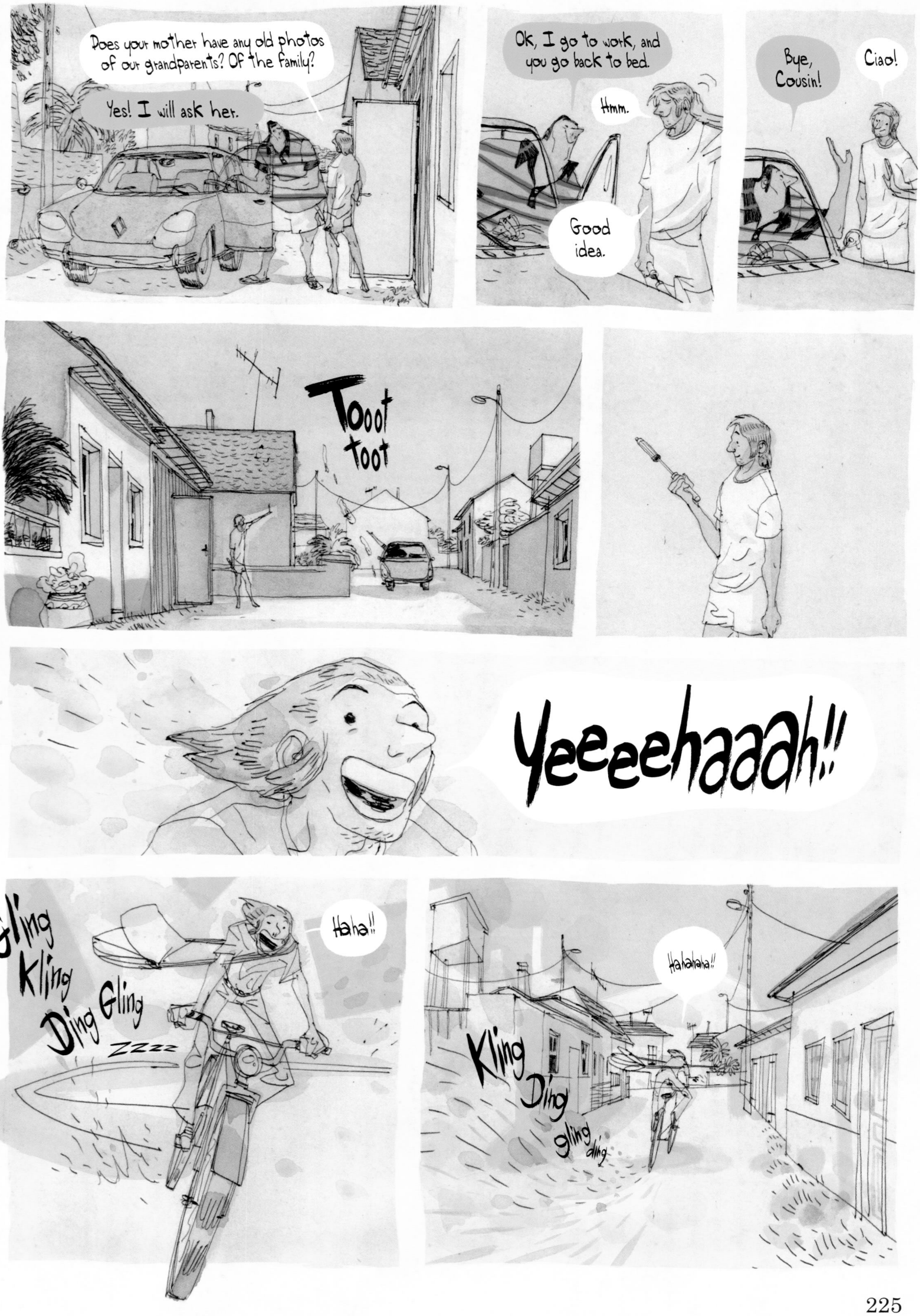

Does your mother have any old photos of our grandparents? Of the family?
Yes! I will ask her.
Ok, I go to work, and you go back to bed.
Hmm.
Good idea.
Bye, Cousin!
Ciao!
Tooot toot
Yeeeehaaaah!!
Gling Kling Ding Gling
Zzzz
Haha!!
Hahahaha!!
Kling Ding gling

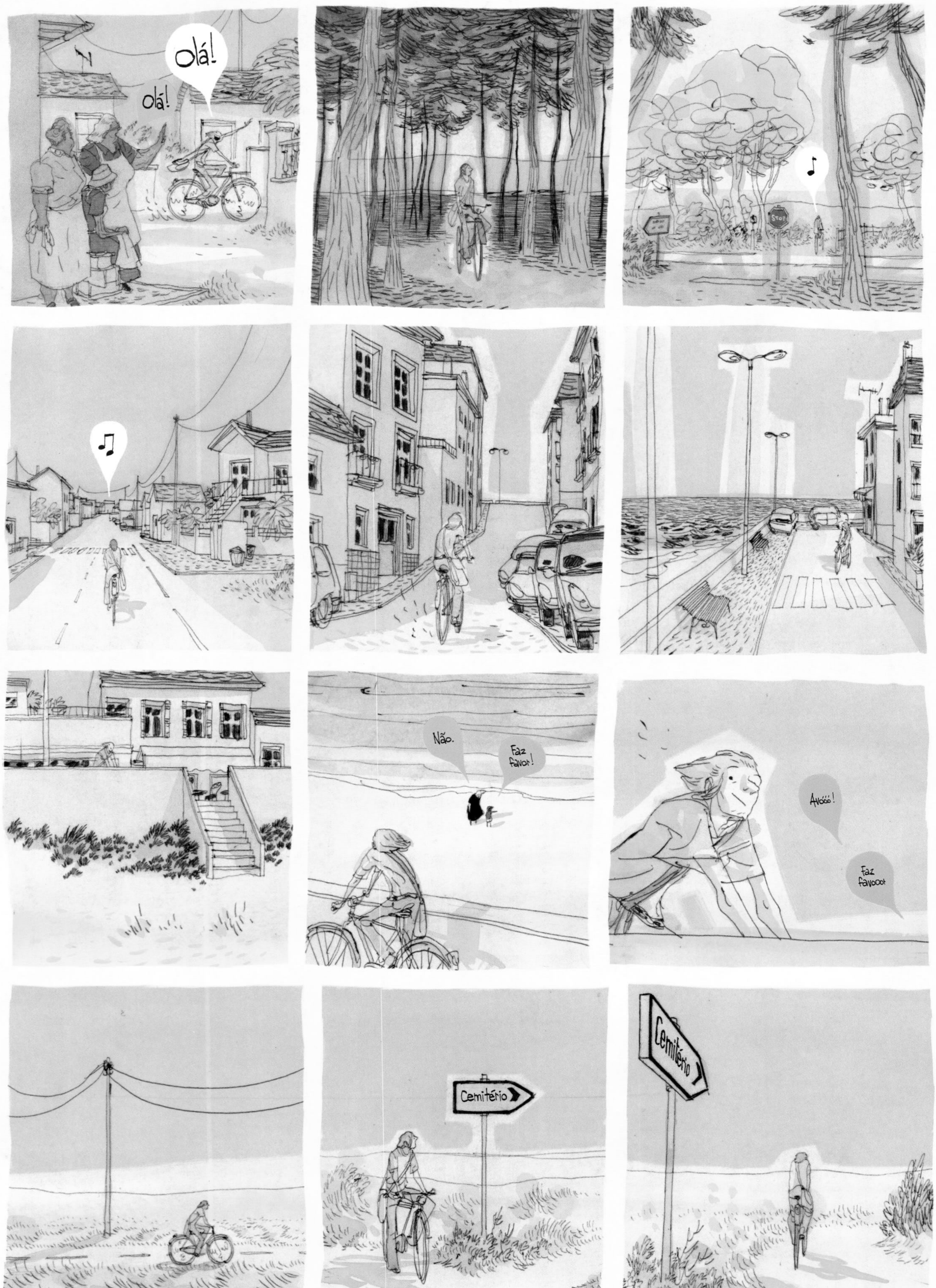
Olá!
Olá!
STOP
Não.
Faz favor!
Avóóó!
Faz favooor
Cemitério
Cemitério

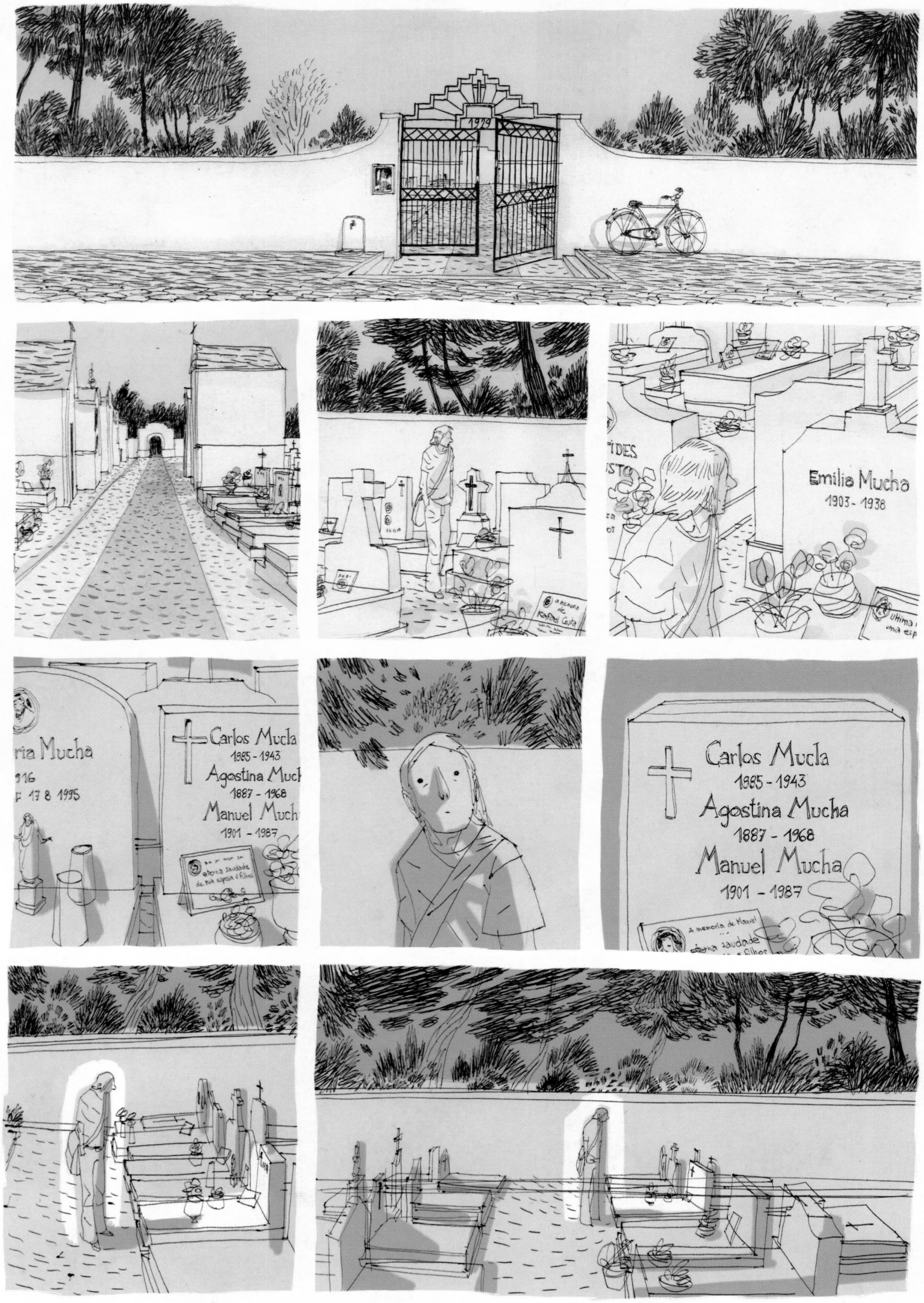

1979
Emilia Mucha
1903 - 1938
ria Mucha
17 8 1995
Carlos Mucla
1885 - 1943
Agostina Mucha
1887 - 1968
Manuel Mucha
1901 - 1987
eterna saudade
Carlos Mucla
1885 - 1943
Agostina Mucha
1887 - 1968
Manuel Mucha
1901 - 1987
A memoria de Manuel
eterna saudade

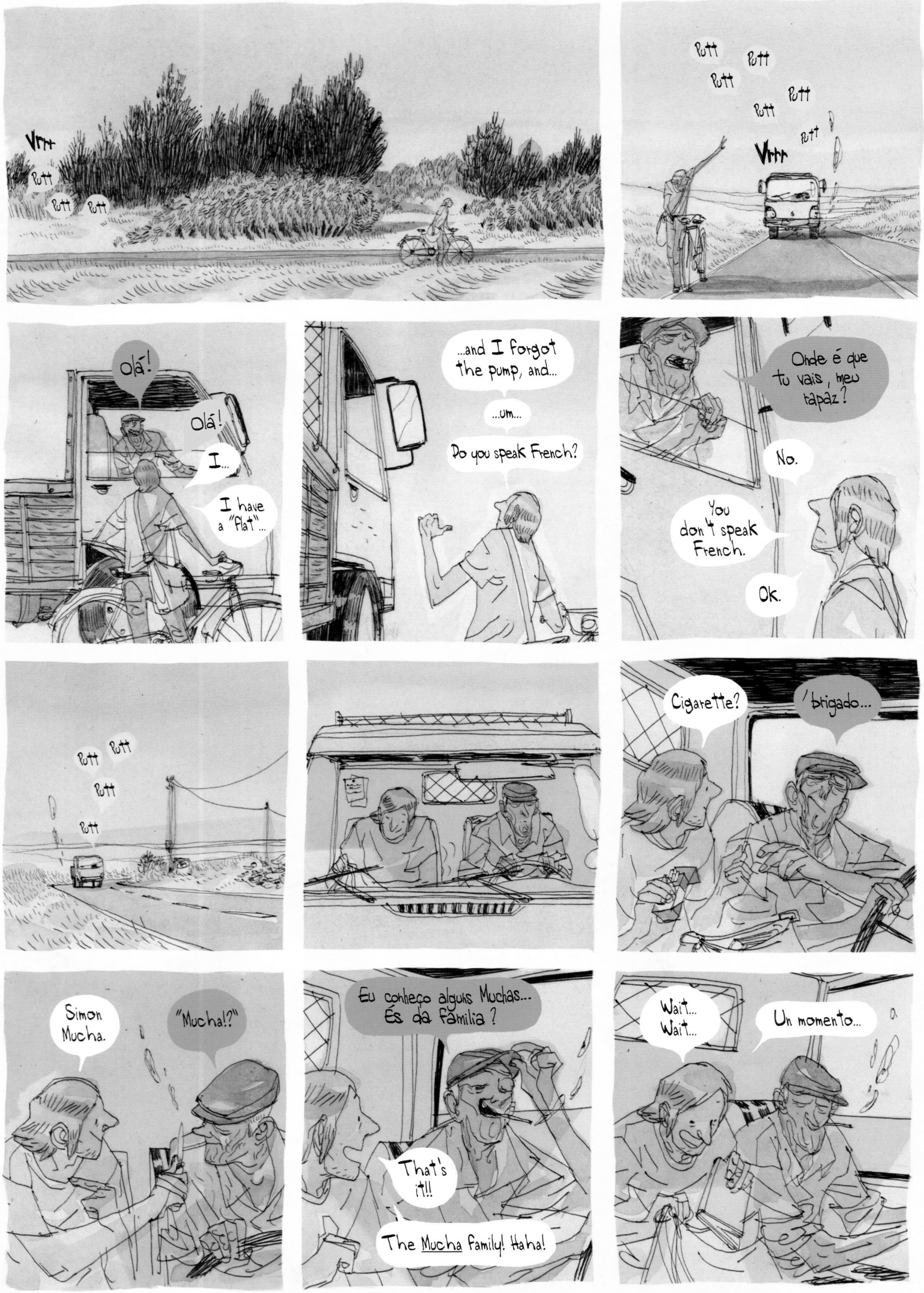
Vrrr
Putt
Putt
Putt
Putt
Putt
Putt
Putt
Putt
Putt
Vrrr
Olá!
Olá!
I...
I have a "flat"...
...and I forgot the pump, and...
...um...
Do you speak French?
Onde é que tu vais, meu rapaz?
No.
You don't speak French.
Ok.
Putt
Putt
Putt
Putt
Cigarette?
'brigado...
Simon Mucha.
"Mucha!?"
Eu conheço alguns Muchas... És da família?
That's it!!
The Mucha family! Haha!
Wait... Wait...
Un momento...

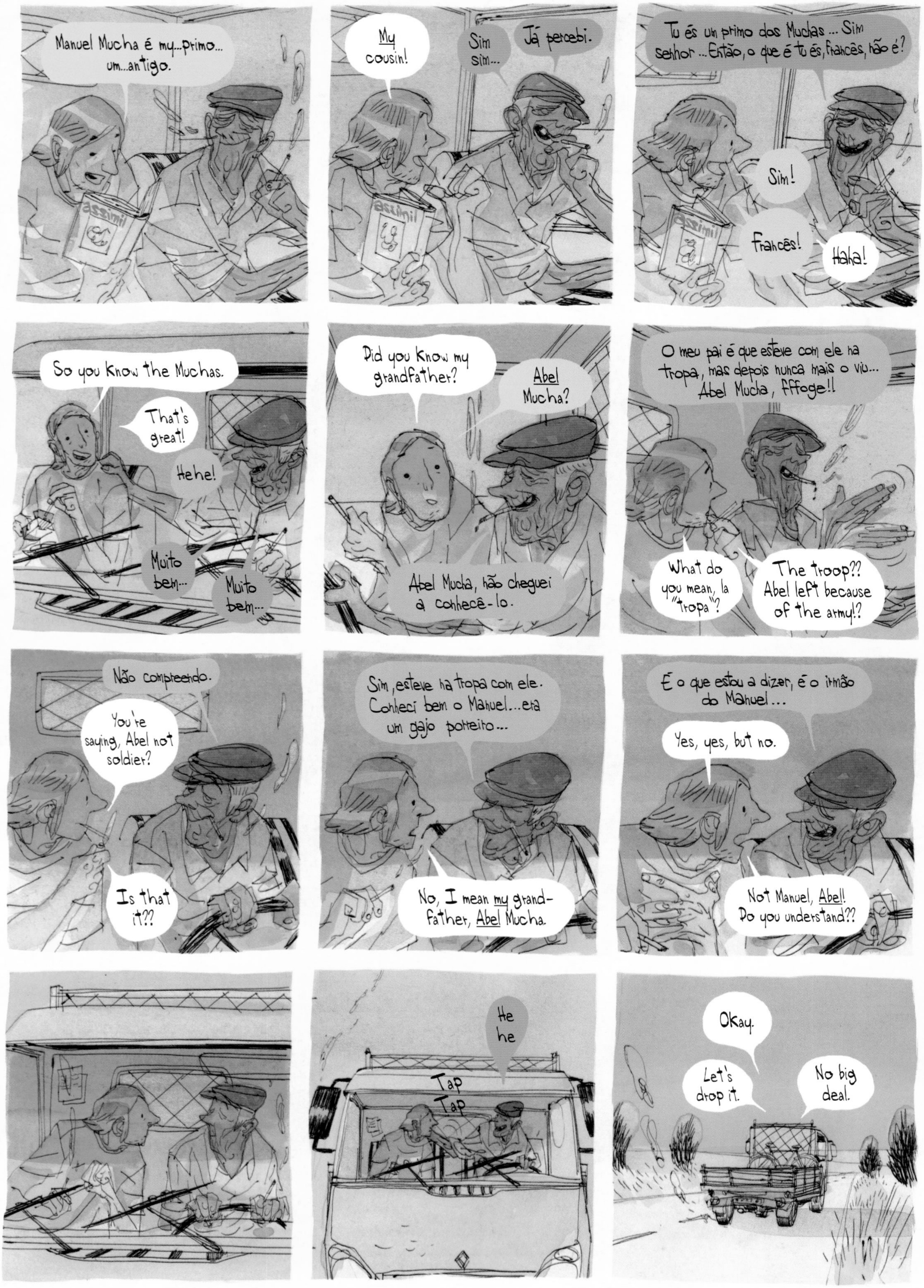
Manuel Mucha é my...primo... um...antigo.
My cousin!
Sim sim...
Já percebi.
Tu és um primo dos Muchas ... Sim senhor ... Então, o que é tu és, francês, não é?
Sim!
Francês!
Haha!
So you know the Muchas.
That's great!
Hehe!
Muito bem...
Muito bem...
Did you know my grandfather?
Abel Mucha?
Abel Mucha, não cheguei a conhecê-lo.
O meu pai é que esteve com ele na tropa, mas depois nunca mais o viu... Abel Mucha, fffoge!!
What do you mean, la "tropa"?
The troop?? Abel left because of the army!?
Não compreendo.
You're saying, Abel not soldier?
Is that it??
Sim, esteve na tropa com ele. Conheci bem o Manuel...era um gajo porreiro...
No, I mean my grand-father, Abel Mucha.
É o que estou a dizer, é o irmão do Manuel...
Yes, yes, but no.
Not Manuel, Abel! Do you understand??
He he
Tap Tap
Okay.
Let's drop it.
No big deal.

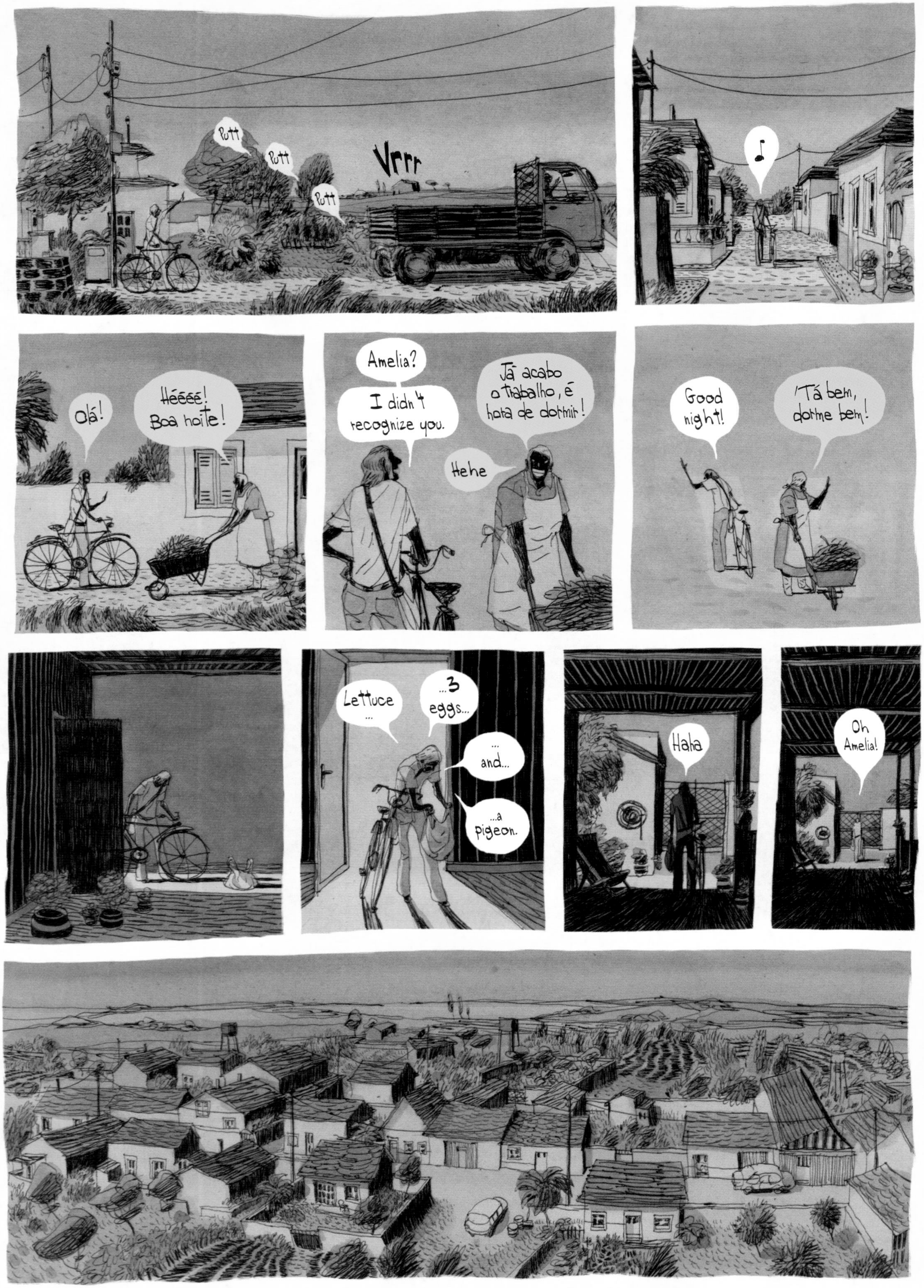
Putt
Putt
Putt
Vrrr
Olá!
Hééé! Boa noite!
Amelia?
I didn't recognize you.
Já acabo o trabalho, é hora de dormir!
Hehe
Good night!
'Tá bem, dorme bem!
Lettuce ...
...3 eggs...
... and...
...a pigeon.
Haha
Oh Amelia!

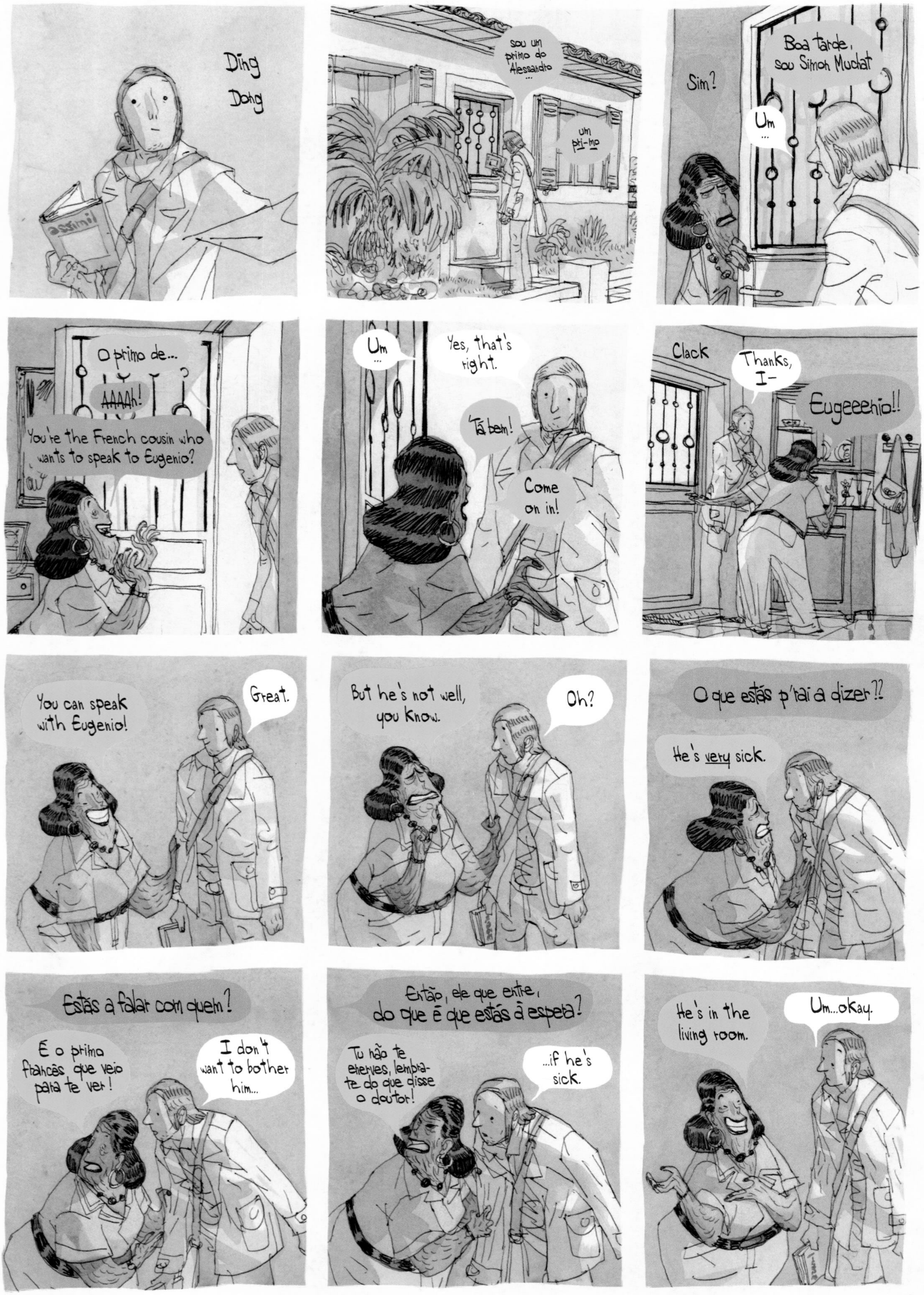
Ding
Dong
sou um primo do Alessandro ...
um pri-mo
Sim?
Boa tarde, sou Simon Muchat
Um ...
O primo de...
AAAAh!
You're the French cousin who wants to speak to Eugenio?
Um ...
Yes, that's right.
'Tá bem!
Come on in!
Clack
Thanks, I-
Eugeeenio!!
You can speak with Eugenio!
Great.
But he's not well, you know.
Oh?
O que estás p'rai a dizer??
He's very sick.
Estás a falar com quem?
É o primo francês que veio para te ver!
I don't want to bother him...
Então, ele que entre, do que é que estás à espera?
Tu não te enerves, lembra-te do que disse o doutor!
...if he's sick.
He's in the living room.
Um...okay.

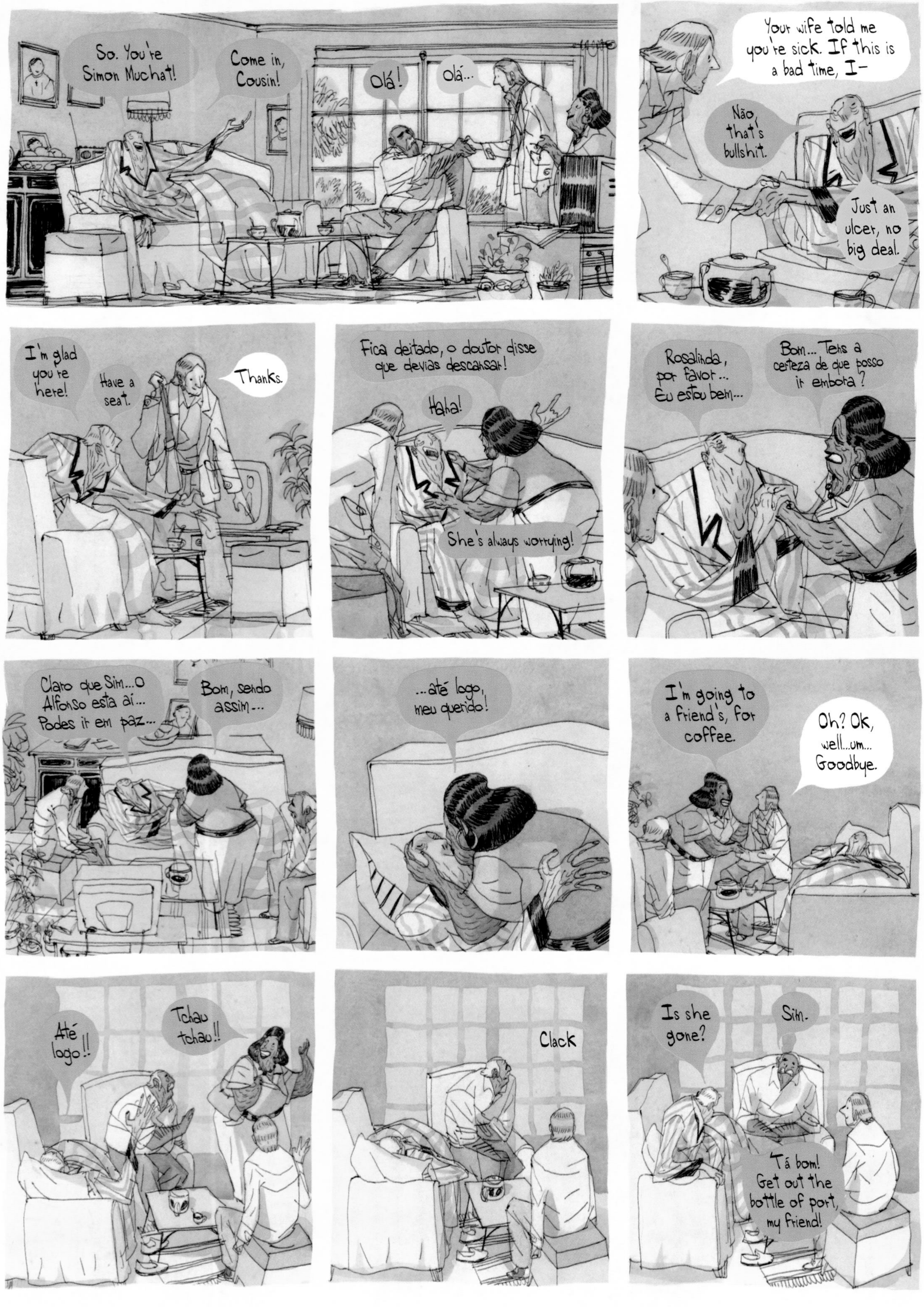
So. You're Simon Muchat!
Come in, Cousin!
Olá!
Olá...
Your wife told me you're sick. If this is a bad time, I–
Não, that's bullshit.
Just an ulcer, no big deal.
I'm glad you're here!
Have a seat.
Thanks.
Fica deitado, o doutor disse que devias descansar!
Haha!
She's always worrying!
Rosalinda, por favor... Eu estou bem...
Bom... Tens a certeza de que posso ir embora?
Claro que Sim...o Alfonso esta aí... Podes ir em paz...
Bom, sendo assim...
...até logo, meu querido!
I'm going to a friend's, for coffee.
Oh? Ok, well...um... Goodbye.
Até logo!!
Tchau tchau!!
Clack
Is she gone?
Sim.
Tá bom! Get out the bottle of port, my friend!

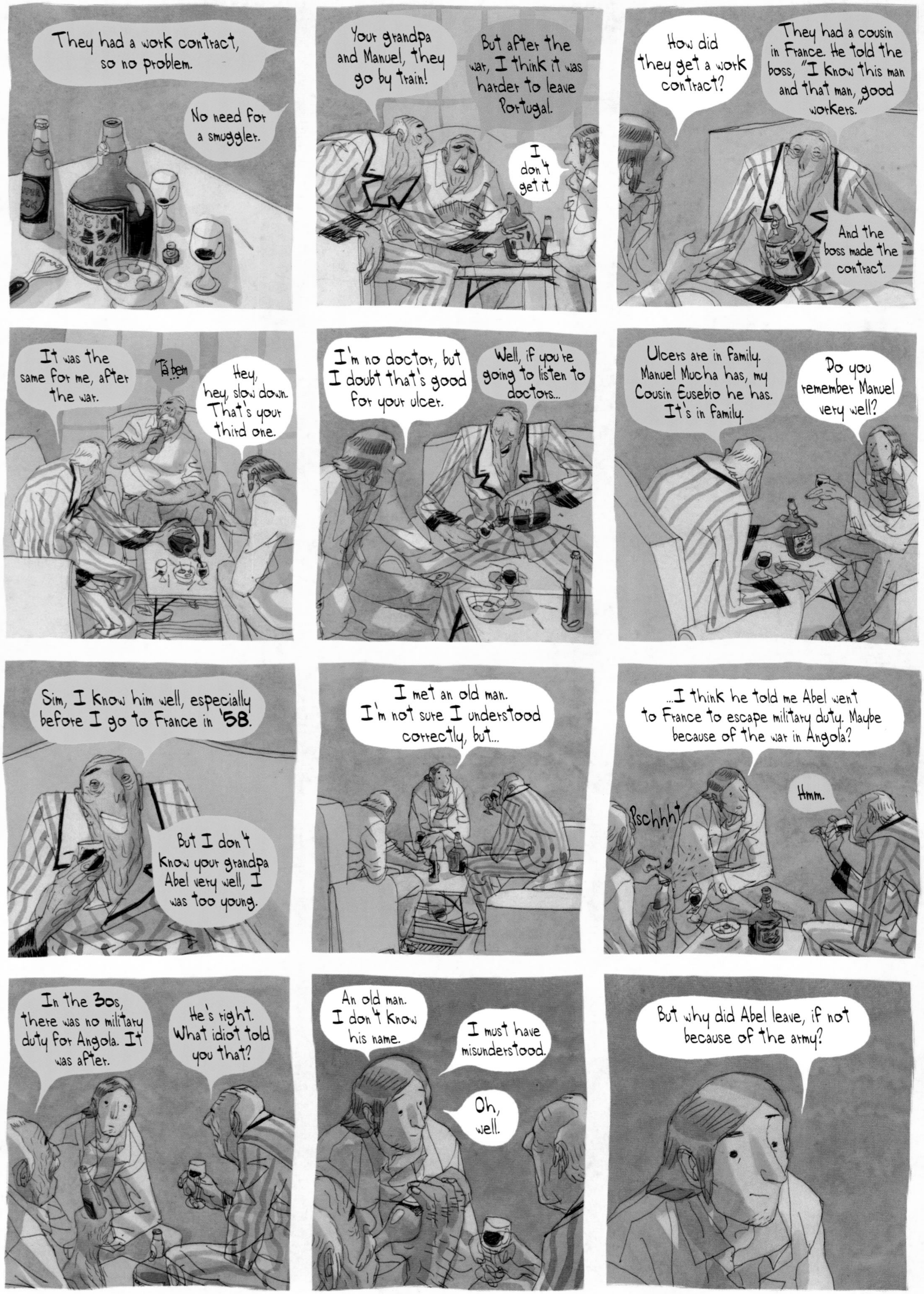
They had a work contract, so no problem.
No need for a smuggler.
Your grandpa and Manuel, they go by train!
But after the war, I think it was harder to leave Portugal.
I don't get it.
How did they get a work contract?
They had a cousin in France. He told the boss, "I know this man and that man, good workers."
And the boss made the contract.
It was the same for me, after the war.
Tá bem...
Hey, hey, slow down. That's your third one.
I'm no doctor, but I doubt that's good for your ulcer.
Well, if you're going to listen to doctors...
Ulcers are in family. Manuel Mucha has, my Cousin Eusebio he has. It's in family.
Do you remember Manuel very well?
Sim, I know him well, especially before I go to France in '58.
But I don't know your grandpa Abel very well, I was too young.
I met an old man. I'm not sure I understood correctly, but...
...I think he told me Abel went to France to escape military duty. Maybe because of the war in Angola?
Pschhht
Hmm.
In the 30s, there was no military duty for Angola. It was after.
He's right. What idiot told you that?
An old man. I don't know his name.
I must have misunderstood.
Oh, well.
But why did Abel leave, if not because of the army?

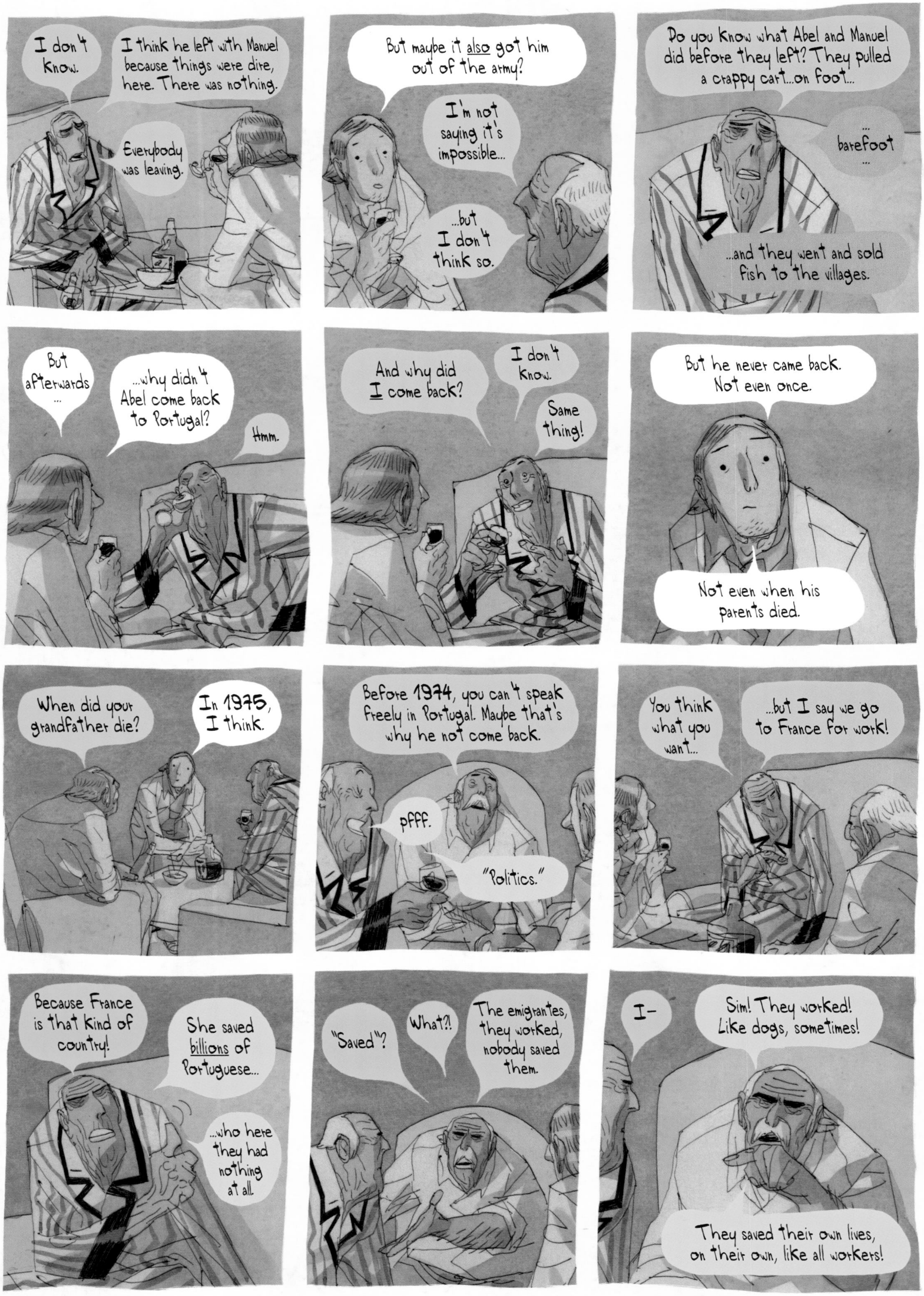

I don't know.
I think he left with Manuel because things were dire, here. There was nothing.
Everybody was leaving.
But maybe it also got him out of the army?
I'm not saying it's impossible...
...but I don't think so.
Do you know what Abel and Manuel did before they left? They pulled a crappy cart...on foot...
... barefoot ...
...and they went and sold fish to the villages.
But afterwards ...
...why didn't Abel come back to Portugal?
Hmm.
And why did I come back?
I don't know.
Same thing!
But he never came back. Not even once.
Not even when his parents died.
When did your grandfather die?
In 1975, I think.
Before 1974, you can't speak freely in Portugal. Maybe that's why he not come back.
pfff.
"Politics."
You think what you want...
...but I say we go to France for work!
Because France is that kind of country!
She saved billions of Portuguese...
...who here they had nothing at all.
"Saved"?
What?!
The emigrantes, they worked, nobody saved them.
I-
Sim! They worked! Like dogs, sometimes!
They saved their own lives, on their own, like all workers!

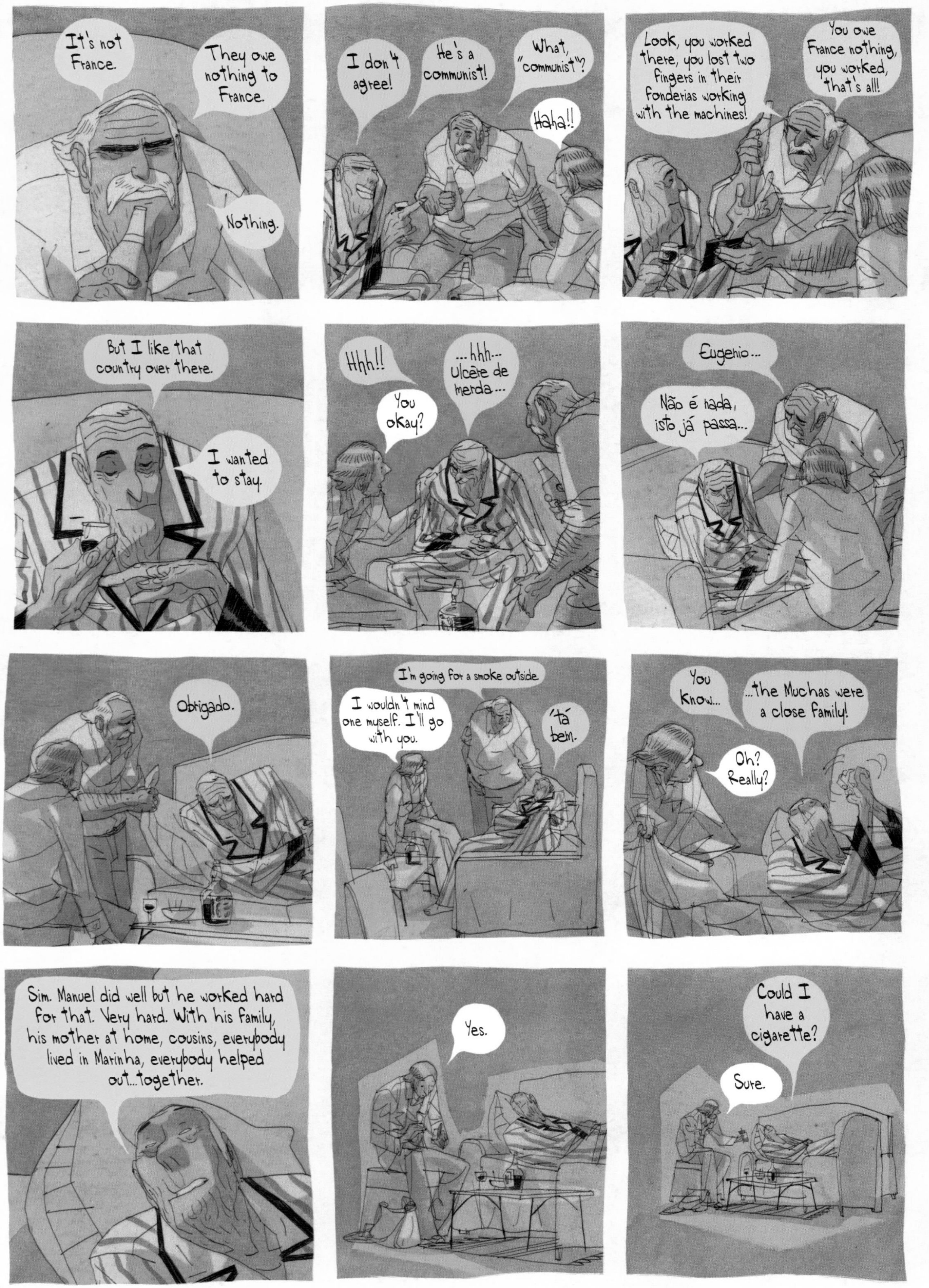
It's not France.
They owe nothing to France.
Nothing.
I don't agree!
He's a communist!
What, "communist"?
Haha!!
Look, you worked there, you lost two fingers in their fonderias working with the machines!
You owe France nothing, you worked, that's all!
But I like that country over there.
I wanted to stay.
Hhh!!
...hhh... Ulcère de merda...
You okay?
Eugenio...
Não é nada, isto já passa...
Obrigado.
I'm going for a smoke outside
I wouldn't mind one myself. I'll go with you.
'tá bem.
You know...
...the Muchas were a close family!
Oh? Really?
Sim. Manuel did well but he worked hard for that. Very hard. With his family, his mother at home, cousins, everybody lived in Marinha, everybody helped out...together.
Yes.
Could I have a cigarette?
Sure.

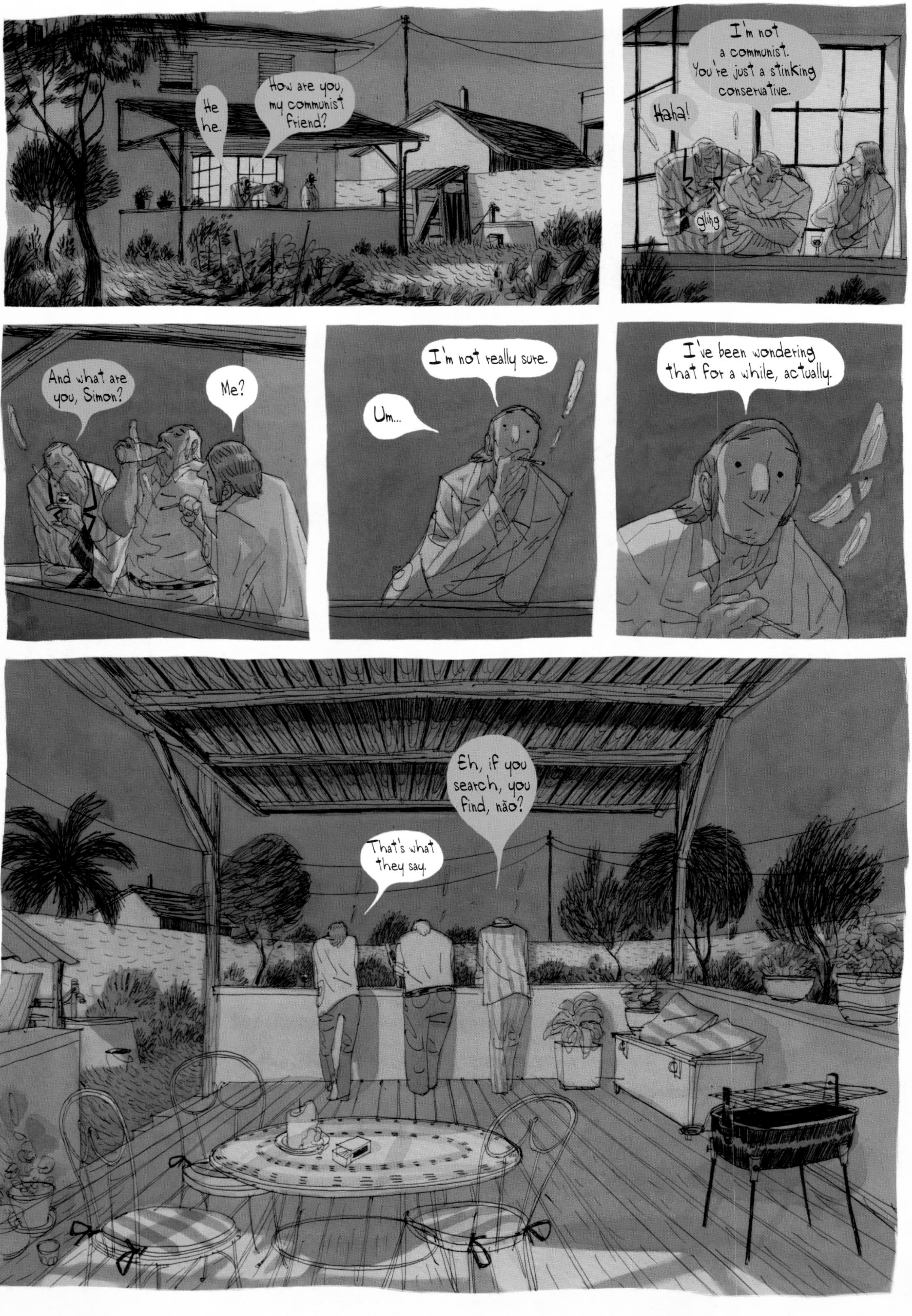
He he.
How are you, my communist friend?
I'm not a communist. You're just a stinking conservative.
Haha!
gling
And what are you, Simon?
Me?
Um...
I'm not really sure.
I've been wondering that for a while, actually.
Eh, if you search, you find, não?
That's what they say.

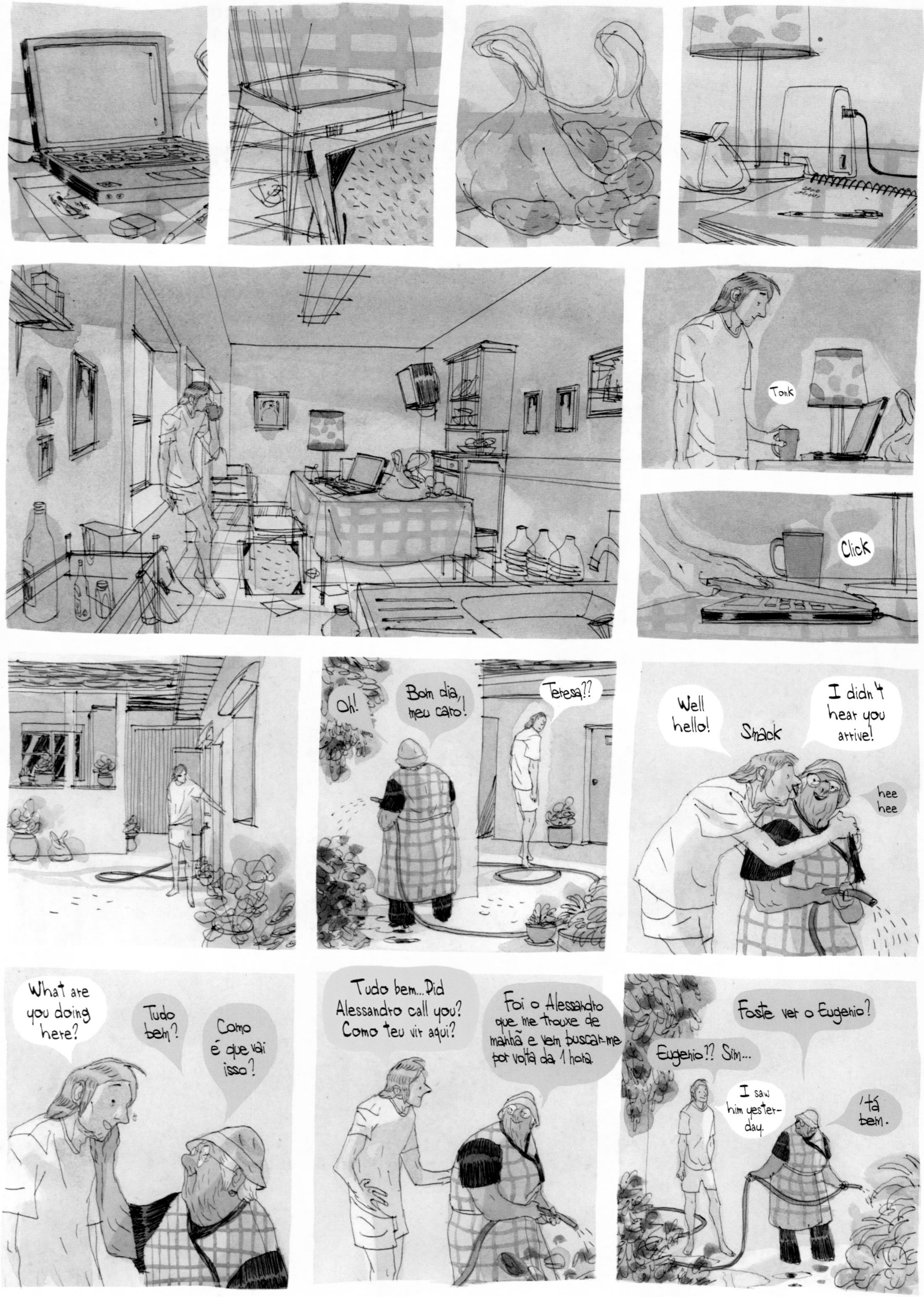
Tonk
Click
Oh!
Bom dia, meu caro!
Teresa??
Well hello!
Smack
I didn't hear you arrive!
hee hee
What are you doing here?
Tudo bem?
Como é que vai isso?
Tudo bem... Did Alessandro call you? Como teu vir aqui?
Foi o Alessandro que me trouxe de manhã e vem buscar-me por volta da 1 hora.
Foste ver o Eugenio?
Eugenio?? Sim...
I saw him yesterday.
'tá bem.

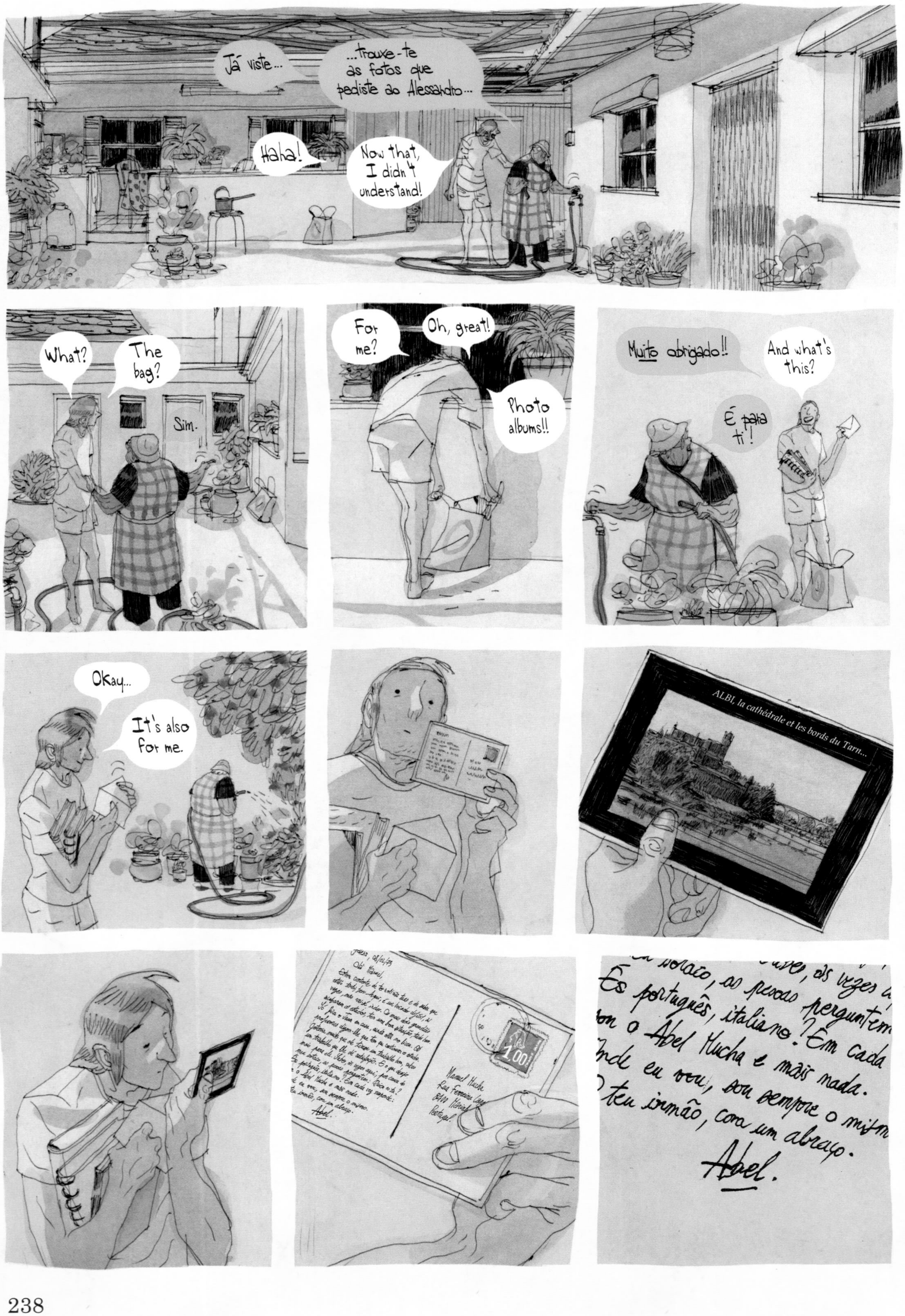
Já viste...
...trouxe-te as fotos que pediste ao Alessandro...
Haha!
Now that, I didn't understand!
What?
The bag?
Sim.
For me?
Oh, great!
Photo albums!!
Muito obrigado!!
And what's this?
É para ti!
Okay...
It's also for me.
ALBI, la cathédrale et les bords du Tarn...
És português, italiano? Em cada
o Abel Mucha e mais nada.
eu vou, sou sempre o mesmo
teu irmão, com um abraço.
Abel.

Teresa tried to gently protest. Alessandro would be there in just a few hours...

está sou eu com o meu irmão e os meus pais...

"Irmão"?

...and she was sure he could talk about the photos a lot better than she could.

...penso que estávamos a chegar a casa...

irmão...

Shit, what does that mean, again?

But I didn't have the patience to wait.

irmão

irmão...

Ah! "Brother".

Plus, I wanted to look through the albums with her.

Sim, Camilo! Meu irmão!

Ok, so Camilo's your brother.

She patiently answered my questions.

Espera...

Wait, let me write this down.

Ca-mi-lo...

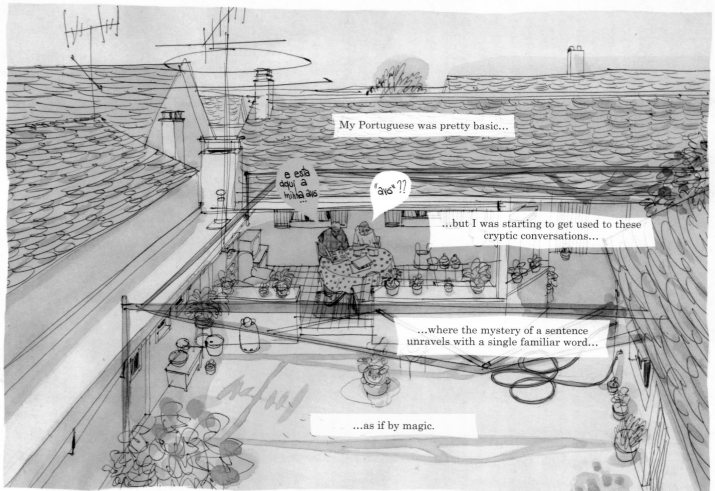

My Portuguese was pretty basic...

e está aqui a minha avó

"avó"??

...but I was starting to get used to these cryptic conversations...

...where the mystery of a sentence unravels with a single familiar word...

...as if by magic.

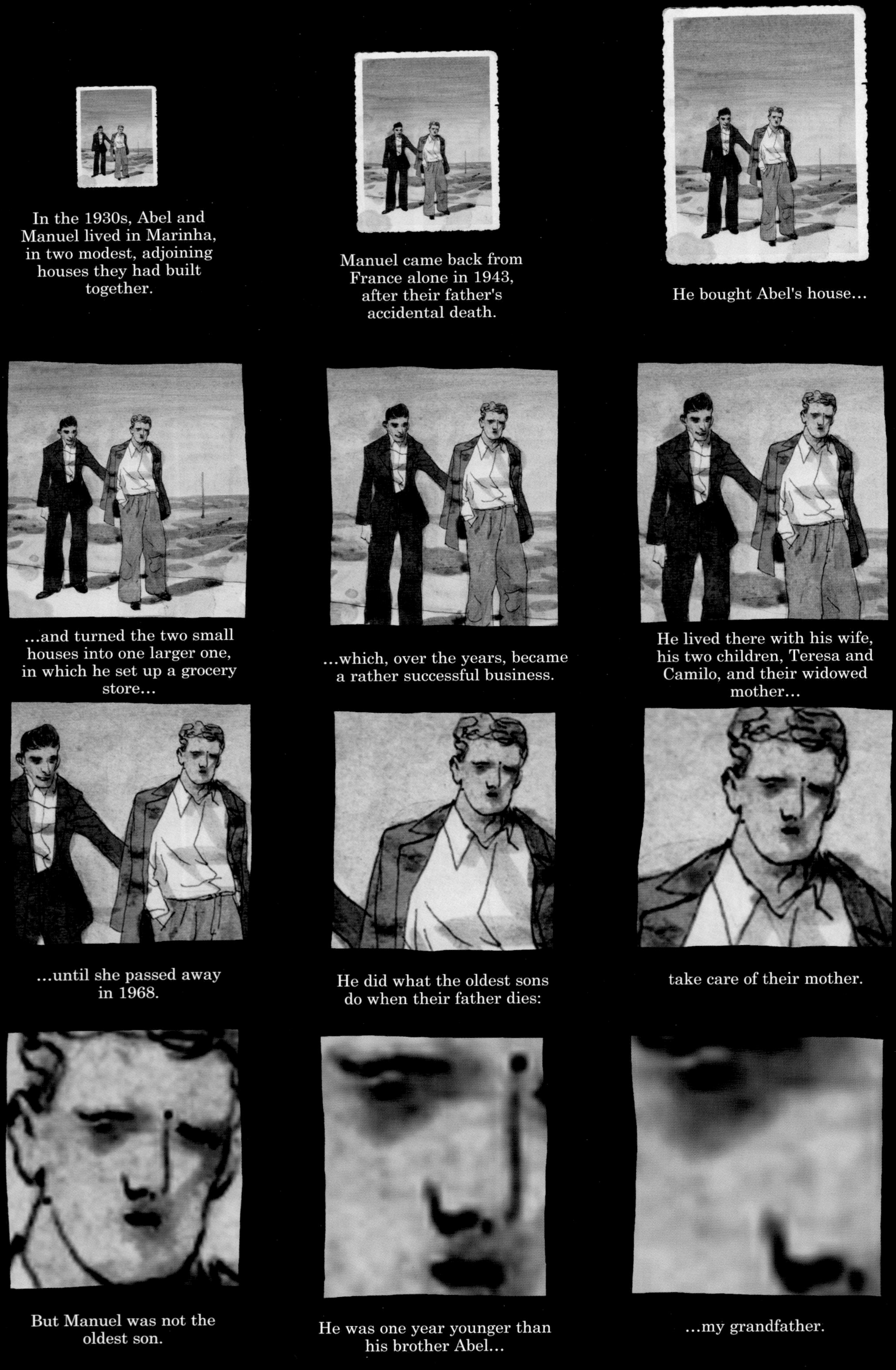
In the 1930s, Abel and Manuel lived in Marinha, in two modest, adjoining houses they had built together.
Manuel came back from France alone in 1943, after their father's accidental death.
He bought Abel's house...
...and turned the two small houses into one larger one, in which he set up a grocery store...
...which, over the years, became a rather successful business.
He lived there with his wife, his two children, Teresa and Camilo, and their widowed mother...
...until she passed away in 1968.
He did what the oldest sons do when their father dies:
take care of their mother.
But Manuel was not the oldest son.
He was one year younger than his brother Abel...
...my grandfather.

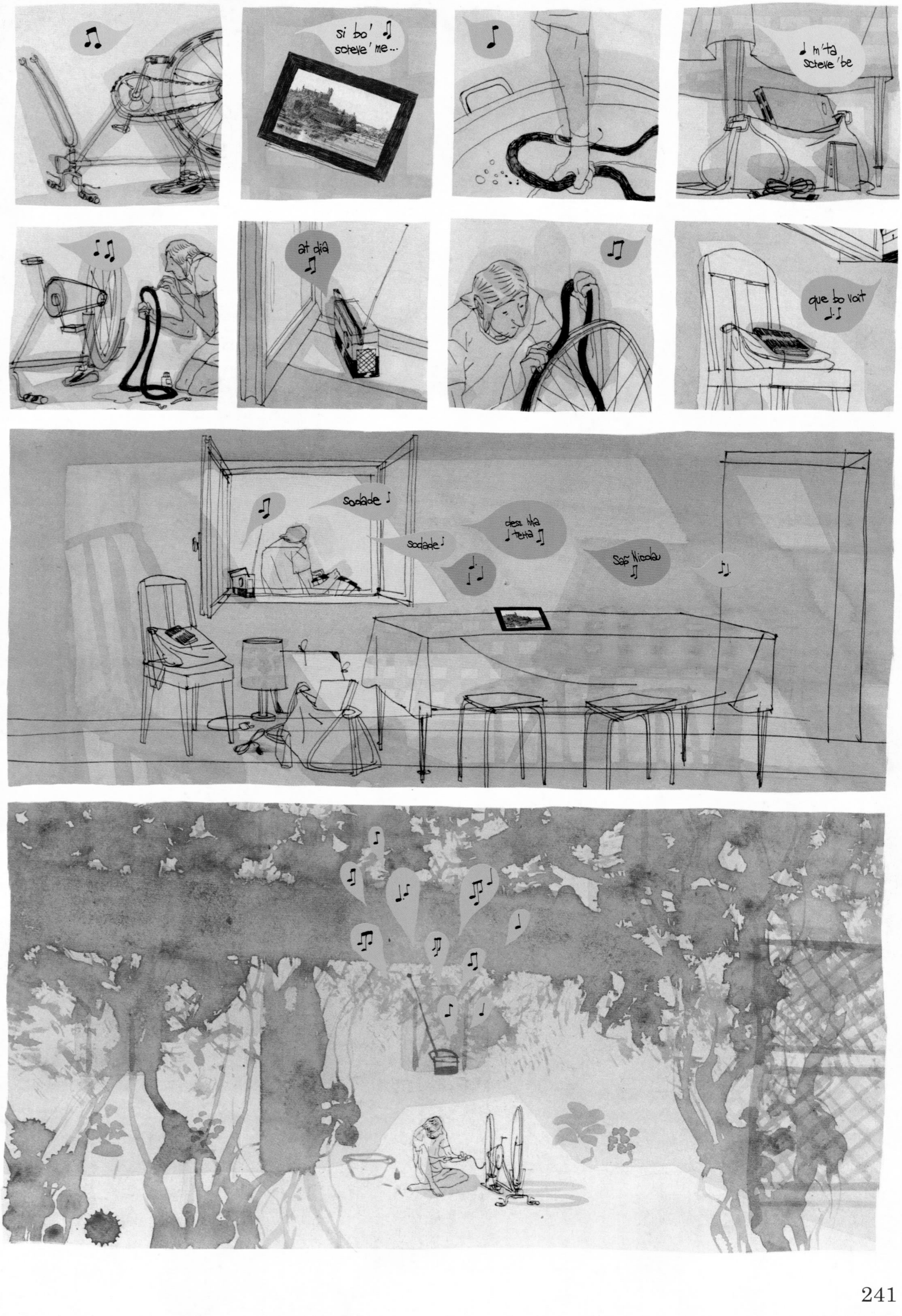
si bo' scteve'me...
m'ta scteve'be
at dia
que bo vait
sodade
sodade
dess nha terra
Saõ Nicolau

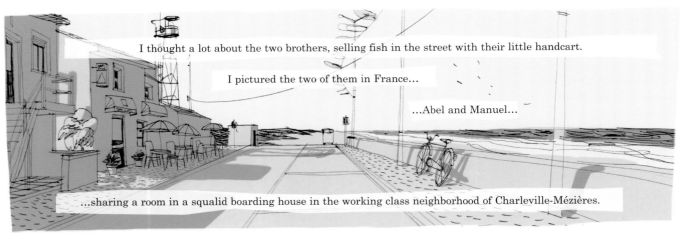

I thought a lot about the two brothers, selling fish in the street with their little handcart.

I pictured the two of them in France...

...Abel and Manuel...

...sharing a room in a squalid boarding house in the working class neighborhood of Charleville-Mézières.

It was probably one evening after work that they received the letter with the bad news.

Telling them of their father's death.

A long, sad evening where dreams were shattered...

...and it all fell apart.

Maybe they made a deal that night.

"You go home and take my house, and I'll stay here."

Or maybe they argued.

Abel not wanting to go home and give up his dreams for the future in the name of duty and family.

Manuel disappointed in his brother and deciding to do it himself.

Maybe that night sealed the slow dilution of our family.

Divisions that continued on through the generations.

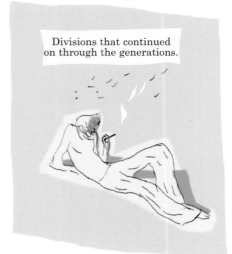

A family in which it is hard to feel free.

Where the men have a hard time living their lives.

242

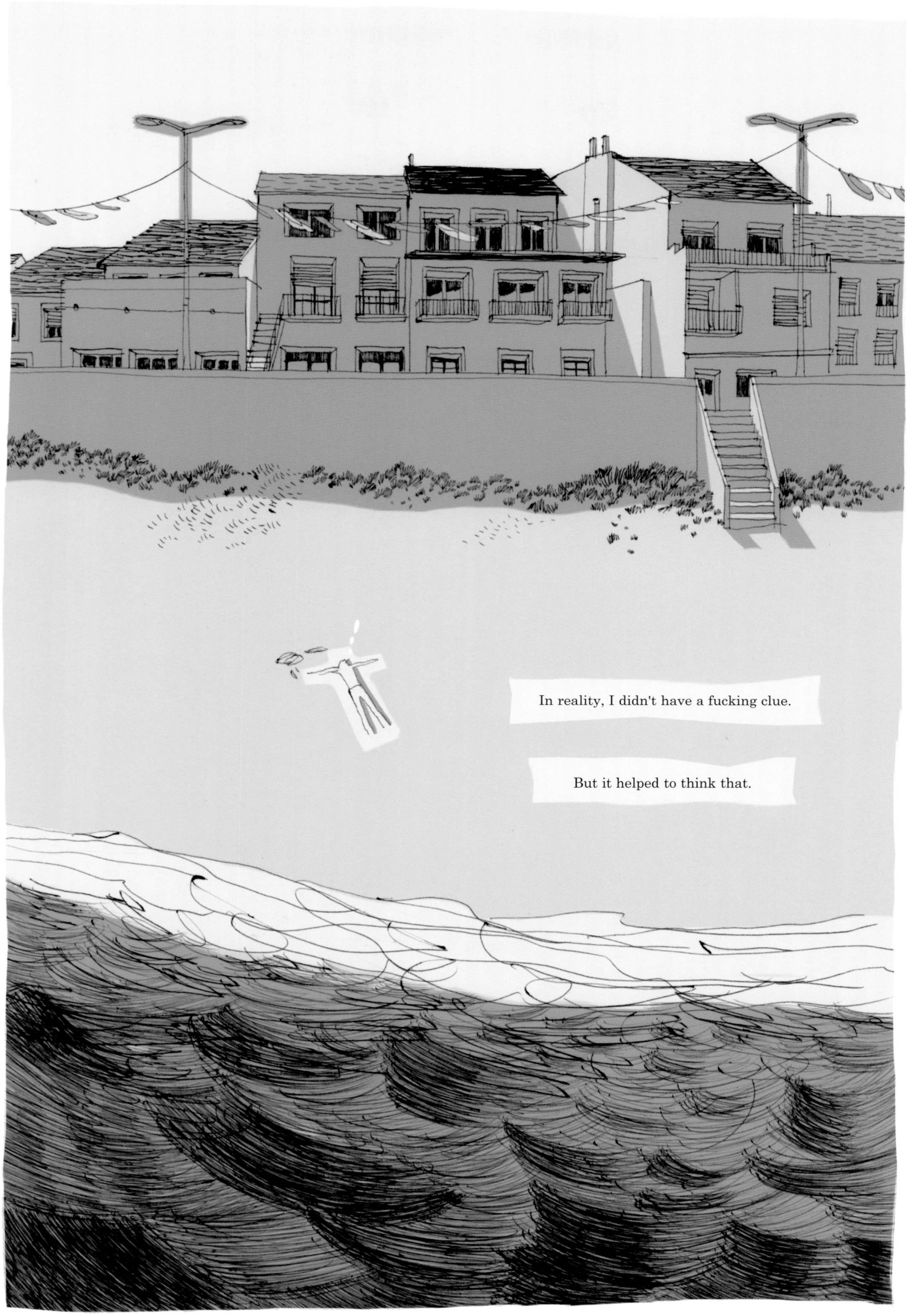
In reality, I didn't have a fucking clue.
But it helped to think that.

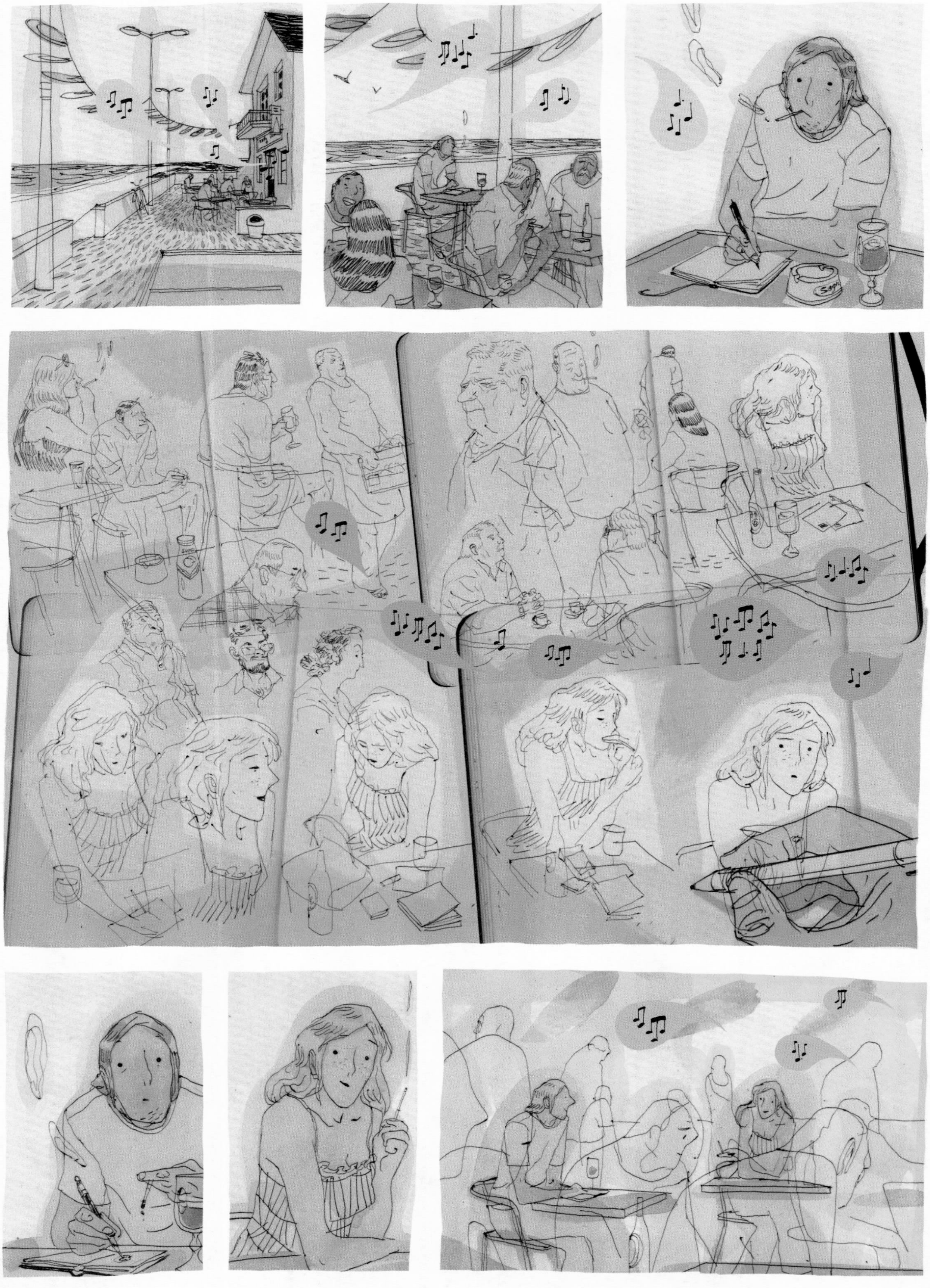

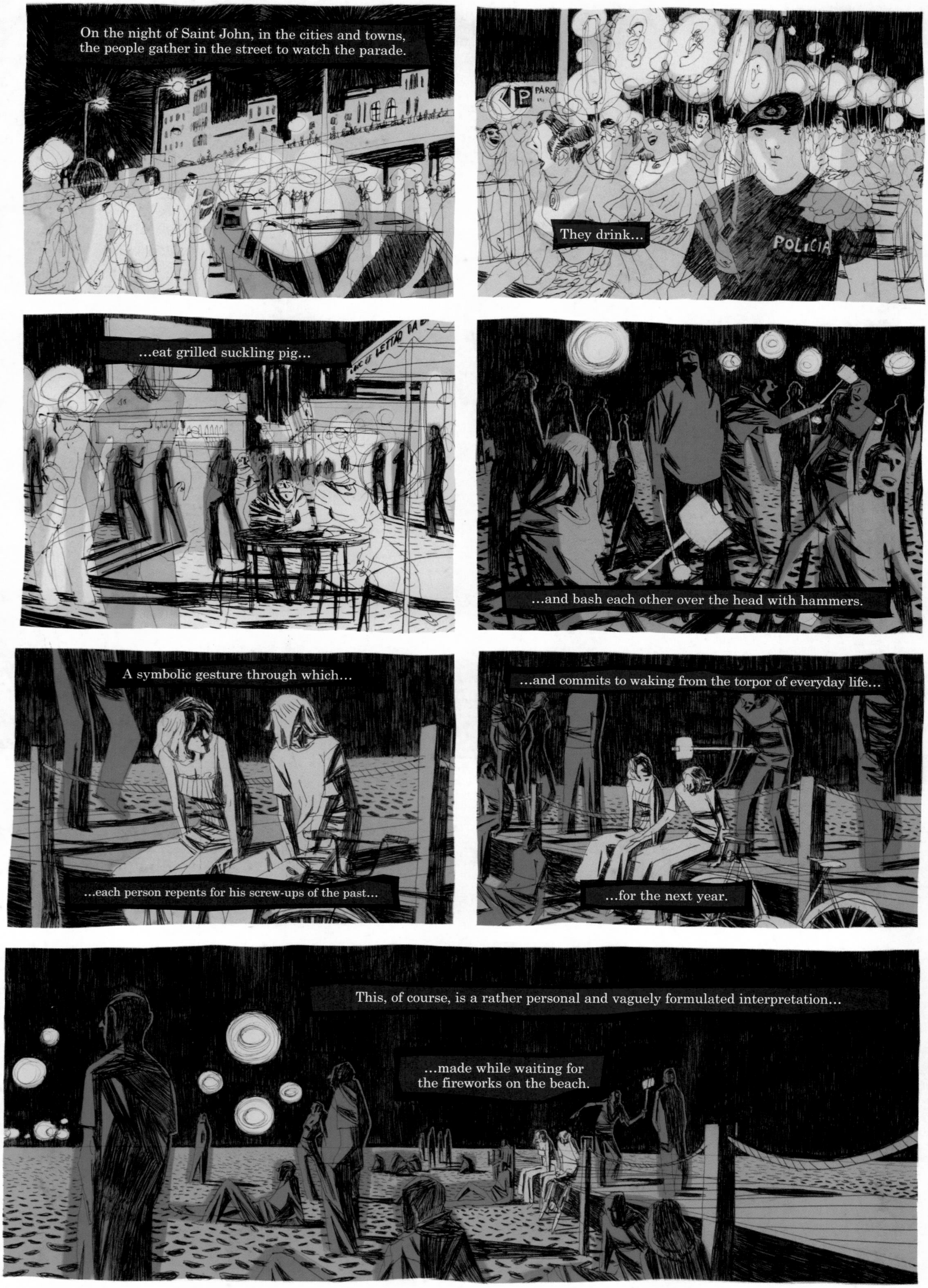
On the night of Saint John, in the cities and towns, the people gather in the street to watch the parade.
They drink...
POLICIA
...eat grilled suckling pig...
...and bash each other over the head with hammers.
A symbolic gesture through which...
...each person repents for his screw-ups of the past...
...and commits to waking from the torpor of everyday life...
...for the next year.
This, of course, is a rather personal and vaguely formulated interpretation...
...made while waiting for the fireworks on the beach.

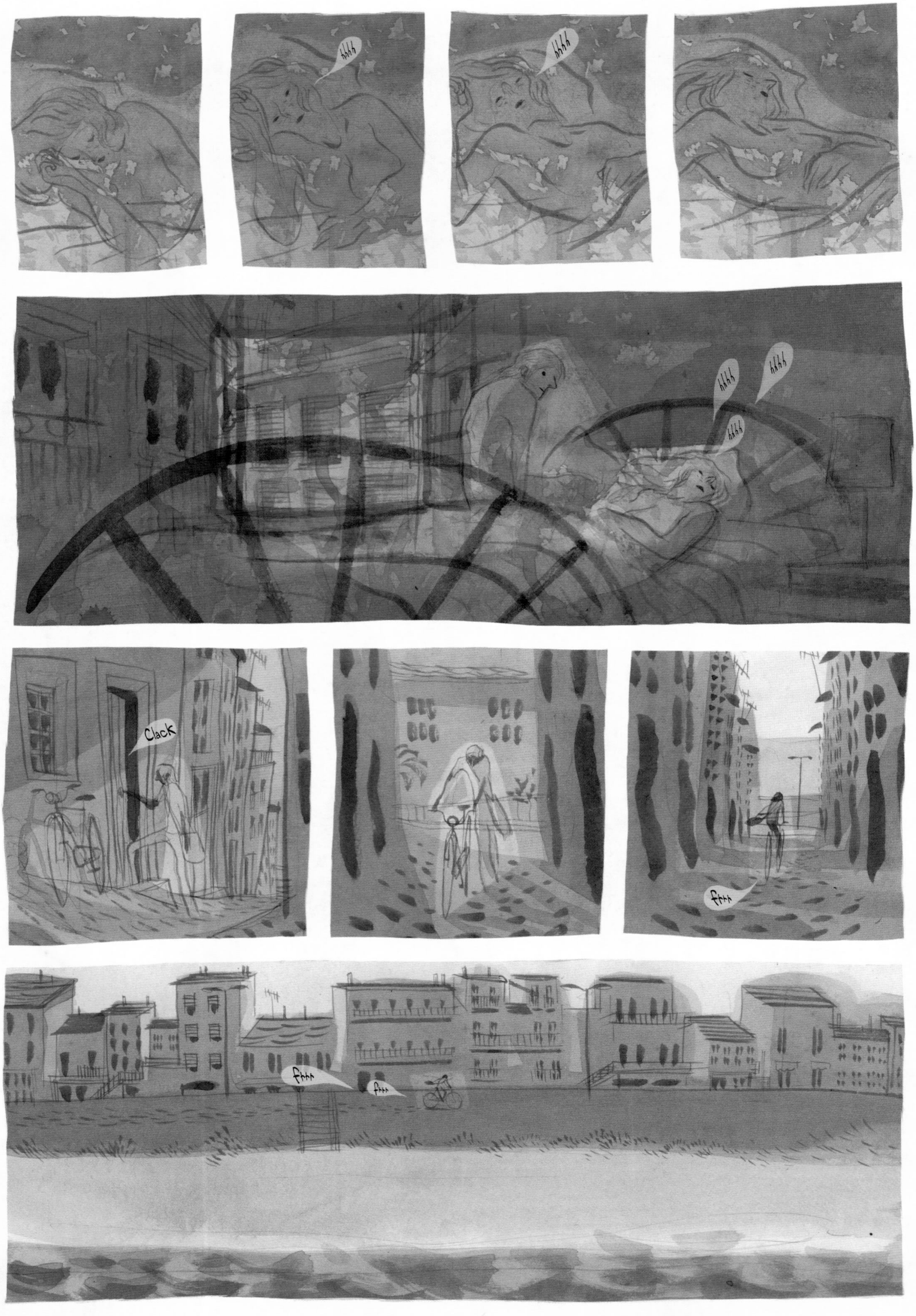
hhhh
hhhh
hhhh
hhhh
hhhh
Clack
frrr
frrr
frrr

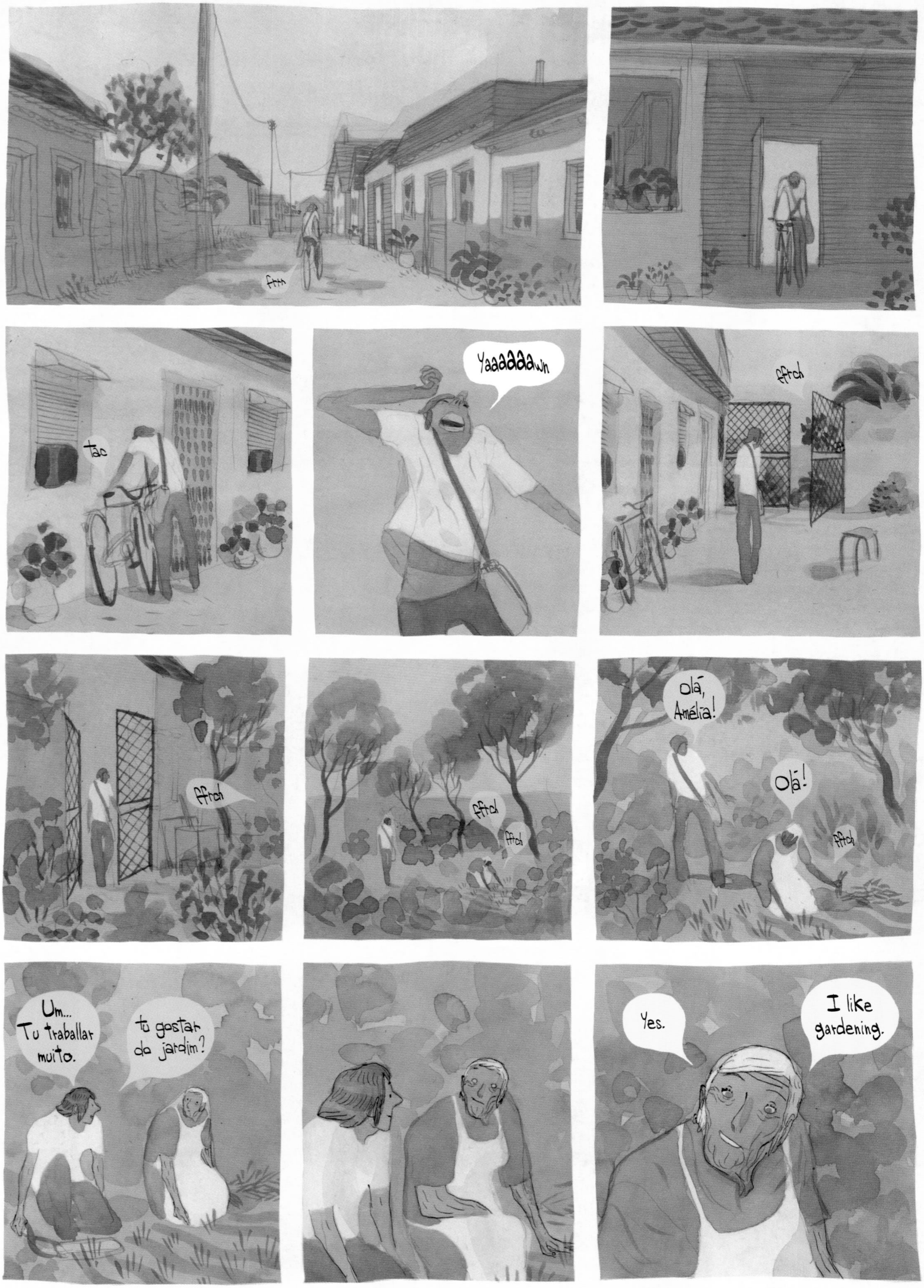
frrr
tac
Yaaaaaawn
ffrch
ffrch
ffrch
ffrch
Olá, Amélia!
Olá!
ffrch
Um... Tu traballar muito.
tu gostar da jardim?
Yes.
I like gardening.

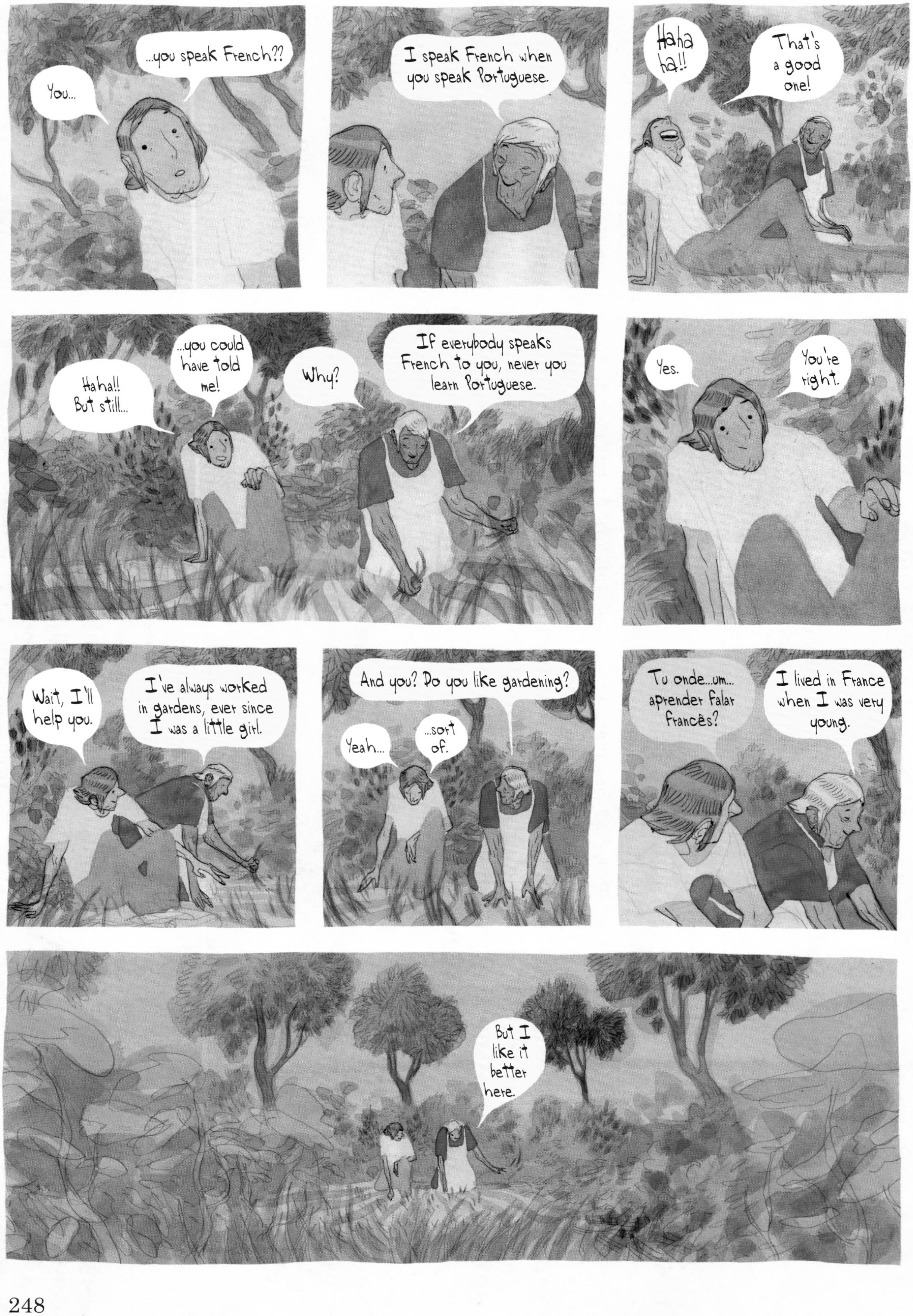
You...
...you speak French??
I speak French when you speak Portuguese.
Haha ha!!
That's a good one!
Haha!! But still...
...you could have told me!
Why?
If everybody speaks French to you, never you learn Portuguese.
Yes.
You're right.
Wait, I'll help you.
I've always worked in gardens, ever since I was a little girl.
And you? Do you like gardening?
Yeah...
...sort of.
Tu onde...um... aprender falar francês?
I lived in France when I was very young.
But I like it better here.

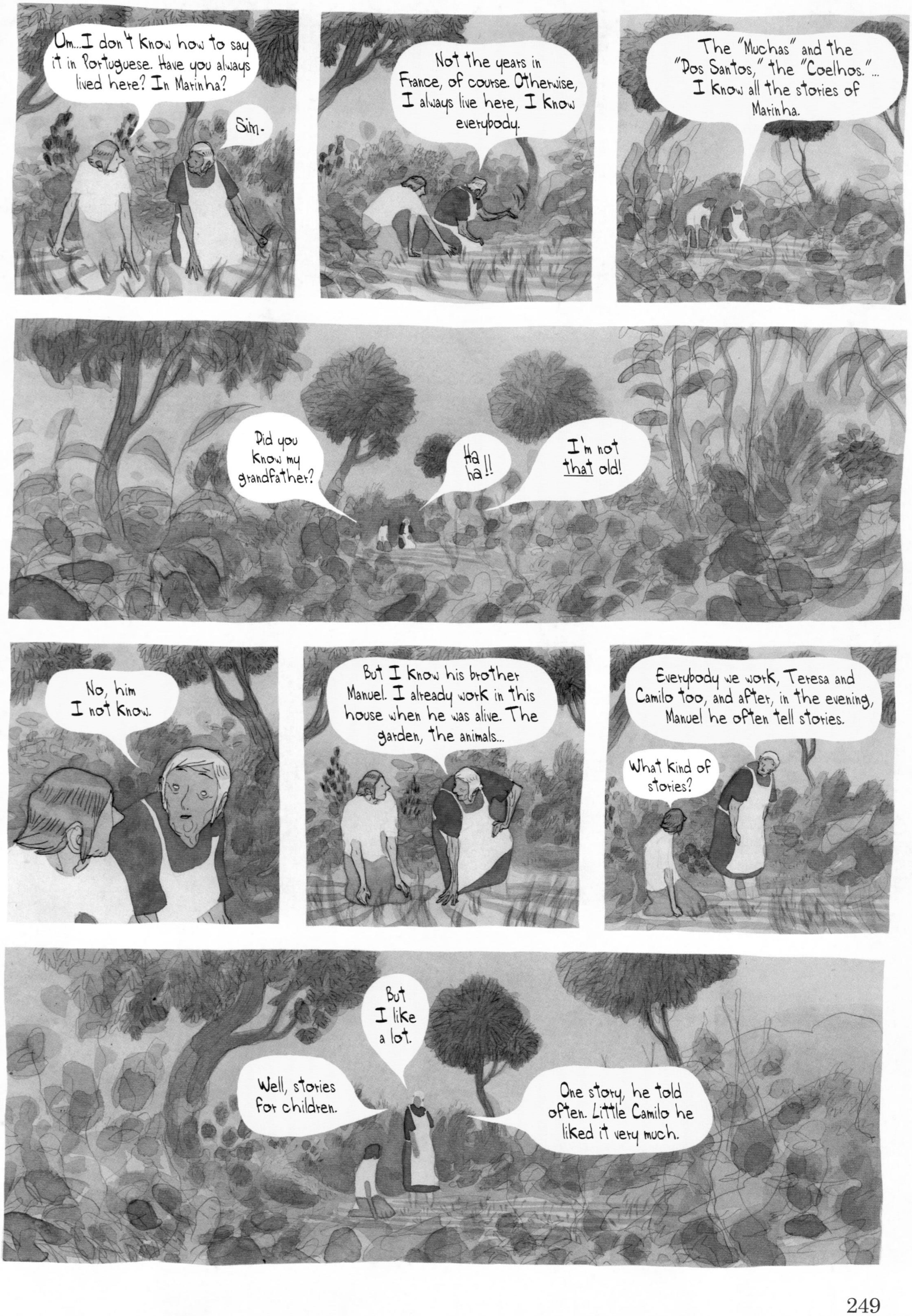
Um...I don't know how to say it in Portuguese. Have you always lived here? In Marinha?
Sim.
Not the years in France, of course. Otherwise, I always live here, I know everybody.
The "Muchas" and the "Dos Santos," the "Coelhos."... I know all the stories of Marinha.
Did you know my grandfather?
Ha ha!!
I'm not that old!
No, him I not know.
But I know his brother Manuel. I already work in this house when he was alive. The garden, the animals...
Everybody we work, Teresa and Camilo too, and after, in the evening, Manuel he often tell stories.
What kind of stories?
Well, stories for children.
But I like a lot.
One story, he told often. Little Camilo he liked it very much.

"It was a long, long time ago…

…when Spain and Portugal were at war."

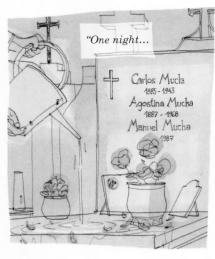

"One night…

Carlos Mucla
1885 - 1943
Agostina Mucha
1887 - 1968
Manuel Mucha
1987

…three exhausted men on horses came knocking at the door of one of the little farms in Marinha da Costa."

"They were Spanish…

…and traveling with a little boy."

"They asked if they could sleep in the barn for the night."

"The farmers, intimidated by the armed men,

didn't dare refuse them hospitality."

"In the early morning, the farmer who had taken them in was worried because they had not yet awoken, and he approached the barn."

Carlos Mucl
1885 - 1943
Agostina Mucha
1887 - 1968
Manuel Mucha
M -

"The horsemen were no longer there."

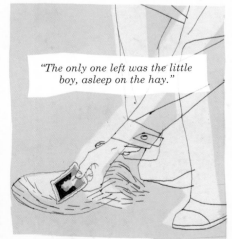

"The only one left was the little boy, asleep on the hay."

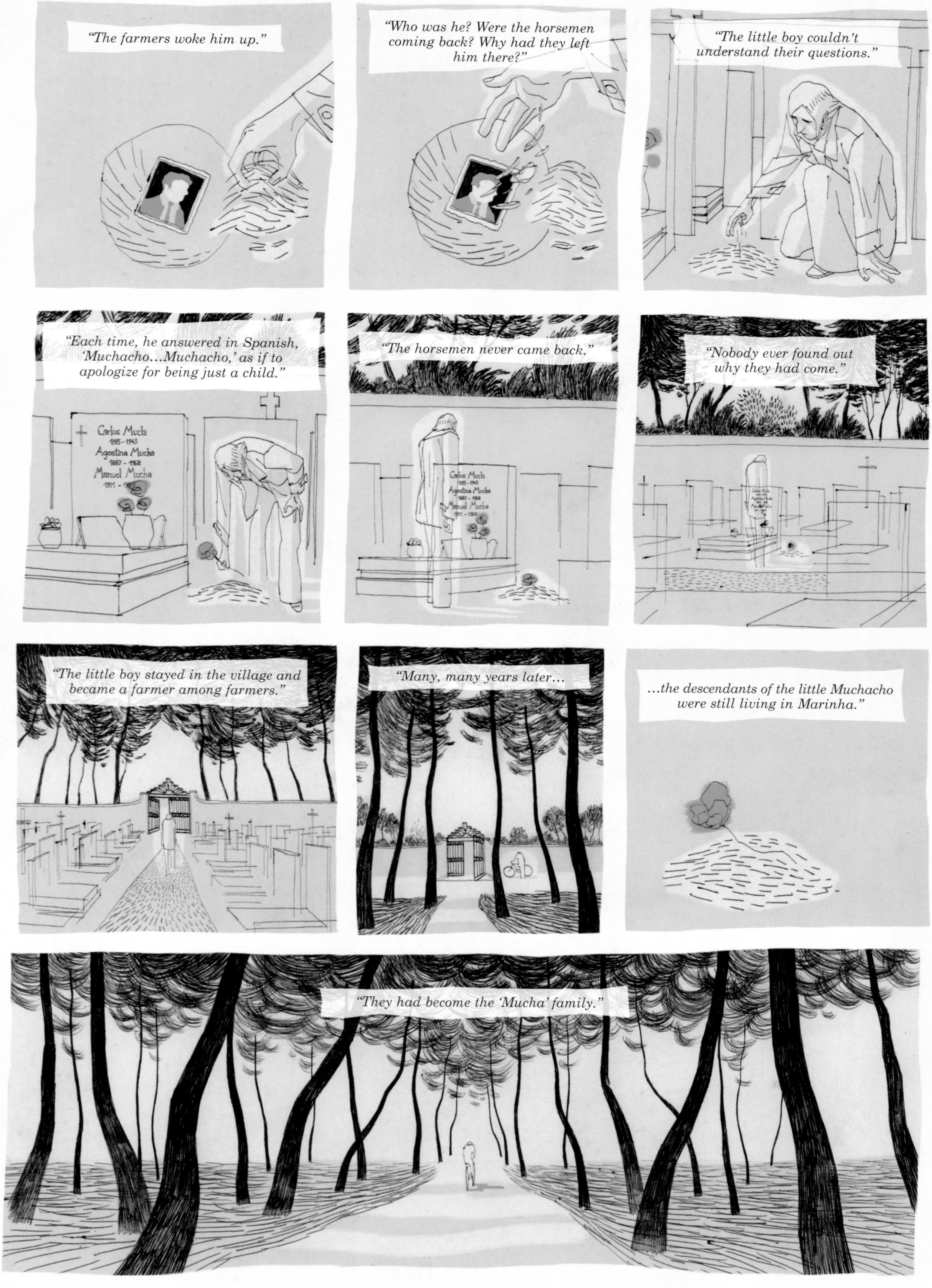
"The farmers woke him up."
"Who was he? Were the horsemen coming back? Why had they left him there?"
"The little boy couldn't understand their questions."
"Each time, he answered in Spanish, 'Muchacho…Muchacho,' as if to apologize for being just a child."
Carlos Mucha
1885 - 1943
Agostina Mucha
1887 - 1968
Manuel Mucha
"The horsemen never came back."
"Nobody ever found out why they had come."
"The little boy stayed in the village and became a farmer among farmers."
"Many, many years later…
…the descendants of the little Muchacho were still living in Marinha."
"They had become the 'Mucha' family."

Epilogue

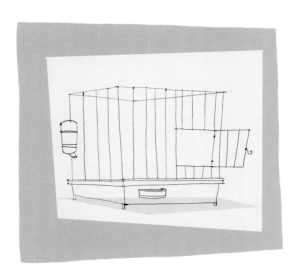

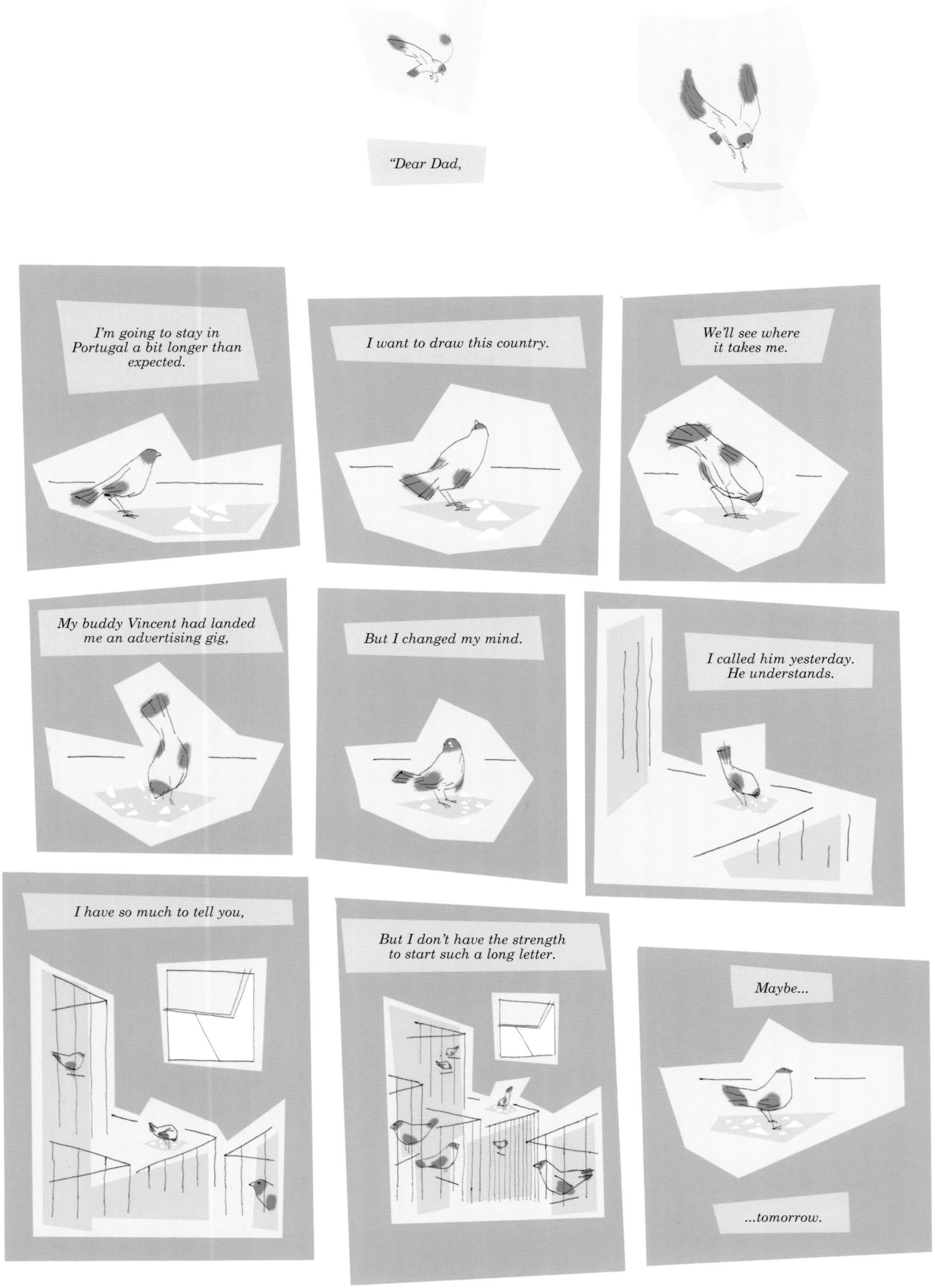
"Dear Dad,
I'm going to stay in Portugal a bit longer than expected.
I want to draw this country.
We'll see where it takes me.
My buddy Vincent had landed me an advertising gig,
But I changed my mind.
I called him yesterday. He understands.
I have so much to tell you,
But I don't have the strength to start such a long letter.
Maybe...
...tomorrow.

I will, however, take the opportunity...

...to enclose this postcard, which Teresa gave me.

Grandpa wrote it.

Alessandro read it to me in French.

I'll leave it up to you to have it translated, if you want to.

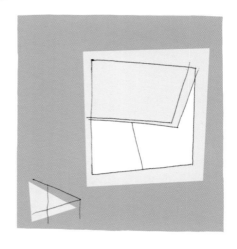

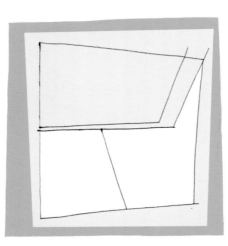

I can't help thinking the postcard was meant for us.

I would really like it if you and I came back here together one day, whenever you want.

All my love,

Simon."

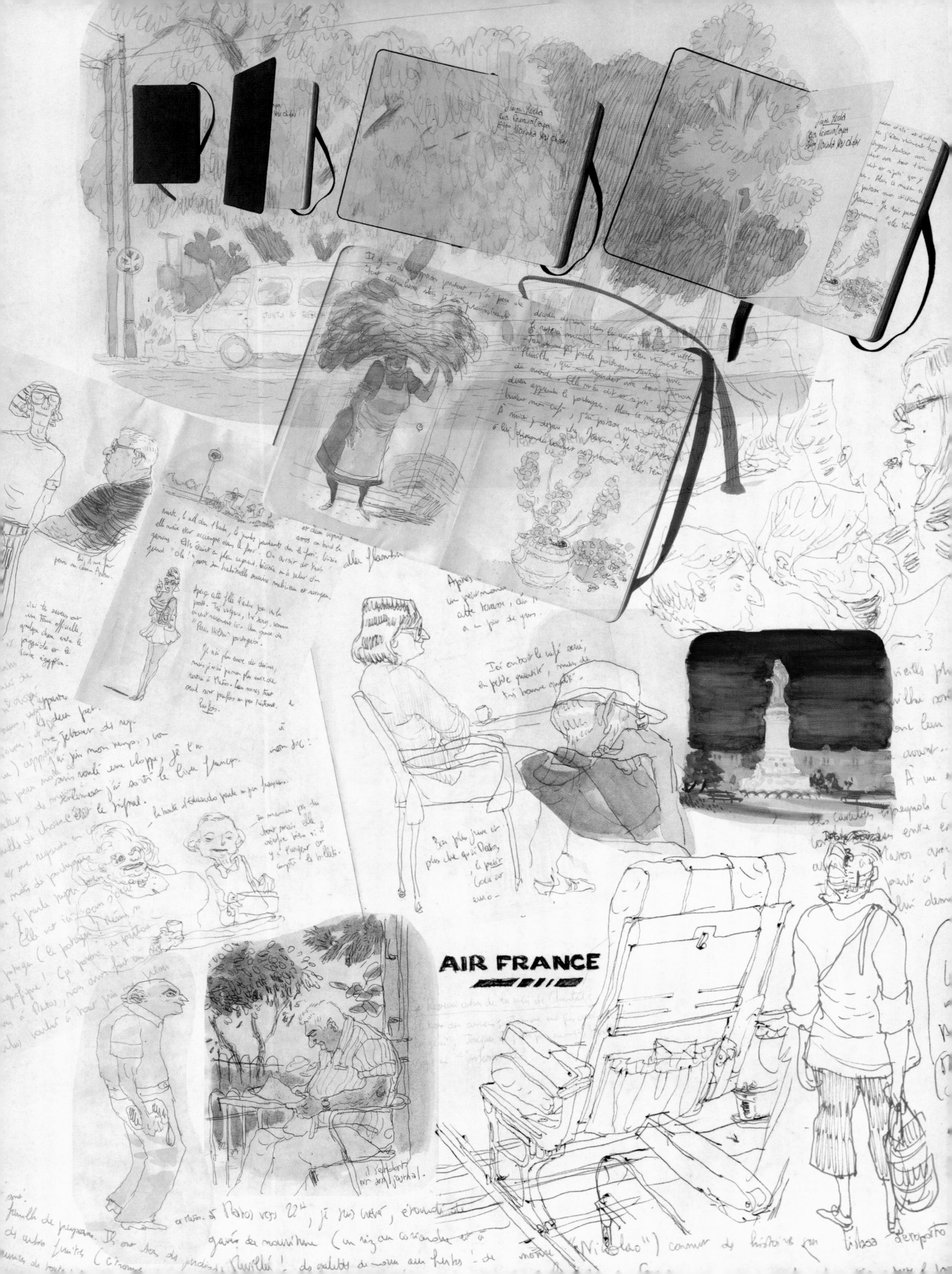
AIR FRANCE

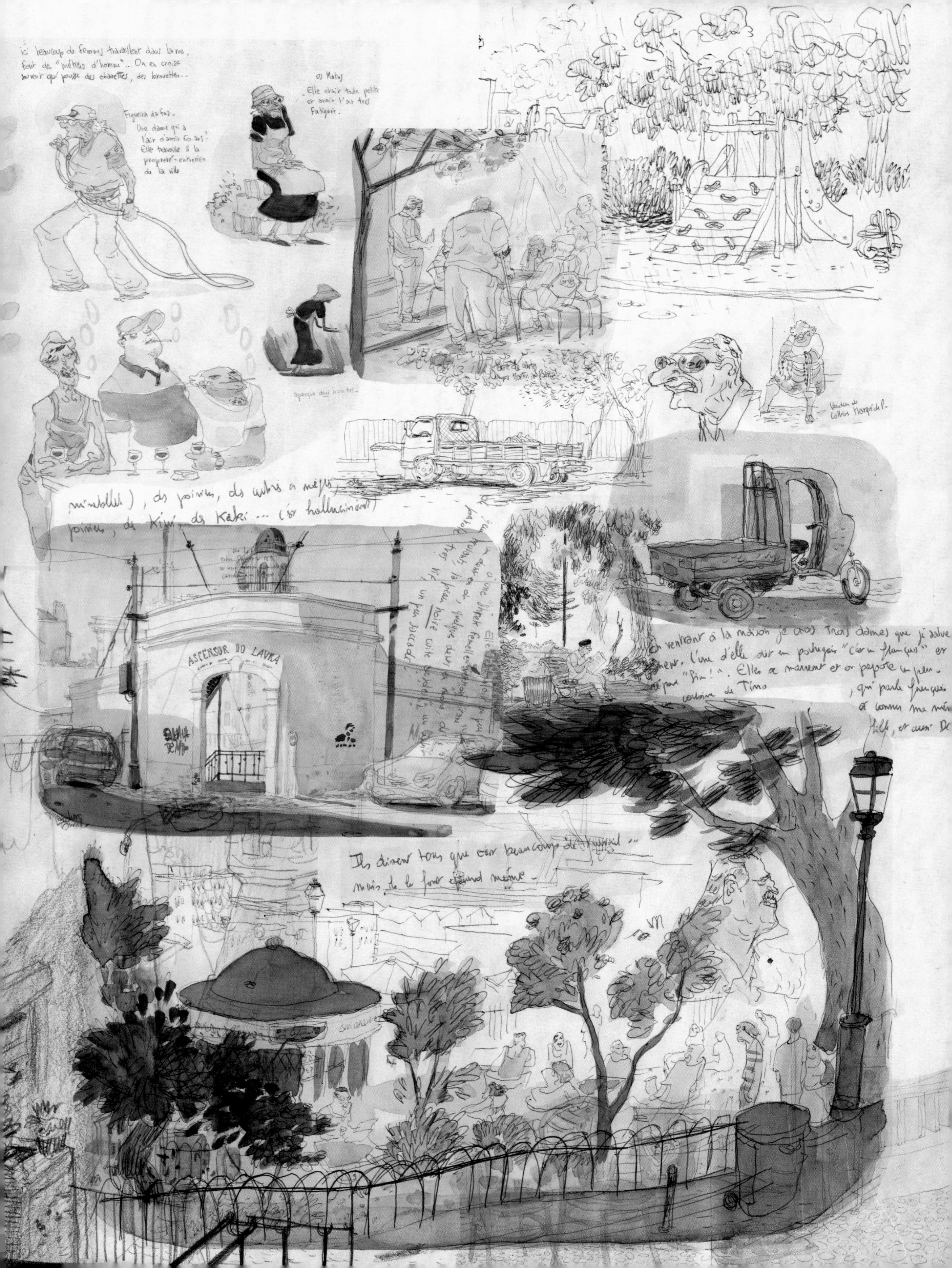
ici beaucoup de femmes travaillent dans la rue, font des "métiers d'homme"... On en croise souvent qui pousse des charettes, des brouettes...
Figueira da Foz.
Une dame qui a l'air d'avoir 60 ans ! Elle travaille à la propreté-entretien de la ville.
Os Matos
Elle était toute petite et avait l'air très fatiguée.
ASCENSOR DO LAVRA
Ils disent tous que c'est beaucoup de travail...
mais de le font quand même.

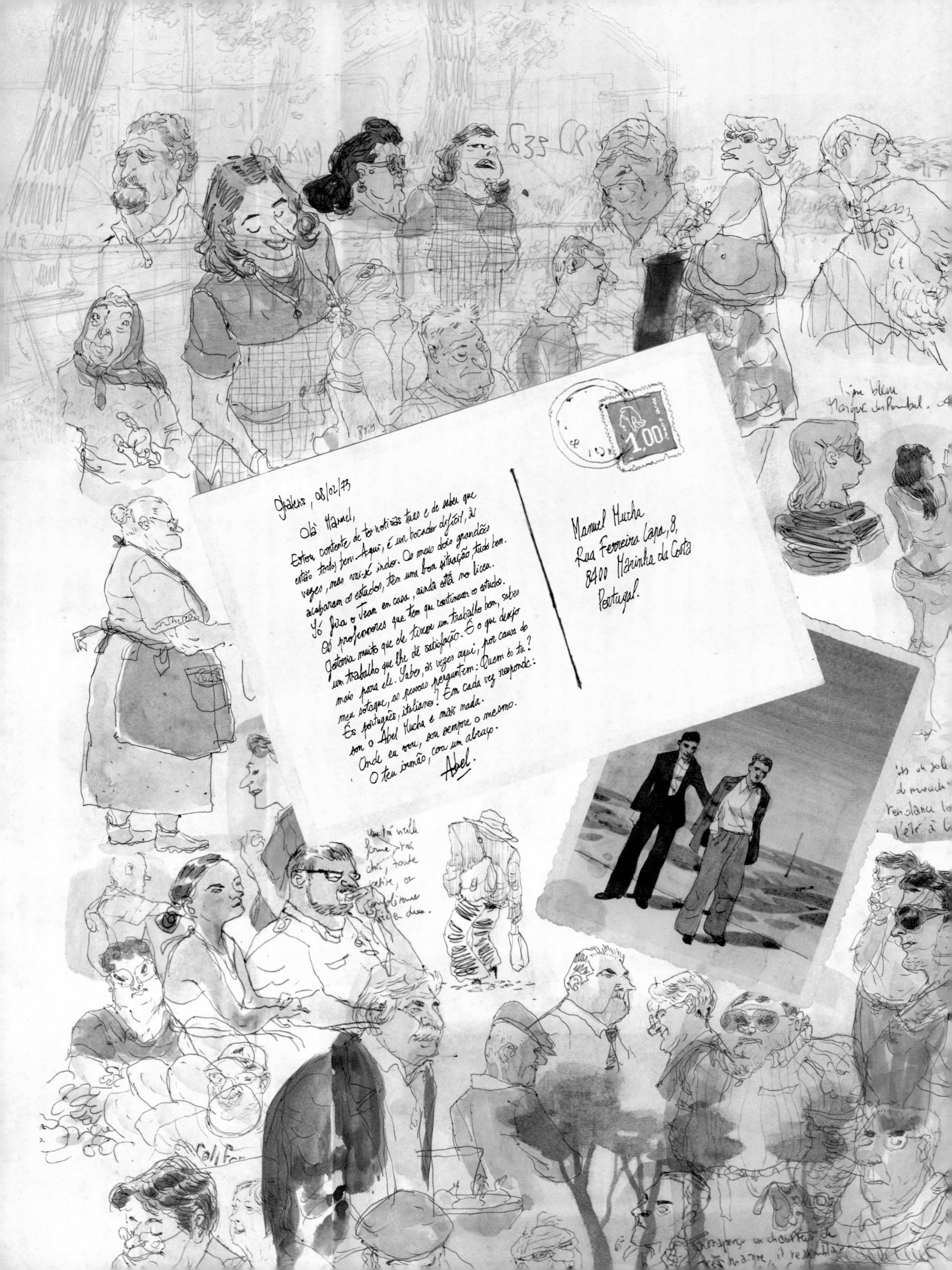

Athens, 08/02/73
Olà Manuel,
Estou contente de ter notícias tuas e de saber que
estão todos bem. Aqui, é um bocado difícil, às
vezes, mas vai-se indo. Os meus dois grandões
acabaram os estudos, têm uma boa situação, tudo bem.
Só fica o Jean em casa, ainda está no liceu.
Os professores que tem que continuar os estudos.
Gostaria muito que ele tivesse um trabalho bom, sabes
um trabalho que lhe dê satisfação. É o que desejo
mais para ele. Sabes, às vezes aqui, por causa do
meu sotaque, as pessoas perguntem: Quem és tu?
És português, italiano? Em cada vez respondo:
sou o Abel Mucha e mais nada.
Onde eu vou, sou sempre o mesmo.
O teu irmão, com um abraço.
Abel.
Manuel Mucha
Rua Ferreira Lapa, 8,
8400 Marinha da Costa
Portugal.
1,00

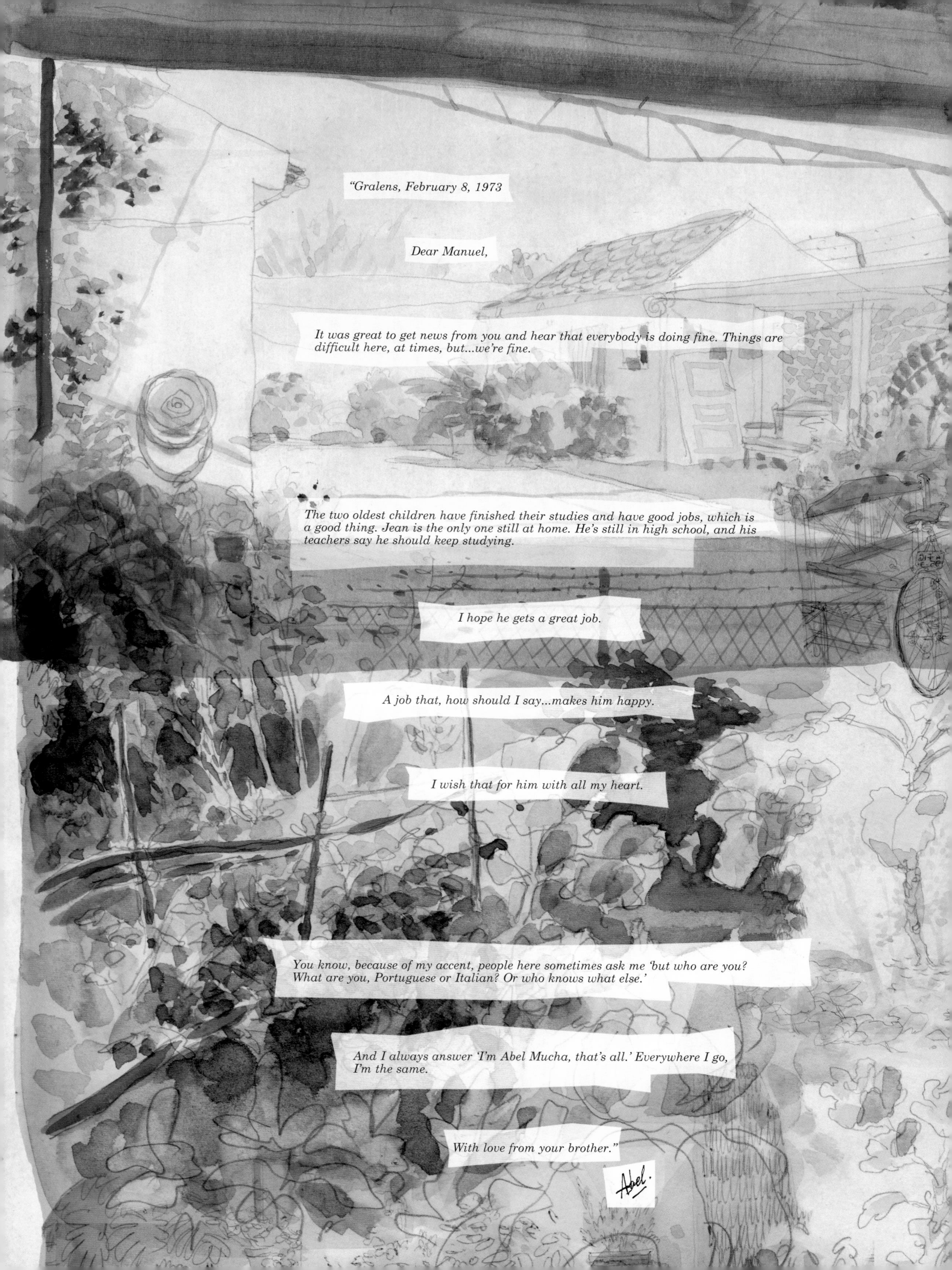
"Gralens, February 8, 1973
Dear Manuel,
It was great to get news from you and hear that everybody is doing fine. Things are difficult here, at times, but...we're fine.
The two oldest children have finished their studies and have good jobs, which is a good thing. Jean is the only one still at home. He's still in high school, and his teachers say he should keep studying.
I hope he gets a great job.
A job that, how should I say...makes him happy.
I wish that for him with all my heart.
You know, because of my accent, people here sometimes ask me 'but who are you? What are you, Portuguese or Italian? Or who knows what else.'
And I always answer 'I'm Abel Mucha, that's all.' Everywhere I go, I'm the same.
With love from your brother."
Abel.

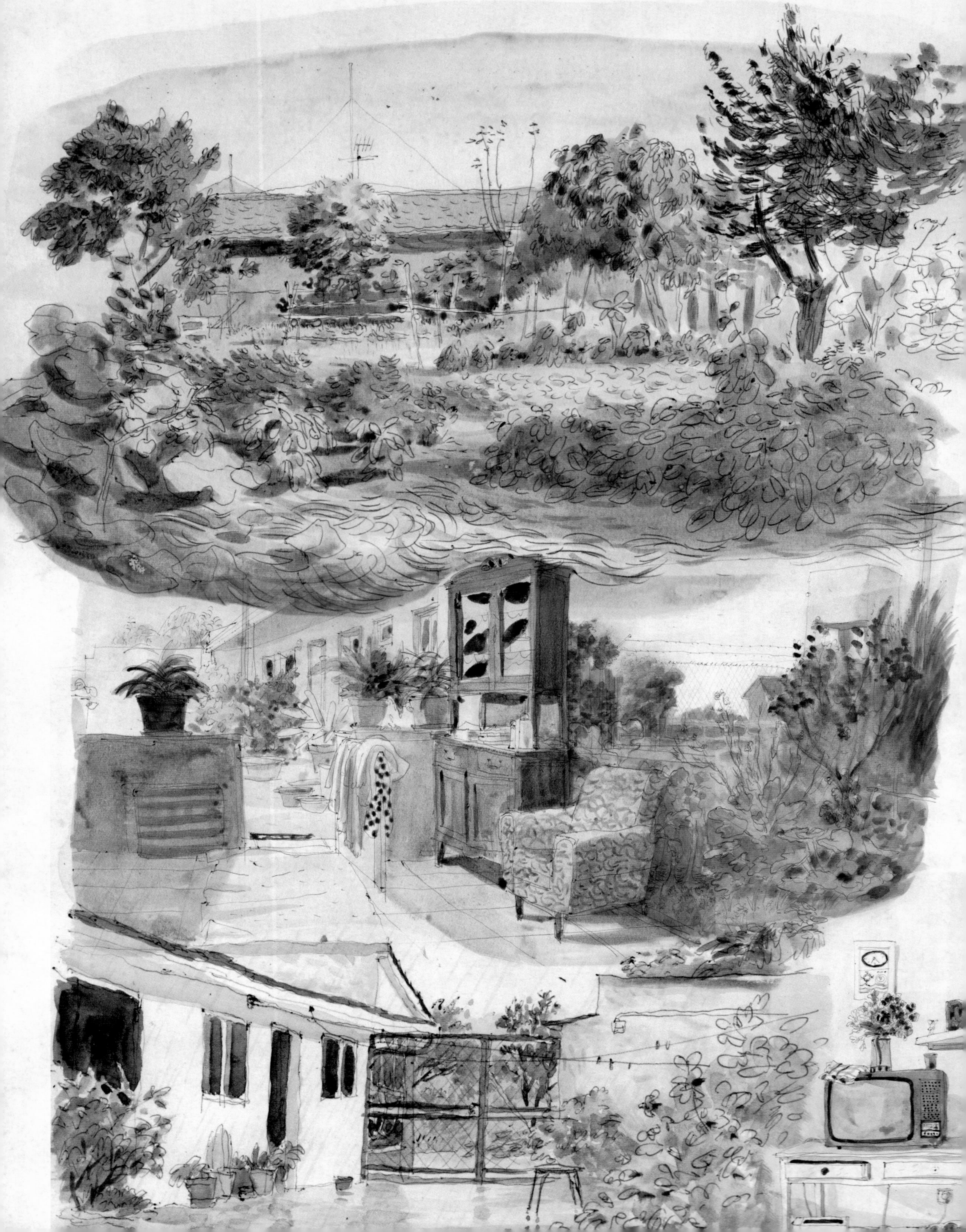

Rue d'Aschariou

For Deosinda, Gracinda, Joaquim,
and all those that leave, sometimes
without ever coming back...

Pedrosa 31/05/11

Born November 22, 1972 in Poitiers (Vienne). A big comic reader during childhood and adolescence, Cyril Pedrosa first went into scientific studies. After some trial and error, he finally studied at the Gobelins animation design, a Parisian establishment dedicated to careers in the moving image. He worked on Disney animated feature films such as "The Hunchback of Notre Dame" and "Hercules." There he acquired a speed of execution and a sense of movement that will later serve him well. Meeting writer David Chauvel inspired him to turn to comics. A "rising star" in graphic storytelling, his unique work is a product of his animation background combined with his literary influences of Borges, Marquez and Tolkien.